The Progresses And Public Processions Of Queen Elizabeth: Among Which Are Interspersed Other Solemnities, Public Expenditures, And Remarkable Events, During The Reign Of That Illustrious Princess, Volume 3...

Anonymous

Nabu Public Domain Reprints:

You are holding a reproduction of an original work published before 1923 that is in the public domain in the United States of America, and possibly other countries. You may freely copy and distribute this work as no entity (individual or corporate) has a copyright on the body of the work. This book may contain prior copyright references, and library stamps (as most of these works were scanned from library copies). These have been scanned and retained as part of the historical artifact.

This book may have occasional imperfections such as missing or blurred pages, poor pictures, errant marks, etc. that were either part of the original artifact, or were introduced by the scanning process. We believe this work is culturally important, and despite the imperfections, have elected to bring it back into print as part of our continuing commitment to the preservation of printed works worldwide. We appreciate your understanding of the imperfections in the preservation process, and hope you enjoy this valuable book.

PROGRESSES,

PUBLIC PROCESSIONS, &c.

OF

QUEEN ELIZABETH.

IN THREE VOLUMES.
VOL. III.

" The splendor and magnificence of ELIZABETH's Reign is no where more strongly painted than in these little Diaries of some of her Summer Excursions to the houses of her Nobility; nor could a more acceptable present be given to the world, than a re-publication of a select number of such details as this of the Entertainment at Elvetham, that at Killingworth, &c. &c. which so strongly mark the spirit of the times, and present us with scenes so very remote from modern manners." PERCY's Reliques of Antient English Poetry, vol. III. p. 64.

Ὡς ΚΕΙ'ΝΗ περὶ κῆρὶ τετίμηταί τε, καὶ ἐστὶν,
Ἐκ λαῶν, οἱ μίν ῥα, θεὸν ὡς, εἰσορόωντες,
Δειδέχαται μύθοισιν, ὅτε στείχησ' ἀνὰ ἄστυ.
Odyss. vii. 69.

When through the street she gracious deigns to move,
(The public wonder, and the public love,)
The tongues of all with transport sound her praise,
The eyes of all, as on a goddess, gaze.
POPE's Odyssey, ver. 90.

THE PRINCESS ELIZABETH.

THE
PROGRESSES
AND
PUBLIC PROCESSIONS
OF
QUEEN ELIZABETH.

AMONG WHICH ARE INTERSPERSED

OTHER SOLEMNITIES, PUBLIC EXPENDITURES, AND REMARKABLE EVENTS,

DURING THE REIGN OF THAT ILLUSTRIOUS PRINCESS.

COLLECTED FROM

Original Manuscripts, Scarce Pamphlets, Corporation Records, Parochial Registers, &c. &c.

ILLUSTRATED WITH HISTORICAL NOTES,

BY JOHN NICHOLS, F. S. A. LOND. EDINB. & PERTH.

A NEW EDITION, IN THREE VOLUMES.

VOLUME III.

LONDON: PRINTED BY AND FOR JOHN NICHOLS AND SON,
(PRINTERS TO THE SOCIETY OF ANTIQUARIES,)
25, PARLIAMENT STREET.
1823.

QUEEN ELIZABETH'S PROGRESSES.

Anno Regni Regine ELIZABETH *tricesimo-primo,* 1588-9.

Newe Yeare's Guiftes gyven to the Queene's Majesty at her Highnes Mannour of Richmond, by these Parsons whose names do hereafter ensewe, the firste daye, the yeare aforesaide [1].

Elizabeth [signature]

By Sir *Christopher Hatton*, Knight, Lord Chancellor of England, a coller of gold, conteyninge 11 peeces, whereof four made like scallop shells garneshed round about with small diamonds and rubyes, one pearle pendaunt and two rubyes pendaunt without foyle, six other longer peeces eche garnesshed with seven pearles, five rubyes of two sorts, sparks of diamonds and two rubyes pendaunt without foyle, having a bigger peece in the middest like a scallopp shell, garneshed with diamonds and rubyes of sundry bignesses, one pearle in the topp, one rock ruby in the middest, having three fishes pendaunt garneshed on th'one side with sparks of diamonds and two rubyes pendaunt, without foyle, and with one peece at eche end of them garneshed with two small rubyes and one pearle, and a paire of braceletts of gold, conteyninge 12 peeces, six like knotts garnesshed with sparks of diamonds, and six like knotts garnesshed with sparks of rubyes, and two pearles in a peece, and two pearles betweene eche peece.

Delivered to Mrs. *Ratcliffe*.

[1] From an orignal Roll in the Lansdown Collection of MSS.

	£.	s.	d.
By the Lorde *Burleigh*, Lord High Treasorer of England, in golde	20	0	0
By the Lord Marques of *Winchester*, in golde - - -	20	0	0

Delivered to Mr. *Henry Sackford*, one of the Groomes of her Majestie's Pryvie Chamber.

EARLES.

By the Earle of *Shrewesbury*, in gold - - - -	20	0	0
By the Earle of *Darby*, in gold - - - -	20	0	0
By the Earle of *Sussex*, in gold - - - -	10	0	0
By the Earle of *Huntingdon*, in gold - - - -	10	0	0
By the Earle of *Bath*, in gold - - - -	20	0	0

By the Earle of *Warwick*, a sarcconet of gold, conteyninge 15 peeces, seven sett with foure rubyes, and one small diamond in the middest, the other seven sett with nyne pearles in a peece sett in gold, having a rowe of small pearles on thupside, and pendaunts of sparks of rubyes, oppalls, and ragged pearles.

Delivered to the said Mrs. *Ratcliff*.

By the Earle of *Hertford*, in gold - - - -	10	0	0
By the Earle of *Lincoln*, in gold - - - -	10	0	0
By the Earle of *Penbrok*, in gold - - - -	20	0	0

Delivered to the said Mr. *Sackford*.

By the Earle of *Ormound*, part of a petticote of carnation satten embrodered with a broade garde or border of antyques of flowers and fyshes of Venis gold, silver, and silke, and all over with a twist of Venis gold.

Delivered to the Roabes.

By the Earle of *Northumberland*, one jewell of golde like a lampe garnesshed with sparks of diamonds and one oppall.

By the Earl of *Cumberland*, a jewell of gold like a sacrifice.

Delivered to the said Mrs. *Ratclife*.

VICOUNTE.

By the Vicounte *Mountague*, in gold - - - -	10	0	0

Delivered to the said Mr. *Sackford*.

MARQUESSE AND COUNTESSES.

By the Lady Marquesse of *Northampton*, a peire of braceletts of gold conteyning 16 peeces, four enamuled white set with one pearle

	£.	s.	d.

in a peece, and four sparks of rubyes a peece, the other foure sett with one dasy and a small ruby in the middest thereof, and four small pearles and eight longe peeces betwene them, ech sett with small diamonds and two sparks of rubyes.
 Delivered to the said Mrs. *Ratcliff.*

By the Countesse of *Shrewsbury*, a safegard with a jhup or gaskyn coate of faire cullored satten, like flames of fire of gold, and garnesshed with buttons, loupes, and lace of Venis silver.
 Delivered to the Roabes.

By the Countesse of *Huntington*, in gold - - - 8 0 0
 Delivered to the said Mr. *Sackford*.

By the Countesse of *Warwick*, a chayne, containing 22 aggetts slytely garnesshed with gold, and 22 bawles of jheat slytely garnesshed over with seede pearles.
 Delivered to the said Mrs. *Ratcliff*.

By the Countesse of *Lyncoln*, widdowe, a longe cloake of murry velvet, with a border rounde aboute of a small cheyne lace of Venis silver, and two rowes of buttons and lowpes of like silver furred thorough with mynnyover and calloper like myll pykes.
 Delivered to the Roabes.

By the Countesse of *Sussex*, widdowe, in gold - - - 10 0 0
By the Countesse of *Sussex*, in gold - - - 10 0 0
By the Countesse of *Penbrok*, in gold - - - 10 0 0
 Delivered to the said Mr. *Sackford*.

By the Countesse of *Bedford*, two large candlesticks of cristall garnesshed with silver gilte paynted, per oz. altogether - - 80 10 0
 Charged upon *John Astelly*, Esquire, Master of our Juells and Plate.

By the Countesse of *Cumberland*, a peire of braselets, conteyninge eight peeces of gold, sett with sparks of diamonds and rubyes, and knotts or rundells of small pearles betwene them, threded.
 Delivered to the said Mrs. *Ratcliff*.

By the Countesse of *Southampton*, in gold - - - 10 0 0
By the Countesse of *Rutland*, in gold - - - 10 0 0
By the Countesse of *Hertford*, in gold - - - 10 0 0
 Delivered to the said Mr. *Sackford*.

By the Countesse of *Ormount*, parte of a petticote of carnačon satten ymbrodered with a broade garde or border of anticks of flowers and fishes of Venis gold, silver, and all over with a twist of Venis gold.
 Delivered to the Roabes.

By the Countesse of *Bath*, a fanne of swanne downe, with a maze £. s. d. of greene velvet, ymbrodered with seed pearles and a very small chayne of silver gilte, and in the middest a border on both sides of seed pearles, sparks of rubyes and emerods, and thereon a monster of gold, the head and breast mother-of-pearles; and a skarfe of white stitche cloth florished with Venis gold, silver, and carnacion silke.

Delivered the fanne to the Roabes; and the skarfe to Mrs. *Carr*.

VICOUNTESSE.

	£	s.	d.
By the Vicountesse *Mountagu*, in gold	10	0	0

Delivered to the said Mr. *Sackford*.

BUSSHOPS.

	£	s.	d.
By the Archbusshopp of *Canterbury* [1], in gold	40	0	0
By the Busshopp of *London* [2], in gold	20	0	0
By the Busshop of *Salisbury* [3], in gold	20	0	0
By the Busshopp of *Winchester* [4], in gold	20	0	0
By the Busshopp of *Lincoln* [5], in gold	20	0	0
By the Busshopp of *Worcester* [6], in gold	20	0	0
By the Busshopp of *Bathe* [7], in gold	20	0	0
By the Busshopp of *Norwich* [8], in gold	20	0	0
By the Busshopp of *Lichfeild and Coventry* [9], in gold and silver	13	6	8
By the Busshopp of *Carleill* [10], in gold	10	0	0

[1] Dr. John Whitgift, Lady Margaret Professor of Divinity, 1560-1; Founder and Master of Pembroke Hall, Cambridge, 1567; and Master of Trinity College in the same year; Dean of Lincoln, 1571; Bishop of Worcester, 1577; translated to Canterbury, 1583; and President of the Society of Antiquaries. He died Feb. 29, 1603-4. See vol. I. p. 384.

[2] Dr. John Aylmer, Archdeacon of Lincoln 1562; Bishop of London 1576; died June 3, 1594.

[3] Dr. John Piers, Dean of Christ Church 1570-1; and of Sarum 1571; Bishop of Rochester 1576; of Salisbury 1578; and Archbishop of York in Feb. 1588-9. He died Sept. 28, 1594.

[4] Dr. Thomas Cowper, Dean of Christ Church 1567; Bishop of Lincoln 1570; of Winchester 1584; died April 29, 1594.

[5] Dr. William Wickham, Dean of Lincoln 1577; Bishop of that Diocese 1584; died Feb. 22, 1594-5.

[6] Dr. Edmund Freak, Dean of Sarum 1570; Bishop of Rochester 1571; of Norwich 1575; of Worcester 1584; died March 21, 1590-1.

[7] Dr. Thomas Godwin, Dean of Canterbury 1566; Bishop of Bath and Wells 1584; died Nov. 19, 1590.

[8] Dr. Edmund Scambler, Prebendary of Westminster and York, both in 1560; Bishop of Peterborough 1560; of Norwich 1584; died May 7, 1594.

[9] Dr. William Overton, Bishop of Lichfield and Coventry 1578; died in April 1609.

[10] Dr. John Mey, Master of Catharine Hall, Cambridge 1559; Prebendary of Ely 1563; Archdeacon of the East Riding of Yorkshire 1569; Bishop of Carlisle 1577; died Feb. 15, 1597-8.

NEW YEAR'S GIFTS PRESENTED TO THE QUEEN, 1588-9.   5

	£.	s.	d.
By the Busshopp of *Peterburrowe*[1], in gold - - -	9	16	6
By the Busshopp of *Chester*[2], in gold - - - -	10	0	0
By the Busshopp of *Rochester*[3], in gold - - -	10	0	0
By the Busshopp of *Exceter*[4], in gold - - - -	10	0	0
By the Busshopp of *St. David*[5], in gold - - -	10	0	0
By the Busshopp of *Chichester*[6], in gold - - -	10	0	0
By the Busshopp of *Gloucester*[7], in gold - - -	10	0	0
By the Busshopp of *Herreford*[8], in gold - - -	10	0	0

Delivered to the said Mr. *Sackford.*

LORDES.

By the Lord *Hunsdon*, Lord Chamberleyne, the nether skirts of the coveringe of a gowne, black stitcht cloth, florished with gold, and some owes.

Delivered to the Roabes.

By the Lord *Howard*, Lord Admirall, a sarceonett of gold, conteyninge fyve peeces garnesshed with sparks of diamounds, foure whereof each a ruby, foure lesse peeces like knotts garnesshed with sparks of diamounds, eight litle pendaunts of diamounds without foile, and nine small pearles pendaunt.

Delivered to the said Mrs. *Ratcliff.*

| By the Lord *Cobham*, in gold - - - - - | 10 | 0 | 0 |
| By the Lord *Darcy of Chiche*, in gold - - - - | 9 | 17 | 6 |

[1] Dr. Richard Howland, Fellow of Peter House, Cambridge; Master of Magdalen College 1575; and of St. John's College 1577; Bishop of Peterborough 1584; died in 1600.

[2] Dr. William Chaderton, Warden of Manchester College; Archdeacon of York 1568; Prebendary of York 1573; of Westminster and Sarum; Fellow of Christ's College, and Master of Queen's, Cambridge; Bishop of Chester 1579; of Lincoln 1594. He died April 10, 1608. See in the Second Volume several Letters from the Queen to this Prelate.

[3] Dr. John Young, Master of Pembroke Hall, Cambridge 1567; Prebendary of Westminster 1572; Bishop of Rochester 1578. He died in 1605.

[4] Dr. John Woolton, Canon-Residentiary of Exeter; Bishop of that diocese 1579; died March 13, 1593-4.

[5] Dr. Marmaduke Middleton, Bishop of Waterford in Ireland 15..; of St. David's 1582. He was deprived in 1592, for contriving and publishing a forged will.

[6] Dr. Thomas Bickley, Warden of Merton College, Oxford 1569; Bishop of Chichester 1585; died April 30, 1596, æt. 90.

[7] Dr. John Bullingham, Prebendary of Worcester; Bishop of Bristol 1581; of Gloucester the same year; died May 20, 1598.

[8] Dr. Herbert Westphaling, Canon of Christ Church 1561; and Canon of Windsor 1577; Bishop of Hereford 1585; died March 1, 1601-2.

	£.	s.	d.
By the Lord *Shandoyes,* in gold	10	0	0
By the Lord *Compton,* in gold	10	0	0
By the Lord *Norris,* in gold	10	0	0
By the Lord *Lumley,* in gold	10	0	0
By the Lord *Wharton,* in gold	10	0	0
By the Lord *Ritch,* in gold	10	0	0
By the Lord of *Buckhurst,* in gold	5	0	0
By the Lord *North,* in gold	10	0	0

Delivered to the said Mr. *Sackford.*

By the Lord *Seymer,* a comfett box of mother-of-pearles, garnesshed with small sparks of rubies.

Delivered to the said Mrs. *Ratcliff.*

BARRONESSES.

By the Barronesse *Burghley,* a porringer of gold with a cover, per oz. 24 oz.
  Charged upon *John Asteley,* Esq.

By the Barrones *Hunsdon,* a peire of bodies for the covering of a gowne of black stitcht cloth, florished with gold and some owes.

By the Barronesse *Howard,* a covering of a gowne of black nett-work, faire florished over with Venis gold.

By the Barrones *Cobham,* a petticote of faire cullored caffa laid with six laces of Venis silver with plate.

By the Barrones *Dakers,* a petticote of white chamlett striped with silver, printed with a border of six broade bone laces of Venis gold and silver plate, and striped all over broade arrowehedwyse, with a lesse lace of like Venis gold and silver plate.

  Delivered to the Roabes.

By the Barrones *Lumley,* a wastecoate of white taffety, imbrodered all over with a twist of flowers of Venis gold, silver, and some black silke.
  Delivered to Mrs. *Skidmore.*

By the Barrones *Shandowes Knolls,* a stoole of wood paynted, the seate covered with murry velvet, ymbrodered all over with pillers arched of Venis gold, silver, and silke.
  Charged upon *Roberte Cotton,* Yeoman of the Wardropp of bedds.

By the Barrones *Shandoyes,* in gold	10	0	0
By the Barronesse *Sainte John Bletzowe,* in gold	10	0	0

	£.	s.	d.

By the Barronesse *Pagett Cary*, in gold - - - - 10 0 0
    Delivered to the said Mr. *Sackford*.

By the Barronesse *Dudley*, two ruffes with rabatines of lawne cut-work made, and one ruff of lawne cutt-work unmade.
    Delivered to Mrs. *Bonne*.

By the Barronesse *Cheney*, a small jewell of gold sett wyth fyve diamounds of sundry cutts without foyle, and three small pearles pendaunt.
    Delivered to the said Mrs. *Ratcliffe*.

By the Barronesse *Wharton*, in gold - - - - 10 0 0
By the Barronesse *Buckhurst*, in gold - - - - 5 0 0
By the Barronesse *Barkeley*, in gold - - - - 10 0 0
By the Barrones *Norris*, in gold - - - - 10 0 0
By the Barronesse *Ritch*, widdowe, in gold - - - 10 0 0
    Delivered to the said Mr. *Sackford*.

By the Barronesse *Sheffield*, one saddle cloth of black velvet, ymbrodered all over with Venis gold, with all the furniture belonginge for a saddle.
    Delivered to the Stable.

By the Barronesse *Rich*, a fore parte of white nettworke like rundells, and buttons florished with Venis gold and owes layde upon purple satten, and lined with white sarsonet.

By the Barronesse *Talbott*, widdowe, a mantle of black stitch cloth florished and seamed with Venis silver.
    Delivered to the Roabes.

LADIES.

By the Lady *Mary Seymer*, wife to Mr. *Rogers*, a standitch of wood covered with silke needlework, garnished with a fewe seede pearles.
    Delivered to the said Mrs. *Skidmore*.

By the Lady *Elizabeth Seymer*, wife to Mr. *Richard Knightley*, a skarfe of black nettwork, florished with silver, and lyned with faire cullored sarsonett.
    Delivered to the said Mrs. *Carre*.

By the Lady *Katheryn Constable*, one longe cushion of black velvett, ymbrodered all over with flowers of silke needle-worke of sundry cullors and sorts, and backed with watchett damaske.
    Delivered to the said *Robert Cotton*.

By the Lady *Stafford*, a peire of braseletts of gold, conteyninge 16 peeces, whereof eight enamuled white, four very small sparks of rubyes in a peece, and one ragged pearle in a peece of eche; the other eight enamuled with five ragged pearles in a peece.

Delivered to the said Mrs. *Ratcliff.*

By the Lady *Walsingham*, one skimskyn of cloth of silver, ymbrodered all over very faire with beasts, fowles, and trees, of Venis gold, silver, silke, and small seed pearles, with fyve buttons of seede pearles, lyned with carnation plushe; a peire of perfumed gloves, the coaffe ymbrodered with seed pearle, and lyned with carnation velvett.

Delivered to the said Mrs. *Carre.*

By the Lady *Hennage*, one shorte cloke of black cloth of silver layde round about with a passmayne before, with buttons and lowpes of like lace of Venis gold and silver, lyned with white plushe.

Delivered to the Roabes.

By the Lady *Carow*, one smock of fyne Holland about wroughte with black silke.

Delivered to the said Mrs. *Skidmore.*

By the Lady *Cheake*, a fore parte of white nettworke florisshed with Venis gold, silver, and carnation silke, layde upon white satten.

Delivered to the Roabes.

By the Lady *Drewry*, a skimskyn of black cipres, florished with Venis gold and small seed pearles, with a border or rowe of seed pearles, with eight buttons of gold, ech of them four small ragged pearles with a garnett in eche of them.

Delivered to the said Mrs. *Carre.*

By the Lady *Leyton*, a waistcote of white sarsnett, ymbrodered round about with a border of eglantyne flowers, and ymbrodered all over with a twist of Venis gold.

Delivered to the said Mrs. *Skidmore.*

By the Lady *Southwell*, a dooblett of lawne cuttwork, florished with squares of silver owes.

Delivered to the Roabes.

	£.	s.	d.
By the Lady *Pawlett*, in gold - - - - -	5	0	0
By the Lady *Jarrett*, in gold - - - - -	10	0	0

Delivered to the said Mr. *Sackford.*

By the Lady *Digby*, one cloke of black silke stitched cloth, florished with silver striped, layd upon faire cullored taffety, lyned with white plushe.

By the Lady *Willoughby*, a fore parte of lawne cuttwork, florished with silver and spangles.

Delivered to the Roabes.

By the Lady *Scroope*, a vaile of white knittwork, striped with rowles and silver plate.

Delivered to the said Mrs. *Carre.*

By the Lady *Gresham*, in gold - - - - - 9 17 6
 Delivered to the said Mr. *Sackford*.

By the Lady *Ratcliff*, a vaile of white stitch cloth striped, florished with Venis gold, silver, and some owes.
 Delivered to the said Mrs. *Carre*.

By the Lady *Souche*, a smock of fyne Holland, wroughte with black silke.
 Delivered to the said Mrs. *Skidmore*.

By the Lady *Weste*, a skimskyn of watched satten, ymbrodered with knotts of Venis gold, and lyned with carnation flushe.

By the Lady *Longe*, a skimskyn of cloth of silver, ymbrodered all over with beasts and flowers and a woman in the middest, lyned with carnation flushe.
 Delivered to the said Mrs. *Carre*.

By the Lady *Harrington*, a wastecote of lawne, faire wroughte with Venis gold and black silke.
 Delivered to the said Mrs. *Skidmore*.

By the Lady *Townesende*, a large ruffe of lawne cuttwork unmade.
 Delivered to the said Mrs. *Bonne*.

KNIGHTS.

	£.	s.	d.
By Sir *Fleaming Knowlls*, Treasorer of the Houshold, in gold	10	0	0
By Sir *James Croftes*, Comptroller of the same, in gold	10	0	0

 Delivered to the said Mr. *Sackford*.

By Sir *Frauncis Walsingham*, Principall Secretary, a cloke and a savegard of faire cullored velvet, laide round aboute and striped downe and eight lowpes in the fore quarters of a broade passamayn lace of Venis gold and silver plate; the cloke lyned with printed cloth of silver, and the savegard lyned with white sarsonett; and a dooblett of white satten cutt, ymbrodered all over with esses of Venis gold, and striped overwhart with a passamayn of Venis gold and plate.
 Delivered to the Roabes.

By Sir *Thomas Hennage*, one jewell of gold, like an Alpha and Omega, with sparks of diamonds.
 Delivered to the said Mrs. *Ratcliff*.

	£.	s.	d.
By Sir *Walter Mildemay*, Chauncellor of thexchequer, in gold	10	0	0
By Sir *Gilberte Jarrett*, Master of the Rowles, in gold	20	0	0
By Sir *Owen Hopton*, Lievtenaunte of the Tower, in gold	10	0	0

 Delivered to the said Mr. *Sackford*.

By Sir *Thomas Layton*, Capteine of Garnsey, a petticote of white sarsnett, imbrodered round about with a broad border like eglantyne flowers, and all over ymbrodered with a twist of Venis gold, and powderings of carnation silke.

By Sir *Robert Sydney*, a dooblett of white satten, embroidered all over like clouds very faire, of scallopp fashion, with flowers and fruits of Venis gold, silver, and silke, betwene them.

Delivered to the Roabes.

	£.	s.	d.
By Sir *Henry Cromwell*, in gold	10	0	0
By Sir *Edwarde Cleare*, in gold	10	0	0

Delivered to the said Mr. *Sackford*.

By Sir *Thomas Cecil*, a Frenche gowne of black silke nettworke, of two sorts, florished with Venis gold, and lyned with white chamlett.

By Sir *Roberte Southwell*, foa reparte of lawne cutwork, florished with squares with owes.

Delivered at the Roabes.

By Sir *John Parrett*, one very small salte of aggett, with a cover and foote gold enamyled, garnished with small sparkes of rubyes and oppalls, the foote garnished with like rubyes, per oz. 1 oz. 3 quarters; and two Irishe mantles, the one murry, th'other russet, the one laced with silver lace and freindge, the other with gold lace and freindge.

The salte charged upon the said *John Asteley*, Esq. and the mantles delivered to *John Whinyard*.

By Sir *Oratio Pavlavizino*, one bodkyn of silver gilte, havinge a pendaunt jewell of gold, like a shipp, garnished with opaulls, sparks of diamonds, and three small pearles pendaunt.

Delivered to the said Mrs. *Ratclife*.

By Sir *George Cary*, a doblett of copp damaske, silver turned freindge lace, wrought with purle, and edged with a passamayn of silver.

Delivered to the Roabes.

CHAPLYN.

John Thorneborow, Clark of the Closett, one small cupp, the bowle, foote, and parte of the cover of aggats, garnished with gold, and sett with small rubyes, pearles, and litle oppalls, per oz. all 5 oz. di. qr.

Charged on the said *John Asteley*.

GENTLEWOMEN.

By Mrs. *Blaunch Aparry*, one long cushion of tawny cloth of gold, backed with taffety.

Delivered to the said *Robert Cotton*.

By Mrs. *Mary Ratcliffe*, a jewell of gold sett with a stone without a foyle, called Icentabella.
Delivered to her owne hande.

By Mrs. *Fraunces Howarde*, a skarf of black stitch cloth, florished with Venis gold and silver.
Delivered to the said Mrs. *Carre*.

By Mrs. *Elizabeth Brooke*, a skarf of white stitcht cloth, striped with black silke and silver, and florished with silver.
Delivered to the said Mrs. *Carre*.

By Mrs. *Elizabeth Throgmorton*, two ruffes of lawne cutwork made.
Delivered to the said Mrs. *Bonne*.

By Mrs. *Edmounds*, a cushen cloth of lawne cutwork like leaves, and a few owes of silver.
Delivered to Mrs. *Skideamore*.

By Mrs. *Skideamore*, parte of a loose gowne of black taffety with a border, ymbrodered with a chayne lace of Venis gold and tufts of white silke.

By Mrs. *Wolley*, a doblett of black stitcht cloth of two sorts, florished with Venis gold and silver.
Delivered to the Roabes.

By Mrs. *Wetston*, a skarf of black silke network, florished with Venis gold and silver, and lyned with faire cullored sarsonett; and two peire of weytinge tables, the one covered with needle-work, the other with crimsonn velvett.
Delivered to the said Mrs. *Carre*.

By Mrs. *Allen*, a ruff of lawne cuttwork unmade.
Delivered to the said Mrs. *Bonne*.

By Mrs. *Dale*, a saveguard of russett satten, florished with gold and silver, with buttons and lowpes downe before of Venis gold and silver, and bound about with a lace of like gold and silver.

By Mrs. *Sackford*, one peece of carnation grogreyne, florished with gold, conteyninge yardes . . . . .
Delivered to the Roabes.

By Mrs. *Wyngfield*, a nightraile of camberick, wroughte all over with black silke.

By Mrs. *Carre*, one sheete of fyne camberick, wrought all over with sundry fowles, beastes, and wormes, of silke of sundry cullers.
Delivered to the said Mrs. *Skidmore*.

By Mrs. *Jane Brizells*, a ruff of lawne cuttwork, with lilies of like cuttwork, sett with small seed pearles.
Delivered to the said Mrs. *Bonne*.

By Mrs. *Vaughan,* one peire of silke stockings and a peire of garters of white sypres.
Delivered to the said Mrs. *Skidmore.*

By Mrs. *Smithson,* two handkerchers of Holland wroughte with black silke.

By Mrs. *Twist,* a peire of sleeves of camberick wrought with black silke.

By Mrs. *Cromer,* a smock of fyne Holland, and the bodyes and sleeves wroughte all over with black silke.

By Mrs. *Fyfield,* a sweete bagge all over ymbrodered, and six handkerchers.

By Mrs. *Huggens,* 24 small sweete baggs of sarsenett of sundry cullors, and six handkerchers of camberick wrought with black silke, and edged with a passamayn of gold.
Delivered to the said Mrs. *Skidmore.*

By Mrs. *Owen,* a gerdle of white sipres, imbrodered at both ends with leaves of faire cullored silk of needle work, friendged with Venis gold, silver, and silke.
Delivered to the said Mrs. *Carre.*

By Mrs. *Jones,* six handkerchers of cambrick wroughte with black silke.

By Mrs. *Robinson,* a quoft and a forehead cloth florished with gold and silver.

By Mrs. *Burley,* six handkerchers of cambrick wrought with black silke.

By Mrs. *Morgan,* two boxes of wood, one cherryes, th'other aberycocks.

By Mrs. *Tomason,* one handkercher of cambrick wrought with black silke.

By Mrs. *West,* one attire of stitched cloth and haire wroughte in eysing puffes.
Delivered to the said Mrs. *Skidmore.*

By Mrs. *Bowne,* one ruff of lawne cuttwork made upp.
Delivered to her Majestie's owne hands.

GENTLEMEN.

By Mr. *Wolley,* one of her Majestie's Secretaries, a round cloke of black cloth of gold, with buttons and lowpes on thinside of Venis gold and black like.

By Mr. *Dyer,* a petticote of white satten, quilted all over with Venis gold and silver, with some plats, with four borders embrodered with gillyflowers and roses of Venis gold, and lyned with white sarsenett.

By Mr. *Bruncker,* one shorte cloke of white stitcht cloth, florished all over with Venis gold, silver, and some carnation silke, layde upon white taffety, and lyned with white plushe; and a skarf of white stitch cloth, and striped with Venis silver.
Delivered to the Robbes, saving the skarf to Mrs. *Car.*

By Mr. *Smith Customer,* one boulte of camberick, and a whole peece of lawne.

By Mr. *Garter King of Armes*, a booke of Armes of the Noblemen in Henry the Fift's tyme.

By Mr. *Newton*, a bodkyn of silver gilte, with a pendaunt like a sonne, enamuled redd, and a moone therein, garnished with sparks of diamounds, and four very small pearles pendaunt.

Delivered to Mrs. *Ratcliffe*.

By Mr. *Henry Brooke*, a petticote of carnation capha florished with silver, with fyne broade passamayn laces of gold, silver, and watched silke.

By a Gentleman unknown, a fanne of sundry collored fethers, with a handle of aggets garnished with silver gilte.

Delivered to the Roabes.

By Mr. *John Stanhop*, a large bagg of white satten, ymbrodered all over with flowers, beasts, and burds, of Venis gold, silver, and silke.

Delivered to the said Mrs. *Skidmore*.

By Mr. *Skidamour*, parte of a loose gowne of black taffety, with a border, imbrodered with a chaine lace of Venis gold, and tufts of white silke.

Delivered to the Roabes.

By Mr. Doctor *Bayly*, a pott of greene gynger, and a pott of the rynds of lemons.

By Mr. Doctor *Gyfford*, a pott of greene gynger, and a pot of the rynds of lemons.

Delivered to the said Mrs. *Skidmore*.

By Mr. Doctor *Lopus*, a peire of perfumed gloves, and a peire of white silke sypres.

Delivered the gloves to Mrs. *Carre*; the sipres to Mrs. *Ratcliffe*.

By Mr. *Fynes*, a longe cushion of purple satten, ymbrodered all over with damaske gold plate, Venis gold, and seed pearles of sundry sorts, with Justice in the middest, backed with yellow satten frenged, buttoned, and tasselld with Venis gold and purple silke.

Delivered to the said *Robert Cotton*.

By Mr. *Spillman*, a small peire of wrytinge tables of glass, garnished with silver gilte.

Delivered to Mrs. *Ratclyff*.

By Mr. *William Huggens*, a large sweete bagg of white satten, ymbrodered all over with Venis gold, silver, and silke of sundry cullors.

Delivered to the said Mrs. *Skidmore*.

By Mr. *Carr*, four stomachers of velvett, trymmed with a passamayn of Venis gold on the toppes; and two bells of jett, the clappers aggetts.

Delivered the stomacher to Mrs. *Skidmore*; the bells to Mrs. *Ratcliff*.

By Mr. *Mountighu*, one smock of fyne Holland cloth, faire wroughte with black silke.

Delivered to the said Mrs. *Skidmore*.

By Mr. Capteine *Crosse*, a faire large looking glasse set in frame, corded with crimson velvett, bound with a passamayn lace of Venis gold.

The glass broken.

By Mr. *Huishe*, one whole peece of lawne.

By Mrs. *Dunston Amys*, a beserte stone.

Delivered to the said Mrs. *Ratclyff*.

By *John Smithson*, Master Cooke, one faire marchpayne, with St. George in the middest.

By *John Dudley*, Sargeante of the Pastry, one faire pye of quinces orringed.

Somma totalis of the money gyven to her Majestie amounteth to £.795 19s. 2d.

Anno Regni Regine ELIZABETH, *nunc tricesimo-primo*, 1588-9.

Neweyeares Guiftes gyven by her Majestie at her Highnes Mannor of Richmond, to these persons whose names doe hereafter ensue, the first of January, the yeare aforesaide.

Signed, " ELIZABETH R."

To Sir *Christofer Hatton*, Knighte Lord Chancellor of England, in gilte plate, Martyn, 400 oz. 3 qrs.

To the Lord *Burghley*, Lord High Treausoror of England, in gilte plate, M. 40 oz.

To the Lord Marques of *Wynchester*, in gilte plate, Keele, 30 oz. 3 qrs.

EARLES.

To the Earle of *Shrewsbury*, in guilte plate, K. 30 oz. di. di. qr.
To the Earle of *Darby*, in guilte plate, K. 30 oz. 3 qrs.
To the Earle of *Sussex*, in gilte plate, M. 20 oz. 3 qrs.
To the Earle of *Huntington*, in gilte plate, M. 20 oz. 3 qrs.
To the Earle of *Bath*, in gilte plate, M. 29 oz.
To the Earle of *Warwick*, in guilte plate, M. 102 oz. qr.
To the Earle of *Heref*, in gilte plate, K. 20 oz. di. di. qr.
To the Earle of *Lincoln*, in gilte plate, K. 20 oz. 3 qrs. di.
To the Earle of *Penbrok*, in guilte plate, K. 30 oz.
To the Earle of *Ormound*, in guilte plate, M. and L. 140 oz. di.
To the Earle of *Northumberland*, in gilte plate, K. 29 oz. di. di. qr.
To the Earle of *Cumberland*, in gilte plate, M. 22 oz. qr. di.

Vicounte.

To the Vicounte *Mountaghu*, in gilte plate, K. 21 oz. qr.

Marquesse and Countesses.

To the Lady Marquesse of *Northampton*, in guilte plate, M. and K. 42 oz.
To the Countesse of *Shrewsbury*, in gilte plate, K. 31 oz.
To the Countesse of *Huntington*, in gilte plate, M. 29 oz. 3 qrs.
To the Countesse of *Warwick*, in gilte plate, K. 56 oz. 3 qrs.
To the Countesse of *Lincoln*, widdowe, in gilte plate, M. 50 oz. qr.
To the Countesse of *Sussex*, in gilte plate, K. 19 oz. qr.
To the Countesse of *Sussex*, in gilte plate, K. 19 oz. di. di. qr.
To the Countesse of *Penbrook*, in guilte plate, K. 29 oz. 3 qrs.
To the Countesse of *Bedford*, in gilte plate, K. 50 oz.
To the Countesse of *Cumberland*, in gilte plate, K. 19 oz. 3 qrs.
To the Countesse of *Southampton*, in gilte plate, K. 20 oz.
To the Countesse of *Rutland*, in gilte plate, K. 19 oz. 3 qrs. di.
To the Countesse of *Herts*, in gilte plate, K. 19 oz. 3 qrs. di.
To the Countesse of *Ormount*, in gilte plate, K. 18 oz. 3 qrs.
To the Countesse of *Bath*, in gilte plate, K. 25 oz. qr.

Vicountesse.

To the Vicountesse *Mountaghu*, in gilte plate, M. 19 oz. di. di. qr.

Busshopps.

To the Archbushopp of *Canterbury*, in gilte plate, M. 45 oz.
To the Bushopp of *London*, in gilte plate, K. 29 oz.
To the Bushop of *Salisbury*, in gilte plate, K. 30 oz.
To the Bushop of *Winchester*, in gilte plate, M. 30 oz.
To the Bushopp of *Lincoln*, in gilte plate, M. 30 oz.
To the Bushopp of *Worcester*, in gilte plate, M. and K. 30 oz. 3 qrs. di.
To the Bushop of *Bathe*, in gilte plate, K. 29 oz.
To the Bushopp of *Norwich*, in gilte plate, M. 30 oz.
To the Bushop of *Lichfield and Coventry*, in gilte plate, K. 20 oz. di. qr.

NEW YEAR'S GIFTS PRESENTED BY THE QUEEN, 1588-9.

To the Bushop of *Carliell*, in gilte plate, M. 14 oz. 3 qrs.
To the Bushop of *Peterborow*, in gilte plate, M. 15 oz. di. di. qr.
To the Bushopp of *Chester*, in gilte plate, M. 14 oz. di. qr.
To the Bushopp of *Rochester*, in gilte plate, K. 15 oz.
To the Bushop of *Exeter*, in gilte plate, M. 14 oz. 3 qrs. di.
To the Busshop of *St. David's*, in gilte plate, M. 14 oz. 3 qrs.
To the Bushop of *Chichester*, in gilte plate, M. 14 oz. 3 qrs. di.
To the Bushop of *Glocester*, in gilte plate, K. 14 oz. qr.
To the Bushop of *Hereford*, in gilte plate, K. 15 oz.

LORDES.

To the Lord *Hunsdon*, Lord Chamberleyne, in gilte plate, K. 30 oz.
To the Lorde *Hawarde*, Lorde Admirall, in gilte plate, M. and K. 104 oz. 3 qrs. di.
To the Lord *Cobham*, in guilte plate, K. 20 oz. di. qr.
To the Lord *Darcey*, in gilte plate, M. 20 oz. qr.
To the Lorde *Shandoyes*, in gilte plate, M. 20 oz. qr.
To the Lord *Compton*, in gilte plate, M. 19 oz. di. di. qr.
To the Lord *Norris*, in guilte plate, M. 19 oz. 3 qrs. di.
To the Lord *Lumley*, in guilte plate, K. 19 oz.
To the Lord *Wharton*, in guilte plate, K. 19 oz. 3 qrs.
To the Lord *Rich*, in gilte plate, K. 19 oz. di. qr.
To the Lord *Buckhurst*, in gilte plate, K. 13 oz.
To the Lorde *North*, in gilte plate, K. 20 oz. di.
To the Lorde *Seymer*, in gilte plate, M. 22 oz. 3 qr.

BARRONESSES.

To the Barrones *Burghley*, in gilte plate, K. 32 oz.
To the Barronesse *Hunsdon*, in gilte plate, M. and K. 29 oz. 3 qrs. di.
To the Barronesse *Howarde*, in gilte plate, M. and K. 25 oz. qr. di.
To the Barronesse *Cobham*, in gilte plate 52 oz.
To the Barronesse *Dakers*, in gilte plate, M. 20 oz. 3 qrs.
To the Barronesse *Lumley*, in gilte plate, K. 20 oz. di. qr.
To the Barronesse *Shandoyes Knolls*, in gilte plate, K. 18 oz. qr. di.
To the Barronesse *Shandoys*, in gilte plate, K. 18 oz. di. di. qr.
To the Barronesse *St. John Bletzo*, in gilte plate, K. 19 oz.
To the Barronesse *Pagett Cary*, in gilte plate, K. 23 oz. di. di. qr.

To the Barronesse *Dudley*, in guilte plate, K. 17 oz. qr.
To the Barronesse *Cheyny*, in guilte plate, M. 35 oz. 3 qrs.
To the Barronesse *Wharton*, in gilte plate, K. 20 oz.
To the Barrones *Buckhurste*, in gilte plate, K. 11 oz. qr.
To the Barrones *Barkeley*, in guilte plate, K. 20 oz. qr. di.
To the Barrones *Talbott*, widdow, in gilte plate, M. 15 oz. qr.
To the Barrones *Norris*, in gilte plate, M. 20 oz. qr.
To the Barrones *Rich*, widdowe, in gilte plate, K. 20 oz. di. qr.
To the Barrones *Rich*, in gilte plate, K. 16 oz.
To the Barrones *Sheffeild*, in gilte plate, M. 21 oz. di.

LADIES.

To the Lady *Mary Seymer*, wife to Mr. Rogers, in gilte plate, K. 12 oz. di.
To the Lady *Elizabeth Seymer*, wife to Sir Richard Knightely, in gilte plate, M. 13 oz. di.
To the Lady *Katheryn Constable*, in guilte plate, K. 14 oz. 3 qrs.
To the Lady *Stafford*, in gilte plate, M. 30 oz. qr.
To the Lady *Walsingham*, in guilt plate, K. 20 oz.
To the Lady *Hennage*, in guilt plate, M. 22 oz. di. qr.
To the Lady *Carowe*, in guilt plate, M. and K. 34 oz. di.
To the Lady *Cheake*, in guilte plate, K. 27 oz.
To the Lady *Drury*, in guilte plate, M. 17 oz. 3 qrs. di.
To the Lady *Leyton*, in guilt plate, K. 20 oz.
To the Lady *Southwell*, in gilte plate, M. 16 oz. di.
To the Lady *Pawlett*, in guilt plate, K. 11 oz. 3 qrs.
To the Lady *Jarrett*, in guilt plate, K. 19 oz.
To the Lady *Digby*, in guilt plate, K. 15 oz. 3 qrs. di.
To the Lady *Willoughby*, Sir Frauncis his wife, in gilt plate, K. 13 oz.
To the Lady *Scroupe*, in gilte plate, K. 16 oz.
To the Lady *Gresham*, in gilte plate, M. 18 oz. 3 qrs. di.
To the Lady *Ratcliff*, in gilte plate, K. 14 oz. di. di. qr.
To the Lady *Souche*, in gilte plate, K. 10 oz.
To the Lady *West*, in guilt plate, M. 17 oz. di. di. qr.
To the Lady *Longe*, in guilt plate, M. 15 oz.
To the Lady *Harrington*, in guilt plate, M. 20 oz.
To the Lady *Townesend*, in guilt plate, M. 16 oz. di. qr.

KNIGHTES.

To Sir *Frauncis Knolls*, Treasurour of the Houshold, in guilte plate, K. 24 oz. di. di. qr.

To Sir *James Crosse*, Comptroller of the same, in guilt plate, K. 24 oz.

To Sir *Frauncis Walsingham*, Principal Secretary, in guilte plate, K. 60 oz. di. qr.

To Sir *Thomas Hennage*, Vice-chamberleyne, in guilt plate, M. 50 oz. di.

To Sir *Walter Mildemay*, Chancellor of thexchequer, in guilt plate, K. 28 oz.

To Sir *Gilbert Jarrett*, Master of the Rowles, in guilt plate, K. 29 oz. di.

To Sir *Owen Hopton*, Lievtenante of the Tower, in guilt plate, M. 23 oz.

To Sir *Thomas Leyton*, Capteine of Garnesey, in guilt plate, K. 30 oz. di.

To Sir *Henry Crumwell*, in guilt plate, M. 20 oz.

To Sir *Edward Cleare*, in guilt plate, M. 19 oz. 3 qrs. di.

To Sir *Thomas Cecill*, in guilt plate M. 30 oz. qr. di.

To Sir *George Cary*, in guilt plate, M. 28 oz. 3 qrs. di.

To Sir *Robert Southwell*, in guilt plate, K. 15 oz. di.

To Sir *John Parrett*, in gilte plate, M. 20. di. di. qr. qr.

To Sir *Robert Sydney*, in guilt plate, K. 23 oz. qr.

To Sir *Oratio Paulavizino*, in guilte plate, K. 23 oz. di. di. qr.

To *John Thorneburrowe*, Clarck of the Closett, in guilte plate, M. 17 oz. di. qr.

GENTLEWOMEN.

To Mrs. *Blanch Aparry*, in guilte plate, M. 17 oz. di.

To Mr. *Mary Ratcliff*, in guilte plate, M. 18 oz. di.

To Mrs. *Frauncis Howard*, in guilt plate, K. 15 oz. di. qr.

To Mrs. *Elizabeth Brooke*, in guilte plate, K. 16 oz. di. qr.

To Mrs. *Elizabeth Throgmorton*, in guilt plate, K. 15 oz. 3 qrs.

To Mrs. *Edmounds*, in guilt plate, K. 15 oz.

To Mrs. *Scudeamour*, in guilt plate, K. 17 oz. di. qr.

To Mrs. *Wolley*, in guilt plate, M. 19 oz. 3 qrs. di.

To Mrs. *Newton*, in guilt plate, K. 16 oz.

To Mrs. *Allom*, in guilte plate, K. 14 oz. 3 qrs. di.

To Mrs. *Dale*, in guilt plate, M. 22 oz.

To Mrs. *Sackford*, in guilte plate, K. 22 oz.

To Mrs. *Winckfield*, in guilt plate, M. 10 oz.

To Mrs. *Carre*, in guilt plate, K. 15 oz.
To Mrs. *Jane Brissells*, in guilt plate, K. 15 oz. di. di. qr.
To Mrs. *Vaughan*, in guilt plate, K. 14 oz. 3 qrs.
To Mrs. *Smithson*, in guilt plate, M. 7 oz.
To Mrs. *Twist*, in guilt plate, K. 7 oz. di.
To Mrs. *Cromer*, in guilt plate, K. 15 oz. di. qr.
To Mrs. *Fyfeyld*, in guilt plate, M. 10 oz.
To Mrs. *Huggens*, in guilt plate, K. 15 oz.
To Mrs. *Over*, in guilt plate, M. 9 oz. 3 qrs.
To Mrs. *Jones*, in guilt plate, K. 10 oz.
To Mrs. *Robinson*, in guilt plate, K. 4 oz. di. di. qr.
To Mrs. *Barley*, in guilt plate, M. 12 oz.
To Mrs. *Morgan*, in guilt plate, K. 5 oz.
To Mrs. *Tomyson*, in guilt plate, K. 4 oz.
To Mrs. *West*, in guilt plate, K. 10 oz.
To Mrs. *Bonne*, in guilt plate, K. 10 oz. 3 qrs. di.

Maides of Honor.

To Mrs. *Katheryn Howard*, in guilt plate, K. 10 oz. qr.
To Mrs. *Ann Hopton*, in guilt plate, K. 10 oz. qr. di.
To Mrs. *Trentham*, in guilt plate, M. 10 oz. qr.
To Mrs. *Elizabeth Mackwilliams*, in guilt plate, K. 10 oz. di. qr.
To Mrs. *Southwell*, in guilt plate, K. 10 oz. di. qr.
To Mrs. *Cavendish*, in guilte plate, K. per oz. 10 oz.
To Mrs. *Jones*, Mother of the Maides, in guilte plate, K. 12 oz.

Gentlemen.

To Mr. *Wolley*, one of her Majesty's Secretaries, in guilt plate, M. 25 oz. di. r.
To Mr. *Dyer*, in guilte plate, M. 13 oz.
To Mr. *Bruncker*, in gilte plate, M. 19 oz. 3 qrs. di.
To Mr. *Smith Customer*, in guilte plate, K. 14 oz. di. di. qr.
To Mr. *Garter King of Armes*, in guilt plate, K. 9 oz. qr.
To Mr. *Newton*, in guilte plate, K. 15 oz. qr.
To Mr. *Henry Brooke*, in guilte plate, K. 20 oz.
To a Gentleman unknown, in guilte plate, M. 12 oz. di.

NEW YEAR'S GIFTS PRESENTED BY THE QUEEN, 1588-9.

To Mr. *Stanhopp*, in gilte plate, M. 14 oz. qr. di.
To Mr. *Skudeamour*, in guilte plate, K. 18 oz. qr.
To Mr. Doctor *Bayless*, in gilte plate, K. 14 oz. 3 qrs.
To Mr. Doctor *Gyfford*, in gilte plate, M. 14 oz. qr.
To Mr. Doctor *Lopus*, in gilte plate, M. 18 oz. di. di. qr.
To Mr. *William Huggens*, in guilte plate, K. 15 oz.
To Mr. *Fynes*, in gilte plate, M. 21 oz. di.
To Mr. *Spillman*, in gilte plate, M. 10 oz. qr.
To Mr. *Mountaghu*, in gilte plate, K. 14 oz.
To Mr. *Huishe*, in guilte plate, M. 13 oz.
To Mr. Capteine *Crosse*, in guilte plate, M. 18 oz. di. di. qr.
To Mr. *Dunston Amis*, in gilte plate, M. 16 oz.
To Mr. *Carr*, in guilte plate, M. 14 oz. qr. di.
To Mr. *Smithson*, in gilte plate, M. 8 oz.
To Mr. *Dudley*, in gilte plate, M 6 oz.

FREE GUIFTS.

To Mr. *John Asteley*, Esquier, Master and Tresorer of her Majesty's Jewells and Plate, in guilte plate, M. 18 oz. 3 qrs. di.

To Mr. *Thomas Gorges*, one of the Groomes of her Highnes Pryvie Chamber, in gilte plate, M. 9 oz.

To Mr. *Thomas Asteley*, Esquier, also Groome of the said Chamber, in gilte plate, M. 9 oz.

To Mr. *Henry Sackford*, also Groome, in gilte plate, K. 9 oz.
To Mr. *Baptest*, also Groome, in gilte plate, M. 9 oz.
To Mr. *Edward Cary*, also Groome, in gilte plate, M. 9 oz.
To Mr. *Middlemour*, also Groome, in gilte plate, M. 9 oz.
To Mr. *Killygrey*, also Groome, in gilte plate, K. 9 oz.
To Mr. *Knevett*, also Groome, in gilte plate, K. 9 oz.
To Mr. *Darsey*, also Groome, in gilte plate, M. 9 oz.
To Mr. *Edward Denny*, also Groome, in gilte plate, M. 9 oz.
To Mr. *Stanhopp*, also Groome, in gilte plate, M. 9 oz.
To Mr. *Ferdynando Richardson*, also Groome, in gilt plate, M. 8 oz.
To *Humfrey Adderley*, Yeoman of the Roabes, in gilte plate, M. 12 oz.
To *Nicholas Bristowe*, Clerck of the Jewells, in guilte plate, M. 10 oz. 3 qrs. di.
To *John Pigeon*, Yeoman of the same office, in gilte plate, M. 10 oz. 3 qrs. di.

22   NEW YEAR'S GIFTS PRESENTED BY THE QUEEN, 1588-9.

To *Stephen Fulwell*, an other Yeoman of the same office, in guilte plate, M. 10 oz. 3 qrs. di.

To *Nicholas Pigeon*, Groome of the said office, in guilte plate, K. 10 oz. 3 qrs. di.

Summa totalis of all the plate gyven away, as aforesaid, amounteth to 4541 oz. 5 qrs. di.

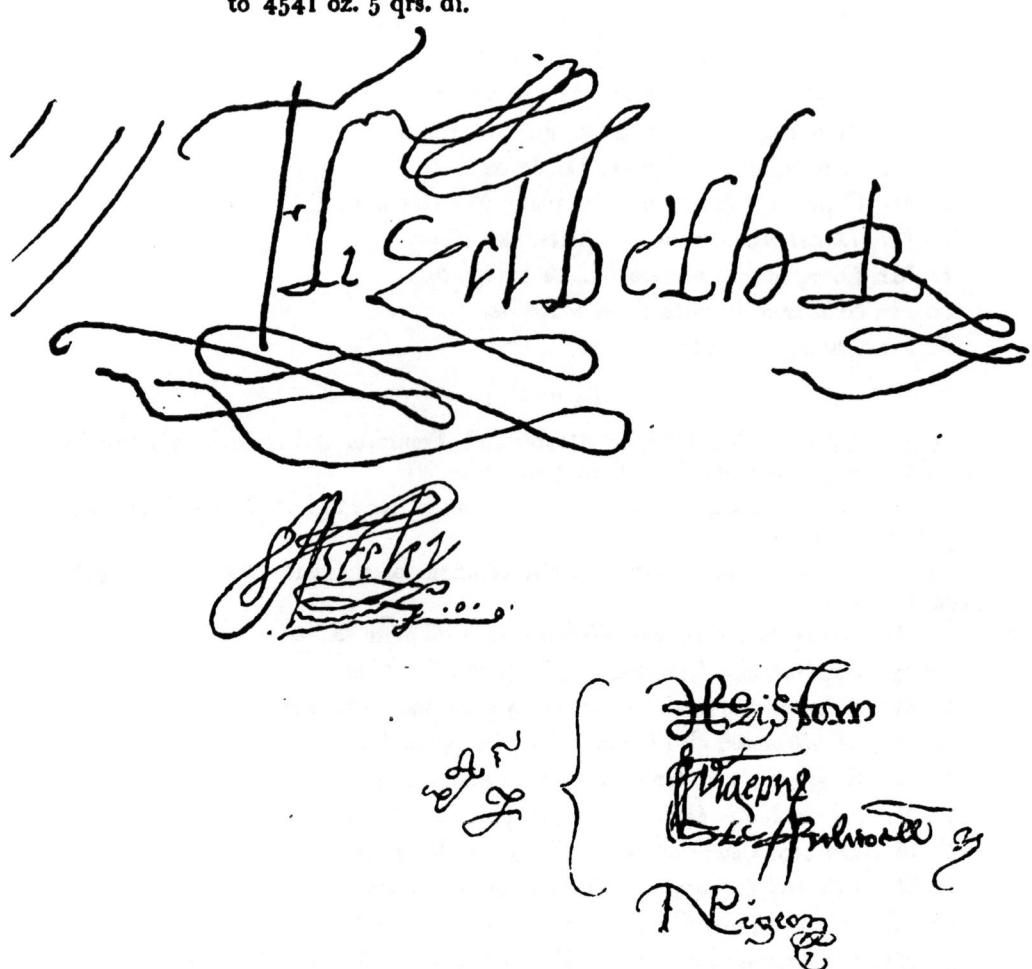

Guiftes given by her Majestie, and delyvered at sundry tymes, in maner and forme followinge, viz. that is to saye,

Gyven by her said Majestie, the 23d of Aprill, anno 30° Regine Elizabeth, &c. unto the Earle of *Ormound*, one George of gold, enamuled white, sett with foure rubyes and five oppalls, of the chardge of John Asteley, Esquier, Master and Treasorer of her Highnes Juells and Plate, per oz. 1 oz. 7 dwt. allo^r.

Item, more gyven to the said Earle, the daye and yeare aforesaid, one garter enamuled white, havinge on the buckell six diamounds and foure rubyes, and on the pendaunte foure diamounds and two rubyes, of the charge of the said John Asteley, per oz. 3 oz. 3 dwts. allo^r.

Item, given by her said Majestie, the daye and yeare above written, unto the Earle of *Essex*, one garter enamuled redd aud white, having one rock ruby with a pearle pendaunt, and seven small rubyes betwene the lres, of the chardge of the said John Asteley, per oz. 3 oz. di. allo^r.

Item, gyven by her said Majestie, the said 23d of Aprill, anno prædicto, unto Sir *Christofer Hatton*, Knighte, Lord Chauncellor of England[1], one George of gold, enamuled white, of the chardge as afore, per oz. 1 oz. 6 dwts. allo^r.

Item, more to him one garter of gold, enamuled white, having on the buckell foure diamounds, and one diamound on the pendaunt, of the chardge of the said John Asteley, per oz. 3 oz. 2 dwts. allo^r.

Item, gyven by her said Majestie, the thurd of June, anno prædicto, unto Sir *Martyn Shinke*, Knighte, parte of a chaine of gold received of Mr. William Killegrewe, of the goodnes of 21 karr. two graynes qr. of the said chardge, per oz. 110 oz. 3 qrs. allo^r.

Item, gyven by her said Majestie, the 11th of June, anno prædicto, unto Mr. *George* ......, servaunte to the Kinge of Denmark, parte of a chaine of gold, received of Mr. Thomas Knyvett, of the goodnes of 21 karr. foure graynes, of the chardge of the said John Asteley, per oz. 10 oz. allo^r.

Item, gyven by her said Majestie, the 25th of September, anno prædicto, at the christening of Sir *Richard Knightley* his sonne, one cupp of silver gilte, bought of Mr. Alderman Martyn, per oz. 23 oz. 3 qrs.

Item, gyven by her said Majestie, the 22d of October, at the marriadge of the Lady *Digby* to Mr. Edward Cordall, one gilte cupp with a cover, bought of the said Alderman, per oz. 60 oz. di. qr.

Item, gyven by her said Majestie, the 27th of October, anno prædicto, at the christeninge of the Earle of *Ormound* his daughter, one bason and ewer gilte, per oz. 119 oz. 3 qrs. di. and one peice of gilte stoopes, per oz. 136 oz. qr. boughte of the said Alderman Martyn, per oz. all, 256 oz. di. qr.

Item, gyven by her said Majestie, the 26th of November, anno 31° Reginæ

---

[1] He was appointed Lord Chancellor April 29, 1587; and held it till May 1592.

Elizabeth, at the christening of the Lord *Rich* his child, one bowle with a cover of silver gilte, boughte of the said Alderman Martyn, per oz. 51 oz. 3 qrs.

Item, gyven by her said Majestie, the thurd of December, anno prædicto, unto Mr. *Jacob Rastropp*, of Juteland, sent from the Kinge of Denmark, parte of a chaine of gold, received of the said Thomas Knyvett, of the chardge aforesaid, per oz. 34 oz. allo^r.

Item, more gyven by her said Majestie, and delivered the thurd of March, anno prædicto, one chaine of gold, unto *Mushac Reyes*, Ambassador from the King of *Hesse*, boughte of the said Alderman, per oz. 45 oz. qr. 1 dwt. and 6 grains.

Item, delivered by her Majestie's comaundment, signified by the Lady Cobham, unto *John Spilman*, Jeweller, by him to be made into buttons for her Majestie's use, two collars of esses and knotts of gold, with two greate roses enamuled in the middest of them, being of the chardge of the said John Asteley, per oz. altogether 71 oz. 3 qrs.

At the bottom of the preceding Roll the following Articles are annexed on a separate piece of vellum.

Anno 31° Reginæ Elizabethæ, &c.

By *Morgan*, the apothecary, a box of wood with prunolyn.

By *Hemyngewaye*, the apothecary, a pott of preserved peares, and a box of manus Christi.

Delivered to Mrs. *Skidmore*.

By *Jaromy*, 24 drinkinge glasses.

By *Petruchio Ubaldino*, a booke covered with vellam of Italian.

Delivered to Mr. *Baptist*.

Ry *Ambrosio Lupo*, a glasse of sweete water.
Delivered to Mrs. *Carre*.

By *Innocent Comy*, a boxe of lute stringes.
Delivered to Mrs. *Richardson*.

By *Jeromy Bassano*, two drinkinge glasses.
Delivered to Mr. *Baptist*.

By *Petro Lupo*, a peire of sweete gloves.

By *Josepho Lupo*, a peire of sweete gloves.

By *Cæsar Caliardo*, a peire of sweete gloves.
Delivered to Mrs. *Carre*.

To *Morgan*, the apothecary, in gilte plate, K. 6 oz. di.

To *Hemingwaye*, the apothecary, in gilte plate, M. 7 oz.

To *Jaromyn*, in gilte plate, K. 5 oz. di. qr.
To *Petruchio Ubaldino*, in gilte plate, K. 5 oz. di.
To *Ambrosio Lupo*, in gilte plate, K. 5 oz. di.
To *Innocente Comy*, in gilte plate, K. 5 oz. di.
To *Jeromy Bassano*, in gilte plate, K. 5 oz. di.
To *Petro Lupo*, in gilte plate, K. 5 oz. di.
To *Josepho Lupo*, in gilte plate, K. 5 oz. di.
To *Cæsar Caliardo*, in gilte plate, K. 5 oz. di.

Summa totalis of the plate gyven as aforesaide cometh to—62 oz. di. qr.

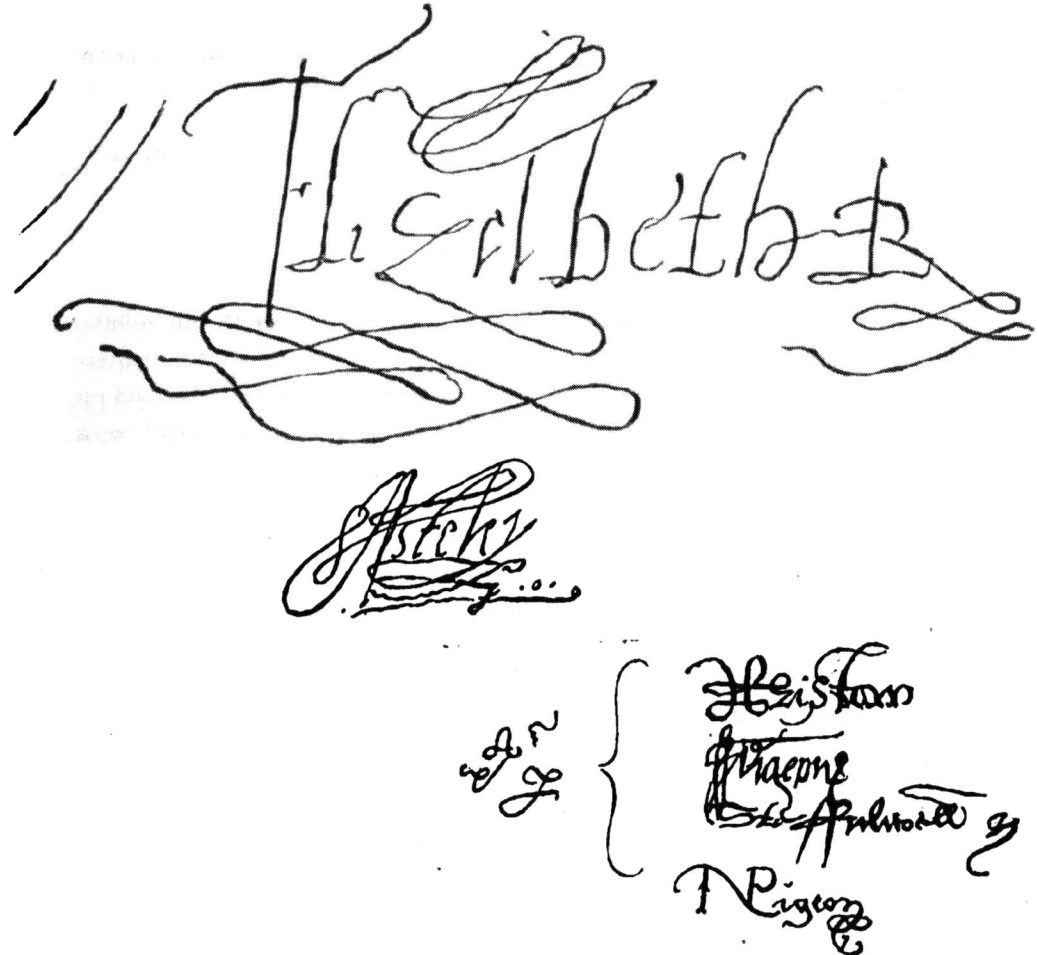

Anno 31° Elizabethæ *Reginæ*.
Plate geven at Newyeres-tide.

Item, two candlestycks of crystall, garnished with sylver guilt, paynted; all together, 91 oz.

Item, a porynger of golde, with a cover. 24 oz.

Item, one very smaull saulte of agathe, with a cover and garnyture of golde enamyoled, garnished with smaull sparcks of rubyes, and the cover garnished with smaull sparcks of rubyes and opaulls. 1 oz. 3 q^a.

Item, one smaull coup, the bolle, foote, and parte of the cover of agatt, garnished with golde, and set with smaull perls, rubyes, and lyttle opaulls, enamelled, 5 oz. dim̃. q^a.

Receyved of Sir Thomas Gorge, Knighte, Gentleman of her Majesties Warderobe of Robes, one bason and a laier of silver guilt, faire wroughte, the backeside of the said bason and the foote of the laier being white, to be guilded. 167 oz.

Ex^r p N. Bristow.

The following Letter may be deemed interesting:

" By the Mayor.

" To the Master and Wardens of the Companye of Stationers.

" Where the Quenc's most excellente Majestie intendith in her Royall psonne to repaire to her Princelie Palace of Whitehall, on Thursdaie next, in thafternoone; and for that I and my bretheren thaldermen are commanded to attend on her Majesties psonne from Chelsey to the Whitehall: Theis therefore shall be in her Majestie's name to require you, that yourselfes, with sixe of the comliest psonages of your said Companye, be redie at the Parke Corner above Sainte James, on horseback, apparelled in velvette coats, with chaynes of gould, on Thursdaie, by twoo of the clocke in thafternoone, to wayte upon me and my bretheren the aldermen to Chelsey, for the recreating of her Majestie accordinglie. And also, that you provide sixe staffe torches lighth if need shall be required. Not failinge hereof, as you will answere the contrarie at your perill. From the Guyldhall, this 28th of Januarie, 1588-9. SEBRIGHTE [1]."

The 30th of January 1588-9, the Queenes Majestie came from Richmond to Chelsey, and so to Westminster; and was received by the Mayor, Aldermen, and Commoners of her Cittie of London, in coates of velvet, and chaines of golde, all on horsebacke, with the Captaines of the Cittie, to the number of fortie, betwixt

---

[1] From the Records of the Stationers' Company, vol. A. p. 56.

five and six of the clock by torch-light.—On this occasion the bells at Lambeth were rung; and again, when the Queen went to my Lord of Warwick's[1], and returned thence to Lambeth.

On the 4th of February, " the Queen went from Whitehall to the College Church[2], and so to the Parliament-house;" on which occasion the bells at Margaret's, Westminster, rang a merry peal.

About this time the Lord Treasurer Burleigh met with the severest stroke in his family that he had ever yet felt, by the death of his beloved wife, April 4, 1589, after they had lived together in the sincerest harmony and affection for three-and-forty years. She is allowed to have been one of the most extraordinary women of her time, in point of piety, learning, and prudence, of which posterity has received many, and those too unexceptionable, testimonies. The loss of her affected the Treasurer to a great degree, as appears plainly by many of his writings, and made a great alteration in his temper; so that, notwithstanding the death of some whom he took to be his adversaries, by which undoubtedly his authority was augmented, and the promotion of his son Robert, who grew daily more and more into the Queen's favour, he became very thoughtful and melancholy, and about two years after, was very earnest and solicitous for leave to quit his employments, that he might spend the remainder of his days in quiet. But the Queen, who saw no decay in his abilities, and who willingly granted all the indulgences possible to his infirmities, would by no means consent to that; on the contrary, as she had formerly rallied him out of a design of the same kind, so she had recourse again to the like method, and, by a paper written with great wit and spirit, diverted him absolutely from this serious purpose[3].

The Earl of Derby, in a Letter to the Earl of Shrewsbury, dated " Channon Row, May 21, 1589," says, " Sir George Carye[4] goeth presently Ambassadour to the Scotyshe King."

On the 26th of May the bells at Lambeth were rung, when the Queen, attended by her whole Court, went from Whitehall to Mr. Secretary Walsingham's

---

[1] This was probably at Chelsea, where the Earl of Warwick had then a house. His Lordship died soon after. See hereafter, p. 39.   [2] The Collegiate Church of St. Peter in Westminster.

[3] See before, in vol. II. pp. 400, 521; and hereafter, under the year 1593.

[4] Eldest son and heir of Henry the first Lord Hunsdon. On the death of his father, July 23, 1596, he became second Lord Hunsdon; but died without issue in 1603, and was succeeded by his brother John, who died in 1617.—Robert Cary, afterwards Lord Lepington and Earl of Monmouth, was the fourth and youngest son of the first Lord Hunsdon.

at Barn-elms; and again, on the 28th, on her return from Barn-elms to Whitehall. This Visit is also recorded by a payment to the Ringers at Fulham.

Lord Talbot, in a Letter dated May 22, to his Father the Earl of Shrewsbury, says, " This daye her Majestie goethe to Barn-ellmes [1], where she is purposed to tarry all day to morrow, being Tewsday, and on Wednesday to return to Whytehall agayne. I am appoynted, among the rest, to attende her Majestie to Barn-ellmes. I pray God my diligent attendance there may procure me a gracious answere in my suite at her return; for, whilst she is there, nothing may be moved but matter of delyghte and to content her, which is the only cause of her going thither."

Sir Francis died in 1590, at his house in Seething Lane, so poor, it is said, that his friends were obliged to bury him late at night, in the most private manner, in St. Paul's Cathedral; in confirmation of which fact, no Certificate of his funeral appears to have been entered at the Heralds' College, as was usual when any person of consequence was interred suitable to his rank.—" There is no tomb or any other monument," says Stow [2], but only this inscription:

" Virtuti & Honori sacrum.

" *Franciscus Walsinghamus*, ortus Familiâ multis seculis illustri, Claritatem Generis, Nobilitate Ingenii præstantibusque Animi Dotibus superavit. Puer, ingenuè domi educatus, generosis Moribus Artibusque optimis Animum excoluit. Adolescens, peregrinatus in exteras Regiones, earum Instituta, Linguas, Politiam,

---

[1] Previously to this Visit, the Queen had taken a lease of the manor of Barn-elms, which was to commence in 1600 after the expiration of Sir Henry Wyatt's. Her interest in this lease she granted by letters patent, bearing date in 1577, to Sir Francis Walsingham and his heirs. On New-year's day 1575-6, " Mr. Secretary Walsingham" presented to the Queen " a collar of gold, being two serpents, the heads being ophal a pyramid of sparks of dyamonds; in the top thereof a strawberry wih a rock ruby; weight $5\frac{3}{4}$ ounces."—In 1577-8, Sir Francis presented " a gown of blue satin, with rows of gold; and two small perfume boxes, of Venice gold, faced with powdered armyns;" and Lady Walsingham gave " two pillow-biers of cambrick, wrought with silk of divers colours, cut." Sir Francis had, in return, $60\frac{1}{2}$ ounces of gilt plate; his Lady $16\frac{1}{4}$ ounces. In the next year Sir Francis gave " a night-gown of tawny satin, all over embroidered, faced with satin like hearecolour;" and his Lady gave " a paire of gloves, with buttons of gold." In return, Sir Francis had three gilt bowls, weighing $59\frac{3}{4}$ ounces; his Lady $16\frac{1}{2}$ ounces of gilt plate. In 1580-1 Lady Walsingham gave " a jewel of gold, being a scorpion of agatha, garnished with small sparks of rubies and diamonds."—Sir Francis and his Lady each presented New-year's Gifts to the Queen in 1588-9, and received each a present of plate in return. See before, pp. 8, 9, 18, 19.

[2] Survey of London, 4to, ed. 1617, p. 1632.

ad civilem Scientiam, Reique publicæ usum didicit. Juvenis, Exilium, *Mariâ* regnante, subiit voluntarium Religionis ergò. Serenissimæ Reginæ *Elizabethæ*, maturâ jam ætate, Orator fuit apud *Gallum*, turbulentissimo tempore, annis compluribus: rursùm bis in *Galliam*, semel in *Scotiam*, semel in *Belgiam*, super gravissimis Principis Negotiis Legatione functus est; eique annis sedecim ab intimis Conciliis & Secretis fuit, ac triennium Cancellarius Ducatûs *Lancastriæ*. Quibus in Muneribus tanta cum Prudentiâ, Abstinentiâ, Munificentiâ, Moderatione, Pietate, Industriâ, & Solicitudine versatus est, ut a multis Periculis Patriam liberârit, servârit Rempublicam, confirmârit Pacem, juvare cunctos studuerit, imprimis quos Doctrina aut bellica Virtus commendârit, seipsum denique neglexerit, quo prodesset aliis, eosque Valetudinis & Facultatum suarum dispendio sublevaret.

" In matrimonio habuit lectissimam Feminam *Ursulam*, è Stirpe *S. Barborum*, antiquæ nobilitatis: è quâ unicam Filiam suscepit, *Franciscam*, *Philippo Sydneio* primùm nuptam; deinde honoratissimo Comiti *Essexiæ*.

Obiit Apr. 6, an. 1590."

"These Verses called Acrosticks (Stow adds) are also there hanged up:"

S hall Honour, Fame, and Titles of Renowne,
  I n Clods of Clay be thus inclosed still?
R ather will I, though wiser Wits may frowne,
  F or to inlarge his Fame extend my Skill.
R ight, gentle Reader, be it knowne to thee,
  A famous Knight doth here interred lye,
N oble by Birth, renown'd for Policie,
  C onfounding Foes, which wrought our Jeopardy.
I n Forraine Countries their Intents he knew,
  S uch was his zeal to do his Country good,
W hen Dangers would by Enemies ensue,
  A s well as they themselves, he understood.
L aunch forth, ye Muses, into Streames of Praise,
  S ing, and sound forth Praise-worthy Harmony;
I n *England* Death cut off his dismall Dayes,
  N ot wrong'd by Death, but by false Trechery.
G rudge not at this unperfect Epitaph;
  H erein I have exprest my simple Skill,
A s the First-fruits proceeding from a Graffe:
  M ake then a better whosoever will.

Disce quid es, quid eris;
Memor esto quod morieris.   E. W."

On the 11th of June the bells at St. Margaret's, Westminster, were rung, when the Queen came from Highgate to Whitehall; and again on the 18th, when she went from Whitehall to Oatlands.

It does not appear to whom the Royal Visit at Highgate was paid; but it was probably at the house thus described by Norden in 1593: "Upon the hill (speaking of Highgate) is a most pleasant dwelling, yet not so pleasant as healthful; for the expert inhabitants there report, that divers who have been long visited with sickness, not curable by physicke, have in a short time repayred their health, by that sweet salutarie aire." And he adds, "At this place —— Cornwalleys, Esquire, hath a very faire house from which he may beholde the statelie Citie of London, Westminster, Greenwich, the famous river of Thamyse, and the country towards the South, verie farre." This Mr. Cornwallis was *Richard*, third son of Sir John Cornwallis (who died in 1544), and father of Sir Thomas Cornwallis, Groom-porter to Queen Elizabeth and King James (who died Nov. 18, 1618, and was buried at Portchester in Hampshire).

Sir William Drury [1], who in 1578 had the honour of entertaining the Queen at Hawsted in Suffolk (see vol. II. p. 119.) was elected one of the Knights of the Shire in 1585; and in 1589 killed in a duel in France. His corpse was brought into England, and interred in the chancel of Hawsted Church, where his memory is preserved by a noble mural monument, consisting of a basement, on which is a sarcophagus of black marble, beneath a double arch, supported by Corinthian pillars. Over the arch, in an oval frame, is a most spirited bust in armour, large as life. The warlike implements on the arch, and the rest of the ornaments, are all in a good taste. This is a performance of Nicholas Stone [2], who received for it £.140 [3].

[1] Sir William Drury, Knight, a most able Commander in the Irish wars, who unfortunately fell in a duel with Sir John Burroughs, in a foolish quarrel about precedency. See Kennett's History, vol. II. p. 449. 457. 473. 557; Pennant's London, 4to, p. 144; and Banks's Extinct Peerage, vol. II. p. 67.

[2] The monument of Mr. Thomas Sutton, the noble founder of the Charter-house, was the work of Nicholas Stone, who (including a little monument to Mr. Law, one of Mr. Sutton's executors, in the same Chapel) had £400 for his performance. Pennant's London, 4to, p. 190. T. G. C.

[3] Anecdotes of Painting in England, vol. II. p. 28; and 4to ed. 1798, vol. III. p. 168.

The oval frame which surrounds the bust is thus inscribed:

MEMORIÆ GULIEL: DRURII EQUIT: AUR:
QUI TRIBUNUS MILITUM OBIIT IN
GALLIA ANNO DOMINI 1589.
HOC MONUMENTUM FIERI JUSSIT
ROBERTUS DRURIUS FIL. EQUES AUR:
UXOR FACIENDUM CURAVIT.

Riot at Bartholomew Fair, 1589.

"In 1589," says Stow, "certain of those furious undaunted spirits" (the Sailors and Soldiers who have been employed by Drake and Norris), "after they had performed many unrulie prankes, in divers shires, began to plot how they might atchieve some speciall act, to relieve their present want, and in the end concluded to surprise Bartholomew Fayre[1], and to that purpose five hundred of them were assembled about Westminster; the Lord Maior having knowledge thereof, uppon the sudden raysed almost two thousand men very well appoynted, and about tenne a clocke at night they marched as farre as Temple Barre, to repulse that rowt; and then the Lord Treasurer sent word by the Chamberlaine of London, that the rabble was dispearst and gone, and then the Citizens returned."

[1] " It is worthy of observation, that every year upon St. Bartholomew's day, when the fair is held, it is usual for the Mayor, attended by the 12 principal Aldermen, to walk in a neighbouring field, dressed in his scarlet gown, and about his neck a chain, to which is hung a Golden Fleece[*], and besides, that particular[†] ornament which distinguishes the most noble Order of the Garter. During the year of his magistracy, he is obliged to live so magnificently, that Foreigner or Native, without any expence, is free, if he can find a chair empty, to dine at his table, where there is always the greatest plenty. When the Mayor goes out of the precincts of the City, a scepter, a sword, and a cap, are borne before him; and he is followed by the principal Aldermen in scarlet gowns, with gold chains, himself and they on horseback: upon their arrival at a place appointed for that purpose, where a tent is pitched, the mob begin to wrestle before them, two at a time; the conquerors receive rewards from the Magistrates. After this is over, a parcel of live rabbits are turned loose among the crowd, which are pursued by a number of boys, who endeavour to catch them, with all the noise they can make. While we were at this shew, one of our company, Tobias Salander, Doctor of Physic, had his pocket picked of his purse, with nine crowns *du soleil*, which without doubt was so cleverly taken from him, by an Englishman who always kept very close to him, that the Doctor did not in the least perceive it." Hentzner.

[*] This probably alluded to the woollen manufacture; Stow mentions his riding through the Cloth Fair, on the Eve of St. Bartholomew, p. 651.
[†] The collar of SS.

On the 15th of November, the bells at St. Margaret's, Westminster, were rung, when the Queen went to Somerset House; and again when she went from Somerset House to Richmond; thence her Majesty came to Lambeth; then to Whitehall; and afterwards to Greenwich.

On the 22d of December, John Stanhope thus writes to Lord Talbot, from Richmond, " My Lo. the Q. is so well as I assure you six or seven gallyards in a mornynge, besydes musycke and syngynge, is her ordinary exercyse [1]."

Orders for Apparel in the several Inns of Court.

The Inner Temple.

In 38 Henry VIII. there was an Order made, that the Gentlemen of this Company should reform themselves in their cut or disguised apparel, and not to have long beards: and that the Treasurer of this Society should confer with the other Treasurers of Court, for an uniform reformation, and to know the Justices opinion therein, and thereupon to perform the same. Whereupon in their Parliament held 5 Maii, 1 and 2 Philip and Mary, there was a decree made that no Fellow of this House should wear his beard above three weeks growth upon pain of 20s. forfeiture.

And for their better regulation in apparel it was ordered, in 36 Eliz. (16 Junii), that if any Fellow in Commons, or lying in the House, did wear either hat, or cloak, in the Temple Church, Hall, Buttry, Kitchin, or at the Buttry-barr dresser, or in the Garden, he should forfeit for every such offence 6s. 8d. And in 42 Eliz. (8 Febr.) that they go not in cloaks, hatts, bootes, and spurrs, into the city, but when they ride out of the town.

So also, in 39 Eliz. (20 Dec.), that no Fellow of this House should come into the Hall with any weapons except his dagger, or his knife, upon pain of forfeiting the summ of five pounds.

[1] Lodge, vol. II. p. 411.

The Middle Temple.

In 4 and 5 Ph. and M. it was ordered, that none of this Society should thenceforth wear any great bryches in their hoses, made after the Dutch, Spanish, or Almon fashion; or lawnd upon their capps; or cut doublets; upon pain of 3s. 4d. forfeiture for the first default, and the second time to be expelled the House. And in 26 Eliz. there was this establishment here made, for reformation in apparel:

1. That no great ruff should be worn.
2. Nor any white colour in doublets or hosen.
3. Nor any facing of velvet in gowns, but by such as were of the Bench.
4. That no Gentlemen should walk in the streets, in their cloaks, but in gowns.
5. That no hat, or long, or curl'd hair be worn.
6. Nor any gowns, but such as were of a sad colour.

In a subsequent page it is stated, that they have no order for their apparell, but every man may go as him listeth, so that his apparell pretend to no lightness, or wantonness in the wearer; for, even as his apparell doth shew him to be, even so shall he be esteemed among them. And their usage in time of Pestilence is thus stated.

If it happen that the Plague of *Pestilence* be any thing nigh their house, they immediately break up their house, and every man goeth home into his country, which is a great loss of Learning; for if they had some house nigh London to resort unto, they might as well exercise their Learning, as in the Temple, untill the Plague were ceased.

Lincoln's Inn.

For decency in apparell, at a Council held on the day of the Nativity of St. John Baptist, 23 H. VIII. it was ordered, that for a continual rule, to be thenceforth kept in this House, no Gentleman, being a Fellow of this House, should wear any cut or pansid hose, or bryches, or pansid doblet, upon pain of putting out of the House. Nay, so regular were they in those days in point of habit, that in 1 and 2 Ph. and M. one Mr. Wyde, of this House, was, by a special Order made upon Ascension-day, fined at five groats, for going in his study gown in Cheapside on a Sunday, about ten of the clock before noon, and in Westminster Hall in the Term time in the forenoon. And in 30 Eliz. they ordered, "That if any Fellow of this House should wear any hat in the Hall or Chappel; or go abroad to London or Westminster without a gown, he should be put out of Commons, and pay such a fine, before his re-admittance, as the Masters of the Bench then in Commons should assess." And likewise, " That if any Fellow of this House should wear long hair, or great ruffs, he should also be put out of Commons, and pay such a fine, before he were re-admitted, as the Masters of the Bench then in Commons should assess." So also, in 8 Elizabeth, " That if any Fellow of this House, being a Commoner or Repaster, should, within the precinct of this House, wear any cloak, boots and spurrs, or long hair, to pay for every offence 5s. for a fine, and also to be put out of Commons." And in 11 Car. I. it was also ordered, " That what Gentleman soever should come into the Hall at meal-time with any other upper garment than a gown, he should be suspended from being a Member of the Society."

Gray's Inn.

In 16 Eliz. 16 Junii, there was an Order made at a Pension then held, that every man of this Society should frame and reform himself for the manner of his apparel according to the Proclamation then last set forth; and within the time therein limited, else not to be accounted of this House. And that none of this Society should wear any gown, doublet, hose, or other outward garment of any light colour, upon penalty of expulsion. And within ten days following, it was also ordered, that none should wear any white doublet in the House after Michaelmass Term ensuing.

In 27 Eliz. (15 Nov.) it was farther ordered, that whosoever, being a Fellow of this House, did thenceforth wear any hat in the Hall, at dinner or supper time, he should forfeit for every time of such his offending 3s. 4d. to be cast into Commons at the next accompt, to the use of the House, without any remission.

So also, in 42 Eliz. (11 Febr.), that no Gentleman of this Society do come into the Hall, to any meal, with their hats, boots, or spurs; but with their caps, decently and orderly, according to the ancient orders of this House, upon pain for every offence to forfeit 3s. 4d. and for the third offence expulsion. Likewise, that no Gentleman of this Society do go into the City, or suburbs, or to walk in the fields, otherwise than in his gown, according to the ancient usage of the Gentlemen of the Inns of Court, upon penalty of 3s. 4d. for every offence; and for the third expulsion, and loss of his Chamber.

In 7 Jac. (27 Nov.) there was an Order made, that all the Gentlemen of this Society, except the Master of the Requests, and the King's Sollicitor, should thenceforth wear caps in the Hall, both in Term time and Vacation, in boots, upon penalty of 12*d.* for each default, and the Butlers to present such defaults. And in 8 Jac. (24 Oct.) that if any Gentleman of this Society should come into the Common Hall of this House, to breakfast, dinner, or supper, or to hear any exercise of Learning, being booted, that then he should be out of Commons *ipso facto*, and not to come into Commons again until they had done their Conges.

Again in 2 Car. I. here was a farther Order made (14 Junii), that every Gentleman of this Society should conform himself to wear a cap in the Hall at dinner and supper time, upon penalty of 12*d.* for every default, according to the ancient Orders of this House [1].

The diffusion of wealth, through the enlargement of commercial intercourse, was accompanied in London by its usual concomitant, luxury, and particularly in dress; so much so, indeed, that several sumptuary laws were at different times enacted to restrain the wear of costly and inordinate apparel, or at least to confine it to the superior ranks. Elizabeth, as well as her predecessors, had recourse to the same questionable policy: and though in a few respects she mitigated the severity of some former statutes, " her good Citizens" were not altogether satisfied with the partial relaxation that had been allowed them [2]. On the plea, therefore, of that decent order and conveniency that was by citizens, officers, and others, thought meet to be used and continued by those who, though they were not of substance and value answerable, by the rates limited by the Book of Subsidy, yet did hold place of such worshipful calling otherwise, as required some larger limitation than was generally prescribed by the Statute and Proclamation.

[1] Dugdale's Origines Juridiciales.
[2] On this subject, see before, in vol. II. p. 543.

The Reign of Queen Elizabeth seems a splendid epoch in the advancing growth of London; and notwithstanding the "dilapidating" Proclamations of the years 1580, 1593, and 1602, both the population and the buildings continued to keep pace with the extension of commerce, and the increase of the working classes, whose numbers had been greatly augmented by the multitudes redeemed by the Reformation from the idleness of the Cloister. The principal ground upon which Elizabeth and her Ministers had recourse to this restraining policy, was the danger of pestilence; and notwithstanding the continued injunctions for the "voiding of inmates" from the Capital, it is most certain, that if London was at any time "overthronged with inhabitants, it appears rather to have had its population decreased by pestilential diseases, than spread over a wider district by civic precaution." In despite, however, as well of plague as of proclamations, the suburbs were greatly extended before the end of Elizabeth's reign; and many of the large mansions of the Nobility and others within the city itself, which now began to be deserted for the more courtly air of Westminster, were either separated into divers tenements, or pulled down to make way for streets of houses[1].

No inconsiderable part of the increase of London in this reign must be attributed to the influx of Foreigners from the Low Countries, which the wise policy of Elizabeth led her to encourage for the advantage of trade, and the introduction of new branches of manufacture. Many hundreds also settled in London of those Protestants who had fled from different parts of France after the fatal Vespers of St. Bartholomew.

According to a Return made in 1580 by order of the Council, the number of resident Foreigners within the City and its Liberties was 6462. This return exhibited an increase of 3762 persons within the course of thirteen years, when a previous Survey had been made.

[1] The first of those Proclamations, dated July 7, 1580, which may serve as a specimen of the whole, may be seen in the "Beauties of England and Wales," vol. X. part II. pp. 50—52. It furnishes abundant evidence of the increase of the people; as an increase which all the authority of the Crown, strengthened as it was in the following century by Parliamentary Statutes, proved wholly inadequate to check. On the swearing in of the new Lord Mayor, Sir John Branch, in the Court of Exchequer in the October following, the Lord Treasurer Burleigh declared to him her Majesty's pleasure as to the course which the City should pursue in respect to the Proclamation; and in consequence of this, at the next Court held by the Mayor, several orders "For New Buildings," &c. were directed to be issued, which may be also seen in the volume above referred to, pp. 52—55.

Extracts from an old book (kept in the chest) in the Church of Chalk, a village situate about two miles from Gravesend, toward Rochester; 1590—1596.

1590. A Note what Cartes dyd . . . .
her Mātie from Greenwich [1] . . . .
this yeare, being in anno 1590 . . . .

Thomas Jennyvar. John Jessopp.

Note. That Robert Rowswelle's cart dyd carry a load of strawe from Chalke to Northefleit the same year, about Shrovetide.

Note. That John Jessopp did carry a load of straw more from the same place to Northfleit, being his owne strawe.

Note also. That George Colt pay'd a load of strawe the same tyme.

Note also. That Thomas Jennyvar carryed a load of strawe from Fylborowe barne in Chalke, the same tyme.

1591. Note. That Robt Rowswell and Henry Patson dyd carry this yeare, from hoell Brookes to Northefleit, two loades of elmnes tymbar, not pay'd for said.

1591. Note. That Robt Rowswell and Thomas Jennyvar dyd carrye the same yeare ij loades of wallnuttry from Chalke to Paynter's Key at Gravesend, not payd for.—Note. That year Robt Rowswell dyd sarve w^t his cart to remove her Mātie^s from Greenwiche to Nonsuche himself alone, and William Jeater and Henry Squiver sarved with one other cart the same tyme, beinge in the yeare of ōr Lord 1591.

---

[1] " A Purveyor having abused the County of Kent, upon her remove to Greenwich, a Countryman watching the time she went to walk, which was commonly early, and being wise enough to take his time when she stood unbent and quiet from the ordinary occasions she was taken up with, placing himself within the reach of her ear, did, after the fashion of his coat, cry aloud, 'Which is the Queen?' whereupon, as her manner was, she turned about towards him, and he continuing still his question, she herself answered, ' I am your Queen, what wouldst thou have with me?' ' You,' replied the fellow ' are one of the rarest women I ever saw, and can eat no more than my daughter Madge, who is thought the properest lass in our parish, though short of you, but the Queen Elizabeth I look for devours so many of my hens, ducks, and capons, as I am not able to live.' The Queen, auspicious to all suits made through the mediation of her comely shape, of which she held a high esteem after her looking-glasses (long laid by before her death) might have confuted her in any good opinion of her face, inquired who was the Purveyor, and, as the story went, suffered him to be hanged."

Osborn's Queen Elizabeth, pp. 373-4.

Note. That Robt Wetherlye and Weddowe Bettes dyd remove her M^{atie} from Greenwiche to Nonsuche, the 25th of Julye, in this year, being in anno 1592.

1593. Note. That Robt Wetherlye dyd carry tymbar from Intare, in Stòke, to Stoke mill, the 15th of Maye, for her Mãtie's ships in anno 1593.

And William Jeator bare halfe his chearge.

Note. That Henry Stephens and Richard Danne dyd sarve the same tyme as ys befor mensyoned, in anno 1593.

William Keynett and George Pattson found a cart to carry tymbar, the same tyme, the daye, and yeare aforesayd.

The 4th of October, 1594. Rychard Danne and John Englyshe dyd remove the Queen's Mãtie with their cartes from Greenwiche to Nonsuche.

The 17 of Decembar, 1594. Saunder Wetherlye and Henry Stephens dyd remove her Mãtie with ther cartes from Somsett howse to Greenwiche.

The 18th of Februarye, 1594. Richard Danne and John Jnglyshe 1 cart, weddowe Newman, John Dove, and William Mathewe, made one other carte, to remove her Mãtie from Greenwiche to Whyt-hall.

Coalles carryed for her Mãtie from Synnocke to Greenwiche in anno 1595.

John Dove carryed a load of hoopes the 9th of Feb$_r$uarye, 1595, for her M^{atie} from in payr wood at Gaddes Hill to Gravesend, and the said Dove had the Queen's pryce, and 2s. 6d. geven by the rest of the p̃ishe.

The 27th of August, 1596, Chalke and Denton dyd send 20s. to remove her Mãtie from Greenwiche to . . . . the said monij was dd to Robert Bowden, beinge then constable of the hondred of Shamell.

Ther was 10s. gathered in Chalke and Denton to hyer a carte to carrye a load of coales from Sennocke to Greenwiche, the Court then dyd lye ther, the 30th of August, in anno 1596.

Anno 32° *Regni Reginæ* ELIZABETHÆ.

Geven to her Majestye on Newyeare's daye, 1589-90.

One jugge of christall, garnished with silver guilte; in all, 19 oz.

DEATH OF AMBROSE DUDLEY, EARL OF WARWICK, 1589.

On the 21st of February, 1589-90, died Ambrose Earl of Warwick, third son of John Dudley, the attainted Duke of Northumberland, and elder brother of Robert Earl of Leicester [1].

[1] This Nobleman's history appears in the following epitaph, which is placed in our Lady's Chapel, adjoining to the Collegiate Church at Warwick, at the head of the monument of Richard Beauchamp:

"Heare under this tombe lieth the corps of the Lord Ambrose Duddely; who, after the decease of his elder brethren without issue, was sonne and heir to John Duke of Northumberlande, to whom Q. Elizabeth, in the first yeare of her reigne, gave the mannour of Kibworth Beauchamp in the county of Lyc', to be held by the service of being pantler to the kings and quenes of this realme at their coronations; which office and manor his said father and other his ancestors earles of War. helde. In the seconde yeare of her reigne the said quene gave him the office of mayster of the ordinaunce. In the 4th yeare of her sayd reigne she created him Baron Lisle and Earl of Warwick. In the same yeare she made him her livetenant generall in Normandy; and duringe the time of his service there he was chosen knt. of the noble order of the garter. In the twelveth yere of her reigne the said erle, and Edward l' Clinton, l. Admerall of England, were made Livetenantes generall joinctely and severally of her Ma'ties army in the North partes. In the thirtenth yeare of her reigne the sayd quene bestowed on him the office of chief butler of Englande; and in the xvth yeare of her reigne he was sworne of her prevye counsell. Who departinge this lief without issue the xxith day of February, 1589, at Bedford howse neare the City of London, from whence, as himself desired, his corps was conveyed, and interred in this place, neare his brother Robert e. of Ley, and others his noble ancestors; which was accomplished by his last and wel-beloved wiefe the lady Anne countes of Warr.; who, in further testimony of her faythful love towardes him, bestowed this monument as a remembrance of him."

The figure of Earl Ambrose is lying on a mat rolled up, and is in plated armour; his hair short and curled, and his beard long; at his feet a muzzled bear.

THE QUEEN AT HACKNEY, AND IN ELY PLACE, 1590.

Of the Queen's Visits in 1590 very little is recorded; but we find by the Churchwardens' Accompts of St. Margaret's, Westminster, that their bells were rung on the 28th of May, "when her Majesty removed from Hackney[1] to my Lord Chancellor's," Sir Christopher Hatton[2], at his then newly-erected mansion.

[1] It is not known to whom this Visit at Hackney was paid; but probably it was to Sir Richard Haywood, when he possessed the manor called "The King's Hold," which he had purchased in 1578 from the Lord Hunsdon.

[2] Fuller, in his "Worthies," in Northamptonshire, says, "Sir Christopher Hatton was born (I recollect at Holdenby) in this county, of a family rather ancient than wealthy, yet of no mean estate. He rather took a bait, then made a meal at the Inns of Court, whilst he studied the laws therein. He came afterwards to the Court in a mask, where the Queen first took notice of him, loving him well for his handsome dancing, better for his proper person, and best of all for his great abilities. His parts were far above his learning, which mutually so assisted each other, that no manifest want did appear; and the Queen at last preferred him Lord Chancellour of England. The Gown-men, grudging hereat, conceived his advancement their injury, that one not thoroughly bred to the laws should be preferred to the place. How could he cure diseases unacquainted with their causes; who might easily mistake the justice of the Common Law for rigour, not knowing the true reason thereof? Hereupon it was that some sullen Serjeants at the first refused to plead before him, until, partly by his power, but more by his prudence, he had convinced them of their errors, and his abilities. Indeed he had one Sir Richard Swale, Doctor of the Civil Laws (and that Law, some say, is very sufficient to dictate equity) his servant-friend, whose advice he followed in all matters of moment. A scandal is raised that he was Popishly affected; and I cannot blame the Romanists, if desirous to countenance their cause with so considerable a person. Yet most true it is, that his zeal for the discipline of the Church of England gave the first being and life to this report. One saith, that he was a meer Vegetable of the Court [*], that sprung up at night, and sunk again at his noon, though indeed he was of longer continuance. Yet it brake his heart, that the Queen (which seldom *gave boons*, and never *forgave due debts*) rigorously demanded the payment of some arrears, which Sir Christopher did not hope to have remitted, but did only desire to be forborn: failing herein in his expectation, it went to his heart, and cast him into a mortal disease. The Queen afterwards did endeavour what she could to recover him, bringing, as some say, cordial broths unto him with her own hands; but all would not do. Thus no pullies can draw up a heart once cast down, though a Queen herself set her hand thereunto. He dyed anno Domini 1591; and is buried, under a stately monument, in the quire of St. Paul's." Fuller's Worthies, vol. II. p. 165, edit. 1811.

Sir Christopher Hatton was a great favourite with Queen Elizabeth who, though averse to all marriage contracts, affected to be greatly struck by his superior personal accomplishments. Sir Christopher's

---

[*] Fragmenta Regalia, in his character.

Justs before the Queen *at the Tilt-yard,* 1590 [1].

The original occasion of these Yearly Triumphs in England is thus related in Segar's "Honors Military and Civil, 1602:"

"Here will we remember also (and I hope without envie so may) that these annuall exercises in Armes, solemnized the 17 day of November, were first begun

fine person and fine dancing were quite as attractive to Elizabeth as his intellectual endowments, which were by no means superficial. After having been for many years Vice-chamberlain to the Queen he was appointed Lord Chancellor April 19, 1587, and discharged his duty with great applause; his modesty, however, prompted by his good sense, never allowed him to act, on any occasion of moment, without the assistance of two able Lawyers.

The site of Hatton's house was that of the orchard and garden of Ely House; and there he died in 1598. By his interest with the Queen, he extorted from the Bishop, Dr. Richard Cox, the ground on which his house was built. The good Bishop for a long time resisted the insolent sacrilege; but the Female Head of the Church soon made him surrender, by the following letter, one of the many glorious privileges of the ever-glorious Reformation.

"Proud Prelate! you know what you was before I made you what you are now. If you do not immediately comply with my request, by God, I will unfrock you. Elizabeth."

What Bishop could resist a demand from so pious and so powerful a Queen? On the 20th of March 1576, the "proud Prelate" granted to Sir Christopher, the fine dancer, "the Gate-house of the Palace, except two rooms used as prisons for those who were arrested, or delivered in execution to the Bishop's Bailiff; and the lower rooms used for the Porter's-lodge; the first Court-yard within the Gate-house to the Long-gallery, dividing it from the second; the Stables there, the Long-gallery with the rooms above and below it, and some others; fourteen acres of land, and the keeping the gardens and orchards for twenty-one years, paying at Midsummer-day, a red rose for the Gate-house and Garden, and for the ground ten loads of hay and £10 *per annum*; the Bishop reserving to himself and his successors free access through the Gate-house, walking in the Garden, and to gather twenty bushels of roses yearly. Sir Christopher undertook to repair and make the Gate-house a convenient dwelling. The sequel of this nefarious transaction was calamitous to Hatton. He had incurred a large debt to the Queen, whose love of money exceeded her love of fine legs and fine dancing; when she demanded the payment, the Chancellor was unable to satisfy the demand. Elizabeth in her usual strains of impatience and insolence, it would seem, reproached her favourite debtor. This so affected him, that he shortly after died of a broken heart; and the avaricious Queen, as in other cases, most bitterly lamented the loss of so able a Judge and Councillor. Hatton House, since that time, has undergone various alterations, and has been devoted to sundry contradictory purposes. It was once a Dancing-academy, and afterwards a Printing-office. The back part of it has been formed into a Chapel, at first for a congregation of the New Jerusalem Church, or Swedenborgians; but it is at present (1822) used as the regular "Caledonian Church."

[1] It appears by Warton's notes on Milton, p. 593, that George Peele wrote "Polyhymnia, the Description of a *Tylt* before the Queen, 1590;" but of this I have not been able to obtain a copy.

and occasioned by the right vertuous and honourable Sir Henry Lee [1], Master of her Highnesse Armorie, and now deservingly Knight of the most Noble Order; who of his great zeale, and earnest desire to eternize the glory of her Majestie's Court, in the beginning of her happy reigne, voluntarily vowed (unlesse infirmity, age, or other accident, did impeach him) during his life, to

[1] This gallant Champion, who was then in his 60th yeare, was honoured in 1592 by a Visit from his Royal Mistress at his mansion in Quarendon, which will be noticed under that year.

In the mean time his personal history may here be gleaned, from the sadly-neglected memorials of antient heroism and worth in the Chapel of Quarendon, where other ancestors of the Earls of Litchfield and their successors in the family possessions, lie entombed.

Quarendon is situated in the nook or corner of a fine meadow in the Eastern part of the Vale of Aylesbury, about two miles and a half distant from that town on the North-west, and between the turnpike roads which respectively lead thence to Bicester and to Winslow. It is also more than two miles from Bierton, to which Vicarage Quarendon is stated by Ecton to be a Chapel of ease; and a small stipend is paid by the inhabitants of the parish of Quarendon to the Vicar of the mother Church.

The building has been suffered to fall into such a state of decay that Divine Service has ceased to be performed in it for several years: and at present it affords a melancholy object of contemplation, not merely from its dilapidated condition, but from the mutilation of some elegant monuments of the former Proprietors of the contiguous estate, which are allowed to moulder into dust, without the least attempt being made to preserve them from the injuries of the weather, and the complete destruction which awaits them when the remainder of the roof shall follow that portion of it which has already fallen down. Not a pane of glass remains in any of the windows; the roof of one half of the body of the Chapel, and a portion of the wall near the South-west corner, has fallen; all the pews and seats, as well as the reading-desk, pulpit, &c. are gone; part of the floor has been dug up, and a breach made in the wall between the body of the Chapel and the small Chancel at its East end. Two octagon pillars on each side, which support the arches that separate the ailes, are, however, still in good preservation, and the outer walls are strong. The roof which remains having lost many of the tiles with which it was formerly covered, is decaying, and the ceiling of the side ailes, which was divided into compartments, and handsomely finished, is fallen amongst the rubbish that covers the floor. At the West end is a strong frame of timber, which may be conjectured to have formerly supported a turret, and perhaps a bell; but no vestige of the upper part of the building at that end can be traced.

There still remain the relicks of three large and apparently very elegant and expensive monuments: two on the North side, and one on the South.

The floor is strewed with fragments of the statues, cornices, and ornaments of the monuments, either accidentally or wantonly broken off, intermingled with the ceiling and walls, and other rubbish.

The most perfect of the three monuments consists of a magnificent sarcophagus, on which is the recumbent effigies of a personage in a coat of mail, and over it the mantle and collar of the Order of the Garter: the whole of alabaster, painted and gilded in a very superb style. The head is towards the altar, resting on a helmet of beautifully polished alabaster; the left arm broken off at the elbow,

present himselfe at the Tilt, armed, the day aforesayd yeerely, there to performe, in honor of her sacred Majestie, the promise he formerly made. Whereupon, the Lords and Gentlemen of the sayd Court, incited by so worthy an example, determined to continue that custome, and not unlike to the antient knighthood della Banda in Spaine, have ever since yeerely assembled

as also part of the right hand, which, from the position of the arm, seems to have grasped (perhaps) a sword, and the point of the beard and nose of the statue are gone. The mantle is thrown back to display the armour; and the collar, as well as the garter, are delicately finished. The azure of the latter, and gold letters upon it, are still quite fresh; but the colour of the mantle is much faded. The feet of the statue have been broken off, and a beautiful cornice which ornamented the canopy or awning over the figure lies in fragments around. This canopy, which is exteriorly carved and painted to resemble small tiles of Delft, is, on the inside, divided into numerous small compartments, ornamented with flowers richly gilt, and rests upon two pilasters within Corinthian capitals, next the wall, and in front upon termini of alabaster, highly finished, with the figures of warriors having on rich crested helmets. On slips of jasper, inserted along the front of the pediment, is the motto FIDE ET CONSTANTIA: and on a dark stone behind the effigies, the following inscription:

Fide et Constantiâ ⎧ Vixi Deo, Patriæ et Amicis, annos [   ].
Fide et Constantiâ ⎨ Christo sp'vm : carnem sepulchro commendavi.
Fide et Constantiâ ⎩ Scio, credo, expecto mortuorum resurrectionem.

On each side trophies in well executed relief.

On the body of the sarcophagus, below, on two tablets, these lines:

"If Fortune's stoore or Nature's wealth commende
They both unto his Vertue praise did lende.
The warres abroade with honnor he did passe,
In courtly Justs his Soveraigne's Knight he was.
Six Princes he did serve, and in the fight
And change of state, still kept himself upright.
With Faith untought, spottlesse and cleere his fame,
So pure that Envy could not wrong the same:
All but his virtue now (so vaine is breath)
Tourn'd dust, lye here in the cold armes of death.
Thus Fortune's gifts and yearthly favours flye
When Virtue conquers Death and Destinie."

Above the monument, against the North wall, is the shield of arms, inclosed by a garter and motto.

Dexter side: quarterly. In the first quarter, Argent, a bar and three crescents Sable. 2d, Gules, a lion rampant Or. 3d, Gules, two wolves (or foxes) passant Or. 4th, Argent, a bar and unicorns' heads Sable.

Sinister side: in the first and fourth quarter, Argent, a bar and three roses Sable. 2d, In a field Azure, powdered with eight stars Or, an escutcheon of pretence Ermine. 3d, within a border Azure, with ten stars Or, a lion rampant Azure, in a field Argent.

in armes accordingly: though true it is, that the Author of that custome, (being now by age overtaken) in the 33 yere of hir Majestie's reigne, resigned and recommended that office unto the right noble George Earle of Cumberland. The ceremonies of which assignation were publiquely performed in presence of her Majestie, her Ladies and Nobilitie; also, an infinite number of people beholding the same, as followeth.

Between this monument and the East end of the Chancel is placed in the wall a tablet within a frame of alabaster, bearing the date 1611, and the letters "Sustinen do pergo," with the following inscription in capital letters.

Memoriæ Sacrum.

"Sir Henry Lee, Knight of the most noble Order of the Garter, sonne of Sir Anthony Lee, and Dame Margaret his wife, daughter to Sir Henry Wiat, that faithful and constant servant and counsellor to the two Kings of famous memory, Henries the VII. and VIII.

"Hee owed his birth and childhood to Kent, and his highly honourable uncle Sir Thomas Wiat, at Alington Castle; his youth to the Courte and Kinge Henry the VIII. to whose service he was sworne at xiiii yeares olde: his prime of manhood, after the calme of that best Prince Edward the Sixt, to the warrs of Scotland in Queen Maries days, till called home by her whose soddeine death gave beginninge to the glorious reigne of Queen Elizabeth. He gave himselfe to Voyage and Travaile into the flourishing States of France, Italy, and Germany, wher soon putting on all those abillities that became the backe of honour, especially skill and proof in armes, he lived in grace and gracing the Courtes of the most renowned Princes of that warlike age, returned home charged with the reputation of a well-formed travellour, and adorned with those flowers of knighthood, courtesy, bounty, valour, which quickly gave forth their fruite as well in the fielde to the advantage (at once) of the two divided parties of this happily united State, and to both those Princes his Sovereignes successively in that expedition into Scotland in the year 1573; when in goodly equipage he repayred to the seige of Edinburgh, ther quartering before the Castle, and commanding one of the batteries, he shared largely in the honor of ravishing that maiden forte; as also in Courte, wher he shone in all those fayer partes became his profession and vowes, honouring his highly gracious M^{ris} with reysing those later Olimpiads of her Courte Justs and Tournaments (thereby trying and treyninge the Courtier in those exercises of armes that keepe the person bright and steeled to hardinesse, that by softe ease rusts and weares) wherein still himself lead and triumphed, carying away great spoyles of grace from the Soveraigne, and renowne from the worlde, for the fairest man at armes and most complete Courtier of his times, till singled out by the choice hand of his Royall M^{ris}, for meed of his worth (after the Lieutenancy of the Royall Manour of Woodstocke, and the office of the Royall Armory), he was called up an Assessour on the Bench of Honour emonge Princes and Peers, receivinge at her Majestie's hands the noblest Order of Garter, whilest the worme of Time gnawinge the roote of this plant, yeldinge to the burden, age, and the industrye of an active youth imposed on him, full of the glorie of the Courte he abated of his sence to pay his better parte, resigned his dignity and honour of her Maj^{ties} Knighte to the adventurous Compt George Earle of Cumberlande, changinge pleasure for ease, for tranquillity honour, making rest his sollace, and contemplation his employment, so as absenting from the world, present

On the 17th day of November, 1590, this honourable Gentleman, together with the Earle of Cumberland, having first performed their service in armes, presented themselves unto her Highnesse, at the foot of the stairs under her gallery window, in the Tilt-yard at Westminster, where at that time her Majestie did sit, accompanied with the Viscount Turyn, Ambassador of France, many Ladies, and the chiefest Nobilitie.

with himself, he chose to loose the fruit of publique use and action for that of devotion and piety, in which time (besides the building of four goodly manors,) he revived the ruines of this Chappell, added these monuments to the honour of his blood and frends, reised the foundation of the adjoining Hospitall *, and lastly, as full of years as of honour, having served *five* †, succeeding Princes, and kept himself reight and steady in many dangerous shockes, and three utter turnes of State, with a body bent to earth, and a mind erected to Heaven, aged 80, knighted 60 years, he met his long attended ende, and now rests with his Redeemer, leavinge much patrimony with his name, honour with the world, and plentifull teares with his friends. Of which sacrifice he offers his part, that beinge a sharer in his blood as well as in many of his honourable favors, and an honourer of his virtues, thus narrowly registreth his spread worth to ensuinge times. WILLIAM SCOTT."

On the opposite side is a large altar-tomb with pillars of Sussex marble (which appear to have been broken and repaired with white stone) supporting a canopy or entablature, under which are recumbent figures as large as life, of an armed knight and his lady. The feet towards the altar: the hands pressed together in a devotional attitude, but the fingers and part of the feet broken off. These figures, as well as the rest of the tomb, are of alabaster, and well sculptured: but the features, as well as the more delicate work of the ornaments, defaced. On a blue stone, at the back of the recess in which the effigies repose, on rolls of well imitated mats, is an inscription much injured by the corrosion of Time and the damp, the following words only being now legible:

" .... Anthony Lee, Knight of worthy name,
Syre .... Sr Henry Lee of noble fame,
Sonne .... Robert .... here tombed lies
Wher .... fame an .... memory never dies;
Grea .... fountaine whence himself did rune,
But greater in the greatnesse of his sone.
His body's here, his soule 'n heaven doth rest,
What scornd the earth canot with earth be prest."

On each side are trophies and fret-work ornaments richly carved.

The front of the tomb is divided into compartments, with tablets corresponding with those on the opposite monument of Sir Henry, and inscribed with about an equal number of lines probably in metre, but so much injured, that the word Margery and some few letters here, and there are all that can be read.

---

* Such is the expression; but as no account is preserved of any such Establishment, it is difficult to understand whether it is meant that he destroyed or began the erection of such a work.

† In the lines of the monument *six* Princes are mentioned.

Her Majesty, beholding these armed Knights comming toward her, did suddenly heare a musicke so sweete and secret, as every one thereat greatly marveiled. And hearkening to that excellent melodie, the earth as it were opening, there appeared a pavilion, made of white taffata, containing eight score elles, being in proportion, like unto the sacred Temple of the Virgin's Vestall. This Temple seemed to consist upon pillars of pourferry, arched like unto a Church, within it were many

Under the canopy, but above the inscription, is a stone shield with the paternal coat of Lee. In a field Argent, a bar and three crescents Sable; impaled with what appears like very antient and uncouth pincers, the blades open by a spring. Above the monument, the same arms, repeated as on Sir Henry Lee's coat, but without the Garter.

The effigies of Sir Anthony Lee lies on a roll of mat; which also supports his head. The head of the Lady reposes on cushions, or pillows, very well executed; represented on the monument in a close head-dress, with a circlet or bandeau of gold richly ornamented with pearls: a chain necklace with square links, and a jewel pendent from it: the gown close, with long stays or body, and a gold chain, also with square links, by way of girdle; and an oval ornament as large as a modern watch (perhaps an etwee case) hanging as low as the knee.

This Lady is called on the tablet belonging to her son Sir Henry's monument (for, excepting the word Margery, nearly the whole of the inscription upon her tomb is illegible) " Dame Margaret the daughter to Sir Henry Wiat, that faithful and constant servant and counsellor to two Kings, Henry VII. and VIII. &c.;" and it is remarkable that in the declaration circulated by Perkin Warbeck, when with the Scottish forces he entered Northumberland to claim the Crown, the name of Henry Wyat is mentioned as one of King Henry the Seventh's especial favourites and advisers. See Lord Bacon's History of the reign of that Monarch, in which the manifesto is reported to be copied from the Cottonian MSS.

There can be no doubt that these personages were the father and mother of Sir Henry Lee, Bart.; but it is not easy to discover for whom the third tomb or monument was erected: the remains of it being only the basis, and the projection of the cornice or arch with some small portions of the pillars of Sussex marble, which formerly decorated as well as supported it. Enough is left to shew that it is of the same workmanship as the others: the materials of which it is composed being the same, but differing in the form of the arch, and the circumstance of its being of considerably smaller dimensions. Neither arms nor inscription can be traced.—It is, however, very probable that it was intended as a memorial of a lady of the name of Vavasour (I do not venture to say of the family once proprietors of an estate at Woughton near Newport Pagnell), who appears to have been the noble Knight's *Dulcinea* in his old age; perhaps after the death of his lady of " illustrious blood and fame," who is buried at Aylesbury, and, not mentioned in the monumental inscriptions at Quarendon. It appears that Chastity and Knighthood were not always concomitants, whatsoever they might have been in the age of Don Quixote, or may be in our own times; and that this Star of Courts, and Rose of Chivalry, was not content with having (according to the pompous display of his achievements upon the tablet in the chapel) " *ravished* the maiden fortress of Edinburgh," and won *her garter* from his Royal Mistress; but, on retiring from the world "to rest and contemplation," he must, forsooth, fall desperately in love with a damsel of such exquisite beauty and accomplishments, that he determined to perpetuate the remembrance of his gallantry by a splendid monument and the following

lampes burning. Also on the one side there stood an altar covered with cloth of gold, and thereupon two waxe candles burning in rich candlesticks; upon the altar also, were layd certaine princely presents, which after, by three Virgins, were presented unto her Majestie.

lines, which Browne Willis copied, and Mr. Lysons (whose account I had overlooked) has quoted from Mr. Willis's papers.

"Under this stone interred lies a fair and worthy dame
Daughter to Henry Vavasor, Ann Vavasor her name!
She living with Sir Henry Lee for love, long time did dwell:
Death could not part them; but here they rest in one cell!"

Whether the noble Knight and the worthy Dame were literally buried in the same grave (and if so, Virgil might have supplied no bad epitaph in

"Speluncam Dido, Dux et Trojanus eandem
Devenient.")

may probably not long remain doubtful; for such is the condition of the Chapel, that, if a few pigs should chance to stray amongst the ruins, as well as "sheep and oxen, and all the beasts of the field," which have free access to it, they may anticipate the researches of the curious and the learned, by unceremoniously opening the hallowed depository of so much valour and beauty!

The Lady of Sir Henry Lee was buried at Aylesbury in 1594, with the following very singular lines inscribed upon her monument:

"If passing by this place thou do desire
    To know what corpse here shry'd in marble lie;
The sum of that which now thou dost require,
    This scle'der verse shal sone to the descrie.
Entombed here doth rest a worthie dame,
    Extract and born of noble house and bloud;
Her sire Lord PAGET hight of worthie fame,
    Whose virtues cannot sinke in *Lethe* floud.
Two brethren had she, Barons of this realme:
    A Knight her freere, Sir Harry Lee he hight,
To whom she bare three impes, which had to name
    John, Henry, Mary, slayn by fortune's spight:
First two bei'g yong, which caus'd their parents mo'e,
    The third in flower and prime of all her years;
All three do rest within this marble stone,
    By which the fickl'ess of worldly joyes appears.
Good friend, stick not to strew with crimson flowers
    This marble stone, wherein her cinders rest;
For sure her ghost lives with the heav'nly powers,
    And guerdon hathe of virtuous life possest."

Before the door of this Temple stood a CROWNED PILLAR[1], embraced by an eglantine tree, whereon there hanged a table, and therein written, (with letters of gold) this Prayer following:

ELIZÆ, &c.
PIÆ POTENTI, FŒLICISSIMÆ VIRGINI,
FIDEI, PACIS, NOBILITATIS VINDICI,
CUI DEUS, ASTRA, VIRTUS,
SUMMA DEVOVERUNT OMNIA.
POST TOT ANNOS, TOT TRIUMPHOS,
ANIMAM AD PEDES POSITURUS TUOS,
SACRA SENEX AFFIXIT ARMA.
VITAM QUIETAM, IMPERIUM, FAMAM
ÆTERNAM, ÆTERNAM,
PRECATUR TIBI,
SANGUINE REDEMPTURUS SUO.
VLTRA COLUMNAS HERCULIS
COLUMNA MOVEATUR TUA.
CORONA SUPERET CORONAS OMNES,
UT QUAM CŒLUM FŒLICISSIME
NASCENTI CORONAM DEDIT,
BEATISSIMA MORIENS REPORTES CŒLO.
SUMME, SANCTE, ÆTERNE,
AUDI, EXAUDI,
DEUS.

[1] See a whimsical allusion to "the Crowned Pillar" in page 51.

The musicke aforesayd was accompanied with these verses, pronounced and sung by Mr. Hales, her Majestie's servant, a gentleman in that art excellent, and for his voice both commendable and admirable.

> My golden locks time hath to silver turn'd,
> (Oh time too swift, and swiftness never ceasing)
> My youth 'gainst age, and age at youth hath spurn'd;
> But spurn'd in vaine, youth waineth by encreasing.
> Beauty, strength, and youth, flowers fading beene,
> Duety, faith, and love, are rootes and ever greene.
>
> My helmet now shall make a hive for bees,
> And lovers songs shall turne to holy psalmes;
> A Man at Armes must now sit on his knees,
> And feed on prayers, that are old ages almes.
> And so from Court to Cottage I depart,
> My saint is sure of mine unspotted hart.
>
> And when I sadly sit in homely cell,
> I 'le teach my swaines this carrol for a song.
> Blest be the hearts that thinke my Sovereigne well,
> Curs'd be the soules that thinke to doe her wrong,
> Goddesse, vouchsafe this aged man his right,
> To be your Beadsman now, that was your Knight.

The gifts which the Vestall Maydens presented unto her Majesty, were these; a vaile of white, exceeding rich and curiously wrought: a cloke and safeguard set with buttons of gold, and on them were graven emprezes of excellent devise: in the loope of every button was a Nobleman's badge, fixed to a pillar richly embrodered.

And here (by way of digression) let us remember a Speech which this noble Gentleman used at such time as these buttons were set upon the garment aforesaid: "I would (quoth he) that all my friends might have bene remembered in these buttons, but there is not roome enough to containe them all; and if I have them not all, then (said hee) those that are left out, may take exception." Whereunto, another standing by, answered: "Sir, let as many be placed as can be, and cause the last button to be made like the character of &c." "Now, Godamercie, with all my heart (quoth the Knight), for I would not have given the *cætera* of my friends for a million of gold."

But to returne to the purpose: These presents and prayer being with great reverence delivered into her Majestie's owne hands, and he himselfe disarmed, offered up his armour at the foot of her Majestie's crowned pillar: and kneeling upon his knees, presented the Earle of Cumberland, humbly beseeching she would be pleased to accept him for her Knight, to continue the yeerely exercises aforesaid. Her Majesty gratiously accepting of that offer, this aged Knight armed the Earle, and mounted him upon his horse. That being done, he put upon his owne person a side coat of blacke velvet, pointed under the arme, and covered his head (in liew of an helmet) with a buttoned cap of the countrey fashion.

After all these ceremonies, for divers dayes hee ware upon his cloake a crowne embrodered, with a certain motto or device; but what his intention therein was, himselfe best knoeth.

Now to conclude the matter of assignation, you shall understand, that this noble Gentleman, by her Majestie's expresse commandement, is yerely (without respect unto his age) personally present at these Military Exercises, there to see, survey, and as one most carefull and skilfull to direct them; for, indeed, his vertue and valour in armes is such as deserveth to command. And touching that point, I will let you know the opinion of Monsieur de Champany, a gentleman of great experience and notable observation; who, at his beeing Embessadour in England for causes of the Low Countreys, and writing to his friends there, in one of his intercepted letters, among other occurrents, these words were found:

"I was (quoth he) one day by Sir Christopher Hatton, Captaine of her Majestie's Guard, invited to Eltham, an house of the Queene's, whereof he was the guardian: at which time I heard and saw three things, that in all my travel of France, Italy, and Spaine, I never heard or saw the like. The first was a consort of musicke, so excellent and sweet as cannot be expressed. The second, a course at a bucke, with the best and most beautifull greyhounds that ever I did behold. And the third, a man of armes excellently mounted, richly armed, and indeed the most accomplished Cavaliero I had ever seene. This Knight was called Sir Henry Lee, who that day (accompanied with the other Gentlemen of the Court), onely to doe me honour, vouchsafed at my returne to Greenwich to breake certaine lances: which action was performed with great dexterity and commendation."

Thus much was the substance (and well neere the whole circumstance) of Sir Henry Lee's lasting taking of armes: wherein he seemed to imitate the aunchent Romanes, who having served a convenient time, and claiming the priviledges due to old souldiers (whome they called *Emeriti*) did come into Campo Martio, every man leading his owne horse; and there offered his armes unto Mars, in presence of the Chiefe Magistrates: which ceremony, Scipio, Cassius, the great Pompey, with many other noble Capteines, disdained not to doe.

Summarily, these annuall Actions have bene most nobly performed (according to their times) by one Duke, 19 Earles, 27 Barons, four Knights of the Garter, and above 150 other Knights and Esquiers.

HER MAJESTIE RESEMBLED TO THE CROWNED PILLAR.

(Ye must read upward.)

Is blisse with immortalitie.
Her trymest top of all ye see,
Garnish the Crowne.
Her iust renowne
Chapter and head.
Parts that maintain
And womanhead,
Her mayden Raigne
In - te - grie - tie.
In ho - nour and
With ve - ri - tie,
Her roundnes stand,
Strengthen the State.
By their increase,
With - out de - bate,
Concord and peace,
Of her sup - port.
They be the base
With stedfastnesse,
Vertue and grace,
Stay, and comfort.
Of Albion's rest,
The sounde Pillar
And seene afarre,
Is plainely exprest,
Tall, stately, and strayt,
By this noble pourtrayt,

R MAJESTIE, FOR MANY PARTS IN HER MOST NOBLE AND VERTUOUS NATURE TO BE FOUND, RESEMBLETH TO THE SPIRE.

(Ye must begin beneath, according to the nature of the Device.)

Skie.
Azur'd
In the
Assur'de
―――――
And better,
And richer,
Much greter
―――――
Crown & empir
After an hier
For to aspire
Like flame of fire,
In forme of Spire,
―――――
To mount on hie.
Con - ti - nu - al - ly
With trauel and teen,
Most gratious Queen
Ye have made a vow,
Shews us plainly how
Not fained but true,
To every man's vew,
Shining cleere in you
Of so bright an hewe,
Even thus vertewe,
―――――
Vanish out of our sight.
Till his fine top be quite
To taper in the ayre,
Endevours soft and faire,
By his kindly nature,
Of tall comely stature,
Like as this faire figure,

A GENERAL RESEMBLANCE OF THE ROUNDEL TO GOD, THE WORLD, AND THE QUEENE.

All and whole, and euer, and one,
Single, simple, eche where alone,
These be counted, as clerkes can tell,
True properties of the Roundell.
His still turning by consequence
And change, doe breede both life and sence.
Time, measure of stirre and rest,
Is also by his course exprest.
How swift the circle stirre aboue,
His center point doeth neuer moue.
All things that euer were or be,
Are closde in his concauitie;
And though he be still turnde and tost,
No roome there wants, nor none is lost.
The Roundell hath no bonch or angle,
Which may his course stay or entangle.
The furthest part of all his spheare,
Is equally both farre and neare.
So doth none other figure fare
Where Nature's chattels closed are;
And beyond his wide compasse
There is no body nor no place;
Nor any wit that comprehends
Where it begins, or where it ends:
And therefore all men doe agree
That it purports eternitie.
God, aboue the Heauens so hie,
Is this Roundell, in world the skie.
Vpon Earth she who beares the bell
Of Maydes, and Queenes, is this Roundell:
All and whole, and euer alone,
Single, sans peere, simple, and one.

A SPECIAL AND PARTICULAR RESEMBLANCE OF HER MAJESTIE TO THE ROUNDELL.

First her authoritie regall
Is the circle compassing all;
The dominion, great and large,
Which God hath geuen to her charge;
Within which most spatious bound
She enuirons her people round,
Retaining them, by oth and liegeance,
Within the pale of true obeysance:
Holding imparked as it were,
Her people like to heards of deere.
Sitting among them in the middes,
Where she allowes, and bannes and bids
In what fashion she list, and when
The seruices of all her men.
Out of her breast, as from an eye,
Issue the rayes incessantly
Of her iustice, bountie, and might,
Spreading abroad their beames so bright,
And reflect not, till they attaine
The fardest part of her domaine,
And makes eche subiect clearely see
What he is bounden for to be
To God, his Prince, and Commonwealth,
His neighbour, kindred, and to himselfe.
The same centre and middle pricke,
Whereto our deedes are drest so thicke,
From all the parts and outmost side
Of her Monarchie large and wide,
Also fro whence reflect these rayes
Twentie hundred maner of wayes,
Where her will is them to conuey
Within the circle of her suruey.
So is the Queene of Briton ground,
Beame, circle, center, of all my round.

HOBBINOLL'S DITTIE IN PRAYSE OF ELIZA QUEENE OF THE SHEEPHEARDS.

 Yee dainty nimphs that in this blessed brooke
   Do bath your brest,
 Forsake your watry bowers, and hether looke
   At my request.
 And you, faire virgins, that on Parnasse dwell,
 Whence floweth Helicon, the learned well,
   Helpe me to blaze
   Her worthy praise,
  Who in her sexe dooth all excell.

 Of faire Eliza by your silluer song;
   That blessed wight:
 The flower of virgins may she flourish long
   In princely plight:
 For shee is Sirinx' daughter, without spot, without spot,
 Which Pan, the Sheepheard's god, on her begot:
   So sprung her Grace
   Of heauenly race:
  No mortal blemish may her blot.

 See where she sits vpon the grassie greene.
   O seemely sight!
 Yclad in scarlet, like a Mayden Queene,
   And ermines white.
 Vpon her head a crimson coronet,
 With daffadills and damaske roses set;
   Bay leaues betweene;
   And primeroses greene
  Embellish the sweete violet.

 Tell me, have ye beheld her angel's face,
   Like Phœbe faire?
 Her heauenly 'hauiour, her princely grace,
   Can well compare

HOBBINOLL'S DITTIE, BY SPENSER.

The red rose medled, and the white yfere,
In eyther cheeke depeincten liuely cheere.
   Her modest eye,
   Her Maiestie,
 Where haue you seene the like but there?

I saw Phœbus thrust out his golden head
   On her to gaze;
But when he saw how broade her beames did spread,
   It did him maze.
He blusht to see another sunne below.
   Let him, if he dare,
   His brightnes compare
With hers, to haue the ouerthrow.

Shew thy selfe, Cinthia, with thy siluer rayes,
   And be not abasht.
When she the beames of her beauty displayes,
   Oh how art thou dasht?
But I will not match her with Latonae's seede;
Such folly great sorrow to Niobe did breede,
   Now she is a stone,
   And makes deadly moane,
Warning all other to take heede.

Pan may be proud, that euer he begot
   Such a Bellibone;
And Sirinx reioyce that euer was her lot
   To beare such a one.
Soone as my younglings cryen for the dam,
To her will I offer a milke-white lamb.
   Shee is my goddesse plaine,
   And I her Sheepheard's swaine,
Albe for-swonck and for-swat I am.

I see Calliope speede her to the place,
   Where my goddesse shines;

HOBBINOLL'S DITTIE, BY SPENSER.

And, after her, the other Muses trace
   With their violines.
Bin they not baie-braunches which they doo beare;
All for Eliza in her hand to weare?
   So sweetly they play,
   And sing all the way,
  That it is a heauen to heare.

Loe! how finely the Graces can it foote,
   To the instrument:
They dauncen deftely, and singen soote,
   In their merriment.
Wants not a fourth *Grace* to make the daunce euen?
Let that roome to my Lady be giuen.
   Shee shall be a *Grace*,
   To fill the fourth place,
  And raigne with the rest in heauen.

And whether runnes this beuie of Ladies bright,
   Ranged in a roe?
They been all Ladies of the lake behight
   That vnto her goe?
Cloris, that is the chiefe nimph of all,
Of oliue-braunches beares a coronall:
   Oliues beene for peace
   When warres doo surcease,
  Such for a Princesse beene principall.

Bring hether the pinke and purple cullumbine,
   With gillyflowers;
Bring sweet carnasions, and sops in wine
   Worne of paramours.
Strew me the ground with daffa-down-dillies,
And cowslips, and king's cups, and loued lillies.
   The pretty paunce,
   And the cheuisaunce,
  Shall match with the faire flower-delice.

Ye Sheepheard's daughters that dwell on the greene,
      Hie you there apace,
Let none come there but such as virgins beene
      To adorne her Grace.
And when you come where as she is in place,
See that your rudenes doo not you disgrace.
      Bind your fillets fast,
        And gird on your wast,
      For more finenesse, with a tawdrie lace.

Now rise up, *Eliza*, decked as thou art,
      In Royall ray.
And now ye, dainty damsels, may depart,
      Each one her way.
I feare I haue troubled your troupes too long:
Let dame *Eliza* thanke you for her song;
      And if you come hether
        When damzins I gather,
I will part them all you among.
                      EDM. SPENSER.

WEBBE, in his "Discourse of English Poetrie," 1586, speaking of different Measures, tells us, "I haue turned the new Poet's [i. e. SPENSER[1]] sweete Song of ELIZA into such homely Sapphick as I coulde."

O ye nymphes most fine, who resort to this brooke,
For to bathe there your pretty breasts at all times;
Leaue the watrish bowres hyther, and to me come
                         at my request nowe.

And ye virgins trymme, who resort to Parnass,
Whence the learned well Helicon beginneth,
Helpe to blase her worthy deserts, that all els
                         mounteth aboue farre.

---

[1] See the original Song before, pp. 55—58.

WEBBE'S IMITATION OF SPENSER'S DITTIE.

Nowe the siluer songes of *Elisa* sing yee,
Princely wight, whose peere not among the virgins
Can be found: that long she may remaine among us
        now let us all pray.

For Syrinx' daughter she is, of her begotten
Of the great god Pan; thus of heauen aryseth
All her exlent race: any mortall harde happe
        cannot aproche her.

See, she sittes most seemely in a grassy greene plott,
Clothed in weedes meete for a pryncely mayden,
Boste with ermines white, in a goodly scarlett
        brauely beseeming.

Decked is that crowne that vpon head standes
With the red rose and many daffadillies,
Bayes, the primrose, and violetts, be sette by: how
        ioyfull a sight ist.

Say, Behold did ye euer her angelike face,
Like to Phœbe fayre; Or her heauenly hauour,
And the princelike grace that in her remaineth?
        Haue yee the like seene?

Medled ist red rose with a white together,
Which in either cheeke do depeincte a trymme cheere,
Her Maiestie and eye to behold so comely, her
        like who remembreth?

Phœbus once peept foorth with a goodly guilt hewe,
For to gaze: but when he sawe the bright beames
Spreade abroade fro her face with a glorious grace,
        it did amaze him.

When another sunne he behelde belowe heere,
Blust he red for shame, nor againe he durst looke:
Would he durst bright beames of his owne with hers match,
        for to be vanquisht.

Shew thy selfe now, Cynthia, with thy cleere rayes,
And beholde her: neuer abasht be thou so:
When she spreades those beames of her heuenly beauty, how
                                thou art in a dump dasht?

But I will take heede that I match not her grace
With the Laton seede, Niobe that once did,
Nowe she doth therefore in a stone repent: to all
                                other a warning.

Pan he may well boaste that he did begit her
Such a noble wight; to Syrinx it is joy,
That she found such lot with a bellibone, trym
                                for to be loaden.

When my younglinges first to the dammes do bleat out,
Shall a milke-white lambe to my lady be offred;
For my goddesse shee is, yea, I myself her heardgrome,
                                though but a rude clowne.

Unto that place Caliope dooth high her,
There my goddesse shines: to the same the Muses
After her with sweete violines about them
                                cheerfully tracing.

Is not it bay braunche that aloft in handes they haue
Eune to giue them sure to my Lady Eliza.
O so sweete they play, and to the same doo sing too
                                heau'nly to heare ist.

See, the Graces trym to the stroake doo foote it,
Deftly dauncing, and meriment doo make them,
Sing to the instruments to reioyce the more. But
                                wants not a fourth Grace.

Then the daunce will be eune, to my Lady therefore
Shalbe geune that place, for a Grace she shall be
For to fill that place that among them in heau'ne, she
                                may be receiued.

Thys beuy of bright nymphes, whether ist goe they now?
Raunged all thus fine in a rowe together?
They be Ladies all i'the lake behight soe?
         They thether all goe.

One that is there chiefe, that among the rest goes,
Called is Chores, of olyues she beares a
Goodly crownett, meete for a Prince that in peace
         euer abideth.

All ye Sheepheardes maides that about the greene dwell,
Speede ye there to her Grace, but among ye take heede
All be virgins pure that aproche to deck her,
         duetie requireth.

When ye shall present ye before her in place,
See ye not your selues doo demeane too rudely:
Bynd the fillets: and to be fine the waste gyrt
         faste with a tawdryne.

Bring the pinkes therewith, many gelliflowres sweete,
And the cullambynes: let us haue the wynesops,
With the carnation, that among the loue laddes
         wontes to be worne much.

Daffadowndillies all along the ground strowe,
And the cowslyppe, with a prety paunce let heere lye,
Kyngcuppe and lyllies, so beloude of all men,
         and the deluce flowre.

" One verse there remaineth untranslated as yet, &c. WEBBE."

A CANZON PASTORALL IN HONOUR OF HER MAIESTIE[1].

Alas! what pleasure now the pleasant Spring
      Hath giuen place
To harsh black frosts, the sad ground couering;
      Can wee poore wee embrace,
When eury bird on eury branch can sing
    Naught but this note of woe alas?
Alas! this note of woe, why should we sound?
With vs as May, September hath a prime;
Then birds and branches your alas is fond,
Which call vpon the absent sommer time:
      For did flowres make our May
      Or the sun-beames your day,
When Night and Winter did the world embrace,
Well might you wail your ill, and sing alas!

Loe, matron-like, the Earth herselfe attires
      In habite graue.
Naked the fields are, bloomelesse are the brires,
      Yet we a Sommer haue,
Who in our clime kindleth these liuing fires,
    Which bloomes can on the briers saue,
No ice doth christallize the running brooke,
No blast deflowres the flowre-adorned field;
Christall is cleere, but cleerer is the looke,
Which to our climes these liuing fires dooth yield:
      Winter though euery where
      Hath no abiding heere:
On brooks and briers she doth rule alone;
The Sunne which lights our world is alwayes one.

                              EDMUND BOLTON.

[1] From England's Helicon, 1600.

ROWLAND'S SONG IN PRAISE OF THE FAIREST BETA [1].

O thou siluer Thames, O clearest christall flood,
Beta alone the Phœnix is of all thy watry brood.
      The Queene of Virgins onely she,
        And thou the queene of floods shalt be.
Let all the nimphs be ioyfull then, to see this happy day:
Thy *Beta* now alone shall be the subject of my lay.

With dainty and delightsome straines of sweetest virelayes,
Come louely sheepheards sit we down, and chaunt our *Beta's* praise;
      And let us sing so rare a verse,
        Our *Beta's* praises to rehearse;
That little birds shall silent be to heare poore shepheards sing,
And riuers backward bend their course, and flow vnto the spring.

Range all thy swannes, faire Thames, together on a ranke,
And place them duly one by one vpon thy stately banke;
      Then set together all a-good,
        Recording to the siluer flood;
And craue the tunefull nightingale to helpe ye with her lay,
The osell and the thrustlecocke, chiefe musique of our May.

O see what troupes of nimphs been sporting on the strauds,
And they been blessed nimphs of peace, with oliues in their hands.
      How merrily the Muses sing,
        That all the flowrie meddowes ring.
And *Beta* sits upon the banke in purple and in pall,
And she the Queene of Muses is, and weares the coronall.

Trim vp her golden tresses with Apollo's sacred tree.
O happy sight vnto all those that loue and honour thee!
      The blessed angels haue prepar'd
        A glorious crowne for thy reward.
Not such a golden crowne as haughty Cæsar weares:
But such a glittering starrie crowne as Ariadne beares.

[1] From England's Helicon, 1600.

Make her a goodly chaplet of azur'd cullumbine,
And wreath about her coronet with sweetest eglantine;
    Bedeck our *Beta* all with lillies,
    And the dainty daffadillies;
With roses damaske, white and red, and fairest flowre-delice;
With cowslips of Jerusalem, and cloaues of Paradise.

O thou faire torch of heauen, the dayes most dearest light,
And thou bright-shining Cinthia, the glory of the night;
    You starres, the eyes of heauen,
    And thou the gliding leuen;
And thou, O gorgeous Iris, with all strange colours dyed;
When she streames foorth her rayes, then dasht is all your pride.

See how the day stands still, admiring of her face,
And Time, loe! stretcheth foorth his armes thy *Beta* to embrace.
    The Sirens sing sweete layes,
    The Trytons sound her praise.
Goe, passe on Thames, and hie thee fast unto the ocean sea,
And let thy billowes there proclaime thy *Beta's* holy-day.

And Water! thou the blessed roote of that greene Oliue tree,
With whose sweete shadow all thy bancks with peace preserved be.
    Laurell for poets and conquerours,
    And mirtle for love's paramours;
That fame may be thy fruite, the boughs preseru'd by Peace,
And let the mournfull cypress die now stormes and tempests cease.

Weele strew the shoare with pearle, where *Beta* walks alone,
And we will paue her princely bower with richest Indian stone.
    Perfume the ayre, and make it sweete,
    For such a goddesse it is meete.
For if her eyes for purity contend with Titan's light:
No meruaile then, although they so doo dazell humaine sight.

Sound out your trumpets then, from London's stately towers,
To beate the stormie winds a-backe, and calme the raging showers.

Set to the cornet and the flute,
　　The orpharion and the lute;
And tune the tabor and the pipe to the sweet violons;
And mooue the thunder in the ayre with lowdest clarions.

Beta, long may thine altars smoake with yeerely sacrifice,
And long thy sacred temples may their sabaoths solemnise!
　　Thy sheepheards watch by day and night,
　　Thy maides attend the holy light,
And thy large empire stretch her armes from East vnto the West,
And Albion on the Appenines aduance her conquering crest!
　　　　　　　　　　　　　　　MICH. DRAYTON.

FRAGMENT OF A PARTHENIAD WRITTEN OF OUR SOUERAIGNE LADY. BY PUTTENHAM[1].

Of siluer was her foreheade hye,
Her browes two bowes of hebenie,
Her tresses trust were to behold
Frizled and fine as fringe of gold.

Two lips wrought out of rubie rocke,
Like leaues to shut and to vnlock.
As Portall dore in princes chamber;
A golden tongue in mouth of amber.

Her eyes, God wot, what stuffe they are!
I durst be sworne each is a starre;
As cleere and bright as woont to guide
The Pylot in his winter tide.

Her bosome, sleake as Paris plaster,
Held up two balles of alabaster;
Eche byas was a little cherrie,
Or els, I thinke, a strawberie.

FRAGMENTS OF TWO PARTHENIADS. BY THE SAME[2].

As falcon fares to bussard's flight,
As egles' eyes to owlates' sight,
As fierce saker to coward kite,
As brightest noone to darkest night;

[1] Arte of Englishe Poesie, p. 234.　　　[2] Ibid. 196.

As summer sunne exceedeth farre
The moone and euery other starre:
So farre my Princesse' praise doeth passe
The famoust Queene that euer was.

Set rich rubie to red esmayle,
The rauen's plume to peacock's tayle,
Lay me the larke's to lizard's eyes,
The duskie cloude to azure skies,
Set shallow brookes to surging seas,
An orient pearle to a white pease;
There shall no lesse an ods be seene
In mine from euery other Queene.

THE NIMPHES, MEETING THEIR MAY QUEENE, ENTERTAINE HER WITH THIS DITTIE.

With fragrant flowers we strew the way,
And make this our cheefe holy-day:
For though this clime were blest of yore,
Yet it was never proud before.
    O beauteous Queene of second Troy [1],
    Accept of our unfayned ioy.

Now th' ayre is sweeter then sweet balme,
And satires daunce about the palme;
Now earth, with verdure newly dight,
Giues perfect signes of her delight.
    O beauteous Queene, &c.

Now birds record new harmonie,
And trees doo whistle melodie;
Now euery thing that Nature breedes
Doth clad itselfe in pleasant weedes.
    O beauteous Queene, &c.   THO. WATSON.

---

[1] It is not observed in the collection from which this poem is transcribed, that it was sung or repeated before Queen Elizabeth; yet from the appellation "Queene of second Troy," (London, in some of our ancient legendary histories, being denominated *Troy Novant*,) it could be addressed to no other person than her Majesty.

THE ZEALOUS POET IN PRAYSE OF THE MAYDEN QUEENE.

Not your bewtie, most gracious Soueraigne,
   Nor maidenly lookes, mainteind with Maiestie;
Your stately port, which doth not match but staine,
For your presence, your Pallace and your traine,
   All Princes courts mine eye could euer see;
Not your quicke wits, your sober gouernaunce;
   Your cleare forsight, your faithfull memorie,
So sweete features in so staid countenaunce:
Nor languages, with plentuous vtterance,
So able to discourse and entertaine:
Not noble race, farre beyond Cæsar's Raigne,
   Runne in right line, and bloud of 'nointed Kings;
Not large empire, armies, treasurs, domaine,
   Lustie liueries of Fortune's dear'st darlings;
Not all the skilles fit for a Princely dame,
   Your learned Muse with vse and studie brings;
Not true honour, ne that immortall fame
   Of mayden Raigne, your only owne renowne,
And no Queene's els, yet such as yeeldes your name
   Greater glory than doeth your treble crowne.
Not any one of all these honor'd parts,
   Your Princely happes, and habites that do moue,
And, as it were, enforcell all the hearts
   Of Christen Kings to quarrell for your loue.
But to possesse at once, and all the good
   Arte and engine, and euery starre aboue
Fortune or kinde, could farce in flesh and bloud,
   Was force inough to make so many striue
For your person, which in our world stoode
   By all consents the minion'st mayde to wiue.

On the 4th of September, 1590, the Queen gave a charter to the Corporation of *Winchester*, declaring it " to be a sole City of itself." In this Charter " the great ruin, decay, and poverty into which it had fallen," are explicitly stated; and, in order to relieve the inhabitants, permission was given them to manufacture particular kinds of cloth.

Sir Julius Cæsar was in this month honoured with a Visit from the Queen of which the following account is given in his own words:

" Tuesday, Sept. 12, the Queen visited my house at Mitcham, and supped and lodged there, and dined there the next day. I presented her with a gown of cloth of silver richly embroidered; a black net-work mantle with pure gold; a taffeta hat, white, with several flowers, and a jewel of gold set therein with rubies and diamonds. Her Majesty removed from my house after dinner the 13th of September to Nonsuch, with exceeding good contentment; which entertainment of her Majesty, with the former disappointment[1], amounted to £700 sterling, besides mine own provisions, and what was sent unto me by my friends[2]."

Queen Elizabeth's arms having been placed in many parts of the manor-house of Streatham gave rise to a tradition that it was one of her palaces; a tradition so prevalent in Salmon's[3] time, that they shewed the Earl of Essex's apartments, and supported it by other circumstantial proofs; yet so destitute of foundation either from history or record, as to make us very cautious of trusting the village tale on such occasions. A curious brick tower at this house is supposed to have been built by Sir George Howland about the year 1600.

On the 23d of October, Thomas Kery, Clerk of the Privy Seal, in a letter to Lord Talbot, says, " Her Matie is at Wyndesor: of her comyng hith^r [to London] no woorde. Marry it is thought to Westm^r, or St. James, the remove will be, against the viith of November, and not before."

In November this year, John Stanhope thus writes to Lord Talbot: "The Q. for healthe is wonderus well, God be thanked; this day comyng from Wyndsor, where on Sunday last she entertayned the Viscount of Turyne openly thoughe he had

---

[1] In a Letter from Rowland White to Sir Robert Sidney, Sept. 30, 1596, the Queen's intention to visit Mitcham is mentioned; at which time, probably, the disappointment here alluded to happened. Lysons, vol. I. p. 354; from Sidney State Papers, vol. II. p. 5.

[2] MSS. of Sir Julius Cæsar, in the British Museum. See Ayscough's Catalogue, N° 4160.

accesse to her in her gallery overnight, dyvers LL^ds and Ladyes beying by. He is very wellcum, in all open showes; and if his aurraunte do not so much importune a p̃sent supply of money, I think his interteynment shalle be better; thoughe, in truthe her Matie be not w^thout good tellyng how she and her estate be interested in the Frenche K. prosperyte or faule. This nyght, God wylling, she wyll to Richmond, and on Saterdaye next to Somerset House; and yf she could overcum her passyon against my Lo. of Essex for his marryadge, no doubt she would be much quyeter; yett both she use yt more temperately then was thought for; and, God be thanked, doth not stryke all she thretes. The Erle doth use yt wth good temper, concealing his marryadge as much as so open a matter may be; not that he denies yt to anie, but, for her M^tie better satisfactyon it plesed y^t my La. shall lyve very retyred to her mother's house. The favors of the Courte be disposed as you left them; and I assure you never a man y^t I know hath cawse to bragge of anye. My Lo. Tresorer hath ben yll of his goute of longe, and so contynues. O^r nue mayd M^rs. Vavasor[1] florishethe lyke the lylly and the rose."

On the 20th of November Richard Brakenbury writes to Lord Talbot: " Yf I should wryt howe muche her Matie this daye dyd make of the lytle Ladye yor doughter, wth often kyssinge (which her Mat^tie seldom usethe to any), and then amendinge her dressinge wth pynns, and styll carynge her wth her Matie in her own barge, and so into the p̃vye lodgings, and so homward from the ronnyng, ye wold scars beleve me: her Matie sayd (as trewe it ys) that she is verye lycke my Lady her grandmother; she behaved herselfe with suche modestye as I pray God she may possess at 20 years old. My Lady Marques dyd tayk onlye cayre of her. Theyse sports weere great, and done in costly sort, to her Ma^t^s great lykinge, and theyr great cost. To expres eṽy part wth sundry devyses, yt ys more fytt for them that delytethe in theme, thene for me who esteemethe lyttel such vanyties, I thanke God. Thene the 19 day, beynge *Saynt Elyzabeth's daye*[2], th' Erle of

---

[1] Mrs. Anne Vavasor, a lady of a Yorkshire family. She was one of the Queen's Maids of Honour, and a very beautiful woman, but the subject of much mirth and scandal among the courtiers on account of her attachment to the old but gallant Sir Henry Lee. Lodge, III. 16. See before, p. 47.

[2] The observation of this day as a Court festival seems to have been one of those absurd pieces of flattery which were so common in this reign: and is perhaps no where mentioned but in the letter before us. Elizabeth was so insignificant a saint, as to have no peculiar service allotted to her in the ancient Rituals, except a short solitary lesson on the 19th of November; and the Reformed Breviary of Pius V. deprives her even of that, and denies her a place in its Calendar. The miracle to which this lady owed her canonization was thus recited in the lesson: " A comely young man, too gayly ha-

Comerland, th' Erle of Essex, and my L. Burge, dyd chaleng all comers, sex courses apeace, whiche was very honorably performed. The French Ymbassadors, as the Vycount Tureyne and the Legere, was at all theys sports. Sence the Vycount his comynge he hathe beene very well interteined at Wyndsor by her Matie, and here in London by my L. Chauncelor (wyther the Quene went secretly, as she thought); but from the fyrst to the last th' Erle of Essex dothe lodge hyme, and the best abowte hyme, and defraythe his dyett. He gothe away about the 23 of this month, and so to Germany, where God send hyme ayd, for his M^r hathe great nede of yt. Her Matie retornethe to Rychmond the 24 daye of this monthe, and theretary Chrystmas. My L. of Essex ys in good favor.

My L. Ormond hath ben very sicke, but nowe well recovered; and was at theyse Tryumphes [1] Erle Marshall, and bare the rod [2]."

bited, coming to visit her, Elizabeth admonished him to despise the vanities of the world. The young man answered her: 'Madam, I beseech you, pray for me.' 'If thou wouldst have me pray for thee,' said Elizabeth, 'go thou and do likewise.' So they began to pray at some distance; till the young man, unable to endure the fervour of her devotion, began to cry aloud, that he should be destroyed by it; whereupon her maidens running to him found him all on fire, so that they could not touch his clothes, but were fain hastily to withdraw their hands, with such vehement heat did he burn. Elizabeth hereupon ceased to pray; and the young man, inspired by this divine warmth, went unto the order of the Franciscans." Reflections upon the Devotions of the Roman Catholic Church, London, 1674.—Our Queen, who resembled the saint only in her name, and in her fondness for practising on the weakness of comely young men, was silly enough to connive at the public recollection of this wretched legend, for the sake of the wretched compliment which her courtiers had founded on it.

[1] See before, pp. 41—52.   [2] Lodge, vol. III. p. 13.

The Palace at *Havering atte Bower* [3] was situated near Havering Green [4]. Part of the walls of this Palace continued standing till very lately, but at the present time not a vestige remains. Havering appears to have been from an early period a favourite residence of our Saxon monarchs and their descendants, probably from the uncommon beauty and variety of its prospects; being situated on an eminence, the view extends over Middlesex, Surrey, Kent, Hertfordshire, and part of Essex, and is enriched with a command of the

[3] Of this Royal Palace, see before, in vol. I. pp. 253, 307.

[4] *Havering Hall*, which adjoins the Green, was purchased in 1808 by my late Friend and Kinsman William Morris, Esq.; and is now the property of the Rev. Thomas Leigh, M. A. in right of his wife, the only surviving daughter and heiress of Mr. Morris.

Thames, for nearly eight miles, with a sight of the ships continually passing to and from London. Edward the Confessor is said, either to have built a Palace here, of free-stone leaded, or improved an old one, as he delighted in the situation: being retired and woody, it was peculiarly suited to his devotional exercises, which the legend describes as having been interrupted by the singing of nightingales, which were very numerous here; however, by his prayers and intercessions with heaven he was so highly favoured, that they were banished from his gardens and park, and were obliged ever after to confine their melody to the outside of his pales [1].

Havering was frequently visited by Queen Elizabeth, in her different Progresses through Essex, Hertfordshire, and Suffolk. During her stay here in 1578, Lord Burghley, one of her Secretaries of State, attending on her Majesty, received the letter from the University of Cambridge which has been noticed in a former page [2]. The reply to this letter is dated "from the Court at Havering."

In Mrs. Elizabeth Ogborne's "History of Essex [3]" is an engraved Plan of part of Havering Palace, which is a reduced copy from the original taken by Lord Burghley, in 1578. The writing and figures are undoubtedly by him; a *fac-simile* is given of them on the Plan. As there appears to be no other delineation of the Royal house than this, it hence becomes a valuable relic, and in part illustrates a curious survey of the Palace, taken in 1596, now in the British Museum, written by Samuel Fox, son of John Fox the Martyrologist, who was made Keeper by Sir Thomas Heneage, to whom the custody of Havering Palace was granted by Queen Elizabeth.

[1] On the East side of the road leading from Havering to London is a very handsome seat, which commands a most extensive and delightful view of the surrounding country. The late Sir John Smith Burges placed in the hall of the mansion a stone, taken from the ruins of the old Palace, with the arms of King Edward III. on it, and the following inscription:

E Reliquiis Ædis Regalis de HAVERING BOWER
in summitate collis sitæ.
Hoc fundavit domicilium JOHANNES BAYNES
Serviens ad Legem,
ut in otia tuta recederet,
et sibi et amicis suaviter vacaret, A. D. 1729.
H. FLITCROFT, Architectus; C. BRIDGMAN, designavit.
Arma Regis Edwardi Tertii super hoc
sculpta saxum vetustatem satis evincunt.

[2] See vol. II. p. 109.

[3] A very elegant Publication in quarto, of which only Three Numbers have appeared; and which, I am sorry to add, has not received that public encouragement which it well deserves.

A noate of suche implements and stuff as was in her Maties house of Haveringe to a view of the repayryne of the lodgynge howses and offyces as they were left by Samuel Foxe, taken the 6th day of May, 1596, by the undernamed:

At the entrance of the Great Chamber: a two leaved doore wth a barre, drawing wyndows of wood. The Lyttell Chamber: at the comyng up w^t a doore, lock, and key; the wyndow glazed. The Great Chamber: a doore w^t a barre, another doore w^t lock and key, all the wyndowes and casements glazed, and wooden wyndowes; two tabells, whereof one is of deal borde w^t tressels, five formes, a cupborde.

The Chappell: a doore w^t a locke and key, another doore to be barred, the wyndowes and casements all glazed; in the claw set, a cupborde, a doore going into the leades w^t locke.

The Presence Chamber: five doores w^t boultes and rings and four double lockes, the wyndowes glazed, only one casement blowen and broken in the wynde, two longe tables w^t tressells and formes.

My Lord Chamberlayne's Lodgynge: a cupborde, a doore with locke and key, three other doores w^t boltes, the wyndowes and casements glazed, and wooden wyndowes.

The Privy Chamber: matted and glazed, the doores w^t double lockes, boltes, stapells and rings.

The Withdrawinge Chamber: matted and glazed and wooden wyndowes, the doors w^t double lockes, boltes, and rings.

The Bed Chamber: matted and glazed, w^t waynscott windows, a doore w^t double locke, stapells, and rings.

The Lobbye, Coffer Chamber, and Gallerye, together with all the Privy Lodgynge, matted and glazed, w^t doores, double lockes, boltes, stapells, and rings; a little closet w^t small shelves.

My Ladye Cobham's Chamber: locke and key. My Lorde Treasurer's Chamber: two doores w^t lockes and keys.

A Portall: and doore of waynscott, wyndowes, and casements glazed, four tressells.

In the Robes: two wyndowes and casement glazed, a doore w^t a locke and key, nine tressels.

The Lodgynges for the Ladyes of the Privy Chamber, by the gardein, w^t doores, lockes, and keyes, and wyndowes glazed.

In the entrie to the Gardein: a doore w^t locke and key. The new lodgings w^t doores, lockes, and keys, wyndowes and casements glazed.

In the Pantrie: an old bynne, a cupboarde, four wooden wyndowes, a doore w^t locke and key, a table and tressells.

In the Cellar and Butterye: stooles to set beere and wyne on, the doors w^t lockes and keys, a pulley, a tabull, a forme. A roome by the buttery w^t a locke and key. A room in the cellar w^t tabull and shelves, the wyndowes glazed. A roome w^t locke and key. In the Privye Kitchen, two doores w^t lockes and keyes, the wyndowes glazed, six planke tabulls or dressers w^t tressels, a dresser, doore bolted and foot stoole. In the Pasterye and Privye Larder: four tabulls w^t tressels, a doore w^t locke and key, the rest w^{t}out, most of the wyndowes glazed. The Wardrobe w^t locke and key.

In the Stable: a bynne for oats, rackes, and mangers whole. In other two stables; mangers whole, racks and planckes, and the walls decayed.

A roome w^t locke and key for the Yeoman of the Butterye. In the salte house; a lock and key. In a chamber over the pasterye, a door w^t a locke and key. In the Spicery a doore w^t locke and key. In the Wett Larder, six plancke boards upon tressells, two doors w^t lockes and keyes, an old pair of stockes.

In the Great Kytchen: four dresser boards upon tressells. In the Bakehouse; a kneading trough, four moulding boards, a doore w^t locke and key. In the L^s Kytchen: two dresser boards upon tressells, three doors w^t lockes and keys, a locke and key to a lofte out of the kytchen. A chamber by the scullerye w^t a locke and key. In the scullerye; a doore w^t locke and key, three plancke boardes upon tressells, the wyndowes glazed.

In the New Kytchen: two dresser boards. In the stow-house; a trouffe to put in nayles, a cupboarde, a hod, a syve, a shovel, a locke and key. At the Well[1] a bucket a chayne, a rope.

In all the Lodgynge over the Gaet next the greene, all the wyndowes and casements glazed, the upper roomes matted, and three new seeled, six doors above steyres w^t lockes and keyes, and five weare taken and are to be put agayne upon the new lodgyngs that want. A waynscott portall w^t two doores, ringes, boltes, and latches.

Duble keyes	6	Short tables	8
Single keyes	18	Formes . . 47 Head of formes	16
Latches	8	Tressels, as many pair as tables.	
Long tables	3	Cupboardes	24

All the howse and out-howses tyled and leaded sufficiently to keep out the rayne.

In the Gardein; three double locks, the alleys and quarters laid out and sett w^t quick-sett and sweet briar, w^t cherye trees, aple trees, and others out of repayre. In the base courte a campe shed pale w^t a doore, locke and key, into the Chappell-yearde, a gaet w^t a padlock into the butterye yearde.

The Chapell-yearde is about w^t cleft pale, all from the new kytchen it is paled with cleft pale all to the stable ende. Between the Chappell and the wall of ye pantrye the pale decayed.

HENRY GRAYE.   + The marke of ROBERT SAKENS.
RICARDUS ATKYNS.   + The marke of RICHARD LOFTON.

[1] This well was discovered in the digging near the chapel-yard, in 1812; in it was found a gold coin of King James I.; the village abounding in water, the well was filled up again.

Anno 33º *Reginæ* ELIZABETHÆ.

Receyved into the Office, and paid for in the Warraunts, 1590-1.
Oone cup with a cover silver guilt, fayer wrought, 749 oz. dim.
Item, one neste of three guilt bolls, with a cover fayre wrought, 257 oz. dim.

Geven to her Majestie in Progresse by the Bishop of *Wynchester* [1].
One cup of golde with a cover, havinge an angell in the toppe thereof, with a skrolle over his hed, VIVAT REGINA ELIZABETHA, 23 OZ.

Received of Mrs. Margaret Vaughain, one of the Chamberers to her Majestie.
One perfume-panne of silver, fayre, parcell guilt, with the Queen's arms graven in the myddest thereof, 27 oz. dim.

On the 11th of February 1590-1, St. Margaret's bells were rung on the Queen's removal from Richmond to Lambeth, on a visit to Archbishop Whitgift; and again on the 13th, when she went from Lambeth to Greenwich.

On the 10th of May 1591, " the Queen came from Hackney to Theobalds[2];" and on the 16th " dined abroad, in the chamber called the Queen's Chamber, in company with the French Ambassador and L."[3]

On this occasion a curious piece of Court flattery[4] was played off, characteristical both of the Statesman and the Queen, as well as of the times. But it seems to have been the compliment rather of Mr. Secretary Cecil the son (afterwards Earl of Salisbury) than of the father (the great Lord Burghley), who was by far the least flatterer and Machiavelian of the two. The Son, we find, was in consequence honoured with Knighthood[5] on the Queen's removing, May 20.

" I suppose you have heard," says Sir T. Wylkes, in a Letter to Sir R. Sydney, June 18, 1591, " of her Majesty's great entertaintment at *Tibbuls*; of her knighting Sir Robert Cecill, and of the expectation of his advancement to the Secretaryship. But so it is (as we said in Court) that the Knighthood must serve for both."

" It would be a very difficult," says Strype[6], " perhaps an impracticable task, should one endeavour to write a commentary capable of explaining the following singular piece, and therefore we shall leave it entirely to the contemplation of the Reader; observing only, that it is a strong piece of irony throughout, in which the Queen seems to rally the pains taken by her Minister, in the more vigorous part of his life, to adorn and beautify the *villa* for the sake of recreation,

---

[1] Dr. Thomas Cowper.
[2] Burghley Papers, vol. II. p. 196.
[3] Qu. who is L. ? Probably Lord Treasurer Burghley.
[4] This is readily explained by the " Conference" printed in p. 76.
[5] Burghley Papers, vol. II. p. 796.
[6] Annals, vol. IV. p. 77.

and when older, and wanting that recreation most, wished to turn it into a gloomy retreat, where he might wear away his lonesome hours in brooding over his cares.

" ELIZABETHA *Anglorum, id est, a nitore Angelorum Regina formosissima & felicissima:* To the disconsolate and retired spryte, the Heremite of Tybole, and to al oother disaffected sowles, claiming by, from, or under, the said Heremit, sendeth greeting: Whereas in our High Coourt of Chanceri it is given us to understand, that you Sir Heremite, the abandonate of Nature's fair works, and servaunt to Heaven's woonders, have, for the space of two years and two moonthes, possessed yoorself of fair Tybollet, with her sweet rosary the same tyme, the recreation of our right trusty and right well beloved Sir *William Sitsilt*, Knt. leaving to him the old rude repoze, wherein twice five years (at his cost) yoor contemplate life was releived, which place and fate inevitable hath brought greefs innumerable (for lover greef biddeth no compare) suffering yoor solitary eye to bring into biz house desolation and moorning, joyes destroyers, and annoye frendes, whereby Paradice is grown Wilderness, and for green grass are comen gray hearz, with cruel banishment from the frute of long laboure, the possession whereof he hath holden many yearz, the want of the mean profit thereof (health and gladness) having been greatly to his hindrance, which tooucheth as much in the interest we have in his faithful servicez, besides the law of his looving neibours and frends infinite, as by the record of their countenaunce most plainly may appear.

"Wee, upon advised consideration, have commanded you Heremit to yoor old cave, too good for the forsaken, too bad for oour worthily belooved Coouncillour. And becauz we greatly tender yoour comfort, we have given poour to oour Chauncillour to make oout such and so many writs, as to him shal be thought good, to abjure desolations and mourning (the consumer of sweetness) to the frozen seas, and deserts of Arabia Petrosa, upon pain of 500 despights to their terror and contempt of their torments, if they attempt any part of yoour hoous again: enjoynyng you to the enjoyment of yoour own hoous and delight, without memory of any mortal accident or wretched adversary.

"And for that you have been so good a servaunt to common tranquility, we command solace to give the ful and pacific possession of al and every part thereof: not departing until oour favour (that ever hath inclined to your meek nature) have assured you peace in the possession thereof. Wherein we command al causez within the prerogative of oour high favour to give you no interruption. And this under the paine aforesaid they shal not omit. Teste meipsa apud Tyboles, 10mo die Maii, Regni nostri 33°.

On the back of this charter, " *Per Chancellor. Angl.* CHR. HATTON."

A Conferrence betweene a Gent. Huisher and a Post, before the QUEENE, *at* MR. SECRETARYE'S *House*[1]. *By* JOHN DAVIES[2].

P. Is Mr. Secretary Cecill heare?—did you see Mr. Secretary?—Gentlemen, can you bring me to Mr. Secretary?

U. Mr. Secretary Cecill is not heare—what business have you with him?

P. Marry, Sir, I have letters that ymport her Majesties service.

U. Then you weare best staye till he come; he was here even nowe; and will be againe by and by, if you have the patience to staye awhile.

P. Staye? The matter requires such post-hast, as I dare not for my lyef staye any where till I have delivered the letters; therefore I praye direct mee where I may fynd him, for without doubt it is busines that espetially concernes the Quenes service.

U. What a busines is here with you?—Yf the letters concerne the Quene, why should you not deliver them to the Quene? You see she is preasant, and you can not have a better opportunity—yf the inteligence be soe important, and concerne herself, as you saye.

P. I cannot tell what I should doe; they concerne the Quenes service indeed; but they tell me they ought to be delivered to one of them to whose place yt is proper to receave them.

U. Quenes service, Post!—what talk you? I know not what you thynke, but I am sure the world thynkes shee dooth herself best service when all is done, for all her morose servaunts, though I confess (for honor's sake) all great Princes must have attendants for their businesses.

P. Is it soe? Why then, I praye thee, tell me what use dooth she make of her servants?

---

[1] A particular description of this fine old mansion, from the pen of its noble Owner, has been given in vol. I. p. 205. It was for many years dilapidated, but the state-parlour, and the room in which King James I. died, were remaining in 1765, and Mr. Gough purchased so much of the chimney-piece of the former as survived the demolition. It is part of a groupe of emblematical figures of James I. under the character of Minerva, driving away the Giants, overthrowing Idolatry, and restoring true Religion, carved in clunch or soft stone, probably by Florentine artists, and was placed by Mr. Gough as an ornament in his spacious library at Forty Hill, Enfield, where it still remains.

[2] From the British Museum, Harl. MSS. 286. folio 248.

U. She makes the same use of them as the mynde makes of the sences. Many things she sees and heares through them; but the judgment and election is her owne.

P. Yf then the use of their service be soe smaule, how comes it that the reward of their service is soe greate?

U. Oh, therein she respecteth her owne greatnes and goodness, which must needs be such as it is, though it fynde noe objecte that is proportionable; as for example, the sun dooth cast his beames upon darke and grosse boodies that are not alike capable of his light, as well as upon cleare and transparent boodies which do more multiplie his beames; or, if thou doost not understand this demonstration, I will gyve thee one that is more familiar.

She dooth in this resemble some gentle mistress of children, whoe, when they gyde the handes of their schollers with their owne handes, and therby doe make them to wryte faire letters, doe yet, to encourage them, give them as much praise as if themselves had done it without direction.

P. Well, I am half perswaded to deliver the letters to her oune hand; but, Sir, they come from the Emperor of China, in a language that she understands not.

U. Why then you are verye symple, Post: though it be soe, yet theise Princes (as the Great Turke and the rest) doe alwaise send a translation in Italian, French, Spainishe, or Latyn; and then all is one to her.

P. Doth shee understand theise languages, and never crost the seas?

U. Art thou a Post, and hast ridden so manie myles, and met with so many men; and hast thou not hard that which all the world knowes, that shee speakes and understands all the languages in the world which are worthy to be spoken or understood?

P. It may bee shee understands them in a sort well for a Ladye, but not soe well as Secretaries should doe, that have been greate travaylers; and it is the parte of every Secretarye's possession to understand so mane languages.

U. Tush, what talkest thou of Secretaryes? As for one of them whome thou most askest for, if he have any thinge that is worth talkinge off, the world knowes well enough where he had it, for he kneles every daye where he learnes a newe lesson: goe on, therefore, deliver thy letters; I warrant thee, shee will read them if they be in any Christian language.

P. But is it possible, that a Lady borne and bred in her owne island, havinge but seene the confynes of her owne kingdomes, should be able without interpreters to gyve audience, and answeare still to all forraigne Embassadors?

U. Yea, Post, we have sene that soe often tryed, that it is here no wonder. But, to make an end, looke upon her. How thinkest thou; doest thou see her? Saye truly, sawest thou ever more majestie, or more perfection, met together in one boodye? Believe me, Post, for wisdome and pollicie, she is as inwardly sutable as externally admirable.

P. Oh—Sir, why nowe I stand back the rather, you have soe daunted my speritts with that worde; for firste, you saye, shee hath Majestie, and that you knowe never likes audacitie. Next, you saye, she is full of pollicie; now, what do I know, if pollicie maye not thinke fytt to hange up a Post if he be too sawcye? Noe, I have learned a better lesson at a grammar-schole: *Non est bonum ludere cum sanctis.* Farewell, good Sir; I will goe to one of the Secretaryes, come what will of yt.

U. Ah, symple Post, thou art the wilfullest creature that lyveth. Dost thou not knowe that, besides all her perfections, all the earth hath not such a Prince for affability; for all is one; come Gentleman, come Servingeman, come Plowman, come Beggar, the hower is yet to come that ever shee refused petition. Will she then refuse a letter when that comes from soe greate an Emperor and for her service? Noe, noe: doe as I bid thee; I should knowe some thinge, that have been a Quarter wayter these 15 yeares; draw nere her, knele downe before her, kisse thy letters, and deliver them, and use noe pratling, while she is readinge; and if ever thou have worse wordes than "God have mercy fellowe!" and "Give him a rewarde!" never trust me while thou lyvest.

P. Well, God blesse me, and God save her. Even God's will be done. I am half of thy belef, and I will prove my destiny.

Faire Queene, here are letters from the Emperor of Chyna, who doth salute you; and I your vassale am joyful to see you, whoe never sawe your Majestie, neither in the East Indies nor in the West, nor any country where there is neither man or beast.

On the second of August Sir Robert Cecil was sworn of the Privy Council at Nonsuch.

THE QUEEN AT THE LORD TREASURER'S HOUSE, 1591.

On the 10th of July the Queen was at the Lord Treasurer Burleigh's house [1] " to see the Earl of Essex's house in Covent Garden."

[1] Burleigh Papers, vol. II. p. 797.

Whenever the Queen shewed marks of condescension, she at the same time supported her own dignity. " Coming once to visit Lord Burleigh, being sick of the gout at Burleigh House in the Strand, and being much heightened with her head-attire (as the fashion then was), the Lord's servant who conducted her through the door said, ' May your Highness be pleased to stoop;' the Queen returned, ' For your Master's sake I will stoop, but not for the King of Spain's.' " Winstanley's Worthies, p. 246.—Of Lord Burleigh's house in Westminster, on or near whose site Exeter 'Change has been since built we have the following descriptions:

" *Burleigh House.* The house of the Right Honourable Lord Burleigh, Lord High Tresorer of England, and by him erected. Standing on the North side of the Stronde, a very fayer house, raysed with brickes, proportionably adorned with four turrets, placed on the four quarters of the house, within it is curiously bewtified with rare devises, and especially the oratory placed in the angle of the great chamber. Unto this is annexed, on the East, a proper house of the honourable Sir Robert Cecill, Knight, and of her Majesties most honourable Prevy Counseyle." Norden's Middlesex, MS.

" In the reign of King Edward VI. Sir Thomas Palmer began to build a house [where Exeter Exchange now stands] of brick and timber, very large and spatious; but afterwards [it] was far more beautifully increased by Sir William Cecil, Lord Burghley, whence it was then called Cecill House; and, after that, Exeter House; from his son and heir Thomas, created Earl of Exeter, 3. Jac. I. After Doctors Commons upon St. Bennet's Hill, London, was burnt down in the fire of London, 1666, this house was taken by the Society of the Doctors of the Civil Law; where, till the year 1672 (that Doctors Commons was rebuilt), the Civilians lodged, and kept their Courts of Arches, Admiralty, and Prerogative. But now of late this house is turned into an Exchange, and called Exeter Exchange." Peck's Desiderata Curiosa, from Newcourt's Repertorium, vol. I. p. 590.

" Cecil House some time belonged to the parson of St. Martin's in the Field, and by composition, came to Sir Thomas Palmer, Knt. in the reigne of Edward the Sixt, who began to build the same of bricke and timber, very large and spacious. But of later time, it hath bin farre more beautifully increased by the late Sir William Cecill, Baron of Burghley, Lord Treasurer, and Great Counsellor of the Estate." Stow, Survey of London, p. 493.

" Exchange Alley, Exeter Street, and Burleigh Street, formerly belonged to Exeter House and Garden, until thus built, being a large house belonging to the Earls of Exeter, and was antiently said to be a Convent, or Monastery, and that Covent Garden, then unbuilt, was the gardens and fields belonging to it. This Exchange contains two walks below stairs, and as many above, with shops on each side, for semsters, milleners, hosiers, &c.; the builders judging it would come in great request; but it received a check in its infancy, I suppose by those of the New Exchange; so that, instead of growing in better esteem, it became worse and worse; insomuch that the shops in the first walk next the street can hardly meet with tenants, those backwards lying useless, and those above converted to other uses; and here the Managers of the Land Bank keep their office." Strype, book IV. p. 119.

A slight sketch of this house may be seen in the Gentleman's Magazine, vol. LVI. p. 1007.

The New Exchange. was built on the site of Durham House; " concerning which," says Anth. Mundy, " it is well known and observed, that the outward part belonging thereto, and standing

On the same day (July 10) Lord Hunsdon, then Lord Chamberlain, writes to Sir William More: "I have thought good to let you understand that her Majesty is resolved to make a Progress this year as far as Portsmouth, and to begin the same the 22 or 23 of this month, and to come to your house. She is very desirous to go to Petworth and Cowdry, if it be possible; but none of us all can set her down any where to lie at between your house and Cowdry. And therefore I am to require you that you will sett this bearer some way for her to pass, and that you will let some one of your own men who is best acquainted with that way, to be his guide, that he may see whether they be fit for her Majesty or no. And whether it will be best going from your house to Petworth, and so to Cowdry, or else from your house to Cowdry. And if you can set her down [at] any place between your house and Cowdry that may serve her for one night, you shall do her a great pleasure, and she will take it very thankfully at your hands. But I have thought good to let you understand that, though she cannot pass by Cowdry and Petworth, yet she will assuredly come to your house, and so towards Portsmouth such other way as shall be set down to her. And therefore, I pray you, advertise me by this bearer of your full knowledge and opinion therein. And so I commit you to God. In haste, July 10, 1591, your very loving frend, HUNNESDON."

North from the houses, was but a low row of stables, old, ruinous, ready to fall, and very unsightly, in so publick a passage to the Court and to Westminster. Upon which consideration, or some more especial respect in the mind of the Right Honourable Robert Earl of Salisbury, Lord High Treasurer of England, it pleased him to take such order in the matter, that (at his own costs and charges) that deformed row of stabling was quite altered, by the erection of a very goodly and beautiful building instead thereof, and in the very same place. Some shape of the modeling, though not in all respects alike, was after the fashion of the Royal Exchange in London, with cellars underneath, a walk fairly paved about it, and rows of shops above, as also one beneath, answering in manner to the other, and intended for the like trades and mysteries. This work was not long in taking down, nor in the erection again; for the first stone was laid on the 10th day of June, 1608, and also was fully finished in the next ensuing November after. Also on Tuesday, being the 10th day of April following, divers of the upper shops were adorned in rich and beautiful manner, with wares most curious to please the eye; so ordered against his Majesty's coming thither to give a name to so good a building. On the day following, it pleased his Highness, with the Queen, Prince, the Duke of York, and the Lady Elizabeth, to come thither, attended on by many great Lords and choice Ladies. Concerning their entertainment there, though I was no eye-witness thereof, yet I knew the ingenuity and mind of the Nobleman to be such, as nothing should want to welcome so great an expectation. And therefore, what variety of devices, pleasing speeches, rich gifts and presents, as then flew bountifully abroad, I will rather refer to your imagination, than any way come short of by an imperfect narration. Only this I add, that it then pleased his most excellent Majesty, because the work wanted a name before, to entitle it "Britain's Burse," or "Buss." Mundy, in Strype, VI. p. 3.

G. Kyter inv.   Printed by Simmons

LETTER FROM SIR WILLIAM MORE TO LORD HUNSDON, 1591.

The following was folded up in the same paper, and appears to be a copy of Sir William More's answer to the above:

"With remembrance of my duty to your hon^ble Lordship. Understanding by your letters her Ma^ty's good pleasure in purposing to visit my poor house, I am most heartly glad thereof, and account myself bound to her Highness' favour therein. And whereas your Lo. doth require to be advertised from me of some fit place between my house and Cowdry for her Ma^ty to lodge in one night, it may please you to understand that there is not any convenient house for that purpose standing near the way from my house towards Petworth or Cowdry: only there is a little house of Mr. Law. Elliott [1], distant 3 miles from mine, the direct way towards either of the said places, and within 10 miles of Petworth, and 11 of Cowdry; to which house I have directed Mr. Constable by a servant of mine who hath viewed the same, and can make report to your Lordship thereof. From thence there is another the like house in Shillinglie [2], of one Bonners, distant 5 miles, the direct way to Petworth, and about a mile out of the way to Cowdry [3]."

Sir William More's daughter Elizabeth married Richard Polsted, Esq. of Aldbury in Surrey, where he died in 1576. She soon after married, secondly, Mr. (afterwards Sir John) Wolley [4], of Pirford in the same County, who died in 1595; and, lastly, in 1596 or 1597, Sir Thomas Egerton, then Lord Keeper.

---

[1] Busbridge, now belonging to Henry Hare Townsend, Esq.   [2] Now the Earl of Winterton's.

[3] The picturesque ruins of this once magnificent seat stand in a valley between two well-covered hills near the borders of the Arun, which runs between them through an extensive park, containing some of the finest chesnut-trees in England. Many good views of Cowdry both in its perfect and dilapidated state, have been engraved by eminent Artists.

[4] This gentleman was a native of Shropshire, and was educated at Merton College in Oxford in 1553; where he took the degree of B. A. Oct. 11, 1553; was elected Fellow the same year; and studied the Canon and Civil Law. He proceeded M. A. July 5, 1557; and in December travelled beyond the seas, where he improved himself much in learning, and in knowledge of men and manners. After the death of Roger Ascham, in 1568, he became Latin Secretary to Queen Elizabeth; and, in 1569, was made (though a Layman) Prebendary of Compton-Dundon in the Church of Wells. In 1576 he had the honour of a Visit from the Queen at his house at Pirford, where Sir William More (whose daughter he soon after married) was knighted.—On New Year's Day 1577-8, Mr. Wolley presented to the Queen "a fork of agathe, garnished with gold;" and received a gilt cup with a cover, weighing 28¼ ounces.—In 1578 he was made Dean of Carlisle; and in 1586 was appointed one of the Commissioners for the Trial of Mary Queen of Scots. In 1588-9 he gave the Queen "a round cloke of black clothe of gold, with buttons and loops on the inside of Venice gold and black silk;" and Mrs. Wolley gave "a doublet of black stitched cloth of two sorts, flourished with Venice gold and silver. In return, they had 45¼ ounces of gilt plate.—In 1589 he was made Chancellor of the Order of the Garter; in 1592 was knighted; and about the same time made one of the Privy

Lady Wolley, in a letter to her father (without date), says, " Since my coming to the Court, I have had many gratious words of her Majesty, and many times bad me welcome with all her heart, ever since I have waited. Yesterday she

Council; being elected also, the year following, one of the Representatives in Parliament for the County of Surrey. He died at Pirford in February or March 1595-6; and was buried in the middle of the Chancel of St. Paul's Cathedral, behind the high altar. Over his grave was soon after laid a flat stone, with an inscription thereon, under which in 1600 was laid his widow Elizabeth (then Lady Egerton), and Sir Francis Wolley, his son and heir, who died in 1611; all whose bodies were removed in 1614, and buried between St. George's Chapel and that of Our Lady, within the precincts of the Cathedral; and a very goodly tomb (as Stowe informs us, Annals, 1617, 4to, p. 633) erected over them thus inscribed:

"JOANNES WOLLEIUS, Eques Auratus,
Reginæ Elizabethæ à Secretioribus Conciliis, Secretarius Linguæ Latinæ,
Cancellarius Ordinis Periscelidis:
Doctrinâ, Pietate, Fide, Gravitate, clarissimus.
Obiit anno 1595.

WOLLEII clarum nomen, Natusque Paterque
Ambo Equites. Natus Franciscus Patre Joanne:
Clarus, ut hæredem virtutis, amoris, honoris
Præstaret, Monumenta sibi hæc; & utrique Parenti
Constituit, generis, qui nominis, unicus hæres.
Tam citò, tàm claros est defecisse dolendum.

Ille Pater, lumen literarum nobile, sydus
Oxoniæ, ex meritis Reginæ accitus Elizæ,
Ut qui à Secretis, cum scriberet illa Latinè,
Atque à Conciliis cum consultaret in Aulâ,
Atque Periscèlidis qui Cancellarius esset.
Tantum ille ingenio voluit, tantum instar in illo.

Non minùs omnimoda virtute illa inclyta Mater
Nobilibus Patre & Fatre illustrissima moris;
Clara domi per se: sed Elizam ascivit Eliza,
Clarior ut fieret Wolleio ornata marito,
Quo, viduata, viro, quo non præclarior alter,
Nubat Egertono, repetat sed mortua primum.

Franciscus tandem, at nimium citò, utrumque sequutus,
Hic jacet ante pedes Eques Illustrissimus, illis,
Hæc poni jussit, seque & tria nomina poni;
Sic voluit, placuit Superis pia, grata voluntas.
Discite mortales, memores sic esse Parentum,
Discite qui legitis, sic sic petit æthera virtus."

wore the gown you gave her¹, and thereby took occasion to speak of you, saying, "Ere long I should find a Mother-in-law," which was herself; but she was afraid of the *two widows*² that are there with you, that they would be angry with her for it; and that she would give ten thousand pounds if you were twenty years younger, for that she hath but few such servants as you are; with many gracious speeches of yourself and my brother."

In another letter, written to her brother Sir George More, dated 5 April, but also without the year, she says, "Her Majesty bad me welcome to the Court, and said I was absent a fortnight, she had kepte a reconninge of the dayes; she verie carefully enquired how my father did, and his *twoe wydowes*², and was verie glad of his health, the contynuance whereof she did praie for."

No particulars of this Visit are found; but it appears by the following paper, that she did go to Loseley, and had been there before.

The abuses of Purveyors of the Royal Household³, in procuring, amongst other things, carriages for removing goods, provisions, and other things, which they took at their own prices, which were less than the real value, and sometimes even that money not paid, occasioned frequent complaints, which were often attended to⁴. On one of those occasions the inhabitants of Merrow, and other places near Guildford, were ordered to make a return of what charges they had been put to

¹ From this circumstance, and what she says of her father's age, this letter was probably written after the Queen's Visit to Loseley in 1591.—Sir W. More died July 20, 1600.

² This allusion is not easily to be explained.

³ On the subject of Purveyors, see the Extracts from Chalk, under 1590, pp. 37, 38.

⁴ When this Queen was at Nonsuch, her purveyor of coals used to make out a warrant to the High Constables of some rape in Sussex, to warn carts for the carriage of coals to Nonsuch, appointing a meeting with them to receive the returns on the warrants. Sometimes the carts went to the places appointed, but found no coals to carry; but in general it was understood that the meeting was the principal purpose, and at that time the Purveyor took a person with him to whom he assigned them over to compound for their carriages. This man would take twelve shillings for every load, and at last raised it to fourteen or fifteen shillings. The Justices of Sussex complained of this to the Green Cloth in 1598.

Queen Elizabeth, by letters patent 14 November, anno 17, granted to Eye of Suffolk, "that the Corporation and inhabitants should be for ever quit of purveyance of all vitayle, and of all quick cattle or other vittaile live or dead."

by the Purveyors. The Constable of Merrow accordingly delivered a paper addressed to Sir William More and the other Justices of the Peace, which states, " that, they being sworn and appointed to bring in a true presentment of all provisions served for her Majesty's Houshold within that parish before Michaelmas 1591," they say; " That in August 1591 they carried 4 bushels of wheat to Guildfold, for her Majesty's use, being paid 2s. 4d. a bushel. At the same place a bushel and half of oats at her Majesty's last being at Loseley. And carried for her use one load of beer or ale from Guildford to Southampton, at her last being at Loseley; and that 5s. 6d. was paid for the carriage[1]."

16 Aug. 1591. The parishioners of Horsell (4 miles North of Guildford) carried 2 loads of beer from Weybridge Mead to Godalming [2].

---

[1] From Merrow to Guildford is a mile and a half, and from thence to Southampton about 52 miles. Can it be supposed that there was no public brewery between Guildford and Southampton, or at the latter place?

[2] There is a similar return from Send and Ripley, 6 miles from Guildford, dated 11 Jan. 1591. (meaning 1591-2), in which are the following articles:

" Item, we have paid for the carriage of 3 lodes of mault from Wickham bushes * to Shalford † when her Maty did lie at Sr Wm More's house.

" Item, Rich. Symon hath carried a tonne of beer from Gildford to Cowdry, for which he was paid 3s. 1d.

" Item, Geo. Stanton hath carried a tonne of wine from the Heath between Cobham and Ripley to Chiddingfold ‡, being paid for the carriage 2s.

" Item, delivered by Geo. Harry, Head Constable of Send, to George Watkins, Purveyor, 18 trusses of hay, and 4 bushels of oats, at the Lyon at Guildford, for which he [was] paid 4d. for every truss of hay, and 6d. for every bushel of oats, when her Majesty lay at Sutton §."

---

* Near Bagshot.

† A mile from Guildford.

‡ Shillinglie house, mentioned in page 81, is in the county of Sussex; but Chiddingfold, in Surrey, extends so near it as to take in part of the garden.

§ The seat of Sir Henry Weston, near Guildford. See hereafter, p. 121.

Expences of Sir HENRY UNTON's[1] Embassy to France[2], 1591.

Her Ma^{tie's} Pasporte, dated the 21st of July, 1591.

ELIZABETH R.

Whereas we have apoynted our trustye and wel-beloved servant Sir Henry Unton, Knyght, to make his repayre into France, ther to be our Ambassador resident with our good brother the French King: we straightly chardge and commaund you, and every of you, not only to suffer him, with his company and trayne, and all his and ther horses and geldings, monye, juells, plate, males, cofers, bagge, and baggages, and all his necessary and household provisions and furniture whatsoever, at all tymes quietly to passe by you, withowte any manner your stay let, or interruption; but also, that all you, and every of you, see him and his sayd trayne furnished, from place to place, to the sea-syde, both of sufficient and

---

[1] Of the Queen's Visit to Sir Edward Unton (otherwise Umpton), Father of this Sir Henry, at Wadley, near Farringdon, see before in vol. I. p. 391.—Sir Henry's character is thus detailed by Fuller in his "Worthies" of Berkshire:

"Henry Umpton, Knight, was born (as by all indications in the Heralds' Office doth appear) at Wadley in this County. He was son to Sir Edw. Umpton, by Anne (the relict of John Dudley, Earl of Warwick, and) the eldest daughter of Edw. Seymour, Duke of Somerset. He was imployed by Queen Elizabeth Embassadour into France, where he so behaved himself right stoutly in her behalf, as may appear by this particular. In the moneth of March, anno 1592, being sensible of some injury offered by the Duke of Gwise to the honour of the Queen of England, he sent him this ensuing challenge. 'Forasmuch as lately, in the lodging of my Lord Du Mayne, and in publick elsewhere, impudently, indiscreetly, and over boldly, you spoke badly of my Soveraign, whose sacred person here in this Country I represent; to maintain both by word and weapon her honour (which never was called in question among people of honesty and vertue): I say you have wickedly lyed in speaking so basely of my Soveraign; and you shall do nothing else but lie, whensoever you shall dare to taxe her honour. Moreover that her sacred person (being one of the most complete and vertuous Princesses that lives in this world) ought not to be evil-spoken of by the tongue of such a perfidious traytor to her law and country as you are. And hereupon I do defy you, and challenge your person to mine, with such manner of arms as you shall like or choose, be it either on horseback or on foot. Nor would I have you think any inequality of person between us, I being issued of as great a race and noble house (every way) as yourself. So, assigning me an indifferent place, I will there maintain my words, and the lie which I gave you, and which you should not endure if you have any courage at all in you. If you consent not to meet me hereupon, I will hold you, and cause you to be generally held, for the arrantest coward and most slanderous slave that lives in all France. I expect your answer.' I find not what answer was returned. This Sir Henry dying in the French King's camp before Lofear, had his corpse brought over to London, and carried in a coach to Wadley, thence to Farington, where he was buryed in the church on Tuesday the 8th of July 1596. He had allowed him a Baron's hearse because dying Ambassador Leigier."

[2] From a contemporary MS.

able horses, and of any other cariages also which he may need, at reasonable pryses. And farther, that ye be also ayding and assisting unto the sayd Sir Henry Unton, for providing him of convenient shipping, for the suer and saffe transportation of him and his trayne, and this likewise at pryses reasonable; not fayling thereof, as you tender our displeasure, and will answer for the contrarye at you perill. And thes our letters shall be your sufficient warrant and dischardge in this behalffe. Geven under our signet, at our mannor of Greenwich, the 20th of July, in the 33d year of our Raigne.

 To all Justices, Mayors, Shrieffes, Bayliffes, Constables, Customers, Controlers, and Searchers, and to all other Officers, Ministers, and Subjects, to whome in this case it may appartayne, and to every of them.   ED. LAKE.

The note of indenture, of the Queen's plate, delivered to my Lo. owte of the Juelle-house, 25 July, 1591.

This indenture, made the 25th day of July, anno 33° Regine Elizabethe, witnessethe, that John Asteley, Esquier, Master and Thrẽr of her Maties juells and plate, hath delivered unto Sir Henry Unton, Knight, Legier Ambassador sent unto Fraunce, thes pcells of silver vessells following;

 First, two great platters, p oz. 86 oz. di. q̃r.
 Itm, fower demy platters, p oz. 119 oz. 3 q̃r.
 Itm, six lesser platters, p oz. 141 oz. q̃r.
 Itm, eight dishes, p oz. 118 oz.
 Itm, nyne demy dishes, p oz. 110 oz.
 Itm, six lesser dishes, p oz. 58 oz. & q̃r.
 Itm, one bassin and ewer of silver, whete, p oz. 62 oz. di. q̃r.
 Itm, six sawcers, p oz. 29 oz.

In wittnes wheroff, the pties abovesayd have to thes p̃sent indentures interchangeably set ther hands, the day and yeare above written.

  Subsc. J. ASTELEY.   Test. N. PIGEON.

A note of the charges Sir Edward Stafford demaunded, every 3 monethes, for intelligence monie; and the words of his warrant were these, as followeth, subscribed under his owne hand, to Mr. Secretarie Walsingham:

For so muche monies by me disborsed, for three monthes, as namely, Aprill, May, and June, for necessarie and especiall causes, for her Ma$^{tie's}$ s̃vice in Fraunce, subscribed by me for 3 monethes before receited, untill the ... of this instant moneth £136.

his rate is demaunded at his goinge out of service.

And he demaunded at his first enterance to the service but £80.

Wares were the causes for thre moneths: by the same reason you may set down more then he did for his 3 monethes.

Wheras I receaved now lately of the Queene's Matie monie by impresse the som of £280, by vertue of her Ma^{ts} Privie Seale, bearinge date the 22d day of July, in the 33d yeare of her Highnesse Raigne; the said som is to be defaulked in allowance of my diet, after the rate of £3. 6s. 8d. the day, which is now expired, the 20th day of March, in manner and forme followinge, and allowinge 28 daies to the moneth:

For my diet of 11 daies in December, beinge on the 20th daie therof, the said daye beinge inclusive.

For 31 daies in Januarie, 29 daies in Februarie, and 13 daies in Marche.

Mr. Petters, I praie you deliver to this bearer my s̃vant, Nicholas Payne, the som of £280, monie nowe dewe to me by imprest by vertue of the Queene's Matie's Privie Seale, bearinge date the 20th daie of July, in the 33rd yeare of her Highnesse's Raigne, for allowance of my diet, from the 20th daie of March exclusive, untill 3 monethes next followinge be expired. Dated at the Camp, the 20th daie of March, 1591, Your verie lovinge frend.

To his verie lovinge frend Mr. Robert Peters, Esquier, Auditor of her Matie's Excheq^r.

The particular chardges of Sir Henry Unton, Knight, her Matie's Ambassador into Fraunce, for his transportations, cariages, and other ordynarye chardges, since his departure, from the 23rd of Julye, untill the 20th of December, in the same yeare, 1591.

	£.	s.	d.
Item, for cariage of some of my stuffe from London to Dover	20	0	0
For 46 post-horses from London to Dover	24	0	0
For the transportation of my horses, stuffe, and servants, from London, wher thei weer shipped, and of myselff and my companye, and other chardges, from Dover to Diepe, with pillotage ther dew	81	0	0
For carying my stuffe from Diepe to Rawnye, beinge 56 leagues	48	0	0
For my horses from Diepe to Rawnye	60	0	0
For the chardges of such as weer with me to convoy me untill comming to the K. and rewarde to them	60	0	0
Sum totall	£293	0	0

Wheras I received now lastlye of the Queene's Maties monye, by impresse, the somme of £500, by vertue of her Maties Privye Seale, bearing date the 22nd day of Julye, in the 33rd yeare of her Maties Raigne: The sayde some is to be defalked in allowaunce of my dyet, after the rate of £3. 6s. 8d. the day, which is nowe expyred, the 20th day of December, in manner and forme followinge, and allowinge 28 dayes the month:

	£	s.	d.
For my dyet of 8 dayes in July, beginning in the 23rd day thereof, the sayd day being inclusive	26	13	4
For 31 daies of August	103	6	8
For 30 daies in September	100	0	0
For 31 in October	103	6	8
For 30 daies in November	100	0	0
For 20 daies in December	66	13	4
Sum	£500	0	0

Mr. Peeters I pray you to deliver to this bearer my servant, Nicholas Payne, the some of £280, mony now dew to me by impresse, by vertue of the Queen's Maties Privie Seale, bearing date the 22nd of July, in the 33rd yeare of her Highnes Raigne, for allowaunce of my dyet, from the 20th day of December till 3 monthes next following be expyred. Dated at the Campe before Roan, the 20th day of December, 1591. Your verye loving frend, HENRY UNTON.

    To his verye loving frend Mr. Auditor Peeter, Esqu^r,
        of her Maties Exchequer.

Wheras I received, &c. *ut supra*:

	£	s.	d.
For my dyet of 11 daies in December, being on the 20th day therof, the sayd daye being inclusive	36	13	4
For 30 dayes in Januarye	103	6	8
For 29 dayes in Feabruarye	96	13	4
For 19 daies in March	63	6	8
Sum totall	£300	0	0

Mr. Peeters, I pray you deliver to this bearer, &c. *ut supra*. Dated the 29th of March, 1591, at Deipe.

EXPENCES OF SIR HENRY UNTON'S EMBASSY TO FRANCE, 1591.

The perticuler chardges of transportations, and other ordinarye chardges, in retourning home to the Courte, the 17th of June, 1592.

	£.	s.	d.
Imprimis, for my transportation, with servants and myselff, from Fere in Tartanoys in Diepe, being 60 leagues - - -	60	0	0
For chardges of 120 horse, which went with me for convoy, and reward to them - - - - - - -	60	0	0
For transportations from Diepe to Dover, of myselff and 22 servants	20	0	0
For transportation of my stuffe, horses, and 26 servants, from Diepe to London - - - - - - -	50	0	0
For 23 post-horses from Dover to London - -	11	10	0
Sum totall -	£210	10	0

The first bill for intelligence monyes.

It may please your Lo. I have sent a bill for such monies as been disbursed by me in especiall and necessarie causes of her Mãtie's service, amounting to the somme of £285, which I humblye beseech your Lo. to subscrybe. In like manner, I have layd owte, for conveyaunce of letters for her Highnes' especiall causes, the some also under-written, which are inclosed in the same bill:

20 Decem. 1591. For espielle and intelligences -	£200	0	0
For sending of letters in August, at sevrall tymes, to Noyon to the French K. and Grymston, by her Matie's speciall order, and your Lo. - - - - - -	20	0	0
For sending of letters in September and October, to her Matie and your Lo. and for her speciall service - -	20	0	0
Sum of the total by me disbursed, from 23rd of July until the 20th of Decembr then next following, amounteth to the some of	£240	0	0

	£.	s.	d.
27 June, 1592. For espyall monye and intelligences, and for sending of letters in April, May, and June, for her Matie's service -	160	0	0
More, for so much monyes by me disbursed, for 3 monthes, as namely, January, February, and March - - -	100	0	0
Sum -	£260	0	

On the 15th of August the Queen, after dining at Farnham Castle, proceeded to Cowdray, where she remained till the 21st, as appears by the following narrative.

The Honorable Entertainment given to her MAJESTIE, *in Progresse, at* COWDRAY *in Sussex, by the Right Honorable the Lord* MONTECUTE, *anno* 1591, *August* 15 [1].

The Queene, having dyned at Farnham, came with a great traine to the Right Honorable the Lord Mountague's, on Saterdaie, being the 15 daie of August, about eight of the clocke at night; where, upon sight of her Majestie, loud musicke sounded, which at her enteraunce on the bridge suddenly ceased. Then was a speech delivered by a personage in armour, standing betweene two porters, carved out of wood, he resembling the third; holding his club in one hand, and a key of golde in the other; as followeth:

Saterday, August 15.

The Porter's Speech.

"The walles of Thebes were raised by musicke: by musick these are kept from falling. It was a prophesie since the first stone was layde, that these walles should shake, and the roofe totter, till the wisest, the fairest, and most fortunate of all creatures, should by her first steppe make the foundation staid, and by the glaunce of her eyes make the turret steddie. I have beene here a porter manie yeeres; many ladies have entred passing amiable, many verie wise, none so happie. These, my fellow-porters, thinking there could be none so noble, fell on sleepe, and so incurde the seconde curse of the prophesie; which is, never againe to awake. Marke how they looke, more like postes then porters, retaining onlie their shapes, but deprived of sences. I thought rather to cut off my eie liddes, then to winke till I saw the ende. And now it is: for the musick is at an end, this house immoveable, your vertue immortall. O miracle of Time, Nature's glorie.

---

[1] "Printed by Thomas Scarlet, and are to bee solde by William Wright, dwelling in Paules Churchyard, neere to the French Schoole. 1591."

FARNHAM PLACE, SURREY.

Fortune's Empresse, the world's wonder! Soft, this is the poet's part, and not the porter's. I have nothing to present but the crest of mine office, this keie: Enter, possesse all, to whom the heavens have vouchsafed all. As for the Owner of this house, mine honourable Lord, his tongue is the keie of his heart: and his heart the locke of his soule. Therefore what he speakes, you may constantly beleeve; which is, that in duetie and service to your Majestie he would be second to none: in praieng for your happinesse equall to anie.

Tuus, O Regina, quod optas explorare favor: huic jussa capescere fas est."

Wherewithall her Highnes tooke the keye, and said, she would sweare for him, there was none more faithfull: then being alighted, she embraced the Ladie Montecute, and the Ladie Dormir her daughter. The Mistresse of the house (as it were weeping in her bosome) said, " O happie time, O joyfull daie!"

That night her Majestie tooke her rest; and so in like manner the next day, which was *Sunday*, being most Royallie feasted. The proportion of breakefast was three oxen, and one hundred and fourtie geese.

Mundaie, August 17.

On Munday, at eight of the clock in the morning, her Highnes took horse, with all her traine, and rode into the parke: where was a delicate bowre prepared, under the which were her Highnesse musicians placed, and a crossebowe by a Nymph, with a sweet song, delivered to her hands, to shoote at the deere, about some thirtie in number, put into a paddock, of which number she killed three or four, and the Countesse of Kildare one.

Then rode hir Grace to Cowdrey to dinner, and aboute sixe of the clocke in the evening, from a turret, sawe sixteene buckes (all having fayre lawe) pulled downe with greyhoundes, in a laund. All the huntinge ordered by Maister Henrie Browne, the Lorde Montague's thirde sonne, Raunger of Windsore forest.

Tuesdaie, August 18.

On Tewsday hir Majestie wente to dinner to the Priory, where my Lorde himselfe kept house; and there was shee and hir Lordes most bountifully feasted[1].

[1] Lord Burghley writes " from the Court at Cowdray, August 18, 1591." Rymer, vol. XVI. p. 116.

After dinner she came to viewe my Lorde's walkes, where shee was mette by a Pilgrime, clad in a coat of russet velvet, fashioned to his calling; his hatte being of the same, with skallop-shelles of cloth of silver, who delivered hir a speach in this sort following:

Pilgrime.

"Fairest of all creatures, vouchsafe to hear a prayer of a Pilgrime, which shall be short, and the petition which is but reasonable. God graunt the worlde maie ende with your life, and your life more happie then anie in the world: that is my praier. I have travelled manie countries, and in all countries desire antiquities. In this Iland (but a spanne in respect of the World) and in this Shire (but a finger in regard of your realme) I have heard great cause of wonder, some of complaint. Harde by, and so neere as your Majesty shall almost passe by, I sawe an Oke, whose statelines nayled mine eies to the branches, and the ornamentes beguiled my thoughtes with astonishment. I thought it free, being in the fielde, but I found it not so. For at the verie entrie I mette I know not with what rough-hewed ruffian, whose armes were carved out of knotty box, for I could receive nothing of him but boxes; so hastie was he to strike, he had no leysure to speake. I thought there were more waies to the wood than one; and finding another passage, I found also a Ladie very faire, but passing frowarde, whose wordes set mee in a greater heate then the blowes. I asked her name? she said it was Peace. I wondred that Peace could never holde her peace. I cannot perswade myselfe, since that time, but that there is a waspe's nest in mine eares. I returned discentent. But if it will please your Highnesse to view it, that rude champion at your faire feete will laie downe his foule head: and at your becke that Ladie will make her mouth her tongues mue. Happelie your Majestie shall finde some content; I more antiquities."

Then did the Pilgrime conduct her Highnes to an Oke not farre off, whereon her Majesties arms, and all the armes of the Noblemen and Gentlemen of that Shire were hanged in escutcheons most beutifull. And a Wilde Man, cladde in ivie, at the sight of her Highnesse, spake as followeth:

The Wilde Man's Speech at the tree.

"Mightie Princesse, whose happines is attended by the Heavens, and whose government is wondered at upon the earth, vouchsafe to heare why this passage is kept, and this Oke honoured. The whole World is drawen in a mappe; the Heavens in a globe; and this Shire shrunke in a tree; and what your Majestie hath often heard off with some comfort, you may now beholde with full content. This Oke, from whose bodie so many armes doe spread, and out of whose armes so many fingers spring, resembles in parte your strength and happinesse: strength, in the number and the honour; happinesse, in the trueth and consent. All heartes of oke, then which nothing surer, nothing sounder. All woven in one roote, then which nothing more constant, more naturall. The wall of this Shire is the sea, strong, but rampired with true hearts, invincible; where every private man's eie is a beacon to discover, everie noble man's power a bulwarke to defende. Here they are all differing somewhat in degrees, not duetie: the greatnes of the branches, not the greenesse. Your Majesty they account the Oke, the tree of Jupiter, whose root is so deeplie fastened, that Treacherie, though she undermine to the centre, cannot finde the windinges; and whose toppe is so highlie reared, that Envie, though she shoote on copheigth, cannot reach her, under whose armes they have both shade and shelter. Well wot they that your enemies lightnings are but flashes, and their thunder, which fills the whole world with a noise of conquest, shall ende with a soft shower of retreate. Be then as confident in your steppes, as Cæsar was in his fortune: his proceedings but of conceit; yours of vertue. Abroad courage hath made you feared, at home honoured clemencie: clemencie which the owner of this grove hath tasted; in such sort, that his thoughts are become his heart's laberinth, surprized with joie and loialtie; joy without measure, loyaltie without end, living in no other ayer, then that which breathes your Majestie's safetie.

"For himselfe, and all these honourable Lords and Gentlemen, whose shieldes your Majestie doeth here beholde, I can say this, that as the veines are dispersed through all the bodie, yet, when the heart feeleth any extreame passion, sende all their bloud to the heart for comfort: so they being in divers places, when your Majestie shall but stande in feare of any daunger, will bring their bodies, their purses, their soules, to your Highnesse, being their Heart, their Head, and their Soveraigne. This passage is kept straight, and the Pilgrime, I feare, hath complained: but such a disguised worlde it is, that one can scarce know a Pilgrime from a Priest, a Tayler from a Gentleman, nor a Man from a Woman; everie man seeming to be that which they are not, onelie doe practise what they should not. The Heavens guyde you, your Majestie governes us: though our peace be envied by them, yet we hope it shall be eternall.—*Elizabetha Deus nobis hæc otia fecit.*"

Then, upon the winding of a cornette, was a most excellent crie of hounds, and three buckes kilde by the bucke hounds, and so went all backe to Cowdrey to supper.

Wednesdaie, August 19.

On Wednesdaie the Lordes and Ladies dined in the walkes, feasted most sumptuously at a table foure and twentie yards long.

In the beginning, her Majestie comming to take the pleasure of the walks, was delighted with most delicate musicke, and brought to a goodlie fish-pond, where was an Angler, that, taking no notice of her Majestie, spake as followeth:

The Angler's Speech.

"Next rowing in a westerne barge well fare angling. I have bin here this two houres, and cannot catch an oyster. It may be for lacke of a bait, and that were hard in this nibling world, where everie man laies bait for another. In the Citie, Merchants bait ther tongues with a lie and an oath, and so make simple men swallow deceitfull wares: and fishing for commoditie is growen so farre, that men are become fishes, for landelords put such sweete baits on rackt rents, that as good it were to be a perch in a pike's belly, as a tenant in theyr farmes. All our trade is growen to trecherie, for now fish are caught with medicins; which are as unwholmsom as love procured by withcraft unfortunate. We Anglers make our lines of divers colours, according to the kindes of waters: so men do their loves, aiming at the complexion of the faces. Thus Merchandize, Love, and Lordships, sucke venom out of vertue. I think I shall fish all daie and catch a frog: the cause is neither in the line, the hooke, nor the bait, but some thing there is over beautifull, which stayeth the verie minow (of all fish the most eager) from biting. For this we Anglers observe, that the shadow of a man turneth backe the fish. What will then the sight of a Goddesse? Tis best angling in a lowring daie, for here the sunne so glisters, that the fish see my hooke through my bait. But soft, here be the Netters; these be they that cannot content them with a dish of fish for their supper, but will drawe a whole pond for a market."

This saide, he espied a fisherman drawing his nettes towarde where hir Majestie was. And calling alowde to him,

" Hoe Sirra (quoth the *Angler*), What shall I give thee for thy draughte?

If there be never a whale in it, take it for a noble, quoth the *Netter*.

Ang. Be there any maydes there?

Net. Maydes, foole! they be sea fish.

Ang. Why?

Net. Venus was borne of the sea, and 'tis reason she should have maydes to attend hir."

Then turned he to the Queene; and after a small pawse, spake as followeth:

" Madame, it is an olde saying, There is no fishing to the sea, nor service to the king: but it holdes when the sea is calme, and the king vertuous. Your vertue maketh Envie blush and stand amazed at your happines. I come not to tell the art of fishing, nor the natures of fish, nor their daintines; but with a poor fisherman's wish, that all the hollow hearts to your Majestie were in my net, and if there be more then it will hold, I woulde they were in the sea till I went thether a fishing. There be some so muddie minded, that they cannot live in a cleere river, but a standing poole: as camells will not drinke till they have troubled the water with their feet, so can they never stanch their thirst, till they have disturbed the state with their trecheries. Soft, these are no fancies for fishermen. Yes, true hearts are as good as full purses, the one the sinues of warre, the other the armes. A dish of fish is an unworthy present for a Prince to accept: there be some carpes amongst them, no carpers of state; if there be, I would they might bee handled lyke carpes, their tongues pulled out. Some pearches there are, I am sure; and if anie pearch higher than in dutie they ought, I would they might sodenly picke over the pearch for me. Whatsoever there is, if it be good it is all yours, most vertuous Ladie, that are best worthie of all."

Then was the net drawen.

The Netter having presented all the fishe of the ponde, and laying it at hir feete, departed.

That evening she hunted.

Thursday, August 20.

On Thursday she dined in the privie walkes in the garden, and the Lordes and Ladies at a table of fortie-eight yardes long. In the evening the countrie people presented themselves to hir Majestie in a pleasaunt daunce, with taber and pipe; and the Lorde Montague and his Lady among them, to the great pleasure of all the beholders, and gentle applause of hir Majestie.

Fryday, August 21.

On Friday she departed towards *Chichester*.

Going through the arbour to take horse, stoode sixe gentlemen, whom hir Majestie knighted; the Lorde Admirall laying the sworde on their shoulders.

The names of the sixe Knights then made were these; *viz.*

Sir George Browne, my Lordes second sonne.

Sir Robert Dormer, his sonne in lawe.

Sir Henry Goaring.

Sir Henry Glemham.

Sir John Carrell.

Sir Nicholas Parker.

So departed hir Majestie to the dining-place, whether the Lord Montague and his sonnes, and the Sheriffe of the Shire, attended with a goodly companie of gentlemen, brought her Highnes.

The escutchions on the Oke remaine, and there shall hange till they can hang together one peece by another.—*Valete.*

The Queen remained some days at Chichester [1]; and of her Majesty's Entertainment in that City there was a full account in one of the Corporation Books; but unfortunately the Book is lost.

Mr. Dallaway, in his "History of the Western Division of the County of Sussex [2]," says, "It is certain that she staid at Petworth [3] and Stanstead."

[1] The Court was at Chichester August 22, whence William Burghley writes of a Monsieur Nocie. Rymer, vol. XVI. p. 117.

[2] Of this valuable work, a part of the second volume was printed, and ready to be delivered by the Printer, Mr. Bensley, when the fire happened at his house, and consumed all but a very few copies of the impression. It is to be feared that this loss will not be supplied, nor the remainder of the work completed.

[3] This place was the property of the Percys Earl of Northumberland, till the extinction of that noble house, when the estate descended by marriage to Charles Seymour Duke of Somerset; and was in like manner carried by his second daughter into the family of Wyndham (since invested with the Earldom of Egremont), and regularly transmitted to the present noble proprietor.

John Lord Lumley prepared a house in the East street near the Cross (now belonging to Mr. Waller) for her reception, with a spacious banqueting-room, still retaining its richly ornamented ceiling, in which she gave audience to the Mayor and Citizens.

In a MS Index of the lost Register, still preserved, is this entry: " 1591. The manner of the Queen's reception and entertainment in the Progresse to Chichester; and rewards given by the City to the Queen's Officers."

When the Queen left Chichester, she probably returned by Petworth and Stanstead[1] to Portsmouth[2], to which place it appears (as stated in page 84) ale was sent from Guildford for her Majesty's use.

Petworth House, the magnificent mansion of the Earl of Egremont, stands close to the town, the back front opening into the church-yard. It was erected on the site of the ancient house by the Duke of Somerset. The front of free-stone, adorned with statues on the top, forms one unbroken range, having twenty-one windows in each story; but the avenues to it want space, as the general effect would have been infinitely heightened by a more gradual approach. The interior arrangements are remarkable for magnificence and elegance, all the principal apartments being decorated with paintings, antique statues, and busts, some of which are of first rate excellence. It is related that many of these antiques, when purchased by the late Earl, were complete invalids, some wanting heads, others hands, feet, noses, or other parts. These mutilations his Lordship supplied by the application of new members, very ill adapted in point of execution to the Grecian or Roman trunks; whence it is observed that this stately fabric excited the idea of an hospital for wounded and disabled statues. —The park is very extensive, the wall being about twelve miles in circumference. In the front of the mansion is a sheet of water, formed at an expence of not less than £30,000, with the springs collected from the neighbouring hills.

[1] Then the seat of John Lord Lumley, now of Lewis Way, Esq.—Stanstead enjoys one of the most delightful situations in the kingdom; the windows of the mansion commanding a complete view of Portsmouth, the Isle of Wight, and the shipping at Spithead, together with an extensive prospect of the sea. The house is of brick. The principal front looks towards the West, and consists of a centre, a quadrangular building, connected with the two wings by a low open colonnade, of the Ionic order. In the middle of the centre building is a balcony, supported by two stages of Ionic columns; and on the top is a small observatory, crowned with a cupola. The wings are handsome quadrangular edifices, adorned with a pediment in the middle of each side, and are also surmounted by light open cupolas.—Stanstead had formerly two parks, one of which has been converted into farms. The present park comprehends 650 acres, exclusive of the forest, a tract of 960 acres, where the lord of the manor has a right of inclosing the land for twenty-one years, on clearing it of timber, and the tenants have at other times a right of common. This tract is now a fine nursery of young timber, the greater part of it having been re-planted with oak. It is a remarkable circumstance, that the spring after the acorns were planted, it was discovered that the mice had eaten holes in the greatest part of the seed; still the trees grew up, and few, if any, of them failed.

[2] No particulars occur of the Queen's Visit to Portsmouth, though there is no doubt of her having visited that noble fortress; to which at a great expence she added many new works. She also placed

From Portsmouth the Queen proceeded to Tichfield House [1], the seat of Henry Wriothesley, Earl of Southampton; and thence to the Town of Southampton [2].

a garrison there, of which some part were to keep watch night and day at the town gates, and others are set at the top of the church tower, where, by ringing of a bell, they can give notice what horse and foot are advancing towards the town, and by waving colours, signify from what quarter they come.

The *Decanter* represented in the annexed Plate was drawn in 1786 by the late very ingenious Mr. Jacob Schnebbelie, from the original, at that time in the possession of the Rev. John Milner, F. S. A. then resident as the Minister of a small Catholic Chapel at Winchester, and now a Bishop *in partibus*, and resident at Wolverhampton, famous for his various Antiquarian and Polemical Publications. The Decanter was given to Mr. Milner by Mr. Knight, who held an office in the Dock-yard at Portsmouth. Mr. Knight had received it as a present from Mr. Thompson, a Surgeon of the Royal Navy, who constantly averred that the curiosity in question had been carefully preserved in his family ever since the days of Elizabeth. Mr. Milner having made enquiries after this gentleman at Portsmouth, had the mortification to hear that he died in the West Indies. The neck of this vessel is one inch three-eighths wide, five three-eighths long; the body four inches high, seven and a half diameter with the ornaments, six and a half without. It is formed into eight pannels, each different, holds upward of two quarts, and is supposed to have been ornamented with diamonds by Queen Elizabeth when in confinement in the reign of her Sister Mary.

[1] On the 2d of September Lord Burghley dates his dispatches from the Court at Tichfield, the seat of the Earl of Southampton. Rymer, vol. XVI. p. 119, from Bibl. Cot. Calig. E. VIII, f. 20, misprinted *Lichfield*, but in the MS. *Tychfeld*.—Tichfield House, which is pleasantly situated on the Western banks of the Tichfield River, near the mouth of Southampton Bay, where it receives the Humble, was built on the spot where formerly stood an Abbey of Præmonstratensian Canons, founded in 1231 by Peter De Rupibus, and granted at the Dissolution by King Henry VIII. to Sir Thomas Wriotheseley, Secretary of State to that King, who, as it appears from Leland's Itinerary, on the site, and probably with the materials of the monastery, erected this mansion. His words are, " Mr. Wriotheseley has builded a right stately house, embateld, and having a goodely gate, and a conduite caste lid in the middle of the court of it, in the very same place wher the late monasterie of Premonstratensians stood caully'd Tichfielde." Sir Thomas was afterwards created by Henry VIII. Lord Wriothesley, or Tichfield, which barony, with the estate, descended to his successors, the Earls of Southampton, who made it their principal seat. Thomas the last Earl dying in 1677 without a male heir, this manor and house went with one of his daughters, to Edmund, first Earl of Gainsborough; whose son leaving no issue, it devolved to one of his daughters, Elizabeth; and she marrying Henry Bentinck, the first Duke of Portland, carried it into that family; and it was by the late Duke sold to Mr. Delme, whose son possessed it in 1793.—In Warner's " Collections for Hampshire," is a neat View of the fine old mansion at Tichfield, and another of Tichfield House Chapel, a venerable remnant of Antiquity.

[2] Though there is no doubt but the Queen visited Southampton both in 1569 and 1591, there is no account of her reception there. See vol. I. pp. 258, 261; and it appears in p. 84, that ale were sent thither from Guildford in August 1591.

Fig. 1
Vol. II p. 325. III. 370.

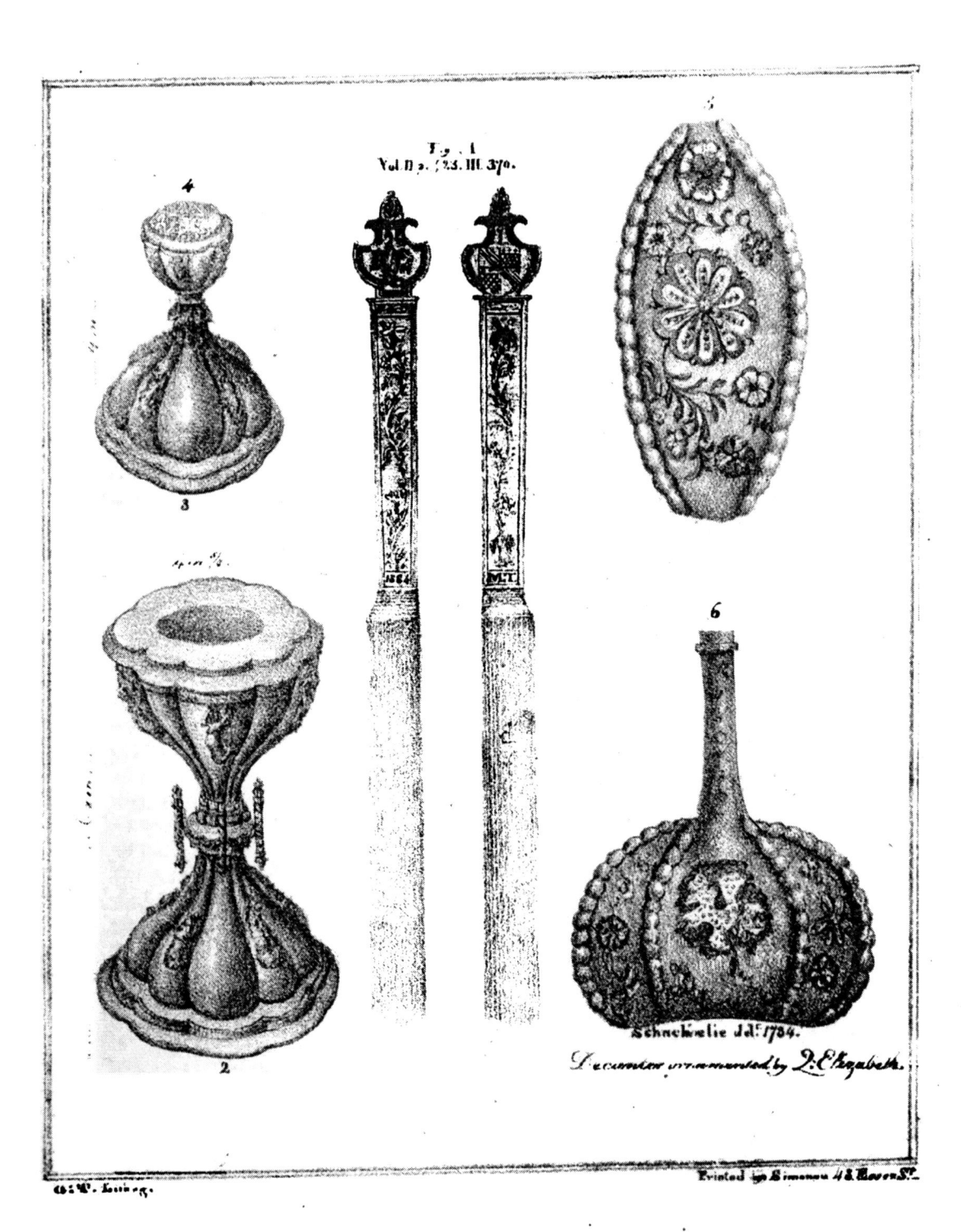

Schnehelie Ad. 1784.
Decanter ornamented by P. Elizabeth.

Though Queen Elizabeth several times honoured the City of Winchester with her presence, the following brief entry of the Visit in 1591, and those with other dates, are all I am able to record [1]:

"A. D. 1591, 33 Eliz. *Custus Panatriæ*,
"Item, pro lavandis linteaminibus post discessum Aulicorum, 3*s*. 6*d*.
"*Custus Necessariorum*,
"Item, pro Vino dat' Famulis Domine Regine, 6*s*. 2*d*.

[1] Previous to the former Edition of these Progresses, by the kindness of Dr. Warton and Mr. Blackstone, the different accompts of the College at Winchester, and the official books of the Town Clerk of that City, have been searched, on the chance of some particulars of Queen Elizabeth's various Visits there being recovered. The only articles that occur in these accounts, or that can be collected from other sources, are these:

In 1560 Queen Elizabeth was first at Winchester.

In 1564 she confirmed the Charter granted to that City by Richard II.

In 1566 she confirmed the College-immunities from payment of subsidies, fifteenths &c.

In 1570 she wrote to the Mayor of Coventry from *Southampton*; and probably passed thither through Winchester.

A. D. 1571. 13 Eliz. *Custus Necessariorum*,   *s. d.*
    Et in Regardis dat' Lusoribus Domine Regine - - - - - 6 8
    Et in Regardis dat' uni Officiar' Domine Regine volenti capere equum Collegii pro cariagiis dicte Domine Regine - - - - - - - - 1 0

"A Proclamation by the Queen's M'tie, for the publishinge and declaringe of the sentence latelie geven against the Queene of Scotts:

"Elizabeth," &c.

The Proclamation is thus endorsed:

"The 10th of December, 1586, betweene the hours of fyve and six of the clocke of the nighte in the afternoone of the same daie, ... Dorington, one of her Majestie's messengers, did deliver unto the Maior and Bailiffs of the City of Winchester this Proclamation within written, and the writt thereunto annexed. And we the said Maior and Bailiffs, callinge unto us the Recorder, Justices, Aldermen, and Citizens of the same Citie, the ninth of this instant month of December 1586, we did proclaim," &c. &c.

In 1589 she became a benefactress, and gave lands and tenements in Hampshire, which she held there.

A. D. 1596, 38 Eliz. *Custus Necessariorum*,
    Item solut' Ministro venienti a Domino Comite de Essex, 5*s*. 6*d*.

On the 13th of September Lord Burghley writes to the English Ambassador " from the Court at Sir Henry Wallop's, at Farley, near Basing[1];" on the 20th from Odiham[2]; and the same day from the Earl of Hertford's at Elvetham[3].

[1] Rymer, vol. XVI. p. 120.—This was from *Farley Wallop*, the seat of the Wallops, from the Reign of Henry VI. when Thomas Wallop acquired it by marriage with Margaret, daughter and coheir of Nicholas de Valoines, whose grandfather Sir William de Valoines lived there temp. Henry III. This noble large structure was the chief residence of the Wallops, till burnt in 1667, and re-built in 1733 by the late Earl of Portsmouth. It was made a garrison for the Parliament in the civil wars, the family monuments plundered, and the Church so ruined that it was obliged to be re-built by the late Earl. Sir Henry Wallop herein was knighted by the Queen at Basyng, 1569, and represented Southampton, a leading member in the House of Commons. On the Irish rebellion breaking out, he raised a company of 100 men, and carried them over; in 1580 he was constituted Vice-treasurer and Treasurer of War in that kingdom, and acted in the Government on the resignation of Lord Grey of Wilton, till the Earl of Desmond's rebellion was crushed in 1582. Upon his return to England, the Queen honoured him with a visit at this his seat in 1591, and was sumptuously entertained with her suite several days. He retired to Ireland, and died at Dublin, April 14, 1599, and was buried in St. Patrick's Church there, having made considerable purchases in that kingdom. His lineal descendant John was created Baron Wallop of Farley Wallop, Viscount Lymington, by George I. 1720, and Earl of Portsmouth by George II. 1742. He died 1762, and was succeeded by his grandson John the second Earl. Collins's Peerage.

[2] Rymer, vol. XVI. p. 121.—Odiham, where the Queen was magnificently entertained till the 23d, is a small corporate town, 41 miles from London, had formerly a Castle, a Royal Palace, and a Park. Some remains of the Castle still exist; the Palace has long since been converted into the residence of a farmer; but still preserves the name of *Place Gate*.—Camden, in the year 1586, says, Odiam is now famous for a Royal Palace, and for the imprisonment of David II. King of Scotland. It was once a free borough of the Bishop of Winchester, whose Castle, in the Reign of John, was gallantly defended for a fortnight by 13 English soldiers against Louis King of France, who had closely beleagured it with his whole army.—Whether the Queen was entertained there in 1591, does not appear, but it is stated in p. 103 to have been at " Odiham House." A neat view of the remains of the Castle, as they appeared in 1761, may be seen in Warner's Collection for Hampshire. Nothing now remained but the Keep, which then was an octagonal building, the North West side nearly demolished.

[3] Rymer, vol. XVI. p. 123.

Vol. III p. 101.

The Honorable Entertainment gieven to the Quene's Majestie, in Progresse, at Elvetham in Hampshire, by the Right Hon'ble the Earle of Hertford, 1591[1].

THE PROEME.

Before I declare the just time or manner of her Majestie's arrivall and Entertainment at Elvetham, it is needful (for the readers better understanding of everie part and processe in my discourse) that I set downe as well the conveniencie of the place, as also the suffising, by art and labour, of what the place in itselfe could not affoord on the sodaine, for receipt of so great a Majestie, and so honourable a traine.

Elvetham House beeing scituate in a parke but of two miles in compasse or thereabouts, and of no great receipt, as beeing none of the Earle's chiefe mansion houses, yet for the desire he had to shew his unfained love, and loyall duetie to her most gratious Highnesse, purposing to visite him in this her late Progresse, whereof he had to understand by the ordinarie gesse, as also by his honorable good frendes in Court neare to her Majestie; his honor with all expedition set artificers a work, to the number of three hundred, many daies before her Majestie's arrivall, to inlarge his house with newe roomes and offices. Whereof I omit to speake now manie were destined to the offices of the Quene's Houshold, and will onlie make mention of other such buildings as were raised on the sodaine, fourteene score off from the house on a hill side, within the said parke, for entertainement of Nobles, Gentlemen, and others whatsoever.

First there was made a roome of estate for the Nobles, and at the end thereof a withdrawing place for her Majestie. The outsides of the walles were all covered with boughs, and clusters of ripe hasell nuttes, the insides with arras, the roofe of the place with works of ivy leaves, the floore with sweet herbes and greene rushes.

[1] " Printed by John Wolfe, and are to bee sold at the Little Shop over against the Great South Dore of Paules, 1591."—A second edition of this Tract was published in the same year, professing to be " Newlie corrected and amended." As a matter of curiosity, I have collated here two copies; and have adopted the variations of the second edition. The orthography is so loose and so various, that it would be endless to mention the instances in which it is changed, sometimes for the worse, but very frequently for the better, or at least much nearer to the present standard. The Family Arms in the title-page and the picture of the Pond are coloured in both Editions.

An Engraving of the Great Pond is here annexed.

Neare adjoining unto this, were many offices new builded, as namely, Spicerie, Larderie, Chaundrie, Wine-seller, Ewery, and Panterie: all which were tyled.

Not farre off was erected a large hall, for the entertainement of Knights, Ladies, and Gentlemen of chiefe account.

There was also a severall place for her Majestie's footemen, and their friends.

Then was there a long bowre for her Majestie's guard.—An other for other servants of her Majestie's house.—An other for my Lord's Steward, to keep his table in.—An other for his Gentlemen that waited.

Most of these foresaid roomes were furnished with tables, and the tables carried twenty-three yards in length.

Moreover on the same hill, there was raised a great common buttrey.—A Pitcher-house.—A large Pastery, with five ovens new built, some of them foureteene foote deepe.—A great Kitchin, with four ranges, and a boyling place for small boild meates.—An other Kitchin, with a very long range, for the waste, to serve all commers.—A Boiling-house, for the great boiler.—A roome for the Scullery.—An other roome for the Cooke's lodgings.

Some of these were covered with canvas, and other some with bordes.

Betweene the Earl's house and the foresayd hill, where these roomes were raised, there had beene made in the bottom, by handy labour, a goodly Pond, cut to the perfect figure of a half moon. In this Pond were three notable grounds, where hence to present her Majestie with sports and pastimes. The first was a *Ship Ile*, of a hundred foot in length, and four-score foote broad, bearing three trees orderly set for three masts. The second was a *Fort* twenty foot square every way, and overgrown with willows. The third and last was a *Snayl Mount*, rising to foure circles of greene privie hedges, the whole in height twentie foot, and fortie foote broad at the bottom. These three places were equally distant from the sides of the ponde, and everie one, by a just measured proportion, distant from the other. In the said water were divers boates prepared for musicke: but especially there was a pinnace, ful furnisht with masts, yards, sailes, anchors, cables, and all other ordinarie tackling, and with iron peeces; and lastly with flagges, streamers, and pendants, to the number of twelve, all painted with divers colours, and sundry devises.

Here follows a description of the Great Pond in Elvetham, and of the properties which it contained, at such time as her Majestie was there presented with faire shewes and pastimes:

Her Majesties presence seate, and traine.—Nereus, and his followers.—The pinnace of Neæra, and her musicke.—The Ship Ile.—A boate with musicke, attending on the pinnace of Neæra.—The Fort Mount.—The Snaile Mount.—The Roome of Estate.—Her Majestie's Court.—Her Majestie's wardrop.—The place whence Silvanus and his companie issued."

To what use these particulars served, it shall evidently appeare by that which followeth. And therefore I am to request the gentle reader, that when any of these places are briefly specified in the sequele of this discourse, it will please him to have reference to this fore-description: that, in avoiding reiterations, I may not seeme to them obscure, whom I studie to please with my plainnesse. For proeme these may suffise: nowe to the matter itselfe: that it may be *ultimum in executione* (to use the old phrase) *quod primum fuit in intentione,* as is usuall to good carpenters; who intending to build a house, yet first lay their foundation, and square many a post, and fasten manie a rafter, before the house be set up: what they first purposed is last done. And thus much for excuse of a long foundation to a short building.

The First Daies Entertainement.

On the twentie day of September, being Mundaie, the Earle of Hertford joyfullie expecting her Majesties comming to Elvetham, to supper, as her Highnesse had promised: the same morning, about nine of the clock, when everie other needful place or point of service was established and set in order for so great an entertainment, called for, and drewe all his servants into the chiefe thicket of the parke: where in fewe wordes he put them in minde what quietnes, and what diligence, or other duetie, they were to use at that present: that their service might first work her Majestie's content, and therby his honor; and lastly, their own credit; with the increase of his love and favour towards them. This done, after dinner, with his traine well mounted, to the number of two hundred and upwardes, and most of them wearing chaines of golde about their neckes, he rode toward Odiham, and leaving his traine and companie orderlie placed, to attende her Majestie's comming out of Odiham Parke, three miles distant from Elvetham: himselfe wayting on her Majestie from Odiham House.

As the Earl in this first action shewed himselfe dutiful, so her Majesty was to him and his most gracious; as also in the sequel, between five and sixe of the clock, when her Highnes, being most honorably attended, entred into Elvetham Parke, and was more than halfe way between the Park-gate and the house, a poet saluted her with a Latine Oration, in heroicall verse: I mean *veridicus vates*, a sooth-saying poet, nothing inferior for truth, and little for delivery of his mind, to an ordinarie Orator. This poet was clad in greene, to signify the joy of his thoughts at her entrance; a laurel garland on his head, to expresse that Apollo was patrone of his studies; an olive branch in his hand, to declare what continual peace and plentie he did both wish and aboade her Majestie: and lastly booted, to betoken that hee was *vates cothurnatus*, and not a loose or lowe creeping prophet, as poets are interpreted by some idle or envious ignorants.

This poet's Boy offered him a cushion at his first kneeling to her Majestie; but he refused it, saying as followeth:

The Poet to his Boy offering him a cushion.

Non jam pulvillis opus est, sed corde sereno:
Nam plusquam solitis istic advolvimur aris.

The Poet's Speach to her Majestie.

Nuper ad Aonium flexo dum poplite fontem
Indulsi placido, Phœbi sub pectine, somno,
Veridicos inter vates, quos Entheus ardor
Possidet, et virtus nullis offusa lituris,
Talia securo cantabant carmina Musæ.
 Aspicis insueto tingentem lumine cœlum
Anglorum nostro majorem nomine Nympham
Os, humerosque Deæ similem, dum tuta Semeri
Tecta petit, qualis dilecta Philæmonis olim
Cannæ Cœlicolum subiit magalia Rector?
Olli tu blandas humili dic ore salutes:
Nos dabimus numeros, numeros dabit ipsus Apollo.
Sed metues tantæ summas attingere laudes:
Nam specie solem, superos virtutibus æquans,
Majestate locum, sacrisque timoribus implet.
Doctior est nobis, et nobis præsidet una:
Ditior est Ponto, Pontum quoque temperat una:
Pulchrior est nymphis, et nymphis imperat una:
Dignior est divis, et divos allicit una.
 En supplex adsum, Musarum numine ductus,
Et meritis (Augusta) tuis, ô dulcis Elisa,

Fronte serenata modicum dignare poetam,
Ne mea vernantem deponant tempora laurum,
Et miser in cantu moriar. Se namque Semeri
Obsequiosa meis condit persona sub umbris:
Qui fert ore preces, oculo fœcundat olivam;
Officium precibus, pacem designat oliva;
Affectum docet officiis, et pace quietem;
Mentes affectu mulcebit, membra quiete.
Hi mores, hæc vera tui persona Semeri,
Cui lætum sine te nihil, illætabile tecum
Est nihil. En rident ad vestros omnia vultus
Suaviter, immensum donec fulgoribus orbem
Elisabetha novis imples: nox invidet una:
Astra sed invidiæ tollunt mala signa tenebras.

   Cætera, qua possunt, sacræ gratantur Elisæ
Lætitia, promptosque ferunt in gaudia vultus.
Limulus insultat per pictos hœdus agellos
Passibus obtortis; et torvum bucula taurum
Blanda petit; tremulus turgescit frondibus arbos,
Graminibus pratum, generosa pampinus uva:
Et tenui latices in arena dulce susurrant,
Insuetumque melos: Te, te, dulcissima princeps,
Terra, polus, fluvii, plantæ, pecudesque salutant:
Dumque tuam cupide mirantur singula formam,
Infixis hærent oculis, nequeuntque tuendo
Expleri; solitis sed nunc liberrima curis,
In placidos abeunt animos: non semina vermes,
Non cervi metuunt cassem, non herba calorem,
Non viscum volucres, non fruges grandinis ictum.
O istos (Augusta) dies, o profer in annos;
Et lustrum ex annis, e lustris sæcula surgant;
E seclis ævum, nullo numerabile motu:
Ut nostros dudum quotquot risere dolores,
Gaudia jam numerent, intabescantque videndo.

En, iter objecto qua clauserat obice livor,
Virtutis famulæ charites, castrique superni
Custodes horæ, blandissima numina, junctim
Jam tollunt remoras, ut arenam floribus ornent.
  Ergo age, supplicibus succede penatibus hospes,
Et nutu moderare tuo: tibi singula parent,
Et nisi parerent tibi singula, tota perirent.
  Dicite Io Pæan, et Io ter dicite Pæan,
Spargite flore vias, et mollem cantibus auram.

Because all our Countreymen are not Latinists, I thinke it not amisse to set this downe in English, that all may bee indifferently partakers of the Poet's meaning.

The Poet's Speech to his Boy offering him a cushion.

Now let us use no cushions, but faire hearts:
For now we kneel to more than usuall Saints.

The Poet's Speech to her Majestie.

  While, at the fountaine of the sacred hill,
Under Apollo's lute I sweetly slept,
Mongst prophets full possest with holy fury,
And with true vertue, void of all disdaine;
The Muses sung, and waked me with these wordes:
  Seest thou that English Nimph, in face and shape
Resembling some great Goddesse, and whose beames
Doe sprinkle Heaven with unacquainted light,
While shee doth visite Semers fraudlesse house,
As Jupiter did honour with his presence
The poore thatcht cottage, where Philæmon dwelt?
See thou salute her with an humble voice;
Phœbus and we will let thee lack no verses.
But dare not once aspire to touch her praise,
Who, like the Sunne for shew, to Gods for vertue,
Fills all with Majesty, and holy feare.
More learned then ourselves, shee ruleth us:
More rich than Seas, shee doth commaund the Seas:

More fair then Nimphs, she governs all the Nimphs:
More worthy then the Gods, shee wins the Gods.
    Behold (Augusta) thy poore supplicant
Is here, at their desire, but thy desert.
O sweete Elisa, grace me with a looke,
Or from my browes this laurell wreath will fall,
And I, unhappy, die amidst my song.
Under my person Semer hides himselfe,
His mouth yeelds prayers, his eie the olive branch;
His praiers betoken duety, th' olive peace;
His duety argues love, his peace faire rest;
His love will smooth your minde, faire rest your body.
This is your Semers heart and quality:
To whom all things are joyes, while thou art present,
To whom nothing is pleasing, in thine absence.
Behold, on thee how each thing sweetly smiles,
To see thy brightnes glad our hemispheare:
Night only envies: whome faire stars doe crosse:
All other creatures strive to shewe their joyes.
The crooked-winding kid trips ore the lawnes;
The milke-white heafer wantons with the bull;
The trees shew pleasure with their quivering leaves,
The meddow with new grasse, the vine with grapes,
The running brookes with sweet and silver sound.
Thee, thee (sweet Princes), heav'n, and earth, and fluds,
And plants, and beasts, salute with one accord:
And while they gaze on thy perfections,
Their eyes desire is never satisfied.
Thy presence frees each thing, that liv'd in doubt:
No seedes now feare the biting of the woorme;
Nor deere the toyles; nor grasse the parching heat;
Nor birds the snare; nor corne the storme of haile.
O Empresse, O draw foorth these dayes to yeares,
Yeeres to an age, ages to eternitie;
That such as lately joyd to see our sorrowes,
May sorrow now, to see our perfect joyes.

Behold where all the Graces, vertues maydes,
And lightfoote Howrs, the guardians of Heav'n's gate,
With joyned forces doe remove those blocks,
Which Envie layd in Majestie's highway.
   Come, therefore, come under our humble roofe,
And with a becke commaund what it containes:
For all is thine; each part obeys thy will;
Did not each part obey, the wholl should perish.
   Sing songs, faire Nymphs, sing sweet triumphal songs,
Fill ways with flowrs, and th'ayr with harmony.

While the Poet was pronouncing this Oration, six Virgins were behind him, busily remooving blockes out of her Majestie's way; which blocks were supposed to bee layde there by the person of Envie, whose condition is to envie at every good thing, but especially to malice the proceedings of Vertue, and the glory of true Majestie. Three of these Virgins represented the three Graces, and the other three the Howres, which by the Poets are fained to be the Guardians of Heaven's gates. They were all attired in gowns of taffata sarcenet of divers colours, with flowrie garlands on their heads, and baskets full of sweet hearbs and flowers upon their armes. When the Poet's Speach was happily ended, and in a scroule delivered to her Majestie (for such was her gracious acceptance, that she deined to receive it with her owne hande); then these sixe Virgins, after performance of their humble reverence to her Highnesse, walked on before her towards the house, strewing the way with flowers, and singing a sweete song of six parts, to this dittie which followeth:

   The Song sung by the Graces and the Houres at her Majesties first arrivall.

With fragrant flowers we strew the way,
And make this our chiefe holliday:
For though this clime were blest of yore,
Yet was it never proud before.
   O beauteous Quene of second Troy,
   Accept of our unfained joy.
Now th'ayre is sweeter than sweet balme,
And Satyrs daunce about the palme:

Now earth, with verdure newly dight,
Gives perfect signe of her delight.
  O beauteous Quene of second Troy,
  Accept of our unfained joy.

Now birds record new harmonie,
And trees doe whistle melodie:
Now everie thing that nature breeds,
Doth clad itselfe in pleasant weeds,
  O beauteous Quene of second Troy,
  Accept of our unfained joy.

This song ended with her Majestie's entrance into the house: and her Majesty alighted from horsebacke at the Hall-dore, the Countesse of Hertford, accompanied with divers honourable Ladies and Gentlewomen, moste humbly on hir knees wecomed hir Highnesse to that place: who most graciously imbracing hir, tooke hir up, and kissed hir, using manie comfortable and princely Speeches, as wel to hir, as to the Earl of Hertford standing hard by, to the great rejoysing of manie beholders. And after hir Majestie's entrance, where shee had not rested her a quarter of an houre, but from the Snail Mount and the Ship Ile in the pond (both being neare under the prospect of her gallerie windowe) there was a long volley of chambers and two brasse peeces discharged. After this, supper was served in, first to her Majestie, and then to the Nobles and others. Were it not that I would not seem to flatter the honorable minded Earle; or, but that I feare to displease him, who rather desired to expresse his loyall dutie in his liberall bountie, then to heare of it againe, I could heere willingly particulate the store of his cheare and provision, as likewise the carefull and kind diligence of his servantes, expressed in their quiet service to her Majestie and the Nobility, and by their loving entertainment to all other, frends or strangers. But I leave the bountie of the one, and the industrie of the others, to the just report of such as beheld or tasted the plentifull abundance of that time and place.

After supper was ended, her Majestie graciously admitted unto her presence a notable consort of six Musitions, which the Earl of Hertford had provided to entertaine her Majestie withall, at her will and pleasure, and when it should seeme good to her Highnesse. Their musicke so highly pleased her, that in grace and favour thereof, she gave a newe name unto one of their Pavans, made long since by Master Thomas Morley, then organist of Paule's Church.

These are the chiefe pointes which I noted in the first daies entertainment. Now therefore it followeth, that I proceed to the second.

The Second Daies Entertainment.

On the next day following, being Tuesday, and Saint Mathewes festivall, there was in the morning presented to her Majesty a faire and rich gift from the Countesse of Hertforde, which greatly pleased and contented hir Highnesse. The forenoone was so wet and stormie, that nothing of pleasure could bee presented her Majestie. Yet it helde up a little before dinner time, and all the day after: where otherwise faire sports would have beene buried in foule weather.

This day her Majestie dined, with her Nobles about her, in the roome of estate new builded on the hil side, above the ponds head. There sate below her many Lords, Ladies, and Knights. The manner of service, and abundance of dainties, I omit upon just consideration; as also the ordinance discharged in the beginning of dinner, a variety of consorted music at dinner time.

Presently after dinner, the Earl of Hertford caused a large canapie of estate to bee set at the ponds head, for her Majestie to sit under, and to view some sportes prepared in the water. The canapie was of greene satten, lined with greene taffeta sarcenet; everie seame covered with a broad silver lace; valenced about, and fringed with greene silke and silver, more then a hand-bredth in depth; supported with four silver pillers moveable; and dekt above head with four white plumes, spangled with silver. This canapie being upheld by foure worthie Knightes (Sir Henrie Greie, Sir Walter Hungerford, Sir James Maruin, and Lord George Caro); and tapestry spread all about the pondes head, her Majestie, about foure of the clocke, came and sate under it, to expect the issue of some devise, being advertised that there was some such thing towards.

At the further end of the ponde, there was a bower, close built to the brinke thereof; out of which there went a pompous array of sea-persons, which waded brest-high or swam till they approched neare the seat of her Majestie. Nereus, the Prophet of the Sea, attired in redde silke, and having a cornerd-cappe on his curlde heade, did swimme before the rest, as their pastor and guide. After him came five Tritons brest-high in the water, all with grislie heades, and beardes of divers colours and fashions, and all five cheerefully sounding their trumpets. After them went two other Gods of the Sea, Neptune and Oceanus, Phorcus and Glaucus, leading betweene them that pinnace whereof I spake in the beginning of this treatise.

In the pinnace were three Virgins, which, with their cornets, played Scottish gigs, made three parts in one. There was also in the saide pinnace an other Nymph of the Sea, named Neæra, the old supposed love of Sylvanus, a God of the Woodes. Neare to her were placed three excellent voices, to sing to one lute, and in two other boats hard by, other lutes and voices, to answer by manner of eccho. After the pinnace, and two other boats which were drawne after it by other Sea-gods, the rest of the traine followed brest-high in the water, all attired in ouglie marine suites, and everie one armed with a huge woodden squirt in his hand; to what end it shall appeare hereafter. In their marching towards the pond, all along the middle of the current, the Tritons sounded one halfe of the way; and then they ceasing, the cornets plaid their Scottish gigs. The melody was sweet, and the shew stately.

By the way, it is needful to touch here many thinges abruptly, for the better understanding of that which followeth.

First, that in the pinnace are two jewels to be presented her Majestie: the one by Nereus, the other by Neæra.

Secondly, that the Fort in the Pond is round environed with armed men.

Thirdly, that the Snayl Mount nowe resembleth a monster, having hornes full of wild-fire, continually burning.

And lastly, that the god Silvanus lieth with his traine not farre off in the woodes, and will shortly salute her Majestie, and present her with a holly scutchion, wherein Apollo had long since written her praises.

All this remembred and considered, I now returne to the Sea-gods; who having, under the conduct of Nereus, brought the pinnace neare before her Majesty, Nereus made his Oration, as followeth; but before he began, hee made a privie signe unto one of his traine, which was gotten up into the Shippe Ile, directly before her Majestie; and hee presently did cast himselfe downe, dooing a summer-sawt from the Ile into the water, and then swam to his companie.

The Oration of Nereus to her Majesty.

Faire Cinthia the wide Ocean's Empresse,
I watry Nereus hovered on the coast,
To greete your Majesty with this my traine
Of dauncing Tritons, and shrill singing Nimphs.
But all in vaine: Elisa was not there;

For which our Neptune grievd, and blamd the star,
Whose thwarting influence dasht our longing hope.
Therefore impatient, that this worthles earth
Should beare your Highnes weight, and we Sea-gods,
(Whose jealous waves have swallowd up your foes,
And to your Realme are walles impregnable,)
With such large favour seldome time are grac't:
I from the deepes have drawen this winding flud,
Whose crescent forme figures the rich increase
Of all that sweet Elisa holdeth deare.
And with me came gould breasted India,
Who, daunted at your sight, leapt to the shoare,
And sprinkling endlesse treasure on this Ile,
Left me this jewell to present your Grace,
For hym, that under you doth hold this place.
See where her ship remaines, whose silke-woven takling
Is turnde to twigs, and threefold mast to trees,
Receiving life from verdure of your lookes;
(For what cannot your gracious looks effect?)
Yon ugly monster creeping from the South
To spoyle these blessed fields of Albion,
By selfe same beams is chang'd into a snaile,
Whose bullrush hornes are not of force to hurt.
As this snaile is, so be thine enemies!
And never yet did Nereus wishe in vaine.
That Fort did Neptune raise, for your defence;
And in this barke, which gods hale neare the shore,
White-footed Thetis sends her musicke maydes,
To please Elisaes eares with harmony.
Hear them, fair Quene: and when their musick ends,
My Triton shall awake the Sylvane gods,
To doe their hommage to your Majesty.

This Oration being delivered, and withall the present whereof he spake, which was hidden in a purse of greene rushes, cunningly woaven together: immediately the three voices in the pinnace sung a song to the lute, with excellent divisions, and the end of every verse was replied by lutes and voices in the other boate somwhat afarre off, as if they had beene ecchoes.

The Song presented by Nereus on the water, sung dialogue-wise, everie fourth verse answered with two Echoes.

Dem. How haps it now when prime is done,
   Another spring-time is begun?
Resp. Our happie soile is overrunne,
   With beautie of a second sunne.
    Eccho. A second sunne.

Dem. What heavenlie lampe, with holie light,
   Doeth so increase our climes delight?
Resp. A lampe whose beams are ever bright,
   And never feares approching Night.
    Eccho. Approching Night.

Dem. Why sing we not eternall praise,
   To that faire shine of lasting daies?
Resp. He shames himselfe that once asssaies
   To fould such wonder in sweete laies.
    Eccho. In sweet laies.

Dem. O yet devoid of envious blame,
   Thou maist unfold hir sacred name.
Resp. 'Tis dread Eliza, that faire name
   Who filles the golden trump of Fame.
    Eccho. Trump of Fame.

Dem. O never may so sweete a Quene,
   See dismall daies or deadly teene.
Resp. Graunt Heavens hir daies may stil be greene,
   For like to hir was never seene.
    Eccho. Was never seene.

This song being ended, Nereus commanded the five Tritons to sound. Then came Sylvanus with his attendants, from the wood: himselfe attired, from the middle downewarde to the knee, in kiddes skinnes with the haire on; his legges, bodie, and face, naked, but died over with saffron, and his head hooded with a goates skin, and two little hornes over his forehead, bearing in his right hand an olive tree, and in his left a scutchion, whereof I spake somewhat before. His followers were all covered with ivy-leaves, and bare in their handes bowes made like darts. At their approche neare her Majesty, Sylvanus spake as followeth, and delivered up his scutchion, ingraven with goulden characters, Nereus and his traine still continuing near her Highnesse.

The Oration of SYLVANUS.

  Sylvanus comes from out the leavy groaves,
To honor her whom all the world adores,
Faire Cinthia, whom no sooner Nature fram'd,
And deckt with Fortunes and with Vertues dower,
But straight admiring what her skill had wrought,
She broake the mould; that never sunne might see
The like to Albion's Quene for excellence.
  Twas not the Tritons ayr-enforcing shell,
As they perhaps would proudly make theyr vaunt,
But those faire beames that shoote from Majesty,
Which drew our eyes to wonder at thy worth.
That worth breeds wonder; wonder holy feare;
And holy feare unfayned reverence.
Amongst the wanton dayes of goulden age,
Apollo playing in our pleasant shades,
And printing oracles in every leafe,
Let fall this sacred scutchion from his brest;
Wherein is writ, " Detur dignissimæ."
O therefore hold what Heaven hath made thy right,
I but in duety yeeld desert her due.

Nereus. But see, Sylvanus, where thy Love doth sit.
Sylvanus. My sweet Neæra, was her eare so neare?
    O set my hearts delight upon this banke,
    That, in compassion of old sufferance,
    Shee may relent in sight of Beauties Quene.

Nereus.   On this condition shall shee come on shoare,
     That with thy hand thou plight a solemne vow,
     Not to prophane her undefiled state.
Sylvanus.   Here, take my hand, and therewithall I vowe,
Nereus.   That water will extinguish wanton fire.

Nereus, in pronouncing this last line, did plucke Sylvanus over head and eares into the water, where all the sea-gods, laughing, did insult over him. In the meane while her Majesty perused the verses written in the scutchion, which were these:

   Aŏniis prior, et Divis es pulchrior alti
      Æquoris, ac Nymphis es prior Idaliis.
   Idaliis prior es Nymphis, ac æquoris alti.
      Pulchrior et Divis, ac prior Aŏniis.

Over these verses was this poesy written:

   Detur dignissimæ.

After that the sea-gods had sufficiently duckt Sylvanus, they suffered him to creep to land, where he no sooner set footing, but crying "Revenge, Revenge," he and his begunne a skirmish with those of the water; the one side throwing their darts, and the other using their squirtes, and the Tritons sounding a pointe of warre. At the last, Nereus parted the fray with a line or two, grounded on the excellence of her Majestyes presence, as being alwaies friend to Peace, and ennemy to Warre. Then Sylvanus, being so ugly, and running toward the bower at the end of the Pound, affrighted a number of the countrey people, that they ran from him for feare, and thereby moved great laughter. His followers retired to the woods; and Neæra his faire Love, in the pinnace, presenting her Majestie a sea-jewell, bearing the forme of a fanne, spake unto her as followeth:

   The Oration of faire NEÆRA.

   When Neptune late bestowed on me this barke,
   And sent by me this present to your Grace:
   Thus Nereus sung, who never sings but truth.
   Thine eyes (Neæra) shall in time behold
   A sea-borne Quene, worthy to governe Kings:
   On her depends the fortune of thy boate,

> If shee but name it with a blisfull word,
> And view it with her life-inspiring beames.
> Her beames yeeld gentle influence, like fayre starres;
> Her silver soundinge word is prophesie.
> Speake, sacred Sibyl, give some prosperous name,
> That it may dare attempt a golden fleece,
> Or dive for pearles, and lay them in thy lap.
> For winde and waves, and all the worlde besides,
> Will make her way, whom thou shalt doome to blisse,
> For what is Sibyl's speech but oracle?

Here her Majesty named the pinnace, The Bonadventure; and Neæra went on with her speech, as followeth:

> Now Neæraes barke is fortunate,
> And in thy service shall imploy her saile,
> And often make returne to thy availe.
> O live in endlesse joy, with glorious fame,
> Sound trumpets, sounde, in honor of her name.

Then did Nereus retire backe to his bower, with all his traine following him, in selfe same order as they came forth before, the Tritons sounding their trumpets one halfe of the way, and the cornets playing the other halfe.

And here ended the second daies pastime, to the so great liking of her Majestie, that her gracious approbation thereof, was to the actors more than a double reward; and yet withall, her Highnes bestowed a largesse uppon them the next daie after, before shee departed.

The Thirde Daies Entertainment.

On Wednesday morning, about nine of the clock, as her Majesty opened a casement of her Gallerie window, there were three excellent Musicians, who, being disguised in aunceient countrey attire, did greet her with a pleasant song of Coridon and Phyllida, made in three parts of purpose. The song, as well for the worth of the dittie, as for the aptnes of the note thereto applied, it pleased her Highnesse, after it had been once sung, to command it againe, and highly to grace it with her chearefull acceptance and commendation.

The Three Mens' Song, sung the third morning, under hir Majesties Gallerie window.

In the merrie moneth of May,
In a morne, by breake of day,
Forth I walked by the wood side,
Where as May was in his pride,
There I spied, all alone,
Phyllida and Corydon.
Much adoe there was, God wot,
He would love, and she would not.
She said, never man was true:
He said, none was false to you.
He said, he had loved her long:
She said, love should have no wrong.
Coridon would kisse her then:
She said, maides must kisse no men,
Till they did for good and all.
Then she made the shepheard call
All the heavens to witnesse truth,
Never lov'd a truer youth.
Thus with many a pretie oath,
Yea and nay, and faith and troth,
Such as silly shepheards use,
When they will not love abuse;
Love, which had beene long deluded,
Was with kisses sweet concluded:
And Phyllida, with garlands gay,
Was made the Lady of the May.

The same day after dinner, about three of the clocke, ten of the Earle of Hertford's servants, all Somersetshire men, in a square greene court, before her Majesties windowe, did hang up lines, squaring out the forme of a tennis-court, and making a crosse line in the middle. In this square they (beeing stript out of their dublets) played, five to five, with the hand-ball, at bord and cord (as they tearme it) to so great liking of her Highnes, that she graciously deyned to beholde their pastime more then an houre and a halfe.

After supper there were two delights presented unto her Majestie: curious fire-works, and a sumptuous banket. The first from the three Ilands in the Pond; the second in a lowe Gallerie in her Majesties Privie-garden. But I will first briefly speake of the fire-works.

First, there was a peale of a hundred chambers discharged from the Snail Mount; in counter whereof, a like peale was discharged from the Ship Ile, and some great ordinance withal. Then was there a castle of fire-works of all sorts, which played in the Fort. Answerable to that, there was in the Snail Mount, a globe of all manner of fire-works, as big as a barrel. When these were spent on either side, there were many running rockets uppon lines, which past between the Snail Mount and the castle in the Fort. On either side were many fire-wheeles, pikes of pleasure, and balles of wilde fire, which burned in the water.

During the time of these fire-workes in the water, there was a banket served, all in glasse and silver, into the lowe Gallerie in the garden, from a hill side foure-teene score off, by two hundred of my Lord of Hertforde's gentlemen, everie one carrying so many dishes, that the whole number amounted to a thousand: and there were to light them in their way a hundred torch-bearers.

The Fourth Daies Entertainment.

On Thursday morning, her Majestie was no sooner readie, and at her Gallerie window looking into the Garden, but there began three Cornets to play certaine fantastike dances, at the measure whereof the Fayery Quene came into the garden, dauncing with her maides about her. Shee brought with her a garland, made in fourme of an imperiall crowne; within the sight of her Majestie shee fixed upon a silvered staffe, and sticking the staffe into the ground, spake as followeth:

The Speech of the Fairy Quene to her Majestie.

I that abide in places under-ground,
Aureola, the Quene of Fairy land,
That every night in rings of painted flowers
Turne round, and carrell out Elisaes name:
Hearing, that Nereus and the Sylvane gods
Have lately welcomde your Imperiall Grace,
Oapend the earth with this enchanting wand,
To doe my duety to your Majestie,

And humbly to salute you with this chaplet,
Given me by Auberon, the Fairy King.
Bright shining Phœbe, that in humaine shape,
Hid'st Heaven's perfection, vouchsafe t' accept it:
And I Aureola, belov'd in heaven,
(For amorous starres fall nightly in my lap)
Will cause that Heavens enlarge thy goulden dayes,
And cut them short, that envy at thy praise.

After this speech, the Fairy Quene and her maides daunced about the Garden, singing a Song of sixe parts, with the musicke of an exquisite consort; wherein was the lute, bandora, base-violl, citterne, treble-violl, and flute. And this was the Fairies Song:

Elisa is the fairest Quene,
That ever trod upon this greene.
Elisaes eyes are blessed starres,
Inducing peace, snbduing warres.
Elisaes hand is christal bright,
Her wordes are balme, her lookes are light.
Elisaes brest is that faire hill,
Where Vertue dwels, and sacred skill,
O blessed bee each day and houre,
Where sweet Elisa builds her bowre.

This spectacle and musicke so delighted her Majesty, that shee commanded to heare it sung and to be danced three times over, and called for divers Lords and Ladies to behold it: and then dismist the Actors with thankes, and with a gracious larges, which of her exceeding goodnesse shee bestowed uppon them.

Within an howre after her Majesty departed, with her Nobles, from Elvetham. It was a most extreame rain, and yet it pleased hir Majesty to behold and hear the whole action. On the one side of her way, as shee past through the parke, there was placed, sitting on the Pond side, Nereus and all the sea-gods, in their former attire: on her left hand Sylvanus and his company: in the way before her, the three Graces, and the three Howres: all of them on everie side wringing their hands, and shewing signe of sorrow for her departure, he being attired as at the first, saving that his cloak was now black, and his garland mixed with ugh branches, to signifie sorrow. While she beheld this dum shew, the poet made her a short oration, as followeth:

The Poet's Speech at her Majestie's departure.

O see, sweet Cynthia, how the watry gods,
Which joyd of late to view thy glorious beames,
At this retire doe waile and wring their hands,
Distilling from their eyes salt showrs of teares,
To bring in Winter with their wet lament:
For how can Sommer stay, when Sunne departs?

See where Sylvanus sits, and sadly mournes,
To thinke that Autumn, with his withered wings,
Will bring in tempest, when thy beames are hence:
For how can Sommer stay, when Sunne departs?

See where those Graces, and those Howrs of Heav'n,
Which at thy comming sung triumphall songs,
And smoothd the way, and strewd it with sweet flowrs,
Now, if they durst, would stop it with greene bowes,
Least by thine absence the yeeres pride decay:
For how can Sommer stay, when Sunne departs?

Leaves fal, grasse dies, beasts of the wood hang head,
Birds cease to sing, and everie creature wailes,
To see the season alter with this change:
For how can Sommer stay, when Sunne departs?

O, either stay, or soone returne againe,
For Sommers parting is the countries paine.

Then Nereus, approching from the ende of the Pond, to hir Majesties coach, on his knees thanked hir Highnesse for hir late largesse, saying as followeth:

Thankes, gracious Goddesse, for thy bounteous largesse,
Whose worth, although it yeelds us sweet content,
Yet thy depart gives us a greater sorrow."

After this, as her Majestie passed through the parke gate, there was a consort of musicions hidden in a bower; to whose playing this dittie of "Come againe" was sung, with excellent division, by two that were cunning.

The Song sung at the gate, when hir Majestie departed. (As this Song was sung, hir Majestie, notwithstanding the great raine, staied hir coach, and pulled off hir mask, giving great thanks.)

>Come againe, faire Nature's treasure,
>Whose lookes yeeld joyes exceeding measure.
>
>Come againe, worlds starre-bright eye,
>Whose presence bewtifies the skie.
>
>Come againe, worlds chiefe delight,
>Whose absence makes eternall Night.
>
>Come againe, sweete lively Sunne,
>When thou art gone our joyes are done.
>
>O come againe, faire Nature's treasure,
>Whose lookes yeeld joyes exceeding measure.
>
>O come againe, heavens chiefe delight,
>Thine absence makes eternall night.
>
>O come againe, worlds star-bright eye,
>Whose presence doth adorne the skie.
>
>O come againe, sweet beauties Sunne:
>When thou art gone, our joyes are done.

Her Majestie was so highly pleased with this and the rest, that she openly said to the Earle of Hertford, that the beginning, processe, and end of this his entertainment, was so honorable, she would not forget the same.

And manie most happie yeares may her gratious Majestie continue, to favour and foster him, and all others which do truly love and honor her.

On the 24th of September the Queen's Court was at Farnham Castle, a Palace of the Bishop of Winchester; and on the 26th she visited Sutton Place[1]; and

---

[1] Sutton Place, built on a rising ground, by Sir Richard Weston, 1529 or 30, of brick, furnished with a double sculptured platband of a yellowish brick earth running round it, with coins and window-cases of the same, was a quadrangle encompassing an acre 80 feet square, entered by a gate adorned with devices of R. W. and a tun. But this side of the quadrangle was taken down in 1784. It is engraved in vol. II. of Bibliotheca Topographica Britannica," and in " Gentleman's Magazine," LIX. p. 108. —The hall on the North-west side 50 feet 9, by 25 feet 5, and 31 feet 6 high. The gallery in South-east front 141¼ feet by 20¼, and 14 feet 4 high. Queen Elizabeth was entertained here in Septem-

then returned to her own Palace at Richmond, from which place the dispatches of Lord Burghley are dated on the 12th of October [1].

In the beginning of November the Queen was at Southwyk [2] with De Beavoir [3] and Mons. de Reaux [4]. On the 11th of that month she went to Ely Place [5],

ber 1591, on the 26th of which month her Letter to Sir Henry Unton, Embassador in France, is dated hence (Rymer, XVI. 122); and shortly after her departure the gallery was burnt, and so remained till 1721, when the wall which had fallen down was rebuilt, and the whole put into proper repair, by John Weston, Esquire; but the four rooms under have not been fitted up. The hall contains many family pictures, and the windows are full of arms, &c. brought from different parts. Among the rest, three camels, the arms of *Camel.* Holland says, the estate was bettered by an heir of T. Camel. The heiress of the Weston family, Melior-Mary Weston, died unmarried 10 June 1782; having devised her estate to John Webbe, Esq. of Sarnsfield Court, Herefordshire, who took the name of Weston, and has made great improvements in the house and grounds.

[1] Rymer, vol. XVI. p. 127.

[2] Burghley Papers, II. 797.—At Southwick was a house of Augustine canons, founded by Henry I. granted at the dissolution to John White, as Tanner: but Magna Britannia, II. 892, says, Henry VIII. exchanged it with the Lord Chamberlain Sir Thomas Wrottesley; but, query if not a mistake? It was afterwards the seat of the Nortons, and hither Charles I. accompanied the Duke of Buckingham on his way to Portsmouth.

[3] His full name was *Beauvoir la Nocle*, and he was an Ambassador from Henry IV. of France. See a letter from him to the English Ambassador, from Hackney, Sept. 27, 1594; Rymer, XVI. 124.

[4] An envoy from the French King.

[5] This London residence of the Bishop of Ely from 1290, was much reduced by Bishop Cox, at the pressing instance of Queen Elizabeth, (see p. 40.) in favour of Sir Christopher Hatton, Lord Chancellor, for whom she in a manner obliged the Bishop to mortgage it to her for £1600, which different circumstances of the succeeding times prevented his successors from redeeming, and the ground so leased was covered with streets. The remaining part, a dark incommodious habitation, entered by a large gateway, or porter's lodge, consisted of a small paved court. On the right hand were some offices supported by a colonnade. On the left, a small garden inclosed by a brick wall. In the front was the venerable old hall, 72 feet by 32, and about 30 feet high, lighted by six Gothic windows, roofed with oak, leaded. At the West end were the chief lodging rooms, and other apartments; and on the North-west a square cloister, 95 feet by 73, round a garden, and over it rooms and galleries. On the North side of the cloister, in a field containing about an acre of ground, walled and planted with trees, stood the Chapel, 91 by 39 feet; the East window large and handsome, and the floor about 10 or 12 feet above the level of the ground, supported by eight strong chesnut posts, and forming a crypt or vault. This Palace, after remaining in the See of Ely near 486 years, in the occupation of 41 Bishops (6 of whom died there), being much decayed, and deemed incapable of further repair, was disposed of to the Crown, by Act of Parliament, 1772, for £6500, and an annuity of £200 *per annum* settled on the Bishop and his successors for ever. The chapel, repaired and fitted up for divine service, remains for the use of the inhabitants of Ely Place; the houses of which occupy the site of the Old Palace.

ELY HOUSE.

then the residence of the Bishop of Ely; and also of Lord Chancellor Hatton, who had been honoured by a Visit there from the Queen in 1589, as noticed in p. 40; and who was now in that illness which terminated fatally on the 20th of this month.—It is to this great man's honour, that he is universally allowed to have deserved all the honours and offices his Mistress lavished on him. If the Queen's eye was pleased with his corporeal perfections, she appears to have been equally so with his mental qualifications; and he is one of the many proofs she gave of her penetration in the choice of her great State Officers. His decrees were unexceptionable, and his speeches full of humility and argument, easy of access, and, in short, the Keeper of the Queen's conscience. His prudence we shall not insist upon, as that slept when he suffered himself to become a debtor to her Majesty, who, his situation might have informed him, never forgave a debt[1]. That ungenerous and avaricious spirit cost the Chancellor his life[2]. He owed the Queen a large sum; she demanded it; he could not raise it; probably Elizabeth reproached him with her former kindness, which was more than his spirits could endure without retiring to the heart; and that too failing, poor Hatton fled to that unknown world where the just are assembled, leaving the Queen in despair that the relief she brought him with her own hands was without efficacy, and bitterly regretting the loss of an upright judge and counsellor.

Among the Publications entered in the Books of the Stationers' Company, is, " A pleasant Conceyt, plainlie set oute, and plainlye presented as a New-yeres Gyfte to the Quenes Majestie at Hampton Court, anno Domini 1591-2."

[1] On the 20th of March, 1576, Richard Cox, Bishop of Ely, granted to Christopher (after Sir Christopher) Hatton, the Gate-house of the Palace (except two rooms, used as prisons for those who were arrested, or delivered in execution to the Bishop's bailiff, and the lower rooms, used for the porter's lodge); the first court-yard within the gate-house, to the long gallery, dividing it from the second; the stables there; the long gallery, with the rooms above and below it, and some others; 14 acres of land, and the keeping of the gardens and orchards, for 21 years, paying at Midsummer-day, a red rose for the gate-house and garden, and for the ground ten loads of hay, and £10 *per annum*; the Bishop reserving to himself and successors free access through the gate-house, walking in the gardens, and gathering 20 bushels of roses yearly; Mr. Hatton undertaking to repair and make the gate-house a convenient dwelling. This lease was confirmed by the Dean and Chapter of Ely.

[2] In the 36th year of the Queen's Reign, Sir William married Lady Elizabeth Cecil, daughter to the Earl of Exeter. In the same year the premises *(inter alia)* were extended to satisfy a debt of £42,139. 5s. due to the Queen from Sir Christopher Hatton, whose rental amounted to no more than £717. 2s. 11d. including Hatton Garden, valued at £10 *per annum* at his decease.

By Inquisition August 29, 1592, Sir Christopher Hatton, was found to be seised in fee of the premises, having died without issue, by which they came to Sir William Hatton.

Anno 34° *Reginæ* ELIZABETHÆ, 1592.

Receyved from the Right Honourable the Lorde of Hunsdon, the Lorde Chamberlaine, the 10th daye of July, one coller of golde of the Order of the Garter, containing 22 knotts, and 22 perles of roses, enamuled within the Garter, having a George of golde hangynge thereat, without stone; which was sent from the late Duke *Casemere*; weyng all together, 36 oz. 3 q^a. diñ.

On the 27th of July the inhabitants of Chalk assisted in removing her from Greenwich to Nonsuch. See before, p. 38.

The only notices of the Queen's removals in the early parts of the year 1592, are by the ringing of the bells:

At St. Margaret's, Westminster, April 7, "when the Queen went from Whitehall.
At Lambeth, "when she went to Sir George Cary's[1]."
At Fulham, " when she went from the Lord Admiral's at Chelsea to Richmond."
At Kingston, " when the Queen was attended on *the Wick*[2]."

The Queen being expected at Bisham[3] in Berkshire, a seat of the family of the Hoby's, Mr. Thomas Posthumus Hoby, younger brother to Sir Edward, wrote to Mr. Anthony Bacon, on the 29th of July, that Lady Hoby was desirous of his and his Brother Francis's company there, where they might have an opportunity of waiting upon her Majesty: and he wrote again to him on the 14th of August, that her Majesty had appointed to be there on that day sennight, where, if his health would permit, he might with most conveniency attend upon her. But he was prevented by his indisposition, or journey to Gorhambury on a visit to his Mother, with whom he resided for several months. And on the 15th Mr. Bacon's servant, George Jenkell, whom he had left in his chambers at Gray's Inn, wrote to inform him that his brother Francis was gone from thence of a sudden to Twickenham, in company of his friends Mr. Dunch, Mr. Cecil, Mr. Gosnold, and Mr. Field[4]." See hereafter, p. 190.

[1] Of whom see before, p. 27.—I do not find where his residence was when visited by the Queen; probably in some part of Surrey, as the Visit is recorded at Lambeth.

[2] Hampton Wick. [3] Of this Visit, see hereafter, p. 130.

The following Extracts are from the Churchwardens' Book for the Parish of Marlow, Bucks:

" 1593. Item, payd J'n Black for mendynge the bells when the Queene came to Bisham, 1*s*. 6*d*.—Item, payd for naylls and dry'ke the same tyme, 1*s*.—Item, rece'd of players for playinge in the church-lofte, 2*s*.—Item, payde to one for the carryinge of the morrys-coats to Maydenhed, 4*d*."

[4] "Probably the same with the author of the celebrated treatise " Of the Church;" chosen in 1594 preacher of Lincoln's Inn, in 1604 made Canon of Windsor, and at last, in 1609, Dean of Gloucester, in which post he died on the 21st of November 1616, at the age of 55." Birch's Memoirs.

In the month of August 1592, Sir Henry Lee[1] was honoured by his Royal Mistress's presence for two days at Quarendon, in the Vale of Aylesbury[2].

[1] Of the Entertainment at Quarendon, see hereafter, p. 193.

A correspondent in the Gentleman's Magazine, who signs "Viator," observes, "Sir Henry Lee's qualifications as a Statesman, or rather a Courtier, seem to have resembled those of his father-in-law, William Lord Paget, who also, like him, enjoyed the confidence of four succeeding Princes, Henry VIII. Edward VI. Mary, and Elizabeth. By what compass the latter Nobleman steered so safe a course through the dangerous commotions which agitated both Church and State in those eventful reigns, may perhaps be gathered from the axioms of his common-place book, now in the possession of his descendant Lord Boston, which thus concludes:

"Fly the courte.	Devise nothing	Lerne to spare.	Pray often.
Speke little.	Never earnest.	Spend in measure.	Live better.
Care less.	In answer cold.	Care for home.	And dye well."

"Nor were such instances of "serpentine prudence," or "columbine simplicity," as Smythe calls them in his History of the Berkeley family, very rare; for, in the character which that writer has drawn of another great Courtier, he tells that "he received like honours and favours from those four Kings, Henry VI. Edward IV. Richard III. and Henry VII. as opposite and discordant among themselves as man might be to man." To be "a willow, and not an oak," was the axiom of Sir William Powlet, first Marquis of Winchester, who also lived and flourished under many Princes of very opposite characters; and, as we have very high authority for saying that *there is nothing new* under the sun, so we shall perhaps find that Prince Talleyrand, and other modern Courtiers, have only possessed themselves of the same clue which conducted these departed Worthies through slippery paths, with honour, safety, and renown. Sir Henry Lee married Anne, daughter of William Lord Paget, from a branch of which family the Marquis of Anglesey is descended, and Lord Paget's two sons were successively Peers of the Realm, *viz.* Henry, created a Knight of the Bath at the coronation of Queen Mary, and summoned to Parliament the 8th of Queen Elizabeth, and who died 1569. His brother succeeded him, and had summons to Parliament the 13th of the same Reign.

"The rewards Sir Henry Lee received from his Sovereigns mentioned in his epitaph, p. 44: in later days his descendant, Sir Edward Henry, was created Viscount Quarendon, and Earl of Lichfield, in 1674, which titles becoming extinct on the decease of George Henry, the last heir male of that family, who was Chancellor of the University of Oxford, and died in 1776, the manor and estate descended to their representative, Henry Augustus Dillon-Lee, Lord Viscount Dillon in Ireland, by whom, in 1802, it was sold to James Dupré, Esq. of Whitton Park, the present possessor."

Another Correspondent to Mr. Urban, "Antiquarius," adds: "The Baronet family of Lee, of Harwell, is descended from the Leghs of the antient house of High Legh, in Cheshire, a different lineage to the Lees, subsequently Earls of Lichfield, Viscounts Quarendon, &c. and there is no cognizance in the armorial bearings of either family that indicate affinity. The Rev. Sir George Lee, Bart. A. M. and F. A. S. Rector of Water Stratford, second and only surviving son of Sir William, fourth Baronet, and his wife, Lady Elizabeth, daughter of Simon, first Earl Harcourt, is the present proprietor of Hartwell House, where Louis XVIII. found a kind asylum during some years of his exile in this Country, which he quitted on the morning of the 20th of April 1814, and made his public entry into London on the evening of the same day."

[2] "Viator," (in Gent. Mag.) says, "The manor of Quarendon was, according to Holinshed, part

Dr. Fuller, nearly two centuries ago, says, "that one entire pasture, called *Beryfield*, in the manor of Quarendon, is let yearly at eight hundred pounds, and the tenant not complaining of his bargain." What must be the present rental!

of the antient possessions of the Fitz-Johns, and came by a female heir to the Beauchamps. This account carries us no higher than to the Reign of Henry III. Whether it were in earlier times in the hands of the Bolebecs, can only be conjectured; but there are some remains of an antient road Eastward of Buryfield, the so much celebrated piece of rich pasturage which still retain the appellation of Bullbeck Gate, and from their vicinity to other considerable estates of that opulent and powerful family, seem to afford some show of probability in support of such an opinion. It is more certain that, on the attainder of Thomas Beauchamp, Earl of Warwick, it was granted, in 1397, to Thomas Mowbray, Duke of Norfolk, who also suffering attainder soon afterwards, it reverted to the Crown, and in 1512 was granted to Robert Lee, Esq. who was a descendant from the younger branch of the Lees of Lea, in Cheshire, [Benedict, fifth son of John, by Elizabeth his wife, the daughter of —— Wood, of Warwickshire, in temp. Edw. III.] seated at Quarendon "as early as the year 1460, and who had been, for some time, lessees under the Crown."

"Quarendon is stated, in the Agricultural Survey of the County of Bucks, to contain 1500 acres of land, of which only 7 or 8 are in arable, and the remainder in pasturage, or meadow. The number of farm-houses 5, of cottages 4, and of inhabitants 55. The average of rents from 40 to 60s. per acre; the whole parish tithe free. The soil is in general a deep rich clay, extremely fertile and productive; and the experience of agriculturists leads them to prefer grazing and feeding oxen, to keeping a dairy of cows. The parish maintains its own poor distinctly from Bierton, to which the Chapel here only was formerly appendant. It is bounded on the North by Hardwick, on the East by Bierton and Aylesbury, on the South by Aylesbury and Stone, and on the South-west and West by Fleet Marston, being separated from the latter by a brook which is formed by the union of several rivulets from the North-west, North, and East (whose divided streams isolate some of the rich pastures, and in wet seasons, by overflowing their banks, perform a sort of natural irrigation), and runs South-west in a tortuous course near Eythrop and Winchendon, until, on the verge of the County, it is dignified with the title of the river Thame.

"The turnpike road leading from Aylesbury to Bicester in Oxfordshire, runs along the border of a portion of the parish of Quarendon on the South; and is supposed to occupy the track of a Vicinal way, which has been often erroneously taken for the Akeman-street, with the course of which, as the Bp. of Cloyne observes, [Lysons, Mag. Brit. vol. I. p. 484,] it by no means agrees. The line of that Vicinal way, however, by whatsoever name it may have been originally called, as laid down in the best maps, appears to have been broken, and no traces of it preserved, from about a mile and half Eastward of Aylesbury, to the distance of more than three miles Westward of that town, in the direction of Quarendon and Fleet Marston. Near the last named place the present road makes a sudden flexure; but whether the antient way ran to the Northward of it, can only be conjectured. In that case it must have passed near the site of Quarendon Chapel; and the old track from Aylesbury to Buckingham, which unquestionably left Hardwick, and the modern line of the turnpike through Winslow, on the right hand, and passed through Claydon, might have branched off from this Vicinal way, and have intersected the Vale of Aylesbury very near the spot before-mentioned, which is still called Bullbank [Bolebec] Gate. The Roman remains in this part of the kingdom are but few, and the materials for its Antient History very scanty; but an attentive examination of the features of the

S.E. VIEW of QUARENDON CHAPEL,
Buckinghamshire.

Interior VIEW of QUARENDON CHAPEL, Bucks.
looking East.

DESCRIPTION OF QUARENDON. 127

Holinshed relates, that in a great Storm, which happened in 1570, Sir Henry Lee is said to have lost 3000 sheep at Quarendon, besides other cattle [1].

So much as been said (pp. 42—47.) of the monuments in Quarendon Chapel, that external and internal representations [2] of that curious building, as it appeared country, even at this distant period, would, I am persuaded, throw much light upon the very imperfect accounts of it which have hitherto appeared, and remove many of the doubts which have been entertained respecting its condition in early times. Unfortunately, those who possess genius enough to qualify them for such researches are often deficient in industry, and those who have sufficient learning are not always impartial. The bias of an Antiquary, and the prejudices of an Historian, are enemies alike to the discovery and to the preservation of Truth."

[1] "It is probable that, at that period, the number of sheep kept there might be more considerable in proportion to heavier stock than of late years; and Drayton, after mentioning the glebe and pasturage of the Vale of Aylesbury, adds,

"That as her grain and grass, so she her sheep doth breed
For burden, and for bone, all others that exceed!" *Polyolbion.*

[2] "It will be unnecessary," says Mr. J. C. Buckler, who furnished these drawings, "to enter into a particular description of the Chapel, or its handsome monuments; or, after what has been said, to offer any comments upon the neglect it has experienced, which is proving so fatal to every part of the building. It is now the common ingress to every passer by, from the Antiquary and Man of feeling, to the Rustic who whistles as he gazes around him within the once-hallowed inclosure, and thoughtlessly deprives the elegant memorials of those distinguished dead, whose ashes rest beneath, of the enrichments which the inclemency of the weather, so long suffered to intrude through various apertures, has left. The construction of Quarendon Chapel throughout is indeed excellent; the masonry regular, and the windows and South door well finished; its plan is uniform, having a centre and side ailes, which are open to each other through elegant pointed arches resting upon octagonal capitals and columns. The roof is handsome, having at its main beams flat arches, which combine numerous mouldings, and stretch across between the windows, resting upon stone brackets, sculptured with human heads, grotesque animals, leaves, &c.; the intermediate spaces are filled with purlings and rafters: but, though the whole is constructed of excellent and substantial Irish oak, the neglect of the external roof has dilapidated some portions of them towards the West end, which is rapidly increasing, and will, ere long, unless some means of preservation are adopted, demolish the whole. The pews, pulpit, &c. have been wholly removed, and very little of the regular stone pavement remains. A plain arch connects the body of the Chapel with the chancel, the latter being very small, and nearly filled with the Monuments already described, p. 42; which gives it more the character of a Sepulchral Chapel, than the service part of the building. It is a remarkable instance of the preference which appears to have been always given by the Founders and Benefactors for these situations of interment; except a few instances in some larger edifices, but the greater number are otherwise: and the unadorned arched recess, to be seen in the chancel walls of many old Churches, doubtless, once contained the plain, uninscribed grave-stone, the ornamented cross, the statue of the founder, or the brass figure."—Another correspondent to Gent. Mag.

in 1815, may not be unacceptable to those who derive pleasure and amusement from the study of these mouldering works of former ages.

"Viator," adds, "The only dates remaining upon the monuments are those of 1573, the period of the expedition into Scotland (the 16th of Elizabeth), and 1611, when it is presumed that Sir Henry Lee died. It is recorded that he attained the age of fourscore, so that, according to the above account, he must have been at the time of the Storm, mentioned in p. 127, in the vigour of life, and perhaps engaged in attendance upon the court or the wars. May it not therefore be supposed that the re-building of the Chapel by this personage had been rendered necessary by the destructive effects of that calamity? for Sir Anthony, his father, having died about the year 1550, it is unreasonable to imagine that his monument (if he had any before the re-building of the Chapel) had become decayed in the short space of twenty years, or that he was buried in a mere heap of ruins. The original Chapel is said to have been founded about the year 1392, by John Farnham; and it was dedicated to St. Peter.

"The Chancel which contains the fragments of sepulchral splendour has two windows, that at the East end consisting of three lights, and a smaller on the South side. Some rude timbers are still remaining within the arched door-way communicating with the Church, and against the partition above; but within the latter are two slender irons, which seem to have been designed to sustain banners or achievements. The shields of arms over the respective monuments appear to have been formerly surmounted with crests, which have probably been broken off: and as the door of the edifice is left open (the lock having been broken), and the building is reported to be occasionally converted to the use of feeding or sheltering cattle within its walls, it may reasonably be expected that every day will diminish the remains of its pristine elegance, and increase the difficulty of ascertaining its antient state. A pretty correct notion may be formed of the general outline and style of the monuments by referring to the construction of those which mark the age of Elizabeth and James the First.

"Of the Hospital alluded to in the inscription on the monument, p. 45, there are no remains; but near the South side of the Chapel, a large piece of meadow, perhaps two acres in extent, is inclosed with banks, which give it the appearance of having been once moated round. Mr. Lysons says, that "the antient seat was pulled down in the early part of the last century; and here may have been the site of it."—Where were situated the "*four goodly mansions*" which Sir Henry Lee built, as recorded in his epitaph, cannot now be traced. At present I find mention made in direct terms of only one of them,—his paternal seat at Burston, in the parish of Aston Abbots, about three miles from Quarendon Eastward. The old mansion there, in which Sir Anthony Lee resided, who was Knight of the Shire, and father of Sir Henry, is said to have been nearly rebuilt by the latter, but left incomplete at his death, and has been since demolished, excepting a portion of the lower part of the walls, which may be still traced in the offices and garden belonging to a farm-house, of late years erected with the materials of the old mansion, and in which a square stone window-case, with mullions, on the South side towards the East end, is also observable as a relick of the former building.—It may be remarked that, if the Knight displayed no better taste in architecture than he seems to have done in the choice of situation, it is not at all surprising that those labours of his life have been suffered to fall into decay, and to moulder with his bones. Burston House was built, if not in

Early in September we find the Queen in Gloucestershire, when she visited John Higford[1], Esq. lord of the manor of Alderton, and also of Dixton (a hamlet within that parish), and conferred on him the honour of Knighthood.

On the 12th of that month her Majesty was at Sudeley Castle[2], the mansion of Giles Lord Chandos; and thence, after resting some days at Woodstock, to Oxford on the 22d.

the very worst situation, certainly in *almost* the very worst, which could have been selected in the whole neighbourhood. It is buried in a valley, without possessing one single imaginable advantage by being so placed, and excluded from the enjoyment of a fine prospect, which even many parts of that valley command, by being hidden close behind a finely swelling hill, whence numerous cheerful and interesting objects, and much pleasing rural scenery, are discernable. It may, however, have been some excuse for such an oversight, if the foundations of the original mansion were regarded as the boundaries or limits of the plan for its re-erection; or if early recollections, much more if filial piety, had any influence in determining the choice of the site. Were neither of these the case, the old Knight must surely have been blinded by love! Besides the house at Burston, it is *probable* that another of the works alluded to might be the mansion at Weedon, formerly the jointured residence of Anne Countess of Lindsey, who was the relict of Sir Francis Lee, and died in 1709; which house having Quarendon Chapel and great part of the Vale of Aylesbury in view from its principal front, occupied the site of Lillies, now the seat of the Lord Grenville, Baron Nugent, being part of the estate which was sold by Lord Dillon in 1801 to George Nugent Grenville Temple, the late Marquis of Buckingham."

[1] " The Higfords have long been in possession of the greatest part of the parish of Alderton; and in 1769 it was held by the Rev. Henry Higford, who had at Dixton a large handsome house built of stone, with many coats of arms in the hall-windows, and near the house a ruined Chapel. William Higford, Esq. who was a Justice of the Peace, and a very ingenious Poet, was much honoured throughout the County. He died in 1657, leaving a large MS. of " Institutions " to his grandson; which were epitomized and published by Clement Barksdale. The family are all buried in Alderton Church, but without monuments or inscriptions." Rudder's Gloucestershire, pp. 220, 221.

[2] It is highly probable that the Queen had before visited Sudeley Castle both in 1574 and 1575. See vol. I. pp. 391. 552.—Some account of this noble mansion, and the Speeches made to the Queen there in 1592 will be found in pages 136. 217. — Sir Thomas Heneage, her Vice-chamberlain, wrote the following Letter to the Lord Keeper Puckering:

" My good Lord,

" Upon the receipt of your letters, I acquainted her Majesty with your joy of her so well passing so long a Progress, and your great desire to know how her Highness did, now at the furthest of her journey, the good news whereof (being so far divided from her Majesty) did give you life, and most contentment. I also shewed her Majesty (as this gentleman, the bearer hereof, told me) how your Lordship had been in Waltham Forest, and was not pleased to take your sport alone, but would have the company of the Ambassador, whom you invited to dinner, and made partner of your pastime. Touching the first, her Majesty willed me to tell you, that she found, by your often sending, your love and great care of her. And for the next, she bad me say, that she found you could not only

Mr. Edward Jones, Secretary to the Lord Keeper Puckering, in a letter dated Stepney, Sept. 12, says, " The Queen is now going to Oxford, where her entertainment is like to be very great. I send you here likewise the gests of her Progress. The Plague[1] increaseth in London, which maketh speech of keeping the term either at Hertford or Reading. My Lord [Keeper] continueth at Stepney, being commanded to have the care of the City; with whom there remain likewise about London my Lord of Canterbury, my Lord Buckhurst, my Lord Cobham, and Mr. Fortescue, to assist."

Speeches delivered to her MAJESTIE *this last Progresse, at the Right Honourable the Lady* RUSSEL's *at Bissam*[2]; *the Right Honourable the Lorde* CHANDOS' *at Sudeley; and the Right Hon. the Lord* NORRIS's *at Ricorte.*

To the Reader.

I gathered these copies in loose papers I know not how imperfect, therefore must I crave a double pardon; of him that penned them, and those that reade them. The matter of small moment, and therefore the offence of no great danger. I. B.

speak well, but also do well, and perform things with judgment and honour: praising you to me exceedingly. For I could not use any one word of just commendation of your Lordship, that she gave not allowance of, and adding too of her own gracious conceiving. Whereof I (that will never be found to deceive you) can assure your Lordship, you have great cause to take comfort. This is the best news that I can either now, or at any time, send to your Lordship. But as soon as any come out of France or Italy worthy the writing, I shall send your Lordship a brief of them. And so, with my humble commendations, rest, assuredly at your Lordship's commandment,   T. HENEAGE.

" At the Court at Sudley, the 12th of September, 1592."

[1] Mr. Francis Bacon, in his Observations upon a Libel published in 1592, refers to this Plague as the only one which the people had felt since the beginning of the Queen's Reign, their universal health never having been so good before for many years, notwithstanding the great pestering of the inhabitants in houses, the great multitude of strangers, and the sundry voyages by seas; all which have been noted to be the causes of pestilence.

[2] Bissam, or Bisham, is a pleasant village in Berkshire, about two miles from Henley, and almost opposite the town of Great Marlow, Bucks. The borders of the Thames in this neighbourhood are decorated with many pleasing seats. The rural villa of Sir George Young is situated in a low valley, encompassed with fertile meadows, and sheltered from the North winds by the majestic hills and beautiful hanging woods of Hedsor, Chiefden, and Taplow. The view on the South-west is very extensive. The manor-house is a very ancient building, but has been repaired and altered at different periods. It appears to have been erected by William Montacute, Earl of Salisbury, in

At the top of the Hill going to Bissam, the Cornets sounding in the Woods, a Wilde Man came forth and uttered this Speech:

I followed this sounde, as enchanted; neither knowing the reason why, nor how to be ridde of it: unusuall to these Woods, and (I feare) to our gods prodigious. *Sylvanus,* whom I honour, is runne into a Cave: *Pan,* whom I envye, courting of the shepheardesse: Envye I thee, *Pan?* No, pitty thee, an eie-sore to chast Nymphes; yet still importunate. Honour thee, *Sylvanus?* No, contemne thee: fearefull of Musicke in the Woods, yet counted the god of the Woods. I, it may bee, more stout than wise, asked, who passed that way? what he or she? None durst answere, or would vouchsafe, but passionate Eccho, who said Shee. And Shee it is, and you are Shee, whom in our dreames many yeares wee Satyres have seene, but waking could never find any such. Every one has tolde his dreame, and described your person; all agree in one, and set downe

---

the year 1338, for Canons regular of the Order of St. Augustine. In 1536 it was surrendered to Henry the Eighth: its revenues at that period were valued at £285. 11s. per annum. The following year it was founded anew by that Monarch, and more amply endowed for the maintenance of thirteen Benedictine Monks, and an Abbot, who was to have the privilege of sitting in Parliament. This was dissolved, however, within three years of its institution; the income at that time amounting to the yearly value of £661. 14s. 9d.; and a pension of £66. 13s. 4d. annually, was bestowed on Cowdrey the Abbot. This Abbey was frequently visited by Henry VIII. and the site of it was granted by King Edward VI. to his Father's repudiated wife, Anne of Cleves, who having surrendered it to the Crown again in 1552, it was then given to Sir Philip Hoby, a zealous Protestant, who had been of the Privy Council to King Henry VIII.— Sir Philip, married Elizabeth, daughter of Sir Walter Stoner, Knight; and after worthy services to his Prince and country, died, without issue, May 31, 1558, aged 53, at his house in London, and from thence was carried to Bisham.—Sir Thomas Hoby, his brother and successor, who published a Translation of " Castiglione's Courtier," married Elizabeth, daughter of Sir Anthony Cooke, of Gidea Hall, Essex, Knight; by whom he had four children; Edward, Elizabeth, Anne, Thomas-Posthumus; and being Embassador for Queen Elizabeth in France, died at Paris, July 13, 1566, at the age of 36, leaving his wife great with child in a strange country; who brought him honourably home, and built the Chapel on the South side of the chancel of Bisham Church; and laid him and his brother in one tomb together. By this Lady, the tomb of her husband and his brother was graced by an elegant Latin inscription, which may be seen in Ashmole's Berkshire, p. 195; and in p. 199 is another Latin epitaph on her two daughters, Elizabeth and Anne, who both died in February 1570, a few days one after the other. Lady Hoby was married, secondly, to John Lord Russel (second son of Francis second Earl of Bedford), who died in 1584, and was buried in Westminster Abbey. He had only one son, Francis, who died an infant in 1580; and two daughters: Elizabeth, who died unmarried in 1600; and Anne, married to Henry Lord

your vertues: in this onely did wee differ, that some saide your Portraiture might be drawen, others saide impossible: some thought your vertues might be numbred, most saide they were infinite: infinite and impossible, of that side was I: and first in humility to salute you most happy I: my untamed thoughts waxe gentle, and I feele in myselfe civility; a thing hated, because not knowen; and unknowen, because I knew not you. Thus Vertue tameth fiercenesse; Beauty, madnesse. Your Majestie on my knees will I followe, bearing this Club, not as a Savage, but to beate downe those that are.

At the middle of the Hill sate Pan, and two Virgins keeping sheepe, and sowing in their samplers, where her Majestye stayed and heard this:

Herbert, son and heir-apparent to Edward Earl of Worcester: she died in 1639.—The elegant and accomplished Lady Russel survived her second husband 25 years. She was buried at Bisham where she has a stately monument inscribed by her son Sir Edward Hoby; but, being without a date, the time of her death has not hitherto been ascertained. The Peerages state it to have happened in 1584; a mistake, arising probably from the circumstance of John Lord Russel's death. Her Greek and Latin epitaphs on her husband and son are printed in Dart's Westminster, p. 115.— Dr. Fuller has also preserved some of her verses, and it is remarkable that she and her two sisters were all good poets. —It is evident that Lady Russel was living when the Queen visited Bisham in 1592; and through the kind attention of my friend Mr. Henry Walter, I have been favoured by the Hon. and Rev. Mr. Melville, who holds the Curacy of Bisham, with the following extract from the Register of the Parish: "The Ladye Elizabeth Russell buryed the second of June, 1609."

Her eldest son Sir Edward Hoby, who entertained the Queen in 1592, was Governor of Queenborough Castle, and a Gentleman of the Privy Chamber. He was a distinguished speaker in the four last Parliaments of Queen Elizabeth. As a writer, he displayed his talents only in controversial divinity: the learned Camden, who dedicated his *Hibernia* to him, has taken more than one opportunity of commending his abilities and acknowledging his friendship. Sir Edward Hoby died in 1617.—In the Chapel is a monument for his wife Margaret; and there is also a window richly ornamented with the arms and quarterings of Hoby.

Bisham Abbey is now the seat of George Vansittart, Esq. many years one of the Knights of the Shire, who purchased it, with the manor, of the widow of Sir John Hoby Mill, Bart. who died in 1780. —There are no remains of the conventual buildings, except an ancient door-way, now the entrance of the house.—There are traditions of the Elizabethan visit at Bisham Abbey; a room there is called her "Presence Chamber;" and a Well in the grounds is called "Queen Elizabeth's Well." It is said she bathed in it. The water of this spring is remarkably cold, too much so for persons in general to use as a bath; perhaps it was the use of such waters that occasioned that frigidity of constitution our Virgin Queen was so famous for.

In the parish of Marlow, in the fields called *The Moors*, is also a Well that still bears the name of "Queen Elizabeth's Well", and seems to be the only remembrance left of her visiting Marlow.

Pan. Prety soules and bodies too, faire Shephardisse, or sweete Mistresse, you know my suite, Love; my vertue, Musicke; my power, a Godhead. I cannot tickle the sheepes gutts of a Lute, *bydd, bydd, bydd,* like the calling of Chickins; but for a Pipe that squeekèth like a Pigg, I am he. How doe you burne time, and drowne beauty, in pricking of clouts, when you should be penning of Sonnets? You are more simple than the sheep you keepe, but not so gentle. I love you both, I know not which best; and you both scorne me, I know not which most. Sure I am, that you are not so young as not to understand love, nor so wise as to withstand it, unlesse you think yourselves greater then gods, whereof I am one. How often have I brought you chestnuts for a love token, and desired but acceptance for a favour. Little did you knowe the misterye, that as the huske was thornye and tough, yet the meate sweete, so though my hyde were rough and hateful, yet my heart was smooth and loving: you are but the Farmer's daughters of the Dale, I the God of the flocks that feede upon the hils. Though I cannot force love, I may obedience, or else send your sheepe a wandring with my fancies. Coynesse must be revenged with curstnesse: but be not agaste, sweet mice: my Godhead cometh so fast upon me, that Majestye had almost overrun affection. Can you love? Will you?

Syb. Alas, poor Pan! Looke how he looketh, Sister, fitter to drawe in a harvest wayne, then talke of love to chaste Virgins. Would you have us both?

Pan. I, for oft I have hearde, that two Pigeons may bee caught with one beane.

Isab. And two Woodcocks with one sprindge.

Syb. And many Dotterels with one dance.

Isab. And all fooles with one faire worde.

Nay, this is his meaning; as he hath two shapes, so hath he two harts; the one of a man wherewith his tongue is tipped, dissembling; the other of a beast, wherewith his thoughts are poysoned, lust. Men must have as manie loves, as they have hart-strings, and studie to make an Alphabet of Mistresses, from A to Y, which maketh them in the end crie *Ay.* Against this, experience hath provided us a remedy, to laugh at them when they know not what to saie; and when they speake, not to beleeve them.

Pan. Not for want of matter, but to knowe the meaning, what is wrought in this sampler?

Syb. The follies of the Gods, who became beastes, for their affections.

Pan. What in this?

Isab. The honour of Virgins, who became Goddesses, for their chastity.

Pan. But what be these?

Syb. Men's tongues, wrought all with double stitch, but not one true.

Pan. What these?

Isab. Roses, egletine, harts-ease, wrought with Queenes stitch, and all right.

Pan. I never hard the odds between men's tongues and weomen's; therefore they may be both double, unlesse you tell mee how they differ.

Syb. Thus, weomen's tongues are made of the same flesh that their harts are, and speake as they thinke: men's harts of the flesh that their tongues, and both dissemble. But prythy, Pan, be packing; thy words are as odious as thy sight, and we attend a sight which is more glorious that the sunne rising.

Pan. What, does Jupiter come this waies?

Syb. No, but one that will make Jupiter blush, as guilty of his unchast jugglings; and Juno dismaide, as wounded at her Majesty. What our mother hath often told us, and fame the whole world, cannot be concealed from thee; if it be, we wil tell thee; which may hereafter make thee surcease thy suite, for feare of her displeasure; and honour virginitye, by wondering at her vertues.

Pan. Say on, sweete soule?

Syb. This way commeth the Queene of this Islande, the wonder of the world, and Nature's glory, leading affections in fetters, Virginitie's slaves: embracing mildnes with justice, Majestie's twinns. In whom Nature hath imprinted beauty, not art paynted it; in whome Wit hath bred learning, but not without labour; Labour brought forth wisedome, but not without wonder. By her it is (Pan) that all our carttes that thou seest are laden with corne, when in other countries they are filled with harneys; that our horses are ledde with a whip, theirs with a launce; that our rivers flow with fish, theirs with bloode; our cattel feede on pastures, they feed on pastures like cattel. One hande she stretcheth to Fraunce, to weaken Rebels; the other to Flaunders, to strengthen Religion; her heart to both Countries, her vertues to all. This is shee at whom Envie hath shot all her arrowes, and now for anger broke her bow; on whom God hath laide all his blessinges, and we for joy clappe our hands. Heedlesse Treason goeth hedlesse; and close Trechery restlesse: Daunger looketh pale, to beholde her Majesty; and Tyranny blusheth to heare of her mercy. Jupiter came into the house of poore Baucis, and she vouchsafeth to visite the bare farmes of her subjects. We, upon our knees, wil entreat her to come into the valley, that our houses may be blessed with her presence, whose hartes are filled with quietnes by her governement. To her wee wish as many yeares as our fieldes have ears of corne, both infinite: and to her enemies, as many troubles as the wood hath leaves, all intolerable. But whilst here she is, run downe, Pan, the hill in all hast; and though thou breake thy necke to give our mother warning, it is no matter.

Pan. No, give me leave to die with wondring, and trippe you to your mother. Here I yeelde all the flockes of these fields to your Highnes: greene be the grasse where you treade: calme the water where you rowe: sweete the aire where you breathe: long the life that you live, happy the people that you love: this is all I can wish. During your abode, no theft shall be in the woods; in the fields no noise, in the vallies no spies: myselfe will keepe all safe. That is all I can offer. And heare I breake my Pipe, which Apollo could never make me doe; and follow that sounde which followes you.

At the bottome of the hill, entring into the house, Ceres with her Nymphes, in an harvest cart, meet her Majesty, having a crown of wheat-ears with a jewell; and after this Song, uttered the Speech following:

> Swel Ceres now, for other Gods are shrinking,
> > Pomona pineth,
> > Fruitlesse her tree;
> > Fair Phœbus shineth
> > Only on mee.
> Conceite doth make me smile whilst I am thinking,
> > How every one doth read my story,
> > How every bough on Ceres lowreth,
> > Cause heaven's plenty on me powreth,
> > And they in leaves doe onely glory,
> > All other Gods of power hereven,
> > Ceres only Queene of Heaven.
> With robes and flowers let me be dressed,
> > Cynthia that shineth
> > Is not so cleare;
> > Cynthia declineth
> > When I appeere,
> Yet in this Ile shee raignes as blessed,

>And every one at her doth wonder,
>And in my ears still fonde Fame whispers,
>Cynthia shalbe Ceres Mistres,
>But first my carre shall rive asunder.
>
>Helpe, Phœbus, helpe; my fall is suddaine;
>Cynthia, Cynthia, must be Sovereigne.

Greater than Ceres receives Ceres' Crowne, the ornament of my plenty, the honour of your peace. Here at your Highnes' feete, I lay down my feined deity, which Poets have honoured, Truth contemned. To your Majesty, whom the heavens have crowned with happines, the world with wonder, birth with dignitie, nature with perfection, we doe all homage, accounting nothing ours but what comes from you. And this muche dare we promise for the Lady of the Farme [1], that your presence hath added many daies to her life, by the infinite joies shee conceyves in her heart, who presents your Highnesse with this toye and this short praier, poured from her hart, that your daies may increase in happines, your happines have no end till there be no more daies.

At her Majestie's entrance into the Castle at *Sudeley*, an olde Shepheard spake this saying:

Vouchsafe to heare a simple Shephard: Shephards and simplicity cannot part. Your Highnes is come into Cotshold, an uneven country, but a people that carry their thoughtes levell with their fortunes; lowe spirites, but true harts; using plaine dealinge, once counted a jewell, nowe beggery. These hills afoorde nothing but cottages, and nothing can we present to your Highnes but Shephards. The country healthy and harmeles; a fresh aier, where there are no dampes, and where a black sheepe is a perilous beast; no monsters; we carry our harts at our tongues ends, being as far from dissembling as our sheepe from fiercenesse; and if in any thing we shall chance to discover our lewdness, it will be in over boldnesse, in gazinge at you, who fils our hearts with joye, and our eies with wonder. As for the honoreble Lord and Lady of the Castle [2], what happines they conceive, I would it were possible for themselves to expresse; then should your Majestie see, that al outwarde entertainment were but a smoake rising from their inward affections, which as they cannot be seene, being in the hart, so can they not be

[1] Lady Russel mother of Sir Edward Hoby. See before, p. 132.
[2] The Lord and Lady Chandos.

smoothred, appearing in their countenance. This lock of wooll, Cotsholdes best fruite, and my poore gifte, I offer to your Highnes; in which nothing is to be esteemed, but the whitenes, Virginitie's colour; nor to be expected but duetye, Shephard's Religion.

Sunday, Apollo running after Daphne, a Shepheard following, uttering this:

Nescis temeraria; nescis
Quem fugias; ideoque fugis.

A short tale, but a sorrowfull; a just complaint, but remedelesse. I loved (for Shephardes have their Saints), long I loved (for Beauty bindeth prentices) a Nymph most faire, and as chast as faire, yet not more faire then I unhappy. Apollo, who calleth himselfe a God (a title among men, when they will commit injuries tearme themselves Gods), pursued my Daphne with bootlesse love, and me with endlesse hate; her he woed, with faire wordes, the flatteries of men; with great gifts, the sorceries of Gods; with cruell threates, the terrefiing of weake damosels. *Nec prece nec pretio nec movet ille minis.* Me he terrified with a monstrous word metamorphosing, saying that he would turne me into a woolfe, and of a Shepheard make me a sheepe-biter; or into a cockatrice; and cause mine eies, which gazed on her, to blind hers, which made mine dazell; or to a molde, that I should heare his flattering speech, but never behold her faire face: *Tantæne animis cœlestibus iræ?* Sometimes would he allure her with sweete musicke, but Harmony is harsh when it is Lust's broaker; often with promise of immortality, but Chastetye is of itselfe immortall; ever pursuing her with swiftnes, but Vertue tying wings to the thoughts of virgins, Swiftnes becommeth surbated. Thus lived he twixt love and jealousy; I twixt love and danger; she twixt feare and vertue. At last and alas, this day, I feare of all my joyes the last, I cannot as a Poet (who describing the Morning, and before he tell what it is make it Night) stand on the time; Love coyneth no circumloquutions; but by the sunne, a Shepheardes diall, which goeth as true as our hearts, it was four of the clocke, when she, flying from his treason, was turned into a tree; which made me stand as though I had bene turned into a stone, and Apollo so enchanted as wounded with her losse, or his owne crueltye: the fingers, which were wonte to play on the lute, found no other instrument then his owne face; the goulden haire, the pride of his heade, pulde off in lockes, and stampt at his feete;

his sweete voice turned to howling; and there sitteth he (long may he sorrowe) wondring and weeping, and kissing the lawrell, his late love, and mine ever. Pleaseth your Majestye to viewe the melancholy of Apollo, my distresse, and Daphne's mischance; it may be the sight of so rare perfection will make him die for griefe, which I wish; or Daphne returne to her olde shape, which must be your wounder; if neither, it shal content me that I have revealed my griefes, and that you may beholde his.

This Speech ended, her Majesty sawe Apollo with the tree, having on the one side one that sung, on the other one that plaide:

> Sing you, plaie you; but sing and play my truth;
> This tree my lute, these sighes my notes of ruth:
> The lawfull leafe for ever shall bee greene,
> And Chastety shal be Apolloes Queene.
> If Gods maye dye, here shall my tombe be plaste,
> And this engraven, " Fonde Phœbus, Daphne chaste."

After these Verses, the Song:

> My heart and tongue were twinnes, at once conceaved;
>   The eldest was my heart, borne dumbe by destenie;
> The last my tongue, of all sweete thoughts bereaved,
>   Yet strung and tunde to play hearts harmonie.
> Both knit in one, and yet asunder placed,
>   What heart would speake, the tongue doeth still discover;
> What tongue doth speake, is of the heart embraced,
>   And both are one to make a new found lover:
> New founde, and onely founde in Gods and Kings,
>   Whose wordes are deedes, but deedes nor words regarded:
> Chaste thoughts doe mount, and she with swiftest wings,
>   My love with paine, my paine with losse rewarded:
> Engrave upon this tree, Daphnes perfection,
>   " That neither men nor gods, can force affection."

The Song ended, the tree rived, and Daphne issued out, Apollo ranne after, with these words:

Nimpha mane, per me concordant carmina nervis.

Faire Daphne, staye, too chaste because too faire,
  Yet fairer in mine eies, because so chaste;
And yet because so chaste, must I despaire?
  And to despaire I yeelded have at last.
Shepheard, possesse thy love, for me too cruell,
  Possesse thy love, thou knowest not how to measure:
A dunghill cock doeth often find a jewell,
  Enjoying that, he knowes not to be treasure.
When broomy bearde to sweepe thy lips presume,
  When on thy necke his rough hewen armes shall move,
And gloate on thee with eies that drizel reume,
  When that his toothlesse mouth shall call thee love;
Nought will I say of him, but pittie thee,
That beauty might, but would no wiser bee.

Daphne, running to her Majestie, uttered this:

I stay, for whither should Chastety fly for succour, but to the Queene of Chastety. By thee was I enterred in a tree, that by crafte, way might be made to Lust: by your Highnes restored, that by vertue there might be assurance in honor. These tables, to set downe your prayses, long since, Sibylla's prophesies, I humbly present to your Majesty; not thinking that your vertues can be deciphered in so slight a volume, but noted. The whole World is drawen in a small mappe, Homer's Illiades in a nutshel, and the riches of a Monarch in a few cyphers; and so much ods, betwext explaining of your perfections and the touching, as is betwixt painting and thinking; the one, running over a little table in a whole day, the other over the whole world in a minute.

With this vouchsafe a poore Virgin's wish, that often wish for good husbands; mine, only for the endlesse prosperity of my Soveraigne.

The Verses, written in the Tables which were given to her Majesty:

> Let Fame describe your rare perfection,
>   Let Nature paint your beauties glory,
> Let Love engrave your true affection,
>   Let Wonder write your vertues story:
> By them and Gods must you be blazed,
> Sufficeth men they stand amazed.

The thirde day should have been presented to her Majestie the High Constable of Cotsholde, but the weather so unfit, that it was not. But this it should have beene; one clothed all in sheepes-skins, face and all, spake this by his interpreter:

May it please your Highnes, this is the great Constable and Commandadore of Cotsholde: he speaks no language but the Rammish tongue; such sheepishe governours there are, that can say no more to a messenger then he *(Bea)*. This therefore, as signifying his duety to your Majesty, and al our desires, I am commanded to be his interpreter, or shepheards starre, pointing directly to Cotshold, and in Cotshold to Sudeley, made us expect some wonder, and of the eldest aske some counsel: it was resolved by the ancientst, that such a one should come by whome all the shepheards should have their flocks in safety, and their own lives, all the country quietnes, and the whole world astonishment. Our Constable commaunds this day to be kept holliday; all our shepheards are assembled; and if shepheards pastimes may please, how joyful would they be if it would please you to see them; which if you vouchsafe not, as pastimes too meane for your Majestie, they meane to call this day the shepherds blacke day. In all humilitie we entreat, that you would cast an eie to their rude devices, and an eare to their harshe wordes; and if nothing happen to be pleasing, the amends is, nothing shal be tedious.

After this Speech, her Majesty was to be brought amonge the Shepheards, amonge whome was a King and a Queene to be chosen, and thus they beganne:

Melibœus. Nisa. Cutter of Cootsholde.

Mel. Cut the cake; who hath the beane, shall be King; and where the peaze is shee shal be Queene.

Nis. I have the peaze, and must be Queene.

Mel. I the beane, and King; I must commaunde.

Nis. Not so; the Queene shall and must commaunde: for I have often heard of a King that coulde not commaunde his subjects; and of a Queene that hath commaunded Kings.

Mel. I yeeld; yet is it within compasse of my authoritie to aske questions; and first I will beginne with you in love, I meane Shepheardes love; for I will not meddle with Gentlefolkes love: which is most constant, the man or the woman?

Nis. It is no question, no more than if you should aske, whether on a steepe hill, a square stone or a globe stoode most steddye.

Mel. Both loving, which is most loving?

Nis. The woman, if she have her right; the man, if he be his own judge.

Mel. Why doth the man ever woe the woman, the woman never the man?

Nis. Because men are most amorous and least chaste; women careless of fonde affections, and when they embrace them, fearfull. But, unlesse your questions were wiser, I commaunde you to silence. You, sirra, that sit as though your wits were a woole-gathering, will you have a question, or a commaundement?

Cut. No question of a Queene, for they are harde to be answered; but anie commaundement, for that must be obeyed.

Nis. Then sing. And you, Sir, a question, or commaundement?

Do. A commaundement I; and glad that I am!

Nis. Then play.

Do. I have plaide so long with my fingers, that I have beaten out of play al my good fortunes.

The Song.

Hearbes, wordes, and stones, all maladies have cured;
   Hearbes, wordes, and stones, I used when I loved;
Hearbes smels, words, winde, stones hardnes have procured;
   By stones, nor wordes, nor hearbes her minde was moved.

I askt the cause: this was a woman's reason,
  Mongst hearbes are weedes, and thereby are refused;
Deceite, as well as Truth, speakes wordes in season,
  False stones by foiles have many one abused.
I sight, and then shee saide my fancie smoaked;
  I gaz'd, shee saide my lookes were follies glauncing;
I sounded deade, shee saide my love was choaked;
  I started up, shee saide my thoughtes were dauncing.
    O, sacred Love! if thou have any Godhead,
    Teach other rules to winne a maidenheade.

Mel. Well song, and wel plaide; seldome so well amonge Shepheards. But call me the Cutter of Cotsholde, that lookes as though he only knew his leripoope; amorous he is, and wise; carying a sheepes eie in a calfs heade.

Nis. Will you three questions, or three commaundments?

Cut. Halfe a dozen of eache. My wits worke like new beare; and they will breake my head, unlesse it vent at the mouthe.

Nis. Sing.

Cut. I have forsworne that since cuckow-time; for I heard one sing all the sommer, and in the winter was all balde.

Nis. Play on the lute.

Cut. Taylers crafte: a knocke on the knuckles will make one faste a fortnight; my belly and back shall not be retainers to my fingers.

Nis. What question shall I aske?

Cut. Any, so it be of love.

Nis. Are you amorous?

Cut. No; but fantasticall.

Nis. But what is love?

Cut. A single Accidens. In love there are eight parties. { Joy, Hope, Truth, Constancy } all tolerable. { Sorrow, Anger, Jelousie, Despaire } all intolerable.

These containe all till you come to the rules; and then in love there are three concords:

1. The first, betwixt a bacheler and a maide.
2. The seconde, betwixt a man and his wife.
3. The thirde, betwixt any he and she that loveth stragling.

Nis. The foole bleeds; it is time to stopp his vaine; for, having wet his foote, he careth not how deepe he wades. Let us attend that which we most expect. The Starr that directs us hither, who hath in Almanacke?

Cut. What meane you, a Starmonger, the quipper of the firmament? Here is one. I ever carrie it, to knowe the hyewaies to everie Good Towne, the Faires, and the Faire Weather.

Mel. Let me see it. The seventh[1] of September Happines was born into the world. It may be the eleventh is some wonder; the Moone at the ful, tis true, for *Cynthia* never shined so bright. The twelfth, the weather inclined to moisture, and shepheards devises to dryenes. The thirteenth, Sommer goeth from hence; the signe in *Virgo*; *Vivat clarissima Virgo.* The diseases shalbe melancholies: some proceeding of necessitie, some of superfluity; many shalbe studying how to spend what they have; more beating their brains to get what they want. Malice shalbe more infectious than the pestilence: and drones more favoured than ants; as for bees, they shal have but theire laboure for their paines; and when their combes be ful, they shalbe stilde; the warre shalbe twixt hemlocke and honie. At foure of the clocke this day, shal appeare the Worldes Wonder, that leades England into every land, and brings all lands into England.

Then, espying her Majesty, he and al the Shepheards kneeling, concluded thus:

This is the day, this the houre, this the Starre; pardon, dread Sovereigne, poore Shepheards pastimes, and bolde Shepheards presumptions. We call ourselves Kings and Queenes, to make mirth; but when we see a King or Queene, we stand amazed. The Sunne warmes the earth, yet loseth no brightnes, but sheweth more force; and Kings names that fall upon Shepheards, loose no dignity, but breede more feare. The pictures are drawn in colours; and in brasse their portraytures engraven. At Chess, there are Kings and Queenes, and they of wood. Shepheards are no more, nor no lesse, wooden. In Theatres, artificers have plaide Emperours; yet the next day forgotten neither their dueties nor occupations. For our boldenes in borrowing their names, and in not seeing your Majesty for our blindnes, we offer these Shepheards weeds; which if your Majestye vouchsafe at any time to weare, it shall bring to our hearts comfort, and happines to our labours.

⁎⁎⁎ The Speeches at RICOT *will be found hereafter, in p.* 168.

[1] This was the Queen's birth-day.

Her Majesty's second Visit to the University of Oxford, is thus described by Anthony Wood, in his " Annals :"

It being now twenty-six years since Queen Elizabeth visited our University, she resolved this year to come again, that she might take her last farewell thereof, and behold the change and amendment of learning and manners that had been in her long absence made. The appointed day therefore appearing, which was the 22d of September, she with a splendid retinew came from Woodstock; and approaching the confines of the University was met by divers Doctors, in their scarlet robes, Heads of Houses, Proctors, and about eighteen Masters of Arts, besides the Vice-chancellor and the three Esquire Bedells. After a Speech was spoken and a gift delivered to her, which she accepted very kindly in the Latin tongue, met her at the end of St. Gyles, the Mayor, Aldermen, Baylives, and others of the thirteen, in their scarlet, who presenting themselves before her, the Recorder spake a Speech, which ended, they in the name of the whole City presented to her a silver-gilt cup with sixty angels therein.

Coming into the City she was received with great acclamations of the people, and from the Northgate to Quatervois and so to Christ Church great gate with that of ' Vivat Regina,' by Undergraduates, Bachelaurs, and Masters of Arts. From the Undergraduates she had an Oration and verses spoken by two of them, and from the Bachelaurs and Masters of the like; all which she with brevity answered in the Latin tongue; and in the conclusion gave them her benediction. At Quatervois, which is the middle way between the North and Christ Church great gate, she was saluted by the Greek Reader with a Greek Oration: for which she thanked him in that language. At length she alighting in Christ Church Quadrangle, the Orator[1] of the University welcomed her in the name of its Members. After which was done, she was conducted into the Cathedral under a

[1] The office therefore of Public Orator, is not, as to the settlement and endowment thereof, ancient in the University, for before the time of Queen Elizabeth nothing of encouragement, only applause, was given thereunto, it being then the custom for the Chancellor or his deputy to court or invite that person that was generally known to have an eloquent pen and tongue to write epistles to great persons, and harangue it before them at their coming to the University for once and no more, unless the said person was willing. But upon a strong rumour that the learned Queen Elizabeth would visit the University, an. 1564, and abide there several days (the event of which came not to pass), a worthy person was then elected to keep the said place for a term of life, and a yearly pension of twenty nobles was allowed to him and his successors.

canopy supported by four Doctors, where she heard Te Deum and other service done by way of thanks for her safe arrival.

As for other ceremonies that were performed in her abode here, which was till the 28th Sept. the same method was used as in an. 1566. Sermons at Christ Church on the Sunday she was here, were preached by the Dean, and Dr. Martin Heton or Mr. John Purefoy, Canons of that Church. Every week day in the morning were ordinary Lectures in the Schools, besides Lectures in every faculty and science by able and selected persons: and on the same mornings also at ten of the clock Quodlibets by ten Masters and ten Bachelaurs of Arts. In most of the afternoons were Disputations at St. Mary's in Philosophy, Law, Physick, and Divinity. In the nights also were sometimes Plays acted in Christ Church Hall by several Students of the University; but what they were, or how applauded, I know not. Every College also provided an Oration to be spoken to the Queen at her entrance into them. Some of which being performed, she answered very readily with great affability in the Latin tongue.

The 25th of September all the Queen's Privy Council, which were with her in Oxford, being invited to dinner to Merton College by Dr. Savile, the Warden, and Fellows, came accompanied with most of the Nobles and other worthy persons belonging to the Court. After they, about 60 in number, had received a sumptuous feast in the Common Hall there (at a table reaching from one end thereof to the other) were pleased to hear certain Divinity Disputations performed by the Fellows on this subject:

" An dissentiones civium sint utiles Reipublicæ?"

The Respondent was Mr. Henry Cuffe, Greek Professor the University. The Opponents, Mr. Thomas French, Mr. Richard Trafford, Mr. Henry Wilkinson, and Mr. Henry Mason. The Moderator was Mr. Thomas Savile, the Senior Proctor of the University; all which performing their respective parts with a general applause from the Auditory (not without great credit to the House of Merton) the Privy Council, with the French Embassador, named Monsieur Beauvoys la Noude, then present, receded to Mr. Jasper Colmer's Chamber to consult about the affairs of the kingdom.

The 26th day were Disputations in Law and Physick, and amongst many questions discussed in the last was this one—" Whether that the air, or meat, or drink, did most change a man?" And a merry Doctor of that faculty, named Richard Ratcliff, lately Fellow of Merton College, but now Principal of St. Alban's Hall, going about to prove the negative, shewed forth a big, large body, a great fat belly, a side waist, all, as he said, so changed by meat and drink, desiring to see any there so metamorphosed by the air. But it was concluded (by the Moderator) in the affirmative, that the air had the greater power of change.

On the next day in the morning divers Nobles and others were created Masters of Arts, and in the afternoon, the French Embassador. After which were Divinity Disputations performed in St. Mary's Church before her Majesty; and at them were present Dr. Westphaling, Bishop of Hereford, who made an eloquent and copious Oration for the conclusion of them. One of the questions was,

"Whether it be lawful to dissemble in cause of religion?"

Which being looked upon as a nice question caused much attention from the courtly auditory. One argument more witty than solid, that was urged by one of the Opponents, was this—" It is lawful to dispute of religion, therefore 'tis lawful to dissemble:" and so going on, said, " I myself now do that which is lawful; but I do now dissemble: *ergo*, it is lawful to dissemble." At which her Majesty and all the auditory were very merry. The Bishop in his Oration concerning the said question, allowed a secresy, but without a dissimulation; a policy, but not without piety, lest men taking too much of the serpent, have too little of the dove. All that then was disliked in him, was the tediousness in his concluding Oration; for the Queen, being something weary of it, sent twice to him to cut it short, because herself intended to make a public Speech that evening; but he would not, or as some told her, could not put himself out of a set methodical Speech for fear he should have marred all, or else confounded his memory.

Wherefore seeing it was so, she forbeared her Speech at that time; and more privately the next morning sending for the Heads of Houses and other Persons, spake to them her mind in the Latin tongue. And among others there present she schooled Dr. John Rainolds for his obstinate preciseness, willing him to follow her laws, and not run before them. But it is seems he had forgotten it when he came to Hampton Court, where he received a better schooling by K. James, an. 1603. After she had done with him, she proceeded to her Oration; and when she was in the midst thereof, she cast her eye aside, and saw the old Lord Treasurer Burleigh (Cecil) standing on his lame feet for want of a stool; whereupon she called in all haste for a stool for him; nor would she proceed in her Speech till she saw him provided of one. Then fell she to it again, as if there had been no interruption. Upon which one that knew he might be bold with her, told her after she had concluded, that she did it of purpose to shew, that she could interrupt her Speech, and not be put out, although the Bishop durst not adventure to do a less matter the day before. As for the Speech itself, you shall have it verbatim as she delivered it.

" Merita et gratitudo sic meam rationem captivam duxerunt, ut facere cogant quæ ratio ipsa negat: Curæ enim regnorum tam magnum pondus habent, ut potius ingenium obtundere, quam memoriam acuere soleant. Addatur etiam hujus linguæ desuetudo, quæ talis et tam diuturna fuit, ut in triginta sex annis, credo vix trigesies me usam fuisse meminerim. Sed fracta nunc est glacies; aut inhærere, aut evadere oportet. Merita vestra, non sunt laudes eximiæ et insignes sed immerita mea: non doctrinarum in multis generibus exercitia quæ declarasse vos cum laude sentio; non Orationes multis et variis modis eruditè et insigniter expressæ: sed aliud quiddam est multò pretiosius atque præstantius, amor scilicet vester, qualis nec unquam auribus, nec scripto nec memoriâ hominum notus fuit: cujus exemplo parentes carent, nec inter familiares cadit: immo nec inter amantes, in quorum sortem non semper fides incidit, experientia ipsa docente, qualem nec persuasiones, nec minæ, nec execrationes delere potuerunt; imo in quem tempus potestatem non habet quod ferrum consumit; quod scopulos minuit id ipsum separare not potuit. Ista sunt ejusmodi, quæ æterna futura putarem, si et ego æterna essem. Ob quæ si mille pro una linguas haberem, gratias debitas exprimere non valerem: tantum animus concipere potest, quæ exprimere nequit. In cujus gratitudinem ab initio regni mei, summa et præcipua mea solicitudo, cura et vigilia fuit; ut Respublica tam externis inimicis, quam internis tumultibus immunis servaretur, ut quod diu et multis sæculis floruisset, sub meis manibus non debilitaretur.

" Post enim animæ meæ tutelam in hoc solo meam perpetuam solicitudinem collocavi, quod si pro totius salute tam semper fuerim vigilans, cum et ipsa Academia pars ejus non minima putetur: quomodo non et in illam extenditur ista cautio, pro qua tanta diligentia usura semper sum, ut nullo stimulo opus sit ad eam excitandam, quæ ex seipsa prompta est promovendam, servandam, et decorandam, illam. Nunc quod ad concilium attinet, tale accipite, quod si sequamini haud dubito quin erit in Dei gloriam, vestram utilitatem, et meum singulare gaudium. Ut diuturna sit hæc Academia, habeatur imprimis cura ut Deus colatur, non more omnium opinionum, non secundum ingenia nimis inquieta exquisita: sed ut lex divina jubet et nostra præcipit, non enim talem principem habetis, quæ vobis quicquam præcipiat quod contra conscientiam vere christianam esse deberet. Scitote me prius morituram quam tale aliquid acturam, aut quicquam jussuram quod in sacris literis vetatur. Si cum corporum vestrorum semper curam suscepi: deseramne animarum? Vetet Deus. Animarum ego curam negligam, pro quarum neglectu anima mea judicabitur? longè absit. Moneo ergo ut non præeatis leges sed sequamini, nec disputetis num meliora possint præscribi, sed observetis quæ lex divina jubet, et nostra cogit. Deinde memineritis ut unusquisque in gradu suo superiori obediat, non præscribendo quæ esse deberent, sed sequendo quod præscriptum est: hoc cogitantes; quod si superiores agere cœperint quæ non decet, alium superiorem habebunt à quo regantur, qui illos punire et debeat et velit. Postremo ut sitis unanimes: cum intelligatis unita robustiora, separata infirmiora, et citò in ruinam casura."

Her Speech being done, she talked with the Vice-chancellor and Doctors a little while, and then retired. In the afternoon she left Oxford, and going through Fish Street to Quatervois, and thence to the East Gate, received the hearty wishes (mixt with tears) of the people; and casting her eyes on the walls of St. Mary's Church, All Souls, University and Magdalen Colleges, which were mostly hung with verses and emblematical expressions of poetry, was often seen to give gracious nods to the Scholars. When she came to Shotover Hill (the utmost confines of the University) accompanied with those Doctors and Masters that brought her in, she graciouslie received a farewell Oration from one of them, in the name of the whole University. Which being done, she gave them many thanks, and her hand to kiss: and then looking wistfully towards Oxford, said to this effect in the Latin tongue: "Farewell, farewell, dear Oxford, GOD bless thee, and increase thy sons in number, holiness, and virtue, &c." And so went towards Ricote [1].

[1] Gutch's Edition of Wood's Annals, 1796, pp. 248—253.

THE QUEEN'S ENTERTAINMENT AT OXFORD, 1592.

The Grand Reception and Entertainment of Queen ELIZABETH at OXFORD in 1592, from a MS account, originally written by Mr. PHILIP STRINGER, one of the two Cambridge Gentlemen [1] who attended Sir William Cecil Lord Burghley (Chancellor of the University of Cambridge), upon that occasion, to Oxford [2]. Communicated to Mr. Peck by the Reverend Samuel Knight, S. T. P. Archdeacon of Berks [3].

On Friday, Sept. 22, 1592, about 3 of the clock in the afternoon, the Queen's Most Excellent Majestie entred into the bounds or precincts of the University of Oxford, at a place called Godstow Bridge, much about a mile from the City of Oxford; where hir Highness was attended for by the Vice-chancellor [Nicholas

---

[1] Mr. Henry Mowtlowe, of King's College, Cambridge, was the other Cambridge Gentleman who attended Sir William Cecil to Oxford. This Mr. Mowtlowe was Senior Proctor of the University of Cambridge, annis 1589 and 1593. The reason of these Gentlemen then going to Oxford was to see and observe what was done there, that (in case of the Queen or any of her successors coming afterwards to Cambridge) that University might know the better how to amend and improve upon what had been done at Oxford. And the University of Oxford, upon the like occasion, observed the same course, for the same reason. Thus, when Queen Elizabeth was at Cambridge in 1564, we find the two Proctors of the University of Oxford there. See the tract above referred to, under that year in vol. I. p. 151. I must add here, that, as this account of Queen Elizabeth's second reception and entertainment at Oxford was written by a Cambridge man, some allowances must be made (where he slurs Oxford, and prefers the conduct of the like matters at Cambridge) to his being a member of that University. And the same rule, or caution, should always be remembred, on such occasions, when the account of any such passages at Cambridge is written by those of Oxford. This Mr. Henry Mowtloe, or Mountlowe, was afterwards LL. D. and elected the first Professor of Civil Law in Gresham College.

[2] The reason of Queen Elizabeth's thus going to Oxford a second time was, "That Lord Buckhurst, coming to the Government of that University, on the death of [Sir Christopher] Hatton he thought himself obliged, and truly with great industry endeavoured, to correct whatever had escaped the knowledge of his predecessor, during his short Chancellorship. And for this end he invited her Majesty again this year to Oxford, as the Earl of Leicester had done before in 1566." Ayloffe, p. 192.

[3] Though Queen Elizabeth was at Oxford in 1592, yet this account of her then entertainment there was not drawn up till after her death (24 March, 1602), when King James I. being expected (soon after his accession) to make a visit to the University of Cambridge, it was (for the reason abovementioned) called for by Dr. John Cowell (LL.D. Master of Trinity Hall, and) Vice-chancellor of the University in 1603.

Bond, S. T. P. President of St. Mary Magdalen's College] and the rest of the Doctors (Heads of Colleges) with the Proctors and Beadles of the University, being allthen on foot in gownes; the Doctors in scarlet; the rest otherwise, as was answerable to their degrees and place.

Upon intelligence of the Vice-chancellor's being ready, with the rest, to present their dutyes unto hir Highness, hir Majestie was pleased to have the coach stayed wherein she was[1]; notwithstanding the foulness of the weather. Whereupon the Vice-chancellor delivered up unto hir Highness the Beadles staves, which were immediately re-delivered unto him by herself, with the signification of hir gracious pleasure to stay the hearing of a Speech wherewithall they were provided (as hir Highness understood) so that it were not too longe. Which being knowne,

---

The following Letter from Mr. Stringer to Dr. Henry Moutloe, dated May 3, 1603, was sent with the Copy of his Account of the Entertainment of the Queen, and praying him to correct any thing amiss in it:

To the Right Worshipful Mr. Dr. MOUTLOE.

Sir, I do assure myself that you did take some notes of the manner of the entertainment of her late Majestie at hir last being in the University of Oxford, and the sum and substance also of that which was then done or shewed by them; and may conceive that you have also set it downe in some order of writing for the use of the University here, if happily it should be required of us that were sent thither. Nevertheless, for that I know not how your leisure and late health hath suffered yow so to do, I have presumed somewhat hastily to put together such notes as I then took therof, in such meane sort as here appeareth; very instantly intreating yow to run over it, and so to alter it, as yow shall finde cause, both for the matter and manner.

My desire was cheefly to set it down truly, according as it was done. Which if it have your allowance (my notes being somewhat worn out of my book of tables) I shall the better satisfy myself in the rest; whose manner is not to be over curiouse in the contenting of those that be curious. And so presuming upon your love and kindness (as ever I have done) I do for the present leave yow, with my true affectionate love recommended unto yourselfe; houlding still a purpose that I have longe had to see yow myselfe as soone as well I may, mine occasions and troublesome infirmities considered. This third of May, 1603.   Yours, in all duty and true affection,   PHI. STRINGER.

I will cause it to be written out somewhat more handsomely, after yow have perused and corrected it; and will so, either deliver it to Mr. Vice-chancellor, or keep it in readiness for him.

[1] "In 1564, William Boonen, a Dutchman (the first who brought the use of coaches into England), became the Queen's coachman; and after awhile divers great ladies, with as great jealousie of the Queen's displeasure, made them coaches, and rid in them up and down the countries to the great admiration of all the beholders." Continuation of Stow's Chronicle by Edmund Howes, p. 867. b.

Mr. [Thomas] Savill, the Senior Proctor [1], being then upon his knees (with the rest of the company) did presently enter into a short Speech. Wherein he first signified, " what great joy the University had conceived by hir Majestie's approaching so near unto them. And then that, in the name of the whole body, for the better manifestinge of their dutifulness, he was to yeld up unto her Majestie the liberties, privileges, howses, colleges, temples, goods, with themselves also, and whatsoever they were by her Majestie's goodness possessed of, with their most instant and dutiful prayers for the longe and blessed preservation of hir Highnes." This done, hir Majestie, with the Nobility, and the rest of her Royal traine, going towards the City, was, within half a mile, received by the Maior of Oxford and his brethren, with a short Speech delivered by their Recorder. Thence, passing by St. John's Colledge, she was there presented with a private Speech in the behalfe of that Colledge (as unto me it seemed). From whence, entring into the City, she passed thorow the streets (the scholers standing in order on both sides of the same) 'till her Highness came to the place which is called Carfax, or Cator Fosey [rectius, *quatre voyes* or *voies*] where she was pleased to hear an Oration in the Greek Tonge, which was offered unto hir by Mr. [Henry Cuffe [2]] then the Greek Reader. Thence she passed along to her lodging (which was provided for her in Christ's Church) the scholars standing on both sydes of the street (as is already said) in their gownes, hoods, and caps, answerable to their several degrees.

In Christ's Church, going in here in [at] the end of the minster (before hir Highnes went up to the roomes provided for her) she was received with an Oration by Mr. Smith (in the behalf of that Colledge, as I then conceived of it); [William James, S. T. P.] the Dean thereof, and the company attending there, for the performance of that dutye.

[1] " This Thomas Savile was brother of Sir Henry, and Fellow of Merton; an accomplished gentleman, and a great philologer. He wrote " Epistolæ variæ ad illustres Viros " (published in 4to, Oxon. 1691, by Dr. Thomas Smith), and died in this his Proctorship 22 Jan. 1592-3, at London, and was after conveyed thence to Oxon, and buried with great solemnity in the choir of Merton College." Ath. Oxon. vol. I. col. 257, 258.

[2] This learned, but unfortunate Gentleman, was hanged at Tyburn, 30 March, 1601, for being concerned in the treason of Robert Earl of Essex, to whom he was then Secretary. Ath. Oxon. vol. I. col. 307, 308. Little John Owen (lib. v. num. 107), has this epigram upon him :

" Doctus eras Græce, felixque tibi fuit Alpha,
" At fuit infelix Omega, *Cuffe*, tuum."

On Satterday then next follwinge, Sept. 23, hir Majestie went to the Church of St. Maryes, betwixt two and three of the clock; being attended upon by hir Nobility hirselfe being in a rich carradge, and the Nobility [riding] upon their foot-clothes.

Hir Majestie being there placed under her cloth of estate, upon a very fayre stage (which was purposely erected for hir in the East end of the Church, nere unto the quire) there was a philosophy act provided for hir Highnes; which was begun upon the signification of hir Highnes pleasure therein, by this only word, "Incipiatis" being uttered by herself. Whereupon the Proctors [Mr. Savile, and Mr. (afterwards Sir) Ralph Winwood[1], of Magdalen] both of them together did, after their usual brief and plain manner, speak unto the first replier, "ad incipiendum." Who, after three congés unto her Majestie, in such sort as is usual, did presently propound the questions unto the Answerer, without any Speech at all unto her Highnes. Hereupon the Answerer, Mr. Thomas Smith[2], then Orator of the University (after his like three congés to hir Highnes) repeated the questions formerly propounded; which were these:

1. "An anima [cujusvis] sit in se præstantior anima alterius?"
2. "An, ob mundi senectam, homines minus sunt heroici nunc quam olim?" and so entred into his position, which continued almost half an hower, hir Majestie thinking it somewhat longe (as it seemed) for that (when hir Speech was ended) the Proctors uttering their accustomed words unto the Replier, *viz.* "Procede, Majister," hir Majestie, supposing it had been spoken to the Answerer, said, that "He had bene already too longe."

Upon these words of the Proctors, one Mr. [Matthew] Gwin[3], the first Replier

---

[1] This memorable person (son of Richard son of Lewis Winwood, sometime Secretary to Charles Brandon, Duke of Suffolk) was born at Ainho, in Northamptonshire, Proctor of this University in 1589; travelled, and returned an accomplished gentleman. He was knighted 28 June, 1607, made Secretary of State in 1614, and died in Oct. 1617. Fasti Oxon. vol. I. col. 133. 139.

[2] This Smith was a Christ's Church man; afterwards Secretary to Robert Earl of Essex, Clerk of the Parliament and Council, and knighted in 1603; Latin Secretary, and one of the Masters of the Requests, to King James. He died 28 Nov. 1609. Ath. Oxon. vol. I. col. 352.

[3] This Matthew Gwin was Fellow of St. John's College, studied physic, poetry, chemistry, &c. and made a great figure in almost every part of Learning. He was chosen Music Professor of this University of Oxford in 1582 (a circumstance unknown to Mr. Wood), though he understood not a tittle either of the theory or practice of that science (as he himself most frankly owns in his inau-

(after his like congés) uttered a premeditate Oration unto hir Highnes; the first [part] being directed unto hirself by way of excuse or supplication concerning his disability [to speak] in that honorable presence, and the rest concerning the questions; wherein his wittie handlinge of the matter, and discreete behavior, seemed much to please hir Majestie.

His Speech continued much about a quarter of an hour; after which he approved an argument in the first cause; and was then cut off by the Proctors.

This done, then stood up one Mr. ——— Sydney (who was placed in the lowest forme) being thereunto required by the Proctors. He forgat his congés, used no Speech at all to hir Majestie, but dealt with the Answerer as though hir Majestie had not bin there. In which Speech he was neither longe nor curiose, nether for matter nor maner; who [after he had] propounded one argument in the first cause, was cut off by the Proctors, *ut ante.*

This so passed over, the Proctors calling for the third Replier (whose name was Mr. ———) willed him to oppose in the second question, which he undertooke (after he had made his congés), beginning with a Speach directed to hir Majestie first, and came after to the handlinge of the question, with a Speach noting the predictions of the death and advancement of divers Princes: and so ended, with one only argument in the second question.

The last Replier (whose name was Mr. [John] Buckridge[1] was willed to dispute only in the second question; [and thereupon] did, without any Speach by way of preface, frame himself thereunto, and did perform at the best purpose (as

guration Speech); but he made good amends for his deficiencies in that science by the elegancies of his Latin Oration in praise of it. It was at the request of one of the Proctors in 1582, that he undertook that lecture. The greatest wound, which music ever received in England, was (as I think Mr. Ant. Wood somewhere observes) from the suppression of Monasteries; after which the Puritans often made it their business to run it down as a relique of popery. For both these reasons, very few Englishmen regarded it in Queen Elizabeth's time. (Her own band of musicians were many of them foreigners (Venecians). See Desiderata Curiosa, vol. I. lib. ii. p. 12 b.) And hence, there being no body of any great learning who then minded it in Oxford, Mr. Gwyn was desired and prevailed on to read upon it. F. P. "At length being designed for an employment of considerable trust, he was created Dr. of Physic [17 July, 1593. Fasti Ox. vol. I. fol. 157.], and soon after went in quality of Physician to Sir Henry Unton, Ambassador to France. After his return, he was designed Physician to the Tower, elected [the first] Medicine Professor of Gresham College, and made one of the College of Physicians." Ath. Ox. vol. I. col. 513.

[1] John Buckridge, now Fellow, and afterwards Master, of St. John's College, and at length Bishop of Rochester. Ath. Oxon. vol. I. col. 557 a.

was supposed) with best likinge unto hir Majestie, as it seemed by hir Highnes gracious countenance, and requiring of him to prosecute his argument (after the Proctors had cut him off) with these hir gracious words, " Imo probeat, si potest, &c."

This argument ended by the last Replyer, Mr. [Henry] Savile, the Master of Martine Colledge, was willed by the Proctors to determine the questions, which he presently did, with a very good Speach, though somewhat longe; endinge that act with thanks unto her Majestie, " for hir great patience in hearinge, and with a longe discourse concerninge such benefit as God, by her Highnes, had bestowed upon us, and upon many forraine nations and Princes, by hir Highnes means." Which done, hir Majestie returned to hir Courte, or lodging, so attended as at hir coming out.

The following certain general passages relate not to one, but to several days.

It is to be remembred, that, besydes this act, there was also an English Sermon especially provided for and preached in another Church in the Town (not far from St. Mary's) by a lerned man of special note amongst them. Which was, in like sort, continued every morning at the same hower and place, by men of like quality, during the time of hir Majestie's remaining there with them. At thes Sermons we [the Cambridge men] could not be [present], by reason of [our] ordinary attendance every morning upon the Lord Treasurer, then our most worthy Chancellor. It is also to be remembered, that the three Esquire Beadles did give their attendance upon hir Majestie's person as oft as she went abroad in state, and had place next before the Serjeants at Arms, beinge in chaines of gold, and in fayre gownes, with the rest of their apparell thereunto according. The entrance into St. Mary's Church was kept by the guard only, standinge without the doors of the Church, with their halberts in their hands, thereby to avoyde the noyse and the knocking at the dores, wherwith hir Majestie was somewhat troubled at the first. Besyds that part of the stage which was new built for hir Majestie, there was a part of their ordinary stage set up on both syds of the Church; but none at all in the West end: thereby to give, as I thinke, the better passage of the air unto hir Majestie, and to avoyde the facing of hir, as it were by an opposition, in respect of the place. The Answerers had their seats and places (as we usually have) in the midst of the Church beneath. And the Disputers in every faculty had their seats in the syde of the Church, somewhat lower than her Majestie, [who] sat under hir cloth of estate. There was none in the end of the stage nere hir Majestie, but such as were necessarily attendant upon hir Highnes, *viz.* the Lord Chamberlayne, the Lady Marquesse [of Winton] and some two or three others of the great honorable Ladies. The going to hir Highnes seat was an easie half paced stayre, which was of good bredth, and cast on the North side of that ende, beginning somewhat without the middle isle of the Church.

On Sunday, Sept. 24, there was a Sermon preached before hir Majestie, by Mr. Dr. [William] James, then Dean of Christ's Church, in the minster Church of that Colledge. At night there was a Comedy acted before hir Highnes in the Hall of that Colledge; and one other on Tuesday at night, being both of them but meanely performed (as we thought), and yet most graciouslye, and with great patience, heard by hir Majestie. The one being called "Bellum Grammaticale," and the other intituled "Rivales."

On Monday, Sept. 25, at eight of the elock in the morning, there was an English Sermon, as is alreadie said. And, at the same hower, their ordinary Lectures of Art were read in the Common Schooles. And, at nine, in the Divinity School was read a Divinity Lecture by Mr. [Dr. Thomas] Holland [1] (her Majestie's Reader in Divinity there), at which were present but a few of the Nobility, and many Scholars. This day, the Lords of the Council dined with Mr. [Henry] Savile, at Merton Colledge, in the Common-hall of that House. Where, after they had dined, they heard a Disputation in Philosophy; the answeringe being performed by Mr. [Henry] Cuffe [abovementioned] of that House; four other of the same House replying unto him. There was but one argument propounded by every one of them. Which being done, the questions were determined by Mr. [Thomas] Savile (then the Senior Proctor), who, in the end of his determination, by reason of one of the questions, *viz.* "An Dissentiones Civium sint Reipublicæ utiles?"—took thereby occasion by name to commend [Sir William Cecil] the Lord Tresurer (who was present), in respect of his greate care in the Government of this Commonwealth. And after him the Lord Chamberlain. And after him the Lord Admiral, his great worth and valiant service at sea. And, lastly, fell into commendation of the Earl of Essex, his honorable, valiant service

---

[1] Thomas Holland, Fellow of Baliol College (which he left in 1583); Divinity Professor in 1589; and Rector of Exeter College in 1592; esteemed by the precise men of his time as another Apostle, so familiar with the Fathers, as if he himself had been a Father; with the Schoolmen, as if he himself had been another Seraphical Doctor. Ath. Oxon. vol. I. col. 377.

in the Low Countryes, in Portugall, and in Fraunce: and so concluded. This done, the Lords went to sit in Counsell. After which there was nothing shewed that day, eyther before hir Majestie publiquely, or privately before the Lords of the Counsell.

On Tuesday, Sept. 26, at eight of the clock in the morning, the ordinary Lectures in Art were read as before. At nine of the clock, Mr. Dr. [John] Reignolds[1] did read a Lecture in Divinity, at the which the Lords of the Counsell and the most of the Nobility were present. At the same hower also there were, in other Common Schooles, Disputations, called " Quodlibets," by Masters of Arts and Bachelors in Art, according to their accustomed manner.

About three of the clock in the afternone of the same day, hir Majestie went again to St. Maryes, accompanyed as on Saturday before; where it pleased hir Highnes to heare a Disputation in Natural Philosophy, which was answered by one Mr. [John] Spencer[2], of Corpus Christi Colledge; who was replyed upon by four Masters of Arts, viz. Mr. [John] Williams[3], of All Souls, Mr. [Humphrey] Pritchard[4], of Christ's Church, Mr. [Edward] Brearewood[5], of Brasen Nose, and Mr. —— Buckhurst, of Magdalen.

This act was determined by one Mr. [Giles] Thompson[6], of All Soules, with a very learned and discreet Speach, (as it was conceived by all that heard him, and the rather in respect of the Lord Treasurer's great commending thereof). He

---

[1] John Rainolds, D. D. Fellow, and afterwards President, of Corpus Christi College. See the life of this great man in Wood's Ath. Oxon. vol. I. col. 339; and his funeral Oration, at the end of Sir Isaac Wake's " Rex Platonicus."

[2] John Spencer (President of Corpus Christi after John Rainolds). He died 3 April 1614. Le Neve.

[3] John Williams, afterwards Margaret Professor, Dean of Bangor, and Principal of Jesus College, Ath. Oxon. vol. I. col. 387.

[4] Humphrey Pritchard, of Bangor, in North Wales, sometime an Oxford Scholar, wrote a large preface before " Cambro-Britannicæ Cymeræcæve Linguæ Institutiones, &c. by John David Rhese. Lond. 1592," fol. Ath. Oxon. vol. I. col. 355.

[5] Edward Brerewood, of Brasen Nose. Afterwards the First Astronomy Professor in Gresham College. A learned man, and a great Anti-Sabbatarian. He wrote (saith my author) the smallest neatest character which mine eyes ever yet behold. Ath. Oxon. vol. I. col. 390, 391.

[6] Giles Thompson. He had a rare gift extempore in all school exercises, and such a happy wit to make use of all occurrences to his purpose, as if he had not taken the occasion as they fell out by accident, but rather had bespoke such pretty accidents to fall out to give him the occasions. He was afterwards Dean of Windsor, Bishop of Gloucester, and one of the translators of the Bible temp. Jacobi I. Ath. Oxon. vol. I. col. 731.

handled the questions principally, and spent no time at all in the commendation of hir Majestie, or of the Nobility, " For that (as he sayd) their vertues were greater then that they could be sufficiently commended by him." His Speach not being above a quarter of an hower in length.

The Replyers were required to put forth each of them one argument without any preface; which they did accordingly: with hir Majestie's very good liking.

This done, and the act concluded by Mr. Thompson, (as is already sayd) there presently succeeded a Disputation in Physicke, which was answered by one Mr. Dr. [Thomas] Dochin [1]; who, after his congés, as afore, and a short preface concerning himself) greatly magnified hir Majestie " for hir gratious favor, in vouchsafing hir presence at this exercise, being so excellent a Prince, and so singularly well seene even in this very faculty, amongst many other hir virtues and great excellency of knowledge and learning, which he wished she might have *in* [2] use of hirself." And so entred into a short exposition of one of the questions; viz. " Quod Aere magis mutantur Corpora humana quam Cibo & Potu ;" wherein he was soon cut off by the Proctors, and the Replyers called for; who were six in number, viz. Dr. [Anthony] Ailesworth [3], —— Dalliber, [Henry] Bust [4], [Edward] Ratcliff [5], —— Bently, and [John] Case [6].

Dr. Ayleworth began with a little preface, somewhat concerning hir Majestie's gratiousness in hearing, and hir other virtues; and the rest concerning the ques-

[1] Thomas Dochyn, of Magdalen College, took his M. D. degree 19 Aug. 1592 [Fasti Oxon. vol. I. col. 143.] He was elected the second Lynacre Lecturer of Physic in Merton College, 4 Nov. 1604, and died 29 Jan. following. Athenæ Oxon. vol. I. col. 21.

[2] in. sic; sed forte, no; i. e. *no occasion for the use of it.*

[3] Anthony Ailesworth, alias Aylworth, of New College, M. D. made Regius Professor of Physic 29 June, 1582. [Le Neve]. He was physician to Queen Elizabeth, and died 18 April, 1619. Fasti Oxon. vol. I. col. 124.

[4] Henry Bust, M. D. of Magdalen College 1578, afterwards Superior Reader of Lynacre's Physic Lecture; he practised in Oxford for many years, with great repute, and died there 17 Feb. 1616. Fasti Oxon. vol. I. col. 117.

[5] Edward Ratcliff, M. D. of Cambridge, was incorporated M. D. of Oxford 4 July, 1600. Fasti Oxon. vol. I. col. 159.

[6] John Case, a chorister, first of New College, and then of Christ Church, Scholar of St. John's in 1564, Fellow, M. A. and the most noted Disputant and Philosopher which ever before set in that College; but, being popishly affected, left his Fellowship, married, and read Lectures in Logic and Philosophy to young men (mostly Romanists) in a private house in Oxford; where he had Disputations, Declamations, and other exercises, as in Colleges. He became M. D. in 1589, and Prebendary of rth Aulton, in the Church of Sarum; and by his practice and reading to Scholars, obtained a fair

tions: but was put to an argument ere he had done. And, the four next using only one argument apeece, Dr. Case would have concluded the busines with a short Speach, (wherein he began to call upon the spirits of certain honorable persons not long since of this Commonwealth) but was very soon cut off, and put to an argumeut in the second cause, *viz.* " An Morbi curantur per Fascinationem & per Dæmones?" Whereupon the Determination being called for by the Proctors, it was presently entred into and performed by Mr. Dr. —— Jeffs, one of hir Majestie's physicians.

It must not be forgotten, that this day, betwene the howers of ten and eleven of the clocke in the forenone, it pleased hir Majestie to heare an Oration made by the Vice-chancellor, in the Chamber of Presence, presenting hir Highnes with two Bibles (the one in Greek, and the other in Latine) in the name of the whole University.

On Wednesday, Sept. 27, the Publique Lectures were read as before, at eight of the clock; and the Queen's Reader in Divinity [Thomas Holland, S. T. P.] above-mentioned, read in Divinity at nine.

There was also, at the same time, a Lecture in Musick, with the practice thereof by instrument, in the Common Schooles [1].

At three of the clock in the afternoone, hir Majestie being again come to St. Marye's (attended, as already sayd), Mr. Dr. —— B—— answered in Law, and four other Doctors replied.

The question which they most stood upon was this; *viz.* " An Judex debet

estate; most whereof he bestowed on pious uses. He died 29 Jan. 1599, and was buried in the Chapel of St. John's College. He was a man of an innocent, meek, religious, and studious life; a lover of Scholars, and beloved by them. Ath. Oxon. vol. I. col. 299, 300.

[1] The Music Lecture at this time was read, I presume, by Dr. Matthew Gwinne, abovementioned. Be that as it will, two famous musicians of Cambridge were now incorporated (the one Edward Gibbons, B. Music, and the other John Bull, D. Music) to the same degrees in that science at Oxford; and one, or both of them, it is like, performed some exercise upon this occasion there. The first of these (Gibbons) " was now, or about this time, the admired organist of Bristol. Fasti Oxon. vol. I. col. 143. The other was that famous Dr. Bull, admitted Bachelor of Music in Oxford in 1586, and would have proceeded in the same place, had he not there met with clowns and rigid puritans, who could not endure Church music." Id. Ib. col. 144. " This Dr. Bull, having a most prodigious hand on the organ, and hearing of a famous musician belonging to a certain Cathedral (St. Omer's, as I have heard) he applied himself as a novice to him to learn something of his faculty, and to see and admire his works. Which musician, after some short discourse, conducted him to a vestry or music-school adjoyning to the Cathedral, and there shewed him a lesson or song of fourty parts, and then made a vaunting challenge to any person in the world, to add only one more part to them. Bull thereupon

judicare secundum allegata & probata, contra Conscientiam?" which (after the Disputation) was concluded in the affirmative by Mr. Dr. (Francis Bevans, LL. D.) Master of Jesus Colledge there, and then Chancellor of Hereford.

After this act, there followed immediately a Disputation in Divinity, which was answered by the Queen's Reader (Dr. Tho. Holland), and opposed against him by the Vice-chancellor (Dr. Nicholas Bond), and the Dean of Christ's Church (Dr. William James). Ten other Doctors being there [also] ready to undertake the same (in their scarlet gowns and silk hoods turned), which they could not do for want of time.

This Act was concluded by Mr. Dr. [Herbert] West[phaling], then Bishop of Hereford, determining this question [in the] negative; *viz.* "An licet in Christiana Republica dissimulare in Causa Religionis?"

His Speech was spent, "First, in thanks to hir Majestie for hir most gratious favour unto himself in particular. Then in proofs, whereby he inferred his conclusion of the question. Next, in petition unto hir Highnes for hir gratious pardon if any thing had unadvisedly passed, wherein they or any of the University had offended. And lastly, in thanks unto hir Highnes, in the name of their Honorable Chancellor, of himself, and the rest of the Doctors, and the whole company of students, for hir most gratious favor in vouchsafing them again hir Highnes presence, after six and twenty years [space,] in that place, and at those exercises, &c."—His Oration was so longe that hir Majestie was somewhat wearied therewith, (as it was thought) and did therefore, without any Speech of hir owne, returne to hir lodginge.

---

desired the use of pen and ink, and music-paper, and prayed the Gentleman to lock him up in the said school for two or three hours; which being done (but not without great disdain by him) Bull, in that time or less, added forty more parts to the said lesson or song. The other, returning at the appointed time, viewed it, tried it, and re-tried it, with great amazement. At length he fell into a downright extasie, and swore by the great God, that he who added those other forty parts must either be the Devil or Dr. Bull. Whereupon Bull making himself known, the other fell down and adored him. Dr. Bull continuing afterwards there for some time, he became so admired in those parts, that he was courted to accept of any preferment suitable to his profession within the dominions of the Emperor, France, or Spain. But tidings thereof coming to Queen Elizabeth, she commanded him home." id. ib. col. 131. "After her death, he became chief Organist to King James I. but then went beyond the seas again, and died; some say at Hamborough, others at Lubec." Id. Ib. col. 144. He was the first Music Professor of Gresham College.

The Nobles and others created M. A. on Wednesday Sept. 27, 1592.

In the Morning. 1. Edward Earl of Worcester. 2. George Clifford, Earl of Cumberland. 3. Henry Herbert, Earl of Pembroke. 4. Sir John Wingfield, Knight. 5. Sir Thomas Coningsby, Knight. 6. Sir William Knollys, Knight; afterwards Earl of Banbury. 7. Michael Stanhop, Esquire; brother to John Lord Stanhop of Harrington. 8. Thomas Knevet, Esquire; afterwards, it seems, Lord Knevet of Escrick. 9. Edward Darcy, Esquire. 10. John Stanhop, Esquire. 11. William Pointz, Esquire. 12. Richard Brakenbury, Esquire. 13. Thomas Lake, Esquire. 14. Anthony Ashley, Esquire. 15. Henry Noel, Esquire[1].

In the Afternoon. Monsieur Beauvoys la Noude, the French Ambassador. 2. Mounsieur Mauditor, or Manditor. 3. Sir Edward Stafford, Knight.

On Thursday, September 28, about ten of the clock in the forenoon, hir Majestie made an Oration to the Vice-chancellor, the Doctors, &c. in hir Highnes Chamber of Presence, in most gracious manner, delivering hir acceptance of that which they had done, &c. as appeareth by the Oration. At which we were not, beinge then in attendance upon our honorable Chancellor, at his lodging, in another part of the Court.

Hir Highnes departed from the University this day, about eleven of the clock in the forenoon, in hir open and princely carriadge. And heard, lastly, a long tedious Oration made unto hir by the Junior Proctor of the University, about a mile from the City, in the very edge of their bounds or liberties towards Shotover.

The Old Rents of every College in Oxford[2], according to which they were taxed for the Entertainment of Queen Elizabeth, in the 34th Year of hir Reign, were reckoned as followeth[3].

1. Christ Church	£.2000	10. Exon College — £.200
2. Magdalen College	1200	11. Oriel College — 200
3. New College	1000	12. Trinity College — 200
4. All Souls	500	13. Lincoln College — 130
5. Corpus Christi College	500	14. University College — 100
6. Merton College	400	15. Baliol College — 100
7. St. John's College	400	16. Jesus College — 70
8. Brazen Nose College	300	17. Wadham Col. ⎱ at that time 100
9. Queen's College	260	18. Pembroke Coll. ⎰ not founded. 100

[1] This whole article is added from Wood's Fasti Oxon. vol. II. col. 144, 145.
[2] See Hentzner's Description of this University in p. 172.
[3] From Gutch's "Collectanea Curiosa."

D. HENRICI SAVILII, τȣ̃ μακαρίτȣ, ORATIO, habita Oxoniæ, Sept. 23, 1592, coram Reginâ ELIZABETHA.

Theses.

I. *Rei Militaris & Philosophiæ studia posse in Republicâ unâ vigere.*
II. *Astrologiam Judiciariam è Civitate benè moratâ esse exterminandam.*

Corpus humanum, Serenissima Princeps, nisi vis aut morbus impulerit, tribus quasi gradibus tendit ad mortem; adolescentiæ, maturitatis, & senectæ: sic respublica, non bellis externis oppressa, non civilibus ante tempus lacerata, naturali certè decursu habet incrementum, statum, & declinationem. Nam & omnia orta occidunt, & maturata defluunt, &, tempore corroborata, tempore labefactantur. Jam artes aliæ sunt necessitatis, aliæ liberalis otii, aliæ eruditi luxûs. Necessitatis, ut, ad depellendam famem, agricultura, pecuaria; ad arcendum frigus, architectura, vestiaria; ad vim propulsandam, ars militaris; otia liberalia (ut gymnastica), musica, & hæc ipsa mater artium Philosophia. Luxûs, ut pictura, statuaria, culinariæ, fucatoriæ artes, aliæque in quas magno corporum, majore animorum, damno sumus ingeniosi. Nec in omnibus reipublicæ temporibus vigent istæ omnes, nec tamen ullum est tempus in quo non aliqua. Sic enim naturâ comparatum est, ut necessitatis inventa tempore prima sint, otii media, extrema luxuriæ; sintque illa nascentis ferè crescentisque reipublicæ, vigentis altera, tertia ruentis. In constituentibus rempublicam, in bella gerentibus pro capite & salute, nasci literarum studia non solent, non possunt. Otium est pacemque nactæ vel pro gloriâ tantùm dimicantis civitatis, alumna Philosophia. Contrà, rei militaris scientia iis reipublicæ temporibus non utilis modò, sed pernecessaria. Ut enim generare naturæ nobilius eóque difficilius est opus quàm augere, quàm conservare: sic majoris animi, ingenii, artis, virtutis, imperium fundare quàm tueri; cùm novam in medio crescentem molem oderint etiam longinquæ nationes, sibi ac posteris suis metuant vicinæ. Secundum est tempus reipublicæ jam constitutæ vigentisque, in quo emicant illa, quæ dixi omnia, oblectationes & otia liberalia, florente etiamnum rei militaris scientiâ. Quòd si idem ardor animorum maneret, idem armorum studium, labor, industria, vigilantia; nempè id in quo deos omnes frustrà votis fatigamus, jamdiu manibus teneremus, immortalem civitatem; facilè enim imperium iis artibus retinetur, quibus initio partum est. Sed nimirùm, cùm nemo jam hostis, nisi quem nos facimus; nulla gens inimica, nisi propter nostras injurias;

cessante necessitate armorum, quæ necessitatis causâ primùm sumta sunt, aciem patimur hebescere. Labente dein paulatìm disciplinâ, cùm, ex superiorum temporum virtute, nihil restet præter opes virtute congestas & instrumenta luxuriæ; spreta jacet res militaris, afflictą divinæ particulâ mentis virtutis imperatoria; eodemque labefactata motu concidunt literarum studia, seu præsidio militari destituta, seu commercii vitiorum voluptatumque pertæsa: ut nemini dubium esse queat, ea studia posse unà vigere, quæ non possunt nisi unà perire. Primâ ætate à Româ conditâ usque ad Annibalem Italiâ Africâque ejectum, tollitur, ut ait Ennius, è medio sapientia, vi geritur res; spernitur orator bonus, horridus miles amatur. Indè ad Augusti maturitatem pono; in quâ eluxerunt illa literarum lumina, Gracchi, Scævolæ, Tuberones, Crassi, Hortensii, Cicerones, Varones. Huic ætati, ingeniorum feracissimæ, debemus Livium, Salustium, Plautum, Lucretium, Virgilium; nec minùs magnos imperatores, Mummium, Mariam, Syllam, Pompeium, Agrippam; & in cœlum ferendos propter summam in utroque genere præstantiam M. Catonem, P. Africanum, & C. Cæsarem. Quæ tamen ætas ita rudis fuit artium ad luxum pertinentium, ita parùm intelligens Græcarum deliciarum, ut Mummius, magnus (ut dixi) imperator, captâ Corintho, cùm maximorum artificum manibus perfectas tabulas ac statuas in Italiam portandas locaret, juberet prædici conducentibus, si eas perdidissent, novas eos reddituros. Post Augustum, deflorescente jam penitùs bellicâ laude, stanteque republicâ non vi suâ, sed rerum priùs gestarum gloriâ, ex domitis nationibus peregrinis hausta infusaque in mores civitatis peregrinitas, ut eadem studia, quasi progressu quodam naturali, idem ubique exitus maneret. Ita dominante luxuriâ, cùm homines beati & locupletes, voluptatibus immersi, literarum studia ad Græculos servos rejicerent, dum putarent se scire quod quisquam in domo suâ sciret: à servilibus ingeniis artes liberales corruptæ, emortuam jam ante rem militarem haud longo intervallo consecutæ sunt; nisi quòd sub Trajano principe, cùm iterùm moveret lacertos imperium, redditâ quasi juventute, bonæ quoque literæ effloruerunt. Testes fero è Græcis Plutarchum, Lucianum; è nostris Plinium, Tacitum: & dubitamus adhuc eas artes posse conjungi, quæ in civitate omnium gentium principe simul floruerunt, simul perîerunt, simulque renatæ sunt? Num apud Græcos secùs? Prima ætas, usque ad Medica tempora, armis exercitatissima, literarum penè rudis. Indè ad Philippum Demetrii altera, literis armisque florens; in quâ Cimon, Alcibiades, Philippus Amyntæ, Alexander, Seleucus, Demetrius, summi imperatores; &, in omni philosophiâ principes, Socrates, Anaxagoras, Plato, Aristoteles, Chrysippus, non est necesse de singulis; nefas tamen fuerit de Pericle, Thucydide, Xenophonte, Socratico, Dione Platonico, qui in utroque genere excelluerunt, silere. Ne in nostrâ quidem republicâ factum est illud, quod plerique putant, literarum & armorum divortium; cùm iis ipsis temporibus, quibus majores tui, Augustissima Regina, terrorem nominis sui in Galliam, Hispaniam, Siciliam, Cyprum, Asiam, Ægyptum intulissent, elucerent domî illa hujus academiæ ornamenta, Europæ lumina, Rogerus Bacon, Walterus Burley, Scotus, Occhamus, Wiclevus; quos, cùm ab omnibus cum ingenii tùm doctrinæ subsidiis fuerint instructissimi, isto orationis flore, quo nunc ferè solùm, certè nimiùm, gloriamur, æquissimo animo patior carere. Quid? quòd nè alterum quidem sine altero horum studiorum potest esse perfectum? Literæ ab imperatore præsidium mutuantur, & tutelam, id est, spiritum & vitam: reddunt multa magnaque & adjumenta belli & ornamenta victoriæ; historiæ veteris notitiam, id est, maximè certam brevemque, maximè multiplicem, minimèque periculosam rerum gerendarum ex gestis scientiam. Do L. Lucullum, qui, Româ profectus rei militaris rudis, rebus gestis legendis in Asiam venit factus imperator; P. Africanum, qui Cyri disciplinam, à Xenophonte scriptam, nunquam solebat ponere de manibus illis gloriosis, quibus Numantia & Carthago, duæ urbes Romani æmulæ fastigii, excisæ sunt. Addo ex Philosophiâ sapientibus sententiis, gravibusque verbis, ornatam orationem; quâ militum animos possit jacentes erigere, ferocientes reprimere, inflammatos restinguere. Addo temperamentum morum & sedationem perturbationum: nequid in bello iratè, in victoriâ superbè, in pace ultra civilem modum; neu cædibus & rapinis assueta mens immanitate efferetur. Quid illa abstrusiora? Astronomia, inquit Plato, imperatori futuro necessaria est ad temporum vicissitudines noscendas; Arithmetica, ad acies instruendas; Geometria, ad castra metanda, loca capienda, figurandos exercitus: hinc urbium muniendarum peritia; hinc bellicorum tormentorum operumque machinatrix. Ab hâc disciplinâ profectus Archimedes, legionum & classium impetum solus perlevi momento luto ludificatus est. Contrà, Philippus, Demetrii scalarum brevitate, id est, ignoratione Geometriæ, à Melitæensium oppido rejectus; Nicius, superstitione lunaris defectûs, id est, ignoratione Astronomiæ, cum exercitu cæsus in Siciliâ. Idem, cùm Sulpitius Gallus in bello cum Perseo provideret, prædiceretque militibus, ne id pro portento acciperent quod, ordine naturali, statis temporibus fiat; magnum momentum ad debellandam Macedoniam, id est, ad Romanum imperium constituendum visus est attulisse. Quare cùm his tot ac tantis adminiculis perficiatur ars imperitoria, neque aliundè sint ea quàm ex mediâ deprompta philosophiâ; concedamus sanè ea studia simul esse posse, quæ, nisi simul, non possunt esse absoluta. Neque tamen non est aliquid, quod contra assertur, Philosophiam avocare animum à sensibus, & contemplationi tradere rerum (dii boni!) maximarum, sed ab hâc consuetudine populari abhorrentium; quarum illecebris, quasi quodam Circæo poculo delinita mens, ad rempublicam tractandam, ad res manu gerendas, nolit accedere, nè possit quidem. Nam, cùm natura, ut ait philosophus, faciat unum ad unum, difficileque sit pluribus in rebus eundem excellere; tum certè difficillimum in tam dissidentibus & naturâ disparatis. Ex humoribus quibus constamus, aptissima ad Philosophiam melancholia, ad arma bilis, ad voluptates sanguis; quartus ille pituita gravis ne ad mala quidem bonus. Plato tres animæ partes ponit sedibus disclusas; rationabilem in capite, irascibilem in corde, concupiscibilem in jecore. Ad rationabilem pertinet Philosophia, ad irascibilem ars militaris, voluptuariæ ad tertium genus. Quòd si possent illi humores ita commisceri, aut istæ sive partes animæ, sive facultates, ita conjungi; aut altera vim alterius non infringeret, non debilitaret; haberemus id quod quærimus, in milite philosophum. Aut, si hoc difficile est, cùm ob alia tum quia utriusque studii eâdem penè ætate, multo sudore, multisque vigiliis facienda sunt tyrocinia: secernamus, si placet, à milite totum hoc philosophari, relinquamus imperatori, ut contemplativis mediocritèr tinctus sit; morali verò civilique philosophiâ, & politiore literaturâ penitùs imbutus. Atque, ut demus vera esse, quæ sunt ab ornatissimis magistris allata, tamen eam vim habent pleraque; non ut in unâ republicâ simul esse non possint, sed ut ne in uno homine: ne nos quidem civitatem ex philosophis constare volumus; quid enim ad vim arcendam foret ineptius? neque ex militibus totam; nam quid turbulentius? Respublica, nimirùm, debet esse unita, non una; cujus dignitas salusque non unâ laude, sed uno omnium rerum laudandarum temperamento, continetur.

Sequitur Astrologia, quam eventis fallacem, usu superstitiosam, à barbaris nationibus importatam, bonis temporibus Græciæ ignotam, etiam malis Româ pulsam, tot senatûsconsultis, tot principum rescriptis damnatam suffragantibus omnium ætatum philosophis (plebeios quosdam excipio) politicisque è republicâ exterminamus: artem, quod in arte turpissimum est, nullis textam principiis, nullâ subnixam demonstratione, nullo constantem syllogismo. Verum est cœlum in hæc inferiora luce, motu, virtute agere; ista omnia fovere, animare; obliquum circulum causam esse ortûs & interitûs; à sole & homine generari hominem; sed ab homine, ut causâ propinquâ propriâque, quæ materiam suppeditet; à sole, ut inter efficientes coadjuvante, remotâque, & generali; qui uno & eodem calore, & semen aconiti animat ad venenum, & brassicæ ad alimentum, & rhabarbari ad medicinam; non naturam aliquam inserendo, sed ea in actum, in lucem producendo, quæ priùs in materiæ potentiis delitescebant. Itaque sanus an morbosus sim, acutus an hebes, albus an ater, nihil ad cœlum stellasque, quæ eodem lumine, eodem cœli situ, eodem momento, omnibus iisdem agentia, & ex materiâ sanè dispositâ sanum producunt infantem, & ex morbosè morbosum. Quid illa externa? pauper an dives, honoribus clarus an secùs? quæ rerum fortuitarum temerario intercursu, nostræque voluntatis libero motu, infinitis modis varieta, nullum habent cum cœlo commercium. Sed de Astrologiâ facilius est tacere quàm pauca dicere.

Reliquæ sunt, Augustissima Regina, partes officii nostri maximis tuis immortalibusque in nos, in rempublicam, in orbem Christianum, meritis debitæ atque consecratæ. Patere igitur, ut id unus pro omnibus dicam, quod isti omnes de tuâ Majestate taciti sentiunt. Patere tuam in obtinendo imperio fœlicitatem, in constituendo sapientiam, in tuendo fortitudinem, in administrando constantiam, cæteras virtutes tuas, quæ omnium gentium literis & linguis commemoratæ sunt, tuorum quoque, ad quos tantarum virtutum fructus propiùs pertinet, voce celebrari. Cùm essent omnia fato quodam superiorum temporum plena suspicionum domi, forìs bellum certum, aut pax infida; cùm in oculis, in visceribus nostris hæreret, ex illo infœlici conjugio contractum, pertinax malum, Hispanorum dominatio; cùm effusum essét ærarium, imminuti fines imperii, præsidia milite, arces tormentis denudatæ; in his tot tantisque difficultatibus eluxit tua singularis, ac verè divina, sapientia, Divinissima Princeps. Gladium, in illâ rerum mutatione ac transitu, vaginâ vacuum Anglia non vidit: vidit plausus, clamores, exultationes, omnium ordinum, ætatum, hominum, nisi quibus expediret esse malum principem, hoc est, quàm dissimillimum tui. Tu Hispanos à capite, à cervicibus nostris, aut invitos depulisti, aut remisisti volentes. Tu publicam fidem, angustiis ærarii vacillantem prædiorum tuorum, rerumque pretiosissimarum venditione levâsti. Tu oppida amissa, pactis conventis, quod in te fuit, recepisti; obsidum fugâ, & quorundam perfidiâ, quod præstare non poteras, perdidisti; eùmque tuæ castissimæ purissimæque menti nihil placeret fallax, nihil fucatum, tu, nummis adulterinis sublatis, commercia revocâsti, fidem restituisti. Tu religionem, majorum incuriâ collapsam, aut ipso tempore desidentem, incredibili animi fortitudine renovâsti, communemque asylum omnibus gentibus aperuisti: neque dubitasti, nova princeps, cùm omnes propinquæ nationes propter veteres inimicitias essent infensæ, longinquarum quoque odium hâc novitate provocare. Ab his initiis profecta, sedisti deinceps belli pacisque arbitra inter reges Christianos regina; qui, à factiosis civibus vexati, aut potentiorum injuriis per vim pulsi, in tuo consilio, armis, opibus acquiescunt. Testis Valesiorum familia, quorum infantiam consiliis tuis rexisti, ferociam mitigâsti; domumque ruentem, quantum in te fuit, sustinuisti. Testis illustrissima hæc Borboniorum, qui tuis unius freti armis, nixi pecuniis, non aliâ re magis quàm majestate nominis tui stantes, te parentem agnoscunt, te deam venerantur. Testis Lusitania, cujus regem extorrem ejectumque liberalissimo hospitio accepisti. Testis Germania, Dania, Suecia; quæ tuo nutu arma sumunt ponuntque. Quid Christianos dico? cùm ipsi Turcarum imperatores, quibus, ante hujus beatissimi sæculi lumen, ne nomen quidem hujus insulæ unquam fando auditum, tui reverentiâ nominis arma abjecerint, pacemque Polonis, jam ad ultima redactis, te interveniente, concesserint. Dixi de singulis ferè partibus: nunc de universo orbe Christiano, cujus cùm maxima pars, aut hæreditate relicta, aut affinitatibus comprehensa, aut armis devicta, unius jussu regeretur; cùm Galliam per emissarios, Turciam per mercenarios, obtineret; cùm Germania partibus, Polonia bellis, distineretur; cùm omnes omnium gentium principes, proceres, aut socordiâ negligerent, aut timore abscederent, aut avaritiâ inclinarent, quà junctis nuper orientis & occidentis opibus aurum præponderabat, cùm auctâ, ut fit, ex prosperis cupiditate, animus haud obscurè adjectus esset ad imperium universi, omniaque, nemine impediente, in unius sinum casura viderentur: hìc tua divina virtus enituit, hìc invictum animi robur, cum sapientiâ singulari. Quæ, oppressis primùm domesticorum insidiis, quod dii prius omen in ipsum, rupto fœdere Burgundico, quod ipse, immisso in tuam provinciam latrocinio, priùs ruperat, receptis in societatem Belgis, ampliatisque imperii finibus tot urbium accessione, bellum terrâ marique, pro salute omnium susceptum, sola gessisti. Quod cujus manibus administratum sit, non quæro, cùm videam tuis auspiciis, tuis consiliis, provincias adjunctas, urbes captas, naves direptas, classes depressas, non hostium fines, sed urbem sedem imperii tuis signis appetitam, obsessam, oppugnatam. Tuis consiliis Indiæ, quanta terræ totius pars, quantulâ tuorum manu, quàm incredibili celeritate victoriis peragratæ! Tuis, tuis intelligo (quid dicam?) consiliis, tabulis, armisque, completa omnis hæc Oceani ora, constrata cadaveribus litora. Tuis auspiciis Hispania Anglum non vidit nisi victorem, aut victoriæ immortuum; Anglia Hispanum nisi captivum. Itaque stant tuorum objectu armorum, tuorum oppositu laterum, quot sunt in Europâ regna, principatus; ipsique adeò pontifici, nominis tui infensissimo hosti, unà cum cæteris, absque tuis armis, vel serviendum fuit, vel pereundum. Bonitatem, clementiam, justitiam, æquitatem, ista pervulgata, ac propè decantata, in tantâ principe referre, regiarum & heroïcarum virtutum, quæ in Majestate tuâ elucent, injuria fuerit. Ne id quidem attingam, quæ mala, quam constanti animo privata pertuleris, quæ tamen & gratiorem præsentis fœlicitatis sensum attulerunt tibi, tuisque civibus certissimam salutem, principem habere, quæ & semper cogitet, crebrisque sermonibus usurpet, quid aut noluerit sub alio principe, aut voluerit. Illa commemorabo, quæ vulgo minùs nota, non minùs certè mirabilia ad laudem. Te cùm tot literis legendis, tot dictandis, tot manu tuâ scribendis, sufficias; cùm consiliariorum tuorum, in minimis etiam rebus, sententias dijudices; cùm privatorum precibus, principum legationibus, per te respondeas, de subditorum quoque privatis controversiis sæpissimè cognoscas: in istâ tamen districtissimâ vitâ, non principum (quorum aliæ sunt nostris moribus artes), sed penè mortalium doctissimam evasisse. Te magnam diei partem in gravissimorum autorum scriptis legendis audiendisque ponere. Neminem nisi suâ linguâ tecum loqui; te cum nemine nisi ipsorum aut omnium communibus Latinâ Græcâque. Omitto plebeios philosophos, quos rarò in manus sumis: quoties divinum Platonem animadverti tuis interpretationibus diviniorem effectum! quoties Aristotelis obscuritates, principis philosophorum, à principe fœminarum evolutas atque explicatas! Dicerem liberè, nemini unquam ad sacratissimam Majestatem tuam aditum patuisse semidocto, qui non ex tuis sermonibus discesserit doctissimus, nisi meæ vehementèr me pœniteret tarditatis, qui in tam illustri scholâ tam parùm profecerim. Itaque literas, literatissima Princeps, tuere ac protege; id est, nobis, qui hic vivimus, nostra privilegia, illis quos emisimus suam dignitatem, sua præmia in republicâ, in ecclesiâ, quod facis, conserva. Academiam utramque novis immunitatibus munire, novis legibus fundare, perge. Utraque, à te ornata, in te ornanda certabit; cæteroqui omni genere laudis pares, hoc nostra fœlicior, quòd tuos vultus iterum intuetur, in cujus oculis habitant Gratiæ, in fronte benignitas, in ore majestas, in pectore sapientia, in manibus liberalitas, in toto corpore pulchritudo & venustas dignæ principe, dignæ tantis prognatâ principibus, dignæ imperio: ut tecum, jam propè parens Natura, redeamus in gratiam, quæ cùm parem, effusis hìc viribus, procreare non posses, neminem voluisti ex tantâ principe disparem superesse.

Speeches to the Queen at Rycot.

The 28th of September her Majesty went from Oxforde to Rycot[1] (thus written, *Ricorte*), where an olde Gentleman, sometimes a Souldier, delivered this Speech:

Vouchsafe, dread Soveraigne, after so much smooth speeches of Muses, to heare a rough hewen tale of a souldier: wee use not with wordes to amplifie our conceites, and to pleade faith by figures, but by deedes to shew the loyalty of our harts, and to make it good with our lives. I meane not to recount any service, all proceeding of duety; but to tell your Majesty, that I am past al service, save only devotion. My horse, mine armour, my shielde, my sworde, the riches of a young souldier, and an olde souldiers reliques, I should here offer to your Highnesse; but my foure boies have stollen them from me, vowing themselves to armes, and leaving mee to my prayers: fortune giveth successe; fidelitye courage; chance cannot blemish faith; nor trueth prevent destinye, whatever happen. This is their resolution, and my desire, that their lives maye be imployed wholy in your service, and their deathes bee their vowes sacrifice. Their deathes, the rumor of which hath so often affrighted the Crowe my wife, that her hart hath bene as blacke as her feathers. I know not whether it be affection or fondnes; but the Crowe thinketh her owne birds the fairest, because to her they are dearest. What joies we both conceive, neither can expresse; sufficeth they be, as your vertues, infinite. And although nothing be more unfit to lodge your Majestye then a Crowes neste, yet shall it be most happy to us, that it is by your Highnesse made a Phœnix neste. *Qui color ater erati nunc est contrarius atro.* Vouchsafe this trifle [a faire gowne]; and with this my heart, the greatest gift I can offer, and the chiefest that I ought.

---

[1] Rycot, according to Leland, "longist to one Fulco de Ricote. It then came to the Quatremaine. Richard Quatremain was a merchant of London, and after Custumar there. He built a goodly large Chapel of Ease without the manor-place of Ricot, and founded there two Chauntry Priests. This foundation was begun in the Reign of Henry VI. and endowed in the Reign of Edward IV." He died without issue, and left the chief of his property to Richard Fowler, the son of a man who had been his clerk. This Richard dissipated the fortune thus easily acquired, and the estate of Rycot was purchased by the Heron family, who again sold it to Sir John Williams, afterwards Lord Williams of Thame. In the person of Sir Henry Norris, who married the youngest daughter of Lord Williams, Rycot was constituted a barony, Queen Elizabeth creating him Lord Norris of Rycot. The daughter and grand-daughter were Ladies Baroness by courtesy. James Lord Norris, Baron Norris of Rycot, had the Earldom of Abingdon superadded to that title, both which honours his descendant now enjoys. Rycot Park is an extensive domain, desirably adorned with an alternation of wood and water. The mansion has been recently pulled down by order of the present Earl; but the Chapel remains, and has been repaired to continue as a place of burial for the family; nor are the grounds yet disparked. The house so lately destroyed was partly built by John Lord Williams of Thame, and had the honour of twice receiving Queen Elizabeth. Once she was conducted there by Lord Williams and Sir Henry Bedingfield, when on her way to Woodstock as a prisoner. On the second occasion she voluntarily visited the seat, on quitting Oxford, in 1592.

Rycoll, Oxfordshire.

On Sunday, her Majesty going to the garden, received with sweete musicke of sundry sorts; the olde Gentleman, meeting her, saide this:

Pardon, dread Soveraigne, the greatnes of my presumption, who, having nothing to say, must follow still to wonder; but saft, some newes out of Irelande.

A Letter delivered by an Irish lacque, in which was inclosed a Darte of gold, set with Diamonds; and, after the Letter read, delivered to her Majestye, with this motto in Irish, "I flye onely for my Soveraigne."

My duety humbly remembred. It is saide, the winde is unconstant: I am gladde it is; otherwise had not I heard that which I most wished, and least looked for. The winde blowing stifly in the Weste, on the suddaine turned Easterly, by which meanes I received letters, that her Majestie woulde bee at Rycort; nothing could happen to me more happy, unlesse it were myselfe to be there to doe my duety. But I am a stranger in mine owne countrye, and almost unknowen to my best frends, onely remembred by her Majestie, whose late favours have made me more than fortunate. I should account my ten years absence a flatt banishment, were I not honoured in her Majesties service, which hath bound all my affections prentises to patience. In all humility I desire this Dart to be delivered, an Irish weapon; and this wish of an English hearte, that in whose hart faith is not fastened, a Darte may. I can scarce write for joy; and it is likely this lacque cannot speak for wondring. If he doe not, this is all that I should say, that my life is my dueties bondman; dutie my faiths Soveraigne.

The Dart delivered, a skipper coming from Flanders delivered another Letter, with a Key of golde set with diamonds, with this motto in Dutch, "I onelie open to you."

My duety remembred. The enemy of late hath made many braveadoes, even to the gates of Ostend; but the succese was onely a florish. Myselfe walking on the ramparts to oversee the sentenels, descryed a pink, of whom I enquired where the Court was: he saide, hee knew not; but that the 28th of September her Majesty would be at Ricort. I was overjoyed; and in making haste to remember my duety, I had almost forgot it; for I was shipping myselfe for England with this skipper; but to come without leave, might be to returne without welcome. To signifie that my heart is there, I most humbly entreat, that this Key may be presented; the Key of Ostende, and Ostend the Key of Flaunders. The wards are made of true hearts; Treachery cannot counterfeit the Key, nor Treason herselfe picke the locke. None shal turne it: but whom her Majesty commands none can. For myselfe, I can but wish all happines to her Highnes; and any occasion, that what my toung delivers, my bloud may seal, the end of my service, that in her service my life may end.

The Key delivered, a French Page came with three other Letters; the one written to the Lady Squemish, which, being mistaken by a wrong superscription, was read before her Majestie. In the second was inclosed a Sword of golde, set with diamonds and rubyes, with this motto in French, "Drawen onelie in your defence." In the thirde was inclosed a Truncheon set with Diamonds, with this motto in Spanish, "I do not commaunde but under you."

A Letter written by a Souldier to his Mistris the Lady Squemish.

Faire Lady and sweete Mistris, I seldom write, because I write not well; if I speake, you say I chatter, because I speake so fast; and when I am silent, you thinke me carelesse. You say, love cannot be in soldiers. I sweare it is: only this the difference, that we prove it by the sword; others by their sonets; theirs inke, blacke for colde; ours bloud, redde for heate. Often have you tolde me, that I know not what love is; and often have I tolde you, that this it is, that which makes the head ake, and the heart to; the eies jelous, and the eares to; the liver blacke, and the splen to; the vaines shrinke, and the purse to. Wit is but loves wierdrawer, making of a short passion an endlesse perswasion, yet no more mettall. You object, that I have many Mistresses: I answere, you have ten times as many servants: and if you should picke a quarrel, why should not I bring my Mistresses into the field against your servants? But inconstancy is a soldier's scarre, it is true; but the wound came by constancie. What a patient vertue is staidnes! like a nail in a dore, rusty, because never removed. I cannot be so superstitious as these nice lovers, who make the pax of their Mistris hands: tis flat Popery. I would not purchase love in fee-simple; a lease of two years to me were tedious; I mean not to have my tongue ringed at my Mistris eare like a jewel, alwais whispering of love; I am no earewigg; nor can I endure still to gaze on her face, as though my eies were bodkins to sticke in her haire. Let me have my love answered, and you shall finde me faithfull; in which if you make delaies, I cannot be patient. The winde calls me away, and with the winde awaie shall my affections.

The second Letter.

My duetie to your Ladyship remembred, &c. Being readie to take shipping, I heard that her Majesty would honor Ricort with her presence, which wrought no small content; but to have made it full, I wished I might have seene it. In this place is no choise of anie thing whereby I might signifie my dutifull affection, but that which a souldier maketh his chiefest choise, a Sworde, which most humblie I desire to have presented to her Highnes; with this protestation pourde from my heart, that in her service I will spende the bloud of my heart. Eloquence and I am vowde enemies; loialty and I sworne brothers: what my words cannot effect, my sworde shall.

The thirde Letter from the Sea coast.

My duetie humbly remembred. The same time that I received letters that her Majesty would be at Ricort, the winde served for Bretaigne: I was overjoied with both; yet stoode in a mammering whether I should take the opportunity of the winde, which I long expected; or ride poste to do my duetie, which I most desired. Necessitye controled affection; that bid me, unlesse I could keepe the winde in a bagge, to use the windes where they blew. I obaide; yet wishing that they would turne for a while, to serve my turne. Being unfurnished of al presents, I would have this my excuse, that Cheapside is not in my shippe; and therefore I have nothing to offer but my Trunchion, the honour which I received of her Majestie, by whom I am only to be commaunded; and ever else let me be only miserable and ever.

These Letters read, and the presents delivered, the Olde Man, kneeling downe, ended thus:

That my sonnes have remembered their dueties, it is my hearts comfort; that your Majestie accepteth them, their hearts heaven. If Fortune and Fidelitie had bin twinnes, they might have beene as rich, as faithfull; but this is the jubyle of my life, that their fathers are without spot; and your Majesty, I hope, confident, without suspition. Among my joies there is one grief, that my daughter, the Mistris of a Moole-hil, hath so much forgotten, that most she should remember, duetie. I doubt not her excuse, because shee is a woman; but feare the truth of it, because it must be to her Soveraigne. For myselfe, my Crow, and all our birds, this I promise, that they are all as faithfull in their feathers, as they were in their shels.

This being done, there was sweete musicke, and two sonnets; which ended, her Majesty went in.

On Munday morning, as her Majesty was to take horse, a messenger comming out of Jersey, and bringing a Daysie of golde set with rubies, delivered it to her Majestie, with this Speech:

At length, though very late, I am come from the Lady of the Moold-hill, sent long since, but the passage troublesome; at every miles end a lover; at every sentence end a lie. I staide to heare the conclusions, and found nut-browne gyrles to be cheapned; but none to be bought but the amyable. Thus much for my excuse: now for my Mistris; who, hearing that your Majesty would enter this cabbine, was astonished with joie and doubt: joye, for so great honour done to her father; doubt, by what means shee might shew her duety to your Majesty. At the last, sitting upon the top of a Moole-hill, she espied a red Daysie, the fairest flower that barren place doth yeeld, which, with all humilitie, she presents to your Majestie; it hath no sweetnes, yet manie vertues; her heart no tongue, but infinite affections: in you, she saith, are all vertues, and towards you all her affections.

The following Description, by Paul Hentzner, of the famous City and University of Oxford, and of the Royal Palace of Woodstock, written in 1598, only six years after the Royal Visit we have just described, will be no unsuitable appendage to it.

Oxonium, Oxford, the famed Athens of England; the Glorious Seminary of Learning and Wisdom, whence Religion, Politeness, and Letters, are abundantly dispersed into all parts of the Kingdom: the town is remarkably fine, whether you consider the elegance of its private buildings, the magnificence of its public ones, or the beauty and wholesomeness of its situation; which is on a plain, encompassed in such a manner with hills shaded with wood, as to be sheltered on the one hand from the sickly South, and on the other from the blustering West, but open to the East that blows serene weather, and to the North the preventer of corruption; from which, in the opinion of some, it formerly obtained the appellation of Bellositum. This town is watered by two rivers, the Cherwell, and the Isis, vulgarly called the Ouse; and though these streams join in the same channel, yet the Isis runs more entire, and with more rapidity towards the South, retaining its name till it meets the Thame, which it seems long to have sought, at

Wallingford; thence, called by the compound name of Thames, it flows the Prince of all British rivers; of whom we may justly say, as the ancients did of the Euphrates, that it both sows and waters England.

The Colleges in this famous University are as follow:

In the reign of Henry III. Walter Merton, Bishop of Rochester, removed the College he had founded in Surrey, 1274, to Oxford, enriched it, and named it Merton College; and soon after, William, Archdeacon of Durham, restored with additions that building of Alfred's, now called University College; in the reign of Edward I. John Baliol, King of Scotland, or, as some will have it, his parents, founded Baliol College; in the reign of Edward II. Walter Stapleton, Bishop of Exeter, founded Exeter College, and Hart-Hall; and in imitation of him, the King, King's College, commonly called Oriel, and St. Mary's Hall; next, Philippa, wife of Edward III. built Queen's College; and Simon Islip, Archbishop of Canterbury, Canterbury College; William Wickham, Bishop of Winchester, raised that magnificent structure, called New College; Magdalen College was built by William Wainflet, Bishop of Winchester, a noble edifice, finely situated, and delightful for its walks. At the same time Humphrey Duke of Gloucester, that great encourager of Learning, built the Divinity School very splendidly, and over it a Library, to which he gave an hundred and twenty-nine choice books, purchased at a great price from Italy, but the public has long since been robbed of the use of them by the avarice of particulars: Lincoln College, All-Soul's College, St. Bernard's College; Brazen-Nose College, founded by William Smith, Bishop of Lincoln, in the reign of Henry VII.; its revenues were augmented by Alexander Nowell, Dean of St. Paul's, London: upon the gate of this College is fixed a nose of brass. Corpus Christi College, built by Richard Fox, Bishop of Winchester: under his picture in the College Chapel are lines importing that it is the exact representation of his person and dress.

Christ's Church, the largest and most elegant of them all, was begun on the ground of St. Frideswide's monastery by Thomas Wolsey, Cardinal of York; to which Henry VIII. joined Canterbury College, settled great revenues upon it, and named it Christ's Church. The same great Prince, out of his own treasury, to the dignity of the Town, and ornament of the University, made the one a Bishoprick, and instituted Professorships in the other.

Jesus College, built by Hugh Price, Doctor of Law.

That fine edifice, the Public Schools, was entirely raised by Queen Mary, and adorned with various inscriptions.

Thus far of the Colleges and Halls, which, for the beauty of their buildings, their rich endowments, and copious Libraries, excell all the Academies in the Christian world. We shall add a little of the Academies themselves, and those that inhabit them.

These students lead a life almost monastic; for, as the monks had nothing in the world to do, but, when they had said their prayers at stated hours, to employ themselves in instructive studies, no more have these. They are divided into three tables: the first is called the Fellow's Table, to which are admitted Earls, Barons, Gentlemen, Doctors, and Masters of Arts, but very few of the latter; this is more plentifully and expensively served than the others: the second is for Masters of Arts, Bachelors, some gentlemen, and eminent citizens: the third for people of low condition. While the rest are at dinner or supper in a great hall, where they are all assembled, one of the students reads aloud the Bible, which is placed on a desk in the middle of the hall, and this office every one of them takes upon himself in his turn. As soon as grace is said after each meal, every one is at liberty either to retire to his own chambers, or to walk in the College garden, there being none that has not a delightful one. Their habit is almost the same as that of the Jesuits, their gowns reaching down to their ancles, sometimes lined with fur: they wear square caps. The Doctors, Masters of Arts, and Professors, have another kind of gown that distinguishes them: every student of any considerable standing has a key to the College Library, for no College is without one.

In an out part of the town are the remains of a pretty large fortification, but quite in ruins. We were entertained at supper with an excellent concert, composed of variety of instruments.

The next day we went as far as the Royal Palace of Woodstock, where King Ethelred formerly held a Parliament, and enacted certain laws. This Palace abounding in magnificence was built by Henry I. to which he joined a very large park, enclosed with a wall, according to John Rosse the first park in England. In this very Palace the present reigning Queen Elizabeth, before she was confined to the Tower, was kept prisoner by her Sister Mary; while she was detained here in the utmost peril of her life, she wrote with a piece of charcoal the following verses, composed by herself, upon a window-shutter:

"O Fortune!" &c.[1]

[1] These Verses are already printed in the account of her being at Woodstock, in the First Volume of this Collection, p. 10.

A FEW PLAINE VERSES OF TRUTH AGAINST THE FLATERIE OF TIME, MADE WHEN THE QUEENS MAJESTIE WAS LAST AT OXENFORD[1], 1592.

    Sith silent Poets all, that praise your Ladies so:
My Phenix makes their plumes to fall, that would like peacockes goe.
Some doe their Princes praise, and Synthia some doe like;
And some their Mistresse honour raise, as high as soldier's pike.
Come downe yee doe presmount, the warning bell it sounds,
That cals your Poets to account, for breaking of your bounds.
In giuing fame to those faire flowers that soone doth fade;
And cleane forget the white red rose, that God a Phenix made.
Your Ladies also doe decline, like stars in darkesome night;
When Phenix doth like Phœbus shine, and leands the world great light.
You paint, to please Desire, your Dame in colours gay;
As though braue words, or trim attire, could grace a clod of clay.
My Phenix needs not any art, of Poet's painting quill;
She is her selfe in euerie part, so shapte by kindly skil,
That Nature cannot wel amend, and to that shape most rare,
The gods such speciall grace doth send, that is without compare.
The Heauens did agree, by constellations plaine,
That for her vertue shee should bee, the only Queene to raigne,
(In her most happie days), and carries cleane awaie,
The tip and top of peerlesse prayse, if all the world say nay.
Looke not that I should name her vertues in their place,
But loooke on her true well-won fame, that answers forme and face;
And therein shall you read a world of matter now;
That round about the world doth spread, her heauenly graces throw.
The seas (where cannons rore) hath yielded her her right;
And sent such newes vnto the shore, of enemies foile and flight;
That all the world doth sound, the glorie Phenix gote;
Whereof an eccho doth rebound, in such a tune and note,
(That none aliue shall reatch) of Phenix honor great,
Which shall the Poet's Muses teach, how they of her shold treat:

[1] From "Churchyard's Challenge. London, Printed by John Wolfe, 1592."

O then, with verses sweete, if poets haue good store,
Fling down your pen, at Phenix feet, and praise your nimphes no more.
Packe hence, she comes in place, a stately Royall Queene,
That takes away your Ladies grace, as soon as she is seene.

To the Right Worshipfull my Ladie FORTESCUE, wife to the Right Honourable Sir JOHN FORTESCUE, Knight.

The good turne and great labour, good Madam, your Honourable husband bestowed in my behalf, bindes me so far, as I must not be ingrat to him nor non of his, and chieflie to remember your Ladishippe, with some matter acceptable, I than thinking of the great griefe that manie Soldiours found by the absence of the Queenes Maiestie in time of the Plague, when she laie last at Hampton Court, drewe out some sadde verses of the sorrowe among Soldiers conceiued, and presuming you will accept them, I became so bolde as to present them to your handes. Had I anie worthier worke to offer I would bring better, but hoping these fewe lines shall duetifullie show my good will, I am to craue your fauor in presenting these verses vnto you, desiring God to multiplie his benefites and blessinges in your good Ladishippe.

Verses of value, if Vertue bee seene,
Made of a Phenix, a King and a Queene.

My Phenix once, was wont to mount the skies,
  To see how birdes, of baser feathers flew,
Then did her port and presence please our eies:
  Whose absence now, breeds nought but fancies new,
  The Phenix want, our court, and realme may rue.
Thus sight of her, such welcome gladnes brings,
That world ioies much, when Phenix claps her wings,

And flies abroad, to take the open aire,
  In royall sort, as bird of stately kinde;
Who hates foul storms, and loues mild weather fair,
  And by great force, can bore the blostring wind,
  To shew the grace and greatnes of the minde
My Phenix hath, that vertue growing greene,
When that abroad her gracious face is seene.

Let neither feare of plagues nor wits of men
  Keepe Phenix close, that ought to liue in sighte
Of open world, for absence wrongs us then,
  To take from world the lampe that giues us light.
  O, God forbid, our day were turnde to night;
And shining Sunne, in clowds should shrowded be,
Whose golden rayes the world desires to see.

The Dolphin daunts each fish that swims in seas,
  The Lion feares the greatest beast that goes,
The Bees in hive are glad theyr King to please;
  And to their Lord, each thing their duety knowes.
  But first the King his princely presence showes,
Then subiects stoopes and prostrate fals on face,
Or bowes down head, to giue their maister place.

The Sunne hath powre to comfort flowrs and gras,
  And purge the aire of foule infections all,
Makes ech thing pure, wher his clear beames do passe;
  Draws up the dew, that mists and fogs let fall;
  My Phenix hath a greater gift at call;
For vassals all, a view of her doe craue,
Because thereby, great hope and hap we haue.

Good turnes it brings, and suiters' plaints are heard;
  The poore are pleasde, the rich some purchase gains;
The wicked blush; the worthy wins reward;
  The seruant findes a meane to quit his paines;
  The wronged man, by her some right attaines:
Thus euery one, that helpe and succour needes,
In hard distresse, on Phenix fauour feedes.

But from our view if world doe Phenix keepe,
  Both Sunne and Moone and Stars we bid farewell;
The heauens mourne, the earth will waile and weep,
  The heauy heart, it feeles the paines of hell.
  Woe be to those that in despaire doe dwell.

Was neuer plague, nor pestilence like to this,
When soules of men haue lost such heauenly blisse.

Now suiters all, you may shoote up your plaints,
  Your Goddes now is lockt in shrine full fast:
You may perhaps yet pray vnto her Saints,
  Whose eares are stopt, and hearing sure is past;
  Now in the fire you may such Idols cast:
They cannot helpe, like stockes and stones they bee,
They have no life, nor cannot heare nor see.

Till, that at large our royall Phenix comes,
  Packe hence, poore men, or picke your finger's endes,
Or blow your nailes, or gnaw, and bite your thombs,
  Till God aboue, some better fortune sends.
  Who here abides, till this bad world amends,
May doe full well, as tides doe ebbe and flow,
So fortune turnes, and haps doe come and goe.

The bodies ioy, and all the ioints it beares,
  Lies in the head, that may commaund the rest;
Let head but ake, the heart is full of feares,
  And armes acrosse, we clap on troubled brest;
  With heauy thoughts the mind is so opprest,
That neither legs nor feete haue will to goe,
As man himselfe, were cleane orecome with woe.

The head is it, that still preserues the sence,
  And seekes to saue each member from disease;
Deuise of head is bodies whole defence,
  The skill whereof no part dare well displease:
  For, as the Moone moues up the mighty seas,
So head doth guide the body when it will,
And rules the man by Wit and Reason's skill.

But how should head in deede doe all this good,
  When, at our neede, no use of head we haue;
The head is felt, is seene, and understood.
  Then from disgrace it will the body saue,
  And, otherwise, sicke man drops downe in graue;
For when no helpe, nor vse of head we finde,
The feete fals lame, and gazing eies grow blinde.

The lims waxe stiffe, for want of vse and aide;
  The bones doe dry, their marrow wasts away;
The heart is dead, the body liues afraide;
  The sinnowes shrinke, the bloud doth still decay,
  So long as world doth want the star of day,
So long darke night we shall be sure of heere,
For clowdy skies, I feere, will neuer cleere.

God send some helpe, to salue sicke poore men's sores,
  A boxe of baulme would heale our wounde vp quite;
That precious oyle would eate our rotten cores.
  And giue great health, and man his whole delighte.
  God send some sunne, in frostie morning white,
That cakes of yce may melt by gentle thaw:
And at well head wee may some water drawe.

A Riddle.

Wee wish, wee want, yet haue that wee desire.
Wee freese, we burne, and yet kept from the fire.

[*Then follow* 15 *eight-line stanzas, " taken out of Belleau, made of his own Mistresse." And to those succeed a string of* 22 *verses in praise of the Princely Phœnix, " to be red fiue waies:" but not meriting to be read at all; and therefore are not transcribed.*]

AD SERENISSIMAM ELIZABETHAM ANGLIÆ, FRANCIÆ, ET HIBERNIÆ, REGINAM; CARMEN PANEGYRICUM[1].

Nympha senescentis rarissima gloria mundi:
Respice siderea florentes pace Britannos,
Et populi studia, et cœlo pendentia sceptra.
Aurea fælici redeunt sub principe sæcla:
Jam redit & virgo.   Redeunt quæ tempora prisci
In votis habuere patres.   Leo mitior herbas

---

[1] From Reg. MSS. in the British Museum, 12. A. XLIII.

George Carleton, the Author of this Poem was son of Guy, second son of Thomas Carleton, of Carleton Hall in Cumberland, was born [*] at Norham in Northumberland, at what time his father was Keeper of the Castle there, educated in grammar learning by the care of the Northern Apostle Bernard Gilpin, who also (when he was for the University) sent him to St. Edmund's Hall in the beginning of the year 1576, being then 17 years of age, and exhibited to his studies, and took care that nothing should be wanting to advance his pregnant parts. In the latter end of 1579, he took a Degree in Arts, and forthwith completed it by determination, his disputes being then noted to exceed any of his Fellows that did their exercise in the same Lent. In 1580 he was elected Probationer Fellow of Merton College, wherein he spent almost five years before he proceeded in his faculty. While he remained in that College he was esteemed a good Orator and Poet; but, as years came on, a better Disputant in Divinity, than he had before been in Philosophy. He was also well versed in the Fathers and Schoolmen, and wanted nothing that might make him a complete Theologist. "I have loved him," saith a Learned [†] Author, "In regard of his singular knowledge in divinity, which he professeth, and in other more delightful literature, and am loved again by him." What were his preferments successively after he had left that College I cannot tell, because the register of the acts of that house is altogether silent as to them. Sure I am, that after he had continued many years there, and had taken the Degrees in Divinity, he was promoted to the See of Landaff, upon the translation of Dr. Godwin to Hereford, in the year 1618; and the same year was one of the learned English Divines that were, by his Majesty's command, sent to the Synod of Dort, where he behaved himself so admirably well, to the credit of our Nation, (as some Church Historians will tell you) that after his return, he was, upon the translation of Dr. Harsnet to Norwich, elected to the See of Chichester, confirmed by his Majesty 20 Sept. 1619. He was a person of a solid judgment, and of various reading, a bitter enemy to the Papists, and a severe Calvinist. At length, having lived to a good old age, he concluded his last day in the month of May, 1628, and was buried in the choir, near to the altar, of his Cathedral Church at Chichester, on the 27th of the same month. Wood, Ath. Ox. I. 517: where see a list of his writings.

---

[*] Camden, Britan. in Northumb.   [†] Idem, ibid.

Libat, & objectas socio partitur avenas
Cum bove: jam cicures veniunt ad pocula pardi.
Blandior & posita feritate levaculus agno
Securo comes ire solet; porrectaque poscit
Pabula: nec tenero lupus insidiatur ovili.
Scilicet hæc sacri cecinerunt sæcula vates.
Hæc tibi rex pacis dedit exornata trophæis
Regna novis. Bellis alii, tu pace triumphas,
O sola infando concurrere Virgo tyranno
Ausa animis, ultroque in prælia poscere sacro
Marte lacessendum qui voce lacessit Olympum.
O sola imperio summi famulata tonantis:
Christiadum miserata cruces, miserata labores
Non fandos, Dominique tui miserata dolores
Suscipis ingentem fælix nutricula Christum.
Ille, velut fuerat Judæo crimine passum
Non satis: ecce iterum desertus, nudus, inopsque,
Sedibus expulsus, ferro flammisque petitus,
Heu nimis ingrato peregrinus oberrat in orbe.
Nympha tuis (toto depulsus ab orbe) receptus
Hospitiis, injens populis comitantibus exul.
Quam juvat ad regni communia commoda ferre
Quas tibi regnandi regum rex tradidit artes?
Pectore sollicito quanto stant numine sceptra
Quærere: sincerum populi rapuisse favorem;
Imperio tenuisse modum: regnique saluti
Invigilare tui: tum, quo fælicia surgunt
Sceptra modo, magni monitis parere tonantis.
Nec piget esse piam. Magno sub judice tantæ
Mercedem pietatis habes. En horrida bellis
Sæcula concussum rapiunt ardentibus orbem,
In furias & in arma ruunt: ultricia passim
Fata suo domitas volvunt in sanguine gentes.
Una mali secura manes, regumque ruinas
Inconcussa vides. Medios tranquilla furores

Inter & armorum vesana incendia: nullo,
(ELIZABETHA,) regis nutantia turbine sceptra.
Sola sedes intacta malis, quia celsa potenti
Subjicias tua sceptra deo. Sic otia læta
Et rediviva tuo surgit gens aurea sæclo.
 Est tamen, est sacram qui conturbare quietem
Regni nympha tui, populoque avertere pacem
Molitur. Quis tantum animis tentare nefanda
Concilia: inferna Stygii genitoris ab aula
Quis ferat in lucem tenebrarum edicta referre
Tristia; sanguineasque agitare atrocius artes
Sacrosancta quibus regnorum fœdera rumpat:
Et conturbatis bellorum incendia rebus
Misceat, et sceptris domino proturbet avitis?
 Est quæ Romanis horrendum sibilat antris
Bellua: non illa polluti spiritus oris
Tartarea quisquam de sede nocentior exit,
Quam Babyloniaci velant mysteria scorti.
Celsa sedet meretrix, subjecto vecta dracone;
Cui septemgemino surgunt de vertice cristæ,
Septem orbes versat, septena volumina torquet.
Ebria purpureo sanctorum in sanguine lapsat:
Nec rabies expleta malis: magis effera latrat
Ingluvies, nullis hominum satianda ruinis.
Ebria delitiis, regum quibus illa venenis
Pocula plena suis exhausta fæce propinat
Sed faciem mentita viri mirabile fallit,
Mobilis ancipiti ludit sub imagine forma:
Agnum fronte ferens horrenda voce Draconem.
Stat generis pudor humani, crescitque subactis
Principibus populisque tremor: domitoque minatur
Terribilem mundo monstrum fatale ruinam.
Bellua delusum heu quantum bacchata per orbem,
Exitiis regum regnorum assueta rapinis:
Ecquis io regum qui contra audentior ire?

Ecquis io tantos animos, ac robora dextræ
Pugnacis tentare ferox? trahit una venenis
Tartareis domitos meretrix Babilonia reges?
Totque simul proceres inter sua pocula mersos:
Captivosque duces regnum & servilia sceptra
Una rapit Circe? tanto damnata veterno
Secula degeneres animos, & inertia regum
Corda dabant? veteris virtus oblita decoris
Torpuit: occultis velut incantata venenis.
 Eluitur tandem miseris infamia sæclis.
Egregia ausuros terris dedit Anglia reges:
Anglia magnanimum genetrix fœcunda virorum.
Hæc te, nympha potens, hæredem gloria tangit:
Nam tuus elusi vindex fortissimus orbis
Grassantis rabiem monstri furiamque vagantem
Armipotens genitor primo compresserat auso.
Inde venenati soboles Lernæa Draconis
Fatalem, perculsa, domum, fatalia sceptra
Exhorret, velut in Babylonis nata ruinam.
Perpetuis igitur stimulis agitata furoris,
Innumeras scelerum facies Acheronte petitas
Intentat, versatque nefandæ conscia fraudis
Pectora, deformes sceptris meditata ruinas.
Sed fraudum consulta ruunt, dominoque minantur
(In proprium ruitura caput) conversa ruinam.
Obruit artificem sceleris scelus. Ergo ubi tantas
Jam venti rapuere minas: ubi languida fessus
Viribus absumptis jactaret fulmina papa:
(Nam dixere suo mortales nomine papam
Quem sacris velat Babylonis adultera chartis.)
Ille ubi tot scelerum sensit sine numine cæpta
Ingenio ruitura suo: sua vulnera spectans:
Indignantem animam furibundo in pectore versat
Conciliumque vocat divum pudor, atque hominum fæx.
Carnales glomerant circum subsellia fratres.

Ille dolos recoquens solitos, regumque ruina s
Obvolvens animis, tumido sic pectore fatur.
Quo collapsa loco res sit Romana, videtis,
Romulidæ juvenes, genuivi matris alumni.
Occiduum Romana fides credenda per orbem
Regibus, ac populis fuit unica regula recti.
Et quæ credendi regnandi ea forma reperta est.
Una quibus placuit terras dat Roma regendas.
Nec quenquam fas est veneranda capescere sceptra
Quem non celsa sibi famulantem Roma probarit.
Roma fidem populis, & sceptra regentibus offert.
In terris numen, gentes didicere, supremum
Romanum dominum, Romanam agnoscere matrem.
En tamen hæretici quantum valuere furores:
Anglia Romanas audax contemnere leges,
Pontificum tumidas ridet securior iras:
Excussitque jugum Romæ, proh fata! quid hoc est
Quod superi voluere nefas? miseranda videbit
Roma triumphatos Angla sub virgine Papas?
Quem gentes timuere feræ: qui summa solebam
Arbitrio rapuisse meo, vel ponere sceptra:
Cujus ab imperio quondam conterritus orbis
Intremuit: vix nunc imbellis virginis iras
Sustineo; jam cuncta meis cedentia votis
Sperabam: sed fata retro conversa tulerunt,
Ausaque nostra leves rapuerunt irrita venti.
Dii quibus auspiciis Romana potentia surgit,
Tuque adeo qui tergemino diademate cinctam
Non tibi sed Romæ meruisti Petre coronam:
Et vos, o sanctæ, meriti satis indiga vestri
Quas colit innumera sub imagine Roma, sorores:
Testor ad ornandas sacris insignibus aras
Divorum quos Roma Colit; ne laudis honores
Corruerent vestræ. Ne vestras rarus ad aras
Accedat cultor: nostras discrimina nulla

Impediisse manus: Romanis artibus Anglæ
Principis exitium, regni tentasse ruinam.
Nec veriti regum stabilita resolvere jura,
Reginam imperio excussam, gentemque domandam
Hispano dedimus domino: Didacique novelli
Numinis auspiciis rapiendos vovimus Anglos.
Excitos & in arma duces, populumque rebellem
Traximus in furias media inter viscera regni.
Nobile par quondam Borealis gloria plagæ
Alter in exilium, ac ludibria raptus Iberum
Alter in exitium præceps: tam perdita fata
Ingenio subiere meo. Reparanda ruina est,
Transfugiis tentanda fides. Sanctissima mater
Roma saginandos alit in certissima servos
Funera, qui tentent Anglorum pectora furtim.
Sed quibus occultis est seditionibus Anglos
Sollicitare labor famulos jam Roma probatos
Agnoscit, quamvis miseranda in morte relictos,
Oppressosque omnes rapuerunt invida fata.
Et rapiant, satis est famulos si Roma fideles
Laudet & hæc habeant miseræ solatia mortis.
Quis pudor est, Anglis mactandos ensibus Anglos
In se præcipites per mutua fata ruentes
Tradere? dum Romam non hæc discrimina tangant.
Si scelus est Angli sceleris dant sanguine pœnas.
Heu quibus obruimur fatis? nullis cadet Angla
Obruta virgo dolis? pudet & conamine nullo
Esse nocens potui. Sedet imperterrita princeps
Omnibus indejecta malis, & celsior omni
Invidia, majorem animum, majoraque versans
Pectora, sub nostras surgit felicior iras.
Quid juvat Hispanas toties cumulare ruinas?
Impulimus miseras adversa in prælia gentes,
Traximus armatos populos & in unius omnem
Virginis exitium victum stimulavimus orbem.

Seditio, dolus, ira, scelus, fraus, arma furorque,
Omnia jam tentata ruunt.   Adamantina fata
Circumdant nostris majorem viribus Anglam.
Heu pudet, & domitus teneræ sub virginis armis
Dicor, et innocuum videor mansuescere numen.
At non sic quondam mea virtus viluit orbe
Cum mea tum primum tentans sua robora dextra
Abstulit imperii titulis & jure Leonem.
Ille quidem sacras ausus divellere templis
Divorum statuas; magnis documenta daturus
Principibus: discant moniti non temnere divos.
Quid memorem summo dejectos vertice rerum
Henricum? quid Mamphredum, Fredericon, Othonem?
Imperio quos Papa suo pro numina pulsos
Impulit; et toto dederat spectacula mundo.
Chilpricum sceptris excussum Gallia vidit:
Vidit et ingemuit subitoque exterrita casu
Extimuit simili rueret ne fraude Philippus,
Aragonum tibi Petre: Georgi sceptra Boema
Pontificum sunt rapta manu.   Sic arbiter orbis
Mutatos rerum dominos dare Papa solebam.
Cumque meis domitum rapiam sub viribus orbem:
Sceptra revulsa feram: disrumpam fœdera pacis:
Cum possem miscere polo freta: Tartara terris:
Nil mortale manu stet inexpugnibile nostra:
Hei mihi quod nostris non excindenda sub armis
Angla manet victrix: nostros putat una furores
Innocuos: uni despecta potentia nostra est.
Quodque magis doleat: meretrix Babylonia dicar
Virginea cecidisse manu: sic fabula fiam.
Omnia sunt tentanda prius, licet omnia retro
Lapsa cadant, longique ruant impensa laboris.
Si superos in vota nefas sperare secundos:
Quod restat Stygiis tentabitur artibus Angla.
Hæc fatus Stygios horrendo carmine manes

Sollicitat demens, cæcisque furoribus ardens
Devovet exitio populos, & devovet agros.
Et magico tristes revocat sub murmure diras.
At tibi Nympha magis per tot felicia diras
Cuncta fluunt, ceduntque deo crudelia vota.
Ut Balaamiticas diras, inversaque vota
Grata deo quondam soboles Judæa ferebat
Sic tua qui magno propugnat numine sceptra,
In caput artificis deus impia vota retorquet.
Est deus: & nutu reges ac regna coercet.
Ille tibi populos domat, ordinat ille triumphos,
Regia nympha tuos: bellorumque arbiter ingens
Obruit innumeris domitos tibi cladibus hostes.
Ille jubet prestent uni tibi regna tenenti
Tranquillem bellis ardentia sæcula pacem.
Ille (viden' quo laus se regia cardine vertit)
Virgo tuis meritis ornatum sustinet orbem.
Regna quot horrisono jam corruitura tumultu
Stant armis innixa tuis? in Scotica regna
Cum ruerent Galli, Guisio stimulante, furores:
Reddita libertas populis: lux aurea regno:
Regibus antiquus rediit, (te vindice) splendor.
Cum jam barbarico super omnia regna tumultu
Hispani insultent, Papa stimulante, furores;
Vulneribusque suis, nimio & confecta dolore
Belgia fortunis timuisset, Gallia sceptris:
Vulneribus medicata suis lenita dolores
Belgia fortunas debet tibi, Gallia sceptra.
Plurima Christiadum per viscera Turcicus ensis
Tristior ire parat: tanti tu sola furores
Expugnare ducis: manibus tu sola cruentos
Extorquere potes gladios: nutuque retenta est
Barbara dextra tuo; tum libera turba tulisse
Fortunas, vitamque tuo de munere gaudet.
Ebria Romano dum gens Hispana veneno

Impia & in cœlos atque in tua sceptra movere
Arma parat: mox infelicibus omnia fatis
Corruitura videt: confusaque sanguine regna.
Illa suo fidat gladio: tu numine vincis.
At tu dum populos, tua sacra, ac regna tueris:
Arma volente deo victrix victricia tractas.
Straverat innumeris tua Celtiber æquora velis,
Ille tibi populisque tuis horrenda minatus:
(Scilicet) extorquere manu tua sceptra potenti:
Aris atque focis Anglas extrudere gentes:
Cuncta armis miscere suis: in sanguine matrum
Commaculata nurus: natorum in cæde natantes
Accumulare patres: confundere sacra profanis:
Angliadum nomen scelerato excindere ferro:
Quasque solet jactare minas armata libido.
In fumos abiere minæ? Quia justa tuetur
Arma Deus, sacrumque caput sceptrumque verendum
Agminis ætherei superis defenditur armis.
Illa igitur moles Hispanæ incondita classis
Quæ mare, quæ terras, quæ sydera terruit ausu,
Ridiculæ tandem, tenuissima fragmina, turbæ
Reliquias laceras propriis vix intulit oris.
Pars armis oppressa tuis: pars hausta frementis
Fluctibus oceani: rapidis pars perdita flammis.
Terrificis alii circum tua littora rapti
Turbinibus, magnæ redeunt ludibria famæ.
Viribus æquoreis in prælia viribus aucta
Ætheris, o summo princeps dilecta tonanti;
En agit excubias missus tibi miles ab alto,
Et tua vallatis cingit tentoria castris.

    Discite qui regitis populos, quibus orbis habænæ
Sorte sua cedunt, quos celso ab vertice rerum
Ancipiti ostentat sublimes gloria curru:
Discite, de cœlo moniti, pendentia cœlo
In leges cogenda Dei diademata regum.

Sic regit Elizabetha: suis sic jura Britanniæ
Dividit: inviolata subit sic jura tonantis.
Quamne magis salvam populus velit Anglicus: anne
Illa magis regni cupiat populique salutem:
Semper in ambiguo studium mirabile servat.
Impune ergo licet solidæ tibi carpere fructum
Laudis, et exemplum cunctis memorabile sæclis,
Elizabetha, manes. Inter tot ferrea sæcla
Antiquum soli tibi regna feruntur in aurum.
Celtiber en quantis domitus jam cladibus hostis
Exitio tua regna suo tentata fatetur;
En Tartessiaco mersas in pulvere Gades:
Nuper & Hispani quæ propugnacula regni
Nunc armis effracta tuis en fulmen in armis,
Nympha, tuis missum manibus, quo bella gerente
Pressa tuis fatis, animis ducis, omnia cedunt.
Ante tuas acies illum tua bella gerentem
Pone vel Arctoo, vel Phæbo pone sub Indo,
Victor ubique tibi bello est rediturus ab omni.
Auspiciis, regina, tuis Devoraxius ensis.
Terrarum commune decus, nova gloria sæcli,
Regia nympha, tui: nostro lux addita cælo:
Salve sanguineo pacis spes unica sæclo,
Salve sancta parens patriæ. Salvete propago
Inclyta, nobilum gens o veneranda virorum:
Heroum genus omne, quibus vel in arma cruenta
Martiæ flagrantes animos stimulavit Enyo,
Vel qui pacatis magnarum pondera rerum
Consiliis trahitis; felices vivite longum;
Et quo se vertunt populi communia vota,
Principis in sacram longum vigilate salutem.

GEORGIUS CARLETON.

Mr. Francis Bacon's retiring to Twickenham Park, with several of his Friends, has been noticed in p. 124. Dr. Andrews, afterwards Bishop of Winchester, was likewise desired to accompany them, but was prevented by his attendance on his parish of St. Giles, Cripplegate. The reason of their retreat from London was upon a flying report, spread through the City, of a pestilential distemper breaking out, which had likewise occasioned the Law-reader at Gray's Inn to discontinue his office, and mos tof the Gentlemen of that Inn to retire into the country [1].— Mr. Jenkell added, "that some Gentlemen of Furnival's Inn had been apprehended on the Friday before, upon the suspicion of being bad members of the State; but that he had not then heard of any other proceeding against them."— At Twickenham Park, either in this or in the following year [2], through the immediate interest of his steady Patron the Earl of Essex, Mr. Francis Bacon had the

[1] Twickenham Park was demised, in 1574, to Edward Bacon (third son of Sir Nicholas Bacon, Lord Keeper, by his first wife). In 1581 a lease was granted for 30 years to Edward Fitzgarret; in 1595 a farther lease for 21 years, to Francis Bacon, Esq. and John Hibbard. Sir Francis Bacon, whom Voltaire calls the father of experimental philosophy, spent much of his time during the former part of his life in studious retirement at this place, which he thought particularly favourable to his philosophical pursuits.

[2] Mr. Anthony Bacon was with his Brother at Twickenham July 18, 1593, when he wrote to Mr. Thomas Smith, then Secretary to the Earl of Essex. In a letter written the same day, to his Mother, he says, that their most honourable and kind friend the Earl of Essex had been at Twickenham the day before three hours, and most friendly and freely promised to set up his whole rest of favour and credit for Mr. Francis Bacon's preferment before Mr. Edward Coke, whenever the Attorney General Egerton, whom Mr. Coke had succeeded as Solicitor in June 1592, should be removed to the Mastership of the Rolls. His Lordship told me likewise, that he had already moved the Queen for my Brother, and that she took no exception to him, but said, that she must first dispatch the French and Scots Embassadors, and her business abroad, before she thinketh of home matters. On a vacancy soon after of the office of Attorney General great interest was made with the Queen in behalf of Mr. Bacon both by the Earl of Essex and his own Uncle the Lord Treasurer Burleigh; but all proved unavailing, on which occasion Mr. Bacon thus addressed the Queen:

"Madam, Remembring, that your Majesty had been gracious to me, both in countenancing me, and conferring upon me the reversion of a good place, and perceiving that your Majesty had taken some displeasure towards me, both these were arguments to move me to offer unto your Majesty my service; to the end to have means to deserve your favour, and to repair my error. Upon this ground I affected myself to no great matter, but only a place of my profession, such as I do see divers younger in proceeding to myself, and men of no great note, do without blame aspire unto. But if any of my Friends do press this matter, I do assure your Majesty my spirit is not with them. It sufficeth me, that I have let your Majesty know, that I am ready to do that for the service, which I never would do for mine own gain. And if your Majesty like others better, I shall, with the Lacedemonian, be glad that there is such choice of abler men than myself. Your Majesty's favour indeed,

honour of entertaining Queen Elizabeth, where he presented her with a Sonnet in honour of that generous Nobleman [1].

and access to your Royal person, I did ever, encouraged by your own speeches, seek and desire; and I would be very glad to reintegrate in that. But I will not wrong mine own good mind so much as to stand upon that now, when your Majesty may conceive I do it but to make my profit of it. But my mind turneth upon other wheels than those of profit. The conclusion shall be, that I wish your Majesty served answerable to yourself. *Principis est virtus maxima nosse suos.* Thus I most humbly crave pardon of my boldness and plainness. God preserve your Majesty!"

[1] " Mr. Anthony Bacon's ill health, and frequent returns of the gout, prevented him from paying his duty to the Queen, not only at his first return to England, but even for the rest of his life; and this in some measure depriv'd him of the advantages, which his great abilities and qualifications might otherwise have procured both to the public and himself. But his infirmities of body, were not the only cause, why he was less capable of making his fortune at Court; for he met with a still more considerable obstruction from the jealousy of his Uncle the Lord Treasurer, and his Cousin Sir Robert Cecil, who resented his early attachment, as well as that of his Brother, to the Earl of Essex, between whom and the Cecils there was an irreconcilable opposition.—Mr. Francis Bacon asserts, that himself had knit his Brother Anthony's service to be at his Lordship's disposing. But it will be proper to hear Mr. Bacon's own account of the rise of his dependence upon the Earl. ' On the one side,' says he, coming over, " I found nothing but fair words, which make fools fain, and yet even in those no offer, or hopeful assurance of real kindness, which I thought I might justly expect at the Lord Treasurer's hands, who had inned my ten years harvest into his own barn, without any halfpenny charge. And on the other side having understood the Earl of Essex's rare virtues and perfections, and the interest he had worthily in my Sovereign's favour, together with his special noble kindness to my Germain-brother, whereby he was no less bound and in deep arrearages to the Earl, than I knew myself to be free and beforehand with my Lord Treasurer; I did extremely long to meet with some opportunity to make the honourable Earl know how much I honoured and esteemed his excellent gifts, and how earnestly I desired to deserve his good opinion and love, and to acknowledge thankfully my Brother's debt, presuming always, that my Lord Treasurer would not only not dislike, but commend and farther, this my honest desire and purpose.'

" Mr. Francis Bacon's attachment to the Earl was not founded, as he protested, upon the consideration of his Lordship's interest being the likeliest means of his advancement, but a persuasion, that the Earl was the fittest instrument to do good to the State: ' And therefore,' says he, ' I applied myself wholly to him, in a manner, which I think happeneth rarely amongst men. For I did not only labour carefully and industriously in that he set me about, whether it were matter of advice, or otherwise; but neglecting the Queen's service, mine own fortune, and, in a sort, my vocation, I did nothing but devise and ruminate with myself, to the best of my understanding, propositions and memorials of any thing, that might concern his Lordship's honour, fortune or service ... And, on the other side, I must and will ever acknowledge my Lord's love, trust, and favour towards me, and last of all, his liberality.' " Letter to the Earl of Devonshire, as cited in Birch's Memoirs.

Mr. Lodge, in his Life of Bacon, very judiciously remarks, that " he remained long at the Bar, undistinguished but by his talents and his eloquence, and by the extensive practice to which they had conducted him; nor was it till 1588 that he had obtained even the degree of Counsel to the Queen, for he

In Mr. Bacon's memorable " Apology" to the Earl of Devonshire, it appears, that the Queen had a design to dine with him at his lodging at Twickenham Park. He was afterwards resident there occasionally in several successive years; and numerous Letters both from Anthony and Francis Bacon to their various friends are dated from Twickenham Park [1].

had cultivated a strict intimacy with Essex, the Rival, and indeed Enemy, of his powerful Relations, the Cecils, who therefore in a great measure denied him their patronage. It is true that they gave him the reversion of an office of considerable emolument, the Registership of the Star-chamber, and this was perhaps the only instance of their favour ever experienced by him. He waited, however, patiently till the year 1592, when the office of Solicitor-General becoming vacant, Essex and his friends exerted themselves to the utmost to place him in it. They were unsuccessful; and here we meet with a wonderful proof of the romantic generosity and grandeur of that Nobleman's heart. Sympathizing with his disappointed Friend, and stung with anger at the slight which had been put on his own suit, he instantly determined to alienate a part of his estate to Bacon, from whose pen we have a recital of the conversation which occurred when the Earl visited him to declare his intention. ' After the Queen,' says he, ' had denied me the Solicitor's place, for the which his Lordship had been a long and earnest suitor in my behalf, it pleased him to come to me from Richmond to Twickenham Park, and brake with me, and said, ' Mr. Bacon, the Queen hath denied me place for you, and hath placed another. I know you are the least part of your own matter; but you fare ill because you have chosen me for your mean and dependance; yet you have spent your time and your thoughts in my matters: I die (these were his words) if I do not somewhat towards your fortune; you shall not deny to accept a piece of land which I will bestow upon you.' Twickenham Park, here mentioned, was the gift bestowed on him, including one of Essex's highly ornamented mansions, particularly celebrated for its pleasure grounds, which had obtained the name of the ' Garden of Paradise.' Yet Bacon, painful to relate, when that unhappy Nobleman was some years after arraigned, not only pleaded against him at the Bar, but at length published a declaration of his Treasons, with the view of justifying his execution. The Nation shuddered at this ingratitude to its favourite. Bacon was universally execrated, and even threatened with assassination. He addressed an apology, which may be found in his Works, to the Earl of Devonshire, one of Essex's bosom friends, from which the passage just now given is extracted; but the stain which he had cast on himself was then too glaring, and he missed even the sordid reward at which he had aimed; for Elizabeth's Ministers, to whom he had thus sold himself, durst not admit him publicly into their councils." See hereafter, under 1595.

[1] Among the many very valuable MSS. in the British Museum, is a paper, intituled, Instructions from the Lord Chancellor Bacon to his servant Thomas Bushell. It relates to a project he had in view of establishing a corporation for exploring deserted mineral works. On the supposition that such a project would meet with due encouragement, he says, " Let Twitnam Park, which I sold in my younger days, be purchased, if possible, for a residence for such deserving people to study in, since I experimentally found the situation of that place much convenient for the trial of my philosophical conclusions, expressed in a paper sealed to the trust which I myself had put in practice, and settled the same by Act of Parliament, if the vicissitudes of fortune had not intervened and prevented me."

MASQUES:

PERFORMED BEFORE

QUEEN ELIZABETH.

FROM A COEVAL COPY, IN A VOLUME OF MANUSCRIPT COLLECTIONS, BY HENRY FERRERS, OF BADDESLEY CLINTON, IN THE COUNTY OF WARWICK.

IN THE POSSESSION OF WILLIAM HAMPER, ESQ. OF BIRMINGHAM.

"Sol Mundi Borealis erat, dum vixit, Elisa."
Oxford Verses on the Queen's Death, 1603.

[*⁎* These MASQUES were first printed in " Kenilworth Illustrated," the splendid volume noticed under 1575, in vol. I. p. 422, as recently published by Messrs. Merridew and Son, of Coventry; and they are here re-printed, by the permission of my much-valued Friend Mr. Hamper (whose Introduction I preserve unaltered), and the consent of the liberal Proprietors of the above-noticed Volume. J. N.]

INTRODUCTION.

The Author of the following Entertainments is not named in the manuscript from which they are printed; but Gascoigne, in "The Princely Pleasures at Kenilworth Castle," having given some verses "devised and penned by *M.* [Master] *Ferrers,* sometime Lord of Misrule in the Court," and these Masques being preserved in a volume of collections by *Henry Ferrers, Esq.* of Baddesley Clinton, in Warwickshire, his Namesake, if not his Relative; it may be reasonably conjectured, without disparagement to his literary reputation, that they are from the pen of the same well-known and ingenious writer, George Ferrers, whose productions raised him to a conspicuous station amongst the poets of the Elizabethan Age.

He was one of the authors of "the Mirror of Magistrates," and, as Warton observes[1], "appears to have been employed as a writer of metrical speeches or dialogues, to be spoken in character, long after he had left the office of Lord of Misrule. A proof of his reputed excellence in compositions of this nature, and of the celebrity with which he filled that department."

As to the occasion on which these Masques were performed, we are also uninstructed by the manuscript itself; though, from certain expressions and allusions, it is almost beyond doubt that the First Part, commencing with "A Cartell for a Challeng," and ending with "The Supplication of the owld Knight," was exhibited in the Tilt-yard at Westminster, on the 17th of November, 1590, the Anniversary of the Queen's accession, when Sir Henry Lee, her Majesty's personal Champion, resigned his office, through age and infirmity, to George Clifford, Earl of Cumberland; at which time a "*crowned pillar,*" frequently mentioned in the following pages, was one of the ornaments of the splendid scene.

The remainder, beginning with "The Message of the Damsell of the Queene of Fayries," which the Editor has ventured to call Part II. it is extremely probable, was acted when the Queen, either in continuance of the same Fete, or soon after, visited the aged Knight at his own habitation, at Quarendon, near Aylesbury, in Buckinghamshire. That it was acted in the country, is evident from the words of the lively Page, who in bringing tidings of his Master's recovery, speaks of her Majesty's sacred presence having "made the weather fayre and the ground fruitfull, *at this Progress;*" and that the place of performance was at the residence of the gallant old Champion, seems equally certain, from "the Ladies' Thankesgeving," which (being, it is believed, the only part of these Masques hitherto published) is printed in "The Phœnix Nest," A. D. 1593; and also by Nichols[2], from that work, under the title of "An excellent Dialogue between Constancie and Inconstancie, as it was by speech presented to hir Majestie, in the last Progresse, *at Sir Henrie Leighe's House.*"

[1] History of English Poetry, vol. iii. p. 293.
[2] This alludes to the former Edition of the "Elizabethan Progresses." In the present Edition it is of course superseded by this completer copy. J. N.

MASQUES.

[PART I.]

To all the Noble Chosen and Hopefull Gentlemen, in this most notable Assemble; The strange forsaken Knightes send greeting [1], &c.—

Whereas the question hath ben long and often, and yett resteth doubtfull and undiscussed, whether that wch Menne call Loue be good or euill; And that it is manifest that there be manie woorthye Knightes, in this p'sence, to whom Loue is most delightfull, and his lawes no paynes; I bring this scedule, to signifie to all the Gentlemen here, that loue Armes, and list to defend this Cause, that there be three armed and unknowen Knightes, here at hande, of one minde & diuers fortune, that, wth stroke of Arme and dynt of sworde, be come to maintaine against all that will defende the Contrary, that Loue is worse than hate, his Subiectes worse than slaues, and his Rewarde worse than naught: And that there is a Ladie that scornes Loue and his power, of more vertue and greater bewtie than all the Amorouse Dames that be at this day in the worlde.

Sir Henry Lee's challenge before the Shampanie [2].

There is a strange Knight that warres against hope and fortune, who, ouerturned with griefe, hath cast himself into the Crewe of Care: And to maintaine his passion, as an enemie to all that liue in delight, determineth to be here forthwith; and hath sent mee to tell the Procurer of this Assemble, that under the hue of a grene [suit] is couered that unfortunate Carcas that scornes at others Joyes and weepes at all delightes. And knowing that there be manie Seruants to Hope, and Frendes to Fortune (whom he treadeth under foote), meaneth to maintaine, as farr as his posting horse will giue him leaue, that the seruants of Dispaire haue asmuch Vertue, and cary asmuch Goodwill to the guide of his Troupe, as those that serue the other turning and most trustless Goddes.

[1] A Cartell for a Challeng.
[2] Shampanie; i. e. the lists, or field of contention, from the French, *Campagne*.

The Supplication of the owld Knight.

In humble wise, sheweth unto your honorable Lordshipps, and the woorthie Gentelmen of this noble Assembell, and serveres of this English Holiday, or rather Englandes Happie Daye; A poore faithfull feeble Knight, yet once (thowe unwoorthie) your fellowe in Armes, and first Celebrator, in this kinde, of this sacred memorie of that blessed reigne, which shall leaue to this land an eternall monument of Godes fauoure, and greate glorie. That whereas Age, the Foe of Loue and Armes, hath thus disabled me (as you see) to performe with my handes the office of my harte, and hath turned me from a staffe to run with, to a staffe to rest on, making me a glasse for Joylite to looke in, since all strength and bewtie upon Earthe, and whatsoeuer we most lyke and striue for, muste alter and end, eyther soddenlie, by chaunce, or, certainely, by small contynuance: It may please you of your honorable favoures and curtesies, in regard of my past seruice, and present humble sute, to accept to your fellowshippe, in his fathers rome, this oneley sonne of mine, young, and honest, and toward, though I say it; thus shall you incurrage a young gentlemanne in verteouse exercises, that is labouring the waies of Hope, comfort an aged Knight, worne and weried with thoughtes and trauailes, drawing to his ende, and binde him with his force, and me with my prayre, to do you euer the seruice wee are able. And further, least I forfait my tenure (which I would not for my lyfe) of this daies honoring her excellent Ma^{ie}, being not able in person to paye with the launce this rent of my seruice, I must beseeche somme noble or woorthie gentleman, that is most lyke to haue next access to her sacred persone, lowlie to present this little from me, as the yearely fyne of his faith: which no cause shall make light, and no tyme can make less. So the high and mercifull preseruer of all thinges best preserue hir that thus preserues us all, and send you, most noble Gentelmen, and all that be woorth anie thing, best bodies to serue her, best hartes to loue hir, and best happes to honor her, and her most gratiouse Ma^{ie} the longest life, the most felicitie, the heauens did euer giue, or the earth did euer take. Amen. Amen.

[PART II.]

The Message of the Damsell of the Queene of Fayries.

Most fayre and fortunate Princess! To obey the sacred will that bindes mee, and the Inchanted Knight that bade mee, I come to shewe your Matie of strange patienc and hard fortune.

At the celebrating the joyfull remembraunce of the most happie daye of your Highnes entrance into Gouerment of this most noble Islande, howe manie Knightes determined, not far hence, with boulde hartes and broken launces, to pay there vowes and shewe theire prowes, diuers tongued rumors leaues no neede for me to declare: and how manie most desyrouse to doe this sacrifice of theire seruice were dissapoynted by diuers aduentures (which still the world is full), I meane not nowe to shewe you, neyther who that day did best, or was lyked best, is my purpose to reporte. But mine onely Errande to your Excellencie is to lett you understand, that amongst the noble Knightes that there assembled, there was one full hardie & full haples, whoe most hungrie to do you honor and desperate of his owne good, though he knew himself so enchaunted by a chaunce, as he was neyther able to chardge staffe, nor strike blowe; yet, fayre mounted with his staffe on his thighe, did thrust himselfe into the Justes, and as long as horse had anie breath, and anie Knight woulde encounter him, was content to bide the brunt of the strongest Knight, and the blowes of the sturdiest staues (a strainge enduring for a valient man) putting himselfe to the hande of perrill, and the hazard of shame, to doe obseruance to that daie. And nowe hath sent me to your Majestie, most humbly to beseeche you, that as it shall like you to accept the seruice of his sufferinge, and thoe his Armes be locked for a time, from all libertie to performe the office of his desire, in doing you seruice with his bodey, yet his harte is at libertie to pay the homage of his loue.

In token whereof he hath here sent your Matie a simple present of his hartes servis [1]. It is the Image, Madam, of the idoll that so manie serue against theire will, and so manie without reward; who shutes he wotes not where, and hittes he cares not whom, and seldom woundes alike, but soonest striketh the best sighted: which if your excellent Ma^le shall vouchsafe any tyme to weare, the Knight wisheth it may be a watch (better than Scarborows warning) to the Noble Gentel-

---

[1] Cupido in gould and stone.

men of your Courte, to defend them from such blowes as he hath receiued, which may light on them then ere the loke for it, and when they thinke leaste harme, and make a wounde (he knoweth by proofe) more uncurable than is complayned of.

Thus my message being ended; I must, most excellent Ladie, by the commaundement of my mistris, the Queene of the Fayeries, returne to my charge; to follow the inchanted Knight, to beare testimoney of his paines and patience, and so must leaue your sacred Majestie, whom the Almightye make most lasting, as he hath alreadie mad you best and most to be beloved. Amen. Amen.

The olde Knightes Tale.

Now drowsie sleepe, death's image, ease's prolonger,
Thow that hast kept my sences windowes closed,
Dislodge these heauie humors, stay no longer,
For light itself thie darkesom bandes haue losed,
And of mine eies to better use disposed:
    To better use, for what can better be
    Then substance in the steede of shades to see.

O mortall substance of immortall glorie!
To whom all creatures ells are shaddowes demed;
Vouchsafe an eare unto the woeful storie
Of him who, whatso eare before he semed,
Is nowe as you esteme to be estemed:
    And sence himself is of himself reporter
    To all your praise, will make his parte the shorter.

Not far from hence, nor verie long agoe,
The fayrie Queene the fayrest Queene saluted
That euer lyued (& euer may shee see);
What sportes and plaies, whose fame is largelie bruted,
The place and persons were so fitlie shuted:
    For who a Prince can better entertaine
    Than can a Prince, or els a Prince's vaine.

Of all the pleasures there, among the rest,
(The rest were justes and feates of Armed Knightes),
Within hir bower she biddes her to a feast,
Which with enchaunted pictures trim she dightes,
And on them woordes of highe intention writes:
 For he that mightie states hath feasted, knowes
 Besides theire meate, they must be fed with shewes.

Manie there were that coulde no more but vewe them,
Manie that ouer curious nearer pride,
Manie would conster needes that neuer knewe them,
Some lookt, som lyked, som questioned, some aymed,
One asked them too who should not be denied:
 But she that thwarted, where she durst not strugle,
 To make her partie good was fayne to juggle.

Forthwith the Tables were conveied hither,
Such power she had by her infernall Arte;
And I enjoyned to keepe them altogether,
With speciall charge on them to set my harte,
Euer to tarrie, neuer to departe:
 Not bowing downe my face upon the grounde.
 Beholding still the Piller that was crounde.

I whom in elder tyme she dearelie loued,
Deare is that loue which nothing can disgrace,
I that had ofte before her favor proued,
But knewe not howe such fauoure to embrace,
Yea, I am put in trust to warde this place:
 So kinde is loue, that being once conceauid,
 It trustes againe, although it were deceaued.

Seruant, quoth shee, looke upward and beware
Thou lend not anie Ladie once an eye;
For diuers Ladies hither will repaire,
Presuming that they can my charmes untie,
Whose misse shall bring them to unconstancie:
 And happie art thou if thou haue such heede,
 As in anothers harme thine owne to reede.

But loe unhappie I was ouertaken,
By fortune forst, a stranger ladies thrall,
Whom when I sawe, all former care forsaken,
To finde her ought I lost meeself and all,
Through which neglect of dutie 'gan my fall:
  It is the propertie of wrong consenting
  To ad unto the punishment lamenting.

With this the just revengefull Fayrie Queene,
As one that had conceaued Anger deepe,
And therefore ment to execute her teene,
Resolvde to caste mee in a deadlie sleepe,
No other ———[1] coulde decorum keepe:
  For Justice sayth, that where the eie offended,
  Upon the eye the lawe should be extended.

Thus haue I longe abode, without compassion,
The rygor which that wrathefull Judge required;
Till now a straung and suddaine alteration
Declares the date of my distres expired:
O peareles Prince! O presence most desired!
  By whose sole resolution this ys found,
  That none but Princes, Princes mindes expounde.

In lue whereof, though far beneath your merrit,
Accept this woorthles meede that longes thereto,
It is your owne, and onlie you may weare it,
The Farry Queene geue euerie one his due,
For she that punisht me rewardeth you;
  As for us heare, who nothing haue to paie,
  It is ynough for poore men if they pray.
      Cœlumq' solumq' beavit.

[1] A blank in the original.

FINIS.

The Song after Dinner at the two Ladies entrance.

> To that Grace that sett us free,
> Ladies let us thankfull be;
> All enchaunted cares are ceast,
> Knightes restored, we releast;
> Eccho change thie mournefull song,
> Greefes to Groues and Caues belong;
> Of our new deliuerie,
> Eccho, Eccho, certifie.
> Farwell all in woods that dwell,
> Farwell satyres, nymphes farewell;
> Adew desires, fancies die,
> Farwell all inconstancie,
> Nowe thrice welcom to this place,
> Heauenlie Goddesse! prince of grace!
> She hath freed us carefull wightes,
> Captiue Ladies, Captiue Knightes.
> To that Grace that set us free,
> Ladies let us thankfull bee.

Finis.

The Ladies Thankesgeuing for theire deliuerie from Unconstancie[1].

Most excellent! shall I saie Ladie or Goddess! whom I should enuie to be but a Ladie, and can not denie to haue the power of a Goddesse; vouchsafe to accept the humble thankfulnes of the late distressed Ladies, the pride of whose witts was justlie punished with the unconstancie of ouer willes, wherebie we were carried to delight, as in nothing more than to loue, so in nothing more than to chaunge louers; which punishment, though it were onlie due to our desertes, yet did it light most heauily upon those Knightes, who, following us with the heate of theire affection, had neither grace to gett us, nor power to leaue us. Now since, by that mortall power of your more than humane wisdome, the enchaunted tables

---

[1] This Dialogue, as has been observed in the Introduction, is printed, with some variations, in the Phœnix Nest, 1593, where the interlocutors are called *Constancie* and *Inconstancie*, but here by the abbreviations of *Co.* and *Li.*) they seem to be intended for *Constancy* and *Liberty*.

are read, & both they & we released, let us be punished with more than unconstancie if we fayle eyther to loue Constancie, or to eternize your memorie.

Li. Not to be thankfull to so greate a person, for so greate a benefite, might argue as little judgement as ill nature; and therefore, though it be my turne to speake after you, I will striue in thankfulnes to goe before you, but rather for my lybertie, because I may be as I lyste, than for anie minde I haue to be more constant than I was.

Co. If you haue no minde to be constant, what ys the benefite of your deliuerie?

Li. As I sayd before, my liberties, which I esteeme as deare as my selfe, for, though I esteme unconstancie, yet I must hate that which I loue best, when I am once inforced unto yt; and, by your leaue, as dayntie as you make of that matter, you would hate euen your owne selfe yf you were but wedded unto your selfe.

Co. Selfe loue ys not that loue that we talke of, but rather the kinde knitting of twoe hartes in one, of which sorte yf you had a faithfull louer what should you lose by being unconstant unto him?

Li. More than you shall gett by being so.

Co. I seeke nothing but him to whom I am constant.

Li. And euen him shall you lose by being constant.

Co. What reason haue you for that?

Li. No other reason than that which is drawen from the comon places of Loue, which are for the most parte Reason beyond Reason.

Co. You may better call them Reason without Reason, if they conclude that faith & loue the more they are the lesse they shall finde.

Li. Will you beleue your owne experience?

Co. Far beyonde your reason.

Li. Haue you not then founde among your louers that they woulde flie you when you did most followe them, & follow you when you did most fly them?

Co. I graunt I haue founde it true in some, but nowe I speake of a constant Louer in deede.

Li. You may better speake of him, than finde him, but the onlie way to haue him is to be unconstant.

Co. How so?

Li. I haue heard Philosophers saye that *Acquisitio termino cessat motus.* There is no motion, and you know Loue is a motion, but it resteth, or rather dieth when it hath gotten his end. Now Loue ys dull without feare of loosing, which can not be where there are no rivalls.

Co. It were against nature for her, which is but one, to loue more than one; and if it be a fault to beare a double harte, what is it to devide the harte among manie?

Li. I aske no other judge than Nature, especiallie in this matter of Loue, than the whiche there is nothing more naturall; and, as farr as I can see, Nature is delighted in nothing so muche as in varietie. And it were harde that sence she hath appoynted varietie of coullers to please the eye, varietie of soundes for the eare, variete of meates for euerie other sence, she should binde the harte, to the which all the rest do seruice, to the loue of one; rather than the eye to one couller, the eare to one sounde, or the mouth to one kinde of meate.

Co. Neyther doth she denie the harte varietie of choyce, she onely requireth Constancie when it hath chosen.

Li. What yf we comitt an error in our choyse?

Co. It is no error to chuse where wee like.

Li. But if our lyking varrie may we not be better aduised?

Co. When you haue once chosen, you must tourne your eyes inwarde to looke onlie on him that you haue placed in your harte.

Li. Whie then I perceaue you haue not yet chosen, for your eyes looke outwardes; but, as long as your eyes do stande in your heade as they doe, I doubt not but to finde you inconstant.

Co. I doe not denie but I loke upon other men, besides him that I loue best, but they are all as dead pictures unto me, for anie power they haue to touch mine harte.

Li. If they were as you account them, but dead pictures, they were lykelie to make another Pigmalion of you, rather than you would be bounde to the loue of one. But what if that one do proue inconstant?

Co. I had rather the fault should be his than mine.

Li. It is a coulde comforte to saie the fault is his, when the losse ys youres. But how can you avoyde the fault that may helpe it, & will not?

Co. I see no way to helpe it, but by breach of faithe, which I holde dearer than my lyffe.

Li. What is the band of thy faith?

Co. My worde.

Li. Your worde ys winde, & no sooner spoken than gonne.

Co. Yet doth it binde to see what is spoken donne.

Li. You can do lyttle yf you cannot maister your worde.

Co. I should do lesse yf my worde did not maister me.

Li. It maisters you indeede, for it makes you a slaue.

Co. To none but one whome I chuse to serue.

Li. It is basenes to serue though it be but one.

Co. More base to dissemble with more than one.

Li. When I loue all alyke I dissemble with none.

Co. But if I loue manie will anie loue me?

Li. No doubt they will, & so much the more by howe much the more they are that serue for you.

Co. But the harte that is euerie where, is in deede no where.

Li. If you speake of a manes harte I graunt it: but the harte of a woman is lyke a soule in a bodie: *Tota in toto, et tota in qualibet parte.* So that, although you had as manie louers as you haue fingers and toes, you might be one among them all, and yett wholy euerie ones. But, sence I perceive you are so peruersely deuoted to the could synceritie of ymaginarie constancie, I leaue you to be as you maye, minding meeselfe to be as I liste.

Neuerthelesse to your Matie by whom I was sett at libertie, in token of my thankfullnes, I offer this simple woorke of mine owne handes, which you may weare as you please; but I made them to be worne, after mine owne minde, loose.

Co. And I, who by your coming am not only sett at libertie, but made partaker also of Constancie, do present you with as woorthie a wark of mine owne handes; which yett I hope you will better accept, because it may serue to binde the loosenes of that inconstant Dames token.

Li. To binde the loosenes & that of an inconstant Dame! Say no more than you know, for you cannot knowe so much as I feele. Well may we betray ourselues betweene ourselues, and thinke we haue neuer sayde enough, when we haue said all. But now a greater power than eyther your or my reason woorketh in me, & draweth me from the fancies to the centre of true Loue; there representing unto me what contentment it is to loue but one, & howe the heart is satisfied with no number, when once it loueth more than one. I am not, I cannot be, as I was; the loane that I take of myselfe, & to chaunge, or rather to be chaunged, to that state which admitteth no change, by the secrett power of her who though she were content to lett us be carried almost owt of breth by the winde of Inconstancie, dothe nowe with her scilence put mee to scilence; & with the gloriouse beame of her countenaunce, which disperceth the flying cloudes of vaine conceites, enforceth me to wishe others, & to be myselfe, as shee is—Semper eadem.

Finis of this Dialogue.

The last Songe.

Happie houre, happie daie,
That Eliza came this waie!
    Greate in honor, great in place,
    Greater yet in geving grace,
    Greate in wisdome, great in minde,
    But in bothe aboue her kinde,
    Greate in vertue, greate in name,
    Yet in power beyond her fame.

Happie houre, happie daie,
That Eliza came this waie!
    She, with more than graces grace,
    Hath made proude this humble place,
    She, with more than wisdomes head,
    Hath enchaunted tables read,
    She, with more than vertues mighte,
    Hath restorid us to right.

Happie houre, happie daie,
That Eliza came this waie!
    Heauie harted Knightes are eased,
    And light harted Ladies pleased,
    Constant nowe they vowe to be,
    Hating all inconstancie,
    Constant Piller, constant Crowne,
    Is the aged Knightes renowne.

Happie houre, happie daie,
That Eliza came this waie!

FINIS.

[PART III.]

The second daies woorke where the Chaplayne maketh this Relation.

Da mihi quicquid habes, animumqu' fidemq' manumq'
Hec tria si mihi des, das mihi quicquid habes.

Elizæ laudes, et vox et lingua loquntur.

The Oration.

Most excellent Princes! Princes of excellencie! whom God framed in heauen to grace his woorkmanshippe on earth, and whose gratiouse abiding with us belowe is priuileged by the singular grace of God aboue! Vouchsafe, I beseeche you, from the matcheles heighte of your Royall graces, to loke downe on the humble dwelling of an owlde Knight, now a newe religiouse Hermite; who, as heretofore he professed the obedience of his youthe, by constant seruice of the worldes best Creature, so at this present presentethe the deuotion of his yeares, by continuall seruing of the worldes onlie Cretor. In theone, kind judgment was the usher, & beleefe the follower of his sounde loue: in the other, meditation is the forerunner, & zeale the usher, of this streite lyfe. This solitary man, Loricus, for such is his condicion & so is he called, one whose harde adventures were once discouered, and better fortune foreshewed, by a good father of his owne coate, not farr from this Coppies, rann the restles race of desire, to seeke content in the state of perfections; comaunding his thoughtes & deedes to tender theire dutie & make solemne sacrifices to the Idoll of his harte, in as manie partes as his minde had passions, yet all to one ende, because all from one grounde, to wit the consent of his affections. Sometymes he consorted with couragious Gentelmen, manifesting inward joyes by open justes, the yearlie tribute of his dearest Loue. Somtimes he summoned the witnesse of depest conceiptes, Himnes & Songes & Emblemes, dedicating them to the honor of his heauenlye Mistres. Sometymes by lyking drawen to looking, he lost himselfe in the bottomles vewe of unparragonized vertues, eche good ymagination ouertaking other with a better, and the best yelding a degree aboue the best, when they all were deemed too weake for her woorth which ouerweyeth all worthinesse.

Thus spent he the florishe of his gladdest dayes, crauing no rewarde ells, but that he might loue, nor no reputation beside but that he might be knowne to Loue; till the two enimies of Prosperitie, Enuie and Age, (the one greuing at him, & the other growing on him,) cutt him off from the following the Cowrte, not from goyng forwarde in his course. Thence, willingly unwilling, he retired his tyred lymes into a corner of quiet repose, in this Countrie, where he lyued priuate in cœlestiall contemplation of manie matters together, and, as he once told me, seriouslie kept a verie courte in his owne bosome, making presence of her in his soule, who was absent srom his sight. Amongst manie other exercises (whereof feruent desire ys not scant) he founde it noe small furtheraunce of diuine speculation to walke thorow by-pathes & uncoth passages, under the coole shaddowes of greene trees.

And one daie aboue the rest, as he ranged abrode, hauing forgotten himself in a long sweet rauishment, his feete wandring astray, when his mind went right, he hit by chaunce on a homelie Cell of mine which had helde a little space, to my greate solace, & taking mee on a soddaine at my ordinarie Orisons;—By your leaue, verteouse Sir, quoth he, where lyes the highe-waie I pray you. Marry here, gentell Knight (sayde I) looking on my booke with mine eyes, & poyntyng up to heauen with my finger; it is the very Kinge's hie-waye. You saye true in deede (quoth he) the verie Queene's hie-waye, which my harte inquired after though my tongue asked for another. And so, as it is the use with fellowe humors when they fortunately meete, we light bothe upon one argument, the universall fame of that miraculouse gouernment, which by truthe & peace, the harbengers of heauen, directeth us the verie way to eternall blessedness. Much good discourse had we more, of the vanitie of the world, the uncertainetie of frendes, the unconstancie of fortune; but the upshoot of all was this, that he would become an Heremite, I should be his Chaplaine, & both joyntlie joyne in prayers for one Prince, & the prayses of one God. To which purpose, because this plott pleased him, hee here forthwith erected a poore Loddging or twoe, for me, himselfe, & a page, that wayteth on him, naming it when he had donne the Crowne Oratory; and therefore aduaunsed his deuise on the entrance after the Romaine fashion in a Piller of perpetuall remembraunce. But, alas! whilst he seekes to raise one buylding, hee sees the rewins of another; & whilst he shapes a monument for his minde, he feeles the miserie of his bodie, whose roofe was roughe with the mosse of greene haires, whose sides were crased with the tempestes of sicknes, whose foundacion shooke under him with the weight of an unwildye carcasse: and when he perceaued his olde house in a manner past reparacions, considering his owne unablenes, he recomended the care thereof to the conningest Architect of Worlde, who onlie was able to pull it downe unto the earth, & raise it anewe, in better glorie than it stoode before. Then began I to call him to his former preceptes, & his latter practizes, shewing him in fewe woordes (for he conceaued much) that nowe was the time of tryall. A good sayler was better seene in a storme than in a calme. It was no straunge thing to lyue; for slaues lyue, and beastes lyue too. Nature had provided him comforte, who made that most common which shee had made most greeuouse; to the ende the equallnes might aleye the egernes of death. To which he mildelie replied that my motions fytlie touched him, he was as desirouse to encounter with Death, as to heare of Death, for Fortitude still abode his bed-fellowe. Extremitie thought it could not be ouercom yet it might be ouerborne, since his minde had secured him by fearing nothing, and oueriched him by desiring nothing. Hee had longe lyued in the Sea, and ment now to die in the Hauen. Hauen (saide I). Yea! the Hauen (quoth he); lett me be carried into the Hauen. Which Hauen I supposed he hadd spoken idellie, but that he eftsones repeted it, and wished to be brought to this poore houell before the gates. What thatt odde corner (saide I). Yes (quoth he) that corner; and angerlie broke of with this sentence: Subsilire in cœlum ex Angulo licet.

So we speedilie remoued him hither, wher being softely layed he uttered these Speeches softelie:—Before I was olde, I desyred to lyue well, and now I am olde, I desire to die well: and to die well is to die willinglie. Manie there be that wish to lyue, yet wott not how to die: lett me be theire example yf they lyke not lyfe, to lyue, to die with lyking, who neither embraced Fortune when shee flew unto mee, nor ensued Fortune when she fled from mee, nor spared niggardlie, nor spent lavishlie, whatsoeuer she bestowed on me: but since it was my singuler hope to lyue beholding to the Crowne, I accompt it my speciall joye to dye beholding the Crowne. Holy Crowne! hallowed by the sacrament, confirmed by the fates; thou hast been the Aucthor of my last Testament. So calling for pen and inke (which were neuer far off) he drew a formall draught of his whole will, signed & subscribed by himselfe, but witnessed by us, the compassionate spectators of that lamentable action which he had no sooner entituled by wayes of truste, & geuen me charge for the safe deliuering thereof, but he fell soddenlye speecheles, & so continueth to this houre. The stile runnethe thus: *To the most renouned Queene owner of the best Crowne & crowned with the best desertes, the lyuing loue of dying Loricus.* Now, most peereles Princes, sence there is none can laie challenge to this title, except they should also challenge your vertues, which were to complaine of Nature for robbing herselfe to do you right, accept I beseeche you the offer of him who dares not offer it to anie other; & one daie no doubt but the Knight himselfe, if happilie he recouer (as what may not so sacred a Prince promise), will say it is in a good hand, & proue the best expounder of his owne meaning. In the meane season, thoughe myne endevors must be employed about your sick seruant, yet my prayers shall not ceasse for your most gratiouse Majestie, that as you haue ouer liued the vaine hope of your forraine enemies, so you may outlast the kinde wishes of your loyall subjectes, which is to last to the last euerlasting. Amen.

Finis.

To the most renowned Queene,
Owner of the best Crowne, & crowned with the best desertes, the lyuing Loue of dying Loricus.

> I Loricus, Bodie sicke,
> Sences sounde, Remembraunce quicke,
> Neuer crauing, euer seruing,
> Little hauing, lesse deseruing,
>
> Though a hartie true wellwiller
> Of the Crowne & crowned Piller,
> To that Crowne, my lyues content,
> Make my Will & Testament.
>
> Soule! goe first to heauenlie rest;
> Soule the Bodies heauenlie gueste,
> Where, both Host & Inn decaying,
> Yeld the gueste no quiet staying.
>
> Bodie! back againe, departe;
> Earth thou wast, & Earth thou arte.
> Mortall creatures still be jurneing,
> From the earth to earth returning.
>
> As for anie wordlie lyuing
> Nothing haue I woorth the geeuing:
> Let the baser indeed take them,
> We which follow God forsake them.

> But if anie wishe to dwell,
> As I did, in homely Cell,
> Let him pull his Castells downe,
> And as I did serue the Crowne,
> Serue the Crowne, O Crowne deseruing,
> Better that Loricus seruing.
>
> In witness whereof I haue set to my hande & harte.
>
> LORICUS, Columnæ coronatæ Custos fidelissimus.

In presence of us whose names are underwritten,

> STELLATUS, Rectoriæ Coronatæ Capellanus.
> RENATUS, Equitis Coronati Servus obseruantissimus.

The Page bringeth tydings of his Maister's Recouerie, & presenteth his Legacie.

The suddaine recouerie of my distressed Maister, whome latelie you left in a Traunce (Most excellent Princes!) hath made me at one tyme the hastie messenger of three trothes, your miracle, his mending, & my mirthe. Miracles on the sicke are seldom seene without theire mending: & mending of the good ys not often seene without other mens mirth. Where your Majestie hath don a miracle, & it can not be denied, I hope I may manifest, & it shall not be disliked: for miracles are no miracles unlesse they be confessed, & mirth is no mirth yf it be concealed.

May it therefor please you to heare of his life who lyues by you, & woulde not liue but to please you; in whom the sole vertue of your sacred presence, which hath made the weather fayre, & the ground fruitfull at this progresse, wrought so strange an effect and so speedie an alteration, that, whereas before he seemed altogether speechles, now Motion (the Recorder of the Bodies Commonwealth) tells a lyuelie tale of health, and his Tongue (the Cocheman of the Harte) begun to speake the sweete language of affection. So tourning him selfe about to the ayre & the lyght, O wretched man [quoth he] callamities storie, lyfes delay, & deathes prisoner: with that he pawsed a while & then fixing his eyes on the Crowne, he sayd Welcom be that blessed Companie, but thrise blessed be her coming aboue the rest, who came to geue me this blessed rest!

Hereat Stellatus, his Chappelaine, besought him to blesse God onelie, for it was Gods spirite who recouered his spirites. Truthe (quoth he again) yet whosoeuer blesseth her, blesseth God in her: and euer blessed be God for her.—The conferrence continued long, but louinglie, betwixt them; till at length upon question to whom the Will was directed, with knowledge how it was deliuered, Loricus publiklie acknowleged the right performance of his true meaning unto your Royall Majestie, to whom he humblie recommended the full execution thereof, & by me hath sent your Majestye this simple Legacie, which he disposed the rather whilst he yet lyueth, than lefte to be disposed after his deathe, that you might understande how he alwaies preferred the deed. Thus much your diuine power hath performed to him, thus far his thankfulnes hath brought mee to your Majestie. As for anie other Accomplementes, whatsoeuer Dutie yeldes to be debt, Deuotion offers to be dischardged; and if my Maister's best payment be onlie good prayers, what need more than the Pages bare woorde, which is allwaies—Amen.

The Legacye.

Item. I bequethe (to your Highnes) THE WHOLE MANNOR OF LOUE, and the appurtenaunces thereunto belonging:

(Viz.) Woodes of hie attemptes,
   Groues of humble seruice,
   Meddowes of greene thoughtes,
   Pastures of feeding fancies,
   Arrable Lande of large promisses,
   Riuers of ebbing & flowing fauours,
   Gardens hedged about with priuate, for succorie, & bordered with tyme: of greene nothing but hartesease, drawen in the perfect forme of a true louers knott.
   Orchards stored with the best fruit: Queene Apples, Pome Royalls, & Soueraigne Peare.
   Fishing for dayntie Kisses with smyling countenances,
   Hawking to springe pleasure with the spanniells of kindenes.
   Hunting that deare game which repentance followeth.
      Ouer & beside the Royaltie: for
   Westes of fearefull dispaire,
   Strayes of wandring conceiptes,
   Fellons goods of stolne delightes,

Coppie Holders which allure by witte writinges,
Or Tennantes at will who stand upon good behauiour.
The Demaines being deepe sighes,
And the Lordes House a pittifull harte.
And this Mannor is helde in Knightes seruice,
As may be gathered from the true Receauour of fayre Ladies, and seene in the auncient deedes of amorouse Gentelmen.
All which he craueth may be annexed to his former Will, & therewith approued in the Prerogatiue Courte of Your Majesties acceptance.

  In witnes whereof I haue putt to my hande & seale;

    LORICUS, Columnæ coronatæ Custos fidelissimus.

  In the presence of us whose names are here under written:

    STELLATUS, Rectoriæ coronatæ Capellanus.
    RENATUS, Equitis coronati Servus obseruantissimus.

    FINIS.

The following extracts from the "Memoirs of Robert Cary Earl of Monmouth," furnish some interesting traits of the Queen and her Court:

In 1592 I married a Gentlewoman [1] more for her worth than her wealth, for her estate was but five hundred pounds a yeare jointure, and she had betweene five and six hundred pounds in her purse. Neither did she marry me for any great wealth, for I had, in all the world, but one hundred pounds a yeare pension out of the Exchequer, and that was but during pleasure, and I was neere a thousand pounds in debt; besides, the Queene was mightily offended with me for marrying, and most of my best Friends; only my Father was no ways displeased at it, which gave great content. After I was married, I brought my Wife to Carlisle, where we were so nobly used by my Lord [2], that myself, my Wife, and all my servants, were lodged in the Castle, where wee lived with him, and had our diet for ourselves, our servants, and horses, provided for as his owne were. Wee had not long lived thus, but a sodaine occasion called mee up to the Terme, which then was at St. Alban's [1592], by reason of a great plague that yeare in London, the Queen lying then at Windsor. Having ended my businesse, I meant to retourne to Carleil againe. My Father wrote to me from Windsor, that the Queene meant to have a great Triumph there on her Coronation-day, and that there was great preparation making for the course of the Field and Tourney [3]. Hee gave mee notice of the Queen's anger for my marriage, and said it may bee, I being so neere, and to retourne without honouring her day, as I ever before had done, might be a cause of her further dislike; but left it to myselfe to do what I thought best. My businesse of Law therefore being ended, I came to Court, and lodged there very privately; only I made myselfe known to my Father and some few friends besides. I here tooke order and sent to London to provide mee things necessary for the Triumph. I prepared a present for her Majestie, which, with my caparisons, cost me above four hundred pounds. I came in to the Triumph unknown of any. I was the forsaken Knight, that had vowed solitarinesse; but hearing of this great Triumph, thought to honour my Mistresse with my best service, and then to retourne to pay my wonted mourning. The Triumph ended, and all things well passed over to the Queene's liking, I then made myselfe knowne

[1] Elizabeth, daughter of Sir Hugh Trevanion.
[2] Thomas Lord Scroop, who succeeded his father in the Government of the Castle at Carlisle.
[3] Plays, masques, triumphs, and tournaments, which the author calls Tourneys, were small branches of those many spreading allurements which Elizabeth made use of to draw to herself the affections and admiration of her subjects. She appeared at them with dignity, ease, grace, and affability.

in Court; and for the time I stayed there was daily conversant with my old companions and friends: but I made no long stay [1].

My Brother Sir John Cary, that was then Marshal of Berwick, was sent to by the King of Scottes, to desire him that he would meet his Majestie at the bound rode at a day appointed, for that he had a matter of great importance to acquaint his Sister the Queene of England withall, but he would not trust the Queene's Embassadour with it, nor any other, unless it were my Father, or some of his Children. My Brother sent him word he would gladly wait on his Majestie, but durst not untill hee had acquainted the Queene therewith, and when he had received her answer, hee would acquaint him with it. My Brother sent notice to my Father of the King's desire. My Father shewed the letter to the Queene. She was not willing that my Brother should stir out of the towne [2]; but knowing (though she would not know) that I was in Court, she said, " I heare your fine Sonne, that has lately married so worthily, is hereabouts; send him if you will to know the King's pleasure." My Father answered, hee knew I would be glad to obey her commaundes. " No (said she) do.you bid him go, for I have nothing to do with him." My Father came and told me what had passed betweene them. I thought it hard to be sent, and not to see her; but my Father told mee plainly, that she would neither speak with mee nor see me. " Sir," said I, " if she be on such hard termes with mee, I had need be wary what I do. If I go to the King without her licence, it were in her power to hang me at my retorne, and that, for any thing I see, it were ill trusting her [3]." My Father merrily went to the Queene, and told her what I said. She answered, " If the gentleman be so mistrustfull, let the Secretary make a safe-conduct to go and come, and I will sign it." Upon these terms I parted from Court, and made all the haste for Scotland. I stayed but one night with my wife at Carleil, and then to Barwick, and so to Edenborough, where it pleased the King to use me very graciously; and after three or foure dayes spent in sport and merriment, he acquainted mee with what he desired the Queene should know; which when I understood, I said to his Majestie, " Sir, betweene subject and subject, a message

[1] The Queen was undoubtedly advertised that her forsaken Knight (for such indeed he was) had issued forth from his solitariness to bask himself in the sunshine of her luminous countenance, and to gather courage and prowess from the beams of her bright eyes. Nothing, not even trifles, passed abroad or at home, with which she was not acquainted. But as she had no immediate occasion for the service of Sir Robert Cary, her Majesty was determined still to continue the outward shew of her resentment till she wanted him.

[2] The town of Berwick, from whence the Queen would not have him stir, because she did not deem him to be a proper messenger, knowing there was a better within call.

[3] By this expression may be seen the terror in which this mighty Princess governed her subjects. By the tightness with which she grasped the reigns of Government, she was at once beloved and feared.

may be sent and delivered without any danger: between two so great Monarches as your Majestie and my Mistresse, I dare not trust my memory to be a relatour, but must desire you would be pleased to write your minde to her. If you shall think fitt to trust mee with it, I shall faithfully discharge the trust reposed in me." He liked the motion, and said it should be so, and accordingly I had my dispatch within foure dayes. I made all the haste I could to Court, which was then at Hampton Court. I arrived there on St. Stephen's day in the afternoone. Dirty as I was, I came into the presence, where I found the lords and ladies dancing. The Queene was not there. My Father went to the Queene, to let her know that I was retourned. She willed him to take my message or letters, and bring them to her. Hee came for them; but I desired him to excuse mee, for that which I had to say, either by word or by writing, I must deliver myselfe. I could neither trust him, nor much less any other therewith. He acquainted her Majestie with my resolution. With much adoe I was called for in: and I was left alone with her. Our first encounter was stormy and terrible, which I passed over with silence. After shee had spoken her pleasure of mee and my wife, I told her, that, " shee herselfe was the fault of my marriage, and that if she had but graced mee with the least of her favours, I had never left her nor her Court; and seeing shee was the chief cause of my misfortune, I would never off my knees till I had kissed her hand, and obtained my pardon." She was not displeased with my excuse, and before wee parted wee grew good friends. Then I delivered my message and my papers, which shee tooke very well, and at last gave me thankes for the pains I had taken. So having her princely word that she had pardoned and forgotten all faults, I kissed her hand, and came forth to the presence, and was in the Court as I was ever before[1]. This God did for mee to bring mee in favour with my Soveraigne; for if this occasion had been slipt, it may be I should never have seene her face more. After I had stayed all Christmasse 'till almost Shrovetide, I tooke leave of her Majestie and all the rest of my friends, and made straight for Carleil. Presently after this my Father died; and I had letters sent downe from Secretary Cecill, that it was her Majestie's pleasure I should continue as absolute Warden in my father's place, untill her further pleasure were knowne.

[1] The firmness with which Sir Rob. Cary weathered out this storm, evidently shews in what a school, and under what a Mistress, he had been bred. He well knew that the curious desire of the Queen to be fully informed of every particular relating to the King of Scots, must, after a certain degree of assumed passion, turn into a proper calm, proper at least for hearing his sentiments, if not for expressing some of her own. The effects of his judgment never appeared more conspicuous, than from the beginning to the end of the scene which he has here exhibited.

Extracts from Sir EGERTON BRYDGES's *Introduction to an elegant Edition of the "Speeches at Bissam, Sudeley, and Rycott*[1].*"*

SUDELEY CASTLE

belonged at the Conquest to Harold, son to Ralph Earle of Hereford, son of Walter de Maunt, by Goda, sister to King Edward the Confessor. John, son of this Harold, was father of Ralph Lord of Sudeley; from whom it descended to John Lord of Sudeley, who died 41 Edward III. without issue, leaving Joane his sister and coheir, who married William le Boteler, of Wemme in Shropshire, and had issue Thomas Boteler who inherited Sudeley Castle, and died 22 Richard II. He was succeeded by his brother Ralph Boteler, Lord of Sudeley, who, having served King Henry VI. in the wars in France, and stood firm to the Lancastrian interest, was made Lord Chamberlain of the King's Household 20 Henry VI. and was advanced to the dignity of a Baron of the Realm, by letters patent, the same year, by the title of Lord Boteler of Sudeley.

This Ralph Lord Boteler of Sudeley was the re-builder of the Castle, of which the ruins are yet remaining. It was raised, as it is said, in a style of uncommon magnificence for that age, from the spoils obtained in the wars of France. The windows were glazed with beryl, which is mentioned as a circumstance of extraordinary splendour.

Leland gives the following account of it: "The Castle of Sudeley is about halfe a mile from Winchecombe. —— Boteler, L. Sudeley made this Castle *a fundamentis*; and when it was made, it had the price of all the buildinges in those dayes. I read but of one L. Sudeley of the Botelers, and his name was Thomas, as it appeareth in the glasse windowes at Winchecombe, in St. Peter's Church. Therefore I take it, that it was this Thomas that made the Castle. Yet did Mr. Tracy tell me, that Rafe Boteler builded the Castle; but he shewed noe authoritye why. Indeed, Thomas had a sonne, called Rafe, sette as yongest in order in the glasse windowes in St. Peter's Church.

"The Lord Sudeley that builded the Castle, was a famous man of warre in K. Hen. V. and K. Hen. VI. dayes; and was an Admirall, as I have heard, on sea; whereupon it was supposed and spoken, that it was partly builded *ex spoliis Gallorum*, and some speake of a towre in it called Potmare's Towre, that it should be made of a ransome of his. One thinge was to be noted in this Castle, that part of the windowes of it were glazed with berall. There had been a Manour Place at Sudeley, before the building of the Castle, and the plott is yet seene in Sudeley Parke, where it stoode.

"K. Edw. IV. bore noe good will to the L. Sudeley, as a man suspected to be in heart K. Hen. VI. his man; whereupon by complaints he was attached, and going up to London, he looked from the hill to Sudeley, and sayd, 'Sudeley Castle, thou art a traytor, not I!' After he made an honest declaration and sould his Castle of Sudeley to K. Edw. IV."

[1] See before, pp. 129. 136.

This Ralph Lord Boteler of Sudeley died May 2, 13 Edward IV. leaving two nephews, Sir John Norbury and William Belknap, sons of his sisters Elizabeth and Joan, his heirs. His widow Eleanor Talbot, daughter of the Earl of Shrewsbury, had been pre-contracted to King Edward IV. before he fell in love with and married Elizabeth Woodvile.

Leland goes on, " afterwards K. Henry VII. gave this Castle to his Uncle Jasper D. of Bedford, or permitted him to have the use of it. Now it goeth to ruine; more pittye. The Traceis of Todington were sett up by landes given them by the Botelers.

" There runneth a pretty lake out of Sudeley Park, downe by the Castle, and runneth into Esseburne Brook, at the South side of Winchecombe."

In another place he says, " The Hawle of Sudeley Castle is glazed with round beralls."

After the death of Jasper Tudor, Duke of Bedford, the Castle came again into the hands of the Crown; and was falling fast to ruin, when King Edward VI. granted it to his uncle Thomas Seymour, whom he created Lord Seymour of Sudeley, and made Lord High Admiral of England. The history of this ambitious man is well known. In 1547, he married Katherine Parr, widow of King Henry VIII. He repaired this Castle, and some say, built the Chapel of rich Gothic architecture, of which a sketch is exhibited in the title to the Work[1] from which these extracts are taken; but as it much resembles the best Gothic of King Henry VI's days, it was more probably erected by Ralph Lord Sudeley. Here the widowed Queen hoped to have enjoyed that happiness, which a crown could not confer. But her hopes were short-lived: she escaped the capricious cruelty of a tyrant, to fall a victim to the unprincipled and heartless ambition of a subject. The Admiral is now supposed to have aspired to the hand of the Princess Elizabeth. To this Katharine Parr, while living, formed an insurmountable obstacle. At this time the unhappy Queen was delivered of a daughter; and dying in consequence, a strong suspicion of poison was fixed upon her husband. Indeed, she herself apprehended some unfair dealings; and, on her death-bed, roundly reproached the Admiral for his unkind usage.

She was buried in this Chapel of Sudeley. The late learned Historian of Worcestershire, Dr. Nash, learning this fact from a MS. published in " Rudder's Gloucestershire," determined to examine the now roofless and unpaved chapel for her body. He soon discovered the coffin a little way under ground. The body was in perfect preservation; but, on coming to the air, turned in part to dust[2].

The industrious Mr. Strype, who has filled up so many chasms, and added so much to the writings of those who preceded him in the history of those times, did not know where the Queen was buried: however, he has made some amends in obliging the world with a Latin epitaph, composed in memory of her, by Dr. Parkhurst, one of her domestic Chaplains, and afterwards Bishop of Norwich[3].

[1] Rev. Cooper Willyams's History of Sudeley Castle.
[2] See an account of this discovery in Archæologia, vol. IX. p. 1.
[3] This Epitaph, and a subsequent one referred to in these Extracts, may be seen in the re-publication of Sir Egerton Brydges.

THE CHANDOS FAMILY.

Queen Mary on coming to the Crown in 1553, granted Sudeley Castle to Sir John Bridges, of Coberley in the county of Gloucester, Knt. who had been a strenuous supporter of her succession; and who, on April 8, 1554, was created Baron Chandos of Sudeley, to him and the heirs male of his body.

As the family of Bridges long since attained the highest rank of Nobility, and were of ancient descent and considerable consequence centuries before they attained the Peerage, I may be allowed to give at least a brief account of them here.

Their ancestor, Sir Simon de Bruges, was Lord of the manor of Brugge-upon-Wye in Herefordshire, in the reign of Henry III. Whence this Sir Simon sprung cannot be ascertained by any positive proof; but there is strong circumstantial evidence to induce the belief that he was a branch of the illustrious House of Savoy, who had sometime before obtained a temporary dominion in Flanders, by a marriage with the heiress of the ancient Earls of that country; hence it seems that they took their name, as the cross in their arms, and the leopard's face with which it is charged. This it may be admitted is but conjecture: but there are few old Houses of Europe, either noble or sovereign, which through the darkness of those distant ages stand on better grounds. The number of really ancient families in Britain is not great; and merely Antiquity, without lustre, without high employments civil or military, and without honourable alliances, is surely of slight and humble estimation. In feudal times, birth, in the strictest sense of genealogists, was almost an essential qualification for the attainment of any elevated office, or admission into the upper circles of society. The family of which we are now speaking, filled those offices, and moved in that society. They represented the county of Hereford in Parliament as early as the reign of King Edward II. and the county of Gloucester in the reign of King Henry VI. and King Edward IV. They were Sheriffs of Herefordshire and Worcestershire in the reign of King Edward III. and again in that of King Richard II. and of Gloucestershire in the reign of King Henry VI. and King Henry VII.

In the reign of King Henry IV. Thomas Brydges, son of Sir Baldwin (who was great-grandson of Sir Simon before-mentioned) removed into Gloucestershire by marrying a great heiress, Alice, daughter and coheir of Sir Thomas Berkeley, of Coberley in that county, by Joan, sister and coheir of Sir John Chandos, of Herefordshire, son and heir of Thomas Lord Chandos, who died 49 Edward III. His son, Sir Giles Brydges, of Coberley, who married a Clifford, was father of Thomas, who married a Darell of Littlecot in Wiltshire, and was father of another Sir Giles.

This last Sir Giles Brydges of Coberley was knighted for his valour at the battle of Blackheath, June 22, 1497, and was Sheriff of Gloucestershire 15 Henry VII. He died 1511, and was buried at Coberley. His wife was Isabel, daughter of Thomas Baynham, Esq. The brass plates of their monument are yet remaining in the Church there. He is mentioned by Polidore Vergil the historian, in his account of the attack on Perkin Warbeck at Exeter. His brother Henry Brydges, of Newbury, was father of Sir Richard Brydges, K. B. of Luggershall Castle in Wilts, who died in 1548.

Sir John Brydges, eldest son of Sir Giles Brydges, of Coberley, by Isabel Baynham, was knighted for his valour in the French wars, in 1513; and was with King Henry VIII. at Bulloign, in the 24th year of his reign, when he was one of the Esquires of his Body. In 1537, he was constituted Constable of Sudeley Castle; and again in the 34th year of the same reign. In 1544, for his gallant behaviour at the siege of Bulloign, he was made Deputy Governor of that town; and continued in that post by King Edw. VI. In 1549 he successfully defended the town, as Deputy Governor, against the siege carried on by the French King in person. He was in nomination for the Order of the Garter in 1547, and again in 1550. He was one of the principal persons in the train of Queen Mary, on her entrance into London, and passage to the Tower, when, on her brother's death, she came to assume the Crown; and on that occasion the charge of the Tower was committed to his custody. His rewards were a grant of the Castle and Manor of Sudeley; and a peerage to him and the heirs male of his body, by the title of Lord Chandos of Sudeley. He soon after had the melancholy office of attending to the scaffold the amiable and unfortunate Lady Jane Grey (who was of the same family with his wife, though of another branch); and such were his kind attentions to her, that she gave him as a memorial her prayer-book or table-book, inscribed with several Greek and Latin verses by her own hand. He died March 4, 1556-7, and was buried at Sudeley.

There are few old and considerable families of whom the existing church-memorials are so rare as of this once-opulent, wide-spreading, and indisputably ancient House. Part of this may, perhaps, be attributed to the fate which involved the Chapel of Sudeley in the same ruin with its Castle, though no ancient collector has registered any epitaphs previously inscribed in that building. Coberley church retains a few brass fragments. But at Cornbury in Oxfordshire are several[1]. The Church of Keinsham is, however, full of the monuments of that branch. Epitaphs are justly, perhaps, deemed the dullest of all lore. But there is something so satisfactory in the precise and indisputable proof which they afford of the rank and condition of a family at that distance of time, when the living remembrance of them is long past, that it would be very unwise to forego the use of them, when they can be obtained. A sagacious observer knows the hesitation and reluctance with which any thing that sets forth the lustre and consi-

[1] Which are preserved in the re-publication by Sir Egerton Brydges.

deration of a pedigree is admitted. Mere names and dates, even though exact and in their true order of succession, go but a little way in establishing that importance, which it is the object of genealogists to confer.

I am now to return to the elder branch. It is by alliances that we can estimate, with a near approach to Aristocracy, the sphere in which a family moves. Elizabeth Grey, daughter of William Lord Grey of Wilton, and wife of John the first Lord Chandos, was of an House of numerous and truly ancient Nobility, whose history and origin are only lost where the Norman Annals fade away in the darkness of the remote ages, long before the Conqueror assumed the English throne. The Lords Grey of Ruthen (afterwards Earls and Dukes of Kent); of Rotherfield; of Codnor; and of Groby (afterwards Marquises of Dorset, and Dukes of Suffolk, and now Earls of Stamford); were all scions of the same stock. But the Wilton branch were a race of hardy warriors, whose Castle on the romantic banks of the Wye was often deserted for the perilous glory of the French wars, that seldom allowed them to repose under their paternal turrets, in that old age to which they looked as the reward of their adventures. Their narrow and decaying fortunes never seem to have broken their high spirit, and ambition of dignified employment. They knew their place in the State; and won their way to it in spite of falling mansions and the *res angusta domi*. The minion of King James, George Villiers Duke of Buckingham, afterwards got their old seat and estate at Whaddon in Buckinghamshire; which, after another century, was destined to be the abode of an Antiquary of a different cast, and Browne Willis pursued for a long life his sedentary and whimsical occupations in the spot which for ages had been honoured by the presence of the warlike tribe of haughty GREYS. Arthur Lord Grey of Wilton, the nephew of Lady Chandos, is distinguished among the heroes and statesmen of the Elizabethan story.

George Gascoigne the Poet, who seems to have been the Poet of the family, has written some very excellent lines on the first wife of this Peer, who was a daughter of Lord Zouche of Haringworth.

But Lord Grey's memory is enshrined in more precious and living colours by the immortal Spenser, to whom he was the patron and friend [1].

As to the Kentish branch, about which so much extraordinary dispute has arisen, the alliance with the Asteleys of Maidstone, was a very natural and simple reason for their removing thither. If we judge from the will of the first Lord Chandos, his younger sons were very slenderly provided for: a case that very frequently happened to the younger children of a feudal Peer. How Charles, the second son, was enabled to buy the Wilton Castle estate of his cousin, Arthur Lord Grey, it would now be vain to enquire. He might be luckier than his brothers in the talent, or the opportunity of carving out his own fortune: he might possess more virtue, or more ability; or what is not worse calculated for the purposes of accumulating wealth - - - - *less honesty!* Of

[1] Whose Sonnet to him before "The Fairy Queen" is given in Sir Egerton Brydges's work.

the property of the other brothers I can find very trivial notices. Of Henry strange traditions yet remain in the village where he was buried: and if we could credit those stories, he was almost a free-booter in those latter days of inglorious and unprofitable peace, when men of the sword (and he seems to have been a man of the sword) even of high quality, finding no vent for those habits and acquirements which a Reign of more noble adventure had generated, are said to have indulged in many licences, such as in modern days could scarcely obtain belief.

These Asteleys were not merely high in birth and station, but, what is a far better distinction, in intellect and learning. John Asteley, Esq the father, was as well the congenial as the intimate friend of the celebrated Roger Ascham; and though his writings are unknown among the modern literati, I shall prove that his fame among his cotemporaries was of the first class. This will be so new even to most literary Antiquaries that I am anxious to establish it upon the most irrefragable authorities. I will therefore transcribe every word of the article regarding him in Bishop Tanner's "Bibliotheca."

"Asteley Johannes regiorum jocalium Magister et thesaurarius constituitur, cum feodo quinqueginta librarum per annum 23 Dec. lit. pat. 1 Elizab. Fuit etiam reginæ a camera privata, qui antea tempore Regis Edwardi VI. officio aliquo in familia principissæ Elizabethæ functus erat. Scripsit 'The Art of Riding, Lond. MDLXXXIV.' 4to. Epistolam ad Dom. Rogerum Aschamum præfixam operi ejus de Rebus Germanicis Regnante Carolo imperatore, datam ex ædibus Principissæ Elizabethæ Hatfield 19 Oct. MDLII. in qua multa de amicitia mutua apud Chestonam, Chelseiam, et Hatfield com§ memorat. Obiit ante 20 Februar. 38 Elizabethæ, quo die Dom. Edwardus Carey suscepit curam jocalium ab executoribus ejus: cujus indentura extat inter MSS. Norwic. More 255."

Gabriel Harvey, in his "Pierce's Supererogation, 1593," recommending several works of solid merit, in opposition to the pamphleteers of the day, says, " I cannot forget the gallant discourse of Horsemanship penned by a rare gentleman Mr. John Asteley, Esquire of the Court, whom I dare entitle the English Xenophon."

And the same Critic in the same work continually mentions him in the following company: "Come Divine Poets, and sweet Orators; the silver streaming fountains of flowingest wit, and shiningest art; come Chaucer and Spenser; More and Cheek; Ascham and *Asteley*; Sydney and Dyer; come the dearest sister of the dearest brother, the sweetest daughter of the sweetest Muse!" &c.

Mrs. Asteley, who died in 1601, is commemmorated in the Poem of "The Wizard."

Sir John Asteley, the son, was appointed Master of the Revels on the resignation of Sir George Buck in 1621; "but to whatever cause it was owing," says Chalmers, in his Supplemental Apology, p. 207, "relinquished the management of the Revels to Sir Henry Herbert even before the decease of Sir George Buck."

Edmund Brydges, second Lord Chandos, following his father's example, took early to arms, and served under the Earl of Hertford in France, in the reign of King Henry VIII. and in 1547, behaving himself with great bravery in the famous battle of Muselborough, on Sept. 10, was made Knight-banneret by the Duke of Somerset on the 27th, in the camp at Roxburgh. He was elected one of the Knights for Gloucestershire to the Parliament summoned to meet at Westminster Oct. 5, 1553, and served at the siege of St. Quintin in Picardy, 4 Philip and Mary. In the Reign of Q. Eliz. he was elected a Knight of the Garter, and installed at Windsor June 17, 1572. He died Sept. 11, 1573. His issue by Dorothy, daughter of Edm. Lord Bray, were Giles; William; Katharine, wife to William Lord Sands; and Eleanor, wife of George Giffard [1], Esq. of Chillington.

A poem in praise of the eldest daughter, Katharine Lady Sands, by George Gascoigne, was brought back into notice many years ago, by Dr. Percy, late Bp. of Dromore, in his "Ballads," 1765, vol. II. p. 150.

Dorothy, the widow of Edmund Lord Chandos, married, secondly, Sir William Knowles, afterwards Lord Knowles, Earl of Banbury, and Knight of the Garter. She died Oct. 31, 1605.

Giles third Lord Chandos, eldest son of Edmund the second Peer, was born 1547; elected to Parliament for the County of Gloucester 14 Eliz. in the life-time of his father. He married Lady Frances Clinton, daughter of Edward first Earl of Lincoln, and Admiral of England.

This was the Nobleman who entertained Queen Elizabeth at Sudeley Castle in 1592; when the Speeches here re-printed were delivered to her Majesty [2]. He died Feb. 21, 1593-4, aged 47. His widow survived till 1623, and was buried at Cheneys, in Bucks, in the burial-place of the Bedford family.

Of his two daughters and coheirs, Elizabeth, born 1578, married Sir John Kennedy of Scotland, Kt.; and Katherine, born 1576, married Francis Lord Russell, of Thornhaugh, afterwards Earl of Bedford, and died 1654, leaving a son and heir, William first Duke of Bedford.

The match of Lady Kennedy was unhappy. It appeared that her husband had married a former wife in Scotland; and on this discovery Lord Chandos's daughter (though the first wife was then dead) disputed the validity of her own marriage. It appears that her fortune was £16,500. She died in Oct. 1617. There is a curious passage regarding her death, in the Extracts of Letters among Birch's MSS. in the British Museum, in these words:

"Oct. 18, 1617. Mrs Bridges, alias the Lady Kennedy, died at Westminster a fortnight since, being taken with strange convulsions, which made some, perhaps, suspect more than there was cause; that she had done herself some wrong. She lived of late,

[1] Whom the Queen visited in her way from Killingworth in 1575. See vol. I. p. 532.
[2] An engraving of him from the curious portrait at Woburn adorns Sir Egerton Brydges's work.

and died very poor: her maintenance being little or nothing, but as it were the judicious alms of her friends."

"This," says Dr. Birch in a note, "seems to be The Fair Mrs. Bridges with whom the unfortunate Earl of Essex fell in Love[1], which probably occasioned Q. Eliz. to use her with words and blows of anger; and to banish her the Court for three days[2]." But The Fair Mrs. Bridges appears to me as probably to have been either her father's first cousin, afterwards Lady Astley; or her own first cousin Frances, afterwards Lady Smith and Countess of Exeter.

William succeeded his brother Giles as fourth Lord Chandos. He married Mary, daughter of Sir Owen Hopton, Lieutenant of the Tower, and died Nov. 18, 1602. His daughters were, first, Frances, married, first, to Sir Thomas Smith, Master of the Requests, and Latin Secretary to King James I.; and afterwards the last wife and widow of Thomas Cecil, Earl of Exeter, who died 1621, and whom she survived till 1662, æt. 83. The exquisite portrait of her, engraved by Faithorne, is known to all Collectors;—second, Joan, married to Sir Thomas Turvile, Cup-bearer to Queen Anne, wife of King James I.;—third, Beatrice, married to Sir Henry Poole, of Saperton, in Gloucestershire.

Grey, eldest son, succeeded his father as fifth Lord Chandos. He was made Knight of the Bath, 1604-5, and created A. M. at Oxford the same year. He seems to have a right to a niche in the Temple of Fame raised by Lord Orford in his "Royal and Noble Authors." He is thought to have been the author of a little book, entitled, "Horæ Subsecivæ - - - Observations and Discourses," 1620, 12mo. He married Lady Anne, eldest daughter and coheir of Ferdinando Stanley Earl of Derby, by Alice daughter of Sir John Spencer, of Althorp; which Lady re-married Lord Chancellor Egerton, and whose epitaph is at Harefield in Middlesex. This great Lady was the patroness of Spenser, Milton, and other men of genius; and T. Warton observes, in his "Notes to Milton's Juvenile Poems," that her "Peerage-book" is to be found in the volumes of Poetry of her time.

Grey Lord Chandos was a noble house-keeper; and by a winning behaviour contracted so great an interest in Gloucestershire, and had such numerous attendants when he came to Court, that he was commonly called *The King of Cotswold*. For, having an ample fortune, he expended it in the most generous manner; his house being kept open three days every week for the gentry: and the poor were as constantly fed with the remnants of his hospitable entertainments. In short, his ability and disposition were so exactly proportioned to each other, that it was difficult to determine which had the greatest share in his numberless acts of beneficence. On Nov. 8, 1617, he was appointed to receive and introduce the Muscovite Ambassadors, who had brought rich and costly presents from their master to the King. He died August 10, 1621, aged

---

[1] Sydney Papers, II. 90.   [2] Ibid.

about 40. An Elegy upon him was written by Sir John Beaumont, Bart. of Gracedieu in Leicestershire, author of the poem of "Bosworth Field," who died 1628, aged 46, and was elder brother of Francis Beaumont the Dramatic Writer.

The widow of this great Peer re-married the wretched James Earl of Castlehaven, whose son Earl Mervin married Lord Chandos's eldest daughter Elizabeth. Anne, the other daughter, married —— Torteson.

George, born Aug. 9, 1620, succeeded his father as sixth Lord Chandos. He was an eminent Loyalist, and had three horses killed under him at the battle of Newbury, when the King offered to create him Earl of Newbury, which he declined till happier times.

In 1642 Sudeley Castle was besieged by the Rebels under Massie, and after a long siege and several assaults and batteries, when they were almost smothered by the smoke of the hay and barns, burnt about the house, yielded in January that year. This noble Castle then suffered much of its ruin; but was again recovered by the Royalists.

In 1643, when Gloucester was besieged by the King's forces, and relieved by the Earl of Essex, "all this time," says Lord Clarendon, "the King lay at Sudeley Castle, the house of the Lord Chandois, within eight miles of Gloucester, watching when the Earl's army would retire."

In the following year (1644) when Waller prosecuted his march towards Worcester, where his Majesty then was, he "persuaded," says Lord Clarendon, "rather than forced the garrison of Sudeley Castle, the strong house of the Lord Chandois, to deliver up that place to him.

"The Lord of that Castle was a young man of high spirit and courage; and had for two years served the King very bravely at the head of a regiment of horse, which himself had raised at his own charge; but had lately, out of pure weariness of the fatigue, and having spent most of his money, and without any diminution of his affection, left the King, under pretence of travel; but making London in his way, he gave himself up to the pleasures of that place, which he enjoyed, without considering the issue of the war, or shewing any inclination to the Parliament; nor did he in any degree contribute to the delivery of his house; which was at first imagined, because it was so ill, or not at all, defended. It was under the government of Sir William Morton, a gentleman of the Long Robe; who, in the beginning of the war, cast off his gown, as many other gallant men of the Long Robe did, and served as Lieutenant-colonel in the regiment of horse under the Lord Chandois."

Sir William Morton was unfortunate, though without fault, in giving up that Castle in so unseasonable a conjuncture; which was done by the faction and artifice of an officer within, who had found means to go out to Waller, and to acquaint him with the great wants of the garrison; which indeed had not plenty of any thing: and so, by the mutiny of the soldiers, it was given up; and the Governor made prisoner, and sent to the Tower, where he remained some years after the end of the war.

George sixth Lord Chandos died of the small-pox, æt. 35, in February 1664-5, and was buried at Sudeley, having been twice married, first, to Lady Susan, daughter to Henry Earl of Manchester, by whom he had issue two daughters; Margaret, married to William Brownlow, of Hunby, co. Lincoln, Esq.; and Elizabeth, first, to Edward Lord Herbert of Cherbury, secondly, to William, Earl of Inchiquin of the Kingdom of Ireland, and, thirdly, to Charles Lord Howard of Escrick, and died Feb. 3, 1717-18. His Lordship's second wife was Jane, daughter of John Savage, Earl Rivers, by whom he had three daughters: Jane died unmarried; Lucy, married to Adam Loftus, Lord Viscount Lisburn, in Ireland; and Catherine, who also died single. His Lordship having no male issue, the honour descended to William his brother; but the major part of his estate was settled upon Jane his last wife, in fee, as it seems. The said Jane was afterwards married to George Pitt, of Stratfield-Say, in co. Southampton, Esq. ancestor to the present Lord Rivers, who in her right became possessed of Sudeley Castle, and other lands of great value.

William seventh Lord Chandos so succeeding his brother, died 1676, aged 55, and was buried at Harefield. He had by his wife Susan, daughter and coheir of Gerrat Keere, of London, Gent. a son, William; and three daughters, Mary, Frances, and Rebecca, who all died unmarried in their father's life-time, except Rebecca, who married Thomas Pride (son of Thomas Pride and Elizabeth Moncke), who had by her two sons and three daughters, who died young; and Elizabeth married to William Sherwin, Esq. The Barony then expired in the elder branch [1].

I will not pursue this genealogical detail any farther; for here the connection with Sudeley ends. For many reflexions I have at present neither room nor inclination. To "struggle with the waves of time" is the lot of the unfortunate name that I bear. To have all the pride, without the power, of an illustrious family; fondly to look back on the splendour of the past, and yet to find that it only sharpens the sense of present obscurity and neglect; to be exposed to the insults of a new Aristocracy; who exhibit all the offensive airs, without the justification of those qualities which soften and gild the demands of superiority; to feel all this with morbid acuteness; to be, perhaps, weak and cowardly in feeling it; is what it may be most unwise to confess; but what my incautious temper and unrestrained pen will not allow me to conceal.

Nov. 30, 1815.   E. S. BRYDGES.

---

[1] The Barony of Chandos then descended to Sir James Brydges, of Wilton Castle in Herefordshire, Bart. who was third cousin to Grey Lord Chandos, father of this last Peer. This James eighth Lord Chandos died Oct. 16, 1714, and was father of James first Duke.

Anno 35° *Reginæ* ELIZABETHÆ, 1592-3.

Receyved into the office, and payed for in the warraunte for New-yere's Guiftes,

One payer of guilt flagons, chased in panes, 160 oz. q^a.

Receyved oute of her Majestie's Privye Chamber, from the handes of Mr. Michael Stanhop, the 27th daye of Aprill, anno 35° p̃d'; and geven her in the Progresse before.

One golde posset-bolle, a pott with a handell, and a spone, and a cover of golde, having a globe in thende of the handell, and therein an agatt, and an agatt in the cover, and therein a red roase. Geven by therle of *Pembroke*, 38 oz. 3 q^a.

Item, one cup of golde, with a cover of cutt-worke, the shanke of agatt, and a small agatt upon the toppe of the cover, and a white rose over it, 7 oz. 3 q^a.

Item, one small spone of agatt, slightely garnished with golde, dim̃. oz. dim̃. q^a.

Item, one highe standinge cup of selver guilte, with a cover; standing on the toppe thereof a lyon, holding her Majestie's armes enameled; with an inscription, VIVAT ELIZABETHA REGINA on the outeside of the bodye of the cup, 54 oz. 3 q^a.

August 1, 1593, the Queen, with her Court, was at Windsor, and continued there till November; on the 21st of which month, Mr. Standen informs Mr. Bacon, "that the death of a Page of Lady Scroop (so near the Quene's person as of her bedchamber) of the Sickness the last night, and that in the Keep within the Castle, had caused a great alteration there; so that it was not to be doubted but that her Majesty would remove within a day or two at the farthest, though it was not resolved whither, but the Earl of Essex thought to Hampton Court."—Two days after, he adds, from Windsor, "that the Lords and Ladies, who were accommodated so well to their likings, had persuaded the Queen to suspend her removal from thence, till she should see some other effect; so that, though curts were warned to be ready for the Monday following, yet it was constantly believed that her Majesty would not remove till after Christmas[1]."

[1] Birch's "Memoirs of Queen Elizabeth," vol. I. pp. 153, 154.

The RECORDER[1] *of* LONDON's *Speech to Queen* ELIZABETH, *after the Election of Sir* CUTHBERT BUCKLE *to be* LORD MAYOR, 1593[2].

Most mighty Prince, our most deare and dread Soveraigne, it hath alwaise beene reputed a greate happiness amongst all true-hearted subjects, to behold their natural Prince; but, which is more, if they might be heard of him, and their actions and services by his princely favour approved, then have they attayned the fullnes of their desires, to their exceeding joy and comfort. We your Majestie's most humble and obedient subjects and Citizens of London, the chief Citty of your Highness Realme, the safe and secret chamber of your kingdom, haveing obtayned at this present, by your gracious permission, accesse to your sacred person, cannot but behold the same as the visible majesty of God, to our unspeakable joy and consolation.

If we never heretofore had obtained, or ever hereafter should receave any other benefit, this onely were sufficient to make us spend the rest of our dayes in continuall remembrance and thanksgiving to your most excellent Majesty for the same; but there are to be added so many and greate, soe bountifull and princely priviledges and benefitts, which have proceeded from the fountayne of your Highness' imperiall crown to us present, and all other your Highness' Citizens of London, to the whole body, and to every particular member thereof, that for the multitude they cannot be numbered, much lesse can I make rehearsall of them.

Albeit the least of those benefitts doth exceed the bost of my witt, and skill of my tongue, to exprese the greatness and worthiness thereof; yet, by the present occasion, I am inforced briefly to touche some of them, that otherwise would have rather wished with modest silence to have over passed them, than by the unaptnes of my words, and rudeness of my Speech, have demynished the excellency of them; and I doe most humbly beseech your Majesty, that not being able to set them forthe according to their greatness, nor render to your Highness for them that entire thanks that their hartes for whom I speake do inwardly and unfaynedly yeald, your Highness will vouchsafe to pardon my timorous nature, and unexercised tongue, that would, but cannot expresse in words the greatness of your princely favour, nor the thankefull minds of your faithfull subjects.

[1] Edward Drew, Esq. Serjeant at Law, and afterwards Queen's Serjeant. He was Recorder of London 1592—1594.   [2] From the Harleian MSS. N° 852. p. 1.

Your Highness most noble Progenitors have by their Charters granted, which would little availe us, if your most excellent Majesty by your royall Confirmation had not ratified them, that it should be lawfull for your Highness' Citizens of London " to choose, amongest and of themselves, a Mayor every yeare, which to your Highnesse should be faithfull, a discreate man, and fitt for the government of the Citty."

What benefitt greater, what privilage more excellent? Every word hath his reason, every reason his benefit, which benefitt, tendeth to the comon utility and publique happiness of the whole and every part off a Citty.

The felicity and happiness off a Citty doth not consist in the riches, in the strength, in the multitude off Citizens, but in the wise and moderate government thereoff; there can be no government where there is not one to command and others to obey; one governor, not many; one maister off a ship, and not many maisters; one generall off a field, and not many; one Mayor of a Citty, and not a plurality off Mayors; lest they severally commanding breed confusion, and not government; disorder, and not order.

And so much the more greate is the excellency off this princely grant, in that we are to chuse a Mayor, not from abroade, a forrayner or stranger, ignorant off our customs, not knowing our order, or understanding our constitutions; but *de nobis ipsis*, one of ourselves, off our society and brotherhood, a natural Cittizen, naturally inclined to the publick good off his fellow Cittizens; and that this Chief Officer and Mayor is not perpetuall, but yearly to be elected. It doth bring alsoe many special commodities, the hopes of Cittizens that are cheerfully stirred up with the desire of honour to the study of virtue is continued; the custom off our predecessors, which were wont to promote divers from inferior offices to the highest dignity, is observed; and justice also herein is performed, when the chiefest office of the City is distributed not to one perpetually, but to every deserving, paynfully, and watchfully, as it is said of watchmen in warre by Virgil,

" Succedant serventque vices."

The quallities of the person are alsoe described that must be elected; he must be faythfull to your Majesty, descreet, and fitt for the government off your Highness' Citty, and subjects comitted to his rule and chardge; of which properties, as I will not speake much, yet always the care of the Electors have been as a matter most specially importing them to make their choise off such a one as hath been endued therewith, though not all alike, or after one proportion.

Fidelis, to whom the authority is comitted, whereas perfidie in any person is dangerous, and an offence capitall, much more in that person to whom authority is committed to command others.

Discretus, to discern the difference between good and bad, just and unjust, right and wrong; discretion is not onely vertue, but the moderatrix off all other vertues. *Hanc si tollas, & vitium virtus erit.*

Idoneus, fitt, able, willing, and ready to execute the office, omitting his private business, and attending his public chardge.

By this, and divers other greate liberties and priviledges granted to the Citty, we your Highness' subjects and Cittizens receave and enjoy exceeding greate and manifold benefitts; we are governed by authority drawen from your sacred scepter; we are ruled by justice proceeding from your royal seate; we enjoy our jurisdictions and priviledges derived from your imperial crowne, the onely well-spring of all authority, justice, and jurisdiction. By authority in your Majesty's name we command and are to be obeyed; by justice we punish the evil and are feared; we maynteyne the good, and are honoured. By the benefit of our priviledges we are made able to execute both authority and justice, and by them all we live in plenty, peace, and happiness; by the view of the long and present miseries off Cittizens in other Cities, in forraigne realmes not far from us, we cannot but consider our owne greate bliss and happiness; they tossed in continual troubles, we continue in restfull quietness; their goods spoyled with force, ours preserved by justice; they tasteing the calamities of warres, which are lamentable; we enjoying all blessings off peace, which are inestimable.

These incomparable benefitts, and infinite more we possesse, next after God, by no other meanes then by you our most deare and dread Sovraigne; from your most excellent Majesty we have obtayned them, of your princely goodness we enjoy them, of your abundant favour and love we continue them. With your Highness the happiness began, by you it is mayntayned, and after it we looke for no continuance; we confess with David, "Happy are the people that have God for their Lord," and Queene Elizabeth for their Soveraigne Lady.

And, most mighty Soveraigne, the last yeare being finished, and the time of the last Mayor expired, on the accustomed day, according to our ancient custome, we proceeded to a new election, and have made choise off this greate Cittizen and Alderman Mr. Cuthbert Buckle to serve your Highness as a Lord Mayor within the City of London, a man fearing God, faithful to your Majestie, loveing justice, and hateing iniquity, and one that wholly hath given himself from his private conversation to his public function. Of his moderate and discreat government, we have hitherto good experiance; and of his earnest endeavoures and zealous desire to serve your Highness in his office faithfullie, and to execute it sincerely, we have an assured hope. He hath been presented before your Highness' Officers in that behalf appointed, and hath solemnly sworne his fidelitie to your most excellent Majestie, and taken the accustomed oath for the due execution of his office; yet one thing remayneth, without which our election is unprofitable, and his authority imperfect. The Mayor elected by us is a dimme and senceless body untill he receaves light and sence, which is only to be obtayned from your sacred Majesty, being the consecrated lamp from whome all magistrates doe drawe their light, and the only suprem head from whence all motion and senses are dispersed into every member of the body of this Commonweale, from whence all sense and life doth flowe and proceede, unto every member of the incorporate body whereof your Majestie is the sole and supream head.

We therefore, for ourselves, and in the name of all other your Highness' faithfull Cittizens of London, doe with all humblenes of heart entirely beseech your most excellent Majesty to vouchsafe favourably to accept of this our election, and of your high and princely authority graciously to allow and admitt of this your Lord Mayor elected, whereby your most excellent Majesty shall not onely ratify our election, but especially the authority of the person elected, and give him life and courage bouldly to proceed, and constantly perform the duties of his office religiously towards God, faithfully towards your Majestie, and justly towards your Highness' subjects committed to his chardge. For, with your Highness most gracious acceptation and admission, himself, we present, and all other your Highness' Cittizens absent, shall render to your most excellent Majestie our most humble and hearty thanks, and doe offer our goodes, bodies, liveings, and lives, to be alwayes at your commaundment, and for your Highness' service, according to our most bounden dueties, to be reddy and willing to be imployed and commaunded.

A PLEASANT CONCEITE[1],

PENNED IN VERSE,

Collourably sette out, and humblie presented, on New-yeere's Day last, to the QUEENE'S MAJESTIE, at HAMPTON COURT[2]; anno Domini 1593-4.

To the QUEENE'S most excellent MAJESTIE.

May it please your Majestie, so long as breath is in my breast, life in the hart, and spirit in the heade, I cannot hold the hand from penning of some acceptable Device to your Majestie, not to compare (in mine own over weening) with the rare poets of our florishing age, but rather counterfeyting to sette foorth the workes of an extraordinarie Painter, that hath drawne in a Pleasant Conceite, divers flowers, fruites, and famous townes: which Pleasant Conceite I have presumed (this Newe-yeere's Day) to present to your Majestie, in signe and token that your gracious goodnesse towardes me oftentimes (and cheefely now for my pencyon) shal never goe out of my remembrance, with all dutifull services belonging to a loyall subject. So under your princely favour and protection, praying for your prosperous preservation and Royall estate, I proceede to my purposed matter.

Your Majestie's humble servaunt, THOMAS CHURCHYARD.

[1] First printed at London, by Roger Warde, dwelling in Holburne, at the signe of the Castle.

[2] "A Royal Palace, magnificently built with brick by Cardinal Wolsey, in ostentation of his wealth, where he inclosed five very ample courts; consisting of noble edifices, in very beautiful work: over the gate, in the second area, is the Queen's device, a golden rose with this motto, 'Dieu et mon Droit;' on the inward side of this gate are the effigies of the twelve Roman emperors, in plaister. The chief area is paved with square stone, in its centre is a fountain that throws up water, covered with a gilt crown, on the top of which is a statue of Justice, supported by columns of black and white marble. The chapel of this Palace is most splendid, in which the Queen's closet is quite transparent, having its windows of crystal. We were led into two chambers, called the Presence, or Chambers of Audience, which shone with tapestry of gold and silver and silk of different colours: under the canopy of state are these words, embroidered in pearl, 'Vivat Henricus Octavus.' Here is besides a small chapel, richly hung with tapestry, where the Queen performs her devotions. In her bed-chamber, the bed was covered with very costly coverlids of silk: at no great distance from this room we were shewn a bed, the tester of which was worked by Anne Bullen, and presented by her to her husband Henry VIII. All the other rooms, being very numerous, are adorned with tapestry of gold, silver, and velvet, in some of which were woven history pieces; in others, Turkish and American dresses, all

A PLEASANT CONCEITE.

The Painter thought, to please his owne delite,
    With pictures faire, as poore Pigmalion did:
But staring long, on kindly red and white,
    He found therein a secrete nature hid.
Afrayde to fall, like flie in flaming fire,
    He finely cast, cold water on desire,
So shaping grapes, and graine another while,
    At his owne workes, the Painter gan to smile.

Because with grapes, the byrds were once begield,
    And men might dote, on goodly corne and graine:
At more conceits, this merry man he smield,
    As though he had possest some Poet's veine.
As Petrarch had, who did his tryumphs make,
    In sweetest sorte, for Lady Lawrae's sake.
Thys Painter tooke, in pensell such a joy,
    As hee could make, much matter of a toy.

extremely natural. In the hall are these curiosities; a very clear looking-glass, ornamented with columns and little images of alabaster; a portrait of Edward VI. brother to Queen Elizabeth; the true portrait of Lucretia; a picture of the Battle of Pavia; the History of Christ's Passion, carved in mother of pearl; the portraits of Mary Queen of Scots, who was beheaded, and her daughter; the picture of Ferdinand Prince of Spain, and of Philip his son; that of Henry VIII., under it was placed the Bible curiously written upon parchment; an artificial sphere; several musical instruments; in the tapestry are represented negroes riding upon elephants. The bed in which Edward VI. is said to have been born, and where his mother Jane Seymour died in childbed; in one chamber are several excessively rich tapestries, which are hung up when the Queen gives audience to foreign Ambassadors; there were numbers of cushions ornamented with gold and silver; many counterpanes and coverlids of beds lined with ermine; in short, all the walls of the Palace shine with gold and silver. Here is beside a certain cabinet called Paradise, where, besides that every thing glitters so with silver, gold, and jewells, as to dazzle one's eyes, there is a musical instrument made all of glass, except the strings. Afterwards we were led into the gardens, which are most pleasant; here we saw rosemary so planted and nailed to the walls as to cover them entirely, which is a method exceeding common in England." Hentzner, in 1598.—See vol. I. pp. 75, 274.

    In this account of Hentzner, Mr. Walpole very judiciously remarks, "there are several mistakes."

A rush a reede, a feeble feather light,
   Was ground enough, for him to worke upon:
Whatever came, to mind, to view, or sight,
   Stoode for good cloth, to clap hys collours on.
But his most skill, was how to sette forth flowers,
And showe at full, trym Townes and stately Towers,
Not ev'ry Towne, he meant not now to tuch,
For that their names, cannot availe him much.

NORTH-HAMPTON first, the Painter tooke in hand,
   As cheefest work, his pensel lately drew:
Because the plot, did come from forraine land,
   In that faire forme, as doth appeare to you.
Not roughly heaw'd, as timber is in heast:
But smoothed well, and with great honor graest.
A woorthy peece, of workmanship so rare:
With golden fleece, *North-hampton* may compare.

WARWICKE he drewe, in collours sad and grave,
   In elders dayes, a noble name it bore:
It builded was, on vertues rare and brave,
   As auncient seates, and citties were of yore.
The walles were reard, on constant rock ful fast,
That durst abide, the brunt of Envies blast;
The streetes were pavde, with plainnes mixt with grace,
Where good report, fild up each empty place.

The houses hie, shone bright against the sun,
   And all the walkes, and steps were smooth and cleere:
This famous Towne, great love and laud hath wun,
   As by the brute, of world doth well appeare.
It stands and staies, on Honor's pillers large,
Sure props that can, beare up a greater charge.
When *Warwicke* thus, the Painter sette in frame,
He turnd his hand, to Townes of stranger name.

BEDFORD he made, in goodly sumptuous sort,
    With collours ritch, bedeckt and cleere set out:
Like Towne of state, as strong as warlike Fort,
    With wise advice, well fenced round about;
Not to be won, the watch and ward was such,
Ne fraude nor force, durst not attempt it much.
Bedford is blest, for from that house and soyle,
Sprunge many a branch, that never yet tooke foyle.

Olde LYNCOLNE now, that stands on mighty Mount,
    Yet lowe in earth, the first foundation lyes:
He drew for that, it was of great account,
    And lifted up, in favour to the skyes.
The best we know, did love olde *Lincolne* well,
In former age, her beautie did excell.
Of latter tyme, her credite was not small;
For some doe say, that *Lyncolne* past them all.

KYLDARE came now, to minde among the rest,
    A right fayre seate, and so sette foorth it was:
As Gods above, and Nature had her blest,
    Which seem'd to sight, as cleere as christall-glas.
From Hawthorne bough, whose blossoms bring in May,
Kyldare did come, and joyes therein this day.
Kyldare commaunds, more men than thousands do,
Yet dutie bids, it be commaunded to.

HARTFORD he call'd, unto remembraunce than,
    A Towne where Tearme, is kept as cause doth crave:
It favoured is, and likt of each good man,
    It dooth in world, itselfe so well behave.
Gallant and gay, and gladsome to the sight,
Framde from the stock, that still grows bolt upright,
Most meeke of minde, and plaine in ev'ry part,
Where dutie ought, show love and loyall hart.

A PLEASANT CONCEIT, 1593.

Nowe HUNTINGTON, was drawne in order due,
   As did become, the value of that seate:
The honour olde, the name is nothing new,
   The worth not small, the soyle and place is great.
The buildings fayre, and stately too withall,
Stand strong and sure, as doth a brasen wall.
Full glad to please, both God and man indeede,
And prest to serve, the Prince in time of neede.

WOSTER that once, like Huntington did looke,
   Stoode still farre off, as it would not be knowne:
Yet soft and fayre, in ranke her place she tooke,
   She worthy was, of right to have her owne.
In fame and praise, and worldly honour both,
In noble name, in vertue, grace, and troth.
If Painter had, not toucht this Towne no way,
God knowes thereof, what might good people say.

SOUTH-HAMPTON came, in view and judgment now,
   A Haven towne, of great esteeme and praise:
Of nature good, and well disposed throw,
   And nobly hath, bestowd both yeeres and daies.
A princely Porte, where shyp shall safely ryde,
Against all stormes, how ever turnes the tyde.
From *Mountague*, whose trueth no time might staine,
South-hampton tooke, her forme and manner plaine.

PEMBROKE a pearle, that orient is of kind,
   A *Sidney* right, shall not in silence sit:
A gemme more worth, then all the gold of Ind,
   For she enjoyes, the wise Minervae's wit,
And sets to schoole, our poets ev'ry where:
That do presume, the lawrell crowne to weare.
The Muses Nine, and all the Graces Three
In *Pembroke's* bookes, and verses shall you see.

Nowe SHREWSBRIE shal, be honourd as it ought,
　The seate deserves, a right great honour heere:
That walled Towne, is sure so finely wrought,
　It glads itselfe, and beautifies the Sheere.
Her beautie stands, on bounty many waies,
That never dyes, but gaines immortall praise.
Her honor growes on wished well-won fame:
That people sounds, of *Shrewsbrie's* noble name.

OXFORD came last, like sober Sibbill sage,
　Whose modest face, like faire Lucyna shone:
Whose stayed lookes, decors her youthfull age,
　That glisters like, the alabaster stone.
Her blotlesse life, much laude and glorie gate,
And calld her up, to be a great estate.
The diamond, dooth lose his daintie light,
And waxeth dim, when *Oxford* comes in sight.

These Townes and all, the People dwelling there,
　And all the rest, that love theyr Country well:
And all true harts, and subjects ev'ry where,
　That feare their God, and doe in England dwell,
Salute with joy, and gladnes this new yeere,
Our gracious Queene, and Soveraigne Lady deere.
All wished haps, and welcome fortunes to,
Still waites on her, as handmaides ought to doe.
With long good life, with peace and perfect rest,
And all good gifts, that ever Prince possest.

The Painter stayed so, yet rising from the floore,
To Courte then did he goe, to Presence Chamber doore:
And peeping throw the same, he saw in evening late,
Full many a noble Dame, sitte neere the cloth of state.

Where then stood five faire flowers, whose beauty bred disdaine,
Who came at certain houres, as nymphs of Dian's traine.
Those goodly Nimphes most gay, like Goddesses divine,
In darkest night or day, made all the chamber shine.

Dame kinde with collours new, gave them such lively grace,
As they had tooke theyr hue, from faire bright Phœbus' face,
If such faire flowrs quoth he, in Presence men may find,
In Privey-chamber sure, some faire sweet saints are shrind.
The Painter as he might, with that did him content,
And wondring at the sight, amazed he homeward went.
Where he is drawing still, some works of stranger kind,
If this may gaine good-will, for plaine true meaning mind.

Theyr names are heere, that honour much our state,
Who dwels in Court, or Courtiars were of late:
Who sendes to Court, theyr New-yeeres gifts to show
Our gracious Prince, the homage that they owe.

To the GENERALL READERS.

Reade with good will, and judge it as ye ought,
    And spare such speech, as favour can bestow:
So shall you find, the meaning of his thought,
    That did this work, in clowd and collours show.
    Wrest things aright, but doe no further goe.
In ballance thus, wey words with equall weight,
So wisdom's skill, shall skanne the matter streight.

The booke I calld, of late *My deere adiew*,
    Is now become, my welcome home most kinde:
For old mishaps, are heald with fortune new,
    That brings a balme, to cure a wounded mind.
    From God and Prince, I now such favour find,
That full afloate, in flood my ship it rydes,
At anchor-hold, against all checking tydes.

A PLEASANT CONCEIT, 1593.

The houre is come, the seas do swell againe,
   And weltring waves, come rowling in a pace:
The stormes are calmd, with one sweete shower of raine,
   That brought my Barke unto the Porte of Grace;
   Where clowdes did frowne, now Phœbus shewes his face.
And where warme sunne, shines throwly cleere and faire,
There no foule mists, nor fogs infect the ayre.

The Sayler stayes, at anchor in good roade,
   Till winde blowes ore, ill weather from the seas:
The Pilot wise, will not put out a broade,
   Till winde serves well, and men may sayle with ease.
   The Writer first will his owne fancie please,
Then to the rest, that will no word mistake,
He sends those scrowles that studious man did make.

The learned sort, scanne every labour well,
   But beetle-braines, cannot conceive things right:
And if good works, come where disdaine doth dwell,
   Despight in hast, blots out cleere candles light.
   I hope this Booke comes not in Envie's sight,
Whose staring lookes, may make my betters blush,
Yet all his chat, nor babble worth a rush.

If he mislike, a babe but newly borne,
   It is condemnde, for no offence at all:
Ne wit nor skill, can scape the scowling scorne,
   Of bold male boush, that like ban-dog doth ball.
   The sugar sweet, he turnes to bitter gall.
The vargis sower, hath not so sharpe a tast,
As hath his words, that spite will spend in wast.

No Writer now, dare say the Crowe is blacke,
   For cruell Kytes will crave the cause, and why?
A faire white Goose bears feathers on her backe,
   That gaggles still, much like a chattring Pye.
   The Angell bright, that Gabrill is in sky,

Shall know that Nashe I love, and will doe still,
When Gabril's words scarce winne our world's good will.

No force, my hope lyes not in hatefull men
   That cannot helpe themselves in time of neede:
So I please those that have the gyft of pen,
   Or such as can thinke well of that they reede,
   The bargaine is well made and wonne indeede.
That dogge scarce bites, that daily lowde doth barke:
Each winde beates not true archers from theyr marke.

In roving sort, my feeble shaft so flies,
   Drawne to the head, yet from my head doth goe:
I wish but that my shooting please the wise,
   That looke upon, or do a marke man knoe,
   The rest God mende, let him be friende or foe.
Thus now no more, but as I turne about,
This work I end, till greater Bookes come out.

THE HERMIT'S ORATION AT THEOBALDS, 1593-4.
Penned by Sir ROBERT CECIL[1].

MOST GRACIOUS SOVEREIGN!

I humbly beseech you not to impute this my approching soe neere to your sacred presence, so rudelie at your coming to this howse, to be a presumption of a beggar; for I hope when your Majestie shall be remembered by me, who I am, and how graciously you have heretofore on the like occasion relieved my necessity, your Majestie will be pleased to receive my thanks uppon my knees, with all humility.

I am the poor Hermit your Majestie's Beadman, who at your last coming hither[2] (where God graunt yow may come many years), uppon my compleynt,

---

[1] From MSS. Rawlinson, at Oxford, vol. 1340, No. 55, fol. 19.—The volume is styled on the back " Miscellanea Curiosa Hen. Spelman et aliorum;" and on the leaf which follows the contents is written, in a different hand, " William Howard, 1637." The contents of this volume are, 1. A Letter of Lord Digby to the King, 1626. 2. Earl of Bristol's Petition to the Lords. 3. Earl of Bristol's Petition to the Lord Keeper. 4. Letter of Sir Francis Bacon to the Judges, 1616. 5. Letter of King James to the Judges. 6. King James's Speech 1623, touching the Palatinate, &c. 7. Petition of Lord Viscount Falkland to the King. 8. King Charles's Letter to Parliament, first year of his reign. 9. Hermit's Oration to Queen Elizabeth at Theobalds (here printed). 10. Letter of Sir Robert Carr, after Earl of Somerset, to Henry Howard Earl of Northampton, 1612. 11. Babington's Letter from prison to the Queen. See this Letter in vol. II. p. 482.

[2] See before, under the year 1591, p. 76.—Hentzner, describing Theobalds very soon after this " Oration" was made by the noble owner, says, " Theobalds belongs to Lord Burleigh, the Treasurer. In the gallery was painted the genealogy of the Kings of England; from this place one goes into the garden, encompassed with water, large enough for one to have the pleasure of going in a boat, and rowing between the shrubs: here are a great variety of trees and plants, labyrinths made with a great deal of labour, a *jet d'eau*, with its bason of white marble, and columns and pyramids of wood and other materials up and down the garden. After seeing these, we were led by the gardener into the summer-house, in the lower part of which, built semi-circularly, are the twelve Roman Emperors in white marble, and a table of truck-stone; the upper part of it is set round with cisterns of lead, into which the water is conveyed through pipes, so that fish may be kept in them; and, in summer-time, they are very convenient for bathing. In another room for entertainment, very near this, and joined to it by a little bridge, was a noble table of red marble. We were not admitted to see the apartments of this Palace, there being nobody to shew it, as the family was in town attending the funeral of their Lord." He died Aug. 4, and was buried Aug. 29, 1598. The Queen held her Court here Sept. 5, 1598. In 1765 Mr. Gough made a slight sketch of the poor remains of a gallery at Theobalds, wherein was painted the ancient Pedigree of the Family almost evanescent. Perhaps it is the same above alluded to; and mistaken by Hentzner for the genealogy of the Kings of England.

by your pryncely favor, was restored to my hermitage, by an injunction, when my Founder, uppon a strange conceite, to feed his owne humour, had placed me, contrary to my profession, in his house, amongst a number of worldlings, and retyred

At the time of Mr. Gough's visit, there remained on one of the walls a considerable fragment of a Pedigree of the Cecils, painted in fresco, from which he made a slight sketch, thus decyphered:

The Pedigree sets out with saying that *Robert Sitsilt* came with Robert Fitz-Hamon to the conquest of the countrie of Gla morgan, and after wedded a lady by whom he had   and all the land in H*erefords*hire and Glo*stre*shire. He had a son called James de Sitsil *baron of Beauport in Glamorganshire, slain at the siege of Wallingford castle, 4 Stephen, at which time he* had on him *a vesture wrought with his arms as on the* tombe *of Gerald Sitsilt in Dore abbey.* He left issue *John his son and heir* and fowre daughters.

And the next compartment recites, James de Sits*elt son* of Robert de *Sitsilt, sla* yne at the C*astle of Wal* ingeford *serving* under erle for defence *of it* against kinge right of *Matilda em* presse sole *daughter* and heire *of He* nry the first.

The alliance with Heckington took place in the person of Richard Cecil, first owner of Burleigh, who died in 1552, having married Jane, daughter and heir to William Heckington, of Boune, in the county of Lincoln, Esq. Their grand-daughter Anne married Edward Earl of Oxford, and their grandson Thomas, second Lord Burleigh, married Dorothy, daughter of John Neville, Lord Latymer. The slip on each side the Cecil arms may be thus supplied, " William Cecil baronet, anno 1521, 13 Henry VIII.[*] took to his wyfe Mary daughter of Peter, and sister of John Cheke, knight; and had issue Thomas second Lord Burleigh, and first Earl of Exeter.

Under the arms of Cecil within the Garter [†] was a tablet thus inscribed,

" Robert [‡] Cecill, the eldest sonne and *heire* apparant to Sir William Cecil, lord Burghley, maryed mi sters Dorothe *Nevill,* second dau ghter *and coheir* of the fower *daughters of John Nevill, last Lord Latimer* [§].

---

[*] In the Calendar which was his, since belonging to Peter Le Neve, Norroy, 1707, he himself, in the margin, writes these remarks: " 13 Sept. 1521. 13 H. VIII. *hoc die natus sum Will's Cecill.* 6 *Maii,* 1541, *veni in commeatum apud Greys-inne.*" (Le Neve's MS Notes in Dugdale's Baronage, II. 401.) And with this our inscription perfectly agrees.

[†] These arms, supported by two lions, are probably those of Sir Thomas Cecil, Knight of the Garter 1601, created Earl of Exeter 1605; and the same may be seen on his monument in St. John Baptist's Chapel, Westminster Abbey; but were too indistinct to be better drawn.

[‡] A mis-copy for *Thomas.*   [§] See Dugdale's Baronage, I. 313.

himselfe in my poore cell, where I have ever since by your only goodnes (most peerelesse and powerful Queen) lived in all happines, spending three partes of the day in repentance, the fourth in praying for your Majestie, that as your vertues have been the World's Wonder, so your dayes may see the world's end.

And surely I am of opinion I shall not flatter myselfe, yf I thinke my prayers have not been fruitlesse (though millions have joined in the like), in that, since my restitution, not only all your actions have miraculously prospered, and all your enemies been defeated; but that which most amazeth me, to whose long experience nothing can seem strange, with theis same eyes doe I behold you the self-same Queene, in the same esteate of person, strength, and beautie, in which soe many yeares past I beheld yow, finding noe alteration but in admiration, in soe much as I am perswaded, when I looke aboute me on your trayne, that Time, which catcheth everye body, leaves only you untouched.

And now, most gratious Lady, as I have most humbly thanked yow for that which is past, soe being constraeined to trouble your Majestie with another petition, not much differing from the former, I have presumed to prepare for you an offering, only as a token of my devotion, though meter for an Hermitt to present,

---

The lower part of the Pedigree is painted over and among the doors and windows of the Gallery; and the compartment over the second door is to be read:

" Harold lord of Sudley
married Mawde daughter
of Hugh earle
of Chester, had is
sewe John baron of
Sudley."

This is an alliance unnoticed by our Historians, who say that Hugh Earl of Chester had several sons and daughters by his concubines, but only one legitimate son; so that *Mawd* was probably one of his natural daughters. This marriage is considerably prior to our Pedigrees of the Cecils, and not mentioned in them.

A woman in this plate holds the "*Genealogy* of Ethelred King of England."

Mildred, youngest daughter of James Cecil, third Earl of Salisbury, married a Corbet; but this was above a century after the date of this Pedigree.

There is a very curious picture at Earl Poulet's at Hinton St. George, representing an inside View of Theobalds, with figures of the King and Queen, and the two Earls of Pembroke and Montgomery, William and Philip, probably by Steenwyck, and the figures copied from Vandyke by Polenberg, or Van Bassan. Walpole's Anecdotes, vol. II. p. 103.

An outside view, copied by Mr. Tyson, from a piece of tapestry at Houghton, and another from Daniel King's Sheet of Views, may be seen in Mr. Gough's edition of Camden's Britannia.

as a badge of his solitarie life, than for so great a Monarch to receive; but my povertie cannot amend it.

I am (as your Majestie seeth) an old aged man, apt to be full of doubts; and experience hath taught me that many men's promises are no charters: yet it is not my Founder to be mistrusted, whose worde is a scale to others; and I heare it comonly reported he had no disposition to putt out tennants, so am I most sure he will never remove me whome your Majestie hath placed. Onlie this perplexeth my soule, and causeth cold blood in everie vayne, to see the life of my Founder so often in perill; nay, his desire as hastie as his age to inherit his tombe, being nature's tenant.

But this I heare (which is his greatest comfort, and none of your least vertues) that when his body being laden with yeares, oppressed with sicknes, having spent his strength for public service, desireth to be ridd of worldly cares, by ending his dayes; your Majestie, with a band of princelie kindness, even when he is most greviosly sicke, and lowest brought, holdes him back and ransometh him. In this my anxiety have I addressed myselfe to your sacred person, whom I beseech to consider (it is not rare) that Sonnes are not ever of their Fathers conditions; and it may be, that when my young Master shall possesse this, which now under my Founder I enjoy (whereof I hope there shall be no hast), he may be catched with such liking of my dwelling, as he will rather use it for a place of recreation than of meditation; and then of a Beadman shall I become a Pilgrime.

And therefore, seeing I heare it of all the Countrey folke I meet with, that your Majestie doth use him in your service, as in former tyme you have done his Father my Founder; and that although his expence and judgment be noe way comparable; yett, as the report goeth, he hath something in him like the Child of such a Parent.

I beseech your Majestie to take order, that heis gray haires may be assurances for my aboade, that, howsoever I live obscure, I may be quiet and secure, not to be driven to seeke my grave, which though it may be every where, yet I desire it to be here. This may be done, if you will enjoyne him for your pleasure, whose will is to him a law, not to denye me the favor formerlie procured of his Father at the motion of that Goddesse of whom he holdes himself a second creature.

And now a little further to acquainte your Majestie with my happ (though I must arme myself with patience); my Founder, to leave all free for yow and your trayne, hath comitted to my nest all his unfledged birds, being the comfort of his age, and his pretious jewells, being to some of them Grandfather, to others more, all derived from his good opinion of me. But such a wanton chardge for a poor old man, as now they heare, of the arryvall of such an admirable worke of Nature, a man must pluck their quilles, or els the will daylie fly out to see your Majestie, such is the working of the Grandfather's affection in them, and your vertue and beautie.

To this chardge I will hye me, seeing it is my destiny. And for all your Majesties favor, I can but continue my vowed prayers for you, and, in token of my poor affection, present you on my knees theis poore triffles, agreeable to my profession, by use whereof and by constant faith I live free from all temptation. The first is a bell, not bigg, but of gold; the second is a booke of good prayers, garnished with the same mettall; the third is a candle of virgin's wax, meete for a Virgin Queene. With this booke, bell, and candle, being hallowed in my cell with good prayers, I assure myself, by whomsoever they shall be kept, endued with a constant fayth, there shall never come soe much as an imagination of any spiritt to offend them: The like whereof I will still reteyne in my cell, for my daiely use, in ringing the bell, in singing of my prayers, and giving me light in the night for the increase of my devotion, whereby I may be free to my meditation and prayers for your Maiesties contynuance in your prosperity, in health and princely comfort.

Extract from Memoirs of ROBERT CARY, Earl of MONMOUTH.

I continued [absolute Warden] so about a twelvemonth, and lived at my own charge, which impaired my poor estate very much. In this time God sent me another Son, which was borne and christened at Barwick. I did often sollicite Mr. Secretary for some allowance to support me in my place, but could gett no direct answer. I sued for leave to come up myselfe, but could get none. The March was very quiet, and all things in good order, and I adventured without leave to come up.

The Queen lay at Theobalds, and early in a morning I came thither. I first went to Mr. Secretary, who was much troubled when he saw mee, and by no meanes could I gett him to lett the Queene know that I was there, but counsailed mee to retourne, that she might never know what I had done. When I could do no good with him, I went to my Brother, who then was Chamberlaine, after my Lord Cobham's death. I found him farre worse than the other; and I had no way to save myselfe from some great disgrace, but to retorne without her knowledge of my being there; for by no intreaty could I gett him to acquaint her with it. I was much troubled, and knew not well what to do. The Queene went that day to dinner to Enfield House, and had toiles set up in the parke to shoot at buckes after dinner. I durst not be seene by her, these two Counsaillers had so terrified mee. But after dinner I went to Enfield, and walking solitary in a very private place, exceeding melancholy, it pleased God to send Mr. William Killigrew, one of the Privy Chamber, to pass by where I was walking, who saluted mee very kindly, and bade mee welcome. I answered him very kindly, and he perceiving mee very sad, and something troubled, asked mee why I was so? I told him the reason. Hee made little reckoning of what they had said to mee, but bade me comfort myselfe, for hee would go presently to the Queene, and tell her of my coming up, on such a fashion, as hee did warrant me she would take it well, and bid mee welcome. Away he went, and I stayed for his retourne. Hee told the Queene, that she was more beholden to one man, than to many other that made greater shewe of their love and service. She was desireous to know who it was. Hee told her it was myselfe; who not having seene her for a twelvemonth and more, could no longer endure to be deprived of so great a happinesse; but tooke post with all speede to come up to see your Majestie, and to kisse your hand, and so to retourne instantly againe. Shee presently sent him backe for mee, and received mee with more grace and favour than ever she had done before[1]; and after I had beene with her a pretty while, she was called for to go to her sports. She arose; I tooke her by the arme, and led her to her standing. My brother and Mr. Secretary, seeing this, thought it more than a miracle. Shee continued her favour to mee the time I stayed, which was not long; for shee tooke order I should have five hundred pounds out of the Exchequer for the time I had served; and I had a patent given mee under the great seale to be her Warden of the East March. And thus was I preserved by a pretty jeast, when wise men thought I had wrought my own wracke[2]. For out of weaknesse God can shew strength, and his goodnesse was never wanting to me in any extremity. With grace and favour I retourned to my charge againe: yet before my retourne the Queene was pleased to renew my grant of Norham[3], with the life of both my Sonnes, and the longer liver of us.

[1] She had certainly a sincere regard for so useful and loyal a servant.
[2] The men here hinted at had more wisdom than sincerity.
[3] One of the Castles in Northumberland, built to defend the Marches against the invaders from Scotland. Some crown lands were granted with it.

Extracts from Sir JOHN HARRINGTON'S *Papers, called his "Breefe Notes and Remembrances."*

April 4, 1594. It was bruitede[1] at Cowrte that David Areskine, a Scotish man, had basely reviled the Queenes Majestie, by sayinge "she was cosenede by the devile, and solde her faithe for hypocrisie, in the matter of the Queene of Scotlande's death." It dothe not behoove us ordinarie mene to touche on extraordinarie affaires. "God directethe princelie counciles," saithe Sir William W——[2]; and yet, God wot, Sir William is a shallow wighte. Heav'n defende mortal man from hypocrisie!

I came home to Kelstone, and founde my Mall, my childrene, and my cattle, all well fedde, well taughte, and well belovede. 'Tis not so at Cowrte; ill breeding with ill feedinge, and no love but that of the lustie god of gallantrie, Asmodeus. I am to sende goode store of news from the countrie, for hir Highnesse entertainmente. I shall not leave behinde my neighbour *Cotton's* horn, for a plentifull horn it is. Her Highnesse loveth merrie tales. My howse at Bath I have promisede to younge Sheltone, who may do me kindnesse with his Lorde; and as for his Ladie, I will do my kindnesse as I shall liken myselfe. Must not talke more about Spanish grandeur and well shapen mustachoes.

Sunday, June 14. The Queenes Majestie tastede my wifes comfits, and did muche praise her cunninge in the makinge. Sende no more: for other Ladies' jealousie workethe againste my Mall's *comfits*, and this will not *comforte* her. I will write a damnable storie and put it in goodlie verse about Lord A.[3] he hathe done me some ill turnes. God keepe us from lyinge and slander worke.

The Queene stoode up, and bade me reache forthe my arme to reste her thereon. Oh, what sweete burden to my nexte songe! Petrarcke shall eke out good matter for this businesse.

The sweete Ladies suite to her Majestie I will forwarde. Would God I never had so manie suites of mine owne to forwarde withe Ladies as I have heretofore: *Militavi non sine gloriâ.* The Queene loveth to see me in my last frize jerkin, and saithe *'tis well enoughe cutt.* I will have another made liken to it. I do remember she spit on Sir Mathew's[4] fringed clothe, and said, *the fooles wit was*

---

[1] i. e. *reported*. So Churchill, "Let it be *bruited* all about the Town."
[2] *Wood*, a Clerk of the Council, says Mr. Malone.
[3] Qu. Admiral? probably Charles Howard, Earl of Nottingham.
[4] *Forsan* Sir Matthew Arundel?

gone to ragges. Heav'n spare me from suche jibinge. I talkede muche to the Treasurer on sundrie matters latelie, which hathe been reportede.

> Who livethe in Cowrtes, muste marke what they saie;
> Who livethe for ease had better live awaie.

In August I was much troublede at sundrie grievances from divers menne in high states; but envie dothe haunte manie, and breed jealousie. I will bid adieu to good companie, and leave sueing and seeking at Cowrte; for if I have no more friends nor better at Heaven's Cowrte than at this, I shall beginne to thinke somewhat of breefe damnation.

I have spente my time, my fortune, and almoste my honestie, to buy false hope, false friends, and shallow praise; and be it remembered, that he who castethe up this reckoning of a cowrtlie minion, will sette his summe like a foole at the ende, for not being a knave at the beginninge. Oh, that I coud boaste with chaunter David, *In te speravi, Domine*[1]!

I muste turne my poore wittes towardes my suite for my landes in the Northe. Sir Ralph H——[2] biddethe me move the Queenes Majestie in my behalfe, and that stoutlie; she lovethe plaine dealinges, and I will not lie unto her. The Earle doth tell me one waie, but I shall not abide thearby; I have seen those faile by such devices. I muste go in an earlie hour, before her Highnesse hathe speciale matters broughte up to councel on. I must go before the breakfastinge covers are placede, and stande uncovered as her Highnesse comethe forthe her chamber; then kneel and saie, "God save your Majestie, I crave youre eare at what houre it may suite for youre servante to meete your blessede countenaunce." Thus will I gaine her favoure to followe to the Auditorie.

> Truste not a friende to doe or saie
> In that yourselfe can sue or praie.

Yesterday I was neare drunkene, and to daye am neare sicke, and perchance to morrowe maye bothe sicke and sorrie; my cosin did chide me, and saide, "I bade my man lighte his taper at the moone." It maie be so, Horace saithe,

Coelum ipsum petimus stultitiá.

---

[1] See Psalm lxxi. Much in unison with the pathetic aspiration of Wolsey, at the close of his courtly career, when the tide of Royal favour was turned against him.

[2] *Forsan* Horsey?

I see some men who love gameing, some men who love wenching, some men who love wine, and some who love trencheringe[1]: These ofte finde an emptie purse, runninge reins, an acheinge heade, and grumblinge guttes. Now, what findethe he who lovethe the "pride of life," the Cowrte's vanitie, ambition's puff ball? In soothe, no more than emptie wordes, grinning scoffe, watching nightes and fawning daies. *Felix quem faciunt aliena pericula cautum.*

One Sunday (April last[2]) my Lorde[3] of London preachede to the Queenes Majestie, and seemede to touche on the vanitie of deckinge the bodie too finely. Her Majestie tolde the ladies, that "If the Bishope helde more discorse on suche matters, shee wolde fitte him for heaven, but he shoulde walke thither withoute a staffe, and leave his mantle behind him:" perchance the Bishope hathe never soughte her Highnesse wardrobe, or he woulde have chosen another texte.

I heare I ame markede out for the nexte year's Sherrife for the Countie of Somersette. I will not gibe at the Judge as my neighbour did when he was appointed to that charge, and with more wit than good heed, told the Judge, who complainde of stonie roades, and fearde muche the danger of our western travellinge; "In goode soothe, Sir, it be but faire playe, that you, who so ofte make others feare for theire neckes, shoud in some sorte beginne to thinke of savinge your owne." Herewithe Judge Minos was not well pleasede, but saide, "Goode Maister Sherife, leave alone my necke, and looke to your owne heeles, for you may one daye be laide by them." Nor did his anger here reste, for on very slighte offence in Cowrte, he fined my wittie neighboure five poundes: *felix quem faciunt aliena pericula cautum.* So shall I (when in such companie) make no accounte of my countrie wayes, but looke well to my owne.

I must not forgette to call on the Treasurer: he that dothe not love the *man* will have little favoure with the *Mistresse*, and I am in good likinge withe bothe, praised be God. My Lord of Essex is also my friende, and that not in bad sorte. He bidds me lay goode holde on her Majesties bountie, and ask freely. I will

---

[1] i. e. eating: trenchers being then used instead of plates. See "Orders for Household Servants," in the "Nugæ Antiquæ," vol. I. p. 106.

[2] Though the earliest date in these Extracts is 1594, they evidently consist of fragments written at different periods. The present article, for example, should be dated in 1591, the year in which he was nominated to the office of Sheriff, which agrees with the date in Fuller; and that he was actually Sheriff in 1592 appears by the prefix to "Orders for Household Servants," in the "Nugæ Antiquæ," vol. I. p. 105.—He died in 1612. In two of the Harleian MSS. he is described as a Justice of Peace for Somersetshire, in 1601.

[3] Dr. John Aylmer.

attende to-morrow and leave this little poesie behinde her cushion at my departing from her presence.

To the Queenes Majestie [1].

For ever dear, for ever dreaded Prince,
You read a verse of mine a little since,
And so pronounc'st each word, and every letter,
Your gratious reading grac'st my verse the better:
Sith then your Highnesse doth, by gift exceeding,
Make what you read the better for your reading;
Let my poor muse your pains thus farre importune,
Like as you read my verse, so—*read my Fortune*.

From your Highnesse saucy Godson.

Note here, how muche will a man even benefitte his enemie, provided he dothe put him out of his owne waie? My Lord of Essex did lately want Sir George Carew [2] to be Lord Lieutenante of Ireland, rather than his owne unkle, Sir William Knollys [3], because he had given him some cause of offence, and by thus thrusting him into high office, he would remove him from Cowrte [4]."

On the 4th of September 1590, the City of Bath obtained for Queen Elizabeth a Charter of Incorporation, and in 1592 her Majesty conferred an additional mark of favour on that City, by honouring it with her presence [5]. Sir John Harrington, the Godson and Favourite of Elizabeth, had received the promise of a Royal Visit at his country mansion, at Kelweston [6]; and that he might afford the Queen a proper reception there, had fitted up his house in a style of elegance and magnificence suitable to the taste of the age.—The Queen kept her word, arrived at Sir John's house in her way to Oxford, in 1592, and dined

[1] Printed in his Epigrams, lib. iv. ep. 13, and entitled, "The author to Queene Elizabeth, in praise of her reading."

[2] Lieutenant of the Ordnance.   [3] Comptroller of the Household.

[4] See a continuation of these Extracts under the year 1598.

[5] This article should have been inserted a little earlier, but I was misled by the date of the Extracts from Sir John Harrington inserted in p. 249.

[6] The old house at Kelveston, near Bath, was begun by Mr. John Harrington (of whom see vol. II. p. 261), and finished by his son (afterwards Sir John Harrington), for the reception of the Queen during a summer excursion, who had visited her Godson in her way to Oxford in 1592.

right royally under the fountain which played in the Court. Elizabeth took this opportunity of visiting the City of Bath.—The following letter without date, but published in 1596, clearly evinces she had been there some time previous to that year; and a tradition still exists, which tells us she slept at the Barton-house (an old fashioned mansion, now standing in John-street), then in the possession of Mr. Sherston, who resided there as the first Mayor of Bath:—" The Citie of Bathe, my Lord (probably Lord Burleigh), being both poore enough and proude enough, hath, since her Highnesse being there, wonderfully beautified itselfe in fine houses for victualling and lodging, but decayes as fast as their ancient and honest trades of merchandize and clothing. The fair Church her Highnesse gave orders should be re-edified, stands at a stay; and their common sewer, which before stood in an ill place, stands now in no place, for they have not any at all; which for a Towne so plentifullye served of water, in a countrey so well provided of stone, in a place resorted unto so greatly (being at two times of the yeare as it were the pilgrimage of health to all saints), methinke, seemeth an unworthie and dishonourable thing. Wherefore, if your Lordship would authorise me, or some wiser than me, to take a strict account of the money, by her Majesty's gracious graunt gathered and to be gathered, which, in the opinion of manie, cannot be lesse than ten thousand pounds (though not to wrong them, I thinke they have bestowed upon the point of ten thousand pounds, abating but one cipher) I would not doubt of a ruinate Church to make a reverent Church, and of an unsavorie Town a most sweet Town. This I do the rather write, because your Lordship, and the rest of her Majestie's Most Honorable Counsel, thought me once worthie to be the Steward of that Towne, but that the wiser Counsel of the Towne thought it not meet, out of a deeper reach, lest being already their poore neighbour, this increase might have made my estate too great among them. For indeed the fee belonging to it, and some other commodities annexed, might have been worth to me, *de claro viis & modis, per annum* ccclxxxd. Moreover I am to certify your Lordship, that the spring taken out of the hote bath into the private doth not annoy or prejudice the vertue of the hote bath, as her Majesty hath been lately enformed. And it is not unnecessarie, for some honorable persons that come hither, sometimes to have such a private bath [1] "

[1] Warner's History of Bath, p. 187.

Anno 36° *Reginæ* ELIZABETHÆ, 1594.

Receyved into the office from Mr. William Kyllegrewe, the 12th of August.

One cup of golde, with a cover, having a dove in the toppe thereof, garnished in thone side therof with six sparcks of diamonds, 32 oz. q^a.

Item, one cup of assaye of golde, 5 oz. 3 q^a.

Item, fower trencher plates of golde, 39 oz. dim̃. q^a.

Item, one tankarde of bodde called tamaric, slightely garnished on the foote, lyppe, and cover with silver white, covered with lether; garnished with sundrye counterfett stones, having a frogge in the lydde, and snakes about the bodye. Geven by Mr. *Coxe*.

(Signed)   W. BURGHLEY.
             W. MILDMAY.
             N. BRISTOW.
             EDWA. CARYE.

Remembrance for Furnyture at KEW [*the residence of Sir* JOHN PUCKERING[1], *Lord Keeper of the Great Seal*], *and for her Majestie's Entertainment,* 14 *August,* 1594[2].

A Memorial of things to be considered of, if her Majestie should come to my Lord's house:

1. The manner of receyvinge bothe without the house and within, as well by my Lord as by my Ladye.

2. What present shall be given by my Lord, when and by whom it shall be be presented, and whether any more than one.

3. The like for my Ladye.

4. What presents my Lord shall bestowe on the Ladies of the Privy-chamber

---

[1] Sir John Puckering was appointed Lord Keeper May 28, 1592; and held that high office till May 1596. If this Visit took place, her Majesty was probably well pleased with her entertainment; for it appears by a passage in a letter from Rowland White to Sir Robert Sydney, Dec. 15, 1595, "that she honoured him with one in the ensuing year;" and that she received some handsome presents. See hereafter, under 1595.

We learn from Mr. Norden, that Russel House, near Ivy-bridge, situate upon the banks of the Thames, was the Town residence of the Right Hon. Sir John Puckering, Knight, Lord Keeper of the Privy Seal; and that the house of Lord William Haward, and Rutland House were also near Ivy-bridge.

[2] Harl. MSS. 6850. 90.

or Bed-chamber, the Groomes of the Privye-chamber, and Gentlemen Ushers and other officers, Clerks of the Kitchen, or otherwise.

5. What rewards shall be given to the Footemen, Gardes, and other officers.

6. The purveyed diet for the Queen, wherein are to be used her own cooks, and other officers for that purpose.

7. The diet for the Lords and Ladies, and some fit place for that purpose specially appointed.

8. The allowance for diet for the Footmen and Gardes.

9. The appoyntment of my Lord's officers, to attend in their several offices, with sufficient assistance unto them for that time.

10. The orderinge of all my Lord's servants for their waiting, both gentlemen and yeomen; and how they shall be sorted to their several offices and places.

11. The proporcyon of the diett, fitted to eche place of service; plate, linen, and silver vessels.

12. To furnish how there will be upon a soddeyne provision of all things for that diett made, and of the best kinds, and what several persons shall undertake it.

13. As it must be for metes, so in like sorte for bredd, ale, and wynes of all sortes.

14. The like for banquettynge stuffe.

15. The swetnynge of the howse in all places by any means.

16. Greate care to be had, and conference with the Gentlemen Ushers, how her Majestie would be lodged for her best ease and likinge, far from heate or noyse of any office near her lodging, and how her bed-chamber maye be kept free from anye noyse near it.

17. My Lord's attendance at her departure from his howse and her companye.

Ladie's diet for bed-chamber.

Ladies some lodged besydes ordinarie.

Lord Chamberlayne in the howse.

Lord of Essex nere; and all his plate from me, and dyett for his servants at his lodgyngs [1].

On the 4th of October the carts from Chalk were employed in removing the Queen's Majesty from Greenwich to Nonsuch; and again on the 17th of December from Somerset-house to Greenwich. (See before, p. 38.)

The RECORDER of LONDON's[1] SPEECH, on presenting the Lord Mayor, Sir JOHN SPENCER, to the Lord Chief Baron[2] and his Brethren of the Exchequer, 1594[3].

It is full three years past, my good Lord, that by occasion of God's punishment[4], the Cittizens of London have been constrayned to forbear their comeing to this honourable place, to accomplish their duety they owe to your Lordship and this honourable Court. As their absence by all this time hath beene grievous unto them, so are they this day come out of their Citty with joy and gladness, to give testimony to all people howe thankfull they are to God for His great mercyes, in that it hath pleased Him for His owne mercie's sake to withdraw His punishment from them, to restore them to the free use of their ancient solemnities, and once again to present themselves in this high court and judgment seate, even in the peaceable dayes of our most dread Sovraigne, the continuance of whose dayes is the continuance of our blessings: longe may they continue, and accursed be all those that seek to shorten them.

Besides all those generall blessings and benefitts over this whole realme, whereof we with others, and they with us, are partakers, to the great comfort and profitt of us all, we the Cittizens of London, seperatlie by ourselves, for many excellent and princely grants, liberties, and priviledges, are most specially bound to yeald openly, and in all places, our open and public thanks, as the testamony of our faithfull and thankfull heartes to her most excellent Majestie for the same. And by the present occasion I am enforced, amongest many others, to rehearse one onely priviledge, by the excellency whereof the greatnesse of the residue may be conceaved.

[1] Thomas Flemynge, Esq. succeeded Serjeant Drew as Recorder in 1594; and was in the same year made a Serjeant, but was degraded in 1595. Sir John Crooke succeeded him as Recorder.

[2] Sir William Peryam.   [3] From the Harleian MSS. No. 852, p. 3.

[4] "This year [1592] no Bartholomew fair was kept at London, for the avoiding of concourse of people, whereby the infection of the Plague might have increased, which was then very hot in that City, so that on the 23d of October, deceased Sir William Rowe, then Lord Mayor; the 1st of November, Wm. Elken, Alderman; the 5th of December, Sir Rowland Hayward, Alderman; and the 9th of January, Sir Wolstone Dixie, Alderman. The whole number deceasing this year in the City and suburbs adjoining, from the 29th of December, in the year 1592, until the 20th of December, 1593, was, within the walls, of all diseases, 8,598, where, of the Plague was 5,390; without the walls, and in the liberties, 9,295, of the plague 5,385; so that within the City and liberties, of all diseases, died 17,893, where, of the plague was 10,675." Stow's Chronicle, p. 766.

It is well known to your Lordship, that by the ancient Charters made by her Highness' most noble Progenitors, and by her most Royal Confirmation ratified and allowed, and in this honorable Court recorded, the Cittizens of London have power and authority to elect and choose of themselves every year, a Mayor thus qualified. "Qui nobis sit fidelis, discretus, & idoneus ad regimen civitatis predictæ."

The value of this grant is more estimable, the benefitt more greate then I can express: by it we are continued in unity and mutual society; without it our society would be easily broken, our unitie infringed, and the Citty speedily ruinated.

The happiness, the continuance, and felicity of this City, doth not consist in our enclosed walls, fayre houses, great traffick, rich marchandize, or in multitude of Cittizens which are greate, but in the wise and moderate government thereof.

A Citty is a society of men congregated into one place, not only by mutual helps to live together, but to live well and godlie together; but can they live well without order and government? and what order or government can there be where there is not one to commaund, others to obey, one to rule, and others that submit themselves?

When onely two persons were created on the face of the earth, and they bound by the surest bonds that can be, when they were but one flesh, yet was the husband made the head, to commaund; and the wife the inferior, to obey. Families would not continue unless the parents did rule the children, the maisters the servants; the shippe would make shippwreck without a governor; the army would scatter without a commaunder; and the Citty woulde perrishe without a Magistrate. "Ubi non est gubernatio corruet populus."

If a City cannot stand without a Magistrate, then is that graunt of greate price that authorizeth the free election of a Magistrate.

And soe much the more excellent is the benefitt of this priviledge unto us, in that this Chief Magistrate is not to be emposed upon us, or set over us without our consent and choise, but to be elected by ourselves, to be chosen not from amongest forrayners or strangers, but *de nobis ipsis*, a member of our body, a brother of our brotherhood, a Fellow Cittizen of the same society, whereof himself shall be the chiefest. What grant can be more grateful, or what princely gift more bounteous unto subjects, then for the inferiour to chuse his superior; the members their owne head; the Cittizens their owne Magistrate?

That this Chief Officer is not to remayne, but every *year* to be newly chosen, it hath his due consideration:

To the Magistrate; it putteth him in minde that he is to rule Men, and his Fellow Citizens; to rule them not after his will, but according to the laws; to rule, not alwaise, but for a time, and for no longer tyme then only one yeare; then to lay downe his office, not the richer that he had it, but the more honourable for his well usinge it; and to become a Member, and noe Head, as ready to obey as he was willing to commaund.

To the well-disposed Cittizens; to stirr them up to ascend the same degrees that hath advanced others to that honourable dignity, when they see the self-same way for them as it was for others to attayne to the same, which is from vertue to vertue, from service to service, from one office to another, until they come to the highest office, which is the chiefest honour they Cittizens do bestowe, not upon him that will desire it, but by his vertues shall deserve it. Honour is the reward of vertue.

It is required by the tenour of our charters, that the person to be elected Mayor must be *fidelis, discretus, & idoneus*; all which are so necessary properties to be in every Magistrate, that if he want any of them, he may sitt in the highest roomes of honour, but honourably he cannot govern; faythfull to the Queen's Majestie in well keeping that which is committed to his charge, in well governing it while he hath his charge, in yeelding a faithfull accompt when he shall lay downe his charge.

He that taketh upon him the office of a Magistrate is like to a good man, to whose custody a precious jewell is committed; he taketh it not to retayne and challendge it for his own; nor to abuse it while he hath it; but safely to keep, and faythfully to render it to him that deposed it when he shall be required. He must doe all things, not for his private lucar, but for the publick's good preservation, and safe custody of those committed to his chardge, that he may restore them to him that creditted in a better and more happy state, it may be, then he received them.

A Magistrate must remember, that so much is committed to him by his Prince as is committed and credited; not that power and authority is onely given to doe what he will, but fayth and trust is alsoe reposed to doe what he ought. "Deligimus magistratus quasi reipublicæ villicos," sayth Cicero; if they be Bayliffes, then is there required, not only diligence, labour, care, and vigillancy, but alsoe truth and fayth, that they may alwaies be ready when they shall heare it sayd, *Redde rationem villicationis tuæ;* to appeare profitable and faythfull, that it may be said, unto him, " Come, thou faythfull servant, because thou hast been faythfull over one Citty, I will make thee ruler over many :" faythfulness in a Magistrate is required, commaunded, and rewarded; perfidie is hated, condemned, and severely punished.

He must be discreet; discretion is not soe much a vertue as it is a moderatrix and governess of all vertues, the order of affections, and the mistress of good manners, *Hanc si tollas,* saith Barnard, *& virtus vitium erit.*

What good thing is done with discretion, that is a virtue; what without, is a vice.

Undescreet vertue is reputed for a vice. If in all actions, with all men, discretion ought to bear the chiefe place, to discerne of tyme, place, person, matter, and circumstances; much more in a Magistrate, whose office is to discerne between good and evil, right and wronge, truth and falshood, the just from the unjust, the good from the bad, the qualities of the person, and the moment of the matters, that discerning he may judge rightly, and judging rightly, he may not feare to put it in execution effectually.

It is necessary therefore that a Magistrate be illuminated with the light of discretion, that he doe nothing more, nothing lesse, nothing otherwise, than that religion, justice, and equity commandeth.

He that will be fitt to govern others, must first learne to governe himself.

A Magistrate is like the heart in the body; if it be sound and pure, it giveth life to the whole body; but being corrupted, it bringeth death and destruction to all the members: soe fareth it with the Magistrate, if he live under right reason, truth, and justice, the people under him will doe the same.

As a rule or square, if it be streight and right of itself, it will rightly direct all things by it; for a Ruler, when he first hath learned to rule himself, his mind well inclined, and his behaviour well composed, he shall the better govern those that be under him.

The wise man sayth, in Ecclesiastes, cap. x.

" Qualis est Rector Civitatis, tales inhabitantes in ea."

He then that will benefitt must be voyde of all affections; for anger will not suffer a wise man to discerne rightly, hatred urgeth hard things, love hindreth judgment, will worketh violence, enmities provoke revenge, envy dealeth rashly, coveteousness quencheth zeale, and rewards pervert justice; and instead of these affections he must adorne himself with vertues meete for his place and office; as first and chiefest, feare of God; the feare of God is the begining of wisdom.

And wisdom teacheth the Magistrate that he is the Minister of God's justice, and therefore ought to conforme himself to all integrity, prudence, moderation, and innocency; and not to suffer iniquity to have enterance into his seate, neither any unjust sentence to proceed out of his mouth, nor any evil action to be done by himself, or by his commaundment.

As he must fear God, soe must he not fear the face of man; he must be of courage to beate downe vice, and to execute judgment; he must not beare the sworde in vaine, but punish the evil-doers, and protect the innocent; although he endure hard speeches, much envy, sharpe storms, and many conflicts with many audacious and wicked men, sometymes with mighty persons, yet for the good of the commonwealth he must not feare to doe justice.

Severity is more expedient to repayer a declyning estate than lenity: by severity none is offended; but he that is punished by lenity, the Prince, the Lawe, and the People, are offended; for the Prince is contemned, the Law is despised, and the People are infected by severity; with justice the Prince is honoured, the Lawe observed, and the People preserved.

Justice in a Magistrate is the peace of the People, the safety of the Citty, the security of the multitude, the cure of the diseased, the solace of the poore, the inheritance of the subject, the joy of all men, and unto Magistrates themselves an assured hope of future blessedness.

He must be patient of labour, and refuse no paynes to serve the commonwealth; *omnis honos est onus*, and no honour without labour; it is an unworthy thing to seek honour of his office, and to refuse the labour belonging to it.

Many are the vertues and properties in a Magistrate to make him *idoneus*; labour in business, diligence in dooinge, celerity in performing, counsell in foreseeing, wisdom in preventing, fortitude in dangers, courage in execution, love towards the good, hate towards the evill, justice to every one, and many more which I cannot number, much lesse particularly reherse them: I intend not to instruct the Magistrate what he should be, but, by way of remembrance, to admonish what he ought to be, not to prescribe him what he should doe, but intreate him to doe that he ought to perform.

" Onus virtutis laus in actione."

And haveing made an insufficient rehearsall of her Majestie's benefitts, farre lesse then the excellency of them doeth require, and given publique testimony to all this Assembly of our thankfullness to her most excellent Majestie for the same; it is of duety that I descend to declare to your Lordshippe howe we have proceeded in our election, of the person we have elected, and notify unto your Lordship that he is such a one as by the characters we ought to choose.

Our election was on the usual day, at the place accustomed in the Guildhall of London, where were assembled a greater concourse of Free Cittizens than in many times, who in a most orderly and peaceable maner proceeded in their election; and by their suffrages, with one mutuall consent and one voice, not one dissenting, was chosen this auncient and grave Cittizen, Mr. John Spencer, Alderman, to susteyne the office of Mayoraltie of the Citty of London for this year ensueing; of whome if I should speake too much, it would not be seemely; if too little, I should injure the person; if but the truthe, I hope it will be admitted, and our election justified.

Chilo sayd it was a good Commonwealth where the people harkened more to Lawiers then to Orators; the one handleth things in their substance as they are, the other makes them to showe greater then they bee.

According to my profession, I affirme, my Lorde, for trewe, that he feareth God, and is religious: he is faythfull to her Majestie in hearte and deede for his discretion and moderation; even in government we have had trial and experiance in all other offices and places of government within the Citty, all which he hath borne and past over to his praise and commendations, and we have found him meete to occupy the highest place of honour and government that the Cittizens may exalt him unto by their election, as a reward for his good deserts in publicke service for the Citty; and greater honour they cannot doe to him whome they esteeme and love.

His former acts in other offices, as they are good testimonies of his sufficiency, soe they doe give assured hopes of his future proceedinge in the Mayoraltie to be no lesse honourable then the rest have beene acceptable; and his grave and good purposes which he intendeth to put in use, doe alsoe add certaine assurance to our conceaved hopes; for he gravely considereth that he is to take uppon him the person of a Publick Magistrate, to make an honourable conversion from his former conversation, to seeke the profitt of the Commonwealth with noe less carefullness then he hath done his owne, to lay downe his private affections that may be impedyments, and take unto him for his Counsellors, Religion, Faith, Lawe, Equity, and Justice. All which intentions, as he hath perposed them, soe will he perform them; as his actions shall deserve, soe shall he obtayne either good or evil memory and fame.

Therefore, we haveing triall of his wisdome, and such hopes of his good endeavours, are bound to present him to your Lordshippe, as a man very meete and sufficient to be our Mayor; and doe humbly pray your Lordshippe to give allowance to our election, and to admitt and record him the Mayor of the City of London for this year ensueing, and to minister unto him, as a surer bond for the due execution of this office, the oath accostemed in this behalf, that he may be by your Lordshippe's admission the better encouraged by his oath, the more devoted to the due execution of his office towards God, the Queene, and the Commonwealth, to his own honour, and to the profitt of the aunciant, honourable, and famous City of London.

In October 1594, the Queen wrote the following Letter to Peregrine Bertie, Lord Willoughby [1]:

"GOOD PEREGRINE, We are not a little glad that by your journey you have received such good fruit of amendment; specially when we consider how great vexation it is to a minde devoted to actions of honour, to be restrained by any

[1] Son of Richard Bertie and Katharine Dutchess of Suffolk. Dr. Fuller, from whose "Worthies" this letter is transcribed, thus introduces it: "Reader, I crave a dispensation, that I may, with thy good leave, trespass on the premised laws of this book. His name speaking his foreign nativity, born nigh Hidleberg in the Palatinate. Indeed I am loath to omit so worthy a person. Our histories fully report his valiant atchievements in France and the Netherlands, and how at last he was made Governour of Berwick. He could not brook the obsequiousness and assiduity of the Court; and was wont to say that he was none of the *Reptilia* which could creep on the ground. The camp was his proper element; being a great souldier, and having a suitable magnanimity.

"When one sent him an insulting challenge whilst he lay sick of the gout, he returned this answer, 'that although he was lame of his hands and feet, yet he would meet him with a piece of a rapier in his teeth.'

"Once he took a gennet, managed for the war, which was intended for a present to the King of Spain; and was desired by a trumpeter from the General to restore it, offering this Lord £1000 down for him, or £100 *per annum* during his life, at his own choise. This Lord returned, 'that if it had been any Commander, he freely would have sent him back; but, being but an horse, he loved him as well as the King of Spain himself, and would keep him.' Here I will insert a Letter of Queen Elizabeth, written to him with her own hand: and, reader, deale in matters of this nature, as when indisposition of body, from the following those courses, which, to your own reputation and our great satisfaction you have formerly performed. And, therefore, as we must now (out of our desire of your well doing) cheifly enjoyne you to an especial care to encrease and continue your health, which must give life to all your best endeavours: so we must next as seriously recommend to you this consideration; that in these times, when there is such appearance that we shall have the triall of our best & noble subjects, you seem not to affect the satisfaction of your own private contentation, beyond the attending on that which nature & duty challengeth from all persons of your quality & profession. For if necessarily (your health of body being recovered) you should *elloigne* yourself by residence there from those imployments, whereof we shall have too good store; you shall not so much amend the state of your body, as happily you shall call in question the reputation of your mind & judgment, even in the opinion of those that love you, and are best acquainted with your disposition & discretion.

"Interpret this our plaineness, we pray you, to our extraordinary estimation of you, for it is not common with us to deal so freely with many; and believe that you shall ever find us both ready & willing in all occasions to yield you the fruits of that interest, which your endeavours have purchased for you in our opinion and estimation. Not doubting but when you have with moderation made tryal of the success of these your sundrie *peregrinations*, you will find as great comfort to spend your dayes at home, as heretofore you have done; of which we do wish you full measure, however you shall have cause of abode or return. Given under our signet, at the Mannor of Nonesuch, the seventh of October 1594, in the 37th year of our Reigne.

    Your most loving Soveraign,   E. R."

venison is set before thee, eat the one, and read the other, never asking whence either came, though I profess, I came honestly by a copy thereof, from the original.

" It appears by the premises, that it was written to this Lord when he was at the Spaw in Lukeland for the recovery of his health, when a second English invasion of the Spaniard was (I will not say feared but) expected. Now though this Lord was born beyond the seas accidentally (his parents flying persecution in the reign of Queen Mary), yet must be reputed this country man, where his Ancestors had flourished so many years, and where he was Baron Willoughby in right of his Mother. He died, anno Domini 1601; and lyes buryed under a stately monument at Eresby in this county (Lincolnshire)."

GESTA GRAYORUM;

OR,

THE HISTORY OF THE HIGH AND MIGHTY PRINCE HENRY,

Prince of PURPOOLE, Arch Duke of STAPULIA and BERNARDIA, Duke of HIGH and NETHER HOLBORN, Marquis of ST. GILES and TOTTENHAM, Count Palatine of BLOOMSBURY and CLERKENWELL, Great Lord of the Cantons of ISLINGTON, KENTISH TOWN, PADDINGTON, and KNIGHTS-BRIDGE, Knight of the Most Heroical Order of the HELMET, and Sovereign of the same: who reigned and died A. D. 1594.—Together with a Masque, as it was presented (by his Highness's command) for the Entertainment of Q. ELIZABETH, who, with the Nobles of both Courts, was present thereat. In two Parts [1].

The great number of gallant Gentlemen that Gray's Inn afforded at Ordinary Revels, betwixt All-Hollantide and Christmas, exceeding therein the rest of the Houses of Court, gave occasion to some well-wishers of our sports, and favourers of our credit, to wish an head answerable to so noble a body, and a leader to so gallant a company: which motion was more willingly hearkened unto, in regard that such pass-times had been intermitted by the space of three or four years, by reason of sickness and discontinuances.

After many consultations had hereupon by the youths and others that were most forward herein, at length, about the 12th of December, with the consent and assistance of the Readers and Ancients, it was determined, that there should be elected a Prince of Purpoole, to govern our state for the time; which was intended to be for the credit of Gray's Inn, and rather to be performed by witty inventions than chargeable expences.

Whereupon, they presently made choice of one Mr. Henry Holmes, a Norfolk gentleman, who was thought to be accomplished with all good parts, fit for so

[1] The First Part of this tract was printed in 1688, for W. Canning, at his shop in the Temple Cloysters. The publisher was Mr. Henry Keepe, who published the Monuments of Westminster. The Second Part was first published in the former Edition of these Progresses from a MS. then in the Editor's possession, and afterwards given to Mr. Gough.

great a dignity; and was also a very proper man of personage, and very active in dancing and revelling.

Then was his Privy Council assigned him, to advise of state-matters, and the government of his dominions: his lodging also was provided according to state; as the Presence Chamber, and the Council Chamber. Also all Officers of State, of the Law, and of the Household. There were also appointed Gentlemen Pensioners to attend on his person, and a guard, with their Captain, for his defence.

The next thing thought upon, as most necessary, was, provision of Treasure, for the support of his state and dignity. To this purpose, there was granted a benevolence by those that were then in his Court abiding; and for those that were not in the House, there were letters directed to them, in nature of Privy Seals, to enjoin them, not only to be present, and give their attendance at his Court; but also, that they should contribute to the defraying of so great a charge, as was guessed to be requisite for the performance of so great intendments.

The Form of the Privy Seals directed to the foreigners, upon occasion as is aforesaid:

"Your friends of the Society of Gray's Inn now residing there, have thought good to elect a Prince, to govern the state of the Signiory, now by discontinuance much impaired in the ancient honour wherein heretofore it hath excelled all other of like dignity. These are therefore, in the name of the said Prince, to require you forthwith to resort to the Court there holden, to assist the proceedings with your person; and withal, upon the receipt hereof, to make contribution of such benevolence as may express your good affection to the State, and be answerable to your quality. We have appointed our well-beloved Edward Jones our foreign collector, who shall attend you by himself, or by his deputy.

"Dated at our Court at Graya,   Your loving friend,
 the 13th of December, 1594.   GRAY'S-INN."

If, upon the receipt of these letters, they returned answer again, that they would be present in person at our sports, as divers did, not taking notice of the further meaning therein expressed, they were served with an *alias*, as followeth:

"To our trusty and well-beloved W. B. at L. give these.

"Whereas, upon our former letters to you, which required your personal appearance and contribution, you have returned us answer that you will be present, without satisfying the residue of the contents for the benevolence: these are therefore to will and require you, forthwith, upon the receipt hereof, to send for your part, such supply by this bearer, as to you, for the defraying so great a charge, shall seem convenient: and herein you shall perform a duty to the House, and avoid that ill opinion which some ungentlemanly spirits have purchased by their uncivil answers to our letters directed to them, whose demeanor shall be laid to their charge when time serveth; and in the mean time, order shall be taken, that their names and defaults shall be proclaimed in our publick assemblies, to their great discredit, &c.   Your loving friend,   GRAY's-INN."

By this means the Prince's treasure was well increased; as also by the great bounty of divers honourable favourers of our state, that imparted their liberality, to the setting forward of our intended pass-times. Amongst the rest, the Right Honourable Sir William Cecill, Knight, Lord Treasurer of England, being of our Society, deserved honourable remembrance, for his liberal and noble mindfulness of us, and our State; who, undesired, sent to the Prince, as a token of his Lordship's favour, £10, and a purse of fine rich needle-work.

When all these things sorted so well to our desires, and that there was good hope of effecting that that was taken in hand, there was dispatched from our State a messenger to our ancient allied friend the Inner Temple, that they might be acquainted with our proceedings, and also to be invited to participate of our honour; which to them was most acceptable, as by the process of their letters and ours, mutually sent, may appear.

The Copies of the Letters that passed betwixt the two most flourishing Estates of the *Grayans* and *Templarians*.

" To the most Honourable and Prudent, the Governors, Assistants, and Society of the *Inner Temple*.

" Most Grave and Noble,

" We have, upon good consideration, made choice of a Prince, to be predominant in our State of *Purpoole*, for some important causes that require an head, or leader: and as we have ever had great cause, by the warrant of experience, to assure ourselves of your unfeigned love and amity, so we are, upon this occasion, and in the name of our Prince elect, to pray you, that it may continued; and in demonstration thereof, that you will be pleased to assist us with your counsel, in the person of an Ambassador, that may be resident here amongst us, and be a minister of correspondence between us, and to advise of such affairs, as the effects whereof, we hope, shall sort to the benefit of both our estates. And so, being ready to requite you with all good offices, we leave you to the protection of the Almighty. Your most loving friend and ally, GRAY's-INN."

"Dated at our Court of Graya, this 14th of December, 1594.

"To the most Honourable State of the *Grayans*.

"Right Honourable, and most firmly United,

"If our deserts were any way answerable to the great expectation of your good proceedings, we might with more boldness accomplish the request of your kind letters, whereby it pleaseth you to interest us in the honour of your actions; which we cannot but acknowledge for a great courtesie and kindness (a thing proper to you, in all your courses and endeavours), and repute it a great honour intended towards ourselves: in respect whereof we yield with all good will, to that which your honourable letters import; as your kindness, and the bond of our ancient amity and league, requireth and deserveth. Your assured friend,

"From *Templaria*, the 18th of December, 1594. *The State of Templaria.*"

The Order of the Prince of *Purpoole's* Proceedings, with his Officers and Attendants, at his honourable Inthronization; which was likewise observed in all his Solemn Marches on Grand Days, and like occasions; which place every Officer did duly attend, during the Reign of His Highness's Government.

A Marshal.   A Marshal.
Trumpets.   Trumpets.
Pursuevant at Arms, *Lanye*.
Townsmen in the Prince's Livery, with halberts.   Yeomen of the Guard, three couples.
Captain of the Guard, *Grimes*.
Baron of the Grand Port, *Dudley*.   Baron of the Petty Port, *Williams*.
Baron of the Base Port, *Grante*.   Baron of the New Port, *Lovel*.
Gentlemen for Entertainment, three couples, *Binge*, &c.   Gentlemen for Entertainment, three couples, *Wentworth, Zukendeu, Forrest*.
Lieutenant of the Pensioners, *Tonstal*.

Gentlemen Pensioners, twelve couples, *viz.*

Lawson.	Rotts.	Davison,
Devereux.	Anderson.	
Stapleton.	Glascott.	*cum reliquis.*
Daniel.	Elken.	

Chief Ranger, and Master of the Game, *Forrest.*

Master of the Revels, *Lambert.*
Master of the Revellers, *Tevery.*
Captain of the Pensioners, *Cooke.*
Sewer, *Archer.*
Carver, *Moseley.*
Another Sewer, *Drewry.*
Cup-bearer, *Painter.*
Groom Porter, *Bennet.*
Sheriff, *Leach.*
Clerk of the Council, *Jones.*
Clerk of the Parliament.
Clerk of the Crown, *Downes.*
Orator, *Heke.*
Recorder, *Starkey.*
Solicitor, *Dunne.*
Serjeant, *Goldsmith.*
Speaker of the Parliament, *Bellen.*
Commissary, *Greenwood.*
Attorney, *Holt.*
Serjeant, *Hitchcombe.*
Master of the Requests, *Faldo.*
Chancellor of the Exchequer, *Kitts.*
Master of the Wards and Idiots, *Ellis.*
Reader, *Cobb.*
Lord Chief Baron of the Exchequer, *Briggs.*
Master of the Rolls, *Hetlen.*
Lord Chief Baron of the Common Pleas, *Damporte.*
Lord Chief Justice of the Prince's Bench, *Crew.*
Master of the Ordnance, *Fitz-Williams.*
Lieutenant of the Tower, *Lloyd.*
Master of the Jewel-house, *Darlen.*
Treasurer of the Household, *Smith.*
Knight Marshal, *Bell.*
Master of the Wardrobe, *Conney.*
Comptroller of the Household, *Bouthe.*
Bishop of St. Giles in the Fields, *Dandye.*
Steward of the Household, *Smith.*
Lord Warden of the Four Ports, *Damporte.*
Secretary of State, *Jones.*
Lord Admiral, *Cecill (Richard).*
Lord Treasurer, *Morrey.*
Lord Great Chamberlain, *Southworth.*
Lord High Constable.
Lord Marshal, *Knaplock.*
Lord Privy Seal, *Lamphew.*
Lord Chamberlain of the Household, *Markham.*
Lord High Steward, *Kempe.*
Lord Chancellor, *Johnson.*
Archbishop of St. Andrew's in Holborn, *Bush.*
Serjeant at Arms with the Mace, *Flemming.*
Gentleman Usher, *Chevett.*

The shield of Pegasus, for the Inner Temple, *Scevington.*
Serjeant at Arms with the Sword, *Glascott.*
Gentleman Usher, *Paylor.*
The Shield of the Griffin, for Gray's-Inn, *Wickliffe.*
The King at Arms, *Perkinson.*
The Great Shield of the Prince's Arms, *Cobley.*

The Prince of Purpoole, *Helmes.*
A Page of Honour, *Wannforde.*
Gentlemen of the Privy Chamber, six couples.
A Page of Honour, *Butler (Roger).*
Vice-Chamberlain, *Butler (Thomas).*
Master of the Horse, *Fitz-Hugh.*
Yeomen of the Guards, three couples.
Townsmen in Liveries.

The Family and Followers.

Upon the 20th day of December, being St. Thomas's Eve, the Prince, with all his train in order, as above set down, marched from his lodging to the Great Hall: and there took his place in his throne, under a rich cloth of state: his Counsellors and great Lords were placed about him, and before him; below the halfe pace, at a table, sate his learned Council and Lawyers; the rest of the officers and attendants took their proper place, as belonged to their condition.

Then the Trumpets were commanded to sound thrice; which being done, the King at Arms, in his rich surcoat of arms, stood forth before the Prince, and proclaimed his style, as followeth:

"By the sacred laws of arms, and authorized ceremonies of the same (maugre the conceit of any malecontent) I do pronounce my Sovereign Liege Lord, Sir Henry, rightfully to be the high and mighty Prince of *Purpoole*, Archduke of *Stapulia* and *Bernardia*, Duke of the *High and Nether Holborn*, Marquis of *St. Giles's* and *Tottenham*, Count Palatine of *Bloomsbury* and *Clerkenwell*, Great Lord of the Cantons of *Islington*, &c. Knight of the most honourable Order of the *Helmet*, and Sovereign of the same."

After that the King at Arms had thus proclaimed his style, the trumpets sounded again; and then entred the Prince's Champion, all in compleat armour, on horseback, and so came riding round about the fire; and in the midst of the hall stayed, and made his challenge, in these words following:

" If there be any man, of high degree or low, that will say that my Sovereign is not rightly Prince of *Purpoole*, as by his King at Arms right-now hath been proclaimed, I am ready here to maintain, that he lieth as a false traitor; and I do challenge in combat, to fight with him, either now, or at any time or place appointed: and in token hereof I gage my gauntlet, as the Prince's true Knight, and his Champion."

When the Champion had thus made his challenge, he departed. Then the trumpets were commanded to sound, and the King at Arms blazoned the Prince his Highness's arms, as followeth:

" The most mighty Prince of *Purpoole*, &c. beareth his shield of the highest *Jupiter*. In point, a sacred imperial diadem, safely guarded by the helmet of the great goddess *Pallas*, from the violence of darts, bullets, and bolts of *Saturn*, *Momus*, and the *Idiot*; all environed with the ribband of loyalty, having a pendant of the most heroical Order of Knighthood of the *Helmet*; the word hereunto, *Sic virtus honorem*. For his Highness's crest the glorious planet *Sol*, coursing through the twelve signs of the Zodiack, on a celestial globe, moved upon the two poles *Arctick* and *Antartick*; with this motto, *Dum totum peregraverit orbem*. All set upon a *chapew*: *Mars* turned up, *Luna* mantelled, *Sapphire* doubted pearl, supported by two anciently renowned and glorious *Griffyns*, which have been always in league with the honourable *Pegasus*."

The conceit hereof was to shew, that the Prince, whose private arms were three helmets, should defend his honour by virtue, from reprehensions of male-contents, carpers, and fools. The ribband of blue, with an helmet pendant, in imitation of St. George. In his crest, his government for the twelve days of Christmas was resembled to the Sun's passing the twelve Signs, though the Prince's course had some odd degrees beyond that time; but he was wholly supported by the *Griffyns*; for *Gray's Inn* Gentlemen, and not the Treasure of the House, was charged. The words, *Sic virtus honorem*, that his virtue should defend his honour, whilst he had run his whole course of dominion, without any either eclipse or retrogradation.

After these things thus done, the Attorney stood up, and made a Speech of gratulation to the Prince; and therein shewed what great happiness was like to ensue, by the election of so noble and vertuous a Prince as then reigned over them; rightly extolling the nobility, vertue, puissance, and the singular perfections of his Sovereign: whereby he took occasion also to move the subjects to be forward to perform all obedience and service to his Excellency; as also to furnish his wants, if so be that it were requisite; and, in a word, perswaded the people, that they were happy in having such a Prince to rule over them; and likewise assured the Prince, that he also was most happy, in having rule over so dutiful and loving subjects, that would not think any thing, were it lands, goods, or life, too dear to be at his Highness's command and service.

The Prince's Highness made again this answer: "That he did acknowledge himself to be deeply bound to their merits; and in that regard did promise, that he would be a gracious and loving Prince to so well deserving subjects." And concluded with good liking and commendations of their proceedings.

Then the Sollicitor, having certain great old books and records lying before him, made this Speech to his Honour, as followeth:

"Most Excellent Prince,

"High superiority and dominion is illustrated and adorned by the humble services of noble and mighty personages: and therefore, amidst the garland of your royalties of your crown, this is a principal flower, that in your provinces and territories, divers mighty and puissant potentates are your homagers and vassals; and, although infinite are your feodaries, which by their tenures do perform royal service to your sacred person, pay huge sums into your treasury and exchequer, and maintain whole legions for the defence of your country: yet some special persons there are charged by their tenures, to do special service at this your glorious inthronization; whose tenures, for their strangeness, are admirable; for their value, inestimable: and for their worthiness, incomparable; the particulars whereof do here appear in your Excellency's records, in the book of *Dooms-day*, remaining in your Exchequer, in the 50th and 500th chest there."

The Names of such Homagers and Tributaries as hold any Signiories, Lordships, Lands, Privileges, or Liberties, under his Honour, and the Tenures and Services belonging to the same, as followeth:

Alfonso de Stapulia, and *Davillo de Bernardia,* hold the arch-dukedoms of *Stapulia* and *Bernardia,* of the Prince of *Purpoole,* by grand-serjeantry, and castle-guard of the Castles of *Stapulia* and *Bernardia,* and to right and relieve all wants and wrongs of all ladies, matrons, and maids, within the said arch-dutchy; and rendring, on the day of his Excellency's coronation, a coronet of gold, and yearly five hundred millions sterling.

Marotto Marquarillo de Holborn holdeth the manors of *High* and *Nether Holborn* by cornage *in capite* of the Prince of *Purpoole,* and rendring on the day of his Honour's coronation, for every of the Prince's pensioners, one milk-white doe, to be bestowed on them by the Prince, for a favour, or New-year's-night-gift: and rendring yearly two hundred millions sterling.

Lucy Negro, Abbess *de Clerkenwell*, holdeth the nunnery of *Clerkenwell*, with the lands and privileges thereunto belonging, of the Prince of *Purpoole*, by night-service *in Caudâ*, and to find a choir of nuns, with burning lamps, to chaunt *Placebo* to the Gentlemen of the Prince's Privy Chamber, on the day of his Excellency's coronation.

Ruffiano de St. Giles's holdeth the town of *St. Giles's* by cornage *in Caudâ*, of the Prince of *Purpoole*, and rendring on the day of his Excellency's coronation, two ambling, easie-paced gennets, for the Prince's two pages of honour; and rendring yearly two hundred millions sterling.

Cornelius Combaldus de Tottenham, holdeth the grange of *Tottenham* of the Prince of *Purpoole*, in free and common soccage, by the twenty-fourth part of a night's fee, and by rendring to the Master of the Wardrobe so much cunny furr as will serve to line his night-cap, and face a pair of mittins; and yielding yearly four quarters of rye, and threescore double duckets on the feast of St. Pancras.

Bartholomeus de Bloomsbury holdeth a thousand hides in *Bloomsbury*, of the Prince of *Purpoole*, by escuage incertain, and rendring on the day of his Excellency's coronation one Amazon, with a ring, to be run at by the Knights of the Prince's band, and the mark to be his trophy that shall be adjudged the bravest courser; and rendring yearly fifty millions sterling.

Amarillo de Paddington holdeth an hundred ox-gangs of land in *Paddington*, of the Prince of *Purpoole*, by petty-serjeantry, that when the Prince maketh a voyage royal against the *Amazons*, to subdue and bring them under, he do find, at his own charges, a thousand men, well furnished with long and strong morris-pikes, black bills, or halberts, with morians on their heads; and rendring yearly four hundred millions sterling.

Bawdwine de Islington holdeth the town of *Islington* of the Prince of *Purpoole*, by grand-serjeantry; and rendring, at the coronation of his Honour, for every maid in *Islington*, continuing a virgin after the age of fourteen years, one hundred thousand millions sterling.

Jordano Sartano de Kentish Town holdeth the Canton of *Kentish Town* of the Prince of *Purpoole*, in tail-general, at the will of the said Prince, as of his mannor of *Deep-Inn*, in his province of *Islington* by the Veirge, according to the custom of the said mannor; that when any of the Prince's officers or family do resort thither, for change of air, or else variety of diet, as weary of court life, and such provision, he do provide for a mess of the Yeomen of the Guard, or any of the black-guard, or such like inferior officers so coming, eight loins of mutton, which are sound, well-fed, and not infectious; and for every Gentleman Pensioner, or other of good quality, coneys, pidgeons, chickens, or such dainty morsels. But the said *Jordano* is not bound by his tenure, to boil, roast, or bake the same, or meddle further than the bare delivery of the said cates, and so to leave them to the handling, dressing, and breaking up of themselves: and rendring for a fine to the Prince one thousand five hundred marks.

Markasius Rusticanus, and *Hieronymus Paludensis de Knightsbridge*,' do hold the village of *Knightsbridge*, with the appurtenances in *Knightsbridge*, of the Prince of *Purpoole*, by villenage in base tenure, that they two shall jointly find three hundred able and sufficient labouring men, with instruments and tools necessary for the making clean of all channels, sinks, creeks, and gutters, within all the cities of his Highness's dominions; and also shall cleanse and keep clean all and all manner of ponds, pudules, dams, springs, locks, runlets, becks, water gates, sluces, passages, strait entrances, and dangerous quagmires; and also shall repair and mend all common high and low-ways, by laying stones in the pits and naughty places thereof: and also that they do not suffer the aforesaid places to go to decay through their default, and lack of looking unto, or neglect of doing their parts and duties therein.

The tenures being thus read by the Solicitor, then were called by their names those homagers that were to perform their services, according to their tenures.

Upon the summons given, *Alphonso de Stapulia*, and *Davillo de Bernardia*, came to the Prince's foot-stool, and offered a coronet, according to their service, and did homage to his Highness in solemn manner, kneeling, according to the order in such cases accustomed. The rest that appeared were deferred to better leisure; and they that made default were fined at great sums, and their defaults recorded.

There was a Parliament intended, and summoned; but by reason that some special officers that were by necessary occasions urged to be absent, without whose presence it could not be performed, it was dashed. And in that point our purpose was frustrate, saving only in two branches of it: the one was a subsidy granted by the Commons of his dominions, towards the support of his Highness's port and sports. The other was, by his gracious, general, and free pardon.

HENRY Prince of *Purpoole*, Arch-Duke of *Stapulia* and *Bernardia*, Duke of *High* and *Nether Holborn*, Marquis of *St. Giles's* and *Tottenham*, Count Palatine of *Bloomsbury* and *Clerkenwell*, Great Lord of the Cantons of *Islington, Kentish Town, Paddington,* and *Knights-bridge*, Knight of the most heroicall Order of the *Helmet*, and Sovereign of the same; to all and all manner of Persons to whome these Presents shall appertain; Greeting—

" In tender regard, and gracious consideration of the humble affection of our loyal lords and subjects; and by understanding that by often violating of laudable customs, prescriptions, and laws, divers have incurred inevitable and incurable dangers of lands, goods, life, and members, if it be not by our clemency redressed, respected, and pardoned: We therefore, hoping for better obedience and observation of our said laws and customs, do grant and publish this our General and Free Pardon of all dangers, pains, penalties, forfeitures, or offences, whereunto and wherewith they are now charged, or chargeable, by reason of mis-government, mis-demeanour, mis-behaviour, or fault, either of commission, omission, or otherwise howsoever or whatsover.

" It is therefore Our will and pleasure, that all and every public person and persons, whether they be strangers or naturals, within Our dominions, be by virtue hereof excused, suspended, and discharged from all and all manner of treasons, contempts, offences, trespasses, forcible entries, intrusions, disseisins, torts, wrongs, injuries, over-throws, over-thwartings, cross-bitings, coney-catchings, frauds, conclusions, fictions, fractions, fashions, fancies, or ostentations: also all and all manner of errors, misprisions, mistakings, overtakings, double dealings, combinations, confederacies, conjunctions, oppositions, interpositions, snppositions, and suppositaries: also all and all manner of intermedlance or medlance, privy-searches, routs and riots, incumbrances, pluralities, formalities, deformalities, disturbances, duplicities, jeofails in insufficiencies or defects: also all and all manner of sorceries, inchantments, conjurations, spells, or charms: all destructions, obstructions, and constructions: all evasions, invasions, charges, surcharges, discharges, commands, countermands, checks, counterchecks, and counter-buffs: also all and all manner of inhibitions, prohibitions, insurrections, corrections, conspiracies, concavities, coinings, superfluities, washings, clippings, and shavings: all and all manner of multiplications, inanities, installations, destillations, constillations, necromancies, and incantations: all and all manner of mis-feasance, non-feasance, or too much feasance: all attempts or adventures, skirmages, assaults, grapplings, closings, or encounters: all mis-prisonments, or restraints of body or member: and all and all manner of pains and penalties personal or pecuniary whatsoever, committed, made, or done, against our crown and dignity, peace, prerogatives, laws, and customs, which shall not herein hereafter be in some sort expressed, mentioned, intended, or excepted.

"*Except, and always fore-prized out of this General and Free Pardon,* all and every such person and persons as shall imagine, think, suppose, or speak and utter any false, seditious, ignominious, or slanderous words, reports, rumours, or opinions, against the dignity, or his Excellency's honourable actions, counsels, consultations, or state of the Prince, his court, counsellors, nobles, knights, and officers.

"*Except*, all such persons as now or hereafter shall be advanced, admitted, or induced to any corporal or personal benefice, administration, charge, or cure, of any manner of personage, and shall not be personally resident, commorant, or incumbent in, at, or upon the whole, or some part or parcel of the said benefice, administration, or cure; but absent himself wilfully or negligently, by the space of four-score days, nights, or hours, and not having any special substituted, instituted, or inducted Vicar, incumbent, or concumbent, daily, or any other time, duly to express, enjoy, and supply his absence, room, or vacation.

"*Except*, all such persons as have, or shall have any charge, occasion, chance, opportunity, or possible means to entertain, serve, recreate, delight, or discourse, with any vertuous or honourable lady, or gentlewoman, matron, or maid, publicly, privately, or familiarly, and shall faint, fail, or be deemed to faint or fail in courage, or countenance, semblance, gesture, voice, speech, or attempt, or in act or adventure, or in any other matter, thing, manner, mystery, or accomplishment, due, decent, or appertinent to her or their honour, dignity, desert, expectation, desire, affection, inclination, allowance, or acceptance; to be daunted, dismayed, or to stand mute, idle, frivolous, or defective, or otherwise dull, contrary, sullen, mal-content, melancholy, or different from the profession, practice, and perfection, of a compleat and consummate gentleman or courtier.

"*Except*, all such persons as by any force, or fraud, and dissimulation, shall procure, be it by letters, promises, messages, contracts, and other inveaglings, any lady or gentlewoman, woman or maid, sole or covert, into his possession or convoy, and shall convey her into any place where she is or shall be of full power and opportunity to bargain, give, take, buy, sell, or change; and shall suffer her to escape and return at large, without any such bargain, sale, gift, or exchange performed and made, contrary to former expected, expressed, employed contract or consent.

"*Except*, all such persons as by any slander, libel, word, or note, bewray, betray, defame, or suffer to be defamed, any woman, wife, widow, or maid, in whose affairs, secrets, suits, services, causes, actions, or other occupations, he hath been at any time conversant, employed, or trained in, or admitted unto, contrary to his plighted promise, duty, and allegiance; and to the utter disparagement of others hereafter to be received, retained, embraced, or liked in like services, performances, or advancements.

"*Except*, all intrusions and forcible entries had, made, or done, into or upon any of the Prince's widows, or wards female, without special licence; and all fines passed for the same.

"*Except*, all concealed fools, idiots, and mad-men, that have not to this present sued forth any livery of their wits, nor *ouster le mayne* of their senses, until the Prince have had primer seisin thereof.

"*Except*, all such persons as, for their lucre and gain of living, do keep or maintain, or else frequent and resort unto, any common house, alley, open or privy place of unlawful exercises; as of vaulting, bowling, or any forbidden manner of shooting; as at pricks in common highways, ways of sufferance or ease to market-towns or fairs, or at short butts, not being of sufficient length and distance, or at any roving or unconstant mark, or that shoot any shafts, arrows, or bolts, of unseasonable wood or substances, or without an head, or of too short and small a size, contrary to the customs, laws, and statutes, in such cases made and provided.

"*Except*, all such persons as shall put or cast into any waters, salt or fresh, or any brooks, brinks, chinks, pits, pools, or ponds, any snare, or other engine, to danger or destroy the fry or breed of any young lampreys, boads, loaches, bullheads, cods, whitings, pikes, ruffs, or pearches, or any other young store of spawns or fries, in any flood-gate, sluice, pipe, or tail of a mill, or any other streight stream, brook, or river, salt or fresh; the same fish being then of insufficiency in age and quantity, or at that time not in convenient season to be used and taken.

"*Except*, all such persons as shall hunt in the night, or pursue any bucks or does; or with painted faces, vizards, or other disguisings, in the day-time; or any such as do wrongfully and unlawfully, without consent or leave given or granted, by day or by night, break or enter into any park impailed, or other several close, inclosure, chace, or purliew, inclosed or compassed with wall, pale, grove, hedge, or bushes, used still and occupied for the keeping, breeding, or cherishing of young deer, prickets, or any other game, fit to be preserved and nourished; or such as do hunt, chase, or drive out any such deer, to the prejudice and decay of such game and pass-times within our dominions.

"*Except*, all such persons as shall shoot in any hand gun, demy-hag, or hag butt, either half-shot, or bullet, any fowl, bird, or beast; either at any deer, red or fallow, or any other thing or things, except it be a butt set, laid, or raised in some convenient place, fit for the same purpose.

"*Except*, all and every artificer, crafts-man, labourer, householder, or servant, being a layman, which hath not lands to the yearly value of forty shillings; or any clerk, not admitted or advanced to the benefice of the value of ten pounds *per annum*, that with any grey-hound, mongrel, mastiff, spaniel, or other dogs, doth hunt in other men's parks, warrens, and coney-grees; or use any ferrets, hare-pipes, snarles, ginns, or other knacks or devises, to take or destroy does, hares, or coneys, or other gentlemen's game, contrary to the form and meaning of a statute in that case provided.

"*Except*, all merchant-adventurers, that ship or lade any wares or merchandize, into any port or creek, in any Flemish, French, or Dutch, or other outlandish hoy, ship, or bottom, whereof the Prince, nor some of his subjects, be not possessioners and proprietaries; and the masters and mariners of the same vessels and bottoms to be the Prince's subjects; whereby our own shipping is many times unfraught, contrary unto divers statutes in that case provided.

"*Except*, all owners masters and pursers of our ships, as, for the transportation of freight from one port to another, have received and taken any sums of money above the statute-allowance in that behalf, *viz.* for every dry fatt, 6*d.*; for every bale, one foot long, 1*s.*; for every hogshead, pipe, or tierce of wine 5*s.*

"*Except*, all decayed houses of husbandry, and housewifery, and inclosures, and severalties, converting of any lands used and occupied to tillage and sowing, into pasture and feeding; whereby idleness increaseth, husbandry and housewifery is decayed, and towns are dis-peopled, contrary to the statute in that case made and provided.

"*Except*, all such persons as shall maliciously and wilfully burn or cut, or cause to be burned or cut, any conduit, or trough, pipe, or any other instrument used as means of conveyance of any liquor, water, or other kind of moisture.

"*Except*, all commoners within any forest, chace, moor, marsh, heath, or other waste ground, which hath put to pasture into, or upon the same, any stoned horses, not being of the altitude and heighth contained in the statute in that case made and provided for the good breed of strong and large horses, which is much decayed; little stoned horses, nags, and hobbies, being put to pasture there, and in such commons.

"*Except*, all fugitives, failers, and flinchers, that with shame and discredit are fled and vanished out of the Prince's dominions of *Purpoole*, and especially from his Court at *Graya*, this time of *Christmas*, to withdraw themselves from his Honour's service and attendance, contrary to their duty and allegiance, and to their perpetual ignominy, and incurable loss of credit and good opinion, which belongeth to ingenuous and well-minded gentlemen.

"*Except*, all concealments, and wrongful detainments of any subsidies and revenues, benevolences, and receipts upon privy seals, &c.

"*Except*, all, and all manner of offences, pains, penalties, mulcts, fines, amerciaments, and punishments, corporal and pecuniary, whatsoever."

The Pardon being thus read by the Solicitor, the Prince made a short speech to his subjects, wherein he gave them to understand, that although in clemency he pardoned all offences to that present time; yet, notwithstanding, his meaning thereby was not to give any the least occasion of presumption in breaking his laws, and the customs laudably used through his dominions and government. Neither did he now so graciously forgive all errors and misdemeanours as he would hereafter severely and strictly reform the same. His will was, that justice should be administered to every subject, without any partiality; and that the wronged should make their causes known to himself, by petition to the Master of the Requests: and further excused the causes of the great taxes, and sums of money, that were levied, by reason that his predecessors had not left his coffers full of treasure, nor his crown so furnished, as became the dignity of so great a Prince.

Then his Highness called for the Master of the Revels, and willed him to pass the time in dancing: So his gentlemen-pensioners and attendants, very gallantly appointed, in thirty couples, danced the old measures, and their galliards, and other kinds of dances, revelling until it was very late; and so spent the rest of their performance in those exercises, until it pleased his Honour to take his way to his lodging, with sound of trumpets, and his attendants in order, as is above set down.

There was the conclusion of the first grand night, the performance whereof increased the expectation of those things that were to ensue; insomuch that the common report amongst all strangers was so great, and the expectation of our proceedings so extraordinary, that it urged us to take upon us a greater state than was at the first intended: and therefore, besides all the stately and sumptuous service that was continually done the Prince, in very princely manner; and besides the daily revels, and such like sports, which were usual, there was intended divers grand nights, for the entertainment of strangers to our pass-times and sports.

The next grand night was intended to be upon Innocents-day at night; at which time there was a great presence of lords, ladies, and worshipful personages, that did expect some notable performance at that time; which, indeed, had been effected, if the multitude of beholders had not been so exceeding great, that thereby there was no convenient room for those that were actors; by reason whereof, very good inventions and conceipts could not have opportunity to be applauded, which otherwise would have been great contentation to the beholders. Against which time, our friend, the *Inner Temple*, determined to send their Ambassador to our Prince of State, as sent from *Frederick Templarius*, their Emperor, who was then busied in his wars against the Turk. The Ambassador came very gallantly appointed, and attended by a great number of brave gentlemen, which arrived at our Court about nine of the clock at night. Upon their coming thither, the King at Arms gave notice to the Prince, then sitting in his chair of state in the hall, that there was to come to his Court an Ambassador from his ancient friend the *State of Templaria*, which desired to have present access unto his Highness; and shewed his Honour further, that he seemed to be of very good sort, because he was so well attended; and therefore desired, that it would please his Honour that some of his Nobles and Lords might conduct him to his Highness's presence, which was done. So he was brought in very solemnly, with sound of trumpets, the King at Arms and Lords of *Purpoole* making to his company, which marched before him in order. He was received very kindly of the Prince, and placed in a chair besides his Highness, to the end that he might be a partaker of the sports intended. But first he made a speech to the Prince, wherein he declared how his excellent renown and fame was known throughout all the whole world; and that the report of his greatness was not contained within the bounds of the Ocean, but had come to the ears of his noble Sovereign, *Frederick Templarius*, where he is now warring against the Turks, the known enemies to all Christendom; who, having heard that his Excellency kept his Court at *Graya* this Christmas, thought it to stand with his ancient league of amity and near kindness, that so long had been continued and increased by their noble ancestors, of famous memory and desert, to gratulate his happiness, and flourishing estate; and in that regard, had sent him his Ambassador, to be residing at his Excellency's Court, in honour of his greatness, and token of his tender love and good-will he beareth to his Highness; the confirmation whereof he especially required, and by all means possible would study to increase and eternize: which function he was the more willing to accomplish, because our State of *Graya* did grace *Templaria* with the presence of an Ambassador about thirty years since, upon like occasion.

Our Prince made him this answer: That he did acknowledge that the great kindness of his Lord, whereby he doth invite to further degrees in firm and loyal friendship, did deserve all honourable commendations, and effectual accomplishment, that by any means might be devised; and that he accounted himself happy, by having the sincere and steadfast love of so gracious and renowned a Prince, as his Lord and Master deserved to be esteemed; and that nothing in the world should hinder the due observation of so inviolable a band as he esteemed his favour and good-will. Withal, he entred into commendations of his noble and courageous enterprizes, in that he chuseth out an adversary fit for his greatness to encounter with, his Honour to be illustrated by, and such an enemy to all Christendom, as that the glory of his actions tend to the safety and liberty of all civility and humanity: yet, notwithstanding that he was thus employed in this action of honouring us, he shewed both his honourable mindfulnes of our love and friendship, and also his own puissance, that can afford so great a number of brave gentlemen, and so gallantly furnished and accomplished: and so concluded, with a welcome both to the Ambassador himself and his favourites, for their Lord and Master's sake, and so for their own good deserts and condition.

When the Ambassador was placed, as aforesaid, and that there was something to be performed for the delight of the beholders, there arose such a disordered tumult and crowd upon the stage, that there was no opportunity to effect that which was intended: there came so great a number of worshipful personages upon the stage that might not be displaced, and gentlewomen whose sex did privilege them from violence, that when the Prince and his officers had in vain, a good while, expected and endeavoured a reformation, at length there was no hope of redress for that present. The Lord Ambassador and his train thought that they were not so kindly entertained as was before expected, and thereupon would not stay any longer at that time, but, in a sort, discontented and displeased. After their departure, the throngs and tumults did somewhat cease, although so much of them continued as was able to disorder and confound any good inventions whatsoever. In regard whereof, as also for that the sports intended were especially for the gracing the *Templarians*, it was thought good not to offer any thing of account, saving dancing and revelling with gentlewomen; and after such sports, a Comedy of Errors (like to Plautus his Menechmus) was played by the players. So that night war begun and continued to the end in nothing but confusion and errors; whereupon, it was ever afterwards called, "The Night of Errors."

This mischanceful accident sorting so ill, to the great prejudice of the rest of our proceedings, was a great discouragement and disparagement to our whole state; yet it gave occasion to the lawyer's of the Prince's Council, the next night, after revels, to read a commission of Oyer and Terminer, directed to certain Noblemen and Lords of his Highness's Council, and others, that they should enquire, or cause enquiry to be made, of some great disorders and abuses lately done and committed within his Highness's dominions of *Purpoole*, especially by sorceries and inchantments; and namely, of a great witchcraft used the night before, whereby there were great disorders and misdemeanours, by hurly-burlies, crowds, errors, confusions, vain representations, and shews, to the utter discredit of our state and policy.

The next night upon this occasion, we preferred judgments thick and threefold, which were read publickly by the Clerk of the Crown, being all against a sorcererer or conjurer that was supposed to be the cause of that confused inconvenience. Therein was contained, How he had caused the stage to be built, and scaffolds to be reared to the top of the house, to increase expectation. Also how he had caused divers ladies and gentlemen, and others of good condition to be invited to our sports; also our dearest friend the *State of Templaria*, to be disgraced, and disappointed of their kind entertainment, deserved and intended. Also that he caused throngs and tumults, crowds and outrages, to disturb our whole proceedings. And lastly, that he had foisted a company of base and common fellows, to make up our disorders with a play of Errors and Confusions; and that that night had gained to us discredit, and itself a nickname of Errors. All which were against the crown and dignity of our Sovereign Lord the Prince of *Purpoole*.

Under colour of these proceedings, were laid open to the view all the causes of note that were committed by our chiefest statesmen in the government of our principality; and every officer in any great place, that had not performed his duty in that service, was taxed hereby, from the highest to the lowest, not sparing the guard and porters, that suffered so many disordered persons to enter in at the court-gates: upon whose aforesaid indictments the prisoner was arraigned at the bar, being brought thither by the Lieutenant of the Tower (for at that time the stocks were graced with that name); and the Sheriff impannelled a jury of twenty-four gentlemen, that were to give their verdict upon the evidence given. The prisoner appealed to the Prince his Excellency for justice; and humbly desired that it would please his Highness to understand the truth of the matter by his supplication, which he had ready to be offered to the Master of the Requests. The Prince gave leave to the Master of the Requests, that he should read the petition; wherein was a disclosure of all the knavery and juggling of the Attorney and Solicitor, which had brought all this law-stuff on purpose to blind the eyes of his Excellency and all the honourable Court there, going about to make them think that those things which they all saw and perceived sensibly to be in very deed done, and actually performed, were nothing else but vain illusions, fancies, dreams, and enchantments, and to be wrought and compassed by the means of a poor harmless wretch, that never had heard of such great matters in all his life: whereas the very fault was in the negligence of the Prince's Council, Lords, and Officers of his State, that had the rule of the roast, and by whose advice the Commonwealth was so soundly misgoverned. To prove these things to be true, he brought divers instances of great absurdities committed by the greatest; and made such allegations as could not be denied. These were done by some that were touched by the Attorney and Solicitor in their former proceedings, and they used the prisoner's names for means of quittance with them in that behalf. But the Prince and States-men (being pinched on both sides by both the parties) were not a little offended at the great liberty that they had taken in censuring so far of his Highness's government; and thereupon the prisoner was freed and pardoned, the Attorney, Solicitor, Master of the Requests, and those that were acquainted with the draught of the petition, were all of them commanded to the Tower; so the

Lieutenant took charge of them. And this was the end of our law-sports, concerning the Night of Errors.

When we were wearied with mocking thus at our own follies, at length there was a great consultation had for the recovery of our lost honour. It was then concluded, that first the Prince's Council should be reformed, and some graver conceipts should have their places, to advise upon those things that were propounded to be done afterward. Therefore, upon better consideration, there were divers plots and devices intended against the Friday after the New-year's-day, being the 3d of January: and, to prevent all unruly tumults, and former inconveniences, there was provided a watch of armed men, to ward at the four ports; and whifflers to make good order under the four Barons; and the Lord Warden to over-see them all; that none but those that were of good condition might be suffered to be let into the Court. And the like officers were every where appointed.

On the 3d of January at night, there was a most honourable presence of great and noble personages, that came as invited to our Prince; as namely, the Right Honourable the Lord Keeper, the Earls of Shrewsbury, Cumberland, Northumberland, Southampton, and Essex; the Lords Buckhurst, Windsor, Mountjoy, Sheffield, Compton, Rich, Burleygh, Mounteagle, and the Lord Thomas Howard; Sir Thomas Henneage, Sir Robert Cecill; with a great number of knights, ladies, and very worshipful personages: all which had convenient places, and very good entertainment, to their good liking and contentment.

When they were all thus placed and settled in very good order, the Prince came into the Hall with his wonted state, and ascended his throne at the high end of the Hall, under his Highness's arms; and after him came the Ambassador of *Templaria*, with his train likewise, and was placed by the Prince as he was before; his train also had places reserved for them, and were provided for them particularly. Then, after a variety of musick, they were presented with this device.

At the side of the Hall, behind a curtain, was erected an altar to the Goddess of Amity; her arch-flamen ready to attend the sacrifice and incense that should, by her servants, be offered unto her: round about the same sate Nymphs and Fairies, with instruments of musick, and made very pleasant melody with viols and voices, and sang hymns and prayses to her deity.

Then issued forth of another room the first pair of friends, which were Theseus and Perithous; they came in arm in arm, and offered incense upon the altar to their Goddess, which shined and burned very clear, without blemish; which being done, they departed.

Then likewise came Achilles and Patroclus; after them, Pylades and Orestes; then Scipio and Lelius: and all these did, in all things, as the former; and so departed.

Lastly, were presented *Graius* and *Templarius;* and they two came lovingly, arm in arm, to the altar, and offered their incense as the rest, but the Goddess did not accept of their service; which appeared by the troubled smoak, and dark vapour, that choaked the flame, and smothered the clear burning thereof. Hereat, the archflamen, willing to pacifie the angry Goddess, preferred certain mystical ceremonies and invocations, and commanded the nymphs to sing some hymns of pacification to her deity, and caused them to make proffer of their devotion again; which they did, and then the flame burnt more clear than at any time before, and continued longer in brightness and shining to them than to any of those pairs of friends that had gone before them; and so they departed.

Then the arch-flamen did pronounce *Grayus* and *Templarius* to be as true and perfect friends, and so familiarly united and linked with the bond and league of sincere friendship and amity, as ever were Theseus and Perithous, Achilles and Patroclus, Pylades and Orestes, or Scipio and Lælius; and therewithal did further divine, that this love should be perpetual. And, lastly, denounced a heavy curse on them that shall any way go about to break or weaken the same; and an happiness to them that study and labour to eternize it for ever. So, with sweet and pleasant melody, the curtain was drawn as it was at first.

Thus was this shew ended, which was devised to that end, that those that were present might understand, that the unkindness which was growing betwixt the *Templarians* and us, by reason of the former Night of Errors and the uncivil behaviour wherewith they were entertained, as before I have partly touched, was now clean rooted out and forgotten, and that we now were more firm friends, and kind lovers, than ever before we had been, contrary to the evil reports that some enviers of our happiness had sown abroad.

The Prince then spake to the Ambassador, that the shew had contented him exceedingly; the rather, that it appeared thereby, that their ancient amity was so fresh and flourishing, that no friendship in the world hath been compared to the love and good-will of the *Grayans* and *Templarians*. And to the end that he might shew that the conceipt was pleasing unto him, his Highness offered the Lord Ambassador, and some of his retinue, with the Knighthood of the *Helmet*, an Order of his own institution.

To that end his Excellency called to him his King at Arms, and willed him to place the Ambassador, and some of his followers, and also some of his own Court, that they might receive the dignity at his hands; which being done, and the Master of the Jewels attending with the Collar of the Order, the Prince came down from his chair of state, and took a collar, and put it about the Lord Ambassador's neck, he kneeling down on his left knee; and said to him, " Sois Chivalor:" and so was done to the rest, to the number of twenty-four.

So the Prince and the Lord Ambassador took their places again in their chairs, and the rest according to their condition.

Then *Helmet*, his Highness's King at Arms, stood before the Prince, in his surcoat of arms, and caused the trumpets to sound, and made his speech; as doth follow:

"The most mighty and puissant Prince, Sir Henry, my gracious Lord and Sovereign Prince of *Purpoole*, Archduke of *Stapulia* and *Bernardia*, Duke of *High and Nether Holborn*, Marquis of *St. Giles's* and *Tottenham*, Count Palatine of *Bloomsbury* and *Clerkenwell*, Great Lord of the Cantons of *Islington*, *Kentish Town*, *Paddington*, and *Knight's-bridge*, hath heretofore, for the special gracing of the nobility of his realm, and honouring the deserts of strangers, his favourites, instituted a most honourable Order of Knighthood of the *Helmet*, whereof his Honour is Sovereign, in memory of the arms he beareth, worthily given to one of his noble ancestors, many years past, for saving the life of his then Sovereign; in regard that as the *Helmet* defendeth the chiefest part of the body, the head; so did he guard and defend the sacred person of the Prince, the head of the state. His Highness at this time had made choice of a number of vertuous and noble personages, to admit them into his honourable Society; whose good example may be a spur and encouragement to the young nobility of his dominions, to cause them to aspire to the heighth of all honourable deserts.

" To the honourable Order are annexed strict rules of arms, and civil government, religiously to be observed by all those that are admitted to this dignity. You therefore, most noble Gentlemen, whom his Highness at this time so greatly honoureth with his Royal Order, you must every one of you kiss your helmet, and thereby promise and vow to observe and practice, or otherwise, as the case shall require, shun and avoid all these constitutions and ordinances, which, out of the records of my Office of Arms, I shall read unto you."

Then the King at Arms took his book, and turned to the articles of the orders; and read them, as followeth:

"Imprimis, Every Knight of this honourable Order, whether he be a natural subject, or stranger born, shall promise never to bear arms against his Highness's sacred person, nor his state; but to assist him in all his lawful wars, and maintain all his just pretences and titles; especially, his Highness's title to the land of the *Ama zons.* d the *Cape of Good Hope.*

"Item, no Knight of this Order shall, in point of honour, resort to any grammar-rules out of the books *De Dullo,* or such like; but shall, out of his own brave mind, and natural courage, deliver himself from scorns, as to his own discretion shall seem convenient.

"Item, no Knight of this Order shall be inquisitive towards any lady or gentlewoman, whether her beauty be English or Italian, or whether, with care-taking, she have added half a foot to her stature; but shall take all to the best. Neither shall any Knight of the aforesaid Order presume to affirm, that faces were better twenty years ago than they are at this present time, except such Knights have passed three climacterical years.

"Item, everie Knight of this Order is bound to perform all requisite and manly service, be it night-service, or otherwise, as the case requireth, to all ladies and gentlewomen, beautiful by nature or by art; ever offering his aid, without any demand thereof; and if in case he fail so to do, he shall be deemed a match of disparagement to any his Highness's widows, or wards-female; and his Excellency shall in justice forbear to make any tender of him to any such ward or widow.

"Item, no Knight of this Order shall procure any letters from his Highness to any widow or maid, for his enablement and commendation to be advanced to marriage; but all prerogative, wooing set apart, shall for ever cease, as to any of these Knights, and shall be left to the common laws of this land, declared by the statute, *Quia Electiones liberæ esse debent.*

"Item, no Knight of this honourable Order, in case he shall grow into decay, shall procure from his Highness relief and sustentation, any monopolies or privileges, except only these kinds following: that is to say, Upon every tobacco-pipe, not being one foot wide; upon every lock that is worn, not being seven feet long;

upon every health that is drunk, not being of a glass five foot deep; and upon every maid in his Highness's province of *Islington*, continuing a virgin after the age of fourteen years, contrary to the use and custom in that place always had and observed.

" Item, no Knight of this Order shall have any more than one mistress, for whose sake he shall be allowed to wear three colours: but, if he will have two mistresses, then must he wear six colours; and so forward, after the rate of three colours to a mistress.

" Item, no Knight of this Order shall put out any money upon strange returns or performances to be made by his own person; as, to hop up the stairs to the top of St. Paul's, without intermission; or any other such like agilities or endurances, except it may appear that the same performances or practices do enable him to some service or employment; as, if he do undertake to go a journey backward, the same shall be thought to enable him to be an Ambassador into Turkey.

" Item, no Knight of this Order, that hath had any licence to travel into foreign countries, be it by map, card, sea, or land, and hath returned from thence, shall presume upon the warrant of a traveller, to report any extraordinary varieties; as, that he hath ridden through Venice on horse-back post; or that in December he sailed by the Cape of Norway; or that he hath travelled over the most part of the countries of Geneva; or such like hyperbolies, contrary to the statute, *Propterea quod qui diversos terrarum ambitus errent & vagantur, &c.*

" Item, every Knight of this Order shall do his endeavour to be much in the books of the worshipful citizens of the principal city, next adjoining to the territories of *Purpoole*; and none shall unlearnedly, or without looking, pay ready money for any wares, or other things pertaining to the gallantness of his Honour's Court; to the ill example of others, and utter subversion of credit betwixt man and man.

" Item, every Knight of this Order shall apply himself to some or other vertuous quality or ability of learning, honour, and arms; and shall not think it sufficient to come into his Honour's Presence-Chamber in good apparel only, or to be able to keep company at play and gaming: for such it is already determined, that they be put and taken for implements of household, and are placed in his Honour's Inventory.

" Item, every Knight of this Order shall endeavour to add conference and exrience by reading; and therefore shall not only read and peruse Guizo, the French

Academy, Galiatto the Courtier, Plutarch, the Arcadia, and the Neoterical Writers, from time to time; but also frequent the Theatre, and such like places of experience; and resort to the better sort of ordinaries for conference; whereby they may not only become accomplished with civil conversations, and able to govern a table with discourse; but also sufficient, if need be, to make epigrams, emblems, and other devices, appertaining to his Honour's learned revels.

" Item, no Knight of this Order shall give out what gracious words the Prince hath given him, nor leave word at his chamber, in case any come to speak with him, that he is above with his Excellency: nor cause his man, when he shall be in any public assembly, to call him suddenly to go to the Prince, nor cause any packet of letters to be brought at dinner or supper time, nor say that he had the refusal of some great office, nor satisfy suitors, to say, his Honour is not in any good disposition, nor make any narrow observation of his Excellency's nature and fashions, as if he were inward privately with his Honour; contrary to the late inhibition of selling of smoak.

" Item, no Knight of this Order shall be armed, for the safeguard of his countenance, with a pipe in his mouth, in the nature of a tooth-picker, or with any weapon in his hand, be it stick, plume, wand, or any such like; neither shall he draw out of his pocket any book or paper, to read for the same intent; neither shall he retain any extraordinary shrug, nod, or other familiar motion or gesture, to the same end; for his Highness, of his gracious clemency, is disposed to lend his countenance to all such Knights as are out of countenance.

" Item, no Knight of this Order, that weareth fustian, cloth, or such statute-apparel, for necessity, shall pretend to wear the same for the new fashion's sake.

" Item, no Knight of this Order, in walking the streets, or other places of resort, shall bear his hands in his pockets of his great rolled hose, with the Spanish wheel, if it be not either to defend his hands from the cold, or else to guard forty shillings sterling, being in the same pockets.

" Item, no Knight of this Order shall lay to pawn his Collar of Knighthood for an hundred pounds; and, if he do, she shall be, *ipso facto*, discharged; and it shall be lawful for any man whatsoever, that will retain the same Collar for the sum aforesaid, forthwith to take upon him the said Knighthood, by reason of a secret vertue in the Collar; for in this Order, it is holden for a certain rule, that the Knighthood followeth the Collar, and not the Collar the Knighthood.

" Item, that no Knight of this Order shall take upon him the person of a male-content, in going with a more private retinue than appertaineth to his degree, and using but special obscure company, and commending none but men disgraced, and out of office; and smiling at good news, as if he knew something that were not true; and making odd notes of his Highness's reign, and former governments; or saying, that his Highness's sports were well sorted with a Play of Errors; and such like pretty speeches of jest, to the end that he may more safely utter his malice against his Excellency's happiness; upon pain to be present at all his Excellency's most glorious Triumphs.

" Lastly, all the Knights of this honourable Order, and the renowned Sovereign of the same, shall yield all homage, loyalty, unaffected admiration, and all humble service, of what name or condition soever, to the incomparable Empress of the Fortunate Island."

When the King at Arms had read all these articles of the Order of the Knighthood, and finished the ceremonies belonging to the same, and that every one had taken their places as before, there was a variety of consort-musick; and in the mean while, the Knights of the Order which were not strangers brought into the hall a running banquet, in very good order, and gave it to the Prince, and Lords, and other Strangers, in imitation of the feast that belongeth to all such honourable institutions.

This being done, there was a table set in the midst of the stage, before the Prince's seat; and there sat six of the Lords of his Privy Council, which at that time were appointed to attend, in council, the Prince's leisure. Then the Prince spake to them in this manner:

" My Lords,

" We have made choice of you, as our most faithful and favoured Counsellors, to advise with you, not any particular action of our State, but in general, of the scope and end whereunto you think it most for our honour, and the happiness of our State, that our government be rightly bent and directed: for we mean not to do as many Princes use; which conclude of their ends out of their own honours, and take counsel only of the means (abusing, for the most part, the wisdom of their Counsellors) set them the right way to the wrong place. But we, desirous to leave as little to chance or humour as may be, do now give you liberty and warrant to set before us, to what port, as it were, the ship of our government should be bounden. And this we require you to do, without either respect to our affections, or your own; neither guessing what is most agreeable with our disposition, wherein we may easily deceive you; for Princes' hearts are inscrutable: nor, on the other side, putting the case by yourselves, as if you would present us with a robe, whereof measure were taken by yourselves. Thus you perceive our mind, and we expect your answer."

The First Counsellor advising the Exercise of War.

" Most Excellent Prince,

" Except there be such amongst us, as I am fully persuaded there is none, that regardeth more his own greatness under you, than your great over others, I think there will be little difference in the chusing for you a goal worthy your vertue and power. For he that shall set before him your magnamity and valour, supported by the youth and disposition of your body; your flourishing Court, like the horse of *Troy,* full of brave commanders and leaders; your populous and man-rife provinces, overflowing with warlike people; your coffers, like the Indian mines, when that they are first opened; your store-houses are as sea-walls, like to Vulcan's cave; your navy like to an huge floating city; the devotion of your subjects to your crown and person, their good agreement amongst themselves, their wealth and provision: and then your strength and unrevocable confederation with the noble and honourable personages, and the fame and reputation without of so rare a concurrence, whereof all the former regards do grow: how can he think any exercise worthy of your means, but that of conquest? for, in few words, What is your strength, if you find it not? Your fortune, if you try it not? Your vertue, if you shew it not? Think, excellent Prince, what sense of content you found in yourself when you were first invested in our state: for though I know your Excellency is far from vanity and lightness, yet it is the nature of all things to find rest when they come to due and proper places. But be assured of this, that this delight will languish and vanish; for power will quench appetite, and satiety will endure tediousness. But if you embrace the wars, your trophies and triumphs will be as continual coronations, that will not suffer your glory and contentment to fade and wither. Then, when you have enlarged your territories, ennobled your country, distributed fortunes, good or bad, at your pleasure, not only to particulars, but to cities and nations; marked the computations of time with your expeditions and voyages, and the memory of places by your exploits and victories, in your later years you shall find a sweet respect into the adventures of your youth, you shall enjoy your reputation, you shall record your travels, and after your own time you shall eternize your name, and leave deep foot-steps of your power in the world. To conclude, excellent Prince, and most worthy to have the titles of victories added to your high and deserved titles; remember, the Divines find nothing more glorious to resemble our state unto than warfare. All things in earnest and jest do affect a kind of victory, and all other victories are but shadows to the victories of the wars. Therefore embrace the wars, for they disparage you not; and believe, that if any Prince do otherwise, it is either in the weakness of his mind or means."

The Second Counsellor, advising the Study of Philosophy.

" It may seem, Most Excellent Prince, that my Lord, which now hath spoken, did never read the just censures of the wisest men, who compared great conquerors to great rovers and witches, whose power is in destruction, and not in preservation; else would he never have advised your Excellency to become as some comet, or blazing-star, which would threaten and portend nothing but death and dearth, combustions and troubles of the world. And whereas the governing faculties of men are two, force and reason; whereof the one is brute, and the other divine, he wisheth you for your principal ornament and regality, the talons of the eagle to catch the prey, and not the piercing sight which seeth into the bottom of the sea: but I, contrarywise, will wish unto your Highness the exercise of the best and purest part of the mind, and the most innocent and meriting request, being the conquest of the works of natnre; making his proportion, that you bend the excellency of your spirits to the searching out, inventing, and discovering of all whatsoever is hid in secret in the world, that your Excellency be not as a lamp that shineth to others, and yet seeth not itself; but as the eye of the world, that both carrieth and useth light. Antiquity, that presenteth unto us in dark visions the wisdom of former times, informeth us, that the kingdoms have always had an affinity with the secrets and mysteries of learning. Amongst the Persians, the Kings were attended on by the Magi; the Gymnasophists had all the government under the Princes of Asia; and generally those kingdoms were accounted most happy, that had rulers most addicted to philosophy: the Ptolemies of Egypt may be for instance; and Solyman was a man so seen in the universality of nature, that he wrote an herbal of all that was green upon the earth. No conquest of Julius Cæsar made him so remembered as the Calendar. Alexander the Great wrote to Aristotle upon the publishing of the Physicks, that he esteemed more of excellent men in knowledge, than in empire. And to this purpose I will commend to your Highness four principal works and monuments of yourself: First, the collecting of a most perfect and general library, wherein whatsoever the wit of man hath heretofore committed to books of worth, be they ancient or modern, printed or manuscript, European or of the other parts, of one or other language, may be made contributary to your wisdom. Next, a spacious, wonderful garden, wherein whatsoever plant, the sun of divers climates, out of the earth of divers moulds, either wild, or by the culture of man, brought forth, may be, with that care that appertaineth to the good prospering thereof, set and cherished. This garden to be built about with rooms, to stable in all rare beasts, and to cage in all rare birds; with two lakes adjoining, the one of fresh water, and the other of salt, for like variety of fishes: and so you may have, in a small compass, a model of universal nature made private. The third a goodly huge cabinet, wherein whatsoever the hand of man, by exquisite art or engine, hath made rare in stuff, form, or motion, whatsoever singularity, chance, and the shuffle of things hath produced, whatsoever nature hath wrought in things that want life, and may be kept, shall be sorted and included. The fourth, such a Still-house so furnished with mills, instruments, furnaces, and vessels, as may be a Palace fit for a philosopher's stone. Thus when your Excellency shall have added depth of knowledge to the fineness of spirits, and greatness of your power, then indeed shall you lay a Trismegistus; and then, when all other miracles and wonders shall cease, by reason that you shall have discovered their natural causes, yourself shall be left the only miracle and wonder of the world."

The Third Counsellor, advising Eternizement and Fame, by Buildings and Foundations.

"My Lords that have already spoken, most excellent Prince, have both used one fallacy, in taking that for certain and granted, which was most uncertain and doubtful: for the one hath neither drawn in question the success and fortune of the wars; nor the other, the difficulties and errors in the conclusions of nature: but these immoderate hopes and promises do many times issue from those of the wars, into tragedies of calamities and distresses; and those of mystical philosophy, into comedies of ridiculous frustrations and disappointments of such conceits and curiosities: but, on the other side, in one point my Lords have well agreed, that they both, according to their several intentions, counselled your Excellency to win fame, and to eternize your name; though the one adviseth it in a course of great peril, and the other, of little dignity and magnificence. But the plain and approved way that is safe, and yet proportionable to the greatness of a Monarch, to present himself to posterity, is not rumour and hear-say; but the usual memory of himself, is the magnificence of goodly and Royal buildings and foundations, and the new institutions of orders, ordinances, and societies: that is, that your coin be stamped with your own image; so in every part of your State there may be somewhat new; which by continuance may make the founder and author remembred. It was perceived at the first, when men sought to cure mortality by fame, that buildings was the only way; and thereof proceeded the known holy antiquity of building the Tower of Babel; which, as it was a sin in the immoderate appetite of fame, so was it punished in the kind; for the diversities of languages have imprisoned fame ever since. As for the pyramids, the colosses, the number of temples, colleges, bridges, aqueducts, castles, theatres, palaces, and the like, they may shew us, that men ever mistrusted any other way to fame than this only, of works and monuments. Yea, even they which had the best choice of other means. Alexander did not think his fame so engraven in his conquests, but that he thought it further shined in the buildings of Alexandria. Augustus Cæsar thought no man had done greater things in military actions than himself; yet that which, at his death, ran most in his mind, was his building; when he said, not as some mistake it, metaphorically, but literally, ' I found the City of brick, but I leave it of marble.' Constantine the Great was wont to call with envy the Emperor Trajan ' Wall-flower,' because his name was upon so many buildings; which, notwithstanding, he himself did embrace in the new founding of Constantinople, and sundry other buildings: and yet none greater conquerors than these two. And surely they had reason; for the fame of great actions is like to a land-flood, which hath no certain head or spring; but the memory and fame of buildings and foundations hath, as it were, a fountain in an hill, which continually feedeth and refresheth the other waters. Neither do I, excellent Prince, restrain my Speeches to dead buildings only, but intend it also to other foundations, institutions, and creations; wherein I presume the more to speak confidently, because I am warranted herein by your own wisdom, who have made the first fruits of your actions of state, to institute the honourable Order of the *Helmet*: the less shall I need to say, leaving your Excellency not so much to follow my advice, as your own example."

The Fourth Councellor, advising Absoluteness of State and Treasure.

"Let it not seem pusillanimity for your Excellency, mighty Prince, to descend a little from your high thoughts to a necessary consideration of your own estate. Neither do you deny, Honourable Lords, to acknowledge safety, profit, and power, to be of the substance of policy, and fame and honour rather to be as flowers of well-ordered actions, than as good guides. Now if you examine the courses propounded according to these respects, it must be confessed, that the course of wars may seem to encrease power, and the course of contemplations and foundations not prejudice safety; but if you look beyond the exterior, you shall find that the first breeds weakness, and the latter note peril: for certain it is, during wars, your Excellency will be enforced to your souldiers, and generally to your people, and become less absolute and monarchical than if you reigned in peace; and then if your success be good, that you make new conquests, you shall be constrained to spend the strength of your ancient and settled provinces, to assure you new and doubtful, and become like a strong man, that, by taking a great burden upon his shoulders, maketh himself weaker than he was before. Again, if you think you may not end contemplations with security, your Excellency will be deceived; for such studies will make you retired and disused with your business; whence will follow admiration of your authority; as for the other point, of exercising in every part of your state something new, derived from yourself, it will acquaint your Excellency with an humor of innovation and alteration; which will make your Reign very turbulent and unsettled, and many times your change will be for worse; as in the example last touched, of Constantine, who, by his new translation of his estate, ruinated the Roman Empire. As for profit, there appeareth a direct contrariety betwixt that and all the three courses; for nothing causeth such dissipation of treasure as wars, curiosities, and buildings; and for all this to be recompensed in a supposed honour, a matter apt to be much extolled in words, but not greatly to be praised in conceit, I do think it a loser's bargain. Besides that, many politic Princes have received as much commendation for their wise and well ordered government, as others have done for their conquests and glorious affections. And more worthy, because the praise of wisdom and judgment is less communicated with fortune. Therefore, excellent Prince, be not transported with shews; follow the order of nature, first to make the most of that you possess, before you seek to purchase more. To put the case by a private man (for I cannot speak high), if a man were born to an hundred pounds by the year, and one shew him how with charge to purchase an hundred pounds more, and another should shew him how without charge to raise that hundred pounds unto five hundred pounds, I should think the latter advice should be followed. The proverb is a countrey proverb, but significative, 'Milk the cow that standeth still; why follow you her that flieth away?' Do not think, excellent Prince, that all the conquests you are to make be foreign; you are to conquer here at home the overgrowing of your grandees in factions, and too great liberties of your people, the great reverence and formalities given to your laws and customs, in derogation of your absolute prerogatives; these and such like be conquests of state, though not of war. You want a Joseph, that should by advice make you the only proprietor of all the lands and wealth of your subjects. The means how to strain up your sovereignty, and how to accumulate treasure and revenue, they are the secrets of your State: I will not enter into them at this place; I wish your Excellency as ready to them, as I know the means ready to perform them."

The Fifth Councellor, advising him Vertue, and a Gracious Government.

"Most Excellent Prince,

"I have heard sundry plats and propositions offered unto you severally: one, to make you a great Prince; another, to make you a strong Prince; and another to make you a memorable Prince; and a fourth, to make you an absolute Prince; but I hear of no mention to make you a good and virtuous Prince; which surely my Lords have left out in discretion, as to arise of your own motion and choice; and so I should have thought, had they not handled their own propositions so artificially and perswadingly, as doth assure me their Speech was not formal. But, most worthy Prince, fame is too light, and profit and surety are too low, and power is either such as you have, or ought not so to seek to have; it is the meriting of your subjects, the making of golden times, the becoming of a natural parent to your State: these are the only and worthy ends of your Grace's virtuous Reign. My Lords have taught you to refer all things to yourself, your greatness, memory, and advantage; but whereunto shall yourself be referred? If you will be heavenly, you must have influence; will you be as a standing pool, that spendeth and choaketh his spring within itself, and hath no streams nor current to bless and make fruitful whole tracts of countreys, whereby it reneweth? Wherefore, first of all, most virtuous Prince, assure yourself of an inward Peace, that the storms without do not disturb any of your repairers of State within;

therein use and practise all honourable diversions; that done, visit all the parts of your State, and let the balm distil every where from your Sovereign hands, to the medicining of any part that complaineth, beginning with your seat of State, take order that the fault of your greatness do not rebound upon yourself; have care that your intelligence, which is the light of your State, do not go out, or burn dim or obscure; advance men of virtue, and not of mercenary minds; repress all faction, be it either malign or violent. Then look into the state of your laws, and justice of your land; purge out multiplicity of laws, clear the incertainty of them, repeal those that are snaring, and prize the execution of those that are wholesome and necessary; define the jurisdiction of your Courts, reprize all suits and vexations, all causeless delays and fraudulent shifts and devices, and reform all such abuses of right and justice, assist the ministers thereof, punish severely all extortions and exactions of officers, all corruptions in trials and sentences of judgment. Yet, when you have done all this, think not that the bridle and spur will make the horse to go alone without time and custom. Trust not to your laws for correcting the times, but give all strength to good education; see to the government of your Universities, and all seminaries of youth, and of the private order of families, maintaining due obedience of children towards their parents, and reverence of the younger sort towards the ancient. Then when you have confirmed the noble and vital parts of your realm of State, proceed to take care of the blood and flesh, and good habit of the body. Remedy all decays of population, make provision for the poor, remove all stops in traffick, and all cancers and causes of consumption in trades and mysteries; redress all: but whither do I run, exceeding the bounds of that perhaps I am now demanded? But pardon me, most excellent Prince, for as if I should commend unto your Excellency the beauty of some excellent Lady, I could not so well express it with relation, as if I shewed you her picture; so I esteem the best way to commend a virtuous government, to describe and make appear what it is; but my pencil perhaps disgraceth it: therefore I leave it to your Excellency, to take the picture out of your wise observation, and then to double it, and express it in your government."

The Sixth Councellor, perswading Pass-times and Sports,

"When I heard, most excellent Prince, the three first of my Lords so careful to continue your fame and memory, methought it was as if a man should come to some young Prince, as yourself is; and immediately after his coronation, be in hand with him to make himself a sumptuous and stately tomb. And, to speak out of my soul, I muse how any of your servants can once endure to think of you as of a Prince past. And for my other Lords, who would engage you so deeply in matters of State; the one perswading you to a more absolute, the other to a more gracious Government; I assure your Excellency, their lessons were so cumbersome, as if they would make you a King in a Play; who when one would think he standeth in great majesty and felicity, he is troubled to say his part. What! nothing but tasks? nothing but working-days? No feasting, no music, no dancing, no triumphs, no comedies, no love, no ladies? Let other men's lives be as pilgrimages, because they are tied to divers necessities and duties; but Princes' lives are as Progresses, dedicated only to variety and solace. And if your Excellency should take your barge in a summer evening, or your horse or chariot, to take the air; and if you should do any the honour to visit him; yet your pleasure is the principal, and that is but as it falleth out. So if any of these matters which have been spoken of, fall out in the way of your pleasure, it may be taken; but no otherwise. And therefore, leave your wars to your Lieutenants, and your works and buildings to your Surveyors, and your books to your Universities, and your State-matters to your Counsellors, and attend you that in person which you cannot execute by deputy: use the advantage of your youth, be not sullen to your fortune; make your pleasure the distinction of your honours, the studies of your favourites, the talk of your people, and the allurement of all foreign gallants to your Court. And, in a word, sweet Sovereign, dismiss your five Counsellors, and only take Council of your five senses."

"But if a man should follow your five senses (said the Prince) I perceive he might follow your Lordship, now and then, into an inconvenience. Your Lordship is a man of a very lively and pleasant advice; which though one should not be forward to follow, yet it fitteth the time, and what our own humour inclined oftentimes to, delight and merriment. For a Prince should be of a chearful and pleasant spirit; not austere, hard-fronted, and stoical; but, after serious affairs, admitting recreation, and using pleasures, as sauces for meats of better nourishment."

The Prince's Answer and Conclusion to the Speeches of the Counsellors.

" My Lords,

" We thank you for your good opinions; which have been so well set forth, as we should think ourselves not capable of good council, if, in so great variety of perswading reasons, we should suddenly resolve. Mean while, it shall not be amiss to make choice of the last, and upon more deliberation to determine of the rest; and what time we spent in long consulting, in the end we will gain by prompt and speedy executing."

The Prince, having ended his Speech, arose from his seat, and took that occasion of revelling: so he made choice of a lady to dance withal; so likewise did the Lord Ambassador, the Pensioners and Courtiers attending the Prince. The rest of that night was passed in those pass-times. The performance of which night's work being very carefully and orderly handled, did so delight and please the Nobles and the other auditory, that thereby *Gray's-Inn* did not only recover their lost credit, and quite take away all the disgrace that the former night of Errors had incurred; but got, instead thereof, so great honour and applause, as either the good reports of our honourable friends that were present could yield, or we ourselves desire.

The next day the Prince, accompanied with the Ambassador of *Templaria*, and attended by both trains, took his Progress from his Court of *Graya*, to the Lord Mayor's[1] house, called *Crosby's Place*, in *Bishopsgate-street*; as being, before that time, invited to dine with him. This shew was very stately, and orderly performed; the Prince being mounted upon a rich foot-cloth, the Ambassador likewise riding near him; the Gentlemen attending, with the Prince's officers, and the Ambassador's favourites, before; and the other coming behind the Prince; as he set it down in the general marshalling in the beginning. Every one had his feather in his cap, to distinguish of whether State he was; the *Grayans* using a white, and the *Templarians* using ash-coloured feathers; to the number of fourscore in all, very well appointed, and provided of great horses and foot-cloths, according to their places. Thus they rode very gallantly, from *Gray's-Inn*, through *Chancery-lane*, *Fleet-street*, so through *Cheapside*, *Cornhill*, and to *Crosby's-Place*, in *Bishopsgate-street*; where was a very sumptuous and costly dinner for the Prince, and all his Attendants, with variety of musick, and all good entertainment. Dinner being ended, the Prince and his company having revelled a-while, returned again the same way, and in the same order as he went thither,

[1] Sir John Spencer. See before, p. 254.

the streets being thronged and filled with people, to see the Gentlemen as they passed by; who thought there had been some great Prince, in very deed, passing through the City. So this popular shew through the streets pleased the Lord Mayor and his Commonalty so well, as the great Lords, and others of good condition and civility, were contented with our former proceedings.

Shortly after this shew, there came letters to our State from *Frederick Templarius;* wherein he desired, that his Ambassador might be dispatched with answer to those things which he came to treat of. So he was very honourably dismissed, and accompanied homeward with the Nobles of *Purpoole:* which departure was before the next grand day. The next grand night was upon Twelfth-day at night; at which time the wonted honourable and worshipful company of Lords, Ladies, and Knights, were, as at other times, assembled; and every one of them placed conveniently, according to their condition. And when the Prince was ascended his chair of State, and the trumpet sounded, there was presently a shew which concerned his Highness's State and Government: the invention was taken out of the Prince's arms, as they are blazoned in the beginning of his reign, by the King at Arms.

First, there came six Knights of the Helmet, with three that they led as prisoners, and were attired like monsters and miscreants. The Knights gave the Prince to understand, that as they were returning from their adventures out of Russia, wherein they aided the Emperor of Russia, against the Tartars, they surprized these three persons, which were conspiring against his Highness and his dignity: and that being apprehended by them, they could not urge them to disclose what they were: by which they resting very doubtful, there entred in the two goddesses Virtues and Amity; and they said, that they would disclose to the Prince who these suspected persons were: and thereupon shewed, that they were Envy, Male-content, and Folly: which three had much misliked his Highness's proceedings, and had attempted many things against his State; and, but for them two, Virtue and United Friendship, all their inventions had been disappointed. Then willed they the Knights to depart, and to carry away the offenders; and that they themselves should come in more pleasing sort, and better befitting the present. So the Knights departed, and Virtue and Amity promised that they two would support his Excellency against all his foes whatsoever, and then departed with most pleasant musick. After their departure, entred the six Knights in a very stately mask, and danced a new devised measure; and after that, they took to them Ladies and Gentlewomen, and danced with them their *galliards*, and so departed with musick. Which being done, the trumpets were commanded to sound, and then the King at Arms came in before the Prince, and told his Honour, that there was arrived an Ambassador from the mighty Emperor of Russia and Muscovy, that had some matters of weight to make known to his Highness. So the Prince willed that he should be admitted into his presence; who came in attire of Russia, accompanied with two of his own country in like habit. When they were come in presence of the Prince, the Ambassador made his obeysance, and took out Letters of Credence, and humbly delivered them to the Prince, who gave them to the King at Arms, to be read publicly, as followeth:

" To the most High and Mighty HENRY, Prince of *Purpoole.*

" *Theodore Evanwhich,* the great and mighty Emperor of all *Russia, Valderomia, Muscovia,* and *Novogordia;* King of *Rafan,* and of *Astrakan;* Lord of *Plescoe* and *Sinelescoe;* Prince of *Tnaria, Sogoria, Perma,* [*Vachekey,* and *Bolgaria;* Lord and Great Duke of *Valhadha, Norgordia* in the country of *Cherenega;* and also of *Rescod, Polotzkoe, Ogdor,* and *Belesor;* sole Prince of *Lothekey, Rostow, Geroslave,* the white lake *Liselrund, Owdoria, Condencia,* and *Fludoria;* Great Ruler and Commander of *Siberia,* and of all the North-side; and Lord Governor of many other Countries and Provinces. To the most mighty, and glorious renowned Henry, Prince of *Purpoole,* Archduke of *Stapulia* and *Bernardia,* Duke of *High and Nether Holborn,* Marquis of *St. Giles's* and *Tottenham,* Count Palatine of *Bloomsbury* and *Clerkenwell,* Great Lord of the Cantons of *Islington, Kentish Town, Paddington,* and *Knightsbridge,* Knight of the most heroical Order of tye *Helmet,* and Sovereign of the same; all health and glorious renown. We have thought good, most invincible Prince, upon some accidents of importance happened to our State, wherein the worthiness of some of your subjects remaining here have increased your fame, to dispatch to your Highness our most faithful Counsellor *Faman Bega,* to intreat with you, in our name, of certain important affairs: which, though we must confess, do concern us in policy, to have an effectual regard unto; yet withal, they are such as may minister occasion to your Highness to add beams of honour to your praise and glory, which hath already, in a manner, equalled the light of Heaven in brightness, which is seen throughout the whole world. We refer you herein for the particulars to such instructions as we have, under our own hand, delivered to this our present Ambassador: wherein, as also in any other points wherof he shall treat with your Highness, in our name and affairs, we pray your sacred Majesty to give credit to him, as if ourself were present, and treated with you in person. And so we wish to your Excellency all happiness answerable to your peerless virtue. Dated at our Imperial City of *Mosco*."

When the King at Arms had read this Letter, the Ambassador made this Speech to the Prince:

" Most Excellent Prince,

" Fame seemed to the Emperor, my Sovereign, to do your Highness right, by filling the world with the renown of your Princely virtues, and valour of your brave Court; till of late, the gallant behaviour and heroical prowess of divers your *Knights of the Helmet*, whom the good fortune of Russia, addressed to your cold climate, discovered that Fame to be either envious in suppressing a great part of your valour, or unable to set forth so admirable virtues to their full merits: for by these five Knights (whose greatest vaunts were, that they were your Excellency's servants) an exceeding number of Bigarian Tartars, whose vagabond inroads, and inhumane fierceness infested his borders, captivated his people, burnt his cities, and spoiled whole provinces, was, by a most wonderful victory, repulsed, and beaten back. And withal, by their brave conduct, they surprized another army of Negro Tartars: whose wretched devices ceased not to work the confusion and combustion of our whole country, and diverted their barbarous cruelty where it might do us most damage. These same worthy Knights, before they could receive that honour wherewith my Sovereign intended to adorn their virtues, did withdraw themselves, and are retired, as his Majesty is informed, to your Court. Whereupon, he sent me, partly to congratulate your happiness, who deserve to command over such a number of gallant Gentlemen; but especially to conjure your Excellency (according to the ancient league and amity continued betwixt you) that you would send him these six Knights, accompanied with an hundred other of the same Order; for he doubteth not, but, by their virtues, accompanied and attended with his own forces, who are, in largeness of dominion, and number of people, and all other warlike furniture and provision, inferior to no earthly potentate, that these runagate Tartars shall be again confined to their deserts, with their memorable slaughter, and your common glory and profit: common indeed, both to your Highness and him; inasmuch as his Imperial Majesty, contented only with security and assurance of his people and borders, will permit all those large territories, and bateable grounds, which now serve those vermine for pasturage, be sorted into several governments, and strengthened with forts and castles by your direction, to be holden of your Excellency, as commendations by the Knights of special virtue and merit of your Order. So shall you, with honourable commodity, have a perpetual exercise of your virtues, become a bulwark of Christendom, and by raising continual trophies of strengthened Tartars, keep the glory of your virtue in everlasting flourish. My Sovereign, not doubting but that your resolution will be conformable to your magnanimous virtue, and his honourable demand, charged me only to solicit expedition, such as the necessity of his people and country doth require. In the mean time, he hath sent your Excellency, for a present, a ship laden with divers of the best and fairest fruits, and other richest commodities of our country: not so much, by gifts to draw on your speedy help, to which he knoweth the truth and justice of the case will be a spur sufficient; or for complement of an ordinary and seldom omitted companion of great Embassies: but rather for a seal and testimony of the exceeding honour that he beareth to your matchless vertue, and the great love he beareth to your incomparable person. The present is at your next haven, ready to be offered to your sacred hands at your convenient leisure; together with some small gifts sent to those valiant Knights, whose highly deserving vertues my Sovereign meaneth, at their long expected return to his Court, to crown with a garland more worthy his greatness and their merits."

The Answer of the Prince to the former Speech.

" Russia Lord,

" The Emperor, your Master, is happy in having so honourable a Gentlemen as yourself to do him service. He shall well perceive, that ther is nothing in the world more acceptable to us, than the friendship of a Prince so mighty and illustrious. We account amongst our greatest happinesses this honourable embassage. His presents are so large and bountiful, as we have right good occasion to hold him the most free and magnificent Prince in the world. We joy to hear of his hardy adventures, that by our Knights in those parts have been atchieved. They may be glad that our worthy Brother invited them to so high an enterprize, wherein they may do themselves honour, and his greatness service. Rest and refresh your Lordship this present, for now we bid you welcome: assure yourself your request is already granted, and that in far greater measure than you expected or desired."

When the Prince had thus spoken, the Ambassador was placed in a chair near the Prince; and then was served up a running banquet, for the Prince and the Lords present, and the rest, with variety of music.

Whilst these things were thus a-doing, there came a post-boy with letters of intelligence concerning the state, from divers parts of his Highness's provinces, and delivered them to the Secretary; who made the Prince acquainted therewith, and caused them to be read openly and publicly.

A Letter of Advertisement from *Knightsbridge*, to the Honourable Council.

" I beseech your Honours to advertise his Highness, that in his Excellency's Canton of *Knightsbridge*, there do haunt certain foreigners, that seize upon all passengers, taking from them by force their goods, under a pretence that, being merchants strangers, and using traffic into his Highness's territories of *Clerkenwell*, *Islington*, and elsewhere, they have been robbed of their goods, spoiled of their wares; whereby they were utterly undone: and that his Honour, of his good will, hath been pleased to grant them Letters of Reprisal, to recover their loss of them that come next to their hands: by colour whereof, they lay hold of all that pass by, without respect. Some of their names, as I understand, are, *Johannes Shagbag*, *Robertus Untruss*, *James Rapax*, alias *Capax*. There do reign likewise thereabouts another sort of dangerous people, under the name of Poor Soldiers, that say they were maimed, and lost their limbs in his Honour's service and wars against the *Amazons*; and they pretend to have pass-ports from their Captains. Some of them say, they have served under Sir *Robert Kemp* and Sir *William Cooke*; others under *William Knaplocks*, Lord Marshall, Sir *Francis Marham*, Captain *Crymes*, Captain *Conny*, *Yelverton*, *Hugan*, Sir *Francis Davison*, and some other of good place. Some say, that they were maimed with fire-locks; others, in the trenches; others, in going with their captains to discover ambuscadoes of the enemy, and to view the forts; others, in standing sentry, whilst the captains were busied in entering the breach; others, in the very approach at the first. But the number of them is great, and the same inclined to do much mischief. Another sort there is, that pretend that they have protections to beg, in regard of their losses by shipwreck upon certain rocks of hazard, barred quartertrays, high-men and low-men, bom-cards, the sands of bowle-allies, the shelf of new-cut, the gulf of myne and gill, and such other like places of peril. Some of them are called by the names of *Harry Ordinary*, *Jack Moneyless*, *Will Cog-all*, and *Roger Spend-all*. These aforesaid people do gather together in great numbers; and his Excellency's subjects hereabouts stand in great fear of outrages by them to be committed, except his Highness do prevent the same, and that speedily, by sending some of the Captains aforesaid to disperse them.

"Your Honour's at command,   HENRY BROWNBILL.
" From *Knightsbridge*, Jan. 5, 1594-5."

Another Letter from Sea, directed to the Lord Admiral.

" By my letters given at *Pont-Holborn*, the last of December, I gave your Honour to understand, that his Excellency's merchants of *Purpoole* began to surcease their traffick to *Clerkenwell, Newington,* and *Bank-side,* and such like roads of charge and discharge, because they feared lest certain rovers, which lay hovering about the Narrow Seas, should intercept them in their voyages; since which time, may it please your Honour, I have discovered an huge Armado of French Amazons, to the number of seven hundred caracts, galeasses, great galeasses, and tall ships; besides pinnaces, frigots, carvels, shallops, and such small vessels innumerable; which being dispersed into sundry creeks, work daily much damage to all sorts of people, and adventurers hold in durance; not suffering one man to escape, till he have turned *French*. Divers ensigns, standards, pendants, tilting-staves, short trunchions for the principal officers, and such like provisions for his Excellency's triumphs, they have cast overboard; for no other cause, save that his subjects were bound inward from *Gelderland,* a nation that they have always hated: besides that, they exact so unreasonably of those that trade into *Netherland,* that they leave them neither lands, goods, nor good wares. Also they sink all those that use any dealings with the people of *Cleive,* without respect, whether he be merchant or man of war. To conclude, they burn all those vessels that transport any dry wares into the *Low Countries*. Moreover, I am to advertise your Honour, that, on the 9th day of January, in the Straits of the Gulf of *Clerkenwell,* there was a hot skirmish between a merchant of *St. Giles's,* called Amarpso, and the Admiral of the Amazons, called the Rowse-flower; wherein the merchant having gained the wind, came up with her in such close manner, that he brake his bolt-sprite in her hinder quarter; yet notwithstanding, the fight continued fiercely on either part two long hours and more; in which time our gunner, being a very expert soldier, shot her four or five times under water: then the merchant, perceiving his powder to be spent, was inforced to grapple; and so, with great resolution, laid her a-board on the waste, which he found stoutly defended by the *French;* yet, at length, being driven from their close fight, they were constrained to keep under hatches, where one of the soldiers entring, spied fire in the gun-room; notwithstanding, he descended very desperately. Then the admiral, seeing no hope to escape, fired her powder, and burnt herself, the soldiers, and the ship, which, as I after learned, was of an incomparable burden; insomuch, that she had been known to have borne nine hundred fighting men in her poop. Her chief lading was cochenella, musk, guaiacum, tabaco, and *Le grand Vexolle.* The chief of account that were blown up, were Catharina Dardana, Pecta de Lee, and Maria de Rotulis. The rich Carrick of *Newington,* coming to rescue their admiral, were so close at fight when she was fired, that the flame of the wild-fire caught hold of their captain's inner cabbin: and had not one Barbara de Chirurgia been ready with his syringe, to have cast on water, milk, lotium, and such like cooling liquors, and there quenched the wild-fire betimes, they had been both, doubtless, consumed to ashes; but, by his care and coming, they are both escaped alive, though shrewdly scorched, and are taken prisoners. The whole number of them that perished in this hot conflict, is five hundred fifty-five; and prisoners ninety-nine. Our ship had no other hurt, save that she sprang her main-mast in such sort, as that she is not able to bear any high sail. Thus having advertised your Honour of every particular accident which I could learn, I am humbly to desire your Lordship to acquaint his Excellency and his Privy Council therewith; that such speedy order may be taken therein, as seemeth to their wisdoms most convenient. And so, with all duty, I kiss your hands.

" Your Honour's servants,   JOHN PUTTANEMICO.
" From the Harbour of *Bridewell,* the 10th of January, 1594."

There were also read like letters from *Stapulia* and *Bernardia,* of intelligences, and also from *Low Holborn;* wherein were set forth the plots of rebellion and insurrection, that those his Excellency's subjects had devised against his Highness and State, and some other occurrences in those parts of his Highness's dominions. And when they were read, the Prince made this Speech following:

"These suddain accidents (Lords) would make a Prince of little spirit suspect himself to be unfortunate. The *Stapulian* fallen away; the *Bernardian* holds out! News of tumults, treasons, conspiracies, commotions, treacheries, insurrections! Say our lands were sacked, our wealth spoiled, our friends slain, ourself forsaken, vanquished, captivated, and all the evils that might be were fallen upon us; yet could there be nothing so adverse, but that our fortitude and heighth of courage were able to over-work. These events are not matters of moment, or of substance of our government: these are not misfortunes, but Fortune's jests, that gives them she loves not shews of good luck, that in the end she may do them greater spight: but, when she meaneth good, she prepares men with some little bitterness, that her good turns, when they come, may seem more pleasant and delightful. These events proceed of error in our former government, who should not have put great men, well loved or popular, into so great places of sovereingty; nor one man should possess so great a place, of so great command; by too much authority and greatness, a right good mind is oftentimes corrupted: in this late, we rather allow a severe man, somewhat hated: for better were a little profitable civil dissention, than a league and love that were likely to prove dangerous. Lords, you shall find it an harder matter to keep things once gotten, than at the first to obtain it. Hitherto no Prince in this world hath had better success than ourself. Men say, that sovereignty is uncertain, and an ill security; subject to cares, troubles, envy, treacheries, hate, fear, distrust; we have hitherto found none of those. That a Prince hath no sure friend, no faithful servant, no safe place, no quiet hour, no secure pleasure; all these have we, and more, in great abundance; and these things, which to other Princes have been the occasions of mishap, have been to us the very instruments of pleasure, and much service. What Prince ever found in his subjects, in matters of weight, more love, more loyalty, more readiness, more service? When we have been inclined to solace, what liveliness, what alacrity, what ingenious devices, sports, jollities, what variety of pleasure! How have we been honoured with the presents of divers Princes, Lords, and men of great worth; who, confident in our love, without fear or distrust, have come to visit us; by whose honourable kindness, we are to them for ever devinct, and most firmly bounden: How hath the favourable regard, and bright eyes of brave ladies shined upon our endeavours, which to their honours and service have been ever intended! How have we been gratulated with divers Ambassadors from divers Nations! What concourse of all people hath been continually at our Court, to behold our magnificence! Shall small matters therefore daunt us? Shall a few tumultuary disorders dismay us? Shall ill-guided insurrections trouble us, that are, like mushrooms, sprung up in a night, and rotten before the morning? We are loath to believe that there be such sparks of dissention and mischief: but, if there be, we will make haste to quench them, before they grow into violent flames; for it is no longer consulting, where a man cannot commend the counsel before he hath seen the effect. Nor shall it require the presence of a Prince to settle these small commotions. Lords, we send you to these places where need is; and, as occasion serveth, we will take order that garrisons be planted, citadels erected, and whatsoever else be performed, that shall be convenient to subject and bring under these unsettled provinces. Ourself, with Our chosen Knights, with an army Royal, will make towards Our Brother of *Russia*, with my Lord here, his Ambassador, presently to join with him against his enemies, the *Negarian Tartars*; more dreadful, the *Barbarian Tartars*: And if *Fortune* will not grace Our good attempt, as I am rightful Prince, and true Sovereign of the honourable Order of the *Helmet*, and by all those Ladies whom, in Knightly honour, I love and serve, I will make the name of a *Grayan Knight* more dreadful to the *Barbarian Tartars*, than the *Macedonian* to the wearied *Persians*, the *Roman* to the dispersed *Britains*, or the *Castalian* to the weakened *Indians*. Gentle Ladies, be now benign and gracious to your Knights, that never pleased themselves but when their service pleased you; that for your sakes shall undertake hard adventures, that will make your names and beauties most famous, even in foreign regions. Let your favour kindle the vigour of their spirits, wherewith they abound; for they are the men by whom your fame, your honour, your virtue, shall be for ever advanced, protected, and admired."

When the Prince had concluded, for his farewell he took a lady to dance withal, and so did the rest of the Knights and Courtiers; and after some time spent in revelling, the Prince took his way to his lodging, and so the company dissolved, and made an end of this night's work.

On the next morning his Highness took his journey towards *Russia*, with the Ambassador, and there he remained until Candlemas; at which time, after his glorious conquests abroad, his Excellency returned home again; in which the purpose of the Gentlemen was much disappointed by the Readers and Ancients of the House, by reason of the Term: so that very good inventions, which were to be performed in public at his entertainment into the house again, and two grand nights which were intended at his triumphal return, wherewith his reign had been conceitedly determined, were by the aforesaid Readers and Governors made frustrate, for the want of room in the hall, the scaffolds being taken away, and forbidden to be built up again (as would have been necessary for the good discharge of such a matter) thought convenient; but it shewed rather what was performed, than intended. Briefly, it was as followeth:

Upon the 28th of January, the hall being sate at dinner, with Readers, and all the rest of the House, suddainly sounded a trumpet; which being thrice done, there entered the King at Arms, and, in the midst of them, said as followeth:

"On the behalf of my Sovereign Lord, Sir HENRY, the Right Excellent and all-conquering Prince of *Purpoole*, Archduke of *Stapulia* and *Bernardia*, Duke of *High* and *Nether Holborn*, Marquis of *St. Giles's* and *Tottenham*, Count Palatine of *Bloomsbury* and *Clerkenwell*, Great Lord of the Cantons of *Islington*, *Kentish Town*, *Paddington*, and *Knightsbridge*, Knight of the most heroical Order of the Helmet, and Sovereign of the same; I, his Excellency's King at Arms, dispatched from his royal navy, triumphantly returning from his glorious conquests of the *Negarian Tartars*, do, in his Highness's name, command all his officers, Knights and Pensioners, to give their attendance to his Highness's person, at his port of *Black-wallia*, on the 1st of February. And his Highness hath further commanded me to give notice to all his servants within his dominions, of whatsoever condition, that they be ready to perform all offices of obedience and subjection, as well becometh their loyalty to so gracious a Sovereign."

When this news of the Prince's return out of Russia was thus sent abroad, and that it was known that his Highness was to come by Greenwich, where the Court then lay, it was given the Gentlemen to understand, that her Majesty did expect, that in passing by, our Prince should land, and do his homage; the rather because, in Christmas, there was great expectation of his coming thither, to present her Majesty with some pass-time, and none performed. Whereupon it was determined, that, in passing by, there should be a letter directed to Sir Thomas Hencage, our honourable good friend, that he should excuse us for that time; which letter is hereafter set down.

Upon the 1st of February, the Prince and his train were met at Blackwall; from whence they came up the river of Thames, in a very gallant shew. Being come so near his own country, he left his navy of ships, as not fit for so short a cut, and the matter not being very great or dangerous; and he and his retinue took to them fifteen barges, bravely furnished with standards, pendants, flags, and streamers: there was also in every barge music and trumpets; and in some ordnance and shot. Being thus gallantly appointed, we came on our way by the Stairs at Greenwich, where the ordnance was shot off, and the whole navy made a sail round about;

and the second time, when the Admiral, in which the Prince was, came directly before the Court Stairs, his Highness dispatched two Gentlemen with letters to the Right Honourable Sir *Thomas Heneage.* The copy whereof followeth:

"*Henry* Prince of *Purpoole* to the Right Honourable Sir *Thomas Heneage.*

"Most Honourable Knight,

"I have now accomplished a most tedious and hazardous journey, though very honourable, into *Russia;* and returning within the view of the Court of your renowned Queen, my gracious Sovereign, to whom I acknowledge homage and service, I thought good, in passing by, to kiss her sacred hands, as a tender of the zeal and duty I owe unto her Majesty; but, in making the offer, I found my desire was greater than the ability of my body; which, by length of my journey, and my sickness at sea, is so weakened, as it were very dangerous for me to adventure it. Therefore, most honourable friend, let me intreat you to make my humble excuse to her Majesty for this present: and to certifie her Highness, that I do hope, by the assistance of the Divine Providence, to recover my former strength about Shrovetide; at which time I intend to repair to her Majesty's Court (if it may stand with her gracious pleasure) to offer my service, and relate the success of my journey. And so praying your Honour to return me her Majesty's answer, I wish you all honour and happiness.

"Dated from ship-board, at our *Ark of Vanity,*
"the 1st of February 1594."

The letter being delivered, and her Majesty made acquainted with the contents, her gracious answer was: "That if the letter had not excused his passing by, he should have done homage before he had gone away, although he had been a greater Prince than he was: yet," she said, "she liked well his gallant shews, that were made at his triumphant return." And her Highness added further, "That if he should come at Shrovetide, he and his followers should have entertainment according to his dignity." And the messenger returned answer.

The Prince and his company continued their course until they came to the Tower; where, by her Majesty's commandment, he was welcomed with a volley of great ordnance, by the Lieutenant of the Tower. At the Tower-hill there waited for the Prince's landing, men attending with horses, very gallantly appointed, for all the company, to the number of one hundred; the most of them being great horses, and the rest very choice geldings; and all very bravely furnished with all things necessary. So the Prince being mounted, and his company in order, as before set down, every man according to his office, with the ensign thereof, they rode very gallantly through Tower Street, Fenchurch Street, Gracechurch Street, Cornhill, Cheapside, and so through St. Paul's Church Yard; where, at St. Paul's school, his Highness was entertained with an oration, made by one of the scholars of that school; the copy whereof followeth:

" HENRICO, Illustrissimo & Potentissimo *Purpoolæ* Principi, Archi-duci *Stapuliæ* & *Bernardiæ, Superioris & Inferioris Holborn* Duci, *Sancti Ægidii* & *Tottenham* Marchioni, de *Clerkenwell* & *Bloomsbury* Comiti Palatino, Domino magno Cantonum de *Islington, Kentishtown, Paddington,* & *Knightsbridge,* Heroici Ordinis *Galeolæ* Equiti Aurato, & ejusdem Domino Serenissimo.

" Importunum fortasse fuerit (*Purpooliensis* Princeps Serenissime) apud tantam Majestatem tuam tam intempestivo tempore perorare. Vix enim sperare ausus sum, velle te, qui tantam personam sustines tuumque hunc comitatum vere Aulicum, post victorias partas terra marique maximas, ad vocem puerilem in media instructissimi triumphi solemnitate consistere. Verum per affibilitatem in summis principibus semper laudatissimam, liceat mihi prætereunti celsitudini tuæ musarum nostrarum benevolentiam offerre, & gratulationem hanc meam qualemcunque post tam illustrem tuum & triumphantem, ac per totum orbem divulgatum è *Russia* reditum, hac mea oratione Generosis omnibus testatum relinquere. Quamvis enim subito nobis excidat, & ad tantam Majestatem quasi obstupescat oratio, gratulatio tamen quæ magis sit offerri, quæque sit officii & amoris erga virtutes Generosas plenior afferri certe quidem non potest. Nonne vides civitatem ipsam quasi sedibus suis convulsam ad congratulandum tanto Principi procedere? Quid existimas totum hunc concursum cogitare? In cujus ora vultusque horum omnium oculos conjectos putas? Quem sensum reddis amicorum nostrorum? Quid cupimus? Quid optamus? Quid agimus? Nonne ut tam voluntates nostras testemur, quam victoriis gratulemur tuis? Quid igitur mirum si schola, etiam nostra virtutum Generosarum emula, victoriis & triumphis illustrissimis gratulari gestiat? Perge igitur, & optimis auspiciis perge, Clarissime Princeps, ad *Purpooliense* palatium tuum redito, *Grayorum* oraculum, quo tanquam *Delphici Apollinis* voce fatidica omnes controversiæ dirimuntur. De *Hispano* hoste omnium Principum communi invadendo, consulito. Quàm facile tuus jam sanguine madens *Tartarorum* gladius, præsertim si *Templarios* tibi antiquo fœdere conjunctos in belli novi societatem asciscas, aliorum omnium & strictos gladios retundet, & clypeos excutiet? *Hispani invidia rumpantur ut Ilia Codro.* Interim vero Musæ nostræ & præteritis tuis applaudent victoriis, & *Palladem* suam exorabunt antiquam *Grayorum,* ut te alterum jam *Agamemnonem,* qui multos habes *Achilles* & *Ulysses* Comites tuos, galea sua induat, clypeo protegat, & hasta (hostibus tuis omnibus fusis profligatisque) in perpetuum conservat."

The Oration being ended, the Prince rewarded the boy very bountifully, and thanked them for their good wills, and forwardness to shew the same. Then we marched on our way, as before, by Ludgate, and through Fleet Street; where, as all the way else, the streets were so thronged and filled with people, that there was left but room for the horsemen that were to pass. In this state the Prince was conducted to *Gray's Inn,* where his Excellency was received by a peal of ordnance, and sound of trumpets, and all the good entertainment that all his loving subjects could make, to shew their love and loyalty to his Highness.

The Prince, being thus received, came, after supper, into the hall, and there he danced and revelled among the Nobles, and others of his own Court; and in like manner they spent the day following: but there was no other performance, by reason of want of the stage and scaffolds, till Shrovetide, that they went to the Court: and the things that were then performed before her Majesty, were rather to discharge our own promise, than to satisfie the expectations of others. In that regard, the plot of those sports were but small; the rather, that tediousness might be avoided, and confused disorder, a thing which might easily happen in a multitude of actions; the sports therefore consisted of a mask, and some speeches that were as introductions to it; as followeth:

The Speakers.

An *Esquire* of the Prince's Company, attended by a Tartarian Page.
Proteus the Sea-god, attended by two Tritons.
Thamesis and *Amphitrite*, who likewise were attended by their Sea-nymphs.
These five were musicians, which sung on the first coming on the Stage.

At the first coming on the Stage, the Nymphs and Tritons sung this Hymn following, in praise of Neptune.

Of Neptune's empire let us sing,
  At whose command the waves obey,
  To whom rivers tribute pay,
Down the high mountains sliding:
  To whom the scaly nation yields
  Homage for their chrystal fields,
    Wherein they dwell.
      And every Sea-god praise again,
    Yearly out of his wat'ry cell,
      To deck great Neptune's diadem.

The Tritons dancing in a ring,
  Before his palace-gates, do make
  The waiters with their trumpets quake,
Like the great thunder sounding.
  The Sea-nymphs chaunt their accents shrill,
  And the Syrens taught to kill
    With their sweet voice,
      Make every echoing voice reply
    Unto their gentle mourning noise,
      In praise of Neptune's empery.

Which being ended, the Speakers made their Speeches in order as followeth:

Esquire.   Proteus, it seems you lead a merry life;
  Your music follows you where-e'r you go.
  I thought you Sea-gods, as in your abode,
  So in your nature, had not been unlike
  To fishes; the which, as say philosophers,
  Have so small sense of music's delight,
  As 'tis a doubt not fully yet resolv'd,
  Whether of hearing they have sense or no.

Proteus.   'Twas great discourse of reason, to regard
  The dreaming guess of a philosopher,
  That never held his idle buzzing head
  Under the water half an hour's space,
  More than that famous old received history
  Of good Arion, by a dolphin saved.

Esquire. Well, let that pass, and to the purpose now;
    I thought that you, that are a demy-god,
    Would not have fail'd my expectation thus.

Proteus. Why so, fair 'Squire? Is not my promise kept,
    And duly the appointed time observ'd?

Esquire. Yes; and 'tis that in which I rest deceiv'd:
    I rather deem'd, and not without good cause,
    That those still floating regions where you hide,
    And th' ever changing nature that you have,
    Nought else but breach of promise, promised.

Proteus. 'Twere strange if that my word, which credit keeps,
    In future things, and hidden secrecies,
    Should fondly fail in keeping promise made:
    Fondly indeed, when 'tis for my avail.
    Here are the rocks; your person, or your prize.
    But tell me, 'Squire; where's th' appointed place,
    In which we shall these vaunted wonders see?

Esquire. Well may you wonders term them, Proteus:
    For these are wonders that pass human wit:
    These shall surpass thy wit, though half divine.
    But, for to put you out of further doubt,
    This is the place, where all those promises,
    Agreed upon betwixt the Prince and you,
    Shall be perform'd; and shall be so perform'd,
    So far beyond your doubting expectation,
    So far beyond his modest declaration.
    And you shall say, thrice happy Proteus;
    Whose ears unblessed were to bless mine eyes.

Amphitrite. Your fair set speeches make us two amazed.
    But tell us, 'Squire, what be those promises,
    And those agreed covenants? And whereon
    Did they arise 'twixt Proteus and your Prince?

Esquire. Fair Amphitrite, I will tell you all.
    After the victory at Austrican

Had made an end of the Tartarian war,
And quite dispers'd our vanquish'd enemies
Unto their hords, and huge vast wilderness;
Our noble Prince, and his couragious Knights,
Whose untry'd valour, in the battle fought,
Was rather warm'd, than fully exercis'd,
Finding no enterprise that did deserve
Th' employment of their brave united force,
After assignment of a day and place,
Where both himself and all his Knights should meet,
Dispers'd themselves into many sundry quests,
To seek adventures as they should befal.
The Prince himself, who only was attended
By me his 'Squire, had many strange exploits;
Which, since they shortly shall be put in print,
Join'd with Prince Arthur's famous chronicle,
I shall not now need to repeat at large.
Amongst the rest, when as the time approch'd,
That, as it was assign'd, we should all meet,
It thus fell out: the Prince, one sun-shine day,
Resting himself within a goodly tuft
Of tall streight fir-trees that adorn'd the shore,
Reading a letter, lately sent to him
From one of his brave Knights, that did import,
How he, in token of his duteous love,
And for a trophy of his victories,
Had lately sent him a commodity
Of pigmies, taken in a private conquest,
Resting and residing: suddainly he espy'd
Of porpoises a great unusual flock,
Playing and springing in the climbing waves.
Drawn with this sight still nearer to the shore,
Mounting a little cliff, he soon discern'd
A cave, whose frame seem'd more than natural;
And viewing near with wary heedful eyes,

At length he spy'd this fish hard there asleep;
Whom by his head and haviour he suspected
To be this Proteus; as it was indeed.
Our Prince streight, ready at his Fortune's call,
With easie stealing steps drew near to him:
And being near, with great agility.
Seized suddainly upon this demy-god.
He thus surpris'd, resorted presently
To his familiar arts, and turning tricks.
My Lord, like to a skilful Falconer,
Continu'd still to keep his fast'ned hold.

Thamesis.   The story of those oft transformed shapes,
I long to hear from you that present were,
And an eye-witness of that strange conflict.

Esquire.   And shall fair Thamesis know then, that Proteus,
Viewing the gallant shape and budding youth
Of my brave Lord, the form that first he took,
Was of a goodly Lady, passing fair;
Hoping, belike, that whilst he us'd respect
Due to her matchless beauty, and her sex,
Himself being now unloos'd, might slide away:
But finding him that knew his wily shifts,
Embrace him straiter in that feigned shape,
Next, to a Serpent he transform'd himself,
With fiery eyes, and dreadful blackish scales,
And three-fork'd hissing tongue, that might affright
Th' undaunted Master of dread Cerberus;
Pressing with double strength his scaled crest;
Wherewith the Prince, rather enrag'd than fear'd,
Made him betake him to another form;
Which was, a sumptuous Casket, richly wrought,
Whereout, when it open'd, many diadems,
And rubies of inestimable worth,
Seemed by chance to drop into the sea.

This working nought but scorn, and high disdain,
He lastly shew'd him a sad spectacle,
Which was, the North-east of his valiant Knights.
And best beloved of my Lord, the Prince,
Mangled and prick'd with many a grisly wound,
Welt'ring their valiant limbs in purple goar,
Gasping, and closing their faint dying eyes.
This with the Prince, now us'd to his delusions,
 Prevail'd no more, than did the rest before.
When Proteus then had chang'd his changing weed,
And fix'd himself in his own wonted shape,
Seeing no other means could ought prevail,
He ransom profer'd for his liberty.
And first of all, he offer'd to aread
To him, and unto all his Knights, Fortune's spell.
But when my Lord replyd, that that was fit
For unresolved cowards to obtain;
And how his Fortune's often changing play,
Would lose the pleasure of his chief delight,
If the catastrophe should be before known:
Then offer'd he huge treasures, Ladies' Loves,
Honour and Fame, and famous Victories.
My Lord made answer, "That he never would
Offer his honour so great wrong, to take,
By gift or magic, without sweat or pain,
Labour or danger, Virtue's truest prize,
That which by mortal hand might be atchiev'd;
And therefore willed him, as demy-god,
To offer somewhat that might be above
The lowly compass of an human power."
When Proteus saw the Prince could make his match,
He told him then, that under th' Artic Pole
The Adamantine Rock, the Sea's true Star
Was situate; which, by his power divine,
He, for his ransom, would remove, and plant

Whereas he should appoint: assuring him,
That the wild empire of the Ocean
(If his fore-telling spirit fail'd him not)
Should follow that, wher e'er it should be set.
But then again, he added this condition,
Which, as he thought, would no way be perform'd;
That first the Prince should bring him to a Power,
Which in attractive virtue should surpass
The wondrous force of his Iron-drawing rocks.
My Lord, that knew himself as well assured,
As Proteus thought his own match surely made,
Easily yielded to his covenant;
And promis'd further, on his Princely word,
That he himself, and seven of his Knights,
Wou'd enter hostages into the rock,
Which should be brought to the appointed place,
Till this great Covenant should be perform'd,
Which now rests to be done. Now, Proteus,
Since 'tis a Question of comparison,
Blazon you forth the virtue of your rock.

Proteus. What needeth words, when great effects proclaim
Th' attractive virtue of th' Adamantine Rocks,
Which forceth iron, which all things else commands.
Iron, of metals Prince by ancient right;
Though factious men in vain conspire to seat
Rebellious Gold in his usurped throne.
This, sundry metals, of such strength and use
(Disjoin'd by distance o' th' whole hemisphere)
Continually, with trembling aspect,
True subject-like, eyes his dread Sovereign.
Thus hath this Load-stone, by his powerful touch,
Made the Iron-needle, Load-star of the World,
A Mercury, to paint the gayest way
In Wat'ry Wilderness, and Desert Sands;
In confidence whereof, the assured Mariner

Doth not importune Jove, Sun, or Star.
By his attractive force, was drawn to light,
From depth of ignorance, that new found world,
Whose golden mines Iron found out and conquer'd.
These be the virues, and extend so far,
Which you do take to counterpraise.

Esquire. Proteus, the seas have taught your speech to swell,
Where work of mind doth wat'ry castles make.
But calm awhile your over-weening vaunts:
Prepare belief, and do not use your eyes.

Excellent QUEEN, true Adamant of Hearts;
Out of that sacred garland ever grew
Garlands of Virtues, Beauties, and Perfections,
That Crowns your Crown, and dims your Fortune's beams,
Vouchsafe some branch, some precious flower, or leaf,
Which, though it wither in my barren verse.
May yet suffice to overshade and drown
The rocks admired of this demy-god.
Proteus, stout Iron-homager to your rock,
In praise of Force, and Instruments of Wars,
Hath praise ended: yet place our praises right;
For Force to Will, and Wars to Peace to yield.
But that I'll give you.   This I would fain know,
What can your Iron do without Arms of Men?
And Arms of Men from Hearts of Men do move:
That Hearts of Men hath it, their motion springs.
Lo, Proteus, then, the attractive Rock of Hearts:
Hearts, which once truly touched with her Beams,
Inspiring purest zeal and reverence
As well unto the Person, as the Power,
Do streight put off all temper that is false,
All hollow fear, and schooled flattery,
Turn Fortune's wheel, they ever keep their point,
And stand direct upon the Loyal Line,
Your Rock claims kindred of the Polar Star,

Because it draws the Needle to the North;
Yet even that Star gives place to Cynthia's rays,
Whose drawing virtues govern and direct
The flots and re-flots of the ocean.
But Cynthia, praised be your wat'ry reign,
Your Influence in Spirits have no place.
This Cynthia high doth rule those heavenly tides,
Whose sovereign grace, as it doth wax or wain,
Affections so, and Fortune's ebb and flow:
Sometimes their waves applauding on the Shore,
Sometimes retiring to their narrow depths,
The holy Syrians draw pilgrims from all parts,
To pass the mountains, seas, and desert sands.
Unto this living Saint have Princes high,
Of Foreign lands, made vowed pilgrimage.
What excellencies are there in this frame,
Of all things, which her virtue doth not draw?
The Quintessence of Wits, the Fire of Loves,
The Art of Fame, Metals of Courages,
And by her Virtue long may fixed be
The Wheel of Fortune, and the Carr of Time.
In the Protection of this mighty Rock,
In *Britain* land, whilst tempests beat abroad,
The lordly and the lowly shepherd both,
In plenteous peace have fed their happy flocks.
Upon the force of this inviolate Rock,
The giant-like attempts of Power unjust
Have suffer'd wreck. And, Proteus, for the Seas,
Whose Empire large your praised Rock assures:
Your gift is void, it is already here;
As *Russia*, *China*, and *Negellan's* Strait
Can witness here, well may your presence be
Impressa apt thereof; but sure, not cause.
Fisher divine, congratulate yourself,
Your eyes hath won more than your State hath lost;
Yield Victory, and Liberty, and Thanks.

Proteus. Against the Truth, that's Lands and Seas above,
It fits no Proteus make a vain reply.
The shallop may not with small ships contend,
Nor windy bubble with a billow strive,
Nor earthly things compare with greatest Queen
That hath and shall a regal sceptre sway.
Bless'd be that Prince that forc'd me see this Grace,
Which worldly Monarchies, and Sea-Powers adore.
Take Thanks of Gift, and Liberty of Due.

When these Speeches were thus delivered, Proteus, with his bident striking of adamant, which was mentioned in the Speeches, made utterance for the Prince, and his seven Knights, who had given themselves as hostages for the performance of the Covenants between the Prince and Proteus, as is declared in the Speeches. Hereat Proteus, Amphitrite, and Thamesis, with their attendants, the Nymphs and Tritons, went unto the rock, and then the Prince and the seven Knights issued forth of the rock, in a very stately mask, very richly attired, and gallantly provided of all things meet for the performance of so great an enterprize. They came forth of the rock in couples, and before every couple came two pigmies with torches. At their first coming on the Stage, they danced a new devised measure, &c. After which, they took unto them Ladies; and with them they danced their galliards, courants, &c. And they danced another new measure; after the end whereof, the pigmies brought eight escutcheons, with the maskers devices thereupon, and delivered them to the Esquire, who offered them to her Majesty; which being done, they took their order again, and, with a new strain, went all into the rock; at which time there was sung another new Hymn within the rock.

The second Hymn, which was sung at the departure of the Maskers
into the Rock.

Shadows before the shining Sun do vanish:
Th' iron-forcing Adamant doth resign
His virtues, where the Diamond doth shine,
Pure Holiness doth all Inchantments blemish;
And Councellors of false Principality
Do fade in presence of true Majesty.

Shepherds sometimes in Lion's-skins were cloath'd;
But when the Royal Lion doth appear,
What wonder if the silly swains, for fear,
Their bravery, and Princely pall have loath'd?
The Lion's-skin, that grac'd our vanity,
Falls down in presence of her Majesty.

The Impresses which the Maskers used upon their Escutcheons, for their Devices.

H. Helmes, Prince.	In a bark of a cedar-tree, the character E engraven.	*Crescetis.*
W. Cooke.	In a plain shield, as it were Abrasa tabula.	*Quid ipsa velis.*
Jarvis Tevery.	A tortoise, with his head out of the shell.	*Obnoxia.*
Joh. Lambert.	A torch by the sun.	*Quis furor.*
Molineux.	A river with many turnings, running into the sea.	*Semper ad mare.*
Crimes.	A flag streaming in the wind.	*Famamque fovemus inanem.*
Paylor.	A sail and an oar together.	*Fors & virtus miscentur in unum.*
Campnies.	A flag of fire wavering upwards.	*Tremet & ardet.*

For the present her Majesty graced every one; particularly, she thanked his Highness for the good performance of all that was done; and wished that their sports had continued longer, for the pleasure she took therein; which may well appear from her answer to the Courtiers, who danced a measure immediately after the mask was ended, saying, "What! shall we have bread and cheese after a banquet?" Her Majesty willed the Lord Chamberlain, that the gentlemen should be invited on the next day, and that he should present them unto her. Which was done, and her Majesty gave them her hand to kiss, with most gracious words of commendations to them particularly, and in general of *Gray's-Inn,* as an House she was much beholden unto, for that it did always study for some sports to present unto her.

The same night there was fighting at barriers; the Earl of Essex and others challengers, and the Earl of Cumberland and his company defendants: into which number our Prince was taken, and behaved himself so valiantly and skilfully therein, that he had the prize adjudged due unto him, which it pleased her Majesty to deliver him with her own hands, telling him, "That it was not her gift; for if it had, it should have been better; but she gave it him as that prize which was due to his desert and good behaviour in those exercises; and that hereafter he should be remembred with a better reward from herself." The prize was a jewel set with seventeen diamonds and four rubies, in value accounted worth an hundred marks.

Thus, on Shrove Tuesday, at the Court, were our sports and revels ended: so that our Christmas would not leave us, till such time as Lent was ready to entertain us, which hath always been accounted a time most apt, and wholly dedicated to repentance. But now our Principality is determined, which although it shined very bright in ours and others' darkness, yet, at the Royal Presence of her Majesty, it appeared as an obscured shadow: in this, not unlike unto the Morning-star, which looketh very chearfully in the World, so long as the Sun looketh not on it: or, as the Great Rivers, that triumph in the Multitude of their Waters, until they come unto the Sea. *Sic vinci, sic mori pulchrum!*

GESTA GRAYORUM, PART II.
THE PRINCE OF PURPOOLE'S TITLE:

"The Right High and Mighty HENRY the Second[1], by the free election and consent of the Empire, Prince of the illustrious and potent dominions of *Graia* and *Purpulia*, Archduke of *Stapulia* and *Bernardia*, Duke of the *Superior* and *Inferior Holburnia*, and *Leatherlania*, and *Futulania*, Marques of the new-inhabited Province of *St. George, Knightsbridge, Blomesbury,* and all the adjacent Ilands and Creeks, County Pallantyne of *Pancras,* County of *St. Giles,* Vicount of the plesant and fertile Countryes of the greater and lesser *Cunnilania* and *Midlerowe,* Baron of *Mount Jerome,* and the Cantons of *Islington, Kentishtown, Totnam* and *Paddington,* Great Guardian of the *Amazonian* Forest of *Clarkenwell, Turnbolia,* and *St. John's of Jerusalem,* and of all those spatious Parks, Free-warrens, Chases, and Purlieus towards the *North-East Passage,* General of the invincible Forces against the savage and barbarous incursions of the Vulturine Ballives, and trecherous ambushments of the Harpian Catchpoles, Mam-

---

[1] The Second Part of the "Gesta Grayorum" appears more like a banter on the former Part than an actual Exhibition; and requires some apology for allusions ill-suited to the refinement of the present age. It is taken from a MS. in the Harleian Collection, and is without date. But " Henry the Second, Prince of Graya and Purpulia," occurs in the List of Subscribers to " Minshew's Dictionary, 1617."

pernor and Grand Protector of the distressed Christians, against the Jewish Inquistion of usurious, corrupt Chevisance, and Sovraigne Founder of the most noble Order of the Cressent."

"Heare you this, my Lords, and all true Knights and Gentlemen bearing of arms. That if any shalbe soe hardy as to deny any of those dominions, seigniories, territories, or provinces, to be lawfully subjected to the 'glorious government of the gracious Prince, or shall impeach the true and loyall right of his Excellency to any of his dignities, royaltyes, and titles; his valiant Champion is heare ready to make them good, uppon his person, in single combatte, at the utterance, at the utmost, and doth challinge him to the fight, here profferringe his gauntlet, the gage of his knightly performance thereof, according to the inviolable ordinances of the High Court of Chivalry and the Law of Arms."

[*A Flourish after the Ceremony.*]

Articles to be observed by the Knights of the most noble Order of the Cressent, which his Highness Soveraigne Founder of the same, in his speciall wisdome, and for the preservation of the honour thereof, hath thought fit to annex to the charter of creation, and publish at his solempne installation.

1. Imprimis, You shalbe and continue loyall and trusty to his Excellency your Soveraigne, and Soveraigne of this your Order, having your swords and wills still ready at command, without being Penćoners or Intelligencers of any his neighbour States or Provinces, to discover, or undermyne, his counsells or dissigns.

2. You shall not undertake any single combatt within his Highnes domynions at the sharpe, nor crosse the seas with intent to fight, and return without any performance.

3. If any of you borrow money, it must be done honorably, by great somes, and that upon your worde, repaying it, without fayle, according to the Empire, *Ad Græcas Calendas.*

4. If any of you have vowed service to some great and worthy lady, then doe it honorably, not kissinge her glove when you may kisse her bare hand, nor her bare hand when you may reach her lipp, nor her lipp when you may doe her more knightly service.

5. Although the Amazons of *Turnbolle, Clarkenwell,* and *Cunnelanea,* confederate with the brave and roaringe boyes, have lately rebelled, in the vacancy

of the empire, and done much hurt to the *Natwagi*, his Highnes deer subjects, by burninge, spoylinge, and other outragious courses; let none of you be too hardy, in hostile manner, to enter her by day or by night, or dare the attempt of her subduing; for his Highness is not yet resolved of that great expedition.

6. Noe Knight of this honorable Order shall holde himselfe accomplisate in the attchivemente of his ancestors.

7. No Knight of this Order shall calculate his nativity for the findinge out of his Mistress, nor wooe by Constallation; neither shall he think to merit her favour because her friends have made up the matter.

8. You shall not on purpose be out in any measure, to tread uppon a Ladye's toe; for thereby you shalbe put to enquire out her lodginge, rather otherwise she would find out yours.

9. You shall not sweare to any Lady, but by the ensigne of your honourable Order; soe shall you have like liberty of inconstancy as she hath.

10. You shall not presume to whisper his Highness in the eare, walkinge or sittinge in state, to make his subjects believe you are gracious with him, therby to abuse his loyall subjects in preferringe of suite.

11. It is his Highnes' pleasure, that younger brethren only be capable of this Order; for his Highnes's intention is to advance brave and undertakinge spiritts, to the intent they may be still crescent in performance.

12. Noe Knight shalbe seen in publique without his Crescent, nor be found in his chamber unfurnished with one sufficient launce, a short sword, and pistole charged with two bulletts, to be ready for any sudden service.

13. Every one of you shalbe handsomly quallifyed with one mistress, and no more; for love is the whetstone of valour.

14. You shall take heed you forgett not your respect to the ladie, though her gentlewoman be the handsomer.

15. You shall not be tradinge with sittezen's wives, nor pawne your fleshe for your clothes.

16. None of you shall undertake to right a Lady cladd in steele, for she takes uppon her to rectefy her owne cause.

17. You shall weare bootes and spurs, more to shew your knighthood, than to save silk stockings, garters, and roses.

18. You shall call no Lady cozen to avoyd suspicion in accesse, nor suffer millityes to increse, as far as in you lyeth to prevent them.

19. You shall make no slight inquisition about false or sophisticate haire, teeth, breste, or compleccõns, but beleive each one in her owne arte.

20. You shall not soe much as suspecte a Lady's breath; but, if you finde any thinge faulty, rather in charity attribute it your owne.

21. You shall not, on any festivall or other day, weare any favours ravished from Ladyes, nor father any uppon her bowntyes which come by your owne purchase.

22. You shall keepe no Lady in awe with any scape you knowe by her; nor mistake a blush for a fault, a smile for a consent, or a frowne for a denyall.

23. You shall bestowe playes, coach-hire, suppers, and banquets, freely, without expectance of rewards, for those acquitalls will prove your downefall.

24. You shall judge charitable of a jury of boxes, vialls, and gallipotts, in a Ladyes chamber, gessinge them to be phisicall rather for the body than for the face, and a bed towsed rather than made that day than spoyled in the afternoone.

25. You shall hold noe correspondency with noe foolish Knight because he hath a handsome Lady; for you cannot hope to better him, but you may make her worse.

26. You shall not make an inventory of your good parte to any Lady, nor of any Ladyes good parte to herselfe; but leave that task to both your executors.

27. Let none of you be soe absurde in his discourse with any sublunary bewty, to trouble her with outlandish syllables, or to tell her of Tonningalees, and bushell of leakes, or that an old wife first invented virginall keyes, by striking her tounge in hir singinge against her loose teeth; but rather let him imploy his mother's language in some particular subject in verse, wherein may be required more performance than protestation.

28. You shall carry yourselves courtiously and knightly to all that shall visite this his Highness's Palace of *Purpoole*, and especially to Ladyes and Gentlewomen, givinge that soft sex noe cause of distast, but shewinge yourselves as forward and able to lead a measure in peace, as a march in wars.

This heare you, right valiant and worthy Knights, you in whome for your undoubted prowesses it hath pleased his Excellency, in his especial favour, to conferr the honour of his resplendent Order. These are the articles and observances wherunto you are especially obliged. You are therefore to demeane yourselves right wisly and worthely, observinge each particle of them most inviolably; for if you shall degenerat from your noble originall, and violate your faith towards your Soveraigne, you are with shame and dishonour to be degraded from this illustrious Order, to have your coate-armor reversed, your spurs hewen from your heeles, and an utter disability of bearinge arms shall lye reamediles on you and your posterity for ever.

Claimes of his Highnes' Officers.

1. John Lorde Admirall claimes to holde the Manor of Parbreat of his Highnes, *in capite*, rendringe at every corronation a silver bason and a towell, and holdinge his Highnes's head if he shall chance to fall sea-sick.

2. The said Lorde Admirall claimes to have all egives of barnacles, breedinge uppon old thickes, the carkases for the Menialls of the Houshold, and the quiles for the Clarks of the Admiralty to make pens of.

3. His Highnes Master of the Rolles claimes the office of keepinge all records, as well close as patent, and allsoe by a small charter the custody of the pipe-roles, with this proviso, that all faire Ladyes and Gentlewomen may make search therin without any pecuniary fees.

4. His Highnes Master of Requeste claimes the antient allowance of 20li. weight of quicke silver, for the answeringe of peticions before they be delivered; and that none be admitted to peticion his Highnes in dogge-dayes.

5. His Highnes Master of the Ordinance claimes to have all peece guld in the touch-hole, or broken within the ringe, togeather with all burnt and unsufficient charges and scowringe-sticks, as fees and avayles appendant to his office, and to place the ordinance himselfe against the intended place of battery, but not to enter the breach in person unles it be faire and free from fyer.

6. His Highnes honourable Knights of the Cressent clayme the utter circules, the circuler resolution of a day and a night, when their measures they may change, and then enter into the first quarter of their new measures, and then into the middle, and soe still cressent till there measures come to the full.

7. His Highnes Master of the Ceremonyes claimes the privilige of one complement to sevrall companyes, and the allowance of a congee when the tounge is not at leisure.

8. His Highnes Master of the Revells claimes to daunce with the handsomest Ladye, though she have not her best clothes on: to kisse her first though his betters be in presence, and to take her downe though she be never so high.

9. The Gentlemen Ushers claime that none may come into his Highnes presence

that have eaten any clathms or windy meate, uppon forfeiture of her pompe to his Highnes Revill Admirall.

10. The Gentleman Porter of his Highnes Tower claymes to have the utmost garment of every man committed, and the inmost of every woman, and to take with his owne hand, provided allwayes it have not the marke of the cloth in it.

11. The Vice Admirall claymes, that if any Cittizen's wife consent upon the Narrow Seas to cuckold her husband uppon the land, that her smocke may be forfeited, to make sayles for his Highnes ships, for his Highnes voyage against the Great Turk.

Claimes of Common Persons.

1. Peter Strike-dye claimes the Manor of Game Parke, with the liberty of cheatinge, to hold ymeadiatly uppon his person, by the service of a quick eye and a ready hand, and rendringe a foole to the stocks as often as he shall fayle in his service; and averreth his tennure to be but common, *stockningo in calce,* and not *in capite.*

2. Paxnell Lotrix of Purpulia claimes the Manor of Wash-cleane, to hold by the service of quotidian bed-makinge, rendringe a cleane shirte on Satterday, and travellinge at his owne charge *quoties opus fuerit,* and for his service claymeth to be pumpe-free within his Highnes dominions.

3. Rawbone Dishwash claymes the Manor of Scullion Denn, as parcell of the Manor of Cookinge, to hold in Mutton Fee Farme, and to be quitt of all services, except suit of dresser and delivery of potage, as service in grosse by prescription.

4. Phillipe Sluggutt, a Common Sewer of his Highnes meat and drinke, claimes a large and easy seat in Port Esquilyn, after his table service thereon, to make drope-shote for his Highnes fowle-taker.

5. Thomas Joynter, of his Highnes Pallace of Purpoole, claymes liberty and usage of settinge riding-snares in Cunelania, Rently, Rucette, and Fullwood's Rents loope-holes, with licence to preoccupate any man's servall gaines in any of the places aforesaid.

6. Willfull Desire, knowne bayly of the Honour of Ladyes, claimes suite service of all the Knights of the Cressent, as of common right, that every one of them may beare a man in her moone, and by the swel.ing of her gown be knowne to be a cressent Lady.

7. Jeffrye Wisacres claimes a hide of arable land in Cunelania, by teachinge a goose to singe *salve, salve*, to the Maior of Letherlania, when he rides to take his oath.

8. Captaine Dangerfull claymes to be Captaine of his Highnes Artillery-yarde, by havinge in a readines ten thousand Cittizens well disciplined, all able and sufficient men to fight in feast.

9. Symon Armstronge claimes the waste in Horslydowne, by helpinge his Grace's mistress on horseback when she rydeth a huntinge, provided his hande slipes not.

10. Peter Pricipian, regarder of the forrest of Amazonia, claimes nightly a white doe, and to be free from all tolle except pawninge, for which he is to furnish dayly the hall of his Highnes Pallace of Purpoole with a sufficient number of buckhornes, for the Yeomen of the Garde to hange their hatts.

11. Capringe Kate, of Clarkenwell, claymes to hold of his Highnes five cunyborowes of his Manor of Tornwell, by night-service, to hold play for five Gentlemen Ushers, each of them with a ferret and two tumblers, weekly.

12. Winifride Wagtayle, of Wappinge, claimes to hold of his Highnes a messuage called the Purfleet, in Breech Lane, in smokinge, in cheife, by frayilty *tantum*.

13. Richard Seacole claimes to hold of the Prince, in soccage, the burrowe of New Castle, of the Sincke Port, for the transportinge of complexions to the Great Turk's seraglio, in advancement of his Highnes revenues.

14. Peter Pinchpoole claymes to hold the Manor of Knavesbury *in Petti Serjanti*, by two marks rent, and by beinge his Highnes bayly errant.

15. Ferdinando Fartwell claimes to hold by the demeasnes of Troppington, by one whole service, *viz.* to blow his Recorder backwards in consort at his Highnes corronation.

16. Megg Martiall claimes to hold the free Maner of Pickthatch, as of the forrest of Tinnekolia, rendringe two couples of rich conyes, and one milke white, and one of her seisen.

17. John Chapton claimes the Vicaridge of Pancras, to preach out in a Platonicall yeare.

18. Thomas Tastwell claimes to hold the Manor of Totnam Court, as of the Barrony of Mount Jerome, by beinge ale-caller to his Highnes Houshold.

19. Gregory Partihood claims to hold the Manor of Ferringdon infra, London, as of the Manor of Cockinge, by ringinge Bow-bell at his Highnes corronation.

20. Farhell Leftlege claimes to hold the Piscary of Clarkenwell, as of the Middle-row, rendringe ten dozen of maids and flounders for Highnes tent provision.

21. Truston Slovenbancke claimes to hold the Bayliwicke of Fullilanen, by bearinge a stander in thexpedition against the Amazons of Clarkenwell.

22. Humphry Alechops claimes to hold the Townshipe of Hogsdon, as of the Manor of Pimlico, rendringe messe of creaime, and a cowdy of cake, and all for his Highnes Cittizens on Sundayes and Hollidayes.

23. Lawrence Stronger claimes to hold the Towne of Hockly in the Hole, as of the Manor of Robbinge, by service of repairinge the bridge betwixt the two gulfes, as often as it shalbe broken or decayed by travellinge.

24. Abraham Silliman claimes to holde the Assart of Goathood, by breakinge a Speech of nonesence to his Highnes on New Year's-day, and for that to be exempt, and put out of the jurisdiction of the Court of Wards.

25. Simion the Salter claimes to hold the Manor of Stradlinge and Crincleham, by dancinge of French syncopate at his Highnes corronation.

26. The inhabitants of Upper and Neither Holbornia clayme to holde their houses *in capite*, by ellectinge discreet and wise officers; but they humbly pray to be discharged of that tenure, as of impossibility.

27. The inhabitants of Cunilania holdinge of your Highnes, by rendringe 24 virgins at thinstallation of your Highnes Knights, humbly pray, that because the Savage of Saremia *(vi et armis)* have entred and fyred their freholde, they may be discharged of that tenure for 21 yeares, and ever hereafter to render 24 knowne and tryed women.

28. The inhabitants of Middle-rowe claime to hold the capitall messuage of Scalepelane in cheife, as of his Highnes Manor of Calvaria, rendringe yearly xii Gregorians.

29. The auntient famile of the Woolsacke claimeth to have a victuallinge-house within his Highnes territoryes, rendringe 100 puddings dayly for the victuallinge of his Highnes Guard.

30. The Priories of Cunnington claime to hold as of the Burrow of Greter Cunilania, in Borough English, to finde a ringe for his Highnes Knights to runn, at every corronation.

31. John the Pander claimes to hold of his Highnes, as of the Burrough of Mount Jerrome, two tenements called the Cunyborowes, lyinge in Stinke Court,

by townage *in capite,* to finde three Flanders mares yearly, for sixe of his Highnes Blacke Guard, to ride uppon any Requiem.

32. Nager the Indian claimes to hold a messuage in Smock-rowe, called the Pipps, by petty serjanty, to have ready at all times in the messuage six pipps of sovraigne tobaccoe, well conditioned, and allsoe tenn standers of ale, and two feminine drawers for his Highnes menial servants to repose themselves in the said messuage 24 howers in one day, and noe more.

33. Symon the Rorer claims to hold of his Highnes, in free and common soccage, and without fealty, one antient rowe of houses lyinge in Punck-allye, to provide yearly six reclaimed cheffs to trimme, and to furnish his Highnes carrs, uppon an expedition to be made from his Honour of Justice-hall to his Highnes office of Tiburnia, and also to serve himselfe in the same expedition if occasion serve.

34. The Scribe claimes the manor of Nonerinte, by providing sheepe-skins and calves-skynes to wrape his Highnes wards and idiotts in.

35. Corsive Shippinglasse claimes to hold as of his Highnes, as of the Middle-rowe, by the verge, a shipe ther, called the Lawritt, to have alwayes in readines a volley of water-squirts, if those parts shall be in danger of fyringe.

36. Ananias Nethersole claimes to hold of his Highnes dutchy of Letherlanea, a messuage called the Bristle, rendringe ten paire of upright shoes for the sheriffs men, and as many turne-overs for the landresses of the houshold.

Certayne incertentyes which have lately arisen concerninge his Highnes Prerogative in his Wards, Ideotts, Widowes, Lunaticks, &c. wherin the Master of the Court of Wards desireth the Resolution of the Lords of his Highnes most honorable Privy Councell, and of his Highnes Judge and Councell at Law, for the direction of his Judgment in his Decrees, and the Resolutions theruppon:

Questio. Whether any of his Highnes Wards ought to adjudged of full age during the non-age of his discression, though he hath numbered 21 yeares?

Responsio. The infancie of the nobler part denominats the whole matter, and none ought to be soe fool-hardy to take upon him the performance of Knight-service without an head-peece. 'Tis therfor resolved, that all such wards shalbe sent to travaile in pursuite of their bewtifull mother Experience, with whome Pallas hath left an old rusty helmett; and those that by their service to this great Lady can atteyne that prise, ar to be deemed of full age. 'Tis allsoe resolved, that a ward of 21 yeres, haveinge maryed a widdow lady, ought to be adjudged of full age, for though he want discretion, she can teach him to doe Knight-service; but if he marry a virago, or one wiser than himself, his Highnes may still keepe him as his warde, to prevent his wife from makinge him her foole.

Ques. 2. Whether his Highnes ought by his prerogative to have primer seisin of the heires female of all his tennants in cheife?

Res. All heires female which be either marryed or marred in the life of the ancestor, his Highnes can have no primer seisin; but of such as be neither marryed nor marred at the death of thancestor, if he hold by escuage, if it please his Highnes he may have escuage: if it may not please his Highnes, he may leave it to his Lord Chamberlain when he receiveth their homage, or to the Tastor for his Highnes mouth. But primer seisin *capiendo exitus* (as the statute speaketh) he ought not to have; for his Excellency might soone over-charge his coffers, and soe an heire female beinge granedated, if she take husband uppon it, his Highnes should, against lawe, intitle him to be tennante by curtesy, only uppon a possession in lawe.

Ques. 3. Whether any of his Highnes' wards, which hold by Knight-service, shalbe admitted to sue livery before his valour be found by a faire tryal of ladyes?

Res. For one warde to prove his valour to many ladyes, is an Herculean labor; therfor the tryall by one lady only shall suffice: if she approve his manhood, he may sue his livery; if she finde it not, she shall have only an *Outer le maine.*

Ques. 4. Whether his Highnes' wards, notwithstanding the Statute of Merton, *De villanis sicut burgensibus*, may be marryed to the heires of such citizens as be lined with fox, and will warrant them double guilt, and that the foreman never leade them to the Stillyard to drinke Renish, nor to the suburbs to therrectinge of a May-pole, to eate caks at Pimlico, or to see how the pips lye in the new waterworks?

Res. If the father be lined with black fox, it is no disparagement; for it is a rich furr, and may patch a lion's skin; and tho the father be lined with any other fox, be it Reynarde fox, Canary, Muscadine, or Mamsy fox, yet if the daughters be faced with white lambe, well silvered, and hath noe guilt, it is no disparagement. But if the wief of such cittizen hath ben fured with white bastard, it is a disparagement. Allsoe if the foreman hath lead the daughters to the places in the case mentioned, and it be perceived that like should fox she hath preyed for herselfe, it is a disparagement, unles it be holpen by the statute *Circumspectè agatis.*

Ques. 5. If, uppon survey of his Highnes' widdowes, it be found that any of them be marryed to cover the familiarity of her servant or cosey, which her vertingale could no longer obscure; whether she shall pay a fine for doing it without licence, because it was in case of necessity?

Res. She, notwithstanding such necessity, *casu proviso,* ought to pay a double fine, for that without license she hath had th'use of two of his Highnes subjects; and the husband ought to be punnished uppon the statue of maintenance, for medlinge with a pretensed and broken title.

Ques. 6. If any man playing at Gleeke, in whose hand the knave is an honour, shall make him out into stocke, least that five knaves be found in the packe, whether he ought to be adjudged in the custody of the Court of Wards?

Res. He ought to be adjudged in the protection of that Court, for that in his choice he hath preferred the foole before the knave.

Ques. 7. Whether the covetous shall starve in plenty, and the prodigall that brings himselfe to penury, ought to be adjudged within the survey and governance of his Highnes Court of Wards, as well as ideotts, since they all agree in naturall foolery?

Res. Theise ben formerly imbarked in the shipps of fooles; and if his Highnes admirall hath not seised them as wrecke by sea, the Master of the Wards is to provide for them as ideotts by land.

Ques. 8. The feodary of the superior and inferior Honylania hath certefyed, that whereas the Committee of Dulcebella, one of his Highnes female wards, hath placed them with Libidinosa, an Italian schoolemaster, to learne the languages, he, findinge her capable of soled instruction, taught her rules of gramar, *viz.* the English Syntaxis, and *Propria quæ maribus, &c,* and proceedeth soe farr as *Impliciti laqueis nudus uterque jacet;* whether the Committee shall loose his interest, in regard this disparagement grew *per accedens?*

Res. The Committee in this case shall loose his interest, for, uppon the whole matter, this disparagement grew *per insidias,* and the schoolemaster ought to be schooled by thordinary, uppon the canon *de Clerico venatore.*

Ques. 9. If any offend uppon purpose to be committed to the Tower, whether he ought not rather to be committed to the tuition of the Court of

Wards, with power to be delivered to his Highnes phisicians, untill the mallignity of that humour be purged?

Res. His Highnes is pleased, in comiseration, rather to receive them into his protection of ideotts, than comitte them to the Tower as traytors: yet soe that, if his phisick will not worke, they shalbe admitted to fellowship in the Colledge of Bedlam.

Ques. 10. If any of his Highnes subjects shall sell his land, by takinge up comodityes by rattules and hobbi-horses, or to purchase monopolies; whether he shall pay a fine for such alienation, because that his folly hath procured his Highnes a wiser tenante?

Res. His Highnes Lord Tresurer will see that his Excellency in this case shall have a good fine, because he is not like to have any more fines for such alienation untill the buyer's heire come to fooll age; and his Highnes is plesed, for this exchange, that the seller shalbe Post-maister between Conylania and Foolania.

Ques. 11. A Burgomaster that hath placed his clymatericall yeare maryeth a young inheritrix that holds *per servicium socæ;* whether this intermariage alter the tenure into cornage *in capite*, to give the wardship of his heire; or into dotage, to give the custody of himselfe?

Res. The tenure is exchanged, and he must now hold *pro particula* in cornage *in capite*, and the rest at will, not by the rodd, but by coppy only; yet in his owne land the custome of burgage is not yet altered, but he may devise all to his wife, to make her the better marriage for another of his Highnes more able subjects.

Ques. 12. It is found by office, that one of his Highnes widdowes maryed without license, and afterwards divorsed *Causa sine qua non;* whether his Highnes may seize for a fine notwithstandinge?

Res. The nullity *Causa sine qua non* doth not purge the contracting, but that thescheator may seize for a post fine, *Causa qua supra.*

Ques. 13. A comittee maryeth his ward to a maide borne dumbe; whether this (though a defecte in nature) be any disparagement within the Statute of Merton, because it rendereth much to the peace of the commonwealth, *si partus sequatur ventrem?*

Res. To be marryed to a maide borne dumbe, it cannot be passed *sub silencio* without disparagement; but if she be but tounge-tyed, and in due time may turne from a mute to a consonante, it is noe disparagement, but a rare advancement.

The First Antimask of Mountebanks.

Mountebank's Speech.

The greatest master of medicine Æsculapius preserve and prolonge the saivty of the royall and princely spectators; and if any here present happen to be valitudinary, the blessed finger of the grand master at Paracelsus be at hand, for their speedy reparation. I have heard of a mad fellow, who stiles himselfe a merry Greeke, and goes abroad by the name of Paradox, who, with frisking and dauncing, and new-broached doctrine, hath stollen himselfe this festivall-time of Chrismas into favour at the Court of *Purpoole*, and, haveinge there gotten some approbation for a smale performance, is growne soe audatious as to intrude himselfe into this honored presence.

To prevent whose further growinge fame, I have, with these my fellow artists of severall nations, all famous for the bante, hither made repair, to present unto your view more wholesome, more pleasinge, and more novil delights, which, to avoyde prolixity, I distribute into these followinge common-places."

Names of diseases cured by us; which, being infinite, purposely we omitt, musicall charmes, familiar receipts; singe these songs; *viz.*

Chorus.

What is't you lacke, what would you buy,
  What is it that you need;
Come to me, gallants, taste and buy,
  Heer's that will doe the deed.

1 Songe.

Heer's waters to quench maidens fyres,
Heer's spiritts for old occupiers,
Heer's powder to preserve youth longe,
Heer's oyle to make weake sinewes stronge.
  What is't, &c.

This powder doth preserve from fate.
This cures the maleficiate;
Lost maidenhead this doth restore,
And make them virgins as before.
  What is't, &c.

Heer's cure for tooth-ach, feaver lurdens,
Unlawfull and untimely burthens,
Diseases of all sex, all ages,
This medicine cures, or els asswages,
  What is't, &c.

I have receipts to cure the gout,
To keep pox in, or thrust them out,
To coole hote bloode, cold bloode to warme,
Shall doe you, if noe good, no harme.
  What is't, &c.

The second Mountebank's Songe.

Is any deafe? is any blinde?
Is any bounde or loose behinde?
Is any foule that would be faire?
Would any Lady change her haire?
Does any dreame? does any walke?
Or in his sleep affrighted talke?
  I come to cure whatere you feele,
  Within, without, from head to heele.

Bee drumes or rattles in thy head?
Are not thy brains well tempered?
Does Eolus thy stomacke gnawe?
Or breeds there vermine in thy mawe?
Doest thou desier, and cannot please?
Loe heere's the best cantharides.
  I come, &c.

From all diseases that arise
From ill-disposed crudityes,
From too much study, too much paine,
From lasines, or from a straine,
From any humors doeinge harme,
Be it dry, or moyst, or colde, or warme,
  I come, &c.

Of lasy goute I cure the rich,
I rid the beggar of his itch,
I flegme avoyde both thicke and thinne,
I dislocated joynts put in,
I can old Eson's youth restore,
A doe a thousand wonders more:
    Then come to me whatere you feele, &c.

The Third Mountebank's Songe.

Is any soe spente, that his wief keeps Lent?
  Does any waste in his marrowe?
Is any a lugge? let him tast of my drugg,
  'Twill make him as quicke as a sparrowe.
    My powder and oyle, extracted with toyle,
      By rare sublim'd infusions,
    Have proofe they ar good, by my owne deere blood,
      In many strange conclusions.

Does any consume with salte French rhewme?
  Doth the goute or palsy shake him?
Or hath he the stone, ar a moneth begone
  As sound as a bell I'le make him.
    My powder, &c.

The greife of the spleene, and maids that be greene,
  Or the heate in Ladyes faces,
The grips of the stitch, or the schollers itch,
  In my cures deserve no places.
    My powder, &c.

The webb or the pinn, or the morphew of skine,
  Or the risinge of the mother
I can cure in a trice: oh! then be not nice,
  Nor ought that greeves you smother.
    My powder, &c.

Chorus.

Yet let us not to much lyccor delight,
But roundly singe to all, Goodnight, Goodnight.

We must away, yet our slacke pace may showe,
'Tis by constraint wee this faire orbe forgoe;
Our longer stay may forfeite what but nowe
Love hath obteinde for us: to him we bow;
And to his gentler power, who soe contrived,
That we from sullen shades ar now reprived:
And hither brought, wher favour, love, and light,
Soe gloriously shine, they banish night.
More would we say, but Fate forbids us more:
Our clue is out; Goodnight is gone before.

The Fourth Mountebank's Songe.

1. Maids of the chamber or the kitchin,
    If you be troubled with an itchin,
    Come give me but a kisse or two,
    I'le give you that shall soone cure you.
        Noe Galen or Hypocrites
        Did ever doe such cures as these.

2. Crackt maids, that cannot hold your water,
    Or use to breake winde in your laughter;
    Or be you vext with kibes or cornes,
    I'le cure; or cuckolds of their hornes.
        Noe Galen, &c.

3. If lusty Doll, mayde of the dary,
    Chance to be blewe-nipte by the Fayry,
    For makinge butter with her tayle;
    I'le give her that did never fayle.
        Noe Galen, &c.

4. Or if some worse mischance betyde her,
    Or that the night-mare over-ride her;
    Or if she tell all in a dreame;
    I'le cure her for a messe of creame.
        Noe Galen, &c.

FAMILIAR RECEIPTS.

An approved Medicine against melancholicke feminine.—If any lady be sicke of the sullens she knows not where, let her take a handfull of scimples I know not what, and use them I know not how, applyinge them to the party greeved, I know not who, and she shalbe well I knowe not when.

Against the scurvy.—If any scholler be trobled with an itch, or breakinge out, which in time may prove the scurvy, let him first forbeare clawinge and frettinge meate, and then purge choller, but by noe means upwards.

For restoringe Gentleman Usher's Legge.—If any Gentleman Usher hath the conscumption in his legge, let him feed lustely of veale two moneths in the springe time, and forbeare all manner of mutton, and he shall increase his calfe.

For the tentigo.—If any be trobled with the tentigo, let him travaile into Japan; or because the forrest of Turnbolia is of the same altitude or elevation of the Pole, and at hand, let him hunte ther for his recreation, and it shalbe done in an instante.

For the angina.—If any scholer labor of the angina, a dangerous disease in the throat, soe that he cannot speake an hower togeather once in a quarter of an yeare; let him forbeare all violent exersises, as trottinge to Westminster Hall every Tearme, and all hote liquors and vapours, let him absteine from company, retiringe himselfe, warme clad in his study, foure dayes in a weeke (at first).

For a fellon.—If any be trobled with a fellon on his finger, whereby he hath lost the lawfull use of his hand, let him but once use thexercise of swinginge, and stretchinge himselfe uppon a soveraigne tree of Tiburnia, and it will presently kill the fellon. *Probatum.*

For a timpanie.—If any virgine be soe sicke of Cupid, that the disease is growne to a timpany, let her with all speed possible remove herselfe, changinge ayre fourty weeks at least, keepinge a spare dyet as she travailes, allwayes after usinge lawfull exercises till she be marryed, and then she is past danger.

For barrennes.—If any be longe marryed yet childles, let her first desire to be a mother, and to her breakfast take a new-layde egg in a spoonefull of goat's milk, with a scruple of ambergreece; and at supper feede on a henn trodden but by one cocke; but, above all, let her avoyde hurringe on a carroach on the stones, and assuminge a finer mould than nature ment her; noe doubte she shall fructifye.

For the fallinge sicknes.—If any woman be trobled with fallinge sicknes, let her not travayle Westwardhoe, because she must avoyde the Isle of Man; and for that it is an evill only outward into her, let her for a charme alwayes have her leggs acrosse when she is not walkinge, and this will healpe her.

Now, princely spectators, to lett you see we ar men qualified from head to foote, wee will shew you a peece of our footemanshipe.   DANIELL.

For a rupture.—If any tradsman be trobled within his bowells of his estate, that he cannot goe abroade, let him decocte gould from a pound to a noble, taking the broath therof from six moneths to six moneths, and he shalbe as able a man as ever he was.

Daunce Antemaske.   *Exeunt.*

Enter Paradox.

Health and jovisaunce to this faire assembly, now the thrice-three-leaved sisters forsake mee, if ever I beheld such bewtyes in Athens! You aske, perhaps, whence I am, that thus conceitedly salute you? I am a meere Greeke, and a Sophister of Athens, who, by fame and certaine novill and rare performance undertaken and premised by the gallant sprite of *Graia* drawne hither, have intruded myselfe, sophister-like, in at the backe-dore, to be a spectator, or rather a censor, of ther undertakings. Oh, the shewes, and the songs, and the speeches, and the playes, and the comedyes, and the actings, I have seen at Athens!

Ther was another ende of my cominge; and that was, to gett some of these bewtyes to be my disciples, for I teach them rare doctrine, but delightfull; and if you be true Athenians (that is, true lovers of novaltyes, as I hope you ar all) you will give my hops ther looked-for expectation. Know then, my name is Parradox; a strange name, but purposed to my views; for, I blush not to tell you truth, I am a ship of darknes, my father a Jesuite, my mother an Anabaptist, and my name is strange, soe is my perfection, and the art which I teach, myselfe beinge the first that reduced it to rules.

And Methode breeds my name Parradox. I pray you what is a parradox? it is a *quodlibet*, or straine of witt and invention, scrued above the vulgar conceipt, to begett admiration. And because Methode is the mother of Discipline, I divide my Parradox into these three heads, Masculine, Feminine, and Neuter. And first of the first, for the masculine is mor worthy than the feminine, and the feminine mor worthy than the neuter.

Drawes his booke, and reads:

Masculine.

1. 'Tis better to be a coward than a Captaine, for a goose lives longer than a cocke of the game.

2. A Knight of the Longe Roabe is more honourable than a Knight made in the field; for furrs ar dearer than spurrs.

3. Hee cannot be a cuckold that weares a gregorian; for a perriwige will never fitt such a head.

4. A canniball is the lovingest man to his enemy; for willingly noe man eats that he loves not.

5. A bachelor is but halfe a man, and beinge wedd he may prove more than halfe a monster; for Aries and Taurus rule the head and shoulders, and Capricorne reach as low as the knees.

6. A wittall cannot be a cookold, for a cuckold is wronged by his wife; which a wittall cannot be, for *volenti non sit injuria*.

7. A shoe-maker is the fittest man in the parish to make a constable of; for he, *virtute officii*, may put a man into the stocks, and inlarge him at laste.

8. A prisoner is the best fencer; for he ever lyes at a close warde.

9. An elder brother may be a wise man; for he hath wherewithall to purchase experience at any rate.

10. An Under Sherife thrice may be noe knave; for he doth naught without warrant.

11. A falconer is a better woman's man than a huntsman; for he is busied about castinge of stones, while thother is takinge up in catchinge a fox.

12. A musician will never make a good vintner; for he deales too much with flatts and sharps.

13. A drunckard is a good philosopher; for he thinks aright, that the world goeth rounde.

14. The devill cannot take tobacco through his nose; for Sainte Dunstone hath seared that up with his tonges.

15. 'Prentises ar the nimblest scavengers; for they can clense the Citty stones in one day.

16. A City heire cannot be a prodigall; for *est in juvencis patrum virtus*.

17. Noe native phisician can be excellent; for all excellent simples ar forreiners.

18. A master of fence is more honourable than a master of arte; for good fightinge was before good wrightinge.

19. A Courte foole must needs be learned; for he goes to schoole in a porter's lodge.

20. Burgomasters ought not to weare ther furred gownes at Midsomer; for soe they may bringe in the sweatinge-sicknes againe.

21. Widdowes ar the most contented women; for liberty tasteth swetest after a restrainte.

22. A cut-purse is the surest trade: for his work is no soner done, but he hath his money in his hands.

Feminine.

1. 'Tis better to marry a widdow than a maide; *causa patet*.

2. A blinde man makes the best husband; for what he comes short of in seeinge, he reaches in feelinge, and that is a woman's best sence.

3. A nimble Page is more usuall for a Lady than a longe Gentleman; for a sparrow is more active than a bald bussard.

4. Downeright language is the best rhetoricke to wine a woman; for plaine dealinge is a jewell, and ther is noe Lady but desireth to have her lape full of them.

5. Women are to be commended for loveinge stage-players; for they ar men of knowen actions.

6. If a woman with childe longe to lye with another man, her husband must consent; for if he will not, she will doe it without him.

7. Rich widdowes were ordeined for younger brothers; for they, beinge borne to noe lande, must plough in another man's soyle.

8. A maide should marry before the years of discrition; for *malicia supplet ætatem*.

9. 'Tis dangerous to wed a widdowe; for she hath cast her rider.

10. An English virgine sings sweeter heere than at Brussells; for a voluntary is sweeter than a forced noate.

11. A great Lady may with her honour weare her servant's picture; for a shadow yet never made a cuckold.

12. A painted Lady best fitts a Captaine; for soe both may fight under ther cullers.

13. 'Tis good for a younge poapish wench to marry an old man; for soe she shalbe sure to keepe all-fasten night.

14. A dangerous secreat is safly placed in a woman's bosome; for noe wise man will search for it there.

15. A woman of learninge and toungles is an admirable creature; for a starling that can speak is a present for an Emperor.

16. Ther were never soe many chaste wives as in this age; for now 'tis out of fashion to lye with ther husbands.

17. A great Lady should not weare her owne haire; for that's as meane as a coate of her owne spinninge.

18. A faire woman's necke should stande awrye; for soe she looks as if she were lookinge for a kisse.

19. Women love fish better than flesh; for they will have plaice whatsoever they pay for it.

Newters.

1. Partriges ar harde of digeston; for they are harde to be gotten.

2. Old things ar the beste things; for ther is nothinge new but diseases.

3. The best bodyes should weare the plainest habit; for painted clothes were made to hide bare walls.

4. Dissemblers may safly be trusted; for ther meaninge is ever contrary to their words.

5. Usurers ar necessarye members in a Commonwealth; for they binde men to good dealinge.

6. Musitions cannot be but healthful; for they live by good ayre.

7. An usurere is the best Christian; for *quantum nummum servat in arca tantum habet et fidei.*

8. A flatterer deserves to be loved better than a true frende; for oyle cures better than vineger.

9. None should have licence to marry but rich folke; for *vacuum* is a monster *in rerum natura.*

10. Every lover's ayme is vertuous; for *virtus est in medio.*

11. 'Tis better to seeme than to be honest; for the jay is more bewtifull than the dove.

12. A hare is more subtill than a fox; for she maks more doubles than an old Reynarde.

Epicene.

1. 'Tis better to be a beggar than a marchante; for all the world lies open to his traffique, and yet he payes noe custome.

2. 'Tis more safe to be drunk with the hop than with the grape: for a man should be more inward with the countryman than with the stranger.

3. 'Tis better to buy honour than to desire it; for what is far and deare bought is goode for my Ladie.

4. A man deepe in dett should be deepe in drinke; for Bacchus cancells all manner of obligations.

5. Clay houses are more necessarie in a well governed Commonwealth than publicke scholes; for men are better taught by example than precept.

6. 'Tis better to feed on vulgar and grosse meats than on dayntie and highe dishes; for they that eate onlie partrige and quaile, hatch noe other broode than woodcocke or goose.

7. Taverners are more requisite in a Citie than academies; for 'tis better the multitude weare lovinge than learned.

8. A bullion hose is best to goe a woeinge in; for 'tis full of promisinge promontories.

9. 'Tis better to be a theefe than a serving-man; for they, like dice, if they runne not as their masters would have them, are presently cast away.

10. A tobacco-shope and a stew ar coincident; for a smoake is not without a fyer.

11. An almanacke is a booke more worthy to be studyed than the history of the world; for a man to know himselfe is the most worthy knowledge, and there he hath 12 signes to know it by.

12. Wealth is better than witt; for fewe poets have had the fortune to be chosen Aldermen.

13. Marryinge frees a man from care; for then the wife taks all uppon her.

14. 'Tis better to be idle than industrious; for the grass-hopper lives merryer than the ante.

15. A kennell of hounds is the best consorte; for they need noe tuninge from morninge to night.

16. The Court maks better schollers than the University; for when a King vouchsafeth to be a teacher, every man blushes to be a non-proficient.

Musicke sounds.

Enter Pages.

Ther Songe, Dialogue-wise.

When shall wee finde releife?
Is ther noe ende of greife?
Is ther no comfort lefte?
What cruell chaines berefte?
The patrons of our youthe
Wee must now begge for truth.

Enter Pages.

Kinde pitty is the most
Poore boyes can hope for
Whan ther joyes are loste.

Obscuritie.   Light, I sallute thee, I Obscurity,
The sone of Darkness, and forgetfull (Lethe):
I that envie thy brightness, greet thee now:
Enforc'd by Fate, Fate makes the strongest bowe;
The over youthfull knight, by spells inchainde,
And longe within my study-nooke restrainde,
Must be inlarged; and I then usher bee
To their night-glories: so the Fates agree.
Then put on life, Obscurity, and prove
As light as Light, for awe if not for love.
Soe hear ther tender yeares kinde-harted squires,
Mourning there mistress losse; no new desires
Can traine them from their walks; but heare they wend
From shade to shade, and give their toyle no end.
But now will I releife ther sufferinge care:
Heare me, faire youth, since you soe constant are;
In faith, to your lov'd knights goe hast apace,
And with your bright light guide them to their place:
For if you fall, directly that discente,
Ther wisht approach will further search prevent.
Hast by the vertu of a charminge songe;
While I retrive them, least they lagg too longe.

The Call, or Songe of Obscurity.

Appeare, appeare, you happy knights;
Heare ar severall sorts of lights;
Fire and bewty shine togeather,
Your slow steps invitinge hether.

   Come away, and from your eies
      The old shade remove;
   For now the Destenies
      Release you, at the suite of Love.

Soe, soe, 'tis well! march, march apace;
Two by two, fill up the place:
And then, with voyce and measure,
Greet the Kinge of Love and Pleasure.

Now, Musicke, change thy noate, and meete
Aptly with the dancer's feete;
For 'tis the pleasure of Delight,
That they shall triumph all this night.

The Songe and Dance togeather.

Frolicke measures now become you,
   Over-longe obscured knights:
What if Lethe did benume you,
   Love now waks you to delights.

Love is like a goulden flower,
   Your comly youth adorninge;
Pleasure is a gentle shower,
   Shed in some Aprill morninge.

Lightly rise and lightly fall, in the motion of your feete;
Move not till our noats doe call you, musicke maks the action sweet.
Musicke breathinge blowes the fyer, which Cupid feeds with fuell;
Kindlinge honour and desire, and turning harts most cruell.

   Quickly, quickly, move your paces,
   Nimbly changing measure-graces;

Lively mounted, high aspire,
For joy is only found in fyer.

Musicke is the soule of measure, speeding both in equall grace;
Twines ar they begot of pleasure, when she wishly numbred space.
Nothinge is more olde or newer than number all advancinge,
And noe number can be truer, than musick-wynd with dancinge.

Every kinge electe a bewty, such as may thy hart inflame;
Thinke that her bright eie doth vew thee, and to her thy action frame.
Soe shall none be fainte or weary, though treadinge endles paces,
For they all ar light and merry, whose hopes are fed with graces.

Sprightly, sprightly, mend your paces;
Nimbly changinge measure-graces:
Lively mounted, high aspire,
For joy is only found in fyer.

Obscurity. Servants of Love, for soe its fitt you bee,
Since he alone hath wrought your liberty;
His ceremonies now, and courtly wrights,
Performe with rare and free resolved sprights:
To sullen darkness my dull stepps reflete,
All covet that which nature doth affeete.

The Second Measure, with Dancer's Song to take out the Ladyes.

Come on, brave kings, you have well shewed
  Each his due part in nimble daunces:
These bewties to whose hands ar owed
    You wonder why
    You spare to try.
  Marke how invitinge are there glances!
    Such, such a charme; such faces, such a call,
    Would make old Eson skipp about the hall.

See, see, faire choyce, a starry spheare,
  Might dime bright day, chase here a pleasure,
Please your owne eye; approve you heare,

> Right gentle knights,
> To these softe wrights.
> None talke and teach, but all in measure.
> Far, far from hence be roughness, far a frowne;
> Your faire department this faire night shall crowne.

After they have daunced with the ladies, and set them in their places, fall to their last daunce.

Enter Paradox, *and to him his Disciples.*
Silence.

Lordlings, ladies, and fiddlers, let my toungue twang awhile. I have sene what hath ben shewed; and now give me leave to shew what hath not ben sene, for the honour of Athens. By vertue of this musicall, whilst I will summon my disciples, see obedieuce; heare they ar already: put forward my paradoxicall pupills, methodically and arithmetically, one by one.

1. Behold this principall artist that first encounters me, whose head is honoured by his heeles, for dauncinge in a chorus of tragedy presented at Athens, where he produced such learned variety of foolinge, and disgested it soe orderly and close to the grownd, that he was rewarded with his relique (the Cothurne or Buskine of Sophocles) which, for more eminence, he weares on his head. The paradoxicall vertue therof is, that beinge dipt into the river or spring, it alters the nature of the liquor, and returneth full of wine of Chios, Palermo, or Zante.

2. The second master of the science of footmanshipe (for he never came on horsebacke in all his life) was framed at the Feast of Pallas, when, in dauncinge, he came off with such lofty tricks and twines above grownd, caps, crosse-capers, horse-capers, soe high and soe lofty performed, that he for prize bore away the helmet of Pallas. The paradoxicall vertue of the caske is, that in our travells, if we fall amonge enemies, shew but this, and they suddenly vanish all like fearfull shadowes.

3. Now vewe this third peece of excellency; that is he that put all ther bakes at the Feast of Ceres, and soe daunced there as if he kneeded dough with his feet; wherwith the Goddess was soe tickled, that she in regard set this goodly loafe on his head, and indued with this paradoxicall influence, that cut of it, and eate as often as you please, it straight fills up againe, and is in the instant heald of any wounde hunger can inflicte on it.

4. Approach now thou that course in the reare of my disciples; but many martch in the vantgarde, for the vallidity; for at the celebration of the Feast of Venus Citherea this amarose did exprese such passion with his eyes, such winks, such glaunces, and with his whole body such delightfull gestures, such cringes, such pretty wanton mimicks, that he was the applause of all; and as it was necessary at the feast of the goddesse, he had then a most ample and inflaminge cod-peece, which, with his other graces, purchased him his prize, the smocke of Venus, wrapt turbant-like on his head, the same she had on when she went to bed with Mars, and was taken nappinge by Vulcan. The paradox of it is, that it be hanged on the tope of our May-pole, it drawes to us all the younge laddes and lasses neere adjoyninge, without powder to put to, till we stricke saye ourselves. And now I have named our May-pole, goe, bringe it forth, though it be more troublesome or cumbersome than the Trojan horse, bringe it by force of armes; and see you fix it fast in the midst of this place, least, when you circle it with your caprians daunces, it falls from the foundation, lights uppon some ladye's head, and cuffe off her perriwige. But now for the glory of Athens.

Musicke plaies the Antimaske.

The Disciples dance the first streigne.

We have given you a taste of thexcellency of our Athenian revells, which I will now dignify with my owne person bye ther impediment, wherof beinge freed, I will discend: you author of great wonders, what assent is this? what supernaturall paradox? a wodden May-pole finds thuse of voluntary motion! assuredly, this tree was formerly the habitation of some wood-nymphe. For the Druides (as the poets say) live in trees; and perhaps, to honour my dauncinge, the nymphe hath crept into this tree againe; soe I apprehend it, and will entertain her curtesye.

Paradox, his Disciples, and the May-pole, all dance.

Did ever eye see the like foolinge of a tree? or could any tree but an Athenian tree doe this? or could any nimphe move it but an Athenian nimphe? Faire nimphe, though I cannot arrive at thie lips, yet will I kisse thy wooden maske, that hides thy, noe doubte, amiable face.

Paradox offers to kisse, and a Nimph's head meets him out of the May-pole.

Wonder of wonders! sweet nimph, forbeare! my whole structure tombles! mortallity cannot stand the brightnes of thie countenance: pursue me not, I beseech thee: put up thy face for love's sake: helpe, helpe, Disciples; take away the dismall pole from me; rescue me, rescue me, with all your violence: see, the devill is gone, and I will not stay long after. Lordings, or ladies, if ther be any heer desirous to be instructed in the mistery of paradoxing, you shall have mee at my lodginge in the Blacke and White Courte, at the signe of the Naked Boy: and soe to you all the best wishes of the night.

Enter Mountebancke.

Stay, presumptuous Paradox, I have vewed thy antickes, and thy puppet; which have kindled in mee the fyer of emulation. Looke, am I not in habit as fantasticke as thyselfe? doest thou hope for grace with ladies by thy revell doctrines? am I a man of arte? Witnesse this my charminge rod, wherewith I worke miracles. And wheras thou, like a fabulous Greeke, hast made monsters of thie disciples; soe I will oppose squadron against squadron, and plain truth against painted fiction; now for thy meneinge all singe, but for frightinge the devill out of it.

I could incounter thee with Totnam High-crosse, or Cheap-crosse (though it be new guilte), but I scorne odds; and therfore I will affront thee pole to pole.

Soe, Disciples, usher in our lusty inchaunted motion; and, Paradox, now betake you to your tacklinge, for you deale with men that have agew and fyer in them.

Paradox. Assist me, O thou active Nimph, and you my glorious associates: victory, victory, for Athens.

Mountebancke. Accomplished Greeke, now as wee ar true Mountebancks, this was bravely performed on both parts; and nothinge now remaines but to make these two May-poles better acquainted; but we must give place to the knights appeare.

Enter Obscurity.

Enough of these night sports; part, faire knights,
And leave an edge on pleasure; least these lights
I sodainly dime all; and pray how then
Will these gay ladies shift among you men?
In such confusion, some ther honours may misse;
Obscurity knowes tricks as bad as this.
But make your partinge innocent for me;
I will noe author now of error bee:
Myselfe shall passe with you a frende of light,
Givinge to all this round a King's good-night.

Last Songe.

The howers of sleepy night decayes apace;
And now warme beds are fitter than this place.
All time is longe that is unwillingly spent;
But howers are minitts when they yeld content.
The gathered flowers wee love, that breathe sweet sent;
But loathe them, there sweet odours beinge spente.
    It is a life is never ill,
      To lye and sleep in roses still.

    The rarer pleasure is, it is more sweet;
And frends are kindest when they seldome meet.
Who would not heare the nightingale still singe;
Or who grew ever weary of the Springe?
The day must have her nighte, the Springe her fall;
All is divided, none is lorde of all.
    It were a most delightfull thinge,
      To live in a perpetuall Springe.

SONNET [to his First Love],

Upon presenting her with the Speech of Grayes-Inne Maske, at the Court, 1594; consisting of Three Parts: the Story of Proteus' Transformations[1]; the Wonders of the Adamantine Rocke[2]; and a Speech to her Majestie[3].

> Who in these lines may better claime a part,
>   That sing the prayses of the Maiden Queene:
>   Then you, faire sweet, that onely Soueraigne beene
> Of the poore Kingdome of my faithfull heart?
> Or to whose view should I this Speech impart,
>   Where th' Adamantine Rock's great power is showne;
>   But to your conq'ring eyes, whose force once knowne,
> Makes even yron hearts loath thence to part?
>   Or who Proteus' sundry transformations,
>   May better send you the new-fained story;
>   Then I, whose loue unfain'd felt no mutations,
>   Since to be yours I first receiu'd the glory?
> Accept then of these lines, though meanly pen'd,
> So fit for you to take, and me to send[4].

The two following Poems are by Thomas Campion; who, it appears, was Author of the Hymne sung by Amphitrite, Thamesis, and other Sea Nymphes, in the Graies-Inne Maske[5].

Of his Mistresses face.

> And would you see my Mistresse face!
> It is a flowry garden place:
> Where knots of beauty have such grace,
> That all is worke, and no where space.

---

[1] See before, p. 309. [2] See p. 313. [3] See p. 316.

[4] The above Sonnet, from Davison's "Poetical Rapsodie," third edition, 1611, p. 11, appears to belong to Francis Davison's portion of his own valuable Miscellany; and to have been presented to his Mistress, with extracts from the "Gesta Grayorum." [5] See pp. 310. 316.

It is a sweet delitious morne,
Where day is breeding, neuer borne;
It is a meadow yet vnshorne,
Which thousand flowers do adorne.

It is the Heavens bright reflexe,
Weake eyes to dazle and to vexe;
It is th' idæa of her sexe,
Ennui of whom doth world perplexe.

It is a face of death that smiles;
Pleasing though it kill the whiles:
Where death and love, in pretty wiles,
Each other mutually beguiles.

It is faire beauties freshest youth,
It is a fain'd Elizium's truth;
The spring that wintred harts renu'th,
And that is that my soule pursu'th.

Upon her palenesse.

Blame not my cheeks, though pale with loue they be,
   The kindly heate into my heart is flowne:
To cherish it that is dismaid by thee,
   Who art so cruell and vnstedfaste growne.
     For Nature, cal'd for by distressed hearts,
     Neglects and quite forsakes the outward parts.

But they whose cheekes with carelesse bloud are stain'd,
   Nurse not one sparke of loue within their hearts;
And when they woo, they speake with passions fain'd,
   For their fat loue lies in their outward parts:
     But in their brests, where Love his Court should hold,
     Poore Cupid sits, and blowes his nailes for cold.

THO. CAMPION[1].

[1] From Davison's "Poetical Rapsodie, 1611," p. 185.

Commons at Gray's Inn.

That all the Fellows of the Society, being in Town, keep Commons at least eight weeks every year, in Term-time; *viz.* a fortnight in every Term, or be cast in Commons.

That every Fellow of the Society, having a chamber in the House, be in Commons once in every year, or forfeit his chamber.

That every Fellow of the Society pay for his Commons every fortnight.

That every Fellow of the Society coming in or going out of Commons, or taking repast, give or send notice to the Steward thereof, or be continued in Commons.

That no Fellow of the Society be admitted half Commons, or Repaster in grand weeks, but be put in whole Commons.

That no Fellow of the Society take above two repasts in a week, and pay 10*d.* for dinner, and 8*d.* for supper.

That every Fellow of the Society discharge all Commons and duties before he go out of Commons, or be continued in Commons.

That the cross table be served next after the first mess at the barr; and that afterwards no messes be served out of course.

That when any Fellow of the Society is cast out of Commons, he is not to take Commons in the Hall till he hath redeemed his offence; and yet he is to pay for his Commons in the mean time.

That no Commons be served to chambers, or elsewhere out of the Hall, except to readers.

That no particular parts be served, but at the lower ends of the tables.

That none be served in the Hall after cheese is gone about.

That no Fellow of the Society, under the decree of an Ancient, go within the buttery hatch to drink or wash before meals.

That no Fellow of the Society take any meat from any officer, or go down to the kitchen to fetch up his own meat.

That if any Fellow of the Society, being out of Commons, send for beer or bread into the buttery, he is to be cast into half Commons.

That no Fellow of the Society, under degree of a Barrister, sit at the Barr table in Term time.

That no stranger be suffered to stand in the skreen in meal-times.

That civility and due respect be used by every Fellow of the Society to the Readers and Ancients, and others his Seniors, upon pain of amerciament.

That such Fellows of the Society as come to Commons in the Hall, or to exercises, or to pension, come in their gowns, or be amerst.

That no Fellow of the Society pass up or down the Hall, or from place to place there, with his hat on his head, when the Society is met at meals or exercises, or other public occasions.

That no Fellow of the Society stand with his back to the fire.

That no Fellow of the Society make any rude noise in the Hall at exercises, or at meal times.

That no Fellow of the Society, under the degree of an Ancient, keep on his hat at readings, or moots, or cases assigned.

That if any Fellow of the Society, being summoned to attend the pension to answer to any matter laid to his charge, and shall wilfully refuse to come, he is to be amerst for his first offence; and for the second offence, expelled.

That in all cases of wilful contempts by any Fellow of the Society, against the Orders of the House, and of opposition to execution of the penalties, the punishments are, as the case shall require: Amerciament. Skreening his name. Coming in with Congees. Loss of chamber. Prosecution by Pension Writ. Prosecution by Warrant from the Judges. Suit upon his bond. Expulsion.

That if any Landress, or other servant, empty any stools; or cast any ashes, filth, or dirt, in any of the courts; or empty chamber-pots out of windows; the Master is to be amerst for such offence.

That search be made every Term for lewd and dangerous persons; that no such be suffered to lodge in the house.

CHAPEL.

That every Fellow of the Society receive the Communion in the Chappel every Term, or be amerst; and if he fail above three Terms together, he is to be put out of the House.

That none but Readers, and their assistants, sit in the Readers seats, upon pain of amerciament.

That none but Ancients sit in the two uppermost seats on each side in the body of the Chappel; nor any but Barristers in the three seats on each side next.

That no women or boyes be suffered to come within the Chappel.

That no stranger be admitted to come into the Chappel before the bell cease, unless he be brought in by a Fellow of the Society.

A True Accompt of the most triumphant and Royal Accomplishment of the Baptism of the most Excellent, Right High and Mighty Prince HENRY FREDERICK, *by the Grace of God* PRINCE *of* SCOTLAND, *afterwards* PRINCE *of* WALES; *as it was solemnized the 30th day of August,* 1594 [1].

The noble and most potent Prince of Scotland was born in the Castle of Striviling, upon Tuesday the 19th day of February, 1594-5; upon which occasion the King's Majestie sent for the Nobles of his land, and to all the capitall Burrows thereof, to have their advise how he should proceed for the due solemnization of his Royal Baptisme, and what Princes he should send to: when they were all compeired, with great diligence and goodwill he proponed unto them, that it was necessary to direct our Ambassadours to France, England, Denmarke, Low Countries, the Duke of Brunswicke his brother-in-law, and to the Duke of Magdelburgh, the Queene's Majestie's grand-father, and to such other Princes as should be thought expedient likewise: he thought the Castle of Striviling the most convenient place for the residence of this most noble and mightie Prince, in respect that he was born there; as also it was necessary that sufficient preparation might be made for the Ambassadours that should be invited to come, for honour of the Crown and Countrey. And besides all this, because the Chappell Royall

---

[1] First printed at London, in 1603.—The following Advertisement, intituled, "The Bookseller to the Reader," appears in the front of the MS. from which we now reprint. Whether a second edition of it has ever appeared in Scotland, we really do not know.

This little piece having casually fallen in my hands, formerly printed at London in the year 1603, which contains a succinct account of the solemnity of the Birth and Baptism of a Royal Prince of this Kingdom; (a Prince so much lamented upon his decease, in the flower of his age, that when the women in Scotland, even unto this day, do lament the death of their dearest children, to comfort them, it is ordinarily said, and is past into a proverb, " Did not good Prince HENRY die?" in which the genius, wit, learning, and delicacy of the Scots Court, at so great a distance of time, is epitomized; and if any doubt the matter of fact related, they may be fully convinced by several pieces of the workmanship used upon that signal occasion; and particularly the ship, yet extant, which I have lately seen in the apartment next to the great hall in the Castle of Stirling, where triumphant and Royal Entertainment was kept, a greater and more magnificent upon such an occasion is not recorded to have been performed by any Court at that time in Christendom;) and lest such a piece of curiosity and antiquity, now long out of print, might be lost, I thought it not improper to revive it by this new impression, for the satisfaction and diversion of those that love the Antiquities of this Kingdom.

was ruinous, and too litle, concluded that the old Chappel should be utterly rased, and anew erected in the same place, that should be more large, long, and glorious, to entertain the great number of straungers expected. These propositions at length considered, they all, with a free voluntarie deliberation, graunted unto his Majestie the summe of an hundred thousand pounds money of Scotland. Then was there Ambassadours elected to pass in France, England, Denmarke, the Low Countries, and other places before mentioned, who were all dispatched with such expedition, and their legacies took such wished effect; that first, there came two famous men from the King of Denmarke, the one Christimus Bernkow, the other Stenio Bille; these came to Leyth the 16th of July. The next day after them came Adamus Crusius, Ambassadour for the Duke of Brunswicke; and Joachimus Besseurtius, Ambassadour for the Duke of Magdelburgh, who is grand-father to the noble Princesse Anne, by the Grace of God Queene of Scotland. Thirdly, the 3d day of August, there came Ambassadours from the States of Holand and Zeland, the Barron of Braderod, and the Treasurer of Zeland, called Jacobus Falkius.

There was also a Nobleman directed from England, to wit, the Earle of Cumberland, who even when he had prepared himself richly and honourably in all respects for his voyage to come into Scotland, and divers Noblemen and Gentlemen of renown prepared and commanded for his honourable convoy, it pleased God to visit him with sickness; and in that respect another Nobleman was chosen to supply his place, which was the Earle of Sussex, &c.; and he, in consideration of his short and unexpected advertisement, made such diligence in his voyage, and magnificence for his own person, and honourable convoy, as was thought rare and rich by all men; whereby it fell out, that betwixt the sickness of the one Nobleman, and the hastie preparation, the time was so farre spent, that the very prefixt dayes of the Baptisme were sundrie times delayed; and because the Ambassadour of England was so long a coming; and the Ambassadours of Denmarke, Brunswicke, and Magdelburgh, were feared to be hindered in their voyage by the sea, by reason of the neare approaching of winter; they desired daily of the King's Majestie, dureing their remaining in Edenbrugh, to have some prefixed day to be nominate and certainly kept, that immediately thereafter they might be dispatched, which he granted at the last, although he had divers great impediments to the contrary: the first was, because the Chappell Royal of Striviling was not fully compleit in all such necessaries as was requisite, although he had the supply of the greatest number of artificers in the whole country, convened there of all craftes for that service; and his Majestie's owne person dayly overseer, with large and liberal payment: but the cheifest cause was the long absence of an Ambassadour from England, which his Majestie greatlie respected for many causes; and last of all, expecting that some Ambassadour should have come from France, which fell not out as was looked for. But when the Ambassadour was come from England to Edenbrugh, forthwith his Majestie dispatched one of the Gentlemen of his Highnes' Chalmer, to request him to repaire towards Striviling the next day with all possible diligence (which was the 28th day of August), because he would have had the Baptisme administered the day following. But neither were the propynes sent by the Queen of England, neither her Ambassadour's owne carriage, as then come: therefore the Baptisme was delayed untill the 30th day of August, as ye shall hear particularly hereafter.

But in the meane time it is to be understood, that all these noble Ambassadours before expressed were honourably sustained upon the King's Majestie's owne proper costes, during the whole time of their residence in Scotland, save only the Ambassadour of England, whose whole expences were defrayed by his Sovereigne the Queen of England; and because the rest of the Ambassadours were repaired to Striviling by his Majestie's direction, long before the coming of the English Ambassadour, his Highness bestowed the time with them in magnifique banketting, revelling, and dayly hunting, with great honour.

The King's Majestie, purposing further to decore by magnificence this action, committed the charge thereof to the Lord of Lendores, and M. William Fowler, who, by their travels, diligence, and invention, brought it to that perfection which the shortnesse of time and other considerations could permit: so they having consulted togather, concluded that those exercises that were to be used for decoration of that solemnitie, were to be devided both in field-pastimes with martiall and heroicall exploits, and in houshold with rare shewes and singular inventions.

The field to be used at two several daies: the first to be of three Turkes, three Christian Knights of Malta, three Amazones, and three Moores; but by reason of the absence, or at least the uncertaine presence of the three last gentlemen who should have sustained these personages, it was thought good that the number of that maske should consist of nine actors, nine pages, and nine lackies, which, comming from sundry parts, and at divers times, together with the diversitie of their apparel, should bring some noveltie to the beholders.

The place most expedient for this action was the valey neare the castle, which being prepared for that purpose, both with barrier and scaffold, after the comming of the Queene's Majestie, with her honourable and gallant Ladies, together with the honourable Ambassadors, the field being beset by the brave yonkers of Edinbrugh, with their hagbutes, during the whole time of that pastime.

Then three Christians entered the field with sound of trumpet, who were the King's Majestie, the Earle of Mar, and Thomas Erskine (Gentleman of his Majestie's Chalmer), who made up this number.

A little after followed three apparelled lyke Turkes, very gorgeously attired; and these were the Duke of Lenox, the Lord Home, and Syr Robert Ker of Cesfurde, Knight.

Last of all came in three Amazones in women's attire, very sumptuously clad; and these were the Lord of Lendores, the Lord of Barclewch, and the Abbot of Holy-roote-house: so all these persons being present, and at their entrie making their reverence to the Queene's Majestie, Ambassadours and Ladies, having their pages ryding upon their led horse, and on their left armes bearing their masters' impresse or device.

The King's Majestie's was a lyon's head with open eyes; which signifieth, after a mistique and hierogliphique sense, Fortitude and Vigilancie: the words were, "Timeat & primus & ultimus orbis." The second was a dog's collar, all beset with yron pikes; the wordes were these, "Offendit & defendit." The third of that Christian army was a windmill with her spokes unmoving, windes unblowing on every side; with these words, "Ni sperat immota."

The second faction did carry these: a hart half in fire, and half in frost; on the one part Cupid's torch; and on the other Jupiter's thunder; with these words, "Hinc amor, inde metus." The other page a Zodiacke, and in the same the moone farre opposite to the sunne; with these wordes, "Quo remotior, lucidior;" that is to say, the farther, the fairer. The third of this partie caried painted foure coach-wheeles, the hindermost following the foremost, and yet never overtaking them; with these words, "Quo magis insequor."

The last three Pages bare in their targets the impresses following, a crown, an eye, and a portcullis: the crown betokening the power of God; the eye his providence; and the portcullis his protection; with these words, which were composed in Anagrame, of Walterus Scotus, the Laird of Bacleugh's name, "Clausus tutus ero." The second Page of this party carried on his targe the portraiture of an hand, holding an eill by the tail, alluding to the uncertainty of persons or of times; with these words, " Ut frustra, sic patientur." The last was this, a fire in sight of the sun, burning, and not perceived; with this sentence, " Oblector lumine victus."

And every lackie carying in his hand his master's launce.

They began their pastime by running at the ring and glove; the lawes whereof were these:

1. First, that all the persons of this pastime compeare masked, and in such order as they come into the field, so to run out all their courses.

2. Secondly, that none use any other ring but that which is put up; and use no other launce but that which they have brought for themselves.

3. Thirdly, he that twice touches the ring, or stirres it, winneth as much if he caried away the ring.

4. Fourthly, he that lets his launce fall out of his hand, is deprived of all the rest of his courses.

5. Fifthly, that every one run with loose reins, and with as much speed as his horse hath.

6. Sixtly, that none after his race, in uptaking of his horse, lay his launce upon his shoulder, under the pain of losse of that which he hath done in his course.

7. Seventhly, he that carrieth not his launce under his arme, loseth his course.

8. Eighthly, that none, untill his three courses be ended, chaunge his horse, if he be not hurt, or upon some other consideration moved to change him.

These lawes being seen and approved by the actors, the Queene's Majestie signified unto them, that he who did run best should have for his rewarde a faire and a rich ring of diamonds: and he also who on that same side had best fortune in running, he should be acknowledged with another as fair as the first. The proof hereof being made, the victorie fell to the Duke of Lenox; who, bringing it to his side and partie, had the praise and prise adjudged to himself. Thus the first daye's pastime was ended, with great contentment to the beholders, and commendation of the persons enterprisers.

The second daye's pastime was extended, by reason that the artisans were imployed in other businesse, who should have followed forth that invention given them: and seeing the grace of that exercise consisted in embosserie, and the craftesmen apt for the same otherwise and necessarily busied, it was left off; which if it had been brought to effect, this country had not seen nor pactised a more rarer; for what by the bravery and strange apparell of the persons themselves, and by the divers shapes of the beasts that should have bene born and brought there, in sight had been commendable and wonderfull, by reason that such beastes, as lyon, elephant, hart, unicorne, and the griphon, together with the camel, hydre, crocadile, and dragon (carrying their riders), had carried also with it by the newnes of that invention great contentment and commendation of that exercise. But, I say, some arising lets impeshed this invention; and all things were cast off that might have farther decored this solemnity through other urgent occasions.

And when all the Ambassadours were convened together, and all necessarie materials readie, the Chappell Royall of the Castle of Striviling was richly hung with costly tapestries; and at the North-east end of the same a Royall seat of estate prepared for the King's Majestie; and on his right hand was set a faire wide chaire, with the due ornaments pertaining thereto; over which was set the armes of the King of France.

Next thereunto was a princely travers of crimson taffeta for the Ambassadour of England: and over his head the armes of England; on the desk before him lay a cushion of red velvet: there stood attending on him two Gentlemen Ushers, appointed by the Queene of England for that present service.

Next unto him sat M. Robert Bowes, Ambassadour Ordinary for the Queene of England: on the desk before him was laid a cloth of purple velvote, and a cushion sutable thereunto.

Than sat the Ambassadour of the noble Prince Henricus Julius, Duke of Brunswick; and before him on the desk was laid a cloth of green velvete, with a cushen of the same; and over his head the arms of his Prince.

Next unto him sate the Ambassadours of the Lowe Countries, with a long fair cloth, spread on the desk before them, of blewe velvet, and two cushions suitable thereunto; and over their heads the arms of their countries.

On the King's left hand was placed nearest his Majestie the two Ambassadours of Denmarke, with a large broad cloth, spred on the desk before them, of purple velvet; and the arms of Denmark over their heads.

Next unto them sate the Ambassadour of the noble Prince Udalricus, Duke of Magdelburgh, with his Prince's arms over his head.

In the middest of the Chappell Royall, within the partition, where the King's Majestie, the Ambassadours, and Prince with his convoy, were placed, there was a new pulpit erected; the same was richly hung with cloth of gold: all the pavement within this partition was prince-like laid with fine tapestrey.

Under the pulpit was another deske, wherein sate in the midst M. David Cunningham, Bishop of Abirdene; M. David Lindesay, minister of Leyth; and John Duncanson, one of the ordinary ministers to the King's Majestie; before whom was set a table covered with yealow velvet.

And when all things were in readines as was requisite, there was placed a hundred hagbuters (being onely the yonkers of Edinbrugh bravely apparelled) in order, betwixt the Prince's utter chalmer-doore and the entry to the Chappell Royall, on both the sides of the passage.

Then the King's Majestie, with his Nobles and Counsellors attending on him, entered the Chappell, and there sate downe in his Royall seate of estate.

All the Ambassadours likewise were sent for, and convoyed to the Prince's Chalmer of Presence, where the Prince was lying on his bed of estate, richly decored, and wrought with brodered worke, containing the story of Hercules and his travels.

This bed was erected on a platforme, very artificially, with a footepace of three degrees ascending to it; the degrees being covered with tapestrie, all wrought with golde, and a large cloth of lawne covering both the bed and the degrees, which reached forth a great space over the flore.

Then the old Countesse of Mar with reverence past to the bed; she tooke up the Prince, and delivered him to the Duke of Lennox, who presently rendered him likewise to the Ambassadour of England, to be borne to the Chappell Royall.

The Maister of the Ceremonies, addressing himself to a table in the said chalmer, curiously ordered, whereon stood those ornaments of honour which were to be borne to the Chappell before the Prince, with due reverence delivered them to certaine noblemen, according to the order appointed by his Majestie for the bearing thereof.

In like manner the Prince's robe-royall, being of purple velvote, very richly set with pearle, was delivered to the Duke of Lennox, who put the same about the Prince; the traine whereof was borne up by the Lord Sinclair and the Lord Urquhart: then they removed themselves to the utter chalmer, where there was a fair high pale, made foursquare, of crimson velvote attending, which was laid with rich pasments, and fringed with gold; this pale was sustained by four worshipful Barons, the Laird of Bucleugh, the Constable of Dundee, Sir Robert Ker of Cesfurd, Knight, and the Laird of Traquhair; under the which pale were the Embassadours of England; Robert Earle of Sussex carrying the Prince in his armes, and M. Robert Bowes, Ordinary Embassador for England, assisting him. Next to them was the Duke of Lennox. About the pale were the Ambassadours of Denmark, Magdelburgh, Brunswick, and the Estates. There followed the old Countesse of Mar, Mistris Bowes, diverse Ladies of Honour, with the Mistresse Nurse.

Then the trumpets, sounding melodiously before the Prince and his convoy, went forward; Lyon King of Armes, and the Heraulds his brethren, with their coat-armours, in goodly order following.

Next followed the Prince's honours, borne by these Noblemen: the Lord Sempell, carrying a lavar of water; the Lorde Seton, a fair bason; the Lorde Levingston, a towel; and the Lorde Home, a low crowne competent for a Duke, richly set with diamonds, saphires, rubies, and emeraulds; who, approaching neare the pulpit, where these honors were received from them by the Maister of the Ceremonies, and by him placed on the table before the pulpit; the Noblemen retyring backe to their appointed places.

Lastly, the pale was carried in before the pulpit, where the Ambassador of England rendered the Prince to the Duke of Lennox, who immediately delivered him to the old Countesse of Mar, and she consequently to the Mistresse Nurse; and all the Ambassadors were then set in such order of places as the demonstration of their armories gave notice.

Without the partition were ornate fourmes, all covered with greene, whereupon were placed the Gentlemen of England, Denmarke, Almaine, Flanders, and Scotland. And as all men were thus competently placed, and universal silence made, ntered M. Patrik Galloway, one of his Majestie's ordinary preachers, into the pulpit, who learnedly and godly entreated upon the text of the 21st of Genesis; which being done, the Bishop of Aberdene stoode up in his seate, and taught upon sacrament of Baptisme, first in the vulgar tongue, and next in the Latine, to the end all men might generally understand. This done, the Provost and Prebends of the Chappell Royall did sing the 21st Psalm of David, according to the art of musique, to the great delectation of the noble auditory.

Then they proceeded to the action. The King arose, and came towards the pulpit; the Ambassadours followed in their order; the Barons that carried the pale above the Prince moved towards the pulpit; the Duke of Lennox received the Prince from the Countesse of Marr, and delivered him to the hands of the Earle of Sussex, Ambassadour for England; where hee was named, by all their consents, FREDERIKE HENRY, HENRY FREDERIKE, and so baptized, in the name of the Father, Sonne, and Holy Ghost, by the said names.

This being done, Lyon King of Armes, with a loude voice, repeates these names thrise over: and then after him the rest of his brethren herauldes, with trumpets sounding, confirmed the same.

Then the King's Majestie, Ambassadours, and all removing to their places, the English Ambassador alone, withdrawing himself on the one side, was mette and attended on by two groomes, who humbly on their knees, the one presenting a large rich basen, the other a suitable lavar, repleat with sweete water, wherewith the Ambassadour washed; a gentleman sewer, with humble reverence, presenting him a faire towell, wherewith he dried his hands, and so forthwith returned to his place.

This being done, the Bishop ascended to the pulpitte, where, after that he had delivered in verse a certaine praise and commendation of the Prince; then he converted the rest of his Latine Oration in prose to the Ambassadours, every one in particular, beginning at the Ambassadour of England, and so continuing with the rest; wherein he made mention of the Chronology of each of these Princes; and recited the proximitie and nearnesse of bloud that they had with Scotland; concluding his Oration with exhortation and thanksgiving to God for that good occasion and prosperous assembly.

In conclusion, the blessing being given, Lyon King of Arms cryed with a loud voice, "God save Frederik Henry, and Henry Frederik, by the Grace of God, Prince of Scotland:" the rest of the Heraulds proclaimed the same at an open window of the Chappell Royall with sound of trumpet.

Then the King, the Prince, the Ambassadours, the Nobles, and Ladies of Honor, retyred forth of the Chappel in such order as they entered, and repaired towards the King's Hall; during their passage, the cannons of the Castle roared, that therwith the earth trembled; and other smaller shot mode their harmonie after their kinde.

In the King's Hall the Duke of Lennox received the Prince from the Ambassador of England, and presented him to the King's Majestie, who addubbed him knight. He was touched with the spur by the Earl of Mar: thereafter the King's Majestie presented a ducall crowne on his head, and then was proclaimed, by Lyon King of Arms, "The Right Excellent, High, and Magnanime, Frederik Henry, Henry Frederik, by the grace of God, Knight and Barron of Renfrew,

Lord of the Yles, Earle of Carricke, Duke of Rosay, Prince and Great Steward of Scotland."

These words were repeated by the Heraulds, with a loud voice, at an open window of the Hall.

Then the Prince was carried by the Ambassadour of England to his own chalmer of presence; where the most rich and rare propynes were there presented.

Also there were certain barons snd gentlemen addubbed knights, whose names do follow in order as they were proclaimed: and first their oath.

The Oath of a Knight.

1. I shall fortifie and defend the true Christian Religion, and Christ's Holy Evangel, now presently preached within this realme, to the uttermost of my power.

2. I shall be loyall and true to my Soveraigne Lord the King's Majestie, to all orders of chivalrie, and to noble office of armes.

3. I shall fortifie and defend justice at my power, and that without favour or feed.

4. I shall never flie from my Soveraigne Lord the King's Majestie, nor from his Highnesse Lieutenant, in time of mellay and battell.

5. I shall defend my native realme from all allieners and strangers.

6. I shall defend the just action and quarrell of all Ladies of Honour, of all true and friendless widows, of orphants, and of maidens of good fame.

7. I shall do diligence wheresoever I heare there is any murtherers, traytors, and maisterfull reavers, that oppresseth the King's lieges, and poore people, to bring them to the lawe at my power.

8. I shall maintain and uphold the noble estate of chivalrie, with horse, harnishe, and other knightly abillements; and shall help and succour them of the same order at my power, if they have need.

9. I shall enquire and seeke to have the knowledge and understanding of all the articles and points contained in the book of chivalrie.

All these premises to observe, keep, and fulfil, I oblesse me; so help me my God, by my owne hand; so help me God, &c.

  Sir William Stewart, of Houston, knight.
  Sir Robert Bruce, of Clackmannan, knight.
  Sir John Boswell, of Balmowrow.
  Sir James Schaw, of Salquhy, knight.

Sir John Murray, of Ethilstoun, knight.
Sir William Monteith, of Kerse, knight.
Sir Alexander Fraser, of Fraserburgh, knight.
Sir John Lindsay, of Dunrod, knight.
Sir George Levingston, of Ogilface, knight.
Sir James Forester, of Torwood-head, knight.
Sir Andrew Balfoure, of Strathour, knight.
Sir Walter Dundas, of Over Newlistoun, knight.
Sir John Boswel, of Glasemont, knight.
Sir George Elphingstoun, of Blytherood, knight.
Sir William Levingston, of Darnechester, knight.
Sir David Meldrum, of New-hall, knight.

These names were proclaimed upon the terrase of the forefront of the Castle, with sound of trumpets; and great quantity of divers especes of gold and money cast over amongst the people.

These things being accomplished, the King and Queene's Majesties, with the Ambassadours, addressed themselves to the banket in the great Hall about eight of the clock at night. Then came Lyon King of Arms, with his brethren the Herauldes, and entered the Hall before the King and Queene's meate, the trumpets sounding melodiously before them; with these noblemen bearing office for the present:

The Earl of Mar,	G. Mr. Houshold.	
The Lord Fleming,	G. Mr. Usher.	
The Earl of Montrose,	Carver,	
The Earl of Glencarne,	Copper,	for the King's Majestie.
The Earle of Orknay,	Sewer,	
The Lord Seton,		
The Lord Hume,	for the Queene's Majestie.	
The Lord Sempill,		

This delicate banquet being ordered with great abundance, the King, Queene, and Ambassadours, were placed all at one table, being formed of three parts, after a geometrical figure, in such sort, that every one might have a full sight of the other.

The King and Queen's Majesties were placed in the midst of the table; and on the King's right hand were set the English Ambassadours, the Earle of Sussex, and M. Robert Bowes; next them sat the the Ambassadour from the Duke of Brunswick, and the Ambassadour from the Duke of Magdelburgh.

On the King's left hand, next to the Queene's Majestie, sate the Ambassadour of Denmark, and Ambassadours from the States of Holand and Zeland: betwixt every one of their seates was left a good space.

On the east and west side of the Hall was placed two very long tables; where were set certain Noblemen, Ladies of Honour, and Counsellors of Scotland; and with them the Noblemen and Gentlemen of England, Denmark, Almaine, and Flanders; and betwixt every Nobleman and Gentleman stranger was placed a Lady of Honour, or Gentlewoman.

Now, being thus in a very honourable and comely order set, and after a while having well refreshed themselves with the first service, which was very sumptuous, there came into the sight of them all a Black Moore, drawing (as it seemed to the beholders) a triumphall chariott, and before it the melodious noise of trumpets and howboyes; which chariott entered the Hall: the motion of the whole frame (which was twelve foot long, and seven foot broad) was so artificial within itselfe, that it appeared to be drawne in onely by the strength of a Moore, which was very richly attired. His traces were great chaines of pure gold.

Upon this chariot was finely and artificially devised a sumptuous covered table, decked with all sorts of exquisite delicacies and dainties of patisserie, frutages, and confections.

About the table were placed six gallant dames, who represented a silent comedie; three of them clothed in argentine saten, and three in crimson saten; all these six garments were enriched with togue and tinsal of pure gold and silver, every one of them having a crowne or garland on their heads very richly decked with feathers, pearles, and jewels, upon their loose hair *in antica forma*.

In the first front stood dame Ceres, with a sickle in her right hand, and a handfull of corne in the other; and upon the outmost part of her thigh was written this sentence, " Fundent uberes omnia campi," which is to say, the plenteous fields affoord all things.

Overe against Ceres stood Fœcunditie, with some bushes of chessbolls; which, under an hieroglyphick sense, representeth broodbines, with this devise, " Felix prole divum;" and on the other side of her habite, " Crescant in mille." The first importing that this country is blessed by the child of the Goddes; and the second, alluding to the King and Queene's Majesties, that their generations may grow into thousands.

Next on the other side was placed Faith, having in her hands a basen, and in the same two hands joyned together, with this sentence, "Boni alumna conjugii;" the fortresse and nurse of a blessed marriage.

Over against Faith stood Concorde, with a golden tasse in her left hande, and the horne of aboundance in her right hand, with this sentence, " Plene beant te numina sinu;" the heavenly powers do blesse thee with a full bosome.

The next place was occupied by Liberalitie, who having in her right hand two crownes, and in her left two scepters, with this devise, " Me comite plura quam dabis, accipies;" that is to say, having me thy follower, thou shalt receive more than thou shalt give.

And the last was Perseverance, having in her right hand a staffe, and on her left shoulder an anchor, with this devise, " Nec dubiæ res mutabunt, nec secunda;" neither doubtful, nor more prosperous things shall change your state.

This chariot, which should have been drawne in by a lyon (but because his presence might have brought some feare to the nearest, or that the sight of the lights and torches might have commoved his tamenes); it was thought meete, that the Moore should supply that roome: and so he, in outwarde shewe, pleased to draw that forward, which, by a secret convoy, was brought to the Prince's table; and the whole desert was delivered by Ceres, Fœcunditie, Faith, Concord, Liberalitie, and Perseverance, to the Earles, Lords, and Barons, that were sewers.

Presently after the returning of the chariot, entered a most sumptuous, artificiall, and well-proportioned ship; the length of her keele was 18 foot, and her breadth 8 foote; from her bottome to her highest flagge was 40 foote: the sea shee stood upon was 24 foot long, with bredth convenient: her motion was so artificially devised within hereself, that none could perceive what brought her in. The sea under her was lively counterfeit with all colours; on her foresterne was placed Neptunus, having in his hand his trident, and on his head a crowne; his apparell was all of Indian cloth of silver and silke, which bare this inscription, " Junxi, atque reduxi;" which in sense importeth, that as he joyned them, so he reduced their Majesties.

Then Thetis with her mace, goddesse of the sea, with this devise, " Nunquam abero, & tutum semper te littore sistam;" which signifieth, that by her presence shee alwaies shall be careful to bring them into a safe shore and harborow.

Then Triton, with his wilke-trumpet, was next to her, with this devise, "Velis, votis, ventis;" by sailes, by vowes, by windes.

Round about the ship were all the marine people, as Syrenes (above the middle as women, and under as fishes); and these were Parthenope, Ligea, and Leucosia; who, accommodating their gestures to the voice of the musitions, repeated this verse, " Unus eris nobis, cantandus semper in orbe;" and all the same was decored with the riches of the seas, as pearles, coralls, shelles, and metalls, very rare and excellent.

The bulke of this ship was curiously painted; and her galleries, whereupon stood the most part of the banket in christalline glasse, gilt with gold and azure; her mastes were redde; her tackling and cordage was silke of the same colour, with golden pulleis: her ordnance was 36 pieces of brasse bravely mounted; and her anchors silver gilt; and all her sayles were double, of white taffata; and in her fore sayle, a shippe compasse, regarding the North-starre, with this sentence, " Quascunque per undas;" which is to say, through whatsoever seas or waves the King's Majestie intendeth his course, and project of any rising action, Neptune, as God of the sea, shall be favourable to his proceedings.

On the maine saile, was painted the armouries of Scotland and Denmark; with this devise, competent in the person of the Prince of Scotland, " En quæ divisa beatos efficiunt, collecta tenes;" that is to say, Behold (O Prince!) what doth make these kingdomes severally blessed, jointly (O Prince of hope) thou holdes and hast together.

Her tops were all armed with taffetaes of his Majestie's colours, gold, and jewels; and all her flagges and streamers suitable to the same.

Her mariners were in number six, apparelled all in chaungeable Spainish taffataes; and her pilote in cloth of gold: he alone stood at the helm, who only moved and governed the whole frame, both the ship and her burden, very artificially.

The musitions within the same were 14, all apparelled in taffataes of his Majestie's colours, besides Arion with his harpe.

Beinge thus prepared, at the sounde of trumpets she approached; and at the nexte sounde of Triton's wilke-trumpet, together with the master's whistle, she made sayle till shee came to the table, discharging the ordnance in her sterne by the way: but because this devise carried some morall meaning with it, it shall not be impertinent to this purpose to discover what is meant and propyned thereby.

CEREMONIAL OF THE BAPTISM OF HENRY PRINCE OF SCOTLAND, 1594.

The King's Majestie having undertaken in such a desperate time to saile to Norway, and, like a new Jason, bring his Queene, our gracious Lady, to this kingdome, being detained and stopped by the conspiraces of witches, and such devilish dragons, thought it very meet to follow forth this his own invention; that, as Neptunus (speaking poetically, and by such fictions as the like interludes and actions are accustomed to be decored withall) joyned the King to the Queene;

So after this conjunction hee brought their Majesties as happily hither; and now at this her blessed delivery did bring such things as the sea affoords to decore this festivall time withall, which immediately were delivered to the sewers forth of the galleries of this ship, out of christaline glasse, very curiously painted with gold and azure, all sorts of fishes, as hearings, whitings, flooks, oysters, buckies, lampets, partans, lapstars, crabs, sput-fish, clammes; with other infinite things made of suger, and most lively represented in their own shape. And whilst the ship was unloading, Arion, sitting upon the galey-nose, which resembled the form of a dolphine fish, played upon his harpe; then began her musick in greene kolyne howloyes in fine parts. After that, followed viols with voices in plaine counterpoint to the nature of these hexameter verses :

> " Undique conveniant, quot Reges nomine Christi
> Gaudent, atque suas maturent cogere vires.
> Viribus hos, O Rex, opibusque anteiveris omnes
> Quisque suam jam posse velit tibi cedere sortem.
> Regna, viros aurum, quæ te fuere potentem.
> Omnia conjugii decorant hæc pignora chari:
> Anna precor fælix multos feliciter annos,
> Vive, resume novas, atque annuus anni
> Lustar eat, redeatque novo tibi partus ab ortu.
> Cresce Puer, sacri mens numinis imbibar imbres,
> Semper uterque parens de te nova gaudia captet.
> Scotia, quæ quondam multis tenebrosa vocata est
> Lumina magna nitent in te superantia cœlum,
> Lux verbi, & Rex, & Princeps diademata Regni."

After which ensued a still noise of recorders and fluts; and for the fourth, a general consort of the best instruments.

So this Enterlude drawing neare to an end, in the very last courses was discovered this sentence likewise, " Submissus adorat Oceanus ;" inferring, that the Ocean sea, by offering the shapes of her treasure, humbly adored and honoured the sitters. And when in this time all the banket was done, after thanks being given, there was sung with most delicate dulce voices, and sweet harmonie, in seven partes, the 128th Psalm, with fourteen voyces; and that being done, at the sound of Triton's wilke-trumpet, and the pilote's whistle, she wayed anchor, made saile, and with noise of honboys and trumpets retyred, and then discharged the rest of her ordnance, to the great admiration of the beholders.

After all which pastime and sport, with merrie and joyfull repast, the King and Queene's Majesties, after their offices of honour and respect, place being prepared for the revels, and the persons appointed for the same discharging themselves sufficiently: their Majesties and Ambassadors went to an other hall, most richly and magnificently hung with rich tapestrie, where, for the collation, a most rare, sumptuous, and prince-like desart was prepared; which being ended, after taking leave and good-nights, they departed, about three of the clock in the morning to their night's rest.

The dayes ensueing, so long as leisur might serve, was bestowed by the Ambassadours in banketting of Noblemen and Gentlemen of their acquaintance; and the King in the mean time was solicite and carefull of honourable and magnifike rewards to be bestowed on either of them, which was also princely performed to their great contentment.

And as they were come to Edinbrugh, they were all banketted at some time by divers Noblemen of Scotland, with great honour. Last of all, one Ambassadour banketted another, for commemoration of that joyfull meeting and good successe.

Then the King and Queene's Majesties came to Edenbrugh, where they were invited by the Ambassadours of Denmarke unto a banket within their ship, which lay at anchor in the river of Forth: she was so great that she could not enter the harborow.

The banket was very sumptuous, and the Ambassadours so joyous of their finall dispatch, behaved themselves to their Majesties on a kindly manner, according to the ordinary custome of their countrey, by propining of drink unto them in the name of their Princes, which was lovingly accepted and requitted; in commemoration whereof, the whole artillery of that great vessel were shot in great number.

The three great ships of the Estates, lying in the same road near by, made correspondance and resonance to the number of six score great shot, and thus concluded their *Bein ale.* Then the Castle of Edenbrugh, for performance of the King's honour, as they perceived the ships to lose and to hoise up saile, the Captaine of the Castle saluted every ship, as they shewed themselves in readines by order, with a number of great cannon shot. And so I conclude.

Bishop Aylmer, a worthy and learned Prelate, was principally resident at Fulham, and died there in 1594. The zeal with which he supported the interests of the Establishmed Church exposed him to the resentment of the Puritans, who, among other methods which they took to injure the Bishop, attempted to prejudice the Queen against him, alledging that he had committed great waste at Fulham, by cutting down the elms; and, punning upon his name, they gave him the appellation of *Mar-elms;* " but it was a shameful untruth," says Strype; " and how false it was all the Court knew, and the Queen herself could witness; for she had lately lodged at the Palace, where she misliked nothing, but that her lodgings were kept from all great prospect by the thickness of the trees, as she told her Vice-chamberlain, and he reported to the Bishop."—Bancroft was honoured with a Visit from Queen Elizabeth in 1600, and another in 1602.—King James visited him previously to his Coronation [1].

In January 1594-5 the following entry occurs in the Churchwardens' Accompts of Great Wigston, Leicestershire: " Paid 2d. for a candle on the Coronation-day of our gracious Queen. God long continue her in health and peace to raigne over us. So be it. Amen."

On the 18th of February 1594-5, the carts at Chalk were in requisition for removing the Queen from Greenwich to Whitehall [2].

In 1595 we find the Queen dining " at Kew [3], the house of the Lord Keeper (Sir John Puckering), who had lately obtained of her Majesty his suit of £.100 a-year in land in fee-farm. Her entertainment for that meale was great and costlie. At her first lighting she had a fine fanne with a handle garnished with diamonds. When she was in the middle way between the garden gate and the house, there came running towards her one with a nosegay in his hand, and delivered yt unto her with a short well-penned Speech; it had in yt a

---

[1] Lysons, vol. II. p. 354.
[2] See before, p. 38.
[3] Where " Lodgings" were provided for her in 1594; see p. 252.

very rich jewell, with pendants of unfirled diamonds, valued at £.400 at least. After dinner, in her Privy Chamber, he gave her a faire paire of virginals. In her bed-chamber, presented her with a fine gown and a juppin, which things were pleasing to her Highness; and to grace his Lordship the more, she of herself took from him a salt [1], a spoone, and a forcke of fair agatte [2].

A discharge of the state and degree of Serjeant at the Law to Thomas Fleming (who was then made the Queen's Sollicitor General), 1595.

"ELIZABETH, &c. To our trusty and well-beloved subject Thomas Flemyng, Serjeant at the Law, greeting. Where we were minded, and do intend otherwise to imploy you in our service; know ye that we, aswel in consideration thereof, as divers other good causes and considerations us moving, of our especial grace and mere motion have acquitted, released, and discharged; and by these presents do acquit, release, and discharge you of and for being any more, from henceforth, Serjeant at Law, and of the name, title, and degree of Serjeant at Law; and of and from all attendance and service that you should or ought to give, or do at any time or times, or at any place or places, for and by reason of your being Serjeant at Law, or by reason of the said office, state, or degree of Serjeant at Law. And also we release and dischardge you for wearing of any quoif, commonly called a Serjeant's Quoif, and of and for the wearing of all other apparel, garments, vestures, and habits, that by the laws and customes of this our Realm, ye should or ought to wear or use, for that ye were or be Serjeant at Law; and generally of and for all other things whatsover, that ye by any manner of means, ought or are bound to do, use, or exercise, by reason ye were or be Serjeant at Law, as cleerly and freely to all intents and purposes, as though ye never had been Serjeant at Law, had never taken upon you the office, state, or degree of Serjeant at Law, any statute, law, custome, or use, had, made, or used, to the contrary notwithstanding. In witness, &c. Witness Ourself, at Westminster, the 5th day of November, in the 37th year of our Reign.

[1] The Knife described in vol. II. p. 423, and engraved with the *Decanter* (see before, p. 98), was preserved in the valuable Museum of the late Mr. Greene, of Lichfield, and was probably a present given or taken on some such occasion.—In the same Plate, fig. 2. 3. exhibit a piece of plate of the 16th century, a salt-seller of silver gilt, in the possession of the late Mr. Gough: fig. 4. are the arms enameled on the cover; quarterly, 1. *Berkeley*; 2. *Brotherton*; 3. *Warren*; 4, *Mowbray*, impaling *Viole*.

[2] Rowland Whyte to Sir Robert Sidney, December 15, 1595. Sidney Papers, vol. I. p. 376.

Device exhibited by the Earl of ESSEX[1] *before Queen* ELIZABETH, *on the Anniversary of her Accession to the Throne, November* 17, 1595.

The only particulars we have been able to recover relative to this Entertainment given by the Earl of Essex to his Sovereign, are preserved in the "Letters and Memorials of State of the Sidney Family;" where Mr. Rowland White, in a Letter to Sir Robert Sidney, Nov. 16, 1595, says, "There is great preparation for these triumphs, and such Devises promised as our age hath not seen the like." And on the 22d of November he adds, "My Lord of Essex's Device is much comended in these late triumphs. Some pretty while before he came in himself to the Tilt, he sent his Page with some Speech to the Queen, who returned with her Majestie's glove. And when he came himself, he was met with an old Hermitt, a Secretary of State, a brave Soldier, and an Esquire. The first presented him with a Booke of Meditations; the second with Political Discourses; the third with Oracions of brave fought battles; the fourth was but his own follower, to whom the other three imparted much of their purpose before his coming in. Another devised with him, persuading him to this and that course of life, according to their inclinations. Comes into the Tilt-yard, unthought upon, thordinary Post-boy of London, a ragged villain, all bemired, upon a poor leane jade, gallaping and blowing for liff, and delivered the Secretary a packet of lettres, which he presently offred my Lord of Essex. And with this dumb-shew our eyes were fed for that time. In thafter-supper, before the Queen, they first delivered a well-pend Speach to move this worthy Knight to leave his vaine following of love, and to betake him to hevenly meditacion; the Secretarie's all tending to have him follow matters of State; the Soldier's persuading him to the war. But the Squier answered them all; and concluded with an excellent, but plaine English, that this Knight would never forsake his Mistresse's love, whose vertue made all his thoughts devine; whose wisdom tought him all true pollicy; whose beauty and worth were

---

[1] Norden, speaking of York House in the Strand, says, "Yorke House reteyning still the antient title had of the persons possessing it; his Highness hath now committed the same unto the Right Hon. the Earl of Essex."—This was the House which the Queen went to see, from the Lord Treasurer's, noticed in p. 79. Three other Noble Houses in that neighbourhood are also thus noticed by Norden: "The house called *Durham* or *Dunelme House* is so called for that it sometime apperteyned unto the Bishops of that See. It was builded in the time of Henry III. by Anthony Becke, Bishop of Durham. It is a house of 300 years antiquitye, the hall whereof is stately and high, supported with loftie marble pillars. It standeth upon the Thamise very pleasantly. Her Majesty hath commanded the use thereof to Sir *Walter Rawleigh*."—And "Arondell House is so called of the Earles of Arondell; sometymes the Bishop of Bathe's."—"Leicester House is so called of the late Earl of Leicester, who in his lifetime enjoyed the same; sometime apperteyning to the Bishop of Exeter. There was a Chappell wher now the porter's lodge is at the utter gate, apperteyning to St. Clement's Danes."—See hereafter, p. 414.

at all times able to make him fit to comand armies. He shewed all the defects and imperfections of all their times; and therefore thought his course of life to be best in serving his Mistres. Thold man was he that in Cambridge plaied *Giraldy*; Morley plaied the Secretary; and he that plaied *Pedantiq* was the Soldier; and Toby Mathew[1] acted the Squire's part. The world makes many untrue constructions of these Speaches, comparing the Hermit and the Secretary to two of the Lords; and the Soldier to Sir Roger Williams. But the Queen said, that if she had thought there had bene so moch said of her, she would not have bene their that night; and soe went to bed."

Speeches delivered upon the occasion of the Earl of Essex's Device, drawn up by Mr. Francis Bacon [2].

The Squire's Speech.

Most excellent and glorious Queen, give me leave, I beseech your Majesty, to offer my Master's complaint and petition; complaint, that coming hither to your Majesty's most happy day, he is tormented with the opportunity of a melancholy dreaming Hermit, a mutinous brain-sick Soldier, and a busy tedious Secretary. His petition is, that he may be as free as the rest; and, at least while he is here, troubled with nothing but with care how to please and honour you.

The Hermit's Speech in the Presence.

Though our ends be diverse, and therefore may be one more just than another; yet the complaint of this Squire is general, and therefore alike unjust against us all. Albeit he is angry that we offer ourselves to his Master uncalled, and forgets we come not of ourselves but as the messengers of self-love, from whom all that comes should be well taken. He saith, when we come, we are importunate. If he mean, that we err in form, we have that of his Master, who, being a Lover, useth no other form of soliciting. If he will charge us to err in matter, I for my part will presently prove, that I persuade him to nothing but for his own good. For I wish him to leave turning over the book of Fortune, which is but a play for chil-

---

[1] Eldest son of Dr. Tobie Mathew, Archbishop of York. "At his return from his travels, he was esteemed a well-qualified Gentleman, and to be one well versed in the affairs of other nations, and therefore was taken into the acquaintance of that noted scholar Sir Francis Bacon, of Gray's-Inn; who having an esteem for him, and Mathew for Bacon, there passed between them divers letters." He afterwards turned Jesuit, and died at Ghent 1655. Athen. Oxon. II. 194.

[2] From Bishop Gibson's Papers in the MS. Library at Lambeth, vol. V. No. 118, as published by Dr. Birch, in " Letters, Speeches, &c. of Francis Bacon Lord Viscount St. Alban, &c. 1763," 8vo.

dren; when there be so many books of truth and knowledge, better worthy the revolving; and not to fix his view only upon a picture in a little table, when there be so many tables of histories, yea to life, excellent to behold and admire. Whether he believe me or no, there is no prison to the prison of the thoughts which are free under the greatest tyrants. Shall any man make his conceit, as an anchor, mured up with the compass of one beauty or person, that may have the liberty of all contemplation? Shall he exchange the sweet travelling through the universal variety, for one wearisome and endless round or labyrinth? Let thy master, Squire, offer his service to the *Muses*. It is long since they received any into their Court. They give alms continually at their gate, that many come to live upon; but few they have ever admitted into their Palace. There shall he find secrets not dangerous to know; sides and parties not factious to hold; precepts and commandments not penal to disobey. The gardens of Love, wherein he now placeth himself, are fresh to-day, and fading to morrow, as the Sun comforts them, or is turned from them. But the gardens of the Muses keep the privilege of the golden age; they ever flourish, and are in league with Time. The monuments of wit survive the monuments of power. The verses of a Poet endure without a syllable lost, while States and Empires pass many periods. Let him not think he shall descend; for he is now upon a hill, as a ship is mounted upon the ridge of a wave: but that hill of the Muses is above tempests, always clear and calm; a hill of the goodliest discovery that man can have, being a prospect upon all the errors and wanderings of the present and former times. Yea, in some cliff it leadeth the eye beyond the horizon of time, and giveth no obscure divinations of times to come. So that if he will indeed lead *vitam vitalem*, a life that unites safety and dignity, pleasure and merit; if he will win admiration without envy; if he will be in the feast, and not in the throng; in the light, and not in the heat; let him embrace the life of study and contemplation. And if he will accept of no other reason, yet, because the gift of the Muses will enworthy him in love, and where he now looks on his Mistress's outside with the eyes of sense, which are dazzled and amazed, he shall then behold her high perfections and heavenly mind with the eyes of judgement, which grow stronger by more nearly and more directly viewing such an object.

The Soldier's Speech.

Squire, the good old man hath said well to you: but I dare say, thou wouldst be sorry to leave to carry thy Master's shield, and to carry his books; and I am sure thy Master had rather be a falcon, a bird of prey, than a singing bird in a cage. The Muses are to serve martial men, to sing their famous actions; and not to be served by them. Then hearken to me.

It is the War that giveth all spirits of valour, not only honour, but contentment. For mark, whether ever you did see a man grown to any honourable commandment in the wars, but whensoever he gave it over, he was ready to die with melancholy? Such a sweet felicity is in that noble exercise, that he that hath tasted it thoroughly, is distasted for all other. And no marvell; for if the hunter takes such solace in his chace; if the matches and wagers of sport pass away with such satisfaction and delight; if the looker-on be affected with pleasure in the representation of a feigned tragedy; think what contentment a man receiveth, when they, that are equal to him in nature, from the hight of insolency and fury are brought to the condition of a chaced prey; when a victory is obtained, whereof the victories of games are but counterfeits and shadows; and when in a lively tragedy, a man's enemies are sacrificed before his eyes to his fortune.

Then for the dignity of military profession, is it not the truest and perfectest practice of all virtues? of wisdom, in disposing those things which are most subject to confusion and accident: of justice, in continual distributing rewards: of temperance, in exercising of the straitest discipline; of fortitude, in toleration of all labours and abstinence from effeminate delights: of constancy, in bearing and digesting the greatest variety of fortune. So that when all other places and professions require but their several virtues, a brave leader in the wars must be accomplished with all. It is the wars, that are the tribunal-seat, where the highest rights and possessions are decided; the occupation of Kings, the root of Nobility, the protection of all estates. And, lastly, Lovers never thought their profession sufficiently graced, till they have compared it to a Warfare. All, that in any other profession can be wished for, is but to live happily: but to be a brave Commander in the field, death itself doth crown the head with glory. Therefore, Squire, let thy Master go with me: and though he be resolved in the pursuit of his Love, let him aspire to it by the noblest means. For Ladies count it no honour to subdue them with their fairest eyes, which will be daunted with the fierce encounter of an enemy. And they will quickly discern a Champion fit to wear their glove from a Page not worthy to carry their pantofle. Therefore I say again, let him seek his fortune in the field, where he may either lose his love, or find new argument to advance it.

The Statesman's Speech.

Squire, my advice to thy Master shall be as a token wrapped up in words; but then will it shew itself fair, when it is unfolded in his actions. To wish him to change from one humour to another, were but as if, for the cure of a man in pain, one should advise him to lie upon the other side, but not enable him to stand on his feet. If, from a sanguine delightful humour of love, he turn to a melancholy retired humour of contemplation, or a turbulent boiling humour of the wars; what doth he but change tyrants? Contemplation is a dream; love a trance; and the humour of war is raving. These be shifts of humour, but no reclaiming to reason. I debar him not studies nor books, to give him stay and variety of conceit; to refresh his mind, to cover sloth and indisposition, and to draw to him from those that are studious, respect and commendation. But let him beware, lest they possess nor too much of his time; that they abstract not his judgement from present experience, not make him presume upon knowing much, to apply the less. For the wars, I deny him no enterprise, that shall be worthy in greatness, likely in success, or necessary in duty; not mixed with any circumstance of jealousy, but duly laid upon him. But I would not have him take the alarm from his own humour, but from the occasion; and I would again he should know an employment from a discourting. And for his love, let it not disarm his heart within, as it make him too credulous to favours, nor too tender to unkindnesses, nor too apt to depend upon the heart he knows not. Nay, in his demonstration of love, let him not go too far; for these seely Lovers, when they profess such infinite affection and obligation, they tax themselves at so high a rate, that they are ever under arrest. It makes their service seem nothing, and every cavil or imputation very great. But what, Squire, is thy Master's end? If to make the Prince happy he serves, let the instructions to employ men, the relations of ambassadors, the treaties between princes, and actions of the present time, be the books he reads: let the Orations of wise princes, or experimented counsellors in council or parliament, and the final sentences of grave and learned judges in weighty and doubtful causes, be the lecturers he frequents. Let the holding of affection with confederates without charge, the frustrating of the attempts of enemies without battles, the intitling of the crown to new possessions without shew of wrong, the filling of the Prince's coffers without violence, the keeping of men in appetite without impatience, be the inventions he seeks out. Let policy and matters of state be the chief, and almost the only thing, he intends. But, if he will believe *Philautia*, and seek most his own happiness, he must not of them embrace all kinds, but make choice, and avoid all matter of peril, displeasure, and charge, and turn them over to some novices, that know not manacles from bracelets, nor burdens from robes. For himself, let him set for matters of commodity and strength, though they be joined with envy. Let him not trouble himself too laboriously to sound into any matter deeply, or to execute any thing exactly; but let himself make himself cunning rather in the humours and drifts of persons, than in the nature of business and affairs. Of that it sufficeth to know only so much, as may make him able to make use of other men's wits, and to make again a smooth and pleasing report. Let him entertain the proposition of others; and ever rather let him have an eye to the circumstances, than to the matter itself; for then shall he ever seem to add somewhat of his own; and besides, when a man doth not forget so much as a circumstance, men do think his wit doth superabound for the substance. In his counsels, let him not be confident; for that will rather make him obnoxious to the success; but let him follow the wisdom of oracles, which utterred that which might ever be applied to the event. And ever rather let him take the side which is likeliest to be followed, than that which is soundest and best, that every thing may seem to be carried by his direction. To conclude, let him be true to himself, and avoid all tedious reaches of state, that are not merely pertinent to his particular. And if he will needs pursue his affection, and go on his course, what can so much advance him in his own way? The merit of war is too outwardly glorious to be inwardly grateful: and it is the exile of his eyes, which looking with such affection upon the picture, cannot but with infinite contentment behold the life. But when his Mistress shall perceive, that his endeavours are become a true support of her, a discharge of her care, a watchman of her person, a scholar of her wisdom, an instrument of her operation, and a conduit of her virtue; this, with his diligences, accesses, humility, and patience, may move him to give her further degrees and approaches to her favour. So that I conclude, I have traced him the way to that which hath been granted to some few, *amare et sapere*, to love and be wise.

The Reply of the Squire.

Wandering Hermit, storming Soldier, and hollow Statesman, the inchanting Orators of *Philautia*, which have attempted by your high charms to turn resolved *Erophilus* into a statue deprived of action, or into a vulture attending about dead bodies, or into a monster with a double heart; with infinite assurance, but with just indignation, and forced patience, I have suffered you to bring in play your whole forces. For I would not vouchsafe to combat you one by one, as if I trusted to the goodness of my breath, and not the goodness of my strength, which little needeth the advantage of your severing, and much less of your disagreeing. Therefore, first, I would know of you all, what assurance you have of the fruit whereto you aspire.

You, Father, that pretend to truth and knowledge, how are you assured, that you adore not vain chimæras and imaginations? that in your high prospect, when you think men wander up and down, that they stand not indeed still in their place? and it is some smoke or cloud between you and them, which moveth, or else the dazzling of your own eyes? Have not many, which take themselves to be inward Counsellors with Nature, proved but idle believers, which told us tales, which were no such matter? And, Soldier, what security have you for these victories and garlands, which you promise to yourself? Know you not of many, which have made provision of laurel for the victory, and have been fain to exchange it with cypress for the funeral? of many, which have bespoken Fame to sound their triumphs, and have been glad to pray her to say nothing of them, and not to discover them in their flights?

Corrupt Statesman, you that think by your engines and motions to govern the wheel of Fortune; do you not mark, that clocks cannot be long in temper? that jugglers are no longer in request, when their tricks and slights are once perceived? Nay, do you not see, that never any man made his own cunning and practice (without religion and moral honesty) his foundation, but he overbuilt himself, and in the end made his house a windfall? But give ear now to the comparison of my Master's condition, and acknowledge such a difference as is betwixt the melting hail-stone and the solid pearl. Indeed it seemeth to depend, as the globe of the earth seemeth to hang, in the air; but yet it is firm and stable in itself. It is like a cube, or a die-form, which toss it or throw it any way, it ever lighteth upon a square. Is he denied the hopes of favours to come? He can resort to the remembrance of contentments past. Destiny cannot repeal that which is past. Doth he find the acknowledgement of his affection small? He may find the merit of his affection the greater. Fortune cannot have power over that which is within. Nay, his falls are like the falls of Antæus; they renew his strength. His clouds are like the clouds of harvest, which make the sun break forth with greater force. His wanes are changes like the moon's, whose globe is all light towards the sun, when it is all dark towards the world: such is the excellency of her nature, and of his estate. Attend, you Beadsman of the Muses: you take your pleasure in a wilderness of variety; but it is but of shadows. You are as a man rich in pictures, medals, and crystals. Your mind is of the water, which taketh all forms and impressions, but is weak of substance. Will you compare shadows with bodies, picture with life, variety of many beauties with the peerless excellency of one? the element of water with the element of fire? And such is the comparison between Knowledge and Love.

Come out, Man of War; you must be ever in noise. You will give laws, and advance force, and trouble nations, and remove land-marks of kingdoms, and hunt men, and pen tragedies in blood: and, that which is worst of all, make all the virtues accessary to bloodshed. Hath the practice of force so deprived you of the use of reason, as that you will compare the interruption of society with the perfection of society? the conquest of bodies with the conquest of spirits? the terrestrial fire, which destroyeth and dissolveth, with the celestial fire, which quickeneth and giveth life? And such is the comparison between the Soldier and the Lover.

And as for you, untrue Politique, but truest bondman to *Philautia*, you, that presume to bind Occasion, and to overlook Fortune, I would ask you but one question. Did ever any Lady, hard to please, or disposed to exercise her lover, injoin him so good tasks and commandments, as *Philautia* exacteth of you? While your life is nothing but a continual acting upon a stage; and that your mind must serve your humour, and yet your outward person must serve your end; so as you carry in one person two several servitudes to contrary masters. But I will leave you to the scorn of that mistress whom you undertake to govern; that is, to Fortune, to whom *Philautia* hath bound you. And yet, you Commissioner of *Philautia*, I will proceed one degree farther: if I allowed both of your assurance, and of your values, as you have set them, may not my master enjoy his own felicity, and have all yours for advantage? I do not mean, that he should divide himself in both pursuits, as in your feigning tales towards the conclusion you did yield him; but because all these are in the hands of his mistress more fully to bestow, than they can be attained by your addresses, knowledge, fame, fortune. For the *Muses*, they are tributary to her Majesty for the great liberties they have enjoyed in her kingdom during her most flourishing reign; in thankfulness whereof, they have adorned and accomplished her Majesty with the gifts of all the Sisters. What Library can present such a story of great actions, as her Majesty carrieth in her Royal breast by the often return of this happy day? What worthy Author, or Favourite of the Muses, is not familiar with her? Or what Language, wherein the Muses have used to speak, is unknown to her? Therefore, the hearing of her, the observing of her, the receiving instructions from her, may be to *Erophilus* a lecture exceeding all dead monuments of the Muses. For *Fame*, can all the exploits of the war win him such a title, as to have the name of favoured and selected servant of such a Queen? For *Fortune*, can any insolent Politique promise to himself such a fortune, by making his own way, as the excellency of her nature cannot deny to a careful, obsequious, and dutiful servant? And if he could, were it equal honour to obtain it by a shop of cunning, as by the gift of such a hand?

Therefore *Erophilus's* resolution is fixed: he renounceth *Philautia*, and all her inchantments. For her recreation he will confer with his Muse: for her defence and honour, he will sacrifice his life in the wars, hoping to be embalmed in the sweet odours of her remembrance. To her service will he consecrate all his watchful endeavours, and will ever bear in his heart the picture of her beauty; in his actions, of her will; and in his fortune, of her grace and favour.

In this year the following publications appear among those entered in the Books of the Stationers' Company:

"A triumphant newe Ballad, in honour of the Queenes Majestie and her happie Government, who hath Reigned in great prosperitie 37 years."

"A Ballad, intituled, England's Tryumphe; conteyning diverse of these abundant blessings, wherewith this our Realm hath been blessed by our noble gracious Queene Elizabethe's Reigne."

"A newe Ballad of the honourable Order of running at Tilt at Whitehall, the 17th of November [1595], in the 38th year of her Majesties Reign."

On the 3d of July 1596, died Henry the first Lord Hunsdon, Lord Chamberlain to the Queen [1].

The Landgrave of HESSEN *his princely receiving of her Majesties Embassador* [2] *in August* 1596 [3].

To the Right Honorable the Ladie Marie, Countesse of Warwicke.

Right Honorable, gessing at your Ladyship's acquaintance with the Princesse, and this (blast) being a matter of pleasure, fit for a spare hower in an afternoone,

[1] Henry, only son of Henry Cary, a Gentleman of the Bedchamber to Henry VIII. by Mary, daughter and coheir of Thomas Boleyn, Earl of Wiltshire and Ormond, and sister to the unfortunate Queen Anne. Elizabeth, who seems to have been sincerely attached to this Gentleman, her near relation, and a person of the most unblemished integrity, created him Baron of Hunsdon in Hertfordshire, and gave him the noble mansion Hunsdon House, with its large demesne, in the first year of her reign. He was soon after appointed a Knight of the Garter, Captain of the Band of Pensioners, and a Privy Counsellor; and in 1567 was raised to the important posts of Warden of the East Marches, and Governor of Berwick, with the garrison belonging to which he performed the most essential services in the course of the rebellious year, 1569; first, by assisting Sussex against the Earls of Westmoreland and Northumberland, and afterwards by subduing, with his own troops only, the insurgents under Leonard Dacre. Having remained nearly twenty years on the Borders, he was at length constituted Warden of all the Marches, and soon after succeeded the Earl of Lincoln as Lord Chamberlain of the Household, continuing, however, to hold his military offices. He was pitched upon by Elizabeth for the delicate task of pacifying the King of Scots for the death of his mother, in which he succeeded beyond expectation; for he was a bad politician, a worse courtier, and a man totally illiterate; but it is said that James, whose title to the succession he was well known to favour, had a personal esteem for him. This was the last important circumstance of his public life, unless his commanding the Queen's army in the camp at Tilbury may be mentioned as such. He died at Somerset-house July 23, 1596, aged 71, and was buried in Westminster Abbey, where a superb monument remains to his memory.

Lord Hunsdon married Anne, daughter of Sir Thomas Morgan, Knight, and left issue four sons and three daughters; Sir George (of whom see before, p. 27); Sir John; Sir Edward, whose line failed in the last Lord Hunsdon; and Sir Robert, afterwards created Lord Lepington and Earl of Monmouth. The daughters were, Catherine, wife of Charles Howard, Earl of Nottingham; Philadelphia, married to Thomas Lord Scrope of Bolton; and Margaret, to Sir Edward Hoby, Knight.

[2] Henry Clinton, second Earl of Lincoln of that name, who succeeded his father in 1585, and was one of the Commissioners for the trial of Mary Queen of Scots, which was the only thing memorable that Sir William Dugdale found of him. He married Catharine, daughter of Francis Earl of Huntingdon, by whom he had Thomas his successor; Sir Edward Clinton, Knight; and three daughters.

[3] From a copy " Imprinted at London, by Robert Robinson, 1596.

yet for the manner of it, worth the writing done in so good order, and greatlie to hir Majesties honour by the Landgrave, I have presumed (under correction) to put out and present your Honour the relation of our entertainement in Germanie. Hoping by your Ladyship's protective [1], favourable acceptation of it, to walke betweene these two hils whose perfections and excellencies I cannot highthen, but discover, in the vale of my lownesse and obscuritie, if without thankes for my labour, yet, for my good meaning without blame. Readie to be sacrificed for her service, to whom of duetie we owe ourselves and all our endeavors. Desirous to honour him to whom of love it is due, having honoured her Highnesse her Embassador and his company so much, and to performe all good offices to your Ladyship. Your Honour's ever to command, EDWARD MONINGS [2].

His Lordshippe came to Brunswick the 16th of August, where the next day in the morning met us a Gentleman called Johan von der Bruck sent from the Landgrave to attend and entertaine him. This shewed good intelligence, and care had of his comming; for the 17th day he was with us betimes, commanded, if he mette not the Lo. Embassadour there, to go to Breme. We gave him entertainement, and when his Lordship was readie and called for him, he came and delivered his message in French to this effect. That the Landgrave (his master) giving him his titles [3], had sent him to meet, and in his name to welcome his Honour into this country, declaring how long desired, and therefore verie acceptable his comming was, and therein howe deeply he stoode bounde unto her excellent Majestie, that it pleased her Highness so gratiously to send unto him, and greatlie beholding to my Lord Embassadour, and in regard of the length and danger of the journey, had passed so greate a travaile for his sake, with many other cere-

[1] There was no Mary Countess of Warwick at this time; it is probably a mistake for Anne Countess of Warwick, eldest daughter of Francis Russell, second Earl of Bedford, and wife of Ambrose Dudley, Earl of Warwick, who was much a favourite and companion of Queen Elizabeth. She died without issue Feb. 9, 1603, and is buried in the Bedford chapel at Cheneys, in Bucks, under a hne altar-tomb, with her effigies cumbent in Coronation robes.

[2] Sir Edward Monyns, of Waldershare, in Kent, Knt. son of Richard Monyns, of Sallwood. He married Elizabeth Lovelace, of Kent, and had issue Sir William Monyns, of Waldershare, Knt. Sir Edward was buried at Waldershare Nov. 17, 1601. (See the Monyns Pedigree in book marked Howard, in Coll. Armor.)

[3] " Mauritius, Dei gratia, Langrave Hassiæ, Co. Cattzænelaenbogend Diests, Sigenhau Nidda."

monious and gratulatory speaches, till he came to the pointe, that upon very urgent and necessarie occasion, the childe was christened, telling the time of her birth, the 7th of April, and baptisme the 27th of Julie, with the giving hir the name of Elizabeth, by the Landgrave Ludowicke of Marpurg, the Princes unckle, and eldest of his house, who was appointed Deputy at the Christening, but that the solemnitie was reserved till his Honour's comming, and therefore divers Princes, Lordes, Ladies, and Gentlemen, invited and commaunded to attend at the Court, and waite upon him.

And because the Prince his master had bene given to understande, of his Lordshippes hastening (as he did, and that with the venture of his health in the service) he besought him, to take such easie and convenient journeys as might be best for his Honour's provisions by the way, and to that ende had sent him, to doe his Lordshippe all service and attendance. To which my Lo. making a regratulatory answere, after having given him good wordes, made him good cheere, and the next day we went five leagues to Heldeshem; the 19th, five leagues to Hamel through the mountainous and pleasant woodie parte of the Duke of Brunswick's, and the Bishoppe of Padenborge their lands; and so we came to Hixtunne in the Stift of Corui.

At Hixtunne met ns another ancient grave Gentleman called Rauen von Ama Iuxen, a dweller in those parts, and who came with no message, but was sent to bring my Lorde to a castle of the Princes called Zappenburch.

This castle is seated out of common passage, built upon a hill, in a greate forrest, whither by a craggie and unbeaten way we came late by mooneshine. My Lord Embassador was received with all honor and expectation, who, through the soldiers ranked on both sides (as he be very ceremonious) went in with his coaches to the inner court, where he alighted. Master Mezenburgh, Steward of the Princes house, and before sent Embassador into England, with a troupe of Gentlemen of the Landgraves, met him at the stair foote, carried him up by torchlight to his lodging, and in the great chamber made a long saluting, welcomming, excusing, rejoycing, and thankfull oration in the Princes behalfe, which in few words was fully answered, and so we went to supper. The Princes officers and Gentlemen were appointed to waite; onlie Master Mezenburgh sat with my Lord and his companie to governe the table. His Lordship was served with three courses after our fashion very plentifully, and so were all his servants to the meanest, with distinction of diet, and great regard was had. And this action was in all things as honorably, as wisely, orderlie, and exactly well performed, as was possible; for what the country did afford his Lordship had, or they could devise by art, and order discreetlie was donne to honour him, insomuch that his entertainment was honorable passed measure, as his bountie wisely kept proportion.

Heere his Lordship staied three daies, which was so appointed for his better disposition and refreshing; the first day he rested, and the second was the day of rest, and a Latine sermon was made him; in the morning upon Monday the weather brake up, and for after dinner a hunting was appointed.

From the castle we passed a league downe the forrest into an open vallie, where, the length of half an English mile, the toyles were set up on both sides to keepe in the game: the pleasure of the place was as much as the sport; for we were in sight of divers towns and villages, as Quiddelburge, Rottam, Kellam, &c. and from the hill Schoneberg (a faire hill) out of the wood, fell the game downe into the vallie, where in the middest was a greene tent of cloth, set up for my Lord Embassador with a rowe of bowes, to shaddowe the companie, hide their dogges, and losen them at the deere as they passed by; the country was up on both sides of toyles upon waggons, with their broade bore speares and dogges: in halfe an howre six stags and two wild swine, which were the more spared for being out of season, were cruelly murdered, and so the slaughter ceased, and Master Mezenburgh, taking his leave, went to provide at Cassel. Thus love and bounty still went before us in preparation, and the next day we followed.

The Prince's own coach covered over with a large carpet of blacke velvet, and laid with long cushions drawen with six horses, driven by two coachers suted in greene, after the manner of the Princes of Germanie, was prepared for my Lord, and his own English coach to follow with six horses empty, except his Lordship appointed any to go in it; six besides were made ready for his companie; and thus provided with waggons for our carriadges, readie set forward, the Prince's Gentlemen tooke their horses, being gallantlie mounted, and with convoy of the souldiers in the castell, whome my Lord had rewarded, we were carried through a park adjoining, a league out of the forrest, where with a volly of shotte they tooke their leaves, and so went back to Zappenburch.

We had three leagues to Cassell, and within one the way was strowed at our comming with horsemen, that put forward to meete my Lord Embassador; and still our companie increased, who went the neerest way over meadowes, the ditches levelled and cut downe for the purpose. Great expectation there was on both sides, and we were not frustrated, for within an English mile off the towne, upon a rising ground piked out, going up the hill, we discovered first a straunge fellow mounted upon a cammell, with the manner of a Herald before him; this was a blackmoore of the Prince's, sent a little on the one side before, to discover our comming, and appointed to looke backe for a watchwoord, which when he had done, and kneeled downe afarre off to my Lord Embassador with his beast, like to a cloud rising above the sunne after her set, betweene the light and us, appeared a troupe of horsemen comming up the hill, who in a statelie manner trotted toward us.

They were thus marshaled, threescore swarte Ritters, three and three in a ranke, sternely came before; then followed sixe trumpets in the Prince's colours white and red; after came a gallant sort of Gentlemen, every way well and richlie appointed with jewels, and most of them chains of gold; then followed his emptie horses of honour and maintenance, belonging to his feudatorie Graff-chafftes, caparisonned with white and red tafetie, with plumes and all their furniture suitable; after these six hincshmen, two and two, suted alike with chaines, helmets, and javelins in their handes: then came the Princes and the Nobles, and Master Dorstetell (going before the Dukes of Holstein and Luneberg, who were sent to meete the Lorde Embassador) staied the troupes, which had passed along sidewise of us, till these Princes met; who alighting, my Lord went out of his coach, and this Master Dorstetell came and made his speach in Latin, full of receit, love, and curtesie, shewing that these Dukes were sent to meete and entertaine his Lordship by the way, and to accompany him to the Prince's house, which his Excellency desired him to use for his beeing there as his owne; for which my Lord thanked the Prince very kindlie: and after having embraced the young Dukes, he was intreated to take horse, and they set forward, the great ordinaunce discharged, &c. and with all pettie complements and ceremonies, such as Princes use for ornament, and to make, as their persons are, so their actions to be more estimable to the common world, we entered with as manie Ritters behinde as before, the whole being neere 300 horse, into the Towne of Cassell.

They were up in armes, the captaines and companies of the town standing in order on both sides of the streets, stoutlie picke and gunne, even to the Prince's castell; this his troup dismounted and gon in, my Lord was brought to a statelie upper hall, where at the doore the Landgrave Maurice met and embraced my Lord Embassador. And in this honorable assemblie he delivered his Embassage and his letters; to whome the Prince spake Latin, and after gratious entertainmentes given, carried him to his lodgings, putting my Lord before him, where, after all behaviour becomming so great a person, and wherein he had verie extraordinarie grace and facilitate, he left his Lordshippe.

His lodgings were five rowmes, which tooke up one ende of his house, being a goodlie quadrangle, somewhat more in length than in breadth, and, like the Louvre at Paris, hie and statelie; he had two dining chambers, two drawing, and betweene these two his bed chamber, for his more quiet and private being. His Lordshippe's owne dining chamber was a very curious roome, made no doubt of purpose to entertaine strange Princes, all of marble, the doores, the flower, the sides, windowes, roofe, and all things pertinent, being of carved gray marble; and, for the rarenesse, I will more particularly describe it.

The doores are bordered about with timber to keepe the stone together, and comming in the flower even and smoothly paved, the chamber just square, the sides made like a wenscot, with crestings, indentments, and Italian piller woorke, and heereby devided into 27 panes of carved imagerie, to the halfe proportion of a man, bearing upon their shoulder points escouchons with the blasoned armes of his signories, the Electors Count of Palatine, Duke of Saxonie, Mararquish of Brandenburgh, and other houses of his friends and allies of the Protestant part; over these an other course of indented doors and carved hollow woorkes distinct with pillers; and in this compasse next the roofe, on the fower sides, fower stories carved, of the Creation, the Passion, the Resurrection, and Judgement, verie cunningly done, in length about two yardes, compassed in with a frame of marble, as though they hung loose; the roofe is wrought with knot worke, and thus to see to being in the chamber nothing but marble, whereof he hath the mine in his country: the trouble of his rowme is great in winter, when, to keep the stone from cracking and loosening, the stone is continually kept hotte.

The next rowme to this was a faire square chambre hung with tapestery, where the Gentlemen dined, for commonly at the marble table, where the Dukes of Holstein and Luneburgh, or the Graves of Nassaw and of Zolmes, with Sir Richard Fines, Master Brackenburie, and others, as it pleased his Lordshippe to appoint.

The third was a faire drawing chamber, seated round about, and covered with scarlet; above the seates hung round with a rich smale wrought tapesterie of an elle broad, of embleme worke, and verses written underneath; over this, upon a ledge of wentscot were divers large tables of sundrie devises well painted with their posies to garnish the chamber, and, among all, that was the best which had this motto, " Major autem horum est charitas," for it waxed cold. The roofe was likewise flourished with painting and devises. These rowmes had the through light of fower faire windowes; and in this chamber were two square tables, one richlie covered with a carpet of cloath of gold, and the seate laide rounde with fower long cushions of the same, which was extraordinarelie covered morning and evening for breakfast and banquet; two of the Prince's Groomes appointed alwaies to be heere and waite, and heere they sat sometimes in conference and counsell.

Next to this was my Lord's bedchamber, with two fair damaske field beds, prepared for my Lorde and Master Edwarde Clinton[1] his sonne; the pariture of this rowme was a painted tree that grewe up at the doore, the bodie bulking out very naturally of stone painted barkelike, and the braunches spreading all over the seeling of the chamber, full of fruite, and hanging downe upon the walles, with other pictures to fill up emptie places. The storie taken out of Daniell. There his Lordshippe had, at a little side table, delicate preserves and conserves, set and covered over with a vaile of laune wrought with golde and silke, and all thinges for his chamber very fitlie.

Beyond these fowre was there a faire drawing chamber hung with arras, which parted his Honour's lodging from the other side of the house, that so he might not any way be disturbed. And now I speake of lodgings, I will describe the manner, the strength, and convenience of the Prince's whole lodging, being a thing worthe noting, and then returne unto his entertainment.

His castell standing upon the river of Fuld, betwene the two sides of Casse, joyned with a bridge of stone, generally commaundeth the towne and countrie, and is particularly fortified for his owne dwellinge, for the first. A parcell of grounde of some 100 yardes broad he hath inclosed on both sides, which compasseth the towne, and yet is impropriat to any pleasure or use of his owne, as for his walks, orchards, laying in his provisions of wood, &c. upon the countrie. This is strongly fortified, moated, countermured, mounted, bulwarkt, flankered, and with all possible fortification made so strong, as he is thereby easily able to prevaile against the seige of any outward enemie, and beat them from the fielde, upon the towne, onlie shut up with a single wall, to keepe it private from the townes-men, that they may entende their streets, houses, and trades, standing

---

[1] Sir Edward Clinton, Knt. who married Mary, daughter of Thomas Dighton, of Stourton, in the county of Lincoln. Dugdale, ubi sup.

more upon the credit of their good service, then their libertie. Within this place he hath a goodlie armorie, not much inferiour to the Duke of Saxonie, where his ordinance, armor, weapons, and munition, are kept in greate good order and readinesse upon any occasion, all stratagemical engines and devises which belong to offensive or defensive exploits. Such a kinde of forteresse as this hath the Duke of Saxonie at Dresden, the Duke of Brunswicke at Wollfenbuttel, and the Duke of Werkenberg at Stugord above his castle; for these I have seen; and divers other Princes of Germanie which will be absolute; for they have greate reason, as the Grave of Embden knows by late experience, to be diffident of their subjects that dwell in their great townes.

For his private dwelling, his castle is deepe and broade moated, to countergarde his house within the towne, where upon the rampers twentie and fower are appointed to keepe continual sentinel in order; his gates are kept with a double garde, and two bridges, drawne up every night and garded; the inward part, as I saide, a square long court, paved and vated rounde aboute with a large greate vaute under grounde, which is used for his sellerage, full of vessell, twentie, fortie, and some of an hundred tunne. The lower rowmes are the offices; on the right hand a common large great hall, and other common roemes and lodgings. On the left, the middle storie was upon our side the upper hall, where his Excellencie met my Lord Embassador; on the right side a verie goodly greate chamber; and on the left, a gallerie answerable, which William the Landgrave's father addorned with the pictures of all the Princes in Christendome, from anno 60 unto 88, the number of 140.

The third storie are faire lodging chambers rounde about the upper end from the top to the bottom, being the Prince's owne private lodgings, joyning upon the chappell. The fourth and fifth stories for Gentlemen, servants, &c.

On the backe side he hath faire tilt-yards, places for the quintine, the running at the ring, rideing, and other exercises; for his pleasure, gardens, with banqueting houses, artificiall fountains, and water-works, fish-ponds, &c. With his housed gardens of orange-trees, lemons, pomgranets, and divers outlandish fruites and simples, after the custome of the Germane Princes, who in all outward things are very glorious and apparent.

But to his entertainment, where I left my Lord. After an hour resting in his chamber, the Prince sent two principall of his counsell, to salute him, and to know his Lordship's pleasure where hee would suppe, wishing rather, if it pleased him, to keepe his chamber, after his travaile, than otherwise, and to appoint what hower he would for sermon the next day, which he did at nine.

In the morning Master Brackenburie appointed the ordering of the Chappell for the solemnitie; and Doctor Gregorius Schonfelt, *Concionator aulicus Cassellanus*, who succeeds Master Bartholomæus Meyer in his supreme superintendencie, preached; his sermon was brought over.

At the solemnitie my Lord was very richlie and well appointed, as became him, to her Majesties honour and his owne, and their admiration, sitting alone on the right side of the chappell, in a place prepared for him within a travesse of the Queenes; the rowme hung with crimosin tafetie, with chaires and cushions of crimosin velvet; over against him sat the Prince, with the Dukes of Holstein, Luneburg, and the Graves of Zolmes, Nassaw, and others, who did him all the sermon-time great reverence by much standing. His Lordship performed it gratiously, and master Brackenburie, her Majesties Gentleman Usher, stood all the sermon time at the turning up of the travesse, and, with a lowe reverence, gave him first his praier-book, which Master Cotton of the warderobe had readie. After sermon they proceeded to the solemnitie; and first came Master Edward Clinton, taught by the Gentleman Usher what to doe, with a goodlie rich cup of gold set with stone, wherein were comfits; and, with three reverences, they went both and presented it unto her Majesties Deputie, who took a tast; after they presented it unto the Landgrave and the Dukes, who did the like. Then came Sir Richard Fines, in the same manner, with a cuppe of wine; and last they went both; one held the bason, while the other gave water, and the third the towel. When this was performed in the middest of the chappell, upon a little pause, my Lord Embassador, accompanied with his honourable traine, went towardes the Princesse her chamber, to present the gift; whither before we came, we first passed through (in an utter chamber) a garden of faire yoong ladies and gentlewomen, clad in colours, who stood like the rainebow, and they compassed the one halfe of the roume by which we passed into the Princesse her bedchamber, where were none but Ladies, and a solemn presence. First stood three of the Landgrave's sisters, the Ladie Anna Maria holding the Prince's little sonne Otto by the finger; the Ladie Hedwig and the Ladie Sophia, the other sisters, Elizabeth her Majesties god-daughter: Christina and Sabina being dead. There was the Ladie Anna Countesse of Nassaw, and manie of the Graves wives, of the Landgraves countrie, that waited on the Princesse. And she herselfe, as Horace saith of Julium Sidus, stood by her bedside, *velut inter ignes luna minores*, with her Majesties goddaughter, set uppon the middest of a feeld-bed of greene cloath of tissue, with white and greene plumes all verie richlie embrodered. The Prince went with my Lord Embassador toward this fayre Ladie, and by Master Wroth had speech with her, touching her Majesties good will towards her, and the gratifying her with a present, &c. which Master Mezenburge answered; and while this was doing, the present was brought in, and set upon the cubbart. This doone, the Prince and my Lord Embassador tooke their leaves, and left this sober companie of Ladies and Gentlewomen, as they found them, in their chambers; he brought my Lord to his lodging, and so they parted. Within halfe an hower after he sent him word, it was his pleasure and desire, that his Lordship should dine with him in his great chamber, and sit in state; which my Lord, with some straitning of curtesie, took upon him. He was set alone at the bordes end, the Landgrave and his Ladie sitting beneath him about two yardes, with the young Dukes of Hollun, and the Graves of Nassaw, John, Phillipe, Willelm, and Ludowick, the Grave Phillip of Zolmes of Whittenstein, and others, at the bordes ende. There waited on my Lord, Sir Richard Fines as cup-bearer, who, in his journey, did her Majestie great honour and service at the Paltz-grave's, as he went to Venice. He gave the cup with three curtsies and essay; there waited with him Maister Brackenburie; and thus was there a Royal feast continued, in great solemnitie, and varietie of excellent musicke; and in the middest of dinner, the Prince began a health unto her Majestie, whom he often reverently termed Mother. This health went round, and while it was a drinking, there was a devise of a castell served upon the table in a charger, which had a water running about it, with fish swimming in it, verie artificially donne, which shotte of, of itselfe, its blowes as big as petronell, and all besmoked the roome with gunpowder, which, with sweet perfumes, burnte, was soon avoided. After this royall dinner, the Ladies first withdrewe; and then the Prince brought my Lord again unto his chamber, giving him place, and honoring the Person whom he represented, the most effectually and affectionately he could. He staid not there an hower but Barriers were in hand; which being set crosse the courte, all these states were at windows to see them above; and when the judges were set below, there came in two ensignes of pikes and shotte, that compassed them round, to keepe the peace. Then came 15 to 15 Knights, the one side in gilt armour, the other in silver; who, taking up their ends, the Herauld red their orders, and they went to their sporte, first with the speare, then the sworde, after pele-mele, and brake a marvelous deale of iron-worke; and while these hot Knights were swetting in their harnesse, issues such a furious ambuscado of crackers, that flewe out of the barre, painted over greene to hide the treason, that it parted them. This quarrel ended without bloudshed, and judgements given, the Heraulds proclaimed Triumphs for the day following; and the companie, full of the pleasure, love, and honour, of this solemne meeting, dissolved; the Prince withdrew, and Lord was private.

The next day the Prince sent my Lord, by the High Marshall M. Benneberge, his good morowe, as hee did alwayes, sometimes by one, sometimes by another, greete him with honourable salutations twice or thrice a day; and the Grave of Zip was appoynted to accompany my Lord, who, being a fat corpulent man, had little to doe at their activities. After dinner his Lordship was carried to the Tiltyard, but without the Prince, hee was so busie about his sports, marshaling other men, and putting himselfe in order, beeing an actor in them, the more to honor her Majestie and the day. The first Triumphes were the running at the ring, wherein they had extraordinarie devise of three circles wrought the one within the other, with a crosse parting them, and making differences of hitting, above or below, on the right side or on the left; that in the middest being the compasse of a French crowne, which was the best for wagers; no man might runne for under ten, nor for above a hundred dolors, marie they might run atrust, ther were judges appoynted to decide these great matters, who disposed of prises: and the Lords and Ladies being placed in an open place built for the purpose, the Triumphes began. There came in first, with six staffers and six trumpets, masked, with their devise, the two chalengers, Master Donet, a verie proper horseman, and Master Dorstetell, a Counsellour, who ranne with all the rest, and last one with another, for the prise; then came there seaven companies, which made several entrances, first with musieke, then with devises, their launce-bearers and themselves following; and last their servants, and their emptie trapped and caparisoned horse.

The Duke of Luneburgh brought in the Seaven deadlie Sinnes, and he placed Pride (indeed he used us somewhat strangely). Then came in another companie with the Sciences, and another with the Nine Muses; one came in Post, two masked like the Sunne and the Moone, whose devise was the Seasons of the yeare; but of all, the *Vnbekent riter* came in like a Prince, with his musicke of sackbotes and cornets clade in greene tafetie to the ground, six before and six behind, with the most harmonious noyse that could be, answering one another like an eccho. This kind of musike had a Princely ayre; his devise was, or might be fitlie, the Fowre Cardinall Vertues, carrying the globe of the earth and sphere of heaven among them, and consulting, who after came himself, masked like Jove, riding all in white crowned, and with a tripertite sworde in his hand under a crimson canopie borne over him, whereon was written, at the two ends, *Præmia bonis*, and *Pœna bona malis;* on the one side *Virtute et Consilio*, and on the other the embleme of a fagotte, with *Concordia simul manet*. After the lanciers came, and his emptie horse; this unknowen Knight, after having runne six courses, whereof he missed but one, came up to the Princesse, and kept my Lord Embassadour companie.

The Landgrave in his Triumphes, as in all thinges else, kept so good decorum, that the best was reserved for the last, wherein the Princess her brother, representing Cæsar, came in for his devise, with the fower Kinges of America, Africa, Asia, Europa, so naturally set out, everie countrie in his kinde, for musike, attires of going carried before him in their severall fashions of coches and state as coulde be devised. The credit of the Prince's Triumphs was, that they were costly, all things being made new for this meeting, that they were manie, full of varietie, performed in season, and good order.

After supper, as the manner is upon a Triumph-day, there was a daunse, in the gallerie I spake of. The Prince and my Lord Embassadour being set at the upper end, the Duke of Holstein began with the Princesse, and the Duke of Luneburgh with the Ladie Anna Maria; and so the rest of the Lordes and Ladies in their order, with drum and trumpet for their musick.

After the first setting in, there was a summonning of Knights that were to receive favours of their Ladies, either for their good runninge or their devises that day. And when they had first been thanked, with commendations of their doing, and exhortation with injoynment given them, that as they had donne that by way of exercise and pastimes, to honour the Prince and Ladies, so they should be ready indeed, upon just occasion, to shewe their manhoode in the defence of them both and of their countrie. After they received some reward, and with a cranse with their Ladies gave daunses with them. When these honours were donne the well-deservers this day, the Triumphs for the next day were published; but, to avoide satietie, they were discreetely referred to the day after; a day of pause was put in between both, wherein they mett in counsell. Thus entergreabley the time was passed; and upon Saterday the twentie seaven of August the principall Devise and Triumph was performed.

There came in the morning an Embassadoure from the Countie Palatine, Dercon Sehenberg, who came to invite the Landgrave to be godfather to the Paltzgrave sonne and heire. There came in the afternoone, in the middest of their sportes, the Paltzgrave of Zueienburch, with his Ladie and his little sonne; but their comming was onelie to see the Lord Embassadour.

Without the Towne there was a Castell builte, and the water drawne from the river to moate it about so broade that it bore a boat to and fro; the place for standings and perfourming of this sporte was railed in and made convenient; and the substance of the matter was, of an Enchaunter, that had forsooth dwelt there long, and, by two or three Giants in his Castell, taken divers prisoners Knights and Ladies, and by his doings much endammaged his countrie; whereupon the Knights of Hessen put themselves in armes, and appointed a day for the incountering of the Giants and raising of the Castell, and the giving libertie to a faire Ladie that was prisoner there. Now, for their defence, they kept open tent, and hunge out the flagge of defiance to all Knights that passed, who, if disposed, might, by the sounding of a horn, first come in and trie their valours and their fortunes, for by both these this Ladie was to be delivered, and not otherwise. For triall of their dexteritie and valour, there were fower thinges to doe; first, to runne at the quintin, next the turney, then the tilte without a pale, and last the sword and target, wherein if the Knight were at any overcome, he was prisoner: and for their triall there were Judges; if he went through, yet had he a point of destine to prove, whether it were his fate forsooth to draw the enchaunted sword out of a pillar that stood by the Castell.

The Knights of Hesse came at their daie appointed, not to make devises, but to shewe their manhood: they were many, and verie gallantlie armed, and kepte in such order as (which graced the Triumph) there was alwaies a continued sporte, without intermission or losse of time, and three or fower actions to be sene at once. The places were divided with railes; and as one thing was donne, there were wilde fellowes that losened the chaine of the outer gate, and let them by degrees unto the but Castel; the fates had appointed it for the Dukes of Luneburgh, who drewe out the sworde, delivered the Ladie, and brought out a straunge ugly companie from the Castell: which being gone, the fire-workes began, for straungenesse and admirable device exceeding all the rest, some for mounting, some burning in the water, some for their straunge tearing of the aire upright, some turning here and there after an hundred fashions, brustinge out into such noyses and spectacles, as though heaven and earth had gone together. These and the rest were surely Princely vanities, but betwixt jest and earnest; there were two coronets of horsemen set to keepe the feelde, while these things were a doing, for it was late and night before they ended.

Thus full of entertainment it was time for my Lord (as he did wiselie) to speake of parting, and not to put this royally-minded Prince to too great trouble, who was within fewe daies to goe to Amberg, and to meete the Paltzgrave. There should have been a daunse this night as before; but, being late, it was performed in like manner as I tolde. The next day being Sunday, when the Prince, my Lord, the other Embassador, the Paltzgrave of Zueinburch and his Ladie, dined together in the Landgrave's great chamber, after a private and domestical manner, for by this time the extraordinary company was retired, the Landgrave supped with him in the marble chamber, where he told him, as it was given out before, that the next day morning he ment to ride abroade a-hunting with his Lordshippe.

Before they set out, the Landgrave rode with him about his fortresse, shewed him the secret places of it, with his armorie, appointing dinner to be served in the garden at the banquettinge house; after, in a barge, we crossed the water, where were coches ready, and the Prince went two leagues to Milsungen, where he rejoyced and was exceeding merrie, full of state and grace in speach and behaviour. His answere unto my Lord I noted; who saying to him upon occasion, "that the Prince of Hessen was not there, and therefore woulde he be the bolder." "No, my Lord," quoth the Landgrave (in English); "the Prince of Hessen is not heere, but the greate hunts-master." The next day he carried us to his Towne of Rotenberg, which is so called of the red moulde of the hills; yet betwene them runs a verie rich vale, where this Towne is situated. Heere we stayed two dais, and had a freshe fitte of entertainment, with huntings greater then the first, but in that kinde.

The Prince hath heere a goodlie house, where is one of the five choice things of Germanie; which are, the armorie and stabell at Dresden, the banquettinge house at Stutgart, the hunts kammer of Munchen, and the hall of Rottenberg. Heere called he to his councells his lieftenaunt Baltazar Gedel, a worthy grave wise Gentelman, and whom he imployed upon the borders of the Abbacye of

Fuld, which is the Emperour's. But to speake at length, after a timely observation of this noble Prince, whose rare giftes and vertues, and discretion in the cariadge of himselfe, and mannaging affaires, sufficiently discover him, he is a perfect man (in my opinion) and a most perfect Prince.

First a goodly personage, of stature tall and straght for his proportion, of a good presence and a gallant countenance, manly visaged, with a faire big blacke eie, deepe aburne haire, comlie in behaviour, gratious and persuasive in speach. And this bodie hath a minde sutable unto yt.

For his giftes of nature are great, sharpe to apprehend, and sound in judgment, mingling his gravitie with pleasure, his courtesie with state and honour, love with stoutnes, thereby winning the affection of straungers, and keeping his subjectes in a lovely feare, master of his affections, temperat, bounded, not to change, in whom the upper partes commaund the neather.

His education prince-like; generally knowen in all things, and excellent in many, seasoning his grave and more important studies for ability in judgment, with studies of pastime for retiring, as in poetrie, musike, and the mathemitikes; and for ornament in discourse in the languages, French, Italian, and English, wherein he is expert, reading much, conferring and writting much. He is a full man, a readie man, an exact man, and so excellent a Prince, that a man may say of him without flatterie, as Tullie did of Pompey, *unus in quo summa sunt omnia;* and, for my private opinion, I think there are but fewe such men in the world.

His experience in all good courses, greater then his yeares, though for the inconstancies, advantages, and courses of the bad world, it increase with time in all men; for art doth perfect nature, and is perfected by experience. In his government wise, in himselfe absolutely ruling, vehement, yet loving and beloved of his subjects, void of crueltie or exaction, gentell, gratious, not governed by one nor distracted by many, but advised. And as Trajane the Emperor was called *Pater patriæ* by the Romanes, so hath this Prince a terme among his people of their "Goodnesse without end." For his exercise, given much to horsmanship, and to his lawfull pleasures; in the vaine of his age, more given to spend then to gether. And whereas his grandfather advanced his house by matching with Sophia Duchesse of Saxonie, and his father with Sabina Duchesse of Wirtemberg, he hath married vertue and beautie, following rather the contentment of his mind like a great Prince, then the filling of his purse, or his greater advancement, chusing so vertuous and so beautifull as his Countesse, by whom he had first a sonne named Otto, and now her Majestie's god-daughter Elizabeth. His waies may prosper, for they are right; and his counsels take effect, for they tend to pietie.

After his entertainments here at Rotenberg, he would gladly have carried my Lord Embassador to his best house at Smalecole, for as he is goodnes without end unto his subjectes, so shewed he love without end to her Majestie; but his journey of Amberg would not permit it, therefore we returned back by Spauengberg, from whence he suddainly went from us before, whereat we marvailed; but coming to Cassel, he met my Lord Embassador extraordinarily gallant, and received him so freshly, as though he had but now begun his entertainment. This judgment and discretion he used to the last, embracing this favoure of her Majestie in the most estimable and kinde manner that was possible, and shewing greater parts than of a Dutchman. Upon parting, he presented my Lord with princely giftes, as cuppes of ivory, amber, and christal, and, to fit his humor, with turkes and ginnets, furnished verie richly. What other secret giftes were given between them, I knowe not; but, after mutuall presents and gratuities, dispatching of letters, and preparing for our journey to Breme, the Prince sent one Master Branch for Fruce, who went with us, dined with the Embassador, he, and the Dukes of Luneberg and Holsteine, who, after dinner, in all termes of honour and of courtisie, bad my Lord farewell. And so these Princes parted.

His Lordshippe's Entertainment in the Low Countries.

I cannot but in gratitude insert to this discourse a word or two of my Lorde's bountifull and loving Entertainment going and coming through the Lowe Countries.

Wherein this good people shewed their gratefull minds unto her Majestie, as by whose soveraigne counsel and assistance (to say truly) they live in that peaceable libertie, wealthie, and very flourishing estate that now they are in, which is no little honour to her sacred personne, throughout the world. That this kingdom, which was wont to suffer, and be ledde by others, is in her time become active, so far forth, as through Christendome to be principal, for the setting uppe and maintenance of the truth, not onelie in her Majestie's owne dominions, but abroade, in spite of the world and the devil, *etiam rumpantur ut ilia Codro.* God continue her, for his Christe's sake!

The last of July my Lord embarqued from Yarmouth in a shippe of the Queenes, and landed at the Brill, where by the honourable the Lord Burrough's appointment, Captaine Turner, his Honoures Deputies Governour in the garrison, prevented the Burghmaisters in my Lordes entertainment, who were verie sorie for it, desiring his Lordship to return that way.

We crossed the water to Maidensluse, and went by Scute to Delft, where her Majestie's agent Maister Gilpin, with Captaine Iaxley, and some other gentlemen, met with my Lord, and returned with him presently to the Hague.

The Princes were in service, and at Hulst; but five of the States Generall, one for Gelderland, one for Frizeland, two for Holland, Delft, and Leadon, and one for Overissel, came and entertained my Lord, feasting and accompanying him, defraying all manner of charges, and sent further letters of commendations unto other townes to doe the like, taking order by one Captain Corbet, that when his Lordship came to Delphzill, he should, for his Honour's safe conduct, procure either a shippe of warre, or fiftie souldiers.

My Lord was at the Hague saluted further by the Countie Edgmont and the French Embassador; and being desirous to see her, went and saluted the Princesse of Orange with her young sonne.

From thence we went to Leaden, where my Lord was feasted likewise, and so at Harle and at Amsterdam it cost them two and three hundred guldens at a meale, for there was no spare; and for the most part they defrayed his Lord-shippe's wagons and his carriages.

From Amsterdam we sailed to Enchusen, whither comming late, we came unlooked for, and betimes in the morning went to Harlinoen, and the same day to Lewarden.

His Honour's Entertainment in this Province passed all the rest, for they can better skill of it, Frizeland being the more noble, though Holland be as honest.

At Lewarden, Maister Docomartin, the Here Suasenburch, and others, gave my Lord Embassador courtly and gratious entertainment, besides the cost they bestowed of him, which for his supper came to twentie pounde.

From hence we went to the territorie of Grominoen, where the States keepe in continuall garisonne eight companies, whereof the one halfe salied out at my Lord's comming, and caried him into the towne in greate triumph, the trumpet and a coronet of horsmen going before him to his lodging on the market-place, where, above all that I have yet spoken of in these partes, he was entertained and feasted.

In the morning the Seargant Major caried him about the fortresse, and shewed him of the siege, and manner of taking it, by Grave Maurice: and after dinner, four or five of the principal accompanied him towards Delphzil, appointing Captain Corbet to goe with him, where my Lord was likewise received at the watch master's house.

From hence, after having 'seene the sconce, next morning we crossed the water to Embden, where my Lord staying for answere from the Grave, for his convoy, he was put to cost; and so at Leere, Oldenborge, and Breme, where he staied not, but went to Forden Cel, and so to Brunswicke, travailed at great charge until he came to Zappenburch, and so likewise from Cassel till he came backe to Lewarden.

At our return from Cassel, we came down the Wessel, by Munden, Nuneburg, Minden, Breme, where my Lord mette a man of warre of Frizeland, and with him coasting and crossing the islands, came first to the schonse of Northmer Horne, and went from thence to Dockum.

At Lewarden againe they did him curtesie, and defrayed his charges, where he hoped to have met Grave Willelm, but he was at Groningen; we came the same way we went to Amsterdam, where were the States of Holland at their Provincial Councel, there being a Generall Meeting within few daies after at Lewarden.

From thence his Lordship went to Utrecht, where he had marveilous entertainment: it were a storie alone to report it.

From Utrecht we crossed over againe to the Hague, where Grave Maurice invited his Lordshippe to dinner: here were the Duke of Bullone, the Graves of Hollac Emden, Egmont, and many gallants; returning through, we came to Rotterdam, where he was entertained, and from thence to Dordrech, where likewise he was received verie bountifullie.

At Dordrech my Lord tooke shippe for Middelburgh, having appointed to convoy him two men of warre; where, through Zeland, by the townes of Der Gouse, Zerricher, Camphire, and Arnhem, we arrived, and at the English house my Lorde's charges was borne by the Burger-maisters. We hastened from the sicknes to Flushing, where the Lord Governour Sir Robert Sidney mette and received my Lord into the towne, accompanied with manie gallante captaines and gentlemen, being by, and provided him of shipping and all thinges necessary for our passage, imbarkt the sixt of October, and, with a prosperous wind, the seaventh arived in England.

Ceremony of HENRY *the* FOURTH KING *of* FRANCE, *being invested with the* GARTER, 1596.

The twentie-nine of August, the Duke of Buloine being arrived in England, came to the Court then at Greenewich, and there, by her Majestie's oath, confirmed the league of amity and peace betwixt the two realmes of England and Fraunce; and shortly after souldiers were sent over to ayde the French in their wars against the Spaniards.

Presently, uppon the departure of the Duke of Buloine, the Right Honourable Gilbert Earle of Shrewsbury was sent into France, to take the oath of Henry the Fourth French King, for the confirmation of the said league; as also to invest the said King with the order of the Garter: the manner whereof beeing carefully observed by Master William Segar, then Sommerset Herault, I have set downe according unto his owne description as followeth:

" We departed from Dover on Thursday the 16th day of September, 1596, and arrived at Deepe, in France, the Thursday seven-night following; where both the Ambassadours, the Right Honourable the Earle of Shrewsbury, and Sir Anthony Myldmay, Knight, were very nobly entertayned and feasted the first night by the Commander of Deepe, Monsieur de Chaste, who was invjted the next day to dinner, and requited by the Earle; and so, during the unshipping of their horse, and other their provisions, their Lordshipps passed the time in hunting for two or three dayes.

Monday the 27th following, the Earle set forwarde to Roane, the capitall towne of Normandy, and was mette on the way by Monsieur Feruaques and his trayne, who conducted his Lordship that night to the Castle of Cleere, where he lodged.

Tuesday his Lordship's proceeding on was encountered within two miles of the City of Roan, by the Duke Mountspensier, the King's Lieutenant, and about 200 horse, of nobles and gentlemen his attendants; who bringing his Lordship to his lodging, after some ceremonies of honourable entertainment, tooke his leave: his Lordshipp's lodging was in the market-place, called Le March Veux, in a very fayre house, furnished with rich hangings and tapits, three cloths of estate, and two standing beds.

The Wednesday seven-night following, being the fift of October, the King made his royall entrie into Roan; in which entring, sundrie messages passed betweene the King and the Ambassadours, praying them not to thinke the time long of his comming, for that hee was to attend a preparation, which the townes-men had purposed for his welcome, having never beene in the citty before; the manner whereof (for it was very princely and full of rare devises) I have thought good to insert.

In the suburbe of the towne, on the farther side of the river, was newly erected for the King, a most stately roome, made of plaister of Paris, where his Highnesse stood with his Nobilitie to behould the companies, and several classes both of horse and foote, and to receive the townes-men's submissions as they passed, which was most humbly performed by six of everie company, and of his Majestie most gratiously accepted.

First, the order of the Friers Capuchins followed their crosse, being of wood, uppon which a crowne of thornes and three great nayles were fixed; their habit was russet, all bepatched, girt with hempton cords, shirted with haire-cloath, and bare-footed, wearing sandales only. This order may have but one habit for a man during his life; they feede standing, and sleepe sitting; they live by almes, and are much esteemed of the people.

Secondly, the Gray Friers being Cordelers followed their crosse of silver. This order have a library in their house, containing six and fiftie paces in length, with three rowes of deskes all along, replenished with many excellent bookes both of philosophie and the fathers, the most part manuscript.

Thirdly, followed the Carmelites and Celestines; fourthly, the Jacobins; fiftly, the Augustines. Then proceeded the priests and chauntries of the towne in their surplices, singing, bearing 42 crosses of silver, which was the just number of the parishes and chappels in the towne; and every crosse had a great banner of a saint richly painted thereon; besides two tapers of white ware in aulter candle-sticks borne by youths, and every taper armed with an escutchion of King's armes.

Then followed the mint-masters of Normandy; the merchants of the vicounty-shippe, of the river, receivers, customers, treasurers, advocates, procurators, and other officers of the palace.

Then came Batchelers and Masters of Arts, Doctors of Phisicke, Civil Law, and Divinitie. All these degrees were cloathed in very fayre and reverent garments of damaske satten and blacke velvet, long and large, and for the most part riding uppon mules, distinguished by virgers that made waye before them.

Then followed, in gownes of purple cloth, and hoods of the same, with square cappes on their heads, the officers and counsellors of the Chamber of Normandy, in which is kept their High Court of Chauncerie and Parliament.

Then came riding on mules, to the number of fortie, in scarlet, called *De la robe rouge,* being judges and officers of estate belonging to the said Chamber.

After them tooke place the foure Presidents of Normandie in robes of scarlet, furred with calaber, wearing on their heads great caps of maintenance of blacke velvet.

Then proceeded the several bandes of the towne, contayning foure regiments of foote and three coronets of horse, suted in greene russet, and carnation satten, and velvet, garnished with silver lace, their hatts, plumes, scarfes, and shooes white; the furniture of their muskets, fether staves, and partisants, suitable to their colours; their ensignes, cornets, and standarts all white, emblasoned with the King's armes, and inriched with his devise, which was a Roman H crowned, betweene two branches (as I take it), the one an olive, the other a laurell; his motto or word, " Has dedit, His dabit ultra."

After uppon great coursers rode fortie *Enfants d'Honneur* or Henchmen, the properest and choisest young men of the towne, suted in greene velvet horsemen's coates, richly laced with silver, their caparisons and trappings answerable; their plumes, scarfes, and boots white.

Then came all the gallaunts and young gentlemen of the French Court (corvetting and fetching up their great horse), accompanied with divers of the nobilitie, as Barons, Vicounts, and Earles; the Knights of the *Saint Esprite* were knowne by their blue ribandes, and white crosses hanging thereat.

The Chauncellor, Monsieur Cheverny, rode alone after his mace.

The Archbyshop of Rhemes did ride betweene the Byshops of Anjow and Cureur.

Then marched the Kinges three guardes after their drummes and fifes; the Swisses with shotte and pikes; the Scots and French with halberds; the King's trumpets in horsemen's coats of greene velvet, and very well mounted; then tooke they place, and sounded oftentimes as they passed.

Monsieur Suraine, Master of the Ceremonies, and one of the Captaynes of the Guarde, rode together; after whom followed three Heraultes, Anjow, Picardie, and Brytaine, invested in rich coates of purple velvet, embroidered with the armes of France, each bearing his name in capitall letters of gold upon the left manch.

Then followed two Serjeants of Armes, carrying maces before the person of the King, who that day was mounted on a white courser; his owne apparell, plumes, and horses white; wearing the order of the St. Esprite at a broade blue ribande about his necke. About his person were his guarde of Scots, and certayne footemen in white; and after him followed the Duke de Nevers, Duke de Namours, Duke Joyeuse, and others.

Leave wee the King going to the Cittie; and let us, by the way of preparation, knowe how the same was ordered for his entertaynement.

Some five or sixe dayes before the King made his entrie, the Bailiffes of Roane commaunded by sound of trumpet, that all the streetes through which his Majestie should passe, shoulde bee cleansed, sanded, and their signes taken downe, hanging forth their fairest coverings, and tapits at their windows; and to crie "Vive le Roy," as hee passed. All which beeing in a readinesse, the windowes full of people of all degrees, the streetes guarded with certaine ensignes of muskets, and infinite numbers of common people in every quarter.

His Majesty by this time was come to an utter gate, betweene the bridge and the suburbs, which in the late warre had beene more than halfe ruined. This gate in two or three dayes with plaister of Paris they had halfe repayred, and the other halfe remayned in ruine, for explication of a devise which was thus: On the toppe of the gate were certayne personages made of plaister; some carrying of stones, some morter, some heaving, some leveling, and all so lively, that they seemed to want nothing but very motion. Uppon the arch of the part repayred sat Apollo with his lyre; under whom in goulden letters was written this prophesie: "Henrico totum reparabitur auspice regnum."

And over the portall, "Gallicarum urbium restitutorem."

The King beeing past this gate, hee came to the first gate of the bridge, which was made of twelve columnes about fourteene foote of height; the base bodie, capitoll, freeze, and cornish, after the order *Ionica*. Over the arch whereof, in a table of embossed worke, sat a personage representing Normandy, resting her backe against two leopardes (the armes of the dutchie); in her left hand she held a hart; her right hand she put forth to a figure resembling the King, who seemed to raise her uppe: under her was written, "Da miseræ Dextram;" and over her certayne drops distilling from the heavens; then in golden letters, under the King's armes (which was embrased with low palmes) were verses in French, thus Englished :

> O doubled branches, for conquerors ordain'd,
> If Henrie's name for crownes hath you not gain'd,
>   Bowing downe your topps for to be wreathed,
> You cannot give him your honours triumphant,
> No more than this streame can yeeld water currant,
>   Unlesse from higher spring it be received.

The King, having viewed the device and read the verses, passing further, under the roofe or vault, or gate, over his heade certayne cloudes opened; and there descended upon him the similitude of the Holy Ghost, and an angell presented unto him a sworde, called "The Sworde of Peace;" before the opening of which cloude a voyce was heard, as from God, saying,

> Heavenly mooving spirits! stable intelligences!
>   Cleave through, make way for this Spirit's descent;
> Presenting from one Heaven of thousand influences
>   To one speciall Monarke, one speciall present.
> Henrie's mine annoynted: he fears me; I him love;
>   Yeeld him due honour, the honour shall be mine:
> All Kings are Gods; and, as Myselfe above,
>   Dispose both good and bad on earthly line.

The Angell descending, saith :

> Stay, mighty Monarch, stay; the Heavenly Monarch sends
>   To thee this Sworde of Peace, with good and happy day;
> Take it; but in blisse a modest heart entends;
>   Himselfe who raiseth, falls, and God's love loseth aye.
> He hath given thee the sword in fields victorious,
>   And that which to no other hand would be given so:
> One more of peace did rest for thy hand glorious,
>   Receive it from above for to command below.
> Threefold great by these, thou maist thrice happy make
>   France under thee to yeeld; thy scepter greatnesse bring:
> Pursue this good (therefore) the price for gratious take,
>   The which about thy browes makes thousand laurels spring.

The Angell ascending, saith:

Rejoyce, ye Heavens, since peace which yore hath left
    Returned is on earth, to dwell with Henry,
Who for his neighbours good, of joy bereft,
    Merits for his that men one day be sory.

Earth doe as much; tapet thyselfe with flowers,
    And sundry fruits, that henceforth may increase;
All things without man's art are handy labours,
    For Golden Age is where there raigneth Peace.

Then live thrice happy, and content this Prince,
    Who, chiefe of World and peace is made this day;
Of all the world heele make but one province,
    If there be Kings, these Kings shall him obey.

After these words delivered by the angell, the King proceeded over the bridge of Roane, which was guarded by five or six hundred Swissers, all in bright armour and Spanish pikes, untill hee came to the other gate of the bridge, which entred into the towne; the building of which gate was after the order rustique, rising three degrees, having uppon the one corner of the first degree a hound, with a cupid riding on his backe, under which was written, "Dux Amor est Fidei." And on the other corner, an ox, with another Cupid, subscribed, "Vires frænantur Amore." Upon the corners of the second degree stood four Tritons, or mer-men, with tridents in their hands; and above them, on the third degree, was erected a personage representing Roane, with a lambe standing, and laying one foote uppon the knee of the figure, over which was written, "Nowe." It is to bee understood, the lambe is the armes of the City, which, in an epigram made unto the King, was thus described:

    O, King! your Lambe, before our wretched broile,
        Was wont to beare uppon her humble backe
    The golden fleece, like that of Colchos Ile;
        But certaine new-come, Argonauts (alacke!)
    Have her oft-times so barely cut and shorne,
    That on her body poore and all forlorne,
    You scarce with paine can find at all to pull,
    One simple fleece, or little lock of wooll.

The King passing through this gate, the towne had prepared for him a canapie of purple velvet, richly embrodered with his armes and device, and flower de luces strewed all over; which canapie was carried over him by six henchmen apparelled in one suite. From thence hee went up the streete called La Rue du Pont; where was set up a very stately pyramid, about a hundred foote of height, on which was set forth in painting of copper colours the labours of Hercules; on the toppe whereof was a great sunne of golde, bearing the Kinge crowned H. uppon the points of his beames; the spire of this pyramid was carried from the base, or pedestall, by four sphinxes gilt; and on the one side of the said base was written " Hercules Gallicus;" and on the other side in letters of gold upon sable, French verses, thus Englished:

> Hercules and Henry are semblance
> In vertues, words, and acts,
> But that Hercules is in the fable,
> And Henry in the facts.

Here the Kinge turned downe the streete called Ozon, where were set uppe two statues of plaister upon antique bases, both under named in Greeke characters. The first, called Stable Victory, held in her one hand a palme, and in the other an imperiall crowne and scepter, treading upon armour and other martial engines; the other figure was quick-sighted Justice, holding a sword and ballance, and treading under her feete a number of visors or maskes, signifying falsehoods; betweene them both was written in golden letters uppon azure, certayne French verses to this effect:

> Kings which for honour beare name of August
> (Or happy Cæsars) preserv'd by history,
> Acknowledge Henry more valiant and just,
> Would beare no other but the name of Henry.

So the King's Majesty, riding through the streete named Le Rue de la Viscount, at the streetes end opposite his comming forth into the High-streete, there was raised a Doricke piller about twentie foote of height; on the toppe whereof stood Fame treading downe Death, holding a crowned H in one hand, and a trumpet with a banneroll of France in the other; which, when the King's trumpets in passing by sounded, Fame raised her trumpet to her mouth, and seemed to sound also, turning herselfe rounde about, which motion was most cunningly wrought by an engine below within the base. And uppon the outside of the base, leaning against the pedestall, sate Pallas and Peace, treading uppon Envie, who was set forth like a furie, with haires of Snakes, and a murthering knife in her hand. Over these figures sat Historie writing, and looking up to Fame, under whome were written these Latin verses:

> Delicium historiæ, & famæ sed vera canentis.
> Henricum reges exemplar habete futuri:
> Ut forte populos, & bello, & pace regatis.

> O, future Kings, example take by Henry,
>   Historie's delight, and Fame's most true reporte;
> That you may rule and govern prosperously
>   Your people both in warre and peacefull sort.

Under these verses was painted a lyon breathing forth bees, but without either motto or allusion.

The King passing on through the Diall gate, there was an arbor resembling Apolloe's Temple, curiously wrought of herbage, and fashioned like wreathed pillers; adjoyning to which was a little wood, where on a wall was painted in prospect divers metamorphoses, as, Daphne pursued by Apollo, and turned to a laurell; Pan embracing Siringa as she became reedes; Europa and Jupiter; and such like. In which arbor was excellent musique heard, both for voice and instruments. All which being a while listened unto by his Majesty, he proceeded to the streetes end, turning to our Ladie Church (called Nosterdame), where was erected a most magnificent arch triumphall of plaister, after the order Corinthique; on the top whereof, uppon a great globe of the worlde, stood the figure of the King in his royall robes, supported by two personages; the one Prudentia, who crowned him with a crowne of stars; the other Fortitude, who offered him a sceptre wreathed about with laurell: before him sat Occasion; behind him Clemencie; and round about him lay armours, ensignes, drummes, trumpets, and other martial instruments: at eyther corner sat a huge lyon of gold, supporting the armes of France and Navarre; and on the other side of the gate stood Envy, bound in chaines, feeding of her owne heart; and on the other side a man of armes sitting asleepe on a drumme's head, by whome was written Securitie.

Over the portall gate, under the globe, was written in Latin verses, thus translated:

> To some for feare, to some for clemencie,
> Are prizes given: but fourth King Henrie,
> Excelling other Kings in both, and both conjoyned
> In him by wisedome hath also adjoyned,
> Unto these three, a fourth occasion
> Which, if it stand with lawes probation,
> Hath sworne herselfe to be companion,
> Yoking worlds to France by King Borbonion.

Opposite to this arch triumphall, uppon two rustique pillers (distinguished above 20 foote asunder), stood two figures of plaister; the one of St. Lewis in his kingly robes, holding a scepter in one hand, and a verge in another; on the top whereof was a hand pointing to the King, which stood on the globe, with this verse under written,

> Macte tua virtute mea maxima stirps.

The personage on the other piller was Sambetha, one of the Sibyls, who likewise pointed to the King's proportion, and presented to the beholders a table with a prophesie in Latin, Englished thus:

> Sambetha, I of sibyls chiefe, an Hebrew by offspring,
> Glad oracles bring to the French; and unto thee, O King.
> The earth did never boast herselfe of any childe so much
> As France (O Henry!) shall rejoyce that thou their King art such.
> Peace being to the people brought, a thousand armies strong
> Dreadlesse shall march, and follow farre thy battailes all along;
> Where Tagus and Durias swell with goodly golden sand,
> And where Idumea for thyselfe holdes worthy palmes in hand;
> Thou being Captayne, soldiers shall returne with laden spoiles
> Of Easterne and the Westerne wealths, and shall bring to their soiles
> Triumphant signes and trophies backe: O King, their countrie wonne,
> Fame shall eternall crownes thee give for that which thou hast done.
> Live thou therefore now all our yeers, and Nestor's longest date,
> World's love, to people giving lawes, made quiet by thy State.

The King goeing through this arch triumphall, hee presently entred the Cathedrall Church of Nostredame, with all the ecclesiasticall pompe that might bee;

from whence, after certayne ceremonies, which entertayned him for a time, he returned more privately in his coach to his court, being sometimes a cardinal's house, adjoyning to Saint Owin's Church; and thus the King's entrie ended with the day, being performed with great honour, charge, and applaudements of all sortes of people.

Thursday the seaventh of October, the right honourable Lords London Ambassadours had audience of the King; who almost princely received, embraced, and welcomed them both, as also all other the Lords, Knights, and Gentlemen, their attendants.

Satterday the ninth of October, the fidelitie or oath of confederation betweene the King and the Queenes Majesty of England was very solemnly taken in the Church of Saint Owen, in the presence of the French Nobilitie, Lords spirituall and temporall, who that day tooke the right hand of the quire.

Sunday beeing the morrow after, the Order of the Garter was most royally performed in the saide Church, where both the Princes had their estates and armes erected. The Queenes Majesty, being Soveraigne of the Order, had that day the right hand of the quire; and so had the Right Honourable Earle, her Majesties Ambassador, his armes, stile, and stall, accordingly. Before her Majesties estate sat Master William Dethicke, Garter principall King of Armes, in his robe of the Order; before the Earle stoode William Segar, Somerset Herault; next unto the Earle sat the Lord Ambassadour Lieger; then the Lord Cromwell, the Lord Rich, and all other Knights and Gentlemen, according to their qualitie; on the left hand sat the King betweene the two Bishops of Anjow and Cureur; before the King's estate sate his Chancellor Monsieur Cheverney alone; and before him stoode Anjow, Picardy, and Britany, Heraulds of Armes; in the stalls sat the Knights of the Saint Esprite, who (as far as I doe remember) were these, Duke Montpensiere, Duke de Nevers, Duke de Namours, the Prince de Vaudemont, Duke Montmerancie, Constable, and his brother the Admirall, Duke Joyeuse, Duke de Buloin, the Marshall de Rotz, and the Marshall Matignon.

All things being accomplished with much honor, the King's Majestie invested and sworne, the vespers ended, and the benediction given by a Bishoppe in his *pontificalibus*, the King taking the Earle by the hand, they returned as they came, attended upon by the Nobilitie, who, two and two, proceeded before them. That night the King and the Earle supped together under one estate in the house of Duke Montpensier, where also was a general feast for all the English.

Thursday the 14th of October, the King took the Earle into his coach, and went to the bridge of Roane to see a sea-fight, uppon the river, which was performed by two French shippes, against two supposed Spanish and one Brasilian (large boates armed and prepared for that purpose, with muskets, pikes, and hargubur a crooke) where, after one houres fight, the Brasilian was sunke, and the Spaniards forced to flie, by the French. This pastime was done by the townsmen for the King's more delight.

On Friday the Right Honourable Earle, with his attendants, tooke leave of the King's Majesty, and kissed his hand, departed with great love, honour and reputation.

Saterday the sixteenth of October, his Lordshippe set forth of Roan, and came that night to Deepe, beeing accompanied with the commaunder thereof, Mounsieur de Chaste, where he remained for convenient passage ten days after.

The 29th of October, the Queenes Majesties shipps being come, his Lordship embarked himselfe in the Admirall, and arrived at the Downes neere Dover the day next following.

Rewards given by the Right Honourable Gilbert Earle of Shrewsbury, in his Ambassage of France.

To Monsieur Suraine, a chaine of gold of 100 pound.
To the Chiefe Comptroller, a chaine of 80 pound.
To the Second Comptroller, a chaine of 62 pound.
To the Third Comptroller, a chaine of 58 pound.
To Madam Mattigna, a martiall woman, a jewell of 20 pound.
To Mounsieur Civille, one hundred crownes.
To the cookes and other officers of the King, 300 crownes.
To the musitians 20 pound.
To Sir Henry Palmer, Admirall of the Queenes shippe in which his Lordship went, a jewell of the Queenes picture, and a ring sent to his Lady.
To the mariners of the Queenes shippes, in the way of largesse, amongst them a hundred and fiftie pound.

Rewards given by the King.

To the Earle her Majesties Ambassador, a jewell with a rich diamond therein.
To Master Garter principal of Armes, 100 crownes.
To Somerset Herault 200 crownes.

The Proceeding to the Parliament of Queene Elizabeth, from her Majestie's Royall Pallas of Whitehalle to Westminster, 1596.

First Messengers of the Chamber.

Gentlemen, two and two.

Esquires, two and two.

The six Clearkes of the Chauncery.

Clearkes of the Starre Chamber.

Clearkes of the Signett.

Clearkes of the Privie Counsell.

The Maisters of the Chauncery.

Esquires of the Body.

The trumpetts.

The Queene's Attourney and Soliciter.

Sergeants of the Lawe.

The Queene's Sergeant aloane.

Barons of the Exchequer, two and two.

Pursuivants of Armes. { Judges of the Common Pleas. / Judges of the King's Bench. } Pursuivants of Armes.

The Lord Chiefe Baron, and Lord Chiefe Justice of the Common Pleas.
The Maister of the Roules, and the Lord Chiefe Justice of the King's Benche.

Batcheler Knights.

Knights of the Bathe.

Knights Banneretts.

Knights of the Privie Counsell, two and two.

Knights of the Garter.

The Queene's Majestie's cloake and hatt, borne by a Knight, or an Esquire.
Heraldes.—Noblemen's younger sonnes and heires apparent, two and two.—Heraldes.

The Principall Secretary, being no Baron.

The Vice-chamberlaine.

The Thresorer and Comtroller of the Houshold.
Barons in their roabes, two and two, yongest first.
Bishops in theire roabes, two and two.
The Lord Admirall, and the Lord Chamberlaine of the Houshould togeather, if they be Barons *in pare dignitate*.

Norrey King of Armes.
Viscounts in their roabes, two and two, yongest first.
Earles in their roabes, two and two, yongest first.
Marquesses in their roabes.
Dukes in theire roabes.
The Lord President of the Councell, and the Lord Privie Seale.
Lord Steward of the Queene's house, and the Lord Great Chamberlaine.
Clarenceux King of Armes.
The Almner. The Master of Requests.
The Lord Chauncelor and Lord Thresorer.
The Archbishop of Canterbury and the Archbishop of Yorke togeather.
Sergeants at Armes. Sergeants at Armes.
Garter Chiefe King of Armes, bareheaded.
The capp of estate, borne by the Marquesse of Winchester, and with him on the leafte hand the Earl Marshall of England with the gylte rodde.
The sworde, borne by an Earle.
The Queene's Majestie on horseback, or in her chariot, with her roabes of estate, her trayne borne by a Dutches, or Marchiones.
Then Pensioners on each side of her Majesty, bearing polaxes.
The Lord Chamberlaine and the Vice-chamberlaine on each side of the Queene, if they attend out of their ranckes; but somewhat behinde her.
The Maister of the Horse, leading a spare horse next behinde her Majestie.
Ladies and Gentlewomen according to their estates, two and two.
The Captaine of the Guard, with all the Guard following, two and two.

The 27th of August 1596, Chalke and Denton dyd send xxs. to remove her Majestie from Greenwiche.

The said monij was delivered to Robert Bowden, beinge then Constable of the Hondred of Shamell[1].

---

[1] Ther was xs. gathered in Chalke and Denton to hyer a carte to carry a load of coales from Sennocke to Greenwiche, the Court then dyd lye ther, the 30th of August, in anno 1596.

Rates of Servants, Labourers, and Hirers' Wages, appointed at the General Session for the Peace, within the City of Chester, anno 38° R. Elizabethæ.

	Wages by the Yeare, Meate and Drinke.			Wages by the Yeare without ditto.			Wages by the Day without ditto.
	£	s.	d.	£	s.	d.	d.
Smith	-	1	6	8	5	0	0	2
Wheelewrighte	-	2	0	0	5	10	0	2 ob.
Plowewrighte	-	1	10	0	5	0	0	2
Millwrighte	-	1	3	4	5	10	0	3
Master carpenter	-	2	13	4	5	13	4	4
Servant carpenter	-	1	0	0	3	10	0	1
Joyner	-	1	10	0	4	0	0	2
Rough mason	-	1	6	8	5	0	0	2 ob.
Plaisterer	-	1	0	0	5	0	0	2
Sawier	-	1	8	3	4	10	0	2
Lyme maker	-	1	3	0	4	6	8	2
Bricklayer	-	1	0	0	4	0	0	2
Brickman	-	1	6	0	4	10	0	2
Tyler	-	1	5	0	3	13	4	2
Sclater	-	1	0	0	4	0	0	2
Tylemaker	-	1	10	0	4	0	0	2
Lynen weaver	-	1	0	0	4	0	0	1
Turner	-	0	16	0	3	0	0	1
Wolsey weaver	-	1	8	0	3	13	0	1
Cowper	-	1	10	0	4	0	0	2
Miller	-	1	10	0	4	0	0	2
Fuller	-	1	5	0	3	13	4	1 ob.
Malter	-	1	3	4	4	0	0	1 qr.
Thatcher	-	1	0	0	4	0	0	1
Shingler	-	1	10	0	4	0	0	1
Shoeman	-	1	0	0	3	13	4	1 ob.
Dyer	-	1	6	8	3	13	4	1 ob.
Hosiers	-	1	3	0	3	10	0	1
Sla-makers	-	1	0	0	4	0	0	2
Tanners	-	1	6	0	4	0	0	1
Pewterers	-	1	0	0	3	13	4	2
Bakers	-	0	16	0	3	10	0	1
Brewers	-	1	0	0	3	10	0	1
Glovers	-	1	0	0	3	16	0	1
Cutlers	-	1	7	0	4	10	0	2
Sadlers	-	1	5	0	4	0	0	2 ob.
Spurriers	-	1	5	0	4	0	0	2 ob.
Cappers	-	1	0	0	3	10	0	2

	Wages by the Yeare, with Meate and Drinke.			Wages by the Yeare, without ditto.			Wages by the Day, without ditto.
	£.	s.	d.	£.	s.	d.	d.
Hatmakers	-	1	10	0	4	10	0	2
Bowiers	-	1	8	0	4	0	0	2
Fletchers	-	1	0	0	3	10	0	2
Arrow-head makers	-	0	15	0	3	10	0	1
Butchers	-	1	6	8	3	10	0	2
Cookes	-	1	0	0	3	5	0	2
Bayliff of husbandry	-	2	0	0	4	0	0	3
Mowers of grass	-	-	-	-	-	-	-	4
Taskers	-	-	-	-	-	-	-	4
Reapers	-	-	-	-	-	-	-	2
Mowers of corne	-	-	-	-	-	-	-	4
Servants of the best sorte	-	1	0	0	3	0	0	
Servants of the 2d sorte	-	0	10	0	2	0	0	
Servants of the 3d sorte	-	0	8	0	1	15	0	

Lettre de la REYNE d'ANGLETERRE au ROI HENRI IVme, après sa Conversion [1].

"Quelles douleurs, quels regrets, et gemissemens je senti en mon ame par le son de telles nouvelles, que Morcas m'a apportées. Mon Dieu! est-il possibles qu'aucun mondain respect deust effacer la terreure dont la crainte divine menasse. Pouvons nous par raison attendre une bonne suite d'un acte sy inique. Celui qui vous a maintenu et conservé, pouvez vous imaginer qu'il vous lassie au plus grand besoin. O qu'il est dangereux de mal faire, pour en esperer du bien, encore veux je qe plus saine inspiration vous admondra cependant je ne cesserai de vous mettre au premier rang de mes devotions à ce que les mains d'Esau n'egalent les benedictions de Jacob. Et ou vous me promettez toute amitié et fidelité, je confesse l'avoit cherement merité & conservée & ne m'en departirai-je, pourveu que vous ne changiez de père, autrement ne vous serai-je que Sœur Bastarde. Car j'amerai toujours mieux le naturel que l'adoptiff, come Dieu le connoignt, lequel vous guide en droit chemin de mieux sentir.

"Votre tres assurée sœur je le suis à vielle mode ou à la nouvelle je n'en ay que faire. ELISABETH [2]."

[1] From the original, in Cardinal Mazarin's State Papers, in the Library of the Duke of Brunswick.
[2] This Letter was written in 1594.—In 1596 the French King was solemnly invested with the Order of the Garter; see p. 398.

In the Churchwarden's accompts of St. Margaret's, Westminster, in 1596, are the following entries:

Paid the ringers on the 7th (month not mentioned), for joy of Victory over the Spaniards, 7s. 6d.

Item, for a prayer bell, 1d.

Item, paid the ringers when her Majestie went to the Lord Burrowes [1], 6d.

Item, paid for maimed soldiers, 13s. 4d.

On the 6th of March 1596-7, died William Brooke Lord Cobham, a Nobleman much favoured by the Queen. He succeeded his father in his estate, and as Lord Cobham, in September 1588; and on the 17th of July following entertained his Royal Mistress at Cobham Hall, in the first year of her reign [2], with a noble welcome, as she took her Progress through Kent. He was continually employed by her in different negociations abroad. He was Lord Warden of the Cinque Ports, Constable of Dover Castle, Lord Lieutenant of the County of Kent, one of her Privy Council, and Knight of the Order of the Garter [3].

In this year the bells at Fulham were rung, " when the Queen went to the Lord Burleigh's house at Wimbledon [4];" and also when she " went to the Lord

[1] Thomas Lord Burgh, who resided at Lambeth. See before, under 1586, vol. II. p. 482.

[2] See before, vol. I. p. 73.

[3] He was buried at Cobham on the 5th of April 1597. His son Henry Lord Cobham, the eldest son, was likewise Lord Warden of the Cinque Ports, Constable of Dover Castle, Lord Lieutenant of the County of Kent, and Knight of the Garter. But in the first year of King James I. being accused of having, with his brother George, the Lord Grey of Wilton, Sir Walter Raleigh, and others, conspired to kill the King, and, by an insurrection, to alter religion, subvert the government, and procure an invasion by strangers, they were brought to their trial at Winchester in November following, had judgment of death pronounced against them; George, his brother, was thereupon beheaded, and both of them attainted. But the execution of Lord Cobham and some of the others was, through the King's clemency, superseded, and his estate being forfeited to the Crown, he lived many years afterwards in great misery and poverty, and died in January 1619." Hasted's Kent, vol. I. p. 493.

[4] Sir Thomas Cecil, eldest son of William Lord Burleigh, Lord Treasurer, presented to the Queen, in 1588-9, " a French gown of black silk net-worke, of two sorts, flourished with Venice gold, and lined with white camlet." In return, he had 30¼ ounces of gilt plate.—In 1588 he rebuilt the manor-house at Wimbledon (see Lysons's Environs), which was purchased of Sir Christopher Hatton; and in 1590 the manor of Wimbledon was given him by the Queen, in exchange for an estate in Lincolnshire. On the death of his father, Aug. 4, 1598, he succeeded to the title of Lord Burleigh; and on New Year's Day 1599-1600 he presented to the Queen " a jewel of gold, with a large table sapphire foil,

Admiral's at Chelsea[1], and back again."—The Lord Admiral's town residence was in King-street, Westminster.

At the same time the following Noblemen had houses in that neighbourhood[2]:

Earl of Hertford's, Hertford Howse, in Channon Row.
Earl of Lincolne, Lincoln Howse, in Channon Row.
Earl of Derby, Darby House, in Channon Row.
The Lord Dacres, in Channon Row.
Earl of Sussex, Sussex House, in the Abbey Yard.
The Lord Stafford's, within the New Palace.
The Lord Graye's Howse, in Tootehill Street[3].

having eight small diamonds about it, and one pearl pendant." Lady Burghley gave "a waistcoat of white sarçenet, embroidered with flowers of silk of sundry colours." In return, Lord Burghley had 30¼ ounces of gilt plate; his Lady 28¼ ounces.—He was elected Knight of the Garter, May 26, 1601; and after the accession of King James, May 4, 1605, was created Earl of Exeter. He died Feb. 7, 1621-2, aged 80.

[1] *Chelsea Place* was granted by the Queen in 1592 to Catherine Lady Howard, wife of the Lord Admiral. But this Nobleman appears to have resided at Chelsea previous to this grant, as many of his Letters among the Harleian MSS. are dated from that place in 1589 and 1591. In the Sidney Papers mention is made of the Queen's visits to him here in 1597, 1599, and 1600.—The Lord Admiral was descended from the House of Norfolk by the Mowbrays, was created Earl of Nottingham 22 October 1597, and died Dec. 13, 1624.—His first Countess was Catharine, daughter of Henry Cary, Lord Hunsdon. The second was Margaret, daughter of James Stuart, Earl of Murray. Both these Ladies were buried at Chelsea, as appears by the following entries:—"Catharyne, the Countess of Nottingham, died the 25 day of February at Aronedell House, London, and buried at Chelsey the 28 day of the same, whose funeralls were honorably kepte at Chelsea the 21st of March 1603; and Elizabeth our blessed Quene died at Richmond the 24 day of the same moneth aft'r, in the morninge; after whome, the same day, before 8 of the clock, that most happie and christian Kynge, James the VIth of Scotland, was in good righte by our nobles and states proclaymed James the Firste of Englande, to the admirable peace and comforte of the realme, whose raigne and posteritie God contynew in peace with God's truth, longe and longe among us.—The Ritte Hon'ble Margaret Countess of Nottinghame, died on the 4th day of August, in Commun Garden, Lundon, and buried heare at Chelsey the 19th day of the same month, 1639."

[2] Some others have been noticed before; see p. 371.

[3] Norden, who, in his description of Westminster, notices the above several houses, gives the following note of the difference between *Streets*, *Lanes*, and *Allies*. "A Street is a broad and maine way for horsemen and footmen to passe, and where great store of passengers walk and traveyle to and froe, especially in a Citie or Town: and it differeth from a lane in this, that a lane is not so usually frequented, neither is there any such necessity of the use thereof, and it is far lesse, and yeldeth not like scope for manie people to pass; an alley differeth greatly from them both, in that it yieldeth not passage, but hath a stop, which forceth such as pass into it

The Order of receyveing Queen ELIZABETH *in the Colledge Churche of Westminsteer, the firste Daie of the Parliament, October* 13, 1597 [1].

Imprimis. The Queen's Majestie to be receyved at the Northe dore of the said Churche. But before her entrie into the porche of the said dore a fourme with carpetts and cushions to be laid, where her Majestie is to kneele, and to receyve a scepter of gould, having the image of a dove in the toppe, and to pronounce a praier. The Deane of the said Churche is to delyver the said scepter, and to shewe the said praier.

At her Majestie's entry into the Churche, the Deane of her Majestie's Chappell, with all the Company of the Chappell, and the Deane of Westminster with his brethren, and Company in copes, to meete her Majestie at the North dore of the Churche.

The whole quire then to singe a solempne psalme, going before her Majestie.

The Queen's Majestie to come to the bodie of the Churche, and so to enter in at the Weste dore of the quier, and so uppe to her travase by the communion-table.

Uppon her entrie into her travase *Te Deum* to be sounge; after that the Letanie. Then the Sermon.

After the Sermon a solemne songe with a collecte for the Queene.

That beinge ended, the whole quier to goe before her Majestie singinge to the South-east dore, wheare the Deane kneelinge, with two of his bretheren, is to receyve of her Majestie the golden staffe with the dove in the toppe.

to retire. The word *Allee* cometh of the French word *Aller*, to goe, or to walk; and therefore we used to call our walks in gardens, orchards, and such, *Allees*; places where men goe or walk, and at a kind of stop return; and so they pass and repass at their pleasure. So the *Allees* in Cities and Townes have an entrance whereunto a man may walk, but shall be forced to return again. First, therefore, the principal and main street is called King Street. Although they all be *viæ Regis*, yet this is the proper name of this street, gyven (no doubt) when the Kings used to make their abode at the Old and New Pallaces; then was this street much frequented sometime with the presence of the King's people. And of the continual passage from London to the King's Pallace, it took the name of *King Street*. *Tootehill Street*, lying on the West part of this Cytie, taketh name of a hill near it, which is called Tootehill, in the great feyld near the street. *The Stronde*, a place [very fayre and lardge street, which lyeth between Temple Bar and Charing Cross] which taketh the name of the Strond by reason of the lying thereof upon the Thamise: for *Strond* signifyeth properly the sea-shore, or banks; and this, being the banke, as it were, of the famous river Thamise, aptly beareth the name of Strond; and it was that part of the street without Temple Bar, which lyeth between Strand Lane and Leicester House."

[1] From the British Museum, Donation MSS. 4712.

Embassador from the King of Poland, 1597.

This Summer arrived at London an Orator from the King of Polonia, Sigismond, the third sonne to Duke John of Finland, that after was Kinge of Sweden, and was a longe while here in England. This Embassador was named Paulus de Jaline, a gentleman of that countrie; he brought letters of credence from the King, dated the 19th of May last past, and had audience the 25th of July, at the Court then at *Greenwich;* whose Oration in Latin beginning, " Serenissima Princeps, Domina Clementissima, Sacra Regia Majestas, Poloniæ Dominus meus Clementissimus," &c. The effect of his Speech, after princely congratulations, " what good entertainment her Majestie's subjects had in his dominions, as his owne subjects, and contrary to which, his subjects were in England deprived of all their former olde privileges and liberties of trade, graunted them by her Majestie's predecessors, and consequently were deprived of all trade and traffique in her kingdome, And notwithstanding his subjects have made severall complaints, of the which he must have a care, he coulde not bee mooved to diminish any part of his good-will toward her Majestie and her subjects; but there was of late set foorth certayne edicts and proclamations, by the which, contrary to the law of nature, his subjects were forbidden the navigation and trade into Spayne; and under colour thereof, divers ships of his subjects had bene taken at sea, and their goods made prize, and confiscated, with more the like injuries; all the which were such, that it touched not only his marchantes, of whom he must have a care, but likewise all the universall Nobilitie of his kingdomes and dominions, for that by the trade doth consist all their livings and revenues, so that no greater injurie can be done to the King his master and the states of his kingdoms: yet, for his brotherly love to her Majestie, he hath suspended those meanes of dooing the like to her Majestie's subjects, which means her Majestie doth know he doth not want: he thought good to proceed with patience, and to advertise the Queen's Majestie thereof, as a good neighboure and Prince's dutie doth require. And for that letters hitherto have not beene regarded, hee had now sent him to require her Majestie, according to equitie, to make reparation and restitution, and that the trade westward to Spayne might be free, as it ought to be to all menne, by the Law of Nations; otherwise the Kinge his maister woulde no longer neglect his subject's losses, but to take in hand such necessary meanes as might bee required. As for the Queene's Warres with Spayne, that ought not to hinder his subjects navigation, by the common law of nature; and there was very olde and good friendshippe beetwixt the Kinge his master and the Kinge of Spayne, and betwixt the House of Austria and the Kinge his master, having now renued the olde amitie by marriage with a daughter of Austria, so that hee is bounde to maintayne the friendship with the Kinge of Spayne, as well as with her Majestie, ever. His request bearing such equitie, he doth trust that her Majestie will take regard of his protestations, and commaunde satisfaction," &c. commending withal some particular sutors and causes.

The Polonian Ambassador, being of a blunt and harsh behaviour, delivered his mind accordingly, contrary to all expectation: whereat the Queene, being much amazed, was driven into admiration, and unawares and unprovided on the sodaine what to say, with a sharp look and earnest mind, very learnedly and eloquently spake these words following:

"Oh, quam decepta fui; expectavi legationem, tu vero querelam mihi adduxisti. Per literas accepi te esse legatum, inveni vero heraldum: nunquam in vita mea audivi talem orationem: miror sane, miror talem, et tam insolentem in publico audaciam: neque possum credere si Rex tuus adesset quod ipse talia verba protulisset; sin vero tale aliquid tibi fortasse in mandatis commisit (quod quidem valde dubito) eo tribuendum: quod cum Rex tuus sit juvenis, et non tam jure sanguinis, quam jure electionis, et noviter electus, non tam perfecte intelligat rationem tractandi istiusmodi negotia cum aliis principibus, quam vel majores illius nobiscum observarunt, vel fortasse observabunt alii qui locum ejus posthac tenebunt. Quod ad te attinet, videris mihi libros multos perlegisse, libros tamen principum ne attigisse, sed prorsus ignorare quid inter Reges conveniat. Nam quod juris naturæ et gentium tantopere mentionem facis; hoc scito, juris naturæ gentiumque, ut cum bellum inter Reges intercedit, liceat alteri alterius bellica subsidia undicunque allata intercipere, et ne in damnum suum convertantur percavere: hoc (inquam) est jus naturæ & gentium. Quod novam affinitatem cum domo Austriaca commemores, quam tanti jam fieri velis; non te fugiat ex eadem domo non defuisse; qui Regi tuo Poloniæ regnum præripuisse voluerunt. De cæteris vero, quæ non sunt hujus loci & temporis cum plura sint, et singulatim consideranda; illud expecta quod ex quibusdam meis consiliaris huic Rei designandis, intelliges. Interea vero valeas, et quiescas."

The effect whereof in English followeth:

"Oh, how was I deceived! I looked for an ambassage, but thou hast brought a complaint unto me. I understood by thy letter that thou wert a legate, but I finde thee a herault. Never in my life heard I such an oration; truly I marvell at so great and such unaccustomed bouldnesse in a publique assembly. Neither doe I thinke, if the Kinge were present, that hee would say so much; but if peradventure hee hath committed any such thing to thy charge (which surely I much doubt) this is the cause. That where the Kinge is young, and not by bloude, but by election, and newly elected, doth not so perfectly uunderstand the cause of handling these businesses with other Princes, which eyther his auncestors have observed with us, or perhappes others will observe, that afterward shall succeede in his place. For thy part, thou seemest to mee to have read many bookes, but not to have come unto the bookes of Princes, but altogether to bee ignorant what is convenient amongst Kings. For thou that makest often mention of the Lawe of Nature and Nations, that when warre doth happen amongst Princes, it is lawfull for the one of them to intercept the warlike helpes of the others, brought from any place, and to beeware least they fall to the losse. This, I say, is the Law of Nature and Nations. Whereas thou doest rehearse a new affinitie with the House of Austria, which nowe thou makest so famous; forget not that there have beene of the same house, that woulde have bereft the kingdome of Polonia from thy King. But for the rest, which bee not to bee spoken of at this place and time, because they are manie, and to be considered of one after another: thou shall expect that which thou shalt understande of some of my councell, to whom I will assign this matter. In the meane time farewell, and be quiet."

Shortly after the sayde Orator, or Poland Embassadour, was called before certayne of her Highnesse honorable Privie Counsell, to witte, the Lord Burghley, then High Treasurer, the Lorde High Admirall, Sir John Fortescue, and Sir Robert Cecill, Principall Secretary: to whome, after the sayd Polande Embassadour hadde delivered his Speech which hee made before the Queene in writing, and excused his rough kinde of speaking, shewing that by his commission signed and sealed by the King in the assembly of the States of Polonia, hee was thereunto enjoyned: hee received a large answere in the name of her Majestie; which properly pertayning to the matter of the Hanses, and aunswering fully and very pertinently the question made by them about their olde priviledges, is sett downe to the full in a booke, intituled, "A Treatise of Commerce."

Embassador from the King of Denmark, 1597.

This yeere also, Arnald Whitfield, Chancellor of the Realme of Denmarke, Embassadour, and Christian Barnikan, his assistant, from the King of Denmarke, arrived here, and were lodged in Fanchurch Streete: these had audience at the Court then at *Tibals*[1], in Essex. On the seventh of September, they made certayne requests, which her Majestie presently answered without pause to every point of their embassage. The first he required, " that whereas there hadd remayned a long league of amitie betweene the two crownes of England and Denmarke, both in the life of the late deceased King and his Predecessors; that it might please her Majestie to confirme and continue the same to the King his maister, nowe newly adopted and crowned."

Her Majesty granted thereunto, on condition the King his master would prove no worse then his Progenitors had done; and in all christian love accepted thereof.

His request was, " that whereas there was great and continuall warres betweene her Majestie and the King of Spayne, whereby much christian bloude was shedde, to the Kinge his master and all other christian Kinges great griefe, and to the great domage and daunger of Christendome; that it would please her Majestie, if in her wisedome shee did see it convenient, to give her consent that the Kinge his master might make a motion of peace; and if hee founde both parties thereto adicted, to proceede further for the effecting thereof."

Her Majestie replying, said, " she thought the Kinge his master was too young to knowe the cause of the breach of the league betweene her Majesty and Spayne; and as it was not broken by her royall consent, nor by any of hers, so it shoulde not bee sued nor sought for by her Majestie, nor any in her behalfe; for, sayde she, know now, and bee it knowne to the Kinge your master, and all princes christned or heathen, that the Queene of England hath no neede to crave peace; for I assure you, said shee, that I never endured one houre of feare, since my first comminge to my kingdome and subjects." He was to desire, " if it might stand to her Majestie's good liking, open traffique with Spaine; and that the goods might not be stayed on the Narrow Seas, as it hath been heretofore."

Her Majesty said, " if any his maister's or subject's goods were so stayed, it was to her unknowne; but if he had any such just complaint, he should (the mat-

[1] The Extracts from Sir Robert Cary's Memoirs, in p. 245, are a continuation of those in p. 216; and the "Wardenship" was that of the City of Carlisle. But his Visit to Theobalds was not in 1594, but in 1597, subsequently to the death of Lord Cobham, which happened in March 1596-7.

ter being made to her counsell knowne) have such redresse as should well content his master and subjects."

He was to returne the Garter, that her Majesty had bestowed upon the King lately deceased, as the manner of all foraine princes is to do. Her Majestie accepted thereof; but told him, " she was sorie to receive it of him; for thereby shee was put in minde of the losse of a most honorable brother and loving friend; and so that shee were assured of his King's love and friendship in the like sorte, she would hereafter to the Kinge his master do the like favour."

The Ambassadour having his audience the day that her Majesty was born, tooke thereby occasion to say, " that sithen it had pleased God on that day (which he was informed was her Majestie's birth-day) to glorifie the worlde with so gratious a creature, who had brought so great happiness to the realme, and the neighbour kingdomes, hee doubted not but that the Kinge his maister shoulde in that happy day have an happy answere of his request," &c.

" I blame you not to expect a reasonable answere and a sufficient; but you may thinke it a great miracle, that a Childe borne at foure of the clock this morning should bee able to aunswere so learned and wise a man as you are, sent from so great a Prince as you bee, about so great and waighty affayres you speake of, and in an unknowne tongue, by three of the clocke in the afternoone." After using with him more prudent and gratious wordes, shee ended, and gave him leave to depart.

Letter from the QUEEN *to* MARGARET LADY NORRIS, *on the death of her Son.*

" MY OWN CROW[1], 22d Sept. 1597.

" Harm not yourself for bootless help, but shew a good example to comfort your dolorous yoke-fellow. Although we have deferred long to represent to you our grieved thoughts, because we liked full ill to yield you the first reflection of misfortune, whom we have alwayes rather sought to cherish and comfort; yet knowing now, that necessity must bring it to your ear, and nature consequently must move both grief and passion in your heart; we resolved no longer to smother,

---

[1] Dr. Fuller, in his " Worthies," in Oxfordshire says, Queen Elizabeth used to call this Lady her *own Crow*, being (as it seemeth) *black* in complexion (a colour which no whit unbecame the faces of her *martial issue*).—Again, speaking of the Families of *Norris* and *Knowlls*, he says, " No County in England can present such a *brace of Families* contemporaries, with such a bunch of Brethren on either, for eminent atchievements. So great their states and stomachs, that they often *justled together:* and

neither our care for your sorrow, or the sympathy of our grief for your loss. Wherein, if it be true that society in sorrow work diminution, we do assure you by this true messenger of our mind, that nature can have stirred no more dolorous

no wonder if Oxfordshire wanted room for them, when all England could not hold them together. Let them be considered, root and branch, first severally, then conjunctively.

Father.	Mother.	Father.	Mother.
Henry Lord Norris (descended from the Viscounts Lovels) whose Father dyed in a manner martyr for the Queen's Mother, executed about the businesse of Anna Bullen.	Margaret, one of the daughters and heirs of John Lord Williams of Tame, Keeper of Queen Elizabeth whilst in restraint under her Sister, and civil unto her in those dangerous dayes.	Sir Francis Knowlls, Treasurer to the Queen's Houshold, and Knight of the Garter, who had been an exile in Germany under Queen Mary deriving himself from Sir Robert Knowlls, that conquering Commander in France.	—— Cary, Sister to Henry Lord Hunsdon, and Cousin-german to Queen Elizabeth, having Mary Bullen for her Mother.

Thus Queen Elizabeth beheld them both, not onely with gracious but grateful eyes.

Ricot in this County was their chief habitation.

Their Issue.

1. William, Marshall of Barwick, who dyed in Ireland, and was Father to Francis afterward Earl of Bark-shire.

2. Sir John, who had *three horses* in one day killed under him in a Battel against the Scots. Camden's Elizabeth, in anno 1578.—But more of him hereafter, p. 422.

3. Sir Thomas, President of Munster. Being hurt in a fight, and counting it a *scratch* rather than a *wound*, he scorned to have it plaistered; as if the balsom of his body would cure it self: but it rancled, festered, gangreen'd, and he dyed thereof.

4. Sir Henry, who dyed about the same time in the same manner.

5. Maximilian, who was slain in the War of Britain.

6. Sir Edward, who led the front at the taking of the Groyn; and fought so valiantly at the siege of Ostend. Of all six, he onely survived his Parents.

Thus the husband was allied to the Queen in *conscience* (fellow-sufferers for the Protestant cause); the wife in *kindred*.

Grays in this County was their chief dwelling.

Their Issue.

1. Sir Henry, whose daughter and sole heir was married to the Lord Paget.

2. Sir William, Treasurer of the Houshold to King James, by whom he was created Baron Knowlls May 3, 1603; Viscount Wallingford 1616; and by King Charles I. in the first of his Reign, Earl of Banbury.

3. Sir Robert, Father to Sir Robert Knowlls of Greys, now living.

4. Sir Francis, who was living at, and chosen a Member of, the late Long Parliament; since dead, aged 99.

5. Sir Thomas, a Commander in the Low Countries.

6. Lettice, though of the weaker sex, may well be recounted with her brethren, as the strongest pillar of the family. Second wife she was to Robert Dudley, Earl of Leicester, and (by a former husband) mother to Robert Devereux, Earl of Essex; both prime favourites in their generations.

affections in you as a Mother for a dear Son, than gratefulness and memory of his service past hath wrought in us his Sovereign apprehension of our miss for so worthy a Servant. But now that Nature's common work is done, and he that was born to dye hath paid his tribute, let that Christian discretion stay the flux of your immoderate grieving, which hath instructed you, both by example and knowledge, that nothing in this kind hath happened but by God's Divine Provi-

" The Norrisses were all *Martis pulli*, men of the sword, and never out of military employment. The Knowlls were rather valiant men than any great souldiers, as little experienced in war. Queen Elizabeth loved the Knowlls for themselves, the Norrisses for themselves and herself, being sensible that she needed such martial men for her service. The Norrisses got more honour abroad; the Knowlls more profit at home, conversing constantly at Court; and no wonder if they were the warmest, who sate next to the Fire. " There was once a Challenge passed betwixt them at certain exercises to be tryed between the two fraternities, the Queen and their aged Fathers being to be the spectators and judges, till it quickly became a flat quarrel betwixt them. (Fragmenta Regalia, in *Knowlls.*) Thus, though at first they may be said to have fenced with rebated rapiers and swords buttoned up, in merriment onely to try their skill and strength; they soon fell to it at sharps indeed, seeking for many years together to supplant one another, such the heart-smoking and then heart-burning betwixt them. And although their inclinations kept them asunder, the one brother-hood coming seldom to Court, the other seldomer to Camp, yet the Knowlls are suspected to have done the Norrisses bad offices, which at last did tend to their mutual hurt; so that it had been happy for both, had these their contests been seasonably turned into a cordial compliance.

" Sir John Norris must be resumed, that we may pay a greater tribute of respect to his memory. He was a most accomplished General, both for a Charge which is the Sword, and a Retreat which is the shield of War. By the latter he purchased to himself immortal praise, when in France he brought off a small handfull of English from a great armfull of enemies; fighting as he retreated, and retreating as he fought; so that alwayes his reer affronted the enemy; a retreat worth ten victories got by surprise, which speak rather the fortune than either the valour or discretion of a Generall.

" He was afterwards sent over with a great command into Ireland, where his success neither answered to his own care nor others' expectation. Indeed hitherto Sir John had fought with right-handed enemies in France and the Netherlands, who was now to fight with left-handed foes, for so may the wilde Irish well be termed (so that this great Master of Defence was now to seek a new guard), who could lye on the coldest earth, swim through the deepest water, run over what was neither earth nor water, I mean bogs and marishes. He found it far harder to find out than fight his enemies, they so secured themselves in fastnesses. Supplies, sown thick in promises, came up thin in performances; so slowly were succours sent unto him.

" At last a great Lord was made Lieutenant of Ireland, of an opposite party to Sir John; there being animosities in the Court of Queen Elizabeth (as well as of later Princes), though her general good success rendered them the less to the publick notice of posterity. It grieved Sir John to the heart, to see one of an opposite faction should be brought over his head, in so much that some conceive his working soul broke the cask of his body, as wanting a vent for his grief and anger; for, going up into his chamber, at the first hearing of the news he suddenly dyed, anno Domini 1597."

dence. And let these lines from your loving and gracious Sovereign serve to assure you, that there shall ever appear the lively character of our estimation of him that *was*, in our gracious care of you and yours that *are left*, in valuing rightly all their faithful and honest endeavours. More at this time we will not write of this unpleasant subject; but have dispatched this Gent. to visit both your Lord and you[1], and to condole with you in the true sense of your love; and to pray that the world may see, what time cureth in a weak mind, that discretion and moderation helpeth in you in this accident, where there is so just cause to demonstrate true patience and moderation.

" Your gracious and loving Sovereign,   E. R."

November 14, the Queenes Majesty came to Westminster; and was there, by commandement from her Counsell, most Royally received by the Maior of London, Aldermen, and Sherifs, in scarlet, and a great number of wealthy Citizens in velvet coates, and chaines of gold, all on horsebacke, in the evening, by torch-light.

The following Letter appears to have some affinity to the " Gesta Grayorum." It purports to be from the Society of the Middle Temple to the Earl of Shrewsbury; and is indorsed, " This Privy Seale beynge brought unto me at X'temas 1597, in respect of the Prince d'Amore's kepinge his Revells in y^t In of Courte, I sent him, by the hands of Mr. Davyes of that house £30. GILB. SHREWSBURY."

" Right Honourable Lord, we send you humble and hearty greetinge. For as much as the ordinarie expence of our publique hospitalitie is such, and so great at all times, in the knowledge and view of all men of right understandinge and consideracion, and that, by new unexpected accidentes of forraine charge and enterteinmentes, the same is at this present so greetly augmented and encreased, that without a benevolent largesse and contribution of the Members and well wishers of this House the same cannot be well defraied and dischardged; these are therefore to request of y^r Ho. as you tender the loves of your fellowes and allyes, and the grace and reputation of this fellowship, whereof we repute and hold you a worthy and principall member and favourer, to lend us such a some of money as to your Ho. shall seem convenient, in favour of our pretended extraordinarye designes; wch wee promise to repaye unto you the 30th day of Februarie next, at our threasurie, from whence we bid you heartyly farewell.

Your very loving freindes,   MIDDLE TEMPLE."
" To the Right Honourable Gilbert Earle of Shrewsburye[2]."

[1] " Though nothing more consolatory and pathetic could be written from a Prince, yet his death went so near to the heart of the Lord, his ancient Father, that he died soon after."   [2] Lodge, vol. III. p 91.

The Queen's Court at Greenwich, in 1598, is thus described by Hentzner:

"We arrived next at the Royal Palace of Greenwich, reported to have been originally built by Humphrey Duke of Gloucester, and to have received very magnificent additions from Henry VII. It was here Elizabeth, the present Queen, was born, and here she generally resides, particularly in Summer, for the delightfulness of its situation. We were admitted, by an order Mr. Rogers procured from the Lord Chamberlain, into the Presence Chamber, hung with rich tapestry, and the floor, after the English fashion, strewed with hay [1], through which the Queen commonly passes in her way to Chapel: at the door stood a Gentleman dressed in velvet, with a gold chain, whose office was to introduce to the Queen any person of distinction that came to wait on her: it was Sunday, when there is usually the greatest attendance of Nobility. In the same Hall were the Archbishop of Canterbury, the Bishop of London, a great number of Counsellors of State, Officers of the Crown, and Gentlemen, who waited the Queen's coming out; which she did from her own apartment when it was time to go to prayers, attended in the following manner: first went Gentlemen, Barons, Earls, Knights of the Garter, all richly dressed and bare-headed; next came the Chancellor, bearing the seals in a red-silk purse, between two: one of which carried the Royal scepter, the other the sword of state, in a red scabbard, studded with golden fleurs de lis, the point upwards: next came the Queen, in the sixty-fifth[2] year of her age, as we were told, very majestic; her face oblong, fair, but wrinkled; her eyes small, yet black and pleasant; her nose a little hooked; her lips narrow, and her teeth black (a defect the English seem subject to, from their too great use of sugar); she had in her ears two pearls, with very rich drops; she wore false hair, and that red; upon her head she had a small crown, reported to be made of some of the gold of the celebrated Lunebourg Table[3]. Her bosom was uncovered, as all the English Ladies have it till they marry; and she had on a necklace of exceeding fine jewels; her hands were small, her fingers long, and her stature neither tall nor low; her air was stately, her manner of speaking mild and obliging. That day she was dressed in white silk, bordered with pearls of the size of beans, and over it a mantle of black silk, shot with silver threads; her train was very long, the end of it borne by a Marchioness; instead of a chain, she had an oblong

---

[1] He probably means rushes.

[2] This fixes the period of Hentzner's Visit to the year 1598. She was born Sept. 7, 1533.

[3] At this distance of time, it is difficult to say what this was.

collar of gold and jewels. As she went along in all this state and magnificence, she spoke very graciously, first to one, then to another, whether foreign ministers, or those who attended for different reasons, in English, French, and Italian; for, besides being well skilled in Greek, Latin, and the languages I have mentioned, she is mistress of Spanish, Scotch, and Dutch: whoever speaks to her, it is kneeling[1]; now and then she raises some with her hand. While we were there, W. Slawata, a Bohemian Baron, had letters to present to her; and she, after pulling off her glove, gave him her right hand to kiss, sparkling with rings and jewels, a mark of particular favour; whereever she turned her face, as she was going along, every body fell down on their knees. The Ladies of the Court followed next to her, very handsome and well-shaped, and for the most part dressed in white; she was guarded on each side by the Gentlemen Pensioners, fifty in number, with gilt battle-axes. In the anti-chapel next the Hall, where we were, petitions were presented to her, and she received them most graciously, which occasioned the acclamation of "Long live Queen Elizabeth!" She answered it with, "I thank you, my good people." In the Chapel was excellent music; as soon as it and the service was over, which scarce exceeded half an hour, the Queen returned in the same state and order, and prepared to go to dinner. But while she was still at prayers, we saw her table set out with the following solemnity[2]: a Gentleman entered the room bearing a rod, and along with him another who had a table cloth, which, after they had both kneeled three times with the utmost veneration, he spread upon the table, and after kneeling again, they both retired. Then came two others, one with the rod again, the other with a salt-seller, a plate, and bread; when they had kneeled, as the others had done, and placed what was brought upon the table, they too retired with the same ceremonies performed by the first. At last came an unmarried Lady (we were told she was a Countess) and along with her a married one, bearing a tasting-knife; the former was dressed in white silk, who, when she had prostrated herself three times in the most graceful manner, approached the

[1] Her Father had been treated with the same deference. It is mentioned by Fox, in his Acts and Monuments, that when the Lord Chancellor went to apprehend Queen Catharine Parr, he spoke to the King on his knees. King James I. suffered his courtiers to omit it. Bacon's Papers, vol. II. p. 516.

[2] "The excess of respectful ceremonial used at decking her Majesty's table, though not in her presence, and the kind of adoration and genuflection paid to her person, approach to Eastern homage. When we observe such worship offered to an old woman, with bare neck, black teeth, and false red hair, it makes one smile; but makes one reflect what masculine sense was couched under those weaknesses, and which could command such awe from a nation like England!" WALPOLE

table, and rubbed the plates with bread and salt, with as much awe as if the Queen had been present: when they had waited there a little while, the Yeomen of the Guard entered, bare-headed, cloathed in scarlet, with a golden rose upon their backs, bringing in at each turn a course of twenty-four dishes, served in plate, most of it gilt; these dishes were received by a gentleman in the same order they were brought, and placed upon the table, while the lady-taster gave to each of the guards a mouthful to eat, of the particular dish he had brought, for fear of any poison. During the time that this guard, which consists of the tallest and stoutest men that can be found in all England, being carefully selected for this service, were bringing dinner, twelve trumpets and two kettle-drums made the hall ring for half an hour together. At the end of this ceremonial, a number of unmarried ladies appeared, who, with particular solemnity, lifted the meat off the table, and conveyed it into the Queen's inner and more private chamber, where, after she had chosen for herself, the rest goes to the Ladies of the Court. The Queen dines and sups alone, with very few attendants; and it is very seldom that any body, foreigner or native, is admitted at that time, and then only at the intercession of somebody in power.

Near this Palace is the Queen's park stocked with deer: such parks are common throughout England, belonging to those who are distinguished either for their rank or riches. In the middle of this is an old square tower, called *Mirefleur*, supposed to be that mentioned in the Romance of Amadis de Gaul; and joining to it a plain, where knights and other gentlemen used to meet, at set times and holidays, to exercise on horseback.

Death and Funeral of Lord BURLEIGH.

"August 4, 1598, Sir William Cecil, Knight of the Order [of the Garter], Lord Burghley, Master of the Wards and Liveries, High Treasurer of England, a famous Counsellor to the Queene's Majesty all her raigne, and likewise had been to Edward the Sixt, who, for his singular wisedome, was renowned throughout all Europe, departed this mortall life at his house by the Strande[1]. His body was conveyed to Westminster with solemne funerall; and from thence secretly to Stanford, and there buried amongst his ancestors[2]."

The Register of St. Martin's at Stanford says, " William Cicel Lord Burleigh [was there] buried xxix August, 1598."

" In Mr. Holland's Herωologia Anglicana (after an account of his death, &c. as above), it is said, ' cujus exequiæ magno apparatu & tanto viro dignissimæ, hic [Westmonasterio] sunt celebratæ die xxix ejusdem mensis [Augusti;] corpusque quod in hac ecclesia sex dies requievit, Stanfordiam in ecclesiam S. Martini translatum fuit.' So that it seems his funeral was celebrated on one and the same day, both at Westminster Abby and at Stanford. Whence arises this question. Where then was his corps on the said xxix day of August? At Westminster it seems to be, since Mr. Holland, after relating that his funeral was performed at Westminster on the xxix of August, then speaks (if I understand him right) of his body's being removed to Stanford. At Stanford it seems to be, since the parish register tells us, he was there buried on the said xxix day of August. But at both it could not be at the same time.

" I suppose therefore there was only an empty coffin, carried in great pomp, with a solemn procession of Heralds, Gentlemen, and Noblemen, to Westminster

---

[1] The Queen is said to have held her Court at Theobalds in 1598, being a few days only before the death of Lord Burleigh.—Repeated instances have been given, in various parts of these Volumes, of her Majesty's great esteem for this eminent Nobleman, one of her most trusty and sagacious Counsellors. And one more shall here be added from Harrington's " Nugæ Antiquæ," under the title of " Wordes spoken by the Queen to Master Cecil, afterwards Lord Burleigh:" " I give you this chardge, that you shall be of my Privie Counseille, and content yourself to take paines for me and my realme. This judgement I have of you, that you will not be corrupted with anie maner of guifte, and that you will be faithfull to the State, and that, without respect of my private will, you will give me that counseile that you thinck best; and if you shall know anie thinge necessarie to be declared to me of secreasie, you shall shew it to myself onlie, and assure yourself I will not faile to keep taciturnitie therein. And thearfore hearewith I chardge you."

[2] Stow, p. 787.

Abby, where the said coffin was set in the midst of the Choir, under a herse, adorned with scutcheons, penons, and other ornaments, and there stood six days, attended by heralds and other mourners; at the end of which six days, a solemn service, with the music of the Queen's Chapel (in manner of a funeral), was there performed for the deceased; whose body (being some few days before conveyed privately to Stanford) was there put into the vault on the same day the said funeral was more pompously set forth at Westminster. Stow, indeed, says, 'his bodie was conveied to Westminster with solemn funeral, and from thence to Stanford, and there buried amongst his ancestours [1].'"

Among other commendable actions of this great Statesman, may be recorded his building an Hospital at Stanford, near his house at Burleigh, and endowing it, for the maintenace of thirteen poor men for ever [2].

The following lines are extracted from the Manuscript Letters of Mr. John Chamberlain [3], to Mr. (afterwards Sir Dudley) Carleton:

"September 17th, 1598. The Queen removed on Wednesday [Sept.18] towards Nonsuch, taking Dr. Cæsar [4] [at Mitcham] in her way, who had provided for her *eight* several times."

[1] Peck's Desiderata Curiosa, vol. I. p. 42.

[2] In Peck's Desiderata, vol. I. p. 174, are printed " Ordinances made by Sir William Cecill, Knight of the Order of the Garter, Baron of Burghley, for the Order and Government of xiii Poor Men, whereof one to be Warden of the Hospital of Stanford Baron, in the County of Northampton; to remain in a Chest in a Chamber in the said Hospital, locked up with two several locks, the keys whereof to be in the Custody of the Vicar of S. Martin's and the Bailiff of the Manor. xx Augusti, Anno xxxix Elizabethae Reginae; & Anno Domini 1597."

[3] " Mr. John Chamberlain was a gentleman well accomplished in learning and languages, both ancient and modern, and by the advantages of travelling, and an intimacy with some of the most considerable men of his time, though I can find few circumstances relating to the personal history of him. One indeed of both his names was Member for Clitheroe in Lancashire, in the Parliament which met at Westminster, Nov. 19, 1592; and for St. Germain's in Cornwall, in the Parliament of 1597; but I cannot determine whether this was the Friend of Sir Thomas Bodley and Sir Ralph Winwood, as well as the Correspondent of Sir Dudley Carleton. The last of these he accompanied to Venice, when Sir Dudley was sent thither Ambassador, in September 1610." (Winwood's Memorials, vol. II. p. 213; but he returned to London, 3 Nov.) Dr. Birch, MS.

[4] Julius Cæsar, Doctor of Laws, knighted in 1603, and made Master of the Rolls. In a MS. of his, intituled, " A Short Memorial, or brief Chronicle of things past, concerning my Father, myself,

Extracts from Sir JOHN HARRINGTON'S *" Notes and Observations,"*
continued from p. 250.

" October 1598. I this day wente to the new Lord High Treasurer, Lord Buckhurst. I was not ill receivede; nor, in soothe, so well as I had beene usede to in the daye of Lorde Burleigh. When shall oure realme see suche a man, or when suche a Mistresse have suche a servante: well mighte one weepe when the other diede [1]. This choice doth well assure us, that in the witte of the servante dwellethe the master's fortune, and that all states have thriven better or worse, as the government was given to such as were honest as well as able. If a Kinge hathe not discernmente to chuse a few wise heads, how shall he subdue the many foolish hearts; or how shall the leaves and blossom flourish when the sap is corruptede at the roote of the plante? I coud herewithe cite manie good authorities, both Greek and Latin, to prove this mine opinion, but I do remember what Burleigh did once saye in my hearinge to Walsingham, who had been waiting to confer with him aboute manie great matters, whereof I had borne some parte, in bearinge a message from the Queen to Hatton. When my Lord Treasurer did come in from prayers, Sir Francis Walsingham did in merrie sorte say, that 'he wished himself so goode a servant of God as Lord Burleigh, but that he had not been at church for a week past.' Now my Lord Burleigh did gravely replye thus: 'I hold it meete for us to aske God's grace to keep *us* sounde of hearte, who have so much in our powre, and to direct us to the well doinge of all the people, whom it is easie for us to injure and ruine; and herein, my good friendes, the special blessinge seemethe meete to be discretely askede and wisely worne.' I did not a little marvele at this goode discourse, to see how a good man considerethe his weightie charge,

my Wives, and Children;" he mentions, " that on Tuesday, Sept. 12, 1598, the Queen visited him at his house at Mitcham, and supped and lodged and dined there the next day; and that he presented her with a gown of cloth of silver richly embroidered, a black work mantle with pure gold, a taffeta hat white with several flowers, and a jewel of gold set therein with silver and diamonds.—Her Majesty," adds he, " removed from my house after dinner, the 13th of September, to Nonsuch, with exceeding good contentment. Which Entertainment of her Majesty, with the charges of *five former disappointments,* amounted to £700 sterling, besides mine own provisions, and whatever was sent unto me by my friends."—In a Letter from Rowland White to Sir Robert Sidney, Sept. 30, 1596, the Queen's *intention* to visit Mitcham is mentioned; at which time, probably, one of the five disappointments here alluded to happened. Mr. Chamberlain mentions *eight.*

[1] See the Letters of Mr. Robert Markham and Sir Robert Sidney.

and strivethe to keepe oute Satane from corruptinge the hearte in discharge of his duties. Howe fewe have suche heartes or such heads, and therefore shall I note this for those who read hereafter."

"It is worthie noting, when we finde how little sure happiness is allotted even to the mightie on earthe. Philip II. of Spain reigned fortie-two years in troubles and disquietudes [1], loste his Provinces, whilst he was stringinge to enlarge his possessions, and then in olde age was eaten by lice when livinge. God grante me me no further ambition than to be eaten by wormes when I am deade! and this I said to the Queene."

"The Queene seemede troublede to-daye; Hatton came out from her presence with ill countenance, and pulled me aside by the girdle, and saide in secrete waie, 'If you have any suite to daie, I praye you put it aside, *the sunne dothe not shine.*' 'Tis this accursede Spanishe businesse, so will I not adventure her Highnesse *choller*, lest she should *collar* me also."

"News from the Ambassadours to France. Wilkes [2] died at Paris; God speed Cecil and Herbert, or we shall ill speede at home. It is a base matter of Henrie of France, to make peace withouten his allies and friends: I coude wishe her Highnesse could once rounde him in the eare aboute this matter; she seemethe in apte sorte for such businesse, for she callede him in my hearinge, 'the Antichriste of ingratitude.'" [*See hereafter, p. 443.*]

Sir John Stanhope, in a Letter to Sir Robert Cecil, Nov. 3, 1598, says, "I have been redyng Mr. Edmonds' letter, and y^{rs} to her Ma^{ye}, the wch cam not to my handes tyll six a clocke, for I was all the afternowne wth her Ma^{ye} at my booke, and then, thynkynge to rest me, went in agayne wth yor letter. She was plesed with the filosofer's stone, and had ben all this day reasonably quyett, and hath hearde at lardge the dyscourse of the calamytys of Kerry, expressed by Sr Edward Denys in a very lamentable sorte; where he hath lost houses, ground, corne, cattell, and all his studd of horses, and awereth a revenge, to the wch the Q. hath harted him wth promysse of imployment. Of all the French nues I do not find

[1] He died Sept. 13, 1598.

[2] Sir Thomas Wilkes, from whom several letters occur in the Sydney Papers, vol. I. where some account of him is given. He died in 1598. Sir Robert Cecil was his colleague in his last embassy to France.

anye grete apprehensyon taken, save of the procurynge of the maryadge at Rome betwixt the K. and his M^rs, the wch howe yt can sounde well in a relygus Prince's eares yow can judge. The Q. saeth th' Ymbassador gave her this letter yesterday from the French K. wch importeth some complaints against her subjects: she opened yt, but redd yt not, but wysheth yow to confer wth my Lo. Admyrall about yt, and to sho yt hym, but to take hede yow lose not the seale of yt, wch will scarce stick on. Yt were good some Councelors were sent hether, for this Courte hath not had any one this daye. Mr. Grevell is absent, and I am tyed so as I cannot styrr, but shallbe at the wourse for yt thes two dayes. Yesternight my Lo. of Cumberlande was wth her after supper; then my Lo. Graye, and th' Erle of Rut. wth dyvers others, all nyght tyll 12 a clocke. And so I humbly recommend yow my servyce, and rest yor Honor's,

J. STANHOPE[1]."

"Nov. 20, 1598. The Queen came to Whitehall the last week, being received a mile out of town by the Lord Mayor and his Brethren, accompanied with 400 Velvet Coats and Chains of Gold. *Her day*[2] passed without any extraordinary matter more than running and ringing[3]."

In 1598 John Spilman obtained an exclusive grant from the Queen, "that he only, and no others, should buy lynnen ragges, and make paper[4]."

[1] Lodge, vol. III. p. 95.
[2] Her Accession to the Throne, Nov. 17.
[3] Chamberlain's MS. Letters.
[4] See Churchyard's Verses on Spilman's Paper Mill at Dartford, in vol. II. p. 592.

The Earl of Essex's *Departure for Ireland*, 1599.

The Earl of Essex, of whom the Queene had made speciall choyce of all the Nobilitie, as well for his martiall experience and general love of all sorts of people, as otherwise most fit for that speciall imployment, was as aforesaide sent by her Majesty into Ireland in March, to suppresse the stronge Rebel Hugh Tyrone, whose faction at that time had almost overrunne the whole land.

The ceremony of his departure is thus described:

The twentie-seventh of March, 1599, about two a clocke in the afternoone, Robert Earle of Essex, Vicegerent of Irelande [1], &c. tooke horse in Seeding-lane, and from thence, being accompanied with divers Noblemen and many others, himselfe very plainely attired, roade through Grace-streete, Cornehill, Cheapside,

[1] The total reduction of Ireland being brought upon the tapis, the Earl was pitched upon as the only man from whom it could be expected. This was an artful contrivance of his enemies, who hoped by this means to ruin him; nor were their expectations disappointed. He declined this fatal preferment as long as he could; but, perceiving that he should have no quiet at home, he accepted it, and his commission for Lord Lieutenant passed the Great Seal in March 1598-9. His enemies now began to insinuate, that he had sought this command for the sake of greater things which he then was meditating; but there is a Letter of his to the Queen, preserved in the Harleian collections, which shews, that he was so far from entering upon it with alacrity, that he looked upon it rather as a banishment, and a place assigned him for a retreat from his Sovereign's displeasure, than a potent Government bestowed upon him by her favour:

"To the QUEEN,

"From a mind delighting in sorrow, from spirits wasted with passion, from a heart torn to pieces with care, grief, and travel, from a man that hateth himself, and all things else that keep him alive, what service can your Majesty expect, since any service past deserves no more than banishment and proscription to the cursedest of all islands? It is your rebels pride and succession must give me leave to ransom myself out of this hateful prison, out of my loathed body; which, if it happened so, your Majesty shall have no cause to mislike the fashion of my death, since the course of my life could never please you.

"Happy he could finish forth his fate,
  In some unhaunted desert most obscure
From all society, from love and hate
  Of worldly folk; then should he sleep secure.
Then wake again, and yield God ever praise,
  Content with hips and hawes, and brambleberry;
In contemplation passing out his days,
  And change of holy thoughts to make him merry.
Who when he dies his tomb may be a bush,
Where harmless robin dwells with gentle thrush.

"Your Majesty's exiled servant,   ROBERT ESSEX."

and other high streets; in all which places and in the fieldes the people pressed exceedingly to beholde him, especially in the high wayes for more then foure myles space, crying and saying, "God blesse your Lordship, God preserve your honour," &c. and some followed him untill the evening, onely to beholde him: when hee and his companie came foorth of London, the skie was very calme and cleere; but before hee could get past Iseldon, there arose a great blacke cloude in the north-east, and sodainely came lightning and thunder; with a great shower of haile and raine; the which some helde as an ominous prodigie.

The FORTUNATE FAREWELL to the most forward and Noble Earle of ESSEX, one of the Honorable Privie Counsel, Earle High Marshal of England, Master of the Horse, Master of the Ordinance, Knight of the Garter, and Lord Lieutenant General of all the Queenes Majestie's Forces in Ireland. Dedicated to the Right Honorable the Lord HARRY SEAMER, second sonne to the last Duke of Sommerset.—Written by THOMAS CHURCHYARD, Esquire[1].

To the Right Honorable the Lord HARRY SEAMER, Thomas Churchyard wisheth continuance of vertue, blessednesse of minde, and wished felicitie.

In all duty (my good Lord) I am bold, because your most houorable father the Duke of Sommerset (uncle to the renowmed impe of grace Noble King *Edward* the Sixt) favoured me when I was troubled before the Lords of the Counsell, for writing some of my first verses: in requital whereof ever since I have honored all his noble race; and knowing your Lordship in sea services forward and ready in all honorable manner (sparing for no charges) when the Spanyards approched neere our countrie, I bethought me how I might be thankfull for good turnes found of your noble progenie, though unable; therefore finding my life unfurnished of all things woorthy presentation and acceptance, I tooke occasion of the departure of a most woorthy Earle towardes the service in Ireland, so made a present to your Lordship of his happy farewell as I hope; and trust to live and see his wished welcome home. This farewell onlie devised to stirre up a threefold manly courage to the mercenarie multitude of soldiers that follow this marshall-like Generall, and especially to move all degrees in generall loyally to serve our good

[1] Printed at London by Edm. Bollifant, for William Wood, at the West doore of Powles, 1599.

Queene Elizabeth, and valiantly to go through with good resolution the acceptable service they take in hand. Which true service shall redouble their renowne, and enroll their names in the memoriall booke of Fame for ever. I feare I leade your Lordship too farre with the flourish of a fruitlesse pen, whose blandishing phrase makes many to gaze at, and few to consider well of and regarde. My plot is onely laide to purchase good will of vertuous people; what the rest thinke, let their miscontruing conceites answere their owne idle humors. This plaine present winning your Lordships good liking, shall passe with the greater grace to his honorable hands, that the praiers and power of good men waites willingly upon towards the reformation of wicked rebellion.

Your Lordships in all commandement, THOMAS CHURCHYARD.

The happy Farewell to the fortunate and forward most Noble Earle of ESEX.

Now *Scipio* sails to Affrick far from hoem,
    The Lord of Hoests and battels be his gied;
Now when green trees begin to bud and bloem,
    On Irish seas *Eliza's* ships shall ried:
A warliek band of worthy knights, I hoep,
    Aer armd for fight, a bloedy brunt to bied,
With rebels shall boeth might and manhoed coep,
    Our countreis right and quarrell to be tried:
Right makes Wrong blush, and Troeth bids Falshed fly,
    The sword is drawn, *Tyroens* dispatch draws nye.

A traitor must be taught to know his King;
    When *Mars* shal march, with shining sword in hand,
A craven cock cries creak, and hangs down wing,
    Will run about the shraep and daer not stand.
When cocks of gaem coms in to give a bloe,
    So false *Tyroen* may faint when he would fight,
Thogh now alowd on dunghill duth he croe,
    Traitors wants hart, and often taeks the flight:
When rebels see they aer surpriesd by troeth,
Pack hence, in haest away the rebels goeth.

Proud trecherous trash is curbd and knockt with bloes,
   By loftie mindes with force are beaten down;
Against the right, thought oft rued rebels roes,
   Not oen sped well that did impeach a Crown.
Read the Annaels of all the Princes past,
   Whear treasons still are punisht in their kinde,
Thear shall you see, when faithfull men stand fast,
   False traytors still are but a blast of winde:
For he that first formd Kings and all degrees,
The ruel of Staets and Kingdoms oversees.

Riot and rage this rank rebellion breeds;
   Havock and spoyl sets bloudshed so abroetch,
Roethles attempts their filthy humor feeds;
   Rashnes runs on all hedlong to reproetch:
Wildness begaet theas helhounds all a roe,
   The sons of shaem, and children of Gods wraeth,
With wolvish minds, liek breetchles beares they goe
   Throw woods and bogs, and many a crooked path;
Lying, liek dogs, in litter, dung, and strawe,
Bred as bruet beasts that knoes ne ruel nor lawe.

Fostred from faith, and fear of God or man:
   Unlernd, or taught, of any graces good;
Nurst up in vice, whear falsehed first began;
   Mercyles boern, still sheading giltles blood.
Libertiens lewd, that all good order haets;
   Murtherers viel of women great with childe;
Cruell as kiets, despising all estaets;
   Divlishly bent, boeth currish, stern, and wilde:
Their whoel device is rooet of mischeeves all,
That seeks a plaeg on their own heds to fall.

Will God permit such monsters to beare sway,
   His justice haets the steps of tyrants still;
Their damnable deeds craves vengeance every day,
   Which God doth scourge by his own blessed will.

He planteth force to fling down feeble strength;
  Men of mutch worth to weaken things of noght
Whoes cloked craft shall suer be seen at length,
  When unto light dark dealings shall be broght
Sweet civill Lords shall sawsy fellowes meet,
Who must ask grace on knees at honors feet.

Ruednes may range a while in ruffling sort,
  As witlesse wights with wandring maeks world mues,
But when powre coms to cut prowd practise short,
  And shoe by sword how subjects Prince abues;
Then conshens shall Peccavi cry in feeld,
  Tremble and quaek much liek an aspin leaf;
But when on knees do conquerd captives yeeld,
  The victor turns his hed as he wear deaf:
Rueth is grown cold, Revenge is hot as fier,
And Mercy sits with frowns in angry attier.

World past fosgave great faults, and let them pas;
  Time present loeks on futuer time to come;
All ages sawe their follies in a glas,
  Yet were not taught by Time, nor sound of drom.
This world grows blind, and neither sees nor heers;
  Their senses fail; the wits and reason faints;
Old world is waxt worm-eaten by long yeers;
  And men becom black divels that were saints:
Yet God's great grace this wretched caus reforms,
And from fayr flowrs weeds out the wicked worms.

They com that shall redresse great things amis,
  Pluck up the weeds, plant roses in their place;
No violent thing enduers long as hit is;
  Falsehed flies fast from sight of true men's face;
Traitors do fear the plaegs for them prepard,
  And hieds their heds in hoels when troeth is seen;

Thogh gracelesse gives to duty small regard,
    Good subjects yeelds obedience to their Queen:
In quarrels just do thousands offer lives,
They feel fowl bobs that for their bucklars strives.

This Lord doth bring for strength the fear of God,
    The love of men, and sword of justice both;
Which three is to *Tyroen* an iron rod,
    A birtchin twig, that draws bloed where it goeth.
When *Joab* went to warr in *David's* right,
    He broght hoem peace in spite of emnies beard;
For *Jozias* the Lord above did fight
    With Angels force, that maed the foes afeard;
The world doth shaek and tremble at his frown,
Whoes beck soon casts the brags of rebels down.

Stand fast and suer; false traitors turn their back;
    True subjects veaw maeks haerbrain rebels blush;
Stout heavy bloes maeks highest trees to crack;
    An armed piek may bravely bied a push;
Wheel not about, stand stiff liek brazen wall,
    For that's the way to win the feeld indeed;
Charge the foer front, and see the emnies fall,
    The cowards brag is but a rotten reed:
Victors must beare the brunt of evry shock,
A constant minde is liek a stony rock.

Farewell, sweet Lords, Knights, Captains, and the rest,
    Who goes with you, taeks threefold thankfull pain;
Who sets you forth, is ten times treble blest,
    Who serves you well, reaps glory for their gain;
Who dies, shall live in faem among the best;
    Who lives, shall loek and laugh theas broils to scorn;
All honest harts doth civill war detest,
    And curse the time that ear *Tyroen* was born:
We hoep good hap waits on the fleet that goes,
And Gods great help shall clean destroy our foes

The Earl of Essex having spent all the Summer of 1599 in suppressing and preventing many practises and attempts of Tyrone; and being incensed by some of his inward friends concerning many matters in England, whose instigations were strongly seconded by the opinion of divers about him; besides his owne perticular jelousie, that, during his absence, her Majestie's wonted kindnesse and princely graces were many wayes declined, his friends discountenaunced, and his hope of further preferment frustrated; for redresse whereof hee was much perplexed, and after divers consultations with his sure freinds, who disswaded him from attempting any violent course, because the Earle meant to returne into England with three thousand choyce souldiers and competent leaders; making no doubt to have friends enough at his arrivall, for coroboration against all common encounters: but when hee well perceived it woulde prove a daungerous disturbance of the estate, hee declined.

On the 24th of June the Queen was present at the marriage of Mrs. Mary Hennyngham[1].

On the 26th and 27th days of July the Ringers at Lambeth were paid 5s. 6d. "when the Queen came from Greenwich to Foxehalle[2]; and it is remarked, that "the ringers gave their attendance the first day; and her Majestie came not till the next day."—At the time of this Visit the manor of Foxeshall was held on lease from the Crown by Bartholomew Clarke.

[1] See p. 467.

[2] This shews the orthography of that mansion in the 16th century; but as the etymology of the name, though often the object of discussion, is not generally known, I shall transcribe some observations on it by the Rev. Samuel Denne, a very learned and accurate Antiquary, in his Appendix to the History of Lambeth Parish; premising, however, that Mr. Bray in his "History of Surrey" does not agree with Messrs. Lysons and Denne in the derivation of the name of Faukes-hall: "King John bestowed upon Fouk, alias Faulk (Falcasius) de Brent, a Norman by birth, the very opulent heiress Margaret de Ripariis or Redvers; an union reported to have been to her no less discontentment than discouragement, he being a bastard of mean extraction, and a profligate rogue.—By this marriage he became possessor of the manor in Lambeth, to which Faukshall was annexed; and Mr. Lysons has with probability suggested, that it might be from him the district acquired its appellation. Weight will be added to this surmise, if it be considered, that in Annales Ecclesiæ Wigorniensis, his name, as also that of a brother, is repeatedly spelt *Faukisius;* whence it may be presumed, that in English he was vulgarly called Faukes. According to this annalist he had sacrilegiously pillaged the Church of Worcester, and, trusting to the great riches he had amassed in the troubles of those times, he, in 1224, daringly seized the Castle of Bedford, within which he detained as his prisoner Henry de Breis-

August 1, 1599. Mr. Chamberlain informs us, that "The Queen removed from Greenwich the 27th of the last month; and dined the same day at Mon-

brook, one of the King's Justices. After a siege of eight months, Faukes' brother, who commanded in the castle, was obliged to surrender at discretion, and he and near a hundred of his accomplices were hanged. Fawkes, with all humility, implored mercy of the King, who committed him to the custody of Eustace de Fauconberge, Bishop of London, till judgement should be passed on him. The nobles being soon convoked at Westminster, Henry required them to give sentence, and in consideration of the traitor's former services to the King and his father, a remission was granted as to life and limb, and he ordered to abjure the realm. Being reduced thus low, this distich was written of him:

> Perdidit in mense Fulco, tam fervidus ense,
> Omine sub sævo, quicquid quæsivit ab ævo.

This estate, however, which belonged to Margaret de Ripariis, was not affected by the confiscation; she representing to the King she was taken by violence in a time of hostility, and betrothed unwillingly to Faukes, and urging this as a plea why she ought to be divorced from him.

In the same Reign, Margaret de Ripariis held the manor of Lambeth in dower from her late husband Baldwin Earl of Devonshire, but of the inheritance of Isabel de Fortibus, Countess of Albemarle, sister and heir of Baldwin, styled also de Insula, because he was proprietor of the Isle of Wight."— Passing over some intermediate possessors (which may be seen in Mr. Denne's Appendix, pp. 411—414,) we learn that "Edward the Black Prince had probably from his father, a grant in perpetuity of the manor, he having appropriated it for the maintenance of two priests, who were to officiate in a chantry chapel, called after his name, because founded by him in Canterbury Cathedral. A house in the parish of St. Alphage, a part of which is still to be seen, was allotted for the residence of the priests; and out of the revenues of Faukeshall manor, which was settled on the prior and the convent of Christ Church, was to be allowed, for the maintenance of the priests, a yearly stipend of 40 marks, above all charges of reparation or otherwise.—At the dissolution of the Priory, the manor reverted to the Crown; but, on the establishment of a Dean and Chapter by Henry the VIIIth it was made a parcel of their endowment. The oldest court-roll of the manor now existing is dated 1649, in which it is spelt Faux Hall. Thomas Hardress was steward from 1649 to 1681, under the successive description of Esquire, Serjeant at Law, and Knight. Isaac Bargrave, of Eastry in Kent, was Steward in 1795. Lands in Stockwell, and in the parishes of Streatham and Mitcham, are holden of this manor, and its jurisdiction extends to those districts. There is a court-leet and court-baron, and at the former the annual officers, such as constable for Fauxhall and its dependencies, are sworn into office. The copyhold tenants do not exceed sixty. The fine on admission certain, being only double the small reserved rent to the Lord; and the estates, not being heriotable, are in value equal to a freehold, and in goodness of titles preferable, and descend as Borow English lands, viz. to the younger son. (The Gentleman's Magazine, vol. LVII. pp. 309, 572, from the Court Rolls.)

"The manor-house and contiguous ground have been long demised in two leases; one under the title of Manor, the other styled Fauxhall Wharfe."

Mr. Denne then gives the names of the several tenants both of the Manor and the Wharf from 1564 to 1755, when the late Sir Joseph Mawbey became tenant of the Wharf, as he did soon after of the Manor.—Oliver St. John, gent. was tenant of the Manor in the 6th year of Queen Elizabeth; Bartho-

sieur Caron's [1], and so to the Lord Burleigh's at Wimbledon [2], where she tarried three days, and is now at Nonsuch [3].—On this occasion the following entry occurs in the Churchwardens' Accompts at Kingston: " Paid for mending the wayes when the Queen went from Wimbledon to Nonsuch, 20d [4]."

On the 12th of August the Queen honoured Mr. Coke, then Attorney General, with her presence at the christening of his child [5].

lomew Clarke in the 20th year; William Forster in the 44th; and from him it passed in the same year to Sir Edmund Bowyer.

Of Mr. Clarke no notice is given by Mr. Denne.—The other three tenants are thus mentioned:

Oliver St. John.—Oliver having been a Christian name not uncommon among the St. Johns, who were afterwards ennobled, it is likely that this gentleman might be related to the family. He was an inhabitant of Lambeth, and probably resided in the manor-house. In the Churchwardens' Book of Accompts, under the years 1559 and 1560, he is thus entered as present in Vestry: " Mr. Sen John, and Olyver Sen John, gent." He was purchaser of some of the vestments used in the time of popery, and of the sepulchre cloth, and he was in arrear as long as he lived for a part of the money. He died in 1572, there being in that year's receipts an item for 4s. for a piece of black cloth which was his herse cloth; and there is a charge of 20s. for paving over Mr. St. John's grave in the church.

William Forster.—In the receipts of voluntary contributions towards finishing the seats in the church, is this entry, " anno 1616, of Sir William Foster, knight, deceased, £2."

Sir Edmund Bowyer—did not live in the manor-house in 1623; he is mentioned as resident in Lambeth Deane, for his contribution of 7s. 6d. towards re-building the church-yard wall, &c.

It may be worth while to add, that the Manor-house of Fauxhall (sometimes called Copt-hall), is totally distinct from the well-known Vauxhall, so celebrated for its gardens, which probably owed their origin to Sir Samuel Morland in 1665. See Bray's Surrey, III. 490.

[1] Sir Noel Caron was Ambassador from the States of Holland for twenty-eight years, in the Reigns of Elizabeth and James the First. He built a noble house at South Lambeth, where he had a park for deer, which extended to Vauxhall and Kennington Lane. The house, which was in the form of a Roman H, and on the gate whereof was written " OMNE SOLUM FORTI PATRIA," was pulled down in 1687: and a moderate-sized house was built on the site of it. This was also pulled down in 1810. It appears by the above-cited extract, that, on the 27th of July 1599 he was honoured with a Visit from the Queen; who gave him on the 15th of October following, on his departure out of England, a present of ten chains of gold, weighing together more than 68 ounces. (see p. 467). In 1607 he obtained a lease for 21 years of the Prince of Wales's manor of Kennington, with all the houses, buildings, &c. containing 122 acres, at an annual rent of £16. 10s. 9d. In the same year he gave £10 towards the repairs of Lambeth Church, and £50 to the poor. In 1615 he built an almshouse, by the road leading from Vauxhall to Kingston, for seven poor women; and secured to each of them an annual pension of £4.—His helmet, coat of mail, gauntlets, and spurs, together with his arms (Sable, a bend Azure, semé of fleurs de lis Or), were placed in Lambeth Church, and are still in good preservation. See Nichols's History of that Parish, pp. 92. 114.   [2] See before, p. 413.

[3] From Mr. Chamberlain's Letters.   [4] Lysons, vol. I. p. 251.   [5] See p. 467.

In the month of August, the Queen paid a visit to Sir Francis Carew at Bedington in Surrey, for three days, and again in the same week the ensuing year[1]. The Queen's Oak, and her favourite Wall, are still pointed out; and in the garden was a pleasure-house, on the top of which was painted the Spanish Invasion. Sir Hugh Platt[2] tells an anecdote respecting one of these Visits, which shews the pains Sir Francis took in the management and cultivation of his forest trees: " Here I will conclude," says he, " with a conceit of that delicate Knight Sir Francis Carew, who, for the better accomplishment of his Royal Entertainment of our late Queen Elizabeth of happy memory at his house at Bedington, led her Majesty to a cherry-tree, whose fruit he had of purpose kept back from ripening, at the least one month after all cherries had taken their farewell of England. This secret he performed by so raising a tent or cover of canvas over the whole tree, and wetting the same now and then with a scoop, or horn, as the heat of the weather required; and so by withholding the sun-beams from reflecting upon the berries, they grew both great, and were very long before they had gotten their perfect cherry colour; and when he was assured of her Majesty's coming, he removed the tent, and a few sunny days brought them to their full maturity[3]."

On the 28th of September the Earl of Essex came in private to the Court at Nonesuch, where hee prostrated himselfe before the Queene; who gave him good wordes, and said he was welcome, and willed him to goe to his lodging[4], and rest him after so wearie a journey.—On the second of October he was committed to the custodie of the Lorde Keeper, Sir Thomas Egerton.

In November this year, Michael Stanhope thus writes to Sir Robert Cecil: " I humbly beseytche y^r Honor to gyve me leave to unburden my selfe, and to entreate y^r helpe in that wch I cane nott nowe, as my case is, performe accordynge unto my dutye. These perle my Lo. Keeper presented by mee unto her Majestie, as a small token (in respeckte of her greatnesse) of hys very thankefull mynde for her gratyus caer in maintainyng of hys credytt wherby he is the better enabled to his publycke callynge and sarvés: Her Majestie, lykynge marvelus well of the presente, in respeckte of the goodnesse therof, and better of his Lo' natuer and thankefull mynde, pleased to sae that he was hardely imposed by the

[1] Sydney State Papers, vol. II. pp. 111, 120.
[2] Garden of Eden, p. 165.   [3] Lysons, vol. 1. p. 57.
[4] The Earl of Essex's principal residence was *York House* in the Strand (see before, p. 371); which during his absence in Ireland, was inhabited by Mr. Francis Bacon.

arbytraytors, and noe reason he shulde bee att soe greate a furder chardg. After many speitches and tokens of her good lykynge of the presente, and of her favour touards my Lo. shee wylled mee to gyve his Lo. verye manye thankes, and to signifye unto hym how well shee dyd take hys good regarde of her gratyus dealynge, butt thatt her mynde was as greate to refuse as hys was to gyve; so in her prynsely magnanymité, woulde nedys have me to carré them backe, wth her many and kynde thankes. When I came unto hys Lo. and delyvered her Majestie's plesuer, and that he saw the perle, his countenanse chainged, and I assuer yor Honor he looked upon mee wth a hevye eye, as if I had ether caerlessly or doultyshely performed the trust he comyted unto me; and saed that he was very sorye that the shewe of hys thankefull minde was no moer acceptable unto her Majeste: he saed that in regarde of her greatnesse the guyfte was nothinge, but that hee dyd hope that itt would have plesed her to have accepted his duty- full and thankefull mynde; but for the perle, he woulde nott lae hande of them, butt bad me doo what I woulde wth them [1]."

On the 13th of November, the bells of St. Margaret's, Westminster, were rung "when the Queen came from Richmond to Westminster." And the Mayor, Aldermen, and Sheriffes of London, in scarlet, and the Commons, a great number in velvet coats and chaines of golde, all well mounted on horsebacke, as of late times hadde beene used, for honour of the Queene, by commaundement, received her at Westminster by torch-light.

Rowland White, in a Letter to Sir Robert Sidney, Nov. 15, says, "As the Queen passed by the new building [2], Sir Arthur Gorges presented her with a fair jewell [3]."

[1] Lodge, vol. III. p. 105.

[2] Sir Arthur Gorges, resident at Chelsea, in the house which was formerly Sir Thomas More's, and afterwards the Marquis of Winchester's, appears to have come, soon after 1586, into the possession of Gregory Lord Dacre, who married Anne, daughter of Winifred, the old Marchioness of Win- chester, by her first husband Sir Richard Sackville, and died in 1594. Lady Dacre, who survived him but a few months, bequeathed her house at Chelsea, with all its appurtenances, to the great Lord Burleigh, with remainder to his son Robert, afterwards Earl of Salisbury, and Lord High Treasurer. Sir Robert Cecil is supposed to have re-built the house, the initials of his name, and that of his lady, Elizabeth, were to be seen on the pipes, and in some of the rooms. Sir Robert Cecil sold the house to Henry Fiennes, Earl of Lincoln, from whom it passed to Sir Arthur Gorges, who married his daughter Elizabeth.   [3] Sidney Papers, vol. II. pp. 17, 130, 141, 161.

On the 17th of November, the day whereon shee had beene proclaimed Queene, and hadde now reigned 41 yeers, was great justings and other triumphs, which was not ended in divers dayes after.

On the 29th of November, the Lord Keeper and other Lords of the Counsell (by commandement of the Queene) in the Starre-chamber, persuaded against rumorous talke of the Earle of Essex.

Extracts from Sir JOHN HARRINGTON's *Papers, continued from p. 430.*

"1599. The Irishrie are much given to whoredome, as I saw at Munster, where the souldiers, withouten clothes on their backes or foode in their bellies, were lying under hedges with marvelous ill favourede wenches, whom they woud rather perish for than fighte for; and hereby were much injurie to their cause, for nothing but strypes coud bring them to their dutie. They likewise are abusive in their discourse; and yet they do appeare (in the upper sorte) very kind and hospitable to all new comers, as I did well experience in this countrie, even so muche as (if my own landes were here) I would hazarde my dwellinge with them for life. I was often well entertain'd, and in some sorte got ill will for speakinge in praise of their civil usage amonge our commanders, whome I often tolde that tho' I was sente oute to fighte with some, there did appeare no reason for my not eatinge withe others. I was well usede, and therefore am in duty bounde to speak well of the Irishrie."

"The Queene did once aske my wife in merrie sorte, 'how she kepe my goode wyll and love, which I did alwayes maytaine to be trulye goode towardes her and my childrene?' My Mall, in wise and discreete manner, tolde her Highnesse 'she had confidence in her husbande's understandinge and courage, well founded on her own stedfastness not to offend or thwart, but to cherishe and obey; hereby did she persuade her husbande of her own affections, and in so doinge did commande his.' 'Go to, go to, mistresse,' saithe the Queene, 'you are wisely bente I finde: after such sorte do I keepe the good wyll of all my husbandes, my good people; for if they did not reste assurede of some special love towarde them, they woulde not readilie yielde me suche goode obedience.' This deservethe notinge, as beinge both wise and plesaunte."

"What perylla have I escaped? I was entrusted by Essex, whom I did adventure to visit, with a message to the Queenes Majestie, settinge forthe his contrition and sore grievance for his manie offences. I was righte glade to heare such contrition, and laboured to effecte this matter; but ere I coud beare these tydinges (whiche I was well advysede to do), the Earl's petition reached her hand, and I fear her displeasure too, but herein I bore no parte. I was much encouraged to go throughe this friendlye parte on manie sides, but I saide, ' Charitie did begin at home, and should alwaies sayle with a faire winde; or it was not likelie to be a prosperous voyage.' I had nearly been wrecked on the *Essex* coaste in my last venture, as I told the Queene, had it not been for the sweete calme of her special forgivenesse. I have hearde muche on both handes, but the wiser *he* who reportethe nothinge hereof. Did either knowe what I knowe either have saide, it woulde not worke muche to contentemente or good lykinge."

"It restethe wyth me in opynion, that ambition thwarted in its career, doth speedelie leade on to madnesse; herein I am strengthened by what I learne in my Lord of Essex, who shyftethe from sorrow and repentaunce to rage and rebellion so suddenlie, as well provethe him devoide of goode reason or ryghte mynde. In my last discourse[1] he uttered strange wordes borderinge on such strange desygns, that made me hasten forthe and leave his presence. Thank heaven! I am safe at home; and if I go in suche troubles agayne, I deserve the gallowes for a meddlynge foole. His speeches of the Queene become no man who hath *mens sana in corpore sano*. He hathe ill advysers, and much evyll hath sprunge from this source. The Queene well knowethe how to humble the haughtie spirit, the haughtie spirit knoweth not how to yield, and the man's soule seemeth tossede to and fro like the waves of a troubled sea."

[1] *i. e.* conversation.

Anno Regni Regine Eliz. 42°. 1599-1600.

New Yeare's Guyftes geven to the Quene's Maiestie att her Highnes Mannor of Richmonde, the Firste Day of Januarie, in the Yeare abouesayde, by these Persones whose Names hereafter ensue [1], *viz.*

Elizabeth R

By Sir *Thomas Egerton,* Knight, Lord Keeper of the Greate Seale of Englande, one amuylet of golde, garnished with sparkes of rubyes, pearle, and halfe pearle.
    Delivered to Mrs. *Ratclyf.*

By the Lord *Buckhurste,* Lorde High Threausorer of Englande, in golde, £10.
    Delivered to *Henry Sackforde,* Esquyer, one of the Groomes of her Maiesties Privy Chamber.

By the Lord Marques of *Win',* in golde £20.
    Delivered to Mrs. *Ratclyf.*

EARLES.

By the Earle of *Nottingham,* Lord Admyrall, one karcanett, conteyninge 29 peeces of golde, whereof nyne bigger peeces and tenne lesser, 18 pendantes like mullettes, likewyse garnished with small rubyes and pearle, with a round jewell pendant in the myddest, garnished with one white topaz, and a pearle pendant, and nine small rubyes.
    Delivered to Mrs. *Ratclyf.*

	£.	s.	d.
By the Earle of *Darbye,* in golde	10	0	0
By the Earle of *Sussex,* in golde	10	0	0

[1] From an original Roll, formerly in the possession of Sir William Herrick, of Beaumanor Park in Leicestershire; and still preserved by his immediate Descendant, William Herrick, Esq.

						£.	s.	d.
By the Earle of *Bathe*, in golde	-	-	-	-	10	0	0
By the Earle of *Hartforde*, in golde		-	-	-	10	0	0
By the Earle of *Huntington*, in golde		-	-	-	10	0	0
By the Earle of *Pembrooke*, in golde		-	-	-	20	0	0
By the Earle of *Bedforde*, in golde		-	-	-	10	0	0

Delivered to Mr. *Sackford*.

By the Earle of *Northumberland*, one carcanett of golde, conteyninge nine square peeces, four pendants like mullettes and half moones, garnished with sparkes of dyamondes, rubyes, and pearles, threeded betweene.

Delivered to Mrs. *Ratclyf*.

By the Earle of *Shrewesbury*, parte of a doublett of white satten, embrothered all over like snakes wounde together, of Venyce sylver, with wroughte and puffes of lawne embrothered, with Venyce silver lyke wheate eares.

Delivered to the Robes.

By the Earle of *Cumberland*, one pettycote of white sarcenett, embrothered all over with Venyce silver plate, and some carnacon silke like colombines.

Delivered to the Robes.

By the Earle of *Rutlande*, in golde, £10.

Delivered to Mr. *Sackforde*.

By the Earle of *Worcester*, one hatt of tyffany, garnished with 28 buttons of golde of one sorte, and eight buttones of another sorte, about the band and upp the feather.

Delivered to the Robes.

Marquesses and Countesses.

By the Lady Marques of *Northampton*, two knottes of golde, garnished with sparkes of rubyes and pearles pendant.

Delivered to Mrs. *Ratclyf*.

By the Lady Marques of *Winchester*, wydowe, one sprigge of golde, gar' with sparkes of rubyes, one small dyamonde, and pearles of sondry sortes and bignesses.

Delivered to Mrs. *Ratclyf*.

By the Countes of *Kente*, six hankerchers of cambricke, wrought with blacke silke and edged about with gold lace.

Delivered to the Lady *Scudamore*.

By the Countesse of *Oxenforde*, one rounde kyrtell of silver tabynne, with slyppes of white silke like vellat, and tuftes of carnacon silke, with some golde.

Delivered to the Robes.

By the Countes of *Shrewesbury*, wydowe, in golde, £40.

Delivered to Mrs. *Sackforde*.

By the Countes of *Shrewesbury*, junior, parte of a doublet, unmade, of white satten, embrothered all over like snakes wounde together, of Venyce silver, richly wrought, and puffes of lawne embrothered with Venice silver like wheate eares.
Delivered to the Robes.

	£.	s.	d.
By the Countesse of *Sussex*, in golde	10	0	0

Delivered to Mr. *Sackforde*.

By the Countesse of *Nottingham*, one carcanett of golde, garnished with 15 peeces of golde, set with sparkes of rubyes, and a small dyamond in the myddest of every of them, and seven peeces lyke mullets, with pearles, with a rubye in the myddest of eche of them, and pearles threeded betwene them.
Delivered to Mrs. *Ratclyf*.

By the Countesse of *Huntington*, widowe, in golde	8	0	0
By the Countesse of *Huntington*, junior, in golde	8	0	0
By the Countesse of *Pembroke*, in golde	10	0	0
By the Countesse of *Rutland*, in golde	10	0	0

Delivered to Mr. *Sackforde*.

By the Countes of *Darby*, wydowe, one pettycote without bodyes, of silver tynsell, wrought in squares, with a border of trees of grene sylke needleworke.
Delivered to the Robes.

By the Countes of *Darby*, junior, one goblett of taffetta, embrothered all over with a twyste of Venyce silver and spangles, with flowers of silkewoman's worke.
Delivered to the Robes.

By the Countes of *Warwicke*, fyve sprigges of golde, garnished with sparkes of rubies, pearles pendant, and a half perle.
Delivered to Mrs. *Ratclyf*.

By the Countes of *Bathe*, in golde	10	0	0
By the Countes of *Bedford*, in golde	10	0	0

Delivered to Mr. *Sackford*.

By the Countes of *Bedford*, widowe, seven sprigges of golde, gar' with sparkes of rubies and pearle, and seven pearles pendant, four bigger and three lesser.
Delivered to Mrs. *Ratclyf*.

By the Countes of *Comberland*, one paire of braceletts of golde, conteyninge eight peeces like knottes, and eight rounde peeces garnished with small sparkes of rubyes, pearle, and half pearles.
Delivered to Mrs. *Ratclyf*.

By the Countes of *Southampton*, senior, one vale or mantle of white knytworke florished with silver.
    Delivered to the Robes.
By the Countes of *Northumberland*, one jewell of golde, set with a longe white topaz, and one longe pearle pendante.
    Delivered to Mrs. *Ratclyf.*
By the Countes of *Kildare*, seven buttons of golde of two sortes, garnished with sparkes of rubyes and pearle.
    Delivered to Mrs. *Ratclyf.*
By the Countes of *Worcester*, one ruffe of lawne cutworke, set with 20 small knottes of golde like mullets, gar' with small sparkes of rubyes and perle.
    Delivered to Lady *Scudamore.*

VICOUNTES.

	£.	s.	d.
By the Viscountes *Mountagewe*, widowe, in golde	10	0	0

Delivered to Mr. *Sackforde.*

BYSHOPPES.

	£.	s.	d.
By the Archbyshoppe of *Canterbury*[1], in golde	40	0	0
By the Archbyshopp of *Yorke*[2], in golde	30	0	0
By the Byshopp of *Durham*[3], in golde	30	0	0
By the Byshopp of *Winchester*[4], in golde	30	0	0
By the Byshopp of *London*[5], in golde	20	0	0
By the Byshopp of *Salisbury*[6], in golde	20	0	0
By the Byshopp of *Bathe and Welles*[7], in golde	20	0	0

[1] Dr. John Whitgift. See before, under the year 1588-9, p. 4.

[2] Dr. Matthew Hutton, Lady Margaret's Professor of Divinity at Cambridge, 1562; Prebendary of St. Paul's, 1562; of Westminster, 1565; of Ely, 1567; Dean and Prebendary of York, 1567; Bishop of Durham, 1589; translated to York, 1594. He died Jan. 16, 1604-5.

[3] Dr. Tobias Matthew; Public Orator, 1569; Canon of Christ Church, and Archdeacon of Bath, 1570; Prebendary of Salisbury, and President of St. John's College, 1572; Vice-chancellor, 1579; Chauntor of Salisbury, and Dean of Durham, 1583; Bishop of Durham, 1594; and Archbishop of York, 1606. He died March 28, 1628, æt 82.

[4] Dr. Walter Wickham. See before, p. 4.

[5] Dr. Richard Bancroft, Prebendary of Westminster, 1591; Bishop of London, 1597; translated to Canterbury, 1604. He died Nov. 2, 1611.

[6] Dr. Henry Cotton, Prebendary of Winchester, 15..; Bishop of Salisbury, 1598; died in 1615.

[7] Dr. John Still, Master of St. John's College, Cambridge, 1574; and of Trinity, 1577; Prebendary of Westminster; Bishop of Bath and Wells, 1592. He died Feb. 26, 1607-8.

NEW YEAR'S GIFTS PRESENTED TO THE QUEEN, 1599-1600.   449

	£.	s.	d.
By the Byshoppe of *Norwich* [1], in golde	20	0	0
By the Byshoppe of *Lyncolne* [2], in golde	20	0	0
By the Byshopp of *Worcester* [3], in golde	20	0	0
By the Byshopp of *Lytchfeld and Calventry* [4], in golde	8	6	8
By the Byshopp of *Carlyle* [5], in golde	10	0	0
By the Byshopp of *Rochester* [6], in golde	10	0	0
By the Byshopp of *Chichester* [7], in golde	10	0	0
By the Byshopp of *Peterborowe* [8], in golde	10	0	0
By the Byshoppe of *Glocester* [9], in golde	10	0	0
By the Byshopp of *Heryforde* [10], in golde	10	0	0
By the Byshopp of *St. Davye's* [11], in golde	10	0	0
By the Byshoppe of *Chester* [12], in golde	10	0	0
By the Byshoppe of *Exeter* [13], in golde	10	0	0

Delivered to Mr. *Sackforde.*

LORDES.

By the Lorde *Hunsdon*, Lord Chamberleyne, 10 large buttons of golde, garnished with small rubyes and greate ragged pearle.
Delivered to Mrs. *Ratclyf.*

[1] Dr. William Robinson, Archdeacon of Canterbury; Bishop of Norwich, 1594; died 1602.

[2] Dr. William Chaderton. See p. 5.

[3] Dr. Gervase Babington, Prebendary of Hereford, 1588; Bishop of Landaff, 1591; translated to Exeter, 1594; to Worcester, 1597; died May 17, 1610.   [4] Dr. William Overton. See p. 4.

[5] Dr. Henry Robinson, Provost of Queen's College, Oxford; Bishop of Carlisle, 1598; died Jan. 19, 1616.

[6] Dr. John Young (already noticed in p. 5) was Rector of St. Margaret Fish-street, London, 1554; afterwards of St. Giles, Cripplegate; Prebendary of Westminster, 1560; Master of Pembroke Hall, Cambridge, 1567; Bishop of Rochester, 1577-8; and had a dispensation to hold, *in commendam*, the benefice of St. Muge and Wouldan. He held a Prebend in Westminster Abbey, and one in the Church of Southwell. He died April 16, 1605, æt. 71; and was buried at Bromley.

[7] Dr. Anthony Wilson, Dean of Bristol, 1590; Bishop of Chichester, 1590; died in 1605.

[8] Dr. Richard Howland. See p. 5.

[9] Dr. Godfrey Goldsborough, Prebendary of London, Lichfield, and Worcester; Archdeacon of Salop; Bishop of Gloucester, 1598; died May 26, 1604.   [10] Dr. Herbert Westphaling. See p. 5.

[11] Dr. Anthony Rudd, Dean of Gloucester, 1584; Bishop of St. David's, 1594; died in 1615.

[12] Dr. Hugh Bellot, of St. John's College, Cambridge; Bishop of Bangor, 1585; Bishop of Chester, 1595.

[13] Dr. William Cotton, Canon Residentiary of St. Paul's, 1577; Bishop of Exeter, 1598; died in 1621.

	£.	s.	d.
By the Lord *North*, Threasurer of her Maiestie's Howsholde, in golde	10	0	0
By the Lorde *Norres*, in golde	10	0	0
By the Lorde *Barkeley*, in golde	10	0	0
By the Lord *Wharton*, in golde	10	0	0
By the Lord *Lomley*, in golde	10	0	0
By the Lord *Ryche*, in golde	10	0	0

Delivered to Mr. *Sackford*.

By the Lord *Henry Howard*, one pettycote of white tynsell stryped with three brode laces of golde, with tuftes of watchet and carnacion silke.
Delivered to the Robes.

By the Lorde *Darcy of Chichey*, in golde	10	0	0
By the Lord *Delaware*, in golde	10	0	0

Delivered to Mr. *Sackforde*.

By the Lorde *Audeley*, parte of rounde kyrtell of white clothe of silver, bounde about with a lace of Venice golde, and seven buttons lyke the birdes of Arabia.
Delivered to the Robes.

By the Lorde *Burghley*, one jewell of golde, with a long table sapher without foile, havinge eight small dyamons about yt, and one pearle pendant.
Delivered to Mrs. *Ratclyf*.

By the Lord *Mountioy*, one paire of bracelettes of golde, conteyninge 21 peeces, garnished with opalles and small rubyes, whereof eight of those peeces are lyke snakes.
Delivered to Mrs. *Ratclyf*.

By the Lord *Cobham*, one rounde kyrtell of silver tabyne, with starres and droppes of gold tyssued.

By the Lord *Willoby of Earesby*, Governor of Barwicke, one mantell of networke.
Delivered to the Robes.

BARRONNESES.

By the Barronnes *Pagett Cary*, one lapp mantell of ashe-colored and hearecolored unshorn veluett lozengwise, lyned with crymson unshorne veluett, thone side with a brode passamyne lace of golde, and thother with silver lace.
Delivered to the Robes.

By the Barronnes of *Hunsdon*, wydowe, one loose gowne blacke of networke, florished all over with Venyce golde and silver lyke feathers.
Delivered to the Robes.

By the Barronnes *Hunsdon*, junior, one doublet of white satten, embrodered and razed uppon like flyes, and leaves of Venyce silver, and garnished with white knyttworke.
Delivered to the Robes.

By the Barronnes *Chandoes Knowlys*, one pettycote of white sarcenett, embrothered all over with Venice gold, silver, and silke of dyverse colors like peramydes, with three borders likewise embrothered.
Delivered to the Robes.

By the Barronnes *Lomley*, one rounde kyrtell of silver tynsell stryped with golde and knotted buttons.

By the Baronnes *Scroope*, one loose gowne of blacke tyffany stryped with siluer and lined with sarcenet.
Delivered to the Robes.

By the Barronnes *Delaware*, in golde, £10.
Delivered to Mr. *Sackforde*.

By the Barronnes *Abella*, one skarfe or head-vaile of lawne cutworke florished with silver and silke of sondry colors.
Delivered to Mrs. *Luce Hide*.

By the Barronnes *Ryche*, one rounde white kirtell of tabyne in squares of silver and white tuftes.
Delivered to the Robes.

By the Barronnes *Chandoes*, widowe, one rounde kyrtell of silver chamlett or tabyne, with flowers of golde, silver, and silke of sondrye colors.
Delivered to the Robes.

By the Barronnes *Audeley*, parte of a rounde kyrtell of white cloth of silv' bound about with a lace of Venyce golde, and seven buttons like birds.
Delivered to the Robes.

By the Barronnes *Sheiffeilde Stafforde*, one pettycote without bodyes of sarcnet, embrothered all over with a twyste of Venyce silver and owes.
Delivered to the Robes.

By the Barronnes *Buckhurst*, in golde, £10.

By the Barronnes *St. John of Bletzo*, in golde, £10.
Delivered to Mr. *Sackford*.

By the Barronnes *Burghley*, one wastecote of white sarcenett, embrothered with flowers of silke of sondry colors.
Delivered to the Lady *Scudamore*.

By the Barronnes *Barkeley*, one mantell of lawne cut and florished with silver plate.
Delivered to the Robes.

By the Barronnes *Katheryn Cornewalleis*, one pettycote of ashe-colored China taffeta, embrothered all over like oaken leaves and ackhornes, and slyppes of Venyce golde, silver, and silke.
Delivered to the Robes.

LADYES.

To the Lady *Mary Seamer*, wyfe to Mr. Rogers, one quosyon cloth of fyne cambricke, wrought all over with Venyce golde and silke.
 Delivered to the Lady *Scudamore*.

By the Lady *Elizabeth Seamer*, wyfe to Sir Richard Knyghtley, one snoskyn of crymson satten, laide uppon with perfumed leather, cut embrothered with Venyce golde, silver, and silke.
 Delivered to Mrs. *Hide*.

By the Lady *Guylforde*, parte of a rounde kyrtell of orenge-color tabyne, with slippes and lozenges of ashe-color silke.
 Delivered to the Robes.

By the Ladye *Stafforde*, one paire of braceletts of golde, cont' 12 peeces, whereof 6 bigger and 6 lesser, garnished with pearle and garnetts.
 Delivered to Mrs. *Ratclyf*.

By the Lady *Cheeke*, one jewell of golde lyke a starre, garnished with sparkes of dyamons of sondry cuttes, and one small pearle pendante.
 Delivered to Mrs. *Ratclyf*.

By the Lady *Leighton*, one kyrtell of white knyttworke, tufted all over with pincke-colored silke.
 Delivered to the Robes.

By the Lady *Digbye*, two square cushions, thone silke needleworke chevernwise, backed with orenge-colored satten; thother redde leather, embrothered with flowers of silke.
 Delivered to *Stephen Peerce*, Keeper of the Standing Wardrope att Richmond.

By the Lady *Puckeringe*, in golde £10.

By the Lady *Jarrett*, in golde £10.
 Delivered to Mr. *Sackforde*.

By the Lady *Scudamore*, parte of a loose gowne of ashe-colored taffeta, the sleves, roller, and border, embrothered with leaves of Venyce golde.
 Delivered to the Robes.

By the Lady *Egerton*, one rounde kyrtell of white satten, cutt and embrothered all over like esses of Venyce golde, and a border embrothered like peramydes; and one doublet of silver chamlett, embrothered with puffes lyke leaves, florished with silver.
 Delivered to the Robes.

By the Lady *Southwell*, one loose gowne of tyffany, florished with Venyce silver and small tuftes of golde, with spangles att the ende.
 Delivered to the Robes.

By the Lady *Edmondes*, one rufe of lawne unmade.
Delivered to the Lady *Scudamore*.

By the Lady *Newton*, one doublett and a kyrtell of blacke stryped tynsell with a brode border downe afore, and the bodyes cutt and tacked upp, garnished with Venyce golde.
Delivered to the Robes.

By the Lady *Walsingham*, widowe, one pettycote of white satten, embrothered all over with flyes and branches, with a broade border.
Delivered to the Robes.

By the Lady *Hawkyns*, one snoskyn of clothe of silver, embrothered all over with flowers and braunches of Venyce golde, silver, and silke of sondry colors.
Delivered to Mrs. *Hide*.

By the Lady *Zouche*, one paire of pillowbeares of fine Hollan clothe, wrought with blacke silke drawne-worke.

By the Lady *Longe*, one smocke of fine Hollan, the sleves wrought with blacke silke.

By the Lady *Willoby*, one quosion cloth of lawne cutworke, florished with blacke silke and golde.
Delivered to the Lady *Scudamore*.

By the Lady *Hobby*, one snoskyn of clothe of silver, embrothered all over with flowers of Venyce golde, silver, and silke of sondry colors.
Delivered to Mrs. *Hide*.

By the Lady *Harrington*, one rounde kyrtell of lawne cut in workes like flowers and frutage, laide uppon blacke cypress tufted.
Delivered to the Robes.

By the Lady *Walsingham*, junior, parte of a pettycote of clay-color satten, embrothered all over with branches of silver.
Delivered to the Robes.

KNIGHTS.

By Sir *William Knowlys*, Comptroller of her Maiestie's Howsholde, one rounde kirtell of ashe-colored cloth of silver lyke slyppes of trees of orenge-color silke with 8 buttons, embrothered like coronetts.
Delivered to the Robes.

By Sir *Robert Cecill*, Pryncipall Secretory, 7 sprygges of golde, garnished with sparkes of rubies, dyamons, and perles pendante, and a jewell of golde lyke a honter's horne, with a stone called a . . . . garnished with small rubyes, and a small pearle pendante.
Delivered to Mrs. *Ratclyf*.

	£.	s.	d.
By Sir *John Fortescue*, Chauncelor of thexchequer, in golde -	10	0	0

454   NEW YEAR'S GIFTS PRESENTED TO THE QUEEN, 1599-1600.

                      £. s. d.

  By Sir *John Popham*, Lorde Cheif Justyce, in golde - - 10 0 0
   Delivered to Mr. *Sackforde.*

By Sir *Thomas Leighton*, one cloke of blacke networke, florished with Venyce golde, bounde with a lace of Venice silver.
   Delivered to the Robes.

  By Sir *Henry Cromwell*, in golde - - - - 10 0 0
  By Sir *Edwarde Cleare*, in golde - - - - 10 0 0
   Delivered to Mr. *Sackforde.*

By Sir *Edwarde Stafforde*, one jewell of golde, garnished with two spynnelles and sparkes of dyamondes about yt, and 3 small pendantes with like sparkes of dyamons.
   Delivered to Mrs. *Ratclyf.*

By Sir *John Scudamore*, part of a loose gowne of ashe-colored taffeta, embrothered with leaves of Venice gold.
   Delivered to the Robes.

By Sir *Edwarde Hobbye*, one doublet of white satten cutt and snypped, embrothered with leves of Venyce golde.
   Delivered to the Robes.

By Sir *John Stanhoppe*, two pendantes of golde like gates, garnished with sparkes of rubyes, and eche with 3 small pearles pendante.
   Delivered to Mrs. *Ratclyf.*

By Sir *Edward Dyer*, one pettycote of white satten, embrothered all over like grapes and pyne-apples, and a very broade border likewise embrothered.
   Delivered to the Robes.

By Sir *William Cornewallies*, one pe of pillow-beres of fyne cambricke, wrought all over with Venice gold and silke.
   Delivered to the Ladye *Scudamore.*

By Sir *Henry Gyllforde*, parte of a rounde kyrtell of orenge-colored tabyne, with slyppes and lozenges of ashe-color silke, with a border downe before like hollybery leaves.
   Delivered to the Robes.

By Sir *Henry Bronker*, one pettycote of taffeta scarcenet quylted all over with a border, imbrothered with golde and carnacon silke with poyntes.
   Delivered to the Robes.

By Sir *Thomas Wallsingham*, parte of a pettycote of cley-color satten, embrothered all ov' with branches of silv'.
   Delivered to the Robes.

By *Thomas Jarrett*, one loose gowne of orenge-colored taffeta, the grounde golde tabyne with slyppes of ashe-colored silke.
   Delivered to the Robes.

By Sir *Henry Billingsley*, one whole peece of lawne.
Delivered to Mrs. *Ratclyf*.

GENTLEWOMEN.

By Mistriss *Mary Ratclyffe*, one rounde kyrtell of white china damaske bound about with passamyne lace.
Delivered to the Robes.

By Mrs. *Knevett*, one large quoshion of clothe of silver, with branches of flowers, with silkewoman's worke of Venyce golde, silver, and silke of sondry colors.
Delivered to Mr. *Thomas Knevet*, Keeper of Westm' Palace.

By Mrs. *Carre*, one pendante of golde networke, garnished with small sparkes of garnettes, and one small pearle pendante.
Delivered to Mrs. *Ratclyf*.

By Mrs. *Luce Hyde*, one hatt and a feather of white tyffany, embrothered all over.
Delivered to the Robes.

By Mrs. *Coppyn*, one snoskyn of blacke velvet faire, embrothered with Venice silver and gold, and lyned with white plushe.
Delivered to Mrs. *Hide*.

By Mrs. *Twyste*, one paire of inner sleves of Hollan cloth, wrought with blacke silke.

By Mrs. *Cromer*, one smocke of fyne Hollan cloth, the sleves wrought with blacke silke.

By Mrs. *Huggyns*, widowe, one large swete bagge of sarcenet, embrothered on thone side.

By Mrs. *Frauncys Huggyns*, 6 handkercheves of fine Hollan cloth, wrought with blacke silke.

By Mrs. *Thomazine*, one handkercheve of fyne camericke, faire wrought with Venyce golde and silke.

By Mrs. *Barley*, 6 handkerchevs of fyne Hollan clothe, wrought with black silke, and edged with Venice gold and silv'.

By Mrs. *Elizabeth Grene*, one ruffe of lawne cutworke, florished with a wreath of Venice silver knotted.
Delivered to the Lady *Scudamore*.

By Mrs. *Wingfeilde*, mother of the maydes, 4 ruffes of lawne and a fanne.
Delivered Lady *Scudamore* the ruffes; and the fanne to Mistris *Hyde*.

By Mrs. *Elizabeth Russell*, one skarfe of white cypres, embrothered all over with flowers, and leaves of silke of sondry colors.
Delivered to Mrs. *Hyde*.

By Mrs. *Verney Alley*, one sute of ruffes of fyne lawne cutworke.
Delivered to Lady *Scudamore*.

By Mrs. *Gryffyn*, one vaile of white tyffanye, stryped with silke.
Delivered to the Robes.

By Mrs. *Sackforde*, one loose gowne of blacke networke, stryped with silver, and edged with silver lace.
Delivered to the Robes.

By Mrs. *Norton*, one cappe of cypres, florished with silver plate and spangles.
Delivered to Herself.

By Mrs. *Frauncys Kirkham*, one ruffe of lawne cutworke, and a paire of ruffes.
Delivered to the Lady *Scudamore*.

By Mrs. *Dorathy Speckard*, pte of a heade vaile of stryped networke, florished with carnacōn silke, and some owes.
Delivered to the Robes.

By Mrs. *Huggyns*, Mr. *William* his wyef, one ruffe of lawne cutworke.
Delivered to the Lady *Scudamore*.

By Mrs. *Elizabeth Brydges*, one doublett of networke lawne, cutt and tufted upp with white knytworke, florished with silver.
Delivered to the Robes.

GENTLEMEN.

By Mr. *Foulke Gryvell*, one cloke, and one snoskyn of sylver tabyne, tufted with ashe-color silke, and lyned with white plushe.
Delivered to the Robes; snoskyn delivered to Mrs. *Hide*.

By Mr. *Carre*, one pendant of golde cutworke, garnished with small sparkes of garnettes, and one small pearle pendante.
Delivered to Mrs. *Ratclyf*.

By Mr. *Mountagewe*, one smocke of fyne Hollan, wrought with blacke silke.
Delivered to the Lady *Scudamore*.

By Mr. *Garter Kinge att Armes*, one booke of Heraldry of the Knyghtes of thorder this yere.
Delivered to Mrs. *Ratclyf*.

By Mr. *Carmarden*, two boultes of camericke.
Delivered to Mrs. *Ratclyf*.

By Mr. *John Spillman*, one lyttell garlande of silver, curyously wrought with flowers enamelled.
Delivered to Mrs. *Ratclyf*.

By Mr. Doctor *James*, one pott of grene gynger, and a pott of orenge flowers.

By Mr. Doctor *Browne*, one pott of grene gynger, and a pot of orenge flowers.

By Mr. *Morgan,* Apotycary, one pott of grene gynger, and a pott of orenge flowers.

By Mr. *Hemingway,* Apotycary, one boxe of manus Xp̃i, and a pott of preserved peares.

By Mr. *Weston,* Apotticary, three boxes of preservatiues.

Delivered to the Lady *Scudamore.*

By Mr. *Byshop,* a statyoner, two bookes of Titus Lyvius, in Frenche.
Delivered to Mr. *Thomas Knevett.*

By Mr. *William Cordall,* Maister Cooke, one marchpaine.

By Mr. *Danyell Clarke,* Mr Cooke of the Houshoulde, one marchpane.

By Mr. *Thomas Frenche,* Seriant of the Pastery, one pye of orengado.

By Mr. *Raphe Batty,* one other Seriant of the Pastery, one pye of orengado.

By Mr. *Frauncis Bacon,* one pettycote of white satten, embrothered all over like feathers and billets, with three brode borders, faire embrothered with snakes and frutage.

Delivered to the Robes.

By Mr. *Fraunces Wolley,* one mantell of pinke-colored stryped cobwebbe lawne striped with silver.
Delivered to the Robes.

By Mr. *Thomas Myddleton,* one half peece of lawne, and half a peece of camericke.
Delivered to Mrs. *Ratclyf.*

By Mr. *Thomas Ducke,* Seriant of the Sceller, two bottelles of ypocras.

By Mr. *Abraham Speckard,* pte of a heade vale of stryped networke, florished with carnacõn silke, and some owes.

Delivered to the Robes.

By Mr. *Peter Lupo,* six bottles of sweete water.
By Mr. *Josephe Lupo,* one paire of pfumed gloves.
By Mr. *Thomas Lupo,* Josephe his sonne, one paire of pfumed gloves.
By Mr. *William Warren,* one paire of perfumed gloves.
By Mr. *Peeter Guye,* one paire of pfumed gloves.
By Mr. *Jerolimo Bassano,* one paire of perfumed gloves.
By Mr. *Anthune Bassano,* one paire of pfumed gloves.
By Mr. *Edwarde Bassano,* one paire of pfumed gloves.
By Mr. *Andrewe Bassano,* one paire of pfumed gloves.
By Mr. *Cæsar Gallyardo,* one paire of pfumed gloves.

By Mr. *Trochins,* one paire of perfumed gloves.

By Mr. *Innocent Comye,* one paire of perfumed gloves.

By Mr. *Richard Graves,* one paire of perfumed gloves.

Delivered to Mrs. *Hide.*

By Mr. *William Huggyns* one large swete bagge of ashe-color satten, embrothered all over very faire with a branch of eglentyne tree.

Delivered to the Lady *Scudamore.*

By Mr. *William Goodres,* two glasses of pretyous water.

By Mr. *George Baker,* one glasse of pretyous water.

Delivered to the Lady *Scudamore.*

By Mr. *Walter Pearce,* one paire of pfumed gloves.

By Mr. *Robert Hales,* one paire of pfumed gloves.

By Mr. *Thomas Lupo,* Peter Lupo his sonne, one paire of pfumed gloves.

Delivered to Mrs. *Hyde.*

By Mr. *Randall Bull,* one very lyttle locke made in a garnett.

Delivered to Mr. *Ferdynandes.*

By Mr. *Robert Lane,* one rounde boxe of golde, with dyverse drawinge boxes in yt, the outside enamelled.

Delivered to Mrs. *Ratclyf.*

By Mr. *Richarde Frenche,* one mantell of white curled cypres, with tuftes of silver downe the seames.

Delivered to the Robes.

Summa totalis of all the money gyuen to her Highnes this yeare £754. 6s. 8d.

Signed,   ELIZABETH R.

EDWA. CARYE.
N. BRISTOW.
N. PIGEON.
ROBERT CRANMER.
NICHOLAS HOTTOFTE.

Anno Regni Regine ELIZ. 42°.   1599-1600.

Newe yeares Guyftes geven by the Quene's Maiestie att her Highnes Manner of Richmonde, the firste day of Januarie, in the yeare abouesayde, to these persones whose names hereafter ensue, viz.

Elizabeth [signature]

To Sir *Thomas Egerton*, Knight, Lord Keeper of the Greate Seale of Englande in guilt plate, K. 34 oz. di. qr.

To the Lorde *Buckhurste*, Lord Highe Threausorer of Englande, in guilte plate, 23 oz. di. di. qr.

To the Lorde Marques of *Winton*, in guilte plate, K. 29 oz. 3 qr.

EARLES.

To the Earle of *Nottingham*, Lorde Admyrall, in guilte plate, M. and K. 103 oz. qr.

To the Earle of *Shrewesbury*, in guilte plate, M. 31 oz. qr.

To the Earle of *Darby*, in guilte plate, K. 21 oz. di.

To the Earle of *Sussex*, in guilte plate, K. 20 oz. qr. di.

To the Earle of *Comberlande*, in guilte plate, M. 22 oz.

To the Earle of *Bathe*, in gilte plate, M. 20 oz. di. di. qr.

To the Earle of *Hartforde*, in gilte plate, M. 21 oz. di. di. qr.

To the Earle of *Pembrooke*, in guylte plate, M. 31 oz.

To the Earle of *Northumberland*, in guilte plate, M. 29 oz. qr. di.

To the Earle of *Huntington*, in guilte plate, M. 20 oz.

To the Earle of *Worcester*, in guilte plate, M. 25 oz.

To the Earle of *Bedforde*, in guilte plate, K. 19 oz. di. di. qr.

To the Earle of *Rutlande*, in gilte plate, K. 21 oz. di.

MARQUESSES AND COUNTESES.

To the Lady Marques of *Northampton*, in guilte plate, K. and M. 44 oz. 3 qr.

To the Lady Marques of *Wint'*, widowe, in guilte plate, M. 30 oz.

To the Countes of *Oxeforde*, in guilte plate, K. and M. 34 oz.

To the Countes of *Kente*, in guilte plate, K. 29 oz. 3 qr.

To the Counteis of *Shrewesbury*, widowe, in guilte plate, M. 41 oz. qr. di.

To the Counteis of *Shrewesbury*, junior, in guilte plate, M. 19 oz. di.

To the Counteis of *Nottingham*, in guilte plate, K. 26 oz. qr.

To the Counteis of *Darby*, widowe, in guilte plate, K. 21 oz. di. di. qr.

To the Counteis of *Darby*, junior, in guilte plate, K. 23 oz.

To the Counteis of *Huntington*, widowe, in guilte plate, K. 29 oz. qr. di.

To the Counteis of *Huntington*, junior, in guilte plate, K. 19 oz. qr.

To the Counteis of *Bedforde*, widowe, in guilte plate, M. 51 oz.

To the Counteis of *Southampton*, senior, in guilt plate, M. 22 oz. qr.

To the Counteis of *Pembrooke*, in guilte plate, M. 19 oz. qr.

To the Counteis of *Worcester*, in guilte plate, K. 19 oz. di.

To the Counteis of *Bathe*, in guilte plate, M. 19 oz. di. di. qr.

To the Counteis of *Bedforde*, junior, in guilt plate, K. 19 oz. di. di. qr.

To the Counteis of *Comberlande*, in guilt plate, M. 21 oz. 3 qr.

To the Counteis of *Northumberlande*, in guilte plate, K. 23 oz. qr.

To the Counteis of *Kildare*, in guilte plate, M. 23 oz. qr.

To the Counteis of *Sussex*, in guilte plate, K. 19 oz.

To the Counteis of *Warwicke*, in guilte plate, K. and M. 54. oz. qr. di.

To the Counteis of *Rutlande*, in guilte plate, M. 22 oz. di.

VICOUNTES.

To the Vicounteis *Mountagewe*, widowe, in guilte plate, K. 19 oz. di. di. qr.

BYSHOPPES.

To the Archbyshoppe of *Canterbury*, in guilte plate, K. 45 oz.
To the Archbyshoppe of *Yorke*, in guilte plate, M. 38 oz.
To the Byshoppe of *London*, in guilte plate, M. 30 oz. qr. di.
To the Byshoppe of *Durham*, in guilte plate, M. 38 oz.
To the Byshoppe of *Norwiche*, in guilte plate, M. 30 oz. qr.
To the Byshopp of *Lyncolne*, in guilte plate, K. 30 oz.
To the Byshopp of *Worcester*, in guilte plate, K. 30 oz.
To the Byshoppe of *Salesbury*, in guilte plate, K. 31 oz. di. di. qr.
To the Byshoppe of *Lytchfelde*, in guilte plate, K. 19 oz.
To the Byshopp of *Carlyle*, in guilte plate, K. 17 oz. di. di. qr.
To the Byshoppe of *Rochester*, in guilte plate, K. 15 oz. di.
To the Byshoppe of *Chester*, in guilte plate, M. 17 oz. di.
To the Byshoppe of *Wynchester*, in guilte plate, M. 36 oz. 3 qr.
To the Byshoppe of *Chychester*, aulmer, in guilte plate, K. 19 oz. di. di. qr.
To the Byshoppe of *Peterboroughe*, in guilte plate, M. 15 oz. qr.
To the Byshoppe of *Glocester*, in guilte plate, M. 15 oz. qr.
To the Byshoppe of *Hereforde*, in guilte plate, M. 15 oz. di. di. qr.
To the Byshoppe of *Bathe and Welles*, in guilte plate, K. 30 oz. qr.
To the Byshoppe of *St. Davye's*, in guilte plate, M. 17 oz. 3 qr.
To the Byshoppe of *Exeter*, in guilte plate, K. 16 oz. di. di. qr.

LORDES.

To the Lorde *Hunsdon*, Lord Chamberleyne, in guylt plate, K. and M. 32 oz. di. qr.
To the Lorde *Northe*, in guilte plate, K. 21 oz. 3 qr.
To the Lorde *Lomeley*, in guilte plate, K. 20 oz. qr.
To the Lorde *Cobham*, in guilte plate, K. 30 oz.
To the Lorde *Norreis*, in guilte plate, K. 20 oz. di. qr.
To the Lorde *Willoby*, in guilte plate, K. 21 oz. qr.
To the Lorde *Wharton*, in guilte plate, M. 20 oz. qr.
To the Lorde *Ryche*, in guilte plate, M. 20 oz. qr.
To the Lorde *Burghley*, in guilte plate, M. 30 oz. qr.
To the Lorde *Darcy*, in guilte plate, K. 20 oz. qr.
To the Lorde *Audeley*, in guilte plate, K. 22 oz. qr.

NEW YEAR'S GIFTS PRESENTED BY THE QUEEN, 1599-1600.

the Lorde *Mountioye*, in guilte plate, K. 30 oz. qr. di.
the Lorde *Barkeley*, in guilte plate, M. 20 oz. qr.
the Lorde *Henry Howarde*, in guilte plate, M. 25 oz. di.
the Lord *Delaware*, in guilte plate, K. 24. oz. 3 qr. di.

BARRONNESES.

the Barronnesse *Pagett Cary*, in guilte plate, M. 36 oz. 3 qr. di.
the Barronnesse *Chandoes Knowlys*, in guilte plate, M. and K. 21 oz. di. qr.
the Barronnes *Lumley*, in guilte plate, K. 20 oz. di. qr.
the Barronnes *Hunsdon*, wydowe, in guilte plate, K. 32 oz. di. qr.
the Barronnes *Hunsdon*, junior, in guilte plate, M. 31 oz. di. qr.
the Barronnes *Scroupe*, in guilte plate, K. 17 oz. 3 qr.
the Barronnes *Audeley*, in guylt plate, K. 20 oz.
the Barronnes *Arbella*, in guilte plate, M. 19 oz. 3 qr. di.
the Barronnes *Delaware*, in guilte plate, K. 19 oz.
the Barronnes *Sheiffelde, Stafforde*, in guylte plate, M. 20 oz.
the Barronnes *Ryche*, in guilte plate, M. 21 oz. di. qr.
the Barronnes *Burghley*, in guilte plate, M. 25 oz. 3 qr.
the Barronnes *St. John of Bletzo*, in guilte plate, K. 19 oz. 3 qr. di.
the Barronnes *Chandowis*, widowe, in guilte plate, K. 22 oz. 1 qr.
the Barronnes *Buckhurste*, in guylte plate, M. 21 oz. qr.
the Barronness *Barkeley*, in guilte plate, M. 19 oz. di. qr.
the Barronnes *Katheryne Cornewalleis*, in guylte plate, M. 20 oz.

LADYES.

the Lady *Mary Seamer*, Mr. Rogers his wyef, in guylte plate, M. 12 oz. qr.
the Lady *Elizabeth Seamer*, Sir Richarde Knightley, his wyef, in guilte K. 13 oz. di. qr.
the Lady *Guylforde*, in guylte plate, M. 17 oz. di. di. qr.
the Lady *Stafforde*, in guilte plate, K. and M. 31 oz.
the Lady *Cheeke*, in guilte plate, K. 30 oz. di. qr.
the Lady *Leyghton*, in guylte plate, K. 17 oz. di.
the Lady *Southwell*, in guilte plate, K. 17 oz. qr. di.
the Lady *Scudamore*, in guilte plate, K. 17 oz. 3 qr.
the Lady *Zouche*, in guilte plate, M. 16 oz. di.

To the Lady *Egerton,* in guylte plate, K. 17 oz. 3 qr. di.
To the Lady *Edmondes,* in guilte plate, K. 17 oz. 3 qr.
To the Lady *Newton,* in guilte plate, K. 17 oz. 3 qr. di.
To the Lady *Hawkyns,* in guylte plate, M. 18 oz. di.
To the Lady *Hobby,* in guilte plate, K. 18 oz. di. qr.
To the Lady *Wallsingham,* wydowe, in guilte plate, M. 27 oz. di.
To the Lady *Walsingham,* junior, in guilte plate, K. 16 oz. 3 qr. di.
To the Lady *Dygbye,* in guilte plate, K. 17 oz. qr. di.
To the Lady *Jarrett,* widowe, in guilte plate, M. 18 oz. qr.
To the Lady *Longe,* in guilte plate, K. 18 oz. di. qr.
To the Lady *Harrington,* in guilte plate, K. 19 oz. qr. di.
To the Lady *Puckeringe,* in guilte plate, M. 18 oz.
To the Lady *Willoby,* in guilte plate, M. 15 oz. 3 qr.

KNIGHTS.

To Sir *William Knowlys,* Comptroller of her Maiestie's Housholde, in guilte plate, M. 26 oz. di.
To Sir *John Popham,* Chief Justice, in guilte plate, M. 23 oz. di.
To Sir *John Fortescue,* Chauncelor of thexchequor, in guilte plate, M. 24 oz.
To Sir *Robert Cicell,* Principall Secretory, in guilte plate, M. 26 oz. di.
To Sir *Thomas Leyghton,* in guilte plate, K. and M. 32 oz. di. di. qr.
To Sir *John Stanhoppe,* in guilte plate, M. 25 oz. di. di. qr.
To Sir *Edward Stafford,* in guilte plate, M. 20 oz.
To Sir *John Scudamore,* in guilte plate, M. 20 oz.
To Sir *Edward Dyer,* in guilt plate, M. 23 oz. di. di. qr.
To Sir *Edward Hobby,* in guilte plate, M. 23 oz. 3 qr.
To Sir *Thomas Jarrett,* in guilte plate, M. 22 oz. 3 qr.
To Sir *William Cornewalleis,* in guilte plate, K. 17 oz. di. qr.
To Sir *Henry Cromwell,* in guilte plate, M. 19 oz. qr. di.
To Sir *Edward Cleare,* in guilte plate, K. and M. 19 oz. 3 qr. di.
To Sir *Henry Gyllford,* in guilte plate, K. 21 oz. qr.
To Sir *Henry Bronker,* in guilte plate, M. 24 oz. qr.
To Sir *Thomas Wallsingham,* in guylte plate, K. 21 oz. qr.
To Sir *Henry Billingsley,* in guylte plate, K. 21 oz. di.

Fre Giftes.

To Mistris *Anne Russell*, in guilte plate, K. 11 oz.
To the Lady *Dorathy Hastinges*, in guilte plate, K. 10 oz. qr.
To Mrs. *Marye Fytten*, in guilte plate, K. 9 oz. 3 qr. di.
To Mrs. *Anne Carye*, in guylte plate, K. 10 oz. qr.
To Mrs. *Cordall Anslowe*, in guilte plate, M. 9 oz. di. di. qr.

Gentlewomen.

To Mistris *Marye Ratclyffe*, in guylte plate, K. 18 oz. qr. di.
To Mrs. *Knevett*, in guylte plate, K. 32 oz.
To Mrs. *Carre*, in guylte plate, K. 17 oz. qr. di.
To Mrs. *Luce Hyde*, in guylte plate, M. 17 oz.
To Mrs. *Elizabeth Bridges*, in guylte plate, K. and M. 17 oz. di. di. qr.
To Mrs. *Coppyn*, in guylte plate, K. 17 oz. qr.
To Mrs. *Twyste*, in guylte plate, M. 8 oz. qr. di.
To Mrs. *Alley*, in guylte plate, K. 6 oz. di. di. qr.
To Mrs. *Cromer*, in guylte plate, M. 16 oz. di. di. qr.
To Mrs. *Huggyns*, wydowe, in guylte plate, K. 16 oz.
To Mrs. *Fraunces Huggyns*, in guylte plate, M. 16 oz.
To Mrs. *Huggyns*, Mr. *William* his wyef, in guylte plate, K. 16 oz.
To Mrs. *Thomazine*, in guylte plate, K. 6 oz. 3 qr.
To Mrs. *Barley*, in guylte plate, M. 12 oz.
To Mrs. *Grene*, in guylte plate. K. 5 oz.
To Mrs. *Sackforde*, in guylte plate, M. 20 oz.
To Mrs. *Elizabeth Russell*, in guylte plate, K. 17 oz. 3 qrs. di.
To Mrs. *Gryffen*, in guylte plate, M. 21 oz. 3 qrs.
To Mrs. *Winckfeilde*, Mother of the Maydes, in guylte plate, M. 20 oz. qr. di.
To Mrs. *Fraunces Kirkham*, in guylte plate, M. 17 oz. di. qr.
To Mrs. *Elizabeth Norton*, in guylte plate, K. 16 oz. di. di. qr.
To Mrs. *Dorathy Speckarde*, in guylte plate, K. 8 oz. di. qr.

Gentlemen.

To Mr. *Foulke Gryvell*, in guylte plate, M. 25 oz. qr.
To Mr. *Garter Kinge at Armes*, in guylte plate, K. 8 oz.
To Mr. *Carre*, in guylte plate, K. and M. 19 oz. di. di. qr.

NEW YEAR'S GIFTS PRESENTED BY THE QUEEN, 1599-1600.

To Mr. *Mountague*, in guylte plate, M. 14 oz.
To Mr. *Carmarden*, in guylte plate, K. 17 oz.
To Mr. *John Spillman*, in guylte plate, M. 17 oz. di. qr.
To Mr. Docter *James*, in guylte plate, K. 14 oz. 3 qr. di.
To Mr. Docter *Browne*, in guylte plate, K. 4 oz. 3 qr. di.
To Mr. *Morgan*, Apottycary, in guylte plate, M. 8 oz. di. qr.
To Mr. *Hemyngwaye*, Apotycary, in guylte plate, K. 8 oz. di. qr.
To Mr. *Weston*, Apotycary, in guylte plate, K. 8 oz. qr. di.
To Mr. *William Cordall*, Mr Cooke, in guilte plate, K. 7 oz. di. di. qr.
To Mr. *Danyell Clarke*, Mr Cooke of the Housholde, in guylte plate, K. 7 oz. qr.
To Mr. *Thomas Frenche*, Seriant of the Pastery, in guylte plate, K. 8 oz. qr.
To Mr. *Raphe Batty*, one other Seriant of the Pastery, in guylte plate, K. 8 oz.
To Mr. *Fraunces Bacon*, in guylte plate, M. 33 oz.
To Mr. *Fraunces Wolley*, in guilte plate, K. 22 oz.
To Mr. *Abraham Speckard*, in guylte plate, K. 8 oz.
To Mr. *Peter Lupo*, in guylte plate, K. 5 oz.
To Mr. *Joseph Lupo*, in guylte plate, M. 5 oz.
To Mr. *Thomas Lupo*, sonne to Joseph Lupo, in guylte plate, K. 5 oz.
To Mr. *Thomas Lupo*, sonne to Peter Lupo, in guilte plate, M. 5 oz.
To Mr. *William Warren*, in guylte plate, K. 5 oz.
To Mr. *Jerolymo Bassano*, in guylte plate, M. 5 oz.
To Mr. *Arthure Bassano*, in guylte plate, K. 5 oz.
To Mr. *Andrewe Bassano*, in guylte plate, M. 5 oz.
To Mr. *Edward Bassano*, in guylte plate, K. 5 oz.
To Mr. *Richard Greves*, in guylte plate, M. 5 oz.
To Mr. *Cæsar Gallyardoc*, in guylte plate, K. 5 oz.
To Mr. *Innocent Comye*, in guylte plate, M. 5 oz.
To Mr. *Walter Peerce*, in guilte plate, K. 5 oz.
To Mr. *Robert Hales*, in guylte plate, M. 5 oz.
To Mr. *Trochins*, in guylte plate, K. 5 oz.
To Mr. *Peter Guye*, in guylte plate, M. 5 oz.
To Mr. *William Huggyns*, in guilte plate, K. 18 oz.
To Mr. *Thomas Myddleton*, in guylte plate, K. 15 oz. di. qr.
To Mr. *Byshoppe*, a statyoner, in guylte plate, K. 16 oz. qr.

To Mr. *William Goodres*, in guylte plate, M. 14 oz. qr. di.

To Mr. *George Baker*, in guylte plate, K. 14 oz. di.

To Mr. *Thomas Ducke*, Sergeant of the Sceller, in guilte plate, M. 9 oz. di. di. qr.

To Mr. *Roberte Lane*, in guylte plate, K. 30 oz.

To Mr *Randall Bull*, in guilte plate, M. 10 oz.

To Mr. *Richard Frenche*, in guylte plate, K. 11 oz. qr.

FRE GIFTES.

To Sir *Edwarde Carye*, Mr and Threr of her Maiestie's Jewells and Plate, in gylte plate, M. 18 oz. 3 qr. di.

To Sir *Thomas Gorges*, in guylte plate, M. 10 oz.

To Sir *Edwarde Dennye*, in guylte plate, M. 10 oz.

To Mr. *Henry Sackforde*, in guylte plate, M. 10 oz.

To Mr. *Thomas Knevett*, in guylte plate, K. 10 oz.

To Mr. *Edward Darcye*, in guylte plate, M. 10 oz.

To Mr. *William Kyllegrewe*, in guylte plate, K. 10 oz.

To Mr. *Michaell Stanhoppe*, in guylte plate, K. 10 oz.

To Sir *Edwarde Carye*, one other Grome, &c. in guylte plate, M. 10 oz.

To Mr. *Ferdinando Richardsonne*, in guylte plate, M. 10 oz.

To Mr. *Richarde Nightingale*, Yoman of the Robes, in guilte plate, K. 12 oz.

To Mr. *Nicholas Brystowe*, Clerk of her Maiestie's Jewells and Plate, M. 10 oz. 3 qr. di.

To Mr. *Nicholas Pygeon*, Yoman of her Maiestie's Jewells and Plate, in guilte plate, K. 10 oz. 3 qr. di.

To Mr. *Robert Cranmer*, one other Yoman, in guilte plate, M. 10 oz. 3 qr. di.

To Mr. *Nicholas Hottofte*, Groome, in guylte plate, K. 10 oz. 3 qr. di.

Some totall of all the plate, gyuen in manner and forme abouesayd 4,236 oz. di. qr.

FREE GIFTS PRESENTED BY THE QUEEN IN 1599.

Guifts gyuen by her Maiestie to sondrye Personnes, and delyvered at soundrye tymes, as followeth, *viz.*

Marye Hemynham. Fyrste, gyven by her Hignes, and delivered the 24th daye of June, anno 41° regni regine Elizabethe, &c. att the marryage of Mistris Marye Hemyngham, one guylte boule with a cover, bought of Richarde Martyn, Goldsmythe, per oz. 42 oz. di.

Mr. *Attorney.* Item, gyven by her sayde Highnes, and delyvered the 12th o Auguste, anno pred', at the christeninge of Mr Coke, Attorney General to her Maiestie his childe, one guylte boule with a cover, boughte of the sayde Richard Martyn, per oz. 41 oz. di. di. qr.

Mounser *Caron.* Item, gyven by her sayde Highnes, and delyvered the 15th of October, anno pred', to Mounser *Caron,* Agent for Flaunders, at his departure out of England, parte of one cheyne of golde, bought of Hughe Kaylle, per oz. 35 oz. qr. of the goodness of 21 karretts di. graine, and parte of one other cheyne, bought of the sayde Richard Martyn, per oz. 33 oz. qr. 3 dwt 6 graynes, of the goodnes of 22 karrets di. graine. In toto, 68 oz. di. 3 dwt 6 granes.

Edwa. Carye.
N. Bristow.
N. Pigeon.
Robert Cranmer.
Nicholas Hottofte.

Three Letters to the QUEEN, *from* SIR FRANCIS BACON.

1. A Letter of Ceremony, upon the sending of a New-year's Gift.

" It may please your sacred Majesty, according to the ceremony of the time, I would not forget, in all humbleness, to present your Majesty with a small New-year's Gift: nothing to my mind. And therefore, to supply it, I cannot but pray to God to give your Majesty his New-year's Gift; that is, a new year, that shall be as no year to your body, and as a year with two harvests to your coffers; and every other year prosperous and gladsome. And so I remain,

Your Majesty's loyal and obedient subject, FRANCIS BACON."

2. A Letter of Ceremony, upon the sending of a New-year's Gift.

" Most excellent sovereign Mistress, the only New-year's Gift, which I can give your Majesty, is that which God hath given to me; which is, a mind in all humbleness to wait upon your commandments and business: wherein I would to God, that I were hooded, that I saw less; or that I could perform more: for now I am like a hawk, that bates, when I see occasion of service, but cannot fly because I am tied to another's fist. But, meanwhile, I continue my presumption of making to your Majesty my poor oblation of a garment, as unworthy the wearing, as his service, that sends it: but the approach of your excellent person may give worth to both; which is all the happiness I aspire to. FRANCIS BACON."

3. To the QUEEN.

" It may please your excellent Majesty, I presume, according to the ceremony and good manner of the time and my accustomed duty, in all humbleness to present your Majesty with a simple gift; almost as far from answering my mind, as sorting with your greatness; and therewith wish, that we may continue to reckon on, and ever, your Majesty's happy years of reign: and they that reckon upon any other hopes, I would they might reckon short, and to their cost. And so, craving pardon most humbly, I commend your Majesty to the preservation of the Divine Goodness. FRANCIS BACON."

The Principall Addresse, in Nature of a New-year's Gifte; *seeminge therebye the Author intended not to have his Name knowne* [1].

Parthe I. Thaleia.

Gracious Princesse, where Princes are in place,
   To geve you gold, and plate, and perles of price
   It seemeth this day, save your royall advice
Paper presentes should have but little grace;
   But sithe the tyme so aptly serves the case,
   And as some thinke, youre Highnes takes delighte
     Oft to peruse the styles of other men,
     And oft youre self, with Ladye Sapphoe's pen,
In sweet measures of poesye t' endite
The rare affectes of your hevenly sprighte;
Well hopes my Muse to shape all manner blame,
Utteringe your honours to hyde her owner's name.

The Author choosinge by his Verse to honour the Queen's Majestie of England, Ladye Elizabeth, boldly preferreth his Choise, and the Excellencye of the Subject before all others of anye Poet aunceient or moderne.

Parthe II. Clio.

Greeke Achilles, and his Peeres did enjoye
   Great Homer's troompe for theyr high valiaunce:
   And Maro woulde in stately stile advaunce;
Æneas and that noble reste of Troye
In martiall moodes, Lucane did singe the chaunce,
   End, and pursute, of that lamented warre;
   Of proude allyes, whose envy spredd so farre,
As exilde Roome all egall governance.
Horace, honour'd August, the high'st of names,
   And yet his horte from Mecene never swervde;
   Ovid helde trayne in Venus courte, and servde

[1] From Cotton. MSS. Vespasian, E. 8.

NEW YEAR'S GIFT, ADDRESSED TO THE QUEEN, 1600.

Cheife Secretarye to all those noble dames,
Martyres of love who so broylde in his flames,
   As bothe their trauth and penance well deservde
   All in fine gold to have theyr image kervde,
For cleere recorde of theyr most woorthy fames.
By the bright beames of Cynthia the sheene
   Cupide kendled the fyres of Properse,
   Tibullus teares bayned Neæra's herse;
And Ladye Laura her graces that grow greene;
By Dan Petrarche of Tuskan poets Prince,
   Anacreon sange all in his wanton spleene:
   But proude Pindare he spilde the praises cleene
Of all Liricques that were before or since.

I singe noe bloodd nor battayles in my verse,
   Amorous odes, or elegies in teene,
Churlishe satire as Juvenall and Perse:
   But in chast style am borne, as I weene,
   To blazon foorthe the Briton mayden Queene,
Whose woorthes surmount them all that they reherse.

---

t her Majestie (twoo Things except) hath all the Parts that justly make to be sayd a most Happy Creature in this World.

PARTHE III.   ERATO.

Youthfull bewtye, in body well disposed,
   Lovelye favour, that age cannot deface;
A noble harte where nature hath inclosed
   The fruitfull seedes of all vertue and grace,
Regall estate coucht in the treble crowne,
   Ancestrall all, by linage and by right,
Store of treasures, honor, and just renowne,
   In quiet raigne, a sure redouted might:
Fast frindes, foes few or faint, or overthrowen,
The stranger toonges, and the hartes of her owne,

Breife bothe Nature and Nourriture have doone,
With Fortune's helpe, what in their cunning is
To yelde the erthe, a Princelye Paragon.
   But had shee, oh! the two joys shee doth misse,
A Cæsar to her husband, a Kinge to her soone,
   What lackt her Highnes then to all erthly blisse?

That her Majestie surmounteth all the Princesses of our tyme in Wisedome, Bewtye, and Magnanimitye: and ys a Thinge verye admirable in nature.

PARTHE IV.   THALIA.

Whome Princes servé, and realmes obey,
   And greatest of Bryton Kinges begott,
Shee came abroade even yesterday,
   When such as saw her knew her not:
      For one woold ween that stoode a-farre,
      Shee were as other wemen arre.

In trauthe it fares much otherwise;
   For whilest they thinke they see a Queene,
It comes to passe, ye can devise
   No stranger sight for to bee seene;
      Suche erroure falls in feble eye,
      That cannot view her stedfastlye.

How so? alas! forsooth it is
   Nature that seldome workes amis;
In woman's brest by passinge arte,
   Hath harbourd safe the lyon's harte;
      And featlye fixt, with all good grace,
      To serpente's hedd and angell's face.

That wisedome in a Princesse is to be preferred before Bewtye, Riches, Honour, or Puissaunce: but, where all the Parts comme in one Person, as they doe moste evidently in her Majestie, the same is not reputed an humane, but rather a divine perfection.

Parthe V.   Melpomene.

The Phrygian youth, full ill advised,
   To judge betweene Goddesses three;
All worldly wealth and witt despised,
   And gave the price to cleere beawtee.
      His meede therefore was to win grace
      Of Venus, and hir lovinge race.

The wand'ring Prince and Knightes of Troye,
   Who firste broughte bale to Tyrian towne,
Coulde never finde comforte or joye
   While Juno did uppon them frowne:
      Hir wrathe appeased, they purchaste reste,
      And Lavine lande theire owne beheste.

I am not rapte in Junoe's spheare,
   Nor with Dame Venus lovelye hewe;
But here on earthe I serve and feare,
   O mayde Minerve, thine ydoll true,
      Whose power prevayles in warr and peace,
      So as thy raigne can no tyme cease.

The Addresse.

Princesse, you have the doome that I can give,
   But seldome sitts the judge that may not erre:
Whence, to be sure, I have vowed while I live,
   T' addore all three godheads in your owne starre.

That Vertue ys alwayes subject to Envy, and many times to Perill: and yf her Majesties most notable Prosperities have ever beene maligned, the same hath beene for her only Vertues sake.

Parthe VI. Melpomene.

Fayre Briton maye
Wary and wise, in all thy wayes,
   Never seekinge nor finding peere,
   When ere thy happe shalbe to heere,
My mouth be muet in thy prayse,
    But one whole daye.

   Sweare by thine head,
And thy three crownes it must needes bee,
   Whilest I admire thy rare bewtye,
   I am forespoke in spite of thee,
By some disdaynefull curst feyrye,
    Or sicke, or dead.

   But while thy mighte
Can keepe my harte queavinge or quicke,
   Trust me my lippes shall never lenne
   To power thye prayses to my penne,
Till all thy foes be sorrowe sicke,
    Or dead out-right.

   They saye not soothe,
Of grace and goodnes that mainetayne
   Them to be kinges so safe, so lovelye;
   I see nothinge under the skie
Abide such daunger and disdaine,
    As Virtue doothe.

   Then if theyr bee
Any so canckred harte to grutche
   At your glories, my Queene, in vayne;
   Repininge at your fatall raigne,
It is for that they feel too muche
    Of youre bountee.

A Ryddle of the Princesse Paragon.

Parthe VII. Euterpe.

I saw marche in a meadowe greene,
A fayrer wight then feirye queene;
And as I woulde approche her neere,
Her head yshone lyke christall cleere,
Of silver was her forehead hye,
Her browes twoo bowes of henebye;
Her tresses troust were to beholde,
Frizeld and fine as frenge of golde;
Her eyes, God wott, what stuffe they arre,
I durst be sworne eche ys a starre:
As cleere and brighte as to guide
The pilot in his winter tide.
Twoo lippes wrought out of rubye rocke,
Like leaves to shutt, and to unlocke,
As portall doore in prince's chamber;
A golden toonge in mouth of amber,
That oft ys hard, but none yt seethe
Without a garde of yvorye teethe,
Even arrayed and richelye all,
In skarlett or in fine corrall:
Her cheeke, her chinne, her neck, her nose;
This was a lillye, that was a rose;
Her hande so white as whale's bone,
Her finger tipt with cassidone,
Her bosome sleeke as Paris plaster,
Held upp twoo bowles of alabaster:
Ech byas was a little cherrye,
Or, as I thinke, a strawberrye.
A slender greve swifter than roe,
A pretye foote to trippe and goe,
But of a solemne pace perdye,
And marchinge with a majestye:

Her body shapte as strayghte as shafte,
Disclosed eche limbe withouten craft;
Save shadowed all, as I could gesse,
Under a vayle of silk cypresse.
From toppe to toe yee might her see,
Timber'd and tall as cedar tree,
Whose stately turfe exceedeth farre
All that in frithe and forrest arre.
This markt I well: but loe, anone,
Methought all like a lumpe of stone;
The stone that doth the steele enchaunte,
The dreadful rocke of adamante.
And woorkes the shippe as authors speake,
In salt sea manye a wofull wreake.
Her hart was hidd none might yt see,
Marble or flinte folke weene yt be!
Not flint, I trowe, I am a lyer,
But syderite that feeles noe fier.
Now reed a-right, and do not mis
What jolly dame this ladye is.

The Assoile.

This fleshe and bloode, this head, members, and harte,
   These lively lookes, graces, and bewty sheene,
Make but one masse, by nature and by arte;
   Rare to the earth, rathe to the worlde seene;
Would yee faine knowe her name, and see your parte,
   Hye and behold a-while the Mayden Queene.

The Assoile at large moralized, in three Dizaynes.

PARTHE VIII. THALIA.

A hed harbroughe of all counsayle and witt,
   Where Science dwells, makinge a lively sprighte,
And dame Discourse as in her castell sitt,
   Scanninge causes by minde, and by forsighte;

A cheer where Loove and Majestye doe raigne,
   Both mild and sterne, havinge some secret mighte
   'Twixte hope and dreede in woe, and with delighte
Man's harte in holde, and eye for to detayne;
   Feedinge the one with sighte in sweete desyre,
   Dauntinge th' other by daunger to aspire.

Affable grace, speeche eloquent, and wise;
   Stately presence, such as becometh one
   Who seemes to rule realmes by her lookes alone;
And hath what ells dame Nature coolde devise
   To frame a face, and corsage paragon.
Suche as these blessed sprightes of paradise
Are woonte to assume, or such as lovers weene
   They see sometimes in sleepe and dainty dreame,
In femall forme a Goddesse, and noe Queene,
   Fitter to rule a Worlde then a Realme.

A constante mynde, a courage chaste and colde;
   Where love lodget not, nor love hathe any powres;
Not Venus brandes nor Cupid can toke holde,
Nor speeche prevayle, teares, plainte, purple, or golde;
   Honour n' Empire, nor youth in all his flowers;
This wot ye all full well yf I do lye,
Kinges, and Kinges Peeres, who have soughte farre and nye,
   But all in vayne, to bee her Paramoures.
Since twoo Capetts, three Cezarres assayde,
And bid repulse of the great Britton Mayde.

A verye strange and rufull Vision presented to the Authoure, the Interpretation whereof was left to her Majestie, till by the Purpose discovered.

Parthe IX.

In fruitfull soyle behold a flower sproonge,
   Disdayninge golde, rubyes, and yvorye;
Three buddes yt bare, three stalkes tender and younge
   One moare middle earthe, one toppe that touche the skye.

Under the leaves one branches brade and hye
  Millions of birds sange shrowded in the shade:
I came anone, and saw with weepinge eye,
  Two blossoms falne, the thirde began to fade.
So as within the compass of an houre
Sore withered was this noble deintye flowre,
  That no soyle bredd, nor lande shall loose the like;
Ne no seazon, or soone or sokinge showre,
  Can reare agayne, for prayer ne for meede.
Woe, and alas! the people cry and strike,
  Why fades this flower, and leaves nee fruit nor seede.

Another Vision happened to the same Authoure, as comfortable and recreatyve as the former was dolorous.

Parthe X. Calliope.

A Royall Shippe I sawe by tyde and by winde,
  Single and sayle in sea as sweet as milke;
Her cedar keele, her maste of golde refined,
  Her takle and sayles as silver and silke;
Her fraughte more woorthe than all the wares of Inde;
  Cleere was the coaste, the waves were smooth and still;
The skyes all calme, Phœbus so brighte he shined,
  Æolus in poope gave her wether at will;
Dan Neptune stered while Proteus playde his sporte,
  And Nereus' deinty dauters sange full shrill,
  To slise her sayles, that they mighte swell theyr fill;
Jove from above his pleasant showers powrde:
  Her flagge it beares the flowers of man's comforte:
None but a kinge, or more, may her aboarde;
O gallant peece, well will the lillye afoorde,
  Thow strike mizzen, and anker in his porte.

That her Majestie's most woorthy Renowne cannot perishe while the Worlde shall laste; with certayne Philosophicall Opinions touchinge the beginninge and durabilitye of the Worlde.

Parthe XI. Urania.

O mightye Muse,
   The mignionst mayde of Mounte Parnasse,
   Ever verdurde with flowre and grasse,
Of sundyre hews.
Saye, and not misse,
   How long agone, and whence yt was,
   The fayre round Worlde first came to passe,
As yt now ys?

There be that saye,
   How yt was never otherwise
   Than as we see it with our eyes
This very daye.
There be agayne,
   A secte of men, somewhat precise,
   Beleeve a God did yt devise;
And not in vayne.

Nor long agone,
   Onely to serve Adam's linage
   Some little while, as for a stage
To playe upon:
And by despighte,
   One daye agayne will, in his rage,
   Crush it as a kicksow cage,
And spill it quite.

Some weene it must
   Come by recourse of praty moates,
   Far finer than the smallest groates
Of sand or dust

That swarme in sonne;
　　Clinginge as fast as little clotes
　　Or burres uppon younge childrens' cotes,
That slise and runne.

Other suppose
　　A νᾶς approcht, and by reason
　　Brought it to shape and to season
From a chaos.
But some tech us,
　　By playne proofes, whye yt were begone,
　　Nor never more shalbe undone,
But byde even thus.

Whoorling his whott,
　　An endlesse roundel with a throwe,
　　Swifter than shaft out of a bowe,
Or cannon shott:
O bootlesse carke
　　Of mortall men, searchinge to knowe
　　Or this or that, since he must rowe
The dolefull barke

Which Charon guydes.
　　Frought full of shadows cold and starke,
　　That ferrye to the countryes darke,
Tendinge theyr tydes;
Since stoute nor stronge,
　　Metall nor moulde of worldlye warke
　　Nor writt of any cunninge clarke,
Can last soe longe

To outlast the skye;
　　Honour, empire, nor erthly name,
　　Save my Princesse most woorthye fame,
Which cannot dye!

Purpose.

Howe twoo principall Exploytes of her Majestie since shee came to the Crowne, to weete, Establishment of Religion and Peace, doe assuredly promise her in this life a most prosperous raigne; and after her death, a woorthye and longe lastinge name.

What causes mooved so many Forreigne Princes to be Sutours to her MAJESTIE for Marriage; and what, by Conjecture, hath hitherto mooved her to refuse them all.

PARTHE XII. URANIA.

Not youre bewty, most gratious Soveraigne,
   Nor maydenly lookes, mayntaynde with majestye,
     Your stately porte, which dothe not matche but stayne,
     For your pallas, your presence, and your trayne:
All Prince's Courtes myne eye could ever see,
Not your quicke witts, your sober governance,
   Your cleer forsighte, your faytfull memory,
So sweete features, in soe stayed countenance,
Nor languages, with plenteous utterance,
So able to discourse and entertayne.

Not noble race, farre beyonde Cesar's raigne,
   Runne in right line, and bloode of noynted kinges;
Not large empire, armyes, treasures, domayne,
   Lustye liv'ries of Fortune's deerst derlings;
Not all the skills fitt for a Princely Dame,
   Your lerned Muse with youth and studye bringes;
Not true honoure, ne that immortall fame
   Of Mayden Raigne, your onely owne renowne;
And noe Queene's ells, yet suche as yeeldes your name,
   Greater glorye than dooth your treble crowne.

Not any one of all these honourde partes,
   Your princely happs and habites thot doe move;
Or as it were ensarcell all the hartes
   Of Christen Kinges to quarrell for your love.
But to possesse at once, and all the goode
   Arte and engyn, and every starre above,
Fortune or kinde, coolde farce in fleshe and bloode
   Was force ynoughe to make so many strive
For your person, who in your worlde stoode,
   By all consent the mignonst mayde to wive.

But now, saye they, what crueltye could drive
  By such repulse, your harte harder than stone,
So many hopes of Princes to deprive;
  Forsoothe, what guyftes God from his regall throne
Was woont to deale, by righte distributyve
  Share meale to eche, not all to any one,
O peerles yow, or ells no one alive;
  Your pride serves you to seize them all alone.
    Not pride, Madame, but prayse of your lyon;
    To conquer all, and be conquer'd by none.

PURPOSE.

Conteininge a resolution politique, touchinge the feminyne government in monarchye; with a defensive of her Majestie's honoure and constancye, for not enclininge her courage (after the example of other ordinary women) not yet to the appetite of most great greate Princes, eyther in the affayre of her marriage, or of her manner of regyment.

What Things in Nature, Common Reason, and Cyvill Pollicye goe so fast linked together, as they maye not easilye be soonedered without Prejudice to the Politike Body, whatsoever Evill or Absurdity seeme in them.

PARTHE XIII. THALIA.

Princesse, my Muse though not amys,
To enforme your noble mynde of this.
Sythens ye see all worldlye men,
How they run ryott now and then:
By mistakinge and want of sence,
In thinges of little consequence,
Truly discerned as they maye bee,
By one of royal Majestee.
And deepe discourse and earnest zeale,
As yours is for all our weale;
Or ells it maye full oft befall,
For thinges of no moment at all.

Discorde maye grow by braule and jarre;
Thence faction; thence cyvile warre:
Which when the popular brayn is woodd,
Coold not be stauncht withouten bloodd.
And now betymes ye may prevente,
By this humble advertisemente;
Shewinge the soome and points in cheefe
That wholly make and marre this greefe;
Remove mysterye from religion,
From godly feare all superstition,
Idolatrye from deepe devotion,
Vulgare woorshippe from worlde's promotion;
Take me from hallows ceremonye,
From sects errours, from sayntes hypocrisye,
Orders and habites from graduates and clerkes,
Penaunce from sinne, and merite from good werkes,
Pull people and theyr Prince asoonder,
From games to gaze at, and miracle to woonder:
Forbidde pesauntes theys countrye sporte,
Preache all trothe to the raskall sorte,
Pull prophane Powles out of all yoke,
Let popular preachers beare a stroke;
Remove rigour from human laws,
Credulitye from prophetts' saws;
Let reason range beyonde his creede,
Man's faythe languishe, nor conscience bleede;
Make from olde reliques reverence,
From publique shews magnificence;
Take solemne vows from Princes' leagues,
From sanctuary privileage;
Take me from publique testimonye,
Booke oathe by trouthe or perjurye;
Take pompe from Prelates, and majestee from Kinges,
Solemne circumstance from all these worldly thinges;
We walke awrye, and wander without lighte,
Confoundinge all to make a chaos quite.

PURPOSE.

Conteyninge an invective agaynste the Puritans, with singular commendacion of her Majestie's consyderate judgment and manner of proceedinge in the cause of religion. The daunger of innovations in a commonwelth, the poison of sectaryes, and perillous yt ys to shake religion at the roote by licentious disputes and doctrines.

That amonge Men many Thinges be allowed of Necessitye, many for Ornament, which cannot be misliked nor well spared without blemishe to the Cyvile Life.

PARTHE XIV. CALLIOPE.

Deny honoure to dignity
And triumphe to just victorye;
Pull Puissance from soverayntee,
And creditt from authoritee;
Set magistrate fro counenance,
Part veritye and false semblance,
Wronge and force from invasion,
Fayned speeches from persuasion;
Take hartye love from jelosye,
And fraude from cyvile pollicye;
Moorninge and doles from buryalls,
And obsequies from funeralls;
From holy-dayes, and fro weddinges,
Minstrells, and feasts, and robes, and ringes:
Take fro kinge's courtes entertaynmentes,
From ladyes rich habillimentes,
From country girles gorgious geare,
From banquetts mirthe and wanton cheare;
Pull out of clothe and comelye weede,
The nakt carcas of Adame's seede;
From worldlye thinges take vanitee,
Sleit, semblant, course order and degree:
Princesse, yt ys as if one take away,
Greene wooddes from forrests, and sunne-shine fro the day.

PURPOSE.

Agaynste the same Puritanes, a desire of courtiers, and all auncyent courtly usages, devised as well for the publique intertaynements, as for private solaces and disportes, not scandalously evill or vicious.

That her MAJESTIE is the onlye Paragon of Princes in this oure age.

PARTHE XV.

Builde me of bowghes a little bower,
And sett it by a stately tower;
Set me a new robe by an olde,
And course coppar by duckate golde;
An ape unto an elephante,
Bruckle byrall to diamante:
Set Naples courser to an asse,
Fine emerawde unto greene glasse:
Set rich rubye to redd emayle,
The raven's plume to peacocke's tayle:
Laye me the larke's to the lysarde's eye,
The duskye clowde to azure skye;
Sett shallowe brookes to surginge seas,
An orient pearl to a white pease;
Matche camell's hayre to satten silke,
And alloes with almounde milke;
Compare perrye to Nectar wyne,
Juniper bush to lofty pine:
There shall no lesse an oddes be seene,
In myne from everye other Queene!

PURPOSE.

By the generall commendacion of her Majestie, in the highest degree of prayse, the author sheweth the vertue and envyous nature of a Paragon; and how Excellencye cannot appeere but by comparison.

A Comparison shewing her MAJESTIE's Super-excellencye in all Regall Vertues.

PARTHE XVI. EUTERPE.

 As faulcon fares to bussarde's flighte,
 As egles eyes to owlatts sighte,
 As fierc saker to kowarde knighte,
 As britest noone to darkest nighte,
 As amerike is farre from easte,
 As lyon's lookes fears everye beaste,
 As Soommer-soonne exceedeth farre
 The moone, and every other starre,
 So farre my Prince's prayse doth passe
 The famoust Queene that ever was!

PURPOSE.

All prayse by resemblance ys voyde of offence that by comparison odious be in the superlative (be it never soe true), it savoureth a certayne grosse adulation, which being to her Majestie's naturall modestye nothinge agreeable, the authore seeketh to salve the sore of her opinion, and his suspected sentence, by temperinge the excesse with a prety difference made betweene a bare resemblance and a comparison drawne out of the principles of justice; as yf one should saye, the prayse that ys justlye given ys well given, and ought not be misliked thoughe yt surmounte the common credite and opinion.

 O Pallas, Goddesse soverayne,
 Bredd out of great Jupiter's brayne;
 That thoughe thou be no man mervells,
 All honoure and witt, and nothinge ells,
 Thow, that ner was widowe ne wife,
 But a true virgin all thy life;
 Be it for some rare presidente,
 Of all feuringne govermente;
 Or that thow trowe no godd above
 Was ever woorthye of thy love;
 Thou that rangest battayles in fielde,
 And bearest harnesse, speare, and shielde;

And in thine Universitye,
The peacefull branche of olyve tree;
Lendinge out of thyne endlesse store,
All mortall men both low and lore,
Goddesse, as we poore pilgrimes weene,
Of spinsters, and of poets Queene;
And therfore hast, in solempne wise,
Thy temples and thy sacrifise;
Thine himnes, thy vowes, thy noones, thy clerks,
And all that longes to holy werks;
The whole wide worlde for them to dwell,
And Athens for thye chief chappell:
But O, now twentye yeare agon,
Forsakinge Greece for Albion,
Where thow above dost rule and rayne,
Emperesse and Queene of Great Brittayne;
Leavinge thye lande thy bellsire wan
To the barbarous Ottoman;
And for grief chaunged thy holy hawnte
Of Mounte Parnasse to Troynovaunte;
All Atticke showres for Tems to sydes;
Tems easy for hys easye tydes;
Built all alonge with mannours riche,
Quinborow salt sea, brackish Greenewich;
Then that where Britton rayne beyone,
The Tower of lovely Londone,
Westminster old and new Pallace,
Richemounte not great but gorgias;
Kinge Hampton Court, that hath no peere
For stately roomes and turretts cleere;
Save Windsor set on Barock border,
That temple of thye noble order,
The garter of a lovely dame
Which gave yt first device and name:

O Ladye, hence to hethennesse,
Only umpire of warre and peace;
When Cityes, States, Countryes, and Kinges,
Creepe to the covert of thye winges:
Thow that canst dawnt thy forren foes,
To ridde thye realme of warre and woes:
Purchasing peace without battayle;
So firme an one as cannot fayle;
Thy tyme not yet in tyme to be,
By any signe that man may see:
Thow, that besydes forreyne affayres,
Canst tend to make yeerly repayres;
By Sommer Progresse and by sporte,
To Shire and Towne, Citye and Porte,
To view and compasse all thye lande,
And take the bills with thine owne hande,
Of Clowne and Earle, of Knight and Swayne,
Who list to thee, for right complayne,
And therin dost such justice yeelde,
As in thye sexe folke see but seelde;
And thus to doe arte lesse afrayde,
With houshold trayne a syllye mayde,
Then thyne Auncestours, one of tenne,
Durst do with troopes of armed men:
Thow, that canst tende to reade and write,
Dispute, declame, argewe, endyte,
In Schoole and Universitye,
In prose, and eke in poesye;
In Greek, Latine, and fine Tuscan,
In Frenche, and in Castillian:
So kindlye and quicke, as old and younge
May doubte which ys the mother tongue.
O thow, the lovely Mayde above,
Who hast conquer'd the God of Love,

NEW YEAR'S GIFT, ADDRESSED TO THE QUEEN, 1600.

And skapte his mother's suttle gynne;
Triumphed ore him and all his kinne.
Yf thou be all ys sayde afore,
Or if thou be a great deale more,
Than I can utter any wayes,
Not schiphringe thee of thye just prayse,
How longe ys yt ere we forgett
Thyne erthly name *Elizabet*,
And dresse thee as thou dost deserve,
The titles of Britton's Minerve?
In skye why stall we not thye starre,
Est by the syde of great Cæsar?
Or ells appoynt thy plannett where
Shines Berenice's golden haire?
For we suppose thou hast forswore
To matche with man for evermore.
Whye build we not thye temples hye,
Steeples and towers to touch the skye;
Bestrewe thine altars with flowers thicke,
Sente them with odours Arrabicque:
Perfuminge all the revestryes,
With muske, cyvett, and ambergries?
In thy feast-dayes to singe and dawnce,
With lively leps and countenance;
And twise stoope downe at everye leape,
To kisse the shadowe of thy footstepe?
Thy lyvinge ymage to adore,
Yealding thee all earthly honore.
Not earthlye, no, but all divyne,
Takinge for one thys hymne of myne!

In the Churchwardens' Accompts of Kingston-upon-Thames, amongst many similar entries, is a payment to the ringers, in 1600, " when the Queen dined at the Lodge," the residence of George Evelyn [1], Esq. of Norbiton.

On the 20th of March 1599-1600, the Earl of Essex was permitted to return to his own residence at York House [2].

[1] George Evelyn, Esq. founder of that branch of the Evelyn Family which settled at Wotton in Surrey, first carried the art of making gunpowder to perfection in England, and for the conveniency of his works in that neighbourhood, purchased an estate at Wotton, *i. e.* Woodtown, from the groves and plantations that were about it, of one Mr. Owen. This George Evelyn had a considerable interest at Court, and procured from Queen Elizabeth a grant, in conjunction with Thomas Reeves, of the Rectory of St. Nicholas Coleabbey, in Queenhithe Ward, London.

It was in the latter part of his life, that he came to live at Wotton, which however did not hinder him from planting there, as appears from what his grandson tells us: " In a word, to give an instance of what store of woods and timber of prodigious size there were growing in our little county of Surrey, the nearest of any to London, and plentifully furnished, both for profit and pleasure, with sufficient grief and reluctancy I speak it, my own grandfather had at Wotton, and about that estate, timber that now were worth one hundred thousand pounds, since, of what was left my father who was a great preserver of wood, there has been thirty thousand pounds worth of timber fallen by the axe and the fury of the late hurricane and storm, now no more; Wotton, stripped and naked, ashamed to own his name." He died seised, *inter alia*, of the manor of Norbiton, May 30, 1603, in the seventy-third year of his age, and left his estate at Wotton to his youngest and only surviving son, by his second wife.

[2] The situation of Mr. Anthony [not Francis] Bacon after his removal from Essex-house [see p. 441], does not appear; but that he was then so distressed in his circumstances, that it was apprehended he would be obliged to sell his estate at Gorhambury, is evident from a letter of his Brother to the Queen, written on the 13th of that very month, printed by Mr. Blackbourne in his *Collections* (pp. 57, 58), before his Edition of Lord Bacon's Works in 1730, but omitted in the two subsequent ones of 1740 and 1753, and therefore inserted here.

" MOST GRACIOUS SOVEREIGN,

" I think I should rest senseless of that wherein others have sense restless, and that is of my particular estate and fortune, were it not, that the overthrow of my fortune includeth in it a cutting off that thread which is so fastly wreathed with the thread of my life, that I know they will end together; I mean the thread of my hopes to do your Majesty farther and better service. Which consideration only or chiefly constraineth me to make now this motion to your Majesty for the help of my estate; a motion, wherein nevertheless I will keep this stay, that I will not incur the common precedent of being suitor to your Majesty for a value, whereby the best of your possessions useth to be parcelled and deflowered, but in these parcels only, wherein I am informed, arising to the total of eighty and one pounds, and in all respects ordinary land, which if your Majesty shall be pleased of your benignity and love towards me to confer on me in the richest manner, which is fee simple, I can say no more, but that your Majesty shall in one make me a freeman and a bondman, free to all the world, and only bound to yourself. And I will plainly express unto your sacred Majesty the three thorns, the

ODE TO CYNTHIA[1].

This Song was sung before her Sacred Majestie, at a Shew on horsebacke, wherewith the Right Honorable the Earle of CUMBERLAND[2] presented her Highnesse on May-day, 1600.

> The ancient readers of Heauen's booke,
> Which with curious eye did looke
>   Into Nature's story,
> All things under Cynthia tooke
>   To be transitory.

compunction whereof instanted me to make this motion at this time; holding otherwise all the services which I have done or can do, more than rewarded in your Majesty's only gracious respect. First my love to my Mother, whose health being worn, I do infinitely desire she might carry this comfort to the grave, not to leave my estate troubled and engaged. Secondly, these perpetuities being now overthrown, I have just fear my Brother will endeavour to put away Gorhambury; which, if your Majesty enable me by this gift, I know I shall be able to get into mine own hands, where I do figure to myself, that one day I may have the honour and comfort to bid your Majesty welcome, and to trim and dress the grounds for your Majesty's solace. Thirdly, your Majesty may by this redemption (for so I may truly call it) free me from the contempt of the contemptible, that measure a man by his estate, which I find daily weakening of me both in courage and mean to do your Majesty service. Thus, Madam, your Majesty seeth, tho' I am an ill beggar in person, yet I would make no Proctor; for I never received so much contentment of any man, as I could find it in my mind to make him an author or mediator of my fortune. Only I have used an ancient friend and a man of ordinary access to your Majesty for the delivery of these lines. And so, most humbly craving pardon, I leave all to your Majesty's goodness, and yourself to the daily preservation of the divine Majesty.

"Your Majesty's most humble and entirely devoted subject and servant,   FR. BACON.

"From my tub not yet hallowed by your sacred Majesty, March 13, 1599."

[1] From Davison's "Poetical Rapsodie, 1611," p. 197.

[2] By the "Series of Triumphal Justs," printed in this Volume, p. 41, it will appear that George Clifford, Earl of Cumberland was regularly appointed, in the year 1590, to succeed Sir Henry Lee, Master of the Queen's Armory, as her Majesty's Champion, at the exercise of arms annually solemnized on the 17th of November, the day of her Accession to the Crown. On the New-year's day 1599-1600, he gave the Queen "a petticoat of white sarcenet, embroidered all over with Venice silver plate, and some carnation silk, like columbines." His Lady gave "a pair of gold bracelets, containing eight pieces like knots, and eight round pieces garnished with sparks of rubies, pearls, and half pearls." In return, the Earl had 22 ounces of gilt plate; and the Countess 21 ounces and three quarters.

The late excellent Dr. Whitaker, in his "History of Craven," in describing Skipton Castle, after noticing the Predecessors of this gallant Nobleman, says, "From this period I shall in a great measure, make the Cliffords their own biographers; and shall extract the materials of their history from the celebrated family portrait in Skipton Castle, the long inscription on which was drawn up by Lady

This the learned onely knew,
But now all men finde it true,

Anne Clifford, Countess of Pembroke, assisted, according to tradition, by the celebrated Sir Matthew Hale.—This picture is eight feet four inches high, exclusive of the frame; each end is of the breadth of three feet ten inches. A frame goes round the middle part entirely, and likewise round each end, of the breadth of five inches. This frame is adorned with flower-de-luces, harps, roses, and crowned roses. The middle part contains the picture of George Earl of Cumberland, who stands on your right, as you look at the picture; on his right-hand is the Countess his lady, holding in her left-hand the Psalms of David; on her right-hand stands her eldest son Francis; and on his right her other son Robert. Nearly over the head of the Countess is a half-length, eight inches and three quarters high, seven inches and a half broad, of Elizabeth Countess of Bath, eldest sister to the Countess of Cumberland. On your left, a little distance from it, in the same line, is another, the same size, of Anne Countess of Warwick, eldest sister to both the former. In the same line, almost at the left side of the picture as you face it, is another, the same size, of Frances Lady Wharton, sister to the Earl of Cumberland; and below is one, rather larger, of Margaret Countess of Derby, eldest child to Henry second Earl of Cumberland, by his first lady. An head of Samuel Daniel, Lady Pembroke's tutor, is also introduced. On the right and left edges is a series of arms of the family, with inscriptions under each, reaching from top to bottom. These are too much injured by Time to be transcribed. On the right side of the Countess's head are three books on a shelf, marked, 'A written hand book of Alkimee, Extractions of Distillations, and excellent Medicines. All Senakae's Workes, translated out of Latine into English. The Holy Bible; the Old and New Testament.' A little on the left of the Earl's head is his coat of arms, encircled with the Garter, and surmounted with an Earl's coronet, above which is the following inscription:

"'This is the Picture of George Clifford, third Earl of Cumberland in the male line of his family, the fourteenth Baron Clifford of Westmerland, and Shereiff of that Countye by inheritance, and in the same descent the thirteenth Lord of the honor of Skipton in Craven, and also Lord Vipont and Baron Vescy. He was borne sonne and heire apparent to H. Earl of Cumberland, by his second wife Anne, daughter to William Lord Dacres of the North: he was borne in his father's Castle of Bromeham, in Westmorland, the 6th of August, 1558. At the age of eleven years and five months, lieving then in the house called Battell Abbey, in Sussex, he cam to be Earl of Cumberland, by the decease of his father, who died in the said Castle of Bromeham, about the 8th or 10th of January, 1570, as the yeare begins on New-year's day. When he was almost 19 yeares old he was married in ye Church of Saint Mary Over's, in Southwark, June 24, 1577, to his virtuous and onely Lady, the Lady Margaret Russell, third daughter and youngest child to Francys second Earl of Bedford, by his first wife Margarett St. John, by whom he had two sonnes and one daughter; Frances and Robert, whoe being successively Lords Cliffords, died young, in their father's life-time; and the Lady Ann Clifford, who was just fifteen years and nine months at her father's death, being then his sole daughter and heire. He performed Nine Viages by Sea in his own person, most of them to the West Indies, with great honour to himself, and servis to his Quene and Country, having gained the strong Town of Fiall, in the Zorrous [Azores] Islands, in the yeare 1589, and in his last viage the strong Forte of Portereco in the year 1598. He was made Knight of the Garter by Quene Elizabeth, and Councellor of State by King

> Cynthia is descended
> With bright beames, and heauenly hew,
> And lesser starres attended.

James. He died in the Dutchy House, in the Savoy, London, the 30th of October, 1605, being then of age 47 yeares and 3 months wanting 9 dayes. His bowells and inner partes was buried * in Skipton Church in Craven in Yorkshire, the 13th of March following. By his death the title of Earl of Cumberland cam to his only Brother Sir Francys Clifford. But the ancient right to his baronies, honors, and ancient lands, descended then to his onely daughter and heir, the Lady Ann Clifford, for whose right to them hir worthy mother had, after, great suits at law with his brother Francys Earle of Cumberland. This Earl George was a man of many natural perfections, of a great wit and judgement, of a strong body †, full of agility, of a noble mind, and not subject to pride or arrogance, a man generally beloved in this kingdome. He died of the bloody flux, caused, as was supposed, by the many wounds and distempers he receyved formerly in his sea viages. He died penitently, willingly, and christianly. His onely daughter and heire, the Lady Ann Clifford, and the Countess hir mother, weare both present with him at his death.

" 'This is the picture of the Lady Margaret Russell, Countess of Cumberland, third daughter and youngest child to Francis Russell, second Earl of Bedford, by his first wife Margrett, daughter to Sir John St. John, of Bletnesho. She was borne in the Earle her father's house, in the Citty of Exeter, in Devonshire, formerly a priory, about the 7th of July 1560: her mother dyeing two yeares after of the small-pox, in Wooburne House in Bedfordshire, which was once an abbey. Shee was maried, about the age of 17 yeares, to Georg Clifford, Earle of Cumberland, in St. Mary Over's church, London, by whom she had two sonnes, Francys and Robert, successively Lords Clifford, who died both yong, before they were 6 yeares old, and one onely daughter, the Lady Ann Clifford, who was afterwards sole heire to both her parents. This Countess and hir husband were cozen jermans twice removed by the blood of the St. Johns; for his great-grand-mother Ann St. John, wife to Henry Lord Clifford, was great-aunt to hir mother Margaret St. John, they being both of the House of Bletneshoe. In the year of our Lord God 1593, all hir husband's lands in Westmorland were made to her in jointure by act of parliament. Shee lived his wife 28 yeares and upwards, and his widow ten yeares and seven months, in which tyme of her widowhood, espetially in the 3d and 4th yeares thereof, shee had great suits at law with her brother-in-law Francis, then Earle of Cumberland, for the right of her onely daughter's inheritance, in which business she was much opposed by the King and the great ones of that tyme. But by industry and search of records she brought to light the then unknown title which her daughter had to the ancient baronies, honors, and landes, of the Viponts, Cliffords, and Vescyes. So as what good shall accrew to hir daughter's posteritie, by the said inheritance, must, next under God, be

---

* Something is evidently wanting in the inscription here. The sentence was probably written thus: " His bowells and inward parts was buried in the church of the Savoye, and his body in Skipton church."

† This is proved by his weighty suit of tilting armour, now at Appleby Castle, of which the helmet alone is almost insupportable to modern shoulders. But he must have been of a stature well adapted to bearing great weights; for the whole suit measures only five feet nine inches from the cone of the helmet to the ground. The perpendicular pressure, however, may have occasioned some contraction in the leathern ligaments of the joints.

> Lands and Seas she rules below,
> Where things change, and ebbe, and flow,

attributed unto hir. Shee was of a great naturall wit and judgement, of a swete disposition, truly religious and virtuous, and indowed with a large share of those 4 morall virtues, Prudence, Justice, Fortitude, and Temperance. The death of hir two sonnes did so much afflict hir as that ever after the Booke of Jobbe was her dayly companion. Shee died in her Castle of Bromeham in Westmorland, in her widowhood, 24th May 1616, wherein hir husband was borne into this world, when she was 56 yeares old, wanting 6 weeks, and that very day 25 yeares after the death of hir sonne Robert Lord Clifford. Shee outlived all hir brothers and sisters. Hir bowels and inward partes was buryed in the church called Nine Kirks, hard by wheare she died, and hir body was buried in Appleby Church in Westmerland, the 11th of July following; and when this worthy Countess Dowager of Cumberland died, hir only dau'r Anne Clifford, Countess of Dorsett, did then lie in Knowle-house in Kent; but when hir said moother was buryed, was she present at hir burial in Appleby Church, in Westmerland, for then she lay in Bromeham Castle in that county; but that Countess of Cumberland's only grandchild, the Lady Margaret Sackvile, did lie at Horsley-house in Surrey, both when her grandmother Countess of Cumberland died, and was buried.'

"The eldest son holds in his left hand a scroll containing the following inscription: 'These are the Pictures of the two eldest children of Georg Clifford, Earle of Cumberland, &c. which he had by his worthye wife, the Lady Margarett Russell, Countess of Cumberland. Their first-borne child was Francis Lord Clifford, whom the moother was delivered of in his father's castle of Skipton, in Craven, in Yorkshire, on Friday the 10th of Aprill, anno Domini 1584, his father being then theare; which Francys Lord Clifford, after he had lived five years and eight months, died in the same castle theare, the 10th or 11th day of December 1589, and was presently after buryed in the vault of Skipton church, amongst many of his father's ancestors, the Cliffords and others. When this yong Lord Francis Clifford and his brother Robert lay in Channell-row, by Westminster, with theare father and moother, the spring before this young Lord's death, 1589, he was admired by those who knew him for his goodnes and devotion, even to wonder, considering his childish yeares; his brother Robert and the Countess theire moother were in Skipton Castle at his death, wheare the same Countess was great with childe with her onely daughter, whom she was delivered of in that Skipton Castle, the 30th day of January following; she that was the Lady Ann Clifford, and cam after to be the onely child to her parents. When this Lord Francys died, his said father was then beyond the seas, in the North partes of Ireland, whither he was driven on land by extremity of tempest, and great hazard of life, ten dayes before the death of his said sonne, when that Earle was then in his returne from the Ile Azores, in the West Indies. Their second borne childe was Robert Clifford, whom his mother was delivered of on a Wednesday, the 21st of September, anno D'ni 1585, in Northall-hous in Hartfordshire, wheare she and her husband Georg E. of Cumberland then laye. Which Mr. Robert Clifford, by the death of his elder brother Lord Francys, cam to be Lord Clifford, the 10th or 11th of December, 1589. And as theare was neere a yeare and six months between their births, so was theare neere a year and six months between their deaths; and they both dyed when they came to the age of five yeares and eight months old, and in the same severall houses wherein they were both borne; for this Robert Lord Clifford died in Northall-house in Hartfordshire, on a Whitson Monday, the 24th of

> Spring waxe olde, and perish:
> Onely time, which all doth mow,
> Her alone doth cherish.

May, 1591. After his death, he being opened, his bowells and inward p'ts were buryed in the church at Northall in Hartfordshire; but his dead body was buryed in the vaut of Cheneys Church in Buckinghamshire, with his moother's ancestors, the Russells Earls of Bedford, and others. He was a childe endowed with many perfections of nature for so few yeares, and likely to have made a gallant man. His sorrowfull moother, and her then little daughter and only childe, were in the house at Northall when he died: which Lady Ann Clifford was then but a yeare and four months old, who, by the death of hir sayd brother Ro. Lo. Clifford, cam to be ye sole heire to both hir parents. And when this yong Lord Rob't died, his father Georg E. of Cumberland was in one of his viages on the seas toward Spain and the West Indies.

" ' These eight pictures conteyned in this frame are copies drawne out of the original pictures of theese hon'ble personages, made by them about the begening of June, 1589, and were thus finished by the appointment of Ann Clifford, Countess of Pembrooke, in memoriall of them, in anno D'ni 1646. When these originalls were drawne, did Georg Clifford, E. of Cumberland, with his worthy wife and theire two sonnes, lie in the Lord Philip Wharton's house, in Channell Rowe in Westminster, wheare the said worthy Countess conceyved with childe, the 1st of May, anno D'ni 1589, with her onely daughter the Lady Ann Clifford, who was borne the 30th of January following, in Skipton Castle, Craven, in Yorkshire; shee afterwards being the onely child of hir parents, and is now Countess of Pembroke.'

" Under the picture of the Countess of Derby is the following inscription: ' This is the picture of the Lady Margarett Clifford, Countess of Derby, eldest childe to Hen. Clifford, E. of Cumberland, &c. by his first wife Elianor Brandon, youngest da. to Charles Brandon, Duke of Suffolk, by Mary the French Q. which La. Marg't was the only childe of hir moother that lived any time; for hir two brothers by her moother died infants. Shee was borne in her father's castle, at Bromeham in Westmerland, in anno D'ni 1540. Hir moother dieng theare about seven years after, in Novemb. 1547, but was buried at Skipton, in Craven. Which high-borne Lady Elianor hir grace was grand-child to K. H. VII. and his wife Eliz. and niece to K. H. VIII. and cozen jerman to K. E. VI., Q. M., Q. Eliz. and to James the V. King of Scotland; shee being cozen jerman twice removed to the E. of Cumberland hir husband, by the blood of the St. Johns. This Lady Marg't Clifford was the Lady Elianor's grace hir onely child; was married in the Chappell at Whitehall, the K. and Q. being present, to Henry Stanley Lord Strange, afterwards Erle of Darby, ye 7th of February, and was his wife about 38 yere, and his widow three yeres, and had by him two sonnes, Ferdinando and William, successively Erles of Darby. Which William was father to James now Erle of Darby. This great Countess deceased at her house at Cleveland Row, London, when she was about 56 yeres old, 29th of September, 1596, and was buryed presantly after in the Abbey Church in Westminster, in St. Edmund's Chapell theare. Shee was a virtuous, and noble, and kind-hearted Lady, and full of goodnesse and a deere lover of her brother of the half blood, and his worthy wife and their children.'

" On the same compartment with Lady Pembroke's own portrait, we read as follows: ' This is the picture of the Lady Ann Clifford, now Countess of Pembrooke, who, when shee was Countess Dowager

Time's young houres attend her still,
And her eyes and cheekes do fill
With fresh youth and beauty;

of Dorset, and had lived six years and two months a widow, was maryed in Cheneys Church in Buckinghamshire, the 3d day of June, 1630, to hir husband Philip Herbert, Earle of Pembrooke and Montgomery, Lord Chamberlain of his Majesties Household, and Knight of the most noble Order of the Garter, he being ...... of 45 yeares and three months wanting seven daies, and she being of the age of 40 years and 4 months. Shee lived most part of ye time shee was his wife, first in ye Court at Whitehall, and after at Baynard's Castle in London, Ramsbury, Wilton, Wiltshire; but espetially in Ramsbury Hous and in Baynard Castle. And whilst the said Countess then lay in the said Castle in London, dyed Henry Clifford, E. of Cumberland, in one of the Prebende's houses in York, ye 11th December, 1643; and his wife, Lady Frances Cecill, Countess Dowager of Cumb'land, died in ye same hous, ye 14th of February following. By reason of which Erle's death, without issue male, did ye lands in Westmorland and Craven, which of right belongeth to this Co's of Pembrooke, and were detained from hir by the sayd Erle and his father many yeares, revert and come peaceably to the sayd Countess, though the misery of ye then Civill Warrs kept hir from having the profit of theese landes for a good while after. The 5th of July, 1627, was this Countess of Pembrooke hir youngest daughter by hir first husband, the Lady Isabella Sackville, married in Clerkenwell church, in London, to James Compton, Erle of Northampton.'

" Under an escutcheon containing the arms of Clifford and Hewes is the following inscription: ' Sir Francys Clifford, Knight, fourth Erle of Cumb. in the lyfe-tyme of his bro. G. E. of Cumb. about the yeare 1589, did marry Mrs. Grizel Hewes, dau'r of Thomas Hewes, of Uxbridge, and widow to Edw. Nevell, Lo. Aburgavenny, by whom he had divers children, whereof Hen. Clifford, borne 1592, was fifth Earl of Cumberland, and the last Earle of that familey. This Countess dyed 16th of June, 1613, and hir husband dyed 21 January, 1641.'

" Under an escutcheon containing the arms of Clifford and Cecill, is the following inscription: ' Henry Clifford, E. of Cumberland, in the lyfe-tyme of his father, did mary, the 25th of July 1610, the Lady Frances Cecill, dau. to Rob't. E. of Salisbury, by whom he had divers children; but none lived any tyme but theire onely daughter and heire Eliz. Clifford, wife to the E. of Corck. This Hen. dyed the 11th of December 1643, in Yorke; and his wife died theare the 14th of February after.'

" Under an escutcheon, containing the arms of Boyle and Clifford, is the following inscription: ' Richard Boylle, now Erle of Corck, in the life-tyme of his father, did marry the Lady Eliz. Clifford, daughter and at length sole heire to Henry Clifford, Earle of Cumberland, by which lady the sayd Erle of Corck hath now living five children, two sonnes, and three daughters.'

" Under an escutcheon containing the arms of Tufton and Sackvile, is the following inscription: ' John Tufton, now Earle of Thanet, did, in the life-tyme of his father, ye 21st of April 1629, marry ye Lady Margarett Sackvile, first daughter and coheir of Rich. E. of Dorsett, by his wife the Lady Ann Clifford; which E. of Thanett hath seven children by the said Lady Margarett his wife, now living, five sonnes, and two daughters.'

" Such is the account which this lady has transmitted to posterity of her ancestors, herself, her nuptial alliances, and her immediate descendants. But paint and canvas, when neglected, soon give

> All her lovers olde do grow,
> Cut their hearts they do not so
> In their loue and dutie.

way to the operation of damp. Even now the compartment which contains her own youthful portrait is nearly destroyed. Many of the marginal inscriptions are become almost illegible; and, unless the press and the graver had united to perpetuate these perishing remains, another century might have doubted whether such a monument of the Cliffords was ever in being. The idea of combining so much family history, and so numerous a group of figures upon canvas, was, I think, original.

"The foregoing narration leaves me little to add, with respect to that part of the family to which it extends, but a few gleanings and reflections.

"George Earl of Cumberland was a great but unamiable man. His story admirably illustrates the difference between greatness and contentment, between fame and virtue. If we trace him in the public history of his times, we see nothing but the accomplished courtier, the skilful navigator, the intrepid commander, the disinterested patriot. If we follow him into his family, we are instantly struck with the indifferent and unfaithful husband, the negligent and thoughtless parent. If we enter his muniment-room, we are surrounded by memorials of prodigality, mortgages and sales, inquietude and approaching want. He set out with a larger estate than any of his ancestors, and in little more than twenty years he made it one of the least. Fortunately for his family, a constitution, originally vigorous, gave way, at 47, to hardships, anxiety, and wounds[*]. His separation[†] from his virtuous Lady was occasioned by a Court intrigue: but there are families in Craven who are said to derive their origin from the low amours of the third Earl of Cumberland.

"Among the evidences of the family, I have met with a MS journal of the first voyage, fitted out at his expence; but which he does not seem to have accompanied in person."

Mr. Lodge, in his Biographical Memoir of the Earl of Cumberland, accompanying the "Portraits of Illustrious Persons of Great Britain," after a brief but satisfactory narrative of the Earl's good Voyages to that of 1594 inclusive, adds, His passion for nautical adventure was now at the height. Unable to employ ships of sufficient force to support his hired vessels without borrowing from the Queen, and unwilling to subject himself to the controul under which the use of such loans necessarily placed him, he determined to build a man of war of his own, and accomplished the task. It was of the burthen of nine hundred tons; was launched at Deptford; and named by Elizabeth "The Scourge of Malice," reputed the best and largest ship that had been built by any English subject. He entered it, in the river, on his eighth enterprise, accompanied by three inferior vessels, and had proceeded to Plymouth, when he received the Queen's command, by Raleigh, for his instant return to London, which he obeyed. The squadron, however, proceeded on its voyage to the Spanish main; made some prizes; and returned to take him on board for another cruise thither; in which his great ship was so shattered in a violent storm, which occurred when he had scarcely reached the distance of

---

[*] "He was sick of a bloody flux a month before his death; his wife and child were present a few hourse (only) before." Countess of Pembroke's MS Memoirs.

[†] "But as good natures, through human frailty, are often misled, so he fell to love a lady of quality, which did by degrees draw and alienate his affections from his so virtuous and loving a wife; and it became the cause of many sorrows." Ibid.

Q. Elizabeth to Lady Paget, on the death of her daughter Lady Crompton [1].

" Call to mind, good Kate [2], how hardly we Princes can brook of crossing of our commands; how yreful wyll the hiest power be (may you be sure) when mur-

forty leagues from England, that he was obliged to retrace his course, and to wait, however impatiently, at home till the vessel should be rendered again fit for service. At length, on the sixth of March 1598, he embarked in it, at the head of nineteen others, on his last and most considerable expedition. His expenses in the preparations for it had been enormous, and the expectations of his sanguine mind had kept pace with them. He sailed on the sixth of March for the West Indies, where, for seven months, he incessantly harassed the Spaniards in their settlements, to the great advantage of the public interests of his country, lost two of his ships, and more than a thousand of his men, and received from the produce of his captures about a tenth part of the sum which he had disbursed for the purposes of his voyage. " His fleet, however," says Lloyd, " was bound to no other harbour but the port of honour, though touching at the port of profit in passage thereunto." Such is the outline of his maritime story. At home, his politeness, his courage, and his magnificence, were, in the strictest sense of the word, inimitable; highly tinctured always by the singularity of his mind, they were solely and distinctly his own. He had good parts, but the warmth of his temper, and the punctilious exactness of his notions of honour, rendered him unfit for any concern in public affairs. Elizabeth, who looked narrowly and judiciously into the characters of men, seems therefore to have employed him but on one short service, for which no one could have been better qalified—the reducing to obedience his eccentric compeer, Essex; but she knew, perhaps admired, his foibles, and certainly flattered them. In 1592 she dignified and decorated him with the Order of the Garter. At an audience, upon his return from one of his voyages, she dropped her glove, which he took up and presented to her on his knees. She desired him to keep it for her sake, and he adorned it richly with diamonds and wore it ever after in the front of his hat at public ceremonies. This little characteristic circumstance is commemorated in a very scarce whole-length portrait of the Earl engraved by Robert White. She constituted him, on the resignation of Sir Henry Lee, Knight of the Garter, disabled by age, her own peculiar champion at all tournaments. Sir William Segar has preserved, in his treatise " of Honours Military and Civil," and exact account of the pomp and parade of his admission into that romantic office, [which has been already given in this Volume, p. 41.] The Earl's expences in discharging the duties, if they may be so called, of this fantastic office, in horse-racing, which had then lately become fashionable, and in feasts which rivalled the splendour of Royalty, added to the aggregate loss on the whole of his maritime career, greatly impaired his estate. He was, to say the least, careless of his family, lived on ill terms with his Countess, Margaret, third daughter of his guardian, Francis Earl of Bedford, a woman of extraordinary merit, but perhaps too high spirited for such a husband, and neglected the interests as well as the education of his only surviving child. Of that child, little less remarkable than her father, Anne, wife first to Richard Sackvile, Earl of Dorset, and, secondly, to Philip Herbert, Earl of Pembroke and Montgomery: a memoir by Mr. Lodge may be seen among the Portraits of Illustrious Persons.   [1] From Birch, MSS. 4160. 23.

[2] This good Kate was Catharine, daughter of Henry Knevet, Esq. of Bokenham, in Norfolk, and relict of Henry second Lord Paget, who died Dec. 28, 1568, leaving only an infant daughter, who

merings shall be made of his pleasingst will? Let Nature therefore not hurt herself, but give plase to the giver. Though this leson be from a sely vicar, yet it is sent from a loving Soveraine."

In this year the Queen honoured Lord Herbert with her presence at his marriage; as appears by the following extracts from the Letters of Rowland Wyhte to Sir Robert Sidney [1]:

"The marriage between the other Lord Harbert and Mrs. Anne Russel is at a stay till yt please her Majestie to appoint a day. I find it wilbe honourably solemnized, and many take care to doe her all the possible honor they can devise. The feast wilbe in Blackfriars, my Lady Russel making exceeding preparation for it."

"On the 5th of June the Earl of Essex was called before the Council at the Lord Keeper's; where, for matters laid to his charge, he was suspended from the use of divers offices, and, till her Majesty's pleasure to the contrary, to keep his house."

June 11. "The Queen dined yesterday at my Lady Lumley's in Greenwich, and uses to walke muche in the Parke and great walkes out of the Parke, and about the Parke."

June 15. "Her Majestie is in very good healthe, and purposes to honor Mrs. Anne Russel's marriage with her presence. It is thought she will stay there Monday and Tuesday. My Lord Cobham [2] prepares his house for her Majesty to lye in, because it is near the Bride-house. There is to be a memorable maske of eight ladies. They have a straunge dawnce newly invented: their attire is this: each hath a skirt of cloth of silver, a rich waistcoat wrought with silkes and gold and silver, a mantell of carnacion taffeta cast under the arme, and their haire loose about their shoulders curiously knotted and interlaced. These are the maskers:

died in 1571. Lady Paget was married, secondly, to Sir Edward Cary, of Aldenham, Herts, by whom she was mother of Sir Henry Cary the first Viscount Falkland, and also of Sir Philip Cary, of Caddington, Knt. and of three daughters, Anne, Frances, and Meriall, the latter of whom, the lady lamented by her Royal Mistress, was married to Sir Thomas Crompton, of Driffield, co. York, junior, and died May 15, 1600, and was buried at Aldenham, where she has a Latin Epitaph, in which she is styled "Meriall Domini Edwardi Carey, militis, ex Catherina Domina Paget, filia, nobilis virtuosa et lectissima foemina."

[1] From the Sidney Papers.
[2] Henry Brooke, second Lord Cobham, Warden of the Cinque Ports.—See before, p. 413.

My Lady Doritye, Mrs. Fetton, Mrs. Carey, Mrs. Onslow, Mrs. Southwell, Mrs. Bess Russell, Mrs. Darcy, and my Lady Blanche Somersett. Those eight dawnce to the musiq Apollo bringes; and there is a fine speach that makes mention of a ninth, much to her honor and praise. The preparation for this feast is sumptuous and great; but it is feared that the house in Blackfriars wilbe to little for such a company. The marriage is upon Monday; what els may happen in it I will signifie when it is past."

June 23. "This day se'night her Majestie was at Blackfriars to grace the marriage of Lord Harbert and his wife. The bride met the Queen at the water-side, where my Lord Cobham had provided a lectica, made like a litter, whereon she was carried to my Lady Russell's by six Knights. Her Majesty dined there, and at night went through Dr. Puddin's house (who gave the Queen a fanne) to my Lord Cobham's, where she supped. After supper the masks came in, as I writ in my last; and delicate it was to see eight ladies so pretily and richly attired, Mrs. Fetton leade; and after they had donne all their own ceremonies, these eight ladies maskers chose eight ladies more to dawnce the measures. Mrs. Fetton went to the Queen and woed her to dawnce. Her Majesty asked what she was? *Affection*, she said. *Affection*, said the Queen, is false. Yet her Majestie rose and dawnced: so did my Lady Marquis [of Winchester]. The bride was led to the Church by the Lord Harbert of Cardife and my Lord Cobham; and from the Church by the Earles of Rutland and Cumberland. The gifts given that day were valewed at £1000 in plate and jewels at least. The entertainment was great and plentifull, and my Lady Russell much commended for it. Her Majesty upon Tuesday came backe again to the Court: but the solemnities continued till Wednesday night, and now the Lord Harbert and his faire Lady are in Court."

July 27. "Upon Tuesday the Queen removes, but that she will to Northwiltshire is not knowen. It will be a long Progress, which I must follow, and as often as I can I will find means to send a letter to you of all things that happens during this Progress."

THE QUEEN'S WARDROBE, 1600.

The following Extracts are copied from a thin folio book in the possession of Craven Ord, Esq. F. S. A. intituled, "A Booke of all suche Garments, Jewells, Silkes, and other Stuffe Garnishmentes of Golde, Pearle, and Stone, and also of divers Stones of severall natures and workmanship, as are remayninge in the Offyce of the Garderobe of Robes, the   daye of Julie, in the 42d yeare of the raigne of our Soveraigne Ladie Elizabeth, by the Grace of God, of Englande, Fraunce, and Irelande, Queene, Defender of the Faith, &c. and now in the chardge of Sir Thomas Gorges, Knight, Gentleman of the Robes. At which time the Right Honorable Thomas Lorde Buckhurste, Lorde Highe Treasurer of Englande, George Lorde Hunsdon, Lorde Chamberlaine of her Majestie's House, Sir John Fortescue, Knighte, Chauncellor and Underthreasorer of Thexchequer, and Sir Jñ Stanhope, Knighte, Threasorer of her Highnes Chamber, by vertue of her Highnes cõmission, under the Greate Seale of Englande, bearing date the 4th daie of Julie, in the saide 42d yere of her Highnes raigne, to them, or to any three of them (wherof the Lorde Thrẽar or Lorde Chamblaine to be allwaies one) in that behalfe directed, did repaire to the saide Garderobe of the Robes, as well within the Courte as at the Tower of London, and Whitehall; and there did take a perfecte Survey of all such Robes, Garments, and Jewells, and other P'cells as at that tyme were there founde to remaine. Accordinge to whiche S'vey they have caused to be written twoe severall bookes; the one of whiche bookes is subscribed with the handes of the saide Comissioners, and remaineth for a chardge to the saide Office of the Robes; the other is subscribed by the saide Sir Thomas Gorges, Knight, and remaineth with the saide Lorde Threasorer."

It appears from this account, that the Queen's Wardrobe then [1600] consisted, exclusive of her Coronation, Mourning, Parliament Robes, and those of the Order of the Garter, of

Robes	99	Forepartes	136	Saufegards and Juppes	43
Frenche gownes	102	Peticoates	125	Dublettes	85
Rounde gownes	67	Cloakes	96	Lappe mantles	18
Loose gownes	100	Cloakes and Saufegards	31	Fannes	27
Kirtells	126	Saufegards	13	Pantobles	9

ROBES, LATE KING EDWARDE THE VIth.

Firste, one robe of clothe of silver, lyned with white satten, of thorder of the St. Michell, with a brode border of embrodirie, with a wreathe of Venice [1] gold, and the scallop shell, and a frenge of the same golde, and a small border aboute that; the grounde beinge blew vellat, embrodered with halfe moones of silver, with a whoode and a tippet of crymsen vellat, with a like embroderie, the tippet perished in one place with ratts, and a coate of clothe of silver, with demisleeves, with a frenge of Venice golde.

APPARELL.

Item, one gowne of purple golde tissue, with a brode garde of purple vellat, embrodered with Venice golde, and with wreathes of purles of damaske golde, edged with vellat, unlyned.

Item, one gowne of crimsen satten, enbrodered all over with purles of damaske golde, edged with crimsen, with a short stocke sleeve unlyned.

Item, one frocke of clothe of golde, reized and tissued with golde and silver, with a *billament* lace of Venice golde, lyned with blacke vellat.

Item, one frocke of clothe of silver, chequered with redd silke like birdes eies, with demi-sleeves, with a cutt of crymsen vellat, pursled on with silver, lined with crimsen vellat.

Item, one coate with demi-sleeves of crimsen satten, enbrodered all over with a twisk of golde, and a border of crimson vellat, enbrodered with golde, *and pulled out with tincell*, lyned with vellat.

Item, one jerkine of clothe of silver, with longe cutts downeright [2], bounde with a *billament* lace of Venice silver and blacke silke, lined with satten.

JEWELLES.

Item, one brouche of golde, with a small table rubie in it, and divers p̃sonages [3].

Item, one poynarde, the halfe ivorie with an open pomell, the halfe striped downe with golde; with a knife, the hafte of golde, the locker and shape of golde, having a pece of the shape broken of, with a tassell of blew silke, and a skaberde of leather.

---

[1] *Venys* gold occurs in the Wardrobe Account of Rich. III. communicated by Mr. Astle to the Editor of the Antiquarian Repertory, III. 243.   [2] It was *slasht*.

[3] Figures. One of the finest jewels of this kind belonging to Margaret Countess of Lenox, grandmother of James I. was shewn by Dr. Combe to the Society of Antiquaries, in 1782.

Gownes late Queene Marie's.

Item, one Frenche gowne of blacke vellat, with an edge of purle, and pipes of gold, the wide sleeves turned up all over with like *purle and pipes,* lackinge parte of the pipes on the sleeves and in the border.

Kirtells.

Item, one Frenche kirtle, thoutside of rich cloth of golde tissue, the inside of crimsen cloth of golde, edged with a passamaine [1] lace of golde.

Item, one Frenche kirtle of murrey [2] cloth of tissue golde and silver, let downe with murrey satten, edged with vellat, and lined with crimsen taphata.

Item, one foreparte of a kirtle of white vellat, all over enbrodered with Venice golde, and set with small turquesses, garnets, and *ragged pearle* set in the border.

Robes.

The Coroncõn Robes.

Firste, one mantle of clothe of golde, tissued with golde and silver, furred with powdered armyons [3], with a mantle lace of silke and golde, with buttons and tassells to the same.

Item, one kirtle of the same tissue, the traine and skirts furred with powdered armyons, the rest lyned with sarceonet, with a paire of bodies and sleeves to the same.

The Mourning Robes.

Item, one mantle of purple vellat, with a mantle lace of silke and golde, with buttons and tassells to the same.

Item, one kirtle and sircoate of the same purple vellat, the traine and skirts furred with powdered armyons, the rest lyned with srconet, with a paire of upper bodies to the same.

The Parliament Robes.

Item, one mantle of crimsen vellat, fured througheoute with powdred armyons, the mantle-lace of silke and golde, with buttons and tassells to the same.

Item, one kirtle and sircoate of the crimsen vellat, the same traine and skirts furred with powdered armions, the rest lyned with srconet, with a cappe of mainetenance to the same, striped downe right *with passamaine* lace of gold, with a tassell of golde to the same, furred with powdered armyons, with a whoode of crimsen vellat, furred with powdred armyons, with a paire of bodies and sleeves to the same.

[1] An open work-edging. [2] Black. [3] Query Ermines?

Item, one cappe of mainetenance, striped downright, with a passamaine lace of golde to the same, furred with powdered armyons.

For the Order of the Garter.

Item, one mantle of purple vellat, for the Order of the Garter, lyned with white taphata, with mantle-lacs of purple silke and golde, and tassells of the same.

Item, one Frenche kirtle, with bodies of crimsen vellat, laide with a lace of Venice gold.

Item, one mantle of tawnye satten, bordered with an enbroderie of Venice golde and silver, and enbrodered all over with *bias*[1] *cloudes* and spangles of like golde, faced with white satten, razed with a border enbrodered with like golde.

Item, one mantle of aish-colour *sleve*[2] *silke* networke and golde, with a traine.

Item, one vale of white networke, flourished with golde twist and spangles.

Item, one mantle of white lawne or networke, striped, set with tufts of blacke silke and spangles of silver.

Item, one mantle of blacke networke, florished all over with golde and spangles like waveworke.

Item, one mantle, without a traine, of tawney networke, richeley florished with Venice golde and silver, like starres and *crosse billets*, bounde aboute with a lace of Venice golde.

Item, one vale of blacke networke, florished with Venice silver like flagon-worke, and enbrodered all over with roses of Venice golde, silver, and silke, of colours of silke woman's worke.

Item, one mantle, or loose gowne, of aish-colour network, florished with Venice golde and silver plate billetwise, with *owes* of gold and silver, and a threede of like golde and silver like flames.

Item, one mantle, with a traine, of pale pincke coloured networke, florished all over with silver, like esses[3] and branches billetwise.

Item, one mantle of aish-colour taphata, with two *Burgonyon gardes*, enbrodered all over with gold upon lawne, lyned with white taphata šconet, and set throughoute with ragged pearle.

Item, one mantle of blacke stiched clothe, edged with a *bone lace* of small pearle and bugle[4], and fine fishes of mother of pearle, one set with small ermerodes and garnets.

Item, one mantle of white *sipers*[5], tufted with heare-colour silke, with a small passamaine lace of like coloured silke and Venice silver.

[1] Crooked or wreathed.   [2] Network of single or parted silk.   [3] SS.
[4] Bugles.   [5] Cyprus work. So roses of Cypers, gold of Cyprus.

Item, one mantle of white lawne [1] cut and turned in, enbrodered alover with workes of silver, like pomegranetts, roses, honiesocles, and acornes.

Item, one mantle of silver tincell, *printed* and bounde aboute with *a passamaine* lace of silver.

FRENCHE GOWNES [2].

Item, one Frenche gowne of blacke clothe of golde bordered rounde aboute with a brode border indented-wise, enbrodered within the same like wilde fearne-brakes, upon lawne and golde plate.

Item, one Frenche gowne of clothe of silver, enbrodered with a brode border, like pillars and *essefirmes* of Venice of golde.

Item, one Frenche gowne of blacke vellat, enbrodered all over with *wormes* of silke of sondrie colours, cut upon white sarceonet stained.

Item, one Frenche gowne of heare-colour vellat, richlie enbrodered with Venice golde, silver, and ragged seede pearle, like a dead tree.

Item, one Frenche gowne of blacke satten, with a verie brode garde, enbrodered with an enbroderie like artichokes, with leaves of blacke satten and Venice golde and silver, upon carnačõn satten. Given to Mr. Hide by the Quene, March 7.

Item, one Frenche gowne of clodie colour satten, garded with heare colour vellat, enbrodered with knotts and *galtroppes* [3] of Venice golde onlie before, covered with blacke taphata cutte.

Item, one Frenche gowne of murrey-satten, cut with a skallop cut, and laide with a lace of Venice golde chevernewise all over.

[1] Lawns and cambricks were first brought to England in this reign.

[2] The Queen told Sir James Melvil, that "she had cloaths of every sort; which every day thereafter (says he) so long as I was at her Court she changed. One day she had the English weed, another the French, and another the Italian, and so forth. She asked me which of them became her best: I answered, in my judgment, the Italian dress: which answer I found pleased her well; for she delighted to shew her golden hair, wearing a caul and bonnet as they do in Italy."—Hume says, "Among the other species of luxury, that of apparel began much to increase during this age; and the Queen thought proper to restrain it by proclamation. Her example was very little conformable to her edicts. As no woman was ever more conceited of her beauty, nor more desirous of making impression on the hearts of beholders, no one ever went to a greater extravagance in apparel, or studied more the variety and richness of her dresses. She appeared almost every day in a different habit; and tried all the several modes, by which she hoped to render herself agreeable. She was also so fond of her cloaths, that she never could part with any of them; and at her death she had in her wardrobe all the different habits, to the number of 3000, which she had ever worn in her life-time."

[3] Caltrops are iron spikes fixt in balls, to throw in the way of the enemy's cavalry.

Item, one gowne of horse-fleshe-colour satten, enbrodered all over with owes cut with small cuts, with a brode lace aboute it of Venice golde, the longe sleeves lined with clothe of golde, the gowne lined with orenge-colour srconet.

Item, one Frenche gowne of tawney sattin, embrodered all over with knotts, sonnes, and clouds, of golde, silver, and silke, furred with *luzarnes*[1].

Item, one coveringe for a Frenche gowne of lawne, enbrodered all over with fountaines, snaikes, swordes, and other devises, upon silver chamblet prented.

Item, one Frenche gowne of russet stiched cloth, richlie florished with golde and silver, lyned with orenge-colour taphata, and hanginge sleeves, lyned with white taphata, enbrodered with *antiques*[2] of golde and silke of sonderie colours, called china work.

Rounde Gownes.

Item, one rounde gowne of white cloth of silver, with workes of yellow silke, like flies, wormes, and snailes.

Item, one rounde gowne, of the Irish fashion, of orenge tawney satten, cut and snipte, garded thicke overthawarte with aish-colour vellat, enbrodered with Venice golde and spangles.

Item, one rounde gowne of *Isabella*-colour[3] satten, cut in snippes and raised up, set with silver spangles.

Item, one rounde gowne of beasar-colour[4] satten, with workes of silver like *Gynney* wheate[5] and branches.

Item, one rounde gowne of lawne, cut and snipt, with small silver plates upon aish-colour silver chamblet.

Item, one rounde gowne of dove-colour *caph'a*[6], with workes of golde and orenge-colour silke, like rainebowes, cloudes, and droppes and flames of fire.

Item, one rounde gowne of heare-coloured raised mosse-worke, enbrodered all over with *leaves, pomegranets, and men*.

[1] Luzarn or lucern, a sort of lynx, a Russian animal of the size of a wolf.

[2] *Antics*. Men in fantastical postures, like morris-dancers, not uncommon in old embroidery for hangings or apparel.   [3] Or flax-seed colour.

[4] Q. *beufar*, beaver. Or it may be of the *bezoar* stone, which is of a *brownish* hue.

[5] Indian wheat.

[6] A kind of tiffany. Q. Caffoy, a sort of velvet. Or perhaps only *tapta*, for *taphata*, as before, p. 502; see also p. 510.

Loose Gownes.

Item, one loose gowne of blacke satten, enbrodered all over with roses and *pauncies*[1], and a border of oken leaves, roses, and pauncis, of Venice golde, silver, and silke, with a face likewise embroderen.

Item, one loose gowne of white satten, faced with orenge-colour satten, embrodered all over with *Friers' knotts* and roses, in branches of Venice golde and tawney silke, and cut, with a slight border of Venice silver and orenge-colour sylke.

Item, one loose gowne of *drake's colour* satten, cut and tufted, laide on the seames and rounde aboute with twoe laces of Venice silver, faced and edged with white plushe.

Item, one loose gowne of *ladie-blushe* satten, laide with a bone-lace of Venice golde and silver, with spangles, with buttons downe before of the same lace.

Item, one loose gowne of aish-colour tufte taphata, the grounde silver, furred *with callaber*.

Item, one loose gowne of blacke taphata, with *compas lace* of blacke silke and silver, with a braided lace, with a plate on either side.

Item, one loose gowne of *white curle*, laide with golde lace.

Item, one loose gowne of white *tillyselye*, like grograme, bounde aboute with a small lace of golde, the hanginge sleeves beinge cutt and bounde with like lace and tufts of golde threede, and some golde spangles.

Kirtells[2].

Item, one kirtle of aishe-colour[3] cloth of golde, with workes of snailes, wormes, flies and spiders[4].

Item, one rounde kirtle of white clothe of silver chevernd, with *bluncket*, with lace of golde, and spangles, buttons, and loopes.

Item, one rounde kirtle of white cloth of sylver, bounde aboute with a lace of Venice golde, and seaven buttons, like the *birdes of Arabia*[5], embrodered downe before.

---

[1] Pansies.

[2] The garment under the mantle. The mantle was a loose cloak, covering the arms, and fastened at the neck or breast.   [3] Ash-colour.

[4] I have somewhere seen a whole-length portrait of a Lady in white, embroidered with spiders, or beetles in a large pattern. Perhaps the *black-flies*, mentioned p. 508.   [5] Birds of Paradise.

Item, one Frenche kirtle of white satten cutt, all over enbrodered with *hopes*[1], floweres, and cloudes, of Venice golde, sylver, and sylke.

Item, one rounde kirtle of *claie-colour satten, or terr' sigillata*, enbrodered all over with flowers of Venice silver and blacke silke.

Item, one rounde kirtle of white satten, enbrodered with a slight border like *a ryver of the sea*, and slightlie enbrodered all over with plate, *esses*[2] of plate golde, with a deepe golde frenge.

Item, one rounde kirtle of white satten, enbrodered all over with the work like flames, pescods, and pillars, with a border likewise enbrodered with roses. Given by hir Majestie the 16th Apr. 1600.—A. Walsingham.

Item, one round kirtle of *beasar*-colour silver chamblet, with embrodered golde buttones downe before.

Item, one rounde kirtle of heare-colour tufte taphata, the ground silver, with workes like pomegranets and artichoques.

Forepartes[3].

Item, one foreparte of clothe of sylver, enbrodered all over with rainebowes, cloudes, flames of fyer, and sonnes, of sylke of sondrye colour.

Item, one verie faire foreparte of peache-colour satten, embroidered all over with a faire border, embrodered with sondrie beastes and fowle, of Venice golde and sylke, lyned with greene sarconet.

Item, one foreparte and a dublet of white satten, enbrodered all over with rainebowes, of Venice golde and spangles.

Item, one fore parte of white satten, embrodered all over with bugles, made like flowers upon stalkes, within knotts.

Item, one fore parte of white satten, embrodered with daffadillies of Venice golde, and other flowers.

Item, one fore parte of satten, of sondrie colours, embrodered with the twelve signes, of Venice golde, silver, and silke of sondrie colours, unmade.

Item, one fore parte of white satten, embrodered verie faire with borders of the Sonne, Mone, and other Signes and Planetts, of Venice golde, silver, and silke of sondrie colours, with a border of beastes beneath, likewise embrodered.

[1] *Hoops*, circles.   [2] SS.
[3] What we should call in modern times *stomachers*.

Item, one fore parte of white satten, embrodered all over with a runninge worke like potts, and within them jelleflowers, lined with yellowe šrconett.

Item, one fore parte of white satten, embrodered all over verie faire like seas, with dyvers devyses of rockes, shippes, and fishes [1], embrodered with Venice golde, sylver, and silke of sondrye colours, garnished with some seede pearle.

Item, one fore parte of white satten, embrodered all over with paunceis, little roses, knotts, and a border of mulberies, pillers, and pomegranets, of Venice golde, sylver, and sylke of sondrye colours.

Item, one fore parte of peach-colour satten, embrodered all over verie faire with dead trees, flowers, and a lyon in the myddest, garded with manye pearles of sondry sortes.

Item, one fore parte of white satten, embrodered all over with spiders, flies, and roundells, with cobwebs, of Venice golde and tawnye silke.

Item, one fore parte of greene satten, embrodered all over with sylver, like beastes, fowles, and fishes.

Item, one fore parte of lawne, embrodered with bees and sondrie wormes, lyned with white taphata.

Petticoates.

Item, one peticoate of watchet, or blew satten, embrodered all over with flowers and beasts, of Venice golde, silver, and silke, like a wildernes.

Item, one peticoate of tawney satten, razed all over with fower borders of embroderie of Venice silver, and with *lypes*, lyned with orenge-colour šconet.

Item, one peticoate of white satten, embrodered all over with blacke flies, with a border of fountaines and trees, embrodered rounde aboute it, and waves of the sea.

---

[1] At Hardwick is a whole-length of Queen Elizabeth, in a gown painted with serpents, birds, a sea-horse, swan, ostrich, &c. her hair golden. At Hatfield there two portraits of her; in one she is represented richly dressed in black, sitting at a table on which is a great sword. A spotted ermine, with a crown on its head, and collar round its neck, is represented running up her arm. Mr. Pennant says, "This little beast, being an emblem of chastity, is placed here as a compliment to the Virgin Queen." In the other, her gown is close bodied: on her head is a coronet and long aigret, and a long distended gauze veil; her face young; her hair yellow, falling in two long tresses; her neck adorned with a pearl necklace, her arms with bracelets. The lining of her robe is worked with eyes and ears, and on her left sleeve is embroidered a serpent: all to imply wisdom and vigilance. In the other hand is a rainbow, with this flattering motto, "Non sine sole Iris."

Item, one peticoate of white satten, embrodered all over slightlie with snakes, of Venice golde, silver, and some *owes*, with a faire border, embrodered like seas, cloudes, and rainebowes.

Item, one peticoate of white Turquye satten, embrodered all over with a twiste of Venice golde, and *owes* like knotts.

Item, one peticoate of white satten, enbrodered all over with Venice golde, silver, and silke of divers colours, with a verie faire border of pomegranetts, pyneaple trees, frutidge [1], and the nyne Muses, in the same border.

Item, one peticoate of white sconet, quilted all over with a small threede of Venice golde and silke of colours, with flowers and feathers, embrodered with Carnačon watchet and grene silke, with three borders rounde aboute, embrodered with pauncies, roses, and pillars.

Cloakes.

Item, one Dutche cloake of blacke vellat, embrodered all over with flowers and grashoppers, of Venice golde, silver, and silke, lyned with tawnie sconet, furred with sables.

Item, one cloake of blacke taphata, laide aboute and striped with lace of Venice golde and sylver, wrought wtth *pipes* and *ple* [2], with a *jagge* [3] wrought *byas* [4], with *passamanie* lace of Venice golde and silver, lyned with greene cloth of golde and sylver.

Item, one shorte cloake of perfumed leather [5], enbrodered with three small borders of Venice golde, sylver, and crimsen silke, faced and edged with sables, and furred with *callaber*.

Item, one cloake of heare-colour raized mosseworke, embrodered like stubbes of dead trees, set with fourteen buttons embrodered like butterflies, with fower pearles and one emerode in a pece, lyned with cloth of sylver, prented.

Cloakes and Saufegardes.

Item, one cloake, a saufegarde, and a hatt, of blacke taphata, enbrodered all over with droppes of Venice golde, blacke silke, and spangles.

Item, one cloak and a saufegarde of gozelinge-colour taphata.

---

[1] *Fruitage*, clusters of fruit.   [2] *Q. Pearle.*   [3] Jagged.
[4] Worked in crooked or waving lines. See before, p. 503.
[5] Another cloake of perfumed leather occurs.

Item, one cloake and a saufegarde of taphata, called *pounde cythrone* colour, bounde with a lace and buttons of Venice sylver and watchet silke.

SAUFEGARDES.

Item, one saufegarde and a dublet of dove-colour cloth of golde, bounde aboute and garnished with buttons and loopes, of plate lace of Venice silver.

Item, one saufegarde of blacke vellat, spotted all over with little knotts and *cynques*[1] of small seede pearle, the border embrodered with pillers and butterflies, of like seede pearle.

SAUFEGARDES AND JUPPES.

Item, one juppe and a saufegarde of brasell-colour cloth of silver, with a lace of gold and silver, with spangles upon carnačōn satten.

Item, one juppe and saufegarde of orenge-colour, or marigolde-colour vellat, cut and uncutt, the sleeves and downe before garnished with a lace of Venice sylver, like *essefirmes*, and laide aboute with twoe plate laces of Venice silver.

Item, one juppe and saufegarde of heare-colour *capha*, like golde flames of fire, and garnished with buttons, loupes, and lace of Venice silver, lyned with white plushe.

DUBLETTES.

Item, one doublet of blacke clothe of golde, with dogges of silver.

Item, one dublett of straw-colour satten cut, and lyned with cloth of silver, embrodered upon with knotts, roses, and sonnes, of Venice golde and silver.

Item, one dublet of white satten, embrodered like seas, with fishes, castles, and sonne-beames, of Venice golde, silver, and silke of sondrie colours.

Item, one dublett of *camerike*[2], wrought with Venice golde, silver, and silke of sondrie colours, with white networke, striped with sylver.

LAPPE MANTLES.

Item, one compasse lappe-clothe of white taphata, embrodered all over with sondrie antiques, lined with orenge-colour plushe.

Item, one mantle of white plush, with a *pane*[3] of redd swanne-downe in the middest.

[1] *Q.* Cinqfoils.
[2] A sort of stuff made of camel's hair. In the wardrobe account of Hen. VIII. a doublet set oute with camerike.
[3] A breadth.

SILKES.

Item, towe remnants of blacke *burrell*[1], conteyninge both together 12 yeardes.

Item, one peece of tawney networke florished with golde, called[2] birds in the cage, conteyneing 23 yardes.

Item, two handekercheifes like barbers aprones.

Item, three peeces of *baudekin*[3] of sondrye colours, each peece contayninge vii yardes. 21 yardes.

Item, 19 remnants of white silke *curle*, contayninge in the whole 104 yardes.

FANNES.

Item, one fanne of white feathers, with a handle of golde, havinge two snakes wyndinge aboute it, garnished with a ball of diamondes in the ende, and a crowne on each side within a paire of winges garnished with diamondes, lackinge 6 diamondes.

Item, one fanne of feather of divers colours, the handle of golde, with a bear and a ragged staffe on both sides, and a lookinge glasse on thone side.

Item, one handle of golde enameled, set with small rubies and emerodes, lackinge 9 stones, with a shipp under saile on thone side.

Item, one handle of christall, garnished with sylver guilte, with a worde within the handle.

Item, one handle of elitropia[4], garnished with golde, set with sparks of diamondes, rubies, and sixe small pearles, lackinge one diamonde.

PANTOBLES[5].

Item, one paire of pantobles of cloth of silver, embrodered with a mill.

Item, one paire of pantobles of orenge-colour vellat, enbrodered upon with *essefirmes* and other knotts of seede pearle, and some ragged ple.

SONDRIE P'CELLS.

Item, one little bearinge sworde, with a pommell and hilts of iron, guilte.

Item, one sworde, with a pomell of *sanguimarie*.

---

[1] *Burra*, or *Borra*, is a sort of stuffing or wadding. Du Cange, in voc. Q. is *Burrell* the diminutive from it.

[2] Q. *Gold-coloured.*   [3] Gold brocade. The richest cloth.

[4] *Heliotrope.* A precious stone of green-colour, with red spots, or veins. Ainsworth, ex solino.

[5] *Pantoufles.* Fr. Slippers.

Item, one canapie of crimson capha damaske to carrie over one, striped with lace of Venice golde and sylver, the handle mother-of-ple.

Item, fower lazarnes skines.

JEWELLS.

Item, in colletts of golde, in everie collet one *ballas* [1], one being broken, 23.

Item, one small jewell of golde, like a white lyon, with a flie on his side, standing upon a base or foote, garnished with twoe opalls, twoe verie little pearles, fyve rubies, one rubie pendaunt, and twoe little shorte cheines on the backe of the lyon.

Item, one fearne braunche of golde, having therin a lyzard, a lady cow [2], and a snaile.

Item, one jewell of golde, with a flie and a spider in it upon a rose.

Item, in buttons with camewes [3], 18.

Item, one jewell of golde, like *an Irish darte*, garnished with fower small diamondes.

Jewells receaved by Sir Thomas Gorges, Knight, of the charge of the Ladie Katherine Howarde, Countesse of Nott.

Item, in greate rounde buttons of golde, enameled with sondry colours, each set with small sparks of rubies, and one pearle in the middest called *greate bucklers*, 72.

Item, one jewell of golde like a frogg, garnished with diamondes.

Jewells receaved by Sir Thomas Gorges, Knight, of Mrs. Mary Radcliffe.

Item, in buttons of golde like tortoyses, in each one a pearle, 454.

Item, one jewell of golde like a dasye, and small flowers aboute it, garnished with sparks of diamondes and rubies, with her Majestie's picture graven within a garnet, and a sprigge of three branches, garnished with sparks of rubies, one pearle in the topp, and a small pendaunte of sparks of diamondes.

Memorand. All the jewells before mencõned we receved by Sir Thomas Gorges, Knight, of Mrs. Mary Ratcliffe, were by him delivered over unto the charge of the said Mrs. Ratcliffe the 28th of Maye, 1603, in the presence of us,

EDW. CARYE.   THO. KNYVETT.
FRA. GOTTON.

---

[1] A species of ruby of a vermeil rose-colour.
[2] Q. A *lady-bird*, an insect so called.
[3] Cameos.

July 27, Rowland Whyte, in a letter to Sir Robert Sidney, in 1600, says, "Her Majestie din'd this day at Chelsey at my Lord of Nottingham's; yt is thought she will stay there till Monday; she took with her but the Lord Worcester, Sir John Stanhope, and two or three Ladies [1]."

Again, from Nonsuch, August 8, "Her Majesty is in very good health, and goes abroad every day to ride and Church. This day she dines at my Lady Edmonds', and goes to Oatlands to bed. Some feare her Majestie will goe her intended Progress to North Wiltshire; but it is very like that she will goe to Farnham Castle, where she lies seven daies; it may be, if she like the air, it will be the farthest place of her Progress."

August 12, "Her Majesty removed upon Monday to Tooting [2], and on Wednesday came to Nonsuch, where she stays till Tuesday, and then resolves to go on her Progress to Elvetham, the Earl of Hertford's. The Lords are sorry for it; but her Majesty lets the old stay behind, and the young and able to goe with her. She had just cause to be offended, that at her remove to this place she was so poorly attended, for I never saw so small a train."

August 15, "Her Majesty is very well, I thank God; for since Wednesday she hath bene at Bedington; upon Thursday she dined at Croidon with my Lord of Canterbury, and this day returns to Nonsuch again."

August 26, she was at Oatlands; and Sept. 1, Mr. Whyte writes, "The Court is now given to hunting and sports: the Lords come are gon one waye and another. Upon Thursday her Majesty dines and hunts at Hanworth Parke: upon Tuesday she dines at Mr. Drake's; and this day she huntes in the new lodge in the forest. God be thanked she is very merry and well. Lord Nottingham is in these parts, and Master of her Sports."

September 12, "Her Majesty is very well, and excellently disposed to hunting, for every second day she is on horseback, and continues the sport long; it is thought she will remayne in Oatlands till fowle weather drives her away. Upon Tuesday she dined at Mr. Drake's; upon Wednesday the Embassador of Barbary had audience at Oatlands."

In the same month, the Queen paid a Visit at Hanworth [3], the scene of her

---

[1] Sidney Papers, vol. II. p. 161.

[2] Where probably she was the guest of Sir Henry Maynard, who was then Lord of the Manor.

[3] Camden calls Hanworth a small Royal seat, which Henry VIII. took great delight in, and made the scene of his pleasures. Towards the end of his Reign it was settled in dower upon Queen

juvenile pastimes. She dined there, and partook of the amusement of hunting in the Park.

On Thursday the 13th of November the bells at St. Margaret's, Westminster, were rung " when the Queen went from Westminster."

Katherine Parr, who frequently resided there after the King's death with her second husband Sir Thomas Seymour (the Lord Admiral) and the Princess Elizabeth, whose education was entrusted to her care. The Princess was then in her 15th year; and it was said by the Lord Admiral's enemies, and was made one of the articles of accusation against him in his impeachment, that he endeavoured during their residence at Hanworth and Chelsea, to gain the Princess's affections, intending, if he could get the Queen Dowager out of the way, to marry her, and seat himself upon the Throne. The examinations of Katherine Ashlye and others, relating to these transactions, are printed in the Burleigh Papers. (On this subject see before, in vol. I. p. 23.) It appears by Mrs. Ashlye's testimony, that whatever were the Lord Admiral's intentions, the Queen Dowager was entirely free from any suspicion of the kind; for her Majesty appears to have been a principal party in the familiarities which she describes. "At Hanworth," says she, "he would likewise come in the morning unto her Grace ; but, as she remembereth, at all tymes she was up before, savyng two mornings, the which two mornyngs the Quene came with hym. And this examinate lay with her Grace; and ther thei tytled my Lady Elizabeth in the bed, the Quene and my Lord Admyrall." Again, "Another tyme at Hanworth in the garden he wrated with her, and cut her gown in an hundred pieces, beyng black cloth; and when she came up, this examinate chid with hir; and hir Grace answered, she could not do withall, for the Quene held her while the Lord Admirall cut it." William Earl of Pembroke was Keeper of the Wardrobe, and of the Park at Hanworth, in the first year of Queen Mary. In 1588, the manor of Hanworth was granted for life to Anne Dutchess of Somerset. In 1594, it was leased to William Killegrew for 80 years. Lysons, vol. V. p. 94.

Sir Thomas Seymour, Knt. brother to the Protector, and third son of Sir John Seymour, of Wolf Hall, in Wiltshire, by Margaret, daughter of Sir Henry Wentworth, of Nettlestead in Suffolk. He had served with merit against the French in the wars during the Reign of King Henry VIII. and was appointed Master of the Ordnance for life. Upon Edward's accession, he was constituted Lord High Admiral, and created Baron Seymour, of Sudley in Gloucestershire. After having made an ineffectual proposal of marriage to the Princess Mary, he wedded Queen Katherine Parr, so soon after the King's death, that had she proved pregnant the issue might with some probability have been ascribed to her former husband. This Lady, however, dying Sept. 5, 1548, childless (or, as some have said, leaving an infant daughter who not long survived her), Lord Seymour made his addresses to the Princess Elizabeth with so much warmth that the Council thought it necessary to interfere, and the depositions of several persons taken on that occasion are preserved in Haynes's Cecil Papers, very little to the credit of our Virgin Queen. Every other path to power being now obstructed, he attempted to follow his ambitious views by the overthrow of his brother's authority; and laboured to gain the young King to his interest with so much effect, that the Protector, for his own security, was obliged to concur in his impeachment. He was beheaded March 20, 1548-9, after a very impartial trial in parliament, for high treason. Lodge, vol. I. p. 112.

On the same day, her Majestie being most honorablie attended on by the Prelates, Nobles, and Judges of the Realme, was received neere unto Chelsey, by the Lord Maior of London, with his brethren the Aldermen all in scarlet, besides to the number of 500 Citizens in coats of velvet and chaines of golde, on horsebacke, every of them having two staffe-torches to attend on them; and they all waited on her to her Royall Palace at Westminster.

Ambassador from the Emperor of Russia, 1600.

The Lord Boris Pheodorowich, having by many devices wonne the peoples hearts, after he had, as he supposed, made away Demetrius the immediate heire upon the death of Pheodor Vasilowich, his generall love and reputation was such amongst the common people, together with all other the principall officers of estate, which by his means onely obtained their preferment, who strongly held together to the discountenancing and displacing the aunclent nobility, was, by the vygor of his generall faction, chosen Emperor of Russia; which, after a faint refusal, he accepted. And then, with all expedition, sent his Ambassadors unto such Princes as he knew most imminent and propicious for his present fortunes.

The 18th of September, 1600, his Ambassador, with twentie persons, arryved at London. The 14th of October he had audience, and delivered his letters, wherein the new Emperor, otherwise generally, and more truly tearmed the Great Duke, signified his speciall desire of amitie with her Majestie, with what favours he had done and would do unto her subjectes, confirming their charter, and admitting them free passage under his golden seele, manifesting therewithall, with what a generall consent, or rather compulsion of the whole Nobilitie and Commons, besides the earnest desire of the Reverend Cleargie, and their most Holy Patriarch, hee tooke uppon him that dignitie; arrogating unto himselfe an hereditary interest unto the Crowne. Amongst other things he desired the Queene to send him some men of qualitie, as Doctors of Physicke, Learned Men, and skilfull Artificers, unto whome hee promised kind entertainment and condigne reward. Concerning the rest of this smooth-face usurping tyrant (says Stow), looke in the third yeere of King James: his Ambassador was very honorablie entertained, feasted, and entreated by the Queene, and as kindly used and dyetted for eight moneths space, at the sole charges of the Company of the Moscovie marchants.

Ambassador from the King of BARBARY.

On the 8th of August, there arryved at Dover Mully Hamet Xarife, Secretarie and Principall Ambassador from Abdola Wayhet Anowne King of Barbary, and with him in commission two marchants, to wit, Arealhadgel Messy, and Alhadg Hamet Mimon. These, with thirteene others, by Sir Thomas Gerard, Knight Marshall, divers Gentlemen, and the chiefe Barbary marchants, were brought to London the 15th of the same moneth, being carefully provided and lodged neere the Royall Exchange, in Alderman Ratcliffes house. Within five dayes after that they delivered their letters, and had audience, the Court being then at Nonsuch. The tenth of September they received answere, the Court being then at Otelands. The 17th of November, being the Queenes day, the Queene being then at Whitehall, a speciall place was builded onely for them neere to the Parke doore, to beholde that dayes triumph. Notwithstanding all which kindness shewed them, together with their dyet, and all other provision for sixe moneths space wholly at the Queenes charges: yet such was their inveterate hate unto our Christian Religion and estate, as they could not endure to give any manner of almes, charitie, or reliefe, either in moneie or broken meate, unto any English poore, but reserved their fragments, and solde the same unto such poore as would give most for them. They kild all their owne meate within their house, as sheepe, lambes, poultrie, and such like, and they turne their faces eastward when they kill any thing: they use beades, and pray to saints. And whereas the chiefe pretence of their Embassie was to require continuance of her Majesties favour towardes their King, with like entreatie of her navall ayde, for sundry especial uses, chiefly to secure his treasure from the parts of Guynea, &c. yet the English Marchants helde it otherwise, by reason that during their halfe yeere's abode in London, they used all subtiltie and diligence to know the prises, wayghts, measures, and all kindes of differences of such commodities, as eyther their Country sent hither, or England transported thither: they carryed with them all sortes of English wayghts, measures, and samples of commodities. And being returned, it was supposed they poysoned their Interpretor, being borne in Granado, because he commended the estate and bountie of England: the like violence was thought to be done unto their reverend aged Pilgrime, least he also should manifest England's honor to their disgrace. It was generally judged by their demeanors, that they were rather Espials then honorable Ambassadors; for they omitted nothing that might damnifie the English Marchants.

A True Discourse of the whole Occurrences in the [French] Queenes Voyage[1] from her Departure from Florence, until her Arrivall at the Citie of Marseilles, together with the Triumphs there made at her Entrie: whereto is adjoined her receiving and entrie into Lyons. All faithfully translated out of French, by E. A[2].

My Lord, according to the promise which you enforced of me at my departure from Paris, namely, that I should repair to his Majestie, and upon receit of his command to hasten with all diligence to Marseilles, where I have spent my time in expectation of the so long desired arrivall of the Queene: I doe now write unto you these presents, in full discharge of my said promise: wherby you shall understand, that upon the thirteenth day of October, the Queene departed from the Citie of Florence towards France, and arrived at Livorne the seventeenth day following, where she embarked in the generall galley of the Lord the great Duke, where she was attended with five of the Popes galleyes, five of the galleyes of Malta, and sixe of the sayd Lord Dukes: in all seventeene Galleyes. Her first harbor was at Espetie, where the Embassadours of the State of Genes came to salute her, with tender of their galleyes on the behalfe of the sayde State, for the which shee returned them great thankes. From that harbour shee arrived at Fin, where through tempest and foule weather shee was forced to sojourne nine dayes full: but ordinarily lay in her galley. From Fin shee tooke harbour at Savonne; the next day at Antibe; thence at Saint Maryes; then at Treport; next at Tollon, where shee tooke land, and stayed two days; and from Tollon shee arrived at Marseilles, the third of this moneth of November, betweene five and sixe of the clocke at night, and landed upon a great bridge, purposely erected on the kay, over against the lodging prepared for her: upon the which bridge wayted on the left hand the Lord Cardinalles Joyeuse, Gondy, Giury, and Sourdy, the Archbishops of Arles and Aix, the Bishops of Marseilles, Tolon, and Paris. The Lordes Duke of Guyse, the Constable and Chanceler, assisted with the

[1] Mary de Medicis to Henry IV. of France.

[2] Imprinted at London, by Simon Stafford, for Cuthford Burby; and are to be sold at his shop at the Royal Exchange, 1601.

Councellors of his Majesties councell. On the right hand stood the Ladie Dutchesse of Nemours and Guyse, and Mademoyselle her daughter: the Lady of Vantadour, the Lady Chanceler, the Marquesse of Guyercheuille, and other Ladies.

At the entrie unto the sayde bridge, the foure Consuls of the said Citie of Marseilles, in long scarlet gownes, holding in their handes a canapie of russet violet, upon a ground of silver, upon their knees presented her Majestie with two keyes of gold fastened upon a chaine; which keyes her sayd Majestie immediately delivered to the Lord of Lussan, Captain of her Guard; the Consuls rysed and withdrawne some three or foure steppes backe, the sayd Lord Cardinalles did their obeysance and received her; then the Lords of Guyse, the Constable, and Chanceler. After them came the Duchesse of Nemours, and saluted the Queen; then the Lady of Guyse, and Madamoyselle her daughter; and so consequently all the other Ladies.

This done, her sayde Majestie returned under her canapie; before whom marched the sayde Lord of Guyse, Constable and Chaunceler, ledde by the sayde Lord Cardinalles of Joyeuse and Gondy; then followed the Lady Great Duchesse of Florence, ledde by the Lord Cardinall of Guiry; then the Lady Dutchesse of Mantua, ledde by the Cardinall of Sourdy; after these marched the Ladies Duchesses of Nemours and Guyse, with her daughter; the Ladies of Vantadour, Chanceler, and others, according to their degrees; and so ascending a great stayre that was purposely made, they came to the door of a great chamber prepared for that purpose, for the sayde Lady Queene, and so to the Presence, where many Ladyes wayted for her.

This done, shee entred her chamber, followed by the said Ladies, the great Duchesse, the Duchesses of Mantua, Nemours, and Guyse, and the yong Lady of Guyse, with the other Ladyes; who all made but short stay, but returned to their lodgings, so as there remained with her none but the Princesses and Ladyes that had accompanied her in her journeyes. The Lordes likewise that had accompanied her did depart, namely, Don Iouan, Don Virginio, and Don Antonio, who also had assisted her in all her sayde voyages. Neyther am I able to expresse the magnificent discent out of the sayde galleyes, each taking place according to their degrees, enriched with all kindes of honour, as well in regard of the multitude of the Nobilitie, as for the sumptuousnesse of the furniture of the said galleyes, especially of the Queene's, which was under the conduct of the Lord Marc

Archbishop Whitgift's Hospital at Croydon.

Published as the Act directs by J. Nichols, Sept. 1st 1781.

Anthonio Colicat. Therein were two hundred Knights, that bare the crosse of Florence. The galley-slaves were magnifically apparelled. In them of Malta, under the conduct of Don Peter Mendoza, a hundred and fiftie Knights, and so in the rest; so that in the whole, it is accounted shee had for her conduct at the least seven thousand men, all at the King's pay and expences.

The next day, the fourth of this moneth, all the Ladyes came to help up the Queene, whom they brought to the Chappell purposely prepared neere to the Great Chamber, where she had the Masse celebrated, at what time the Princes, Princesses, Lords, and Ladyes, had their Gentlemen, Pages, and Servants, as proudly apparrelled as may be; nothing but cloth of gold, embrodery, and spangles.

Rowland Whyte informs Sir Robert Sidney, that "Mrs. Mary, upon St. Stephen's day in the afternoon, [December 26,] dawnced before the Queene two gullards with one Mr. Palmer, the admirablest dawncer of this tyme. Both were much commended by her Majesty; then she dawnced with him a corante."

The 3d of February, 1600-1, the Ambassadours from the Emperour of Russia, and other the Muscovites, rode through the Cittie of London, to Marybone Parke, and there hunted at their pleasure, and shortlie after returned homeward.

This yeere the Most Reverend Father John Whitgift, Archbishop of Canterburie, did finish that notable and memorable monument of our time, to wit, his Hospital of the Holy Trinity in Croyden [1], in the Countie of Surrey, by him there founded and builded of stone and bricke, for reliefe and sustentation of certayne poore people; as also a faire school-house for the increase of Literature, together with a large dwelling-house for the schoolmaster his use; and these premises he, through God's favourable assistance, in his owne life-time performed and perfited, for that (as myselfe have heard him say) he would not be to his executors a cause of their damnation.

[1] See before, in vol. I. p. 387.

A Discourse of the receiving and triumphs upon the [French] Queenes Entrie into the Citie of Lyons. Translated out of French.

My Lord, this bringer comming to Paris, I have accompanied with these presents, as wishing in what I might, to make shew of the friendship which continually I have vowed unto you; and in regard thereof to participitate unto you the pleasures whereof myself was an eye-witnesse in this towne, where, through God's grace, hearing of the expected and long-wished approach of the Queene of France, I was forced, upon a desire as well to behold the magnificence thereof, as to write unto you of the whole proceedings, to intermit whatsoever any other affayres.

The Queene therefore upon Saturday last towards the twy-light, arriving in the suburbs called La Guillotier, standing at the end of Rosne Bridge, was lodged at the Crowne, a verie large lodging, and of great receipt.

The next day being Sunday, shee returned two leagues back to a Castle, called La Moth, where shee dined, whither also the inhabitants of Lyons came to see her. After dinner the Burgesses troopes issued out of the towne, and marched to the sayd Castle to meete her, being in number some three or foure thousand gallant and very choyse souldiers. Their chiefe Captaines were all attyred alike, everie man his mandilion of blacke velvet, his white satten doublet, his netherstocks of white silke, his gascognes and buskins of black velvet, all garded with gold parchment lace. Their Lieutenants all in violet velvet, garded likewise with gold parchment lace. The Captaine Ancients all in russet velvet, layd also with gold lace, and bevere hats of the like colour, with feathers, garnished with agate stones, set in gold, oval wise. The Coronell marched before them excellently well appoynted, and mounted upon a mightie courser, barded and garded with gold lace, himself apparrelled in blacke velvet, all covered with gold parchment lace.

Then followed the souldiours, one third part pikes, another third part musqueters, and another third part harquebuziers; the musqueters their cassocks of greene velvet, with the bandoliers of the same, and white doublets, all layd with silver lace. The harquebuziers for the most part white doublets, and cassocks of violet cloth. The pikemen white doublets, with cassocks of black russet cloth, all well layde with lace, and hattes all feathers of one colour, and armed in white armour.

Then came the fourth town watch, armed at all assayes. Next the Serjeants on horsebacke, and the Lawyers. Then the Governours of the Towne, the

Steward, and the Sheriffes, accompanied with thirtie Burgesses, all attyred in violet velvet and foot-cloathes. After them the Italian nation.

The streetes were hanged with tapistrie, from Rosne Gate to the Church of Saint John, which was also hanged, and the sayd streetes gravelled all the way that the French Queen should come.

First entred the troopes that went foorth to meet the Queene in verie good order; then the Burgesses and Nations; then the Governours of the Towne; after them the French and Italian Nobilitie mixed. Next the Queene's bastard brother, accompanied with the chiefest of the Nobilitie, and with them tenne pages, apparelled in cloth of gold. After all followed the Queene, who entred the Citie in an open lictier, about foure of the clocke in the afternoone; her lictier all layde with gold parchment lace. At her entrie into the Towne-gate, she was received under a canopy of cloth of gold, borne by foure of the chiefe Burgesses of the Towne, under the which the sayde Lady Queene passed along the Towne, attired in cloth of gold, set with an infinite number of diamonds and stones that gave such a reverberation as to the beholders seemed a number of Sunnes. Yet was all this nothing, in regard of her own most excellent beauty, whereat all men did much marvaile: and withall, the voyce of the people so sounded forth their blessings and prayers, crying, "God save the Queene," that the verie mountaines about returned an eccho. Her Pages marched before her, with two that guided the lictier, apparelled in cornation cloth of gold, accompanied and followed with Princes, Lords, Cardinals, Bishops, Gentlemen, Princesses, and Ladies, as well French as foreyn, so many, that if I should undertake to describe the whole, it would take a quier of paper. Thus was she brought to the Church of Saint John.

Thus much in breefe have I written unto you, of our Ladie the French Queene's entrie into our Citie of Lyons; whom I beseech God to preserve for us, and shortly to send her some issue, which is the thing that with my heart I doe most desire.

From Lyons, this fourth of December, 1600.

A Copie of my Lord of COMBERLANDE's Speeche[1] to the QUEENE, upon the 17th day of November, 1600.

This Knight (Fairest and Happiest of all Ladies) removyng from castell to castell now rowleth up and downe, in open feild, a field of shaddow, having no other m'rs but night-shade, nor gathering anie mosse but about his own harte. This mallancholly, or rather desperit retirdnes, sommons his memorie to a repetition of all his accions, thoughtes, misfortunes, in the depth of which

[1] In this Speech, which seems to have been delivered by the Earl under the character of a pensive and discontented Knight, at one of those romantic spectacles so fashionable in the reign of Elizabeth, he hints, in a doleful strain, at his services and disappointments. He had (for what great courtier ever had not?) many enemies. He had been superseded in some Naval command; and had probably been refused the government of the Isle of Wight. When he complains that he had thrown his Land into the Sea, he obviously alludes to the great waste he had made of his estates in equipping ships, and even squadrons, at his own expence.

An ample account of this gallant Champion has been given in p. 490; and from the family evidences at Bolton, Dr. Whitaker selected the following original compositions of this great man. There are many others in that collection bearing his name; but they are either written by a Secretary, and merely subscribed by the Earl, or, if wholly indited by himself, relate to subjects of little general interest:

"MY VERY GOOD LORD,

" I have bene, as your Lo. well knowethe, long tyme a suter to her Majesty to bestow sume suche benefit upon me as myght manyfest to the worled her good opinion, and macke me the better able to dooe her such servis as at any tyme she should have cause to com'and me, wch not long sence she did, as I then thought, but beinge of late in the cuntri, where I should have received the benefit of hir gifte, I founde not any, but were ether unable or unwillynge to disburse present muny, soe that I am assured not to be relived by that meanes, wch I then hoped, and her Maj. mente, wherfore I noue most earnestly desier that it would please hir Majesti to lende me tenne thousande pound. I will pay it agayne by a thousand pounde a yeare, and for the assurance ether paune suche land as your Lo. shall lycke, or put soe many jentellmen in bond as shall be thought suffitient, and also resine up agayne her late gifte, wch wilbe more benefit to her then the lone of the mony can be, and more profitt to me then tooe suche sutes, my dayes of payement beinge soe neare, and the forfetures greate, wch I shall faule into, if I be not relived by your Lo. good meanes in this, as I thyncke, my resonable sute, wch I will not move till I knowe your good lykynge, by whom in this, as in everi other thynge, I will be derected. Thus hopinge for your Lo. beste advice and furtheraunce, I protest never to be forgettfull of any favor you shall bestow upon me.

"Your Lo. most assured Frynd,   GEORGE CUMBRELAND.

" From the Courte, this xxiii of September."

"To the ryght honorable my very gord Lord the Lord Burghley, Hey Tresorer of Inglande."

Indorsed, seemingly in Lord Burleigh's hand, "23 Sept. 1586. E. of Cumberland. To borrowe x^{m}li. of her Mai'ty."

discontented, contentednes upon one leaf he writes, *utiliter consenesco*, and musters up all his spirite to its wonted corradge; but in the same minut he kisseth night-shade, and embraceth it, saying, *Solanum Solamen*. Then, having no

"To the Ryght Honorable Francis Walsy'gham, Knyght, hir Maiestye's Schife Secritary.

"Sir,   29 October, 1588.

"Beynge at Plymouthe to water, I harde of a hulcke beten in by foule wether, by Hope, a toune xxiii myle from thence. She was one of the Spanyshe flyte, and it was reported the Ducke was in hir, and great store of treasure, wherfore I ridde thither, with Mr. Cary and Mr. Harris, whoe then were with me, to knowe the truthe of it, where we founde no such thynge as was reported of the Ducke; but a shippe suche and soe furnished as by an examination taken by hus and sent herewith you may perseve. Mr. Cary stayeth at the place, to keepe hir from spoylynge of the cuntry-men till here your further derection. Thus muche the have intreted me to macke knowne to you, and thus in hast I com'itte you to God. From Malborowe, this 29 of October.

"Your lovynge frynde,   George Cumbreland."

An original dispatch to Secretary Walsingham, relating to the defeat of the Spanish Armada, in which this Nobleman bore so considerable a part, will be considered as no small curiosity.—By the Ducke, I suppose is meant the Spanish Admiral, the Duke of Medina Sidonia, who, in one of those rumours, which at such times are flying in every direction was said to have been driven on shore near Plymouth.

"To the Ryght Honorable my very good Lo. the Lo. Hygh Tresorer of Ingland.

"My Good Lo',   20 Feb.

"Upon a letter from her Mai. co'mandyng me to repare with my fleete to the rode of Callis, and to bryng with me all such shipps as I should fynd fitt to dooe hir servis there, I comanded tooe shipps in the harbour of Porchmouth, and three at the Cowes, good shipps, and laden w'th nyne companyes of soulgerrs, out of France, to returne with me. Sir He. Poure, their coronell, writte me word that before ther cu'mynge from the Dounes the Spanyards aryvall at Callis was knowne, yett they were suffered to procede. Soe, doubtinge least I should dooe amisse, I have stayed them, to remayne where they be till further derection cum for them, w'ch I pray your Lo. maye be sent, soe that they depend upon it. My self am nowe gooeinge towardes Douer, wher, if hir Mai. have any thynge to co'mande me, I will be redy to obey it. Your Lo. to co'mand,

"George Cumbreland."

"To my very good Lo. the Lo. High Tresorer of Englande.

"My very good Lo',   1 Sept. 1594.

"Since I last moued your Lo. to favor my Lo. Thomas * in his sute, Sir Jo. Forteskew hath delte with her Ma'ie in it, who, after much speeche (as he sayethe), concluded, not unwyllinglie, to grante what my Lo. desired (but in fee farm), and, for any thynge I can perceve, grew into that eumer by Sir Jo. soe movynge it to hir, wher in he hath donne my Lo. a myghty displeasure; for I assure your Lo. in that kynde it will not be worthe any thynge. To releeve this harme, I hope it will not be

---

* I suppose Lord Thomas Howard. It does not appear what was the particular object of his suit. W.

companye but himselfe, thus he talketh w'th himselfe: that he hath made ladders for others to clymbe, and his feet nayled to the ground not to stirr. That he is lyke him that built ye ancker to save others, and themselves to be drownd.

harde sethe it may be mayde apparante to his Ma. to be as I informe your Lo. and that in grantynge the fee simple she gevethe but £120, and 2 or 3 pound for the lyfe of my Lo. Arundayll and his sunne, than w'ch hir Mai. cannot (gevynge any thynge to suche a man) geve lesse, and that she meanes to him sumthynge is well sene by this sayd already, so as I well hope your Lo. favor nowe showed will easely effecte my Lo. desier macke me muche bound to you for it, and him to you in in lowe, whom I assure your Lo. for his firm disposition, and true honesty, is as well worthe hauynge as any man lywethe. If your Lo. when you ar with the Quine, will but offer speeche that my Lo. Admeraw may be cauled to you, he will faule into my Lo. To. cawse, is instructed well in it, and will (I doubt not) macke very playne to be but a very tryflynge demand, out of which your Lo. if soe you lyke, may tacke best occation to favor him; if not, I pray your Lo. co'mand me to wayte upon youe at your leasuer, and lett me knowe what other cource you will derecte, for my Lo. meaneth hooly to depende upon your derection. Your Lo. to co'mand,   GEORGE CUMBERLAND.

"My Lo. Admeraule is alredy instructed."

"To the Ryght Honorabl. the Lo. Tresorer of Ingland *.

"MY GOOD LO.   24 Nov. 1596.

"If want of health had not stayed me, before this I had waited upon your Lo. and let you knowe boothe what I perseve my Lo. of Darbye's cources ar, and alsoe therrs whoe advise, follow, and depende upon him; to longe and intricate it would be to troble your Lo. w'th nowe, soe I will forbere till more fittyngly I may attend you; but heryng that your Lo. hath apoynted Mr. Ireland to be w'th you this day, I thought good to desier your Lo. to euse him w'th kynd speeches, and not to seeme but that you beleve he hath dealte most honestly in thes cources w'th his Lo.; ela I feare me, in a desperate cumer, he may perhapps dooe what hardly agayne may be helped. And I dare assure your Lo. this conveance effected, though but as it is, other thynges after will easely be effected to your Lo. conttentment. Thus hartely thanckyng your Lo. for your care of him whoe cares not for himselfe, I ende, ever your Lo. to co'mmand,   GEORGE CUMBRELAND."

"To my very good Lo. the Lo. Tresorer of Ingland.

"MY GOOD LO.   26 April, 1597.

"As ever I have found your Lo. willyng to dooe me kindnes, soe I besiche you (nowe in the tyme when muche it may pleasure me boothe in my reputation and estate) to geve me your best furtherance. I here hir Mai. will bestowe the Ile of Wyght upon sum suche as shall ther be resident. To w'ch condicion willyngly I woulde, as is fittyng, tye myself: not w'th such eumers to Sea-journeys as heretofore have carried me; but, by just discorage, setell myselfe to what shall nether gett envi, nor

---

* This letter seems to refer to the great dispute which happened after the death of Ferdinando Earl of Derby, in 1595, between his three co-heiresses and William his brother and successor in the title, with respect to the property of the Isle of Man. In the conclusion, Earl William, who was then very young, is censured by his kinsman, as not "caring for himself." He became in due time, however, a very prudent man, and survived to the year 1642. W.

That then he hath outsriptt manie in desert, he is tript upp by Envy, untill those overtake him that undertooke nothing. He, on the confidence of unspotted honour, leveld all his accions to nurse these twinnes, Labor and Dutie, not knowinge which of these was eldest, both running fast, but neither formost. Then, casting his eyes to heaven, he stands to wonder, at Cinthia's brightness[1], and to looke out his owne unfortunate starr: with deepe syghes he breathes out a two-fold wishe, that the one may never waine while the world waxeth; that the other may be erring, not fixed. Howe the two hath troubled ye sacred eares, mine, with glowing and tingling, are witnesses; but they shall confess that their eyes shall prove their being lyers, being as farr from judgm't as they are from honnor. There is no such thing as night-shade; for wher can there be miste or darkenes where you are, whose beames wrappes up cloudes as whirlewindes dust? Night-shade is falne off, shrinking into ye center of the earth, as not daring to showe blackenes before your brightnes. I cannot excuse my Knighte's error, nor care that he knows it, to thinke he could cover himselfe obscurely in anie desolate retirdness wher your Highnes beautie and vertue could not find him out. These Northeren thoughtes, that measure honour by the acre, and would have his crest a plase, he controwles so farr in his truer hounor, that (he?) contempes them. He now grounds all his accions neither upon hopes, counsell, nor experience; he disdaines envy, and scornes ingratitude. Judgem't shall arm his patience; patience confirme his knowledge, which is that, yourselfe being perfection, knaves measures number and tyme to cause favour wher it shold, and when you please, being onely constant and wyse in waiging with true steadines both the thoughtes of all

geve coler for falce informations. I protest to your Lo. desier of inablyng myselfe for her Maie's servis cheeflyest drew me w'th greedynees to follow thes conrces all this yeare, as your Lo. knowes ther hath bene lycklyhood of my imployment, and generawlly spoken of. Now I here it is otherwyse determyned, to w'ch I willingly submitte meselfe, but soe sensible of the disgrace, as if hir Mai. does not showe me sum other token of hir favor, I shall as often wyshe myselfe dead as I haye houres to lyve. For my fitness to govern that Island, I leave to your Lo. iudgment; but this I voœ, he lyves not that w'th more duty and care shall kepe and defend it then I will; and if by your Lo. good meane it may be obtayned, I shall thyncke hir Mai. deales most gratiusly with me, and ever acknowledge myselfe most bound to your Lo. whom I com'tte to God, and rest your Lo. to command,

"GEORGE CUMBRELAND."

This last letter shews how long the sentiments of chagrin and disappointment, so strongly expressed in the Speech, had been brooding in the mind of the speaker. W.

[1] Queen Elizabeth, " the fairest of all ladies, Cinthia's brightness, &c." had now attained to the age of sixty-seven! W.

men, and their affections, upon w'ch he soe relies, that whatsoever happen to him you are still yourselfe (wonder and hapynes), to w'ch his eyes, thoughts, and actions are tyed, w'th such an indissolvable knott, that neither Death, nor Tyme that triumphs after Death, shall or can unloose it. Is it not, as I have often tould ye, that, after he had throwne his Lande into ye Sea, ye Sea would cast him on the Lande for a wanderer? He that spines nothing but hopes shall weave up nothing but repentance. Let him cast his accompts sinc he was first wheeled about with his will wheele, and what can he reckon, save only he is so manie years elder? Hath not he taken his fall wher others take their rysing, he havinge ye Spanishe proverbe at his backe, that shoulde be sticked to his harte, '*Adelante los Abenstados:*' 'Let them hold the purses with ye mouth downeward that hath filled them with mouth upwards.' He may well entertaine a shade for his m'rs, that walketh in the world himselfe like a shaddow, embracing names instead of thinges, dreames for trouthes, blind prophesais for seeing verities. It becomes not me to dispute of his courses; but yet none shall hinder me from wondring to see him that is not to be, and yet to be that never was. If ye thinke his body too straight for his hearte, ye shall find ye worlde wyde enoughe for his body.

Birth and Baptism of King CHARLES *the First* [1].

Upon Wednesday, betwixt eleven and twelve hours at even, the 19th day of November, 1600, the Queen's Majesty was delivered within the Pallace of Dumfermling of a man-child. God of his Mercy make him his servant; give him long and prosperous days, to live both to God's glory, and to the welfare of the country.

Upon Tuesday the 23d of December, 1600, the King's Majestie came from his chamber to the Chapel Royal, convoyed by theis noblemen, *viz.* the Marquis of Huntley, the Earls of Montrose, Chancellor Cassils, Mar, and Winton, with sundry Lords and other Noblemen. My Lord Lyon, Sir George Douglas, of Ellon, Knight, who supplied the place of William Shaw, Master of the Ceremonies;

[1] Copied from a Manuscript in the Lyon's Office at Edinbrugh; written by John Blinsele, Ilay Herauld, who assisted at the Baptism.

John Blinsele, Ilay Herald; James Brothwick, Rothsay Herald; and Thomas Williamson, Ross Herald; Daniel Graham, Dingwal Pursevant; William Mackeson, Bute Pursevant; and David Gardner, Ormond Pursevant; our coats of arms displayed, trumpets sounding before us, convoyed his Majesty to the Chapel Royal. And there his Majesty was placed on the East geivil of the Chapel; and thereafter my Lord Lyon, and Master of Ceremonies, Heralds, Pursevants, and Trumpets, came to the Queen's chamber; and there was a pall of gold, silver, and silk, very magnificent, wrought (as it was spoken) by his Majestie's Umq' Mother, of good memory, which was sustained and borne by six Knights, viz. the Knight of Edzell, the Knight of Dipdup, at one end; the Knights of Trequair and Ormistoun at the other end; and in the midst of the pall on every side, the Knight of Black Ormiston, called Sir Peter Ker, of Ormiston, and William Ballinden of Broughton; and within the pall the Bairne, borne by Monsieur de Rohan, a Nobleman of Britanny, who bare the Bairne in his arms from the Chamber to the Chapel: and on every side of the said Monsieur de Rohan, his brother, called Monsieur de Soubisa (or Sibbois); and on the other side of him the Marquis of Huntley; and behind him my Lord Livingston, who bare up the Bairn's robe royal of purple velvet lined with damask. The Bairn was covered with cloth of gold and lawn; and behind the Dames of Honour, the Marquis of Huntley's Wife, the Countess of Mar, with the wives of my Lord Treasurer, President, Secretary, and many other Dames of Honour; and before the pall was the Bairn's honours borne, viz. my Lord President bare the crown ducal; my Lord Spinie bare the lavar and towel; my Lord Roxburgh bare the basin; my Lord Lyon, Master of Ceremonies; Heralds with our coats displayed; trumpets sounding before us; with sundry other Noblemen. We ranked to the Chapel till we became before his Majesty; and there, on the North side of the said Chapel, the pall and Bairn was placed: the Lady Marchioness of Huntley bare the Bairn instead of the nourice, within the said pall, all the time of sermon. On the East side of the said pall was two chairs of cramoisy velvet, where the two brothers sat beneath his Majesty on his Majesty's right hand; and upon the West side of the pall sat these Noblemen: the Marquis of Huntley, Chancellor Cassils, Mar, Winton, Treasurer, Secretary, Clerk Register, Advocate, and sundry other Noblemen of the Secret Council. Upon the South side the Chapel, my Lords Livingston, Spynie, President Roxburgh, and sundry other Noblemen; and the servants of the two Frenchmen who were his Majesty's gossips.

The Sermon and Baptism was made by Mr. David Lindsay, Bishop of Ross, and Minister of Leith, which was upon Romans xiii. v. 11. The time of the Sermon being ended, Mr. David Lindsay declared it over again in French to the two Frenchmen that were gossips; and thereafter he proceeded to the Baptism of the Bairn: the pall and Bairn was brought to the pulpit, borne by the said Monsieur de Rohan: and his Majesty came from his place to the said pulpit with the said Noblemen, and the Minister baptized him, naming him CHARLES.

And then, after a Psalm sung, and Blessing said, my Lord Lyon proclaimed his styles, and called him, " My Lord Charles of Scotland, Duke of Albany, Marquis of Ormond, Earl of Ross, Lord of Ardmannogh;" and thereafter Dingwal Pursevant proclaimed his styles out of the West window of the said Chapel, crying with a loud voice, " Largess of the Right High and Excellent Prince my Lord Charles of Scotland, Duke of Albany, Marquis of Ormond, Earl of Ross, Lord of Ardmannogh, Largess, Largess, Largess." And thereafter John Blinsele, Ilay Herald, did cast out of the said window one hundred marks of silver to the poor of the Duke's Largess; trumpets sounding; the castle shot nine cannons; his Majesty ranked from the Chapel to the Chamber, as he did before; the pall, Bairn, and honours were borne; the Lords Dames ranked from the Chapel to the Queen's Chamber; the gossip, Monsieur de Rohan, bare the Bairn, as he did to the Kirk; my Lord Lyon, Master of Ceremonies, Heraulds, Pursevants; trumpets sounding before us.

And thereafter his Majesty passed to the Mickle-hall to supper: his Majesty sat on her Majesty's left hand: beneath his Majesty sat the two brothers Frenchmen, where they were magnificently entertained. My Lord Mar was great Master Houshold, in place of the Earl of Argyle; Sir James Sandilands Master Usher, in place of my Lord Fleming; Sir James Douglas served as Master of Ceremonies, in place of William Shaw; Sir Thomas Erskin Master of the Guards; my Lord Lyon served in his coat at supper; my Lord President served the King at supper as Cupper; my Lord Spynie, Carver; my Lord Roxburgh, Sewer. Upon the West side of the Hall sat sundry Lords and Dames, and the two Frenchmens' servants — Ay, a Nobleman and Dame placed, the Marquis of Huntly, Chancellor Cassils, Mar, Winton, Livingston, with sundry other Noblemen, and Lords of Secret Council at the Board.

Upon Wednesday at even, the two noble Frenchmen and the Nobility supped with his Majesty.

A Dialogue betweene two Shepheards, Thenot and Piers, in praise of ASTREA, [Made by the excellent Lady the Lady MARY Countesse of PEMBROOK [1], at the Queenes Maiesties being *at her house* [2].]

> *Thenot.* I Sing divine Astrea's praise;
> O Muses, helpe my notes to raise,
> And heaue my verses higher.

---

[1] "Third Lady of Henry Earl of Pembroke. She was daughter to Sir Henry, and sister to Sir Philip Sidney. The ties of consanguinity between this illustrious brother and sister were strengthened by friendship, the effect of congenial sentiments, and similitude of manners." GRANGER.

"The Countesse of Pembroke's Arcadia" is dedicated, by Sir Philip, "To my deare Lady and sister, the Countesse of Pembroke." She was herself a person of great literature and genius, as well as patroness of learned men, among whom was Abraham Fraunce the Poet, Daniel, &c. Ballard has of course celebrated this ingenious Lady. "As her genius," says he, "inclined her to poetry, so she spent much of her time in that way. She translated many of the Psalms into English verse, which were bound in velvet, and, as it is said, still preserved in the library at Wilton. In these, it is reported by Sir John Harrington, Wood, and others, she was assisted by Dr. Babington, then Chaplain to the family, afterwards Bishop of Worcester. She translated * from the French, Philip Mornay's "Discourse of Life and Death, dated May 13, 1590," 4to, published in 1600; and "The Tragedie of Antonie, dated at Ramsbury, 26 Nov. 1590," and published in 1595, 4to. She had attained an advanced age at her decease, which happened *at her house in Aldersgate Street, London,* Sept. 25, 1621. She was buried near her husband, in the Cathedral Church of Salisbury; and the following beautiful inscription to her memory is much admired:

"Underneath this marble herse,	Marble piles let no man raise
Lies the subject of all verse,	To her name; for, after daies,
Sidney's sister, Pembroke's mother,;	Some kind woman good as she,
Death, ere thou hast slain another,	Reading this, like Niobe,
Learn'd, and fair, and good as she,	Shall turn marble, and become
Time shall throw his dart at thee.'	Both her mourner, and her tomb."

See Brydges's "Memoirs of the Peers of England in the Reign of James the First, 1803," p. 148.

[2] The Prefix to this Poem, in Davison's "Poetical Rapsodies," ed. 1611, p. 23, is given in 1602; but the Dialogue was probably written in 1600, when the Queen meditated a Progress into North Wiltshire (see p. 513); and was perhaps recited in 1601 in *Aldersgate Street.*—The Queen had visited the Earl of Pembroke at Wilton, in the time of his second Lady, in 1574; see in vol. I. p. 409.

---

* Mr. Park conceives that this version was the joint performance of Sir Philip and his sister. See the Nugæ Antiquæ, vol. II. p. 407, edit. 1804.

DIALOGUE AT THE COUNTESS OF PEMBROKE'S, 1600.

Piers.   Thou needst the truth but plainely tell,
          Which much I doubt thou canst not well,
             Thou art so oft a lyer.

Thenot. If in my song no more I show,
          Then heaven and earth and sea do know,
            Then truely I have spoken.

Piers.   Sufficeth not no more to name,
          But being no lesse, the like, the same,
            Else lawes of truth be broken.

Thenot. Then say, she is so good, so faire,
          With all the earth she may compaire,
            Nor Momus selfe denying.

Piers.   Compare may think where likenesse holds,
          Nought like to her the earth enfolds,
            I lookt to find you lying.

Thenot. Astrea sees with Wisedome's sight;
          Astrea works by Vertue's might:
            And ioyntly both do stay in her.

Piers.   Nay take from them her hand, her mind,
          The one is lame, the other blind,
            Shall still your lying staine her?

Thenot. Soone as Astrea shews her face,
          Straight euery ill avoids the place,
            And euerie good aboundeth.

Piers.   Nay long before her face doth show,
          The last doth come, the first doth go,
            How lowd this lie resoundeth!

Thenot. Astrea is our chiefest joy,
          Our chiefest guard against annoy,
            Our chiefest wealth, our treasure.

Piers.   Where chiefest are, there others be:
          To us none else but only she.
            When wilt thou speake in measure?

Thenot. Astrea may be justly said,
        A field in flowry roabe arraid,
          In season freshly springing.

Piers. That Spring indures but shortest time,
        This never leaues Astrea's clime.
          Thou liest, instead of singing.

Thenot. As heauenly light that guides the day,
        Right so doth shine each louely ray
          That from Astrea flyeth.

Piers. Nay, darkenesse oft that light incloudes,
        Astrea's beames no darknesse shrowdes:
          How loudly Thenot lyeth!

Thenot. Astrea rightly terme I may,
        A manly palme, a maiden bay,
          Her verdure neuer dying.

Piers. Palme oft is crooked, bay is low;
        She still upright, still high doth grow:
          Good Thenot, leave thy lying.

Thenot. Then, Piers, of friendship tell me why,
        My meaning true, my words should lie,
          And striue in vaine to raise her?

Piers. Words from conceit doe onely rise,
        Aboue conceit her honour flies.
          But silence, naught can her praise her.

                      Mary Countesse of Pembrooke.

The RIGHT WAY TO HEAVEN: and the true Testimonie of a faithfull and loyall Subiect: Compiled by RICHARD VENNARD, of Lincolne's Inne [1].

"First seeke the Kingdome of Heaven, and all things shal be given." Matth. vi. 33.

On the back of the Title 12 Acrostical Lines, inscribed, "Salvator Mundi."

DEDICATION.

To the high and mightie Princis Elizabeth, by the Grace of God, Queene of England, France, and Ireland, Defendor of the Faith, &c. Richard Vennard, of Lincolnes Inne, Gent. wisheth all happinesse in this life: and in the world to come celestiall eternitie.

Most renowned Soueraigne, pleaseth it your sacred Maiestie, at the humble hands of your loiall subiect, to accept this little handfull of my hart's labour, wherein my feeling of God's mercies, my knowledge of your gracious goodnesse, and my care of my countrie's well-doeing, have made me take such paines, as if it may be pleasing in your sight, shall breed no little ioy to my soule. Who, kneeling at your royall feete, doe beseech the God of all Glory, to indew your Highnesse with His infinite blessings, and long to preserve your sacred Maiestie in all ioyfull health and prosperous life.

Your Maiestie's most faithfull and loyall subiect, RICHARD VENNARD.

Then follow 28 Six-line Stanzas. "Laudetur Dominus in æternum."

To these succeed the Prose Portion of "The Highway to Heaven;" *containing the following Chapters,* in 41 pages.

Cap. i. He that in Heaven will tast the fruits of Divinitie, must first learne to know himselfe in the Schoole of Humilitie.

Cap. ii. Of our lothsome deformitie through Adam's fall.

Cap. iii. Of the miserie of Adam's posteritie, and vanitie of the world.

Cap. iiii. Of the race of man's life; and certenty of death.

Cap. v. The defence of a Christian souldier.

Cap. vi. Hee that in Heaven will come to ioy with Christ, must first travaile with patience under the crosse of Christ.

Cap. vii. Of true repentance with hir inseparable furniture.

[1] At London: Printed by Thomas Este. 1601.

Cap. viii.   Of true fasting.
Cap. ix.   A briefe exhortation to Christian Religion.
Cap. x.   An exhortation to continue patient in adversitie.
Cap. xi.   A comfortable consolation to the faithfull children of Christ.
Cap. xii.   Of the ioyfull state of God's children, after the last Judgement.
A most godly and comfortable Praier, in time of adversitie.
An Exhortacion to continew all subjects in their dew obedience, together with the reward of a faithful subiect to his Prince.   To the Rev. Lord Bishops and the Clergie.
To the true Nobilitie of this realme.
To the Civile Maiestrates, the Lord Maior, and the Shrifes of London, and other inferiour officers.
To the true and faithfull private Subiect.
What a faithfull Subiect is.

[The remainder of the Volume is here inserted.]

E.

E Exceedings made the Miracle of Nature,
L Love ioin'd with life, to frame a blessed creature:
I Ioie in each part, where wisdome hath expressed,
Z Zeale in the hart, to make the spirit blessed:
A A worke of worth, well worthie admiration,
B Beyond the mount of man's imagination:
E Esteem'd more worth, then any wordly wonder,
T That by desert puts all earth's praises vnder.
H Heau'ns blesse the work, wherin such wonder dwelleth,
A As, all worlds wonder, in such worth excelleth.

R.

R Rare is the substance of this worthie sence,
E Expressing all in onely excellence:
G Giu'ne by the heauens vnto the world a blessing,
I In *Fame's* reporting, and in *Truthe's* confessing:
N Neere are such notes vnto an Angell's nature,
A As makes a Queene a Goddesse, of a creature.

THE MIRACLE OF NATURE.

Among the wonders of this age of ours,
   That eare hath heard, or eie hath ever seene:
Upon the toppe of Honour's highest towers,
   The glorious notes of our most gracious *Queene*:
Through all the world, all worthely confessed,
Shew never kingdome in a Queene so blessed.

First, for her birth, the daughter of a King,
   And such a King, as peerelesse in his praise:
A blessed sprig from such a stocke to spring,
   As doth increase the honour of his daies:
And, in hir selfe, in more than world's perfection,
The Art of Nature by the Heaven's direction.

For Beautie, but behold hir blessed eie,
   Where faire Diana puts foule Venvs downe;
For Wisedome, in true sacred Maiestie,
   The worthie head of an Imperiall Crowne:
For Mercy, who so perfectlie divine?
For Grace, who doth not to hir Grace resigne?

For Bountie, note her liberalitie,
   To maintaine right, and to relieve the wrong:
For Vertue, what true vertuous qualitie
   But may bee sung in hir true praises song?
For Learning, where more in a Princesse seene?
For Language, there was never such a Queene.

For Constancy, who so immutable?
   Whose love to God, no divell can remove;
For Gracious Speach, what Prince so affable?
   To winne the hart of every worthy love:
For Zeale, the tryall of religious truth;
For Patience, read the troubles of hir youth.

Whose minde of truer magnanimitie?
   In daungers to disdaine the thought of feare:
Whose hart more neere unto Divinitie?
   With patience, care, all discontents to beare:
Whose soule more full infused with God's spirit,
Through all the world that doth such wonder merit?

With all these blessings, from the highest blisse,
   Hir care to keepe hir kingdome still in peace,
Shews that hir minde is hardly led amisse,
   That doth such glory to hir Crowne encrease;
That Fame doth sound, in hir most pleasing breath,
But onely England's Queene Elizabeth.

Since then that God doth with that grace inspire hir,
   That shewes hir blessed in the Heavens above:
And all the Princes of the world admire hir,
   For all the wonders worthy Honor's love:
Why should this Earth live ever to forget hir?
But in the soule of love's remembrance set hir.

They that have liv'd, could say while they did live,
   Subiects are blest in such a Sovereigne:
They that now live, may well like witnesse give,
   A gratious Queene doth make a glorious reigne.
They that heereafter live hir Grace to see,
May say on earth not such a Queene as shee.

How hath she kept hir Court in comlinesse!
   Hir State in state of gracious Maiestie!
Hir Peeres in love, hir Church in godlinesse,
   Hir Laws in strength, hir Lords in unitie!
Hir People's awe, in loue's perswasion!
Hir Land, in peace without invasion!

Doth shee giue hearing vnto graue aduise!
   Great is hir wisedome so to guide hir will:
Sounds shee the depth of good, or ill-deuise!
   Blest bee the care, of such a princely skill:
Leaves shee the worst, and onely takes the best!
Blest bee hir choice, so bee shee ever blest.

How hath shee sought to beate offences downe,
   With kinde corrections, not with crueltie!
How hath shee kept the honour of hir Crowne,
   With loue and mercy, not with tiranny!
How hath shee liude, that all the world may know,
Was neuer Queene, whose loue did gouerne so.

What neighbour people hath hir land relieved,
   Who driuen from home, make here their safe aboade?
And, with hir will, what people have ben grieved?
   Except they be the enemies of God.
Within hir Lande how soone all tumults cease;
While Love and Mercy breede continuall peace.

To speake of such particularities,
   As in exceedings, doe set downe hir name;
Which all and some are singularities,
   That make true *Musique* for the trompe of Fame;
Is meete for some Heaven's Muses to indite,
While Angels' pens are fittest for to write.

But, as an eie, that all farre of beholdeth
   An excellence it can not comprehend:
Yet what conceit in secret sence vnfoldeth,
   It hath a will in wonder to commend:
Yet, when it speakes, it wincketh at the light,
As though too weake to speake of such a sight,

So my poore spirit, whose hart's humble eie,
   Sees by the light that it hath power to see,
A world of worth, in wonder all so high,
   As shewes what worth above world's wonders bee;
In hir due praises can set down so little,
As to hir Title, all is but a tittle:

Yet, though mine eie can touch nor Sunne nor Moone,
   Shall I not praise the cleerenesse of the Skie?
And, though my morning be an afternoone,
   Shall I still sleepe, as though I had no eie?
No: give mee leave to say the Sunne is bright,
Although mine eies but dimly see the light.

And, though my knowledge be but ignorance,
   Compar'd to that hir praise should comprehend;
And, such a Muse, as would hir pen advance,
   To write hir worth, should but hir will attend:
Yet, let mee say to them that can say more,
England had never such a Queene before.

Who would but note this foure and forty yeeres,
   How Mercie's Justice hath hir Scepter sway'd:
Of which no Prince, nor Emperour, that heares,
   But is with wonder of hir worth dismaide:
Would say in soule, on earth was never seene
Kingdome so gouern'd by a Virgin Queene.

Now, for hir Counsaile, all admire those wits,
   That with such wisedome doe advise her will:
And, in hir will, thinck what true wisedome sits,
   That is the ground-worke of their gratious skill:
And say, that God that Land a blessing gives,
Where such a Queene, and such a Counsaile lives.

Some malecontented, malecondition'd mindes,
    Where private grudge regards no publique good;
Mistaking reason in malitious kindes,
    Like serpents hatcht of an unkindely broode,
In hate may blot, that better loue commends,
But such ill spirits God send speedy ends.

I pray for few, I hope for none at all,
    Indifference speakes so truly in hir praise:
That, while cold feares unchristian harts appall,
    Faith findes in hir the Phœnix of our daies:
While humble love in loyall harts doth pray,
That shee may live vntill the latter day.

Now, for hir Treasure, how shee doth bestow,
    Hir blessed talent in her Crowne behove,
May witnesse well, that God Himselfe doth show;
    Shee is the faire deere Daughter of His love:
Whom His high hand hath over men so placed,
And so above both men and women graced.

What noble spirit hath true honour proved,
    But hir sweet eie hath graciously regarded:
What vertuous spirit but hir hart hath loved,
    And to the due of best desert rewarded:
For princely kindnesse to hir humble friends,
Fame sounds hir point in praise that never ends.

What should I need to walke my wits about
    A world of wonder, where there is no truth:
When truth itselfe doth bring these wonders out,
    Both in her princely peerless age and youth:
Where olde and young, may all and onely see,
How blest a kingedome in a Queene may be.

THE MIRACLE OF NATURE.

I make no care of fictions, nor of fables,
   Minerva faire, and *Pallas* were but fained:
But Truth may write in her memoriall tables,
   That such a Queene in England never raigned:
As makes all Poets idle spend their breath,
That name a Queene, but in Elizabeth.

I cannot chuse but wonder at those Wits
   That have imploy'd their pennes in Poetrie,
In whose deepe braines, that best invention sits,
   That lookes at Honour with a heavenly eie:
That some, or all their songs and laies,
Have not contended for *Eliza's* praise.

But, it may bee, they found their wits too weake
   To equall will, in writing of their wonder:
Yet such as could of Earth's chiefe praises speake,
   Might say hir praise puts all Earth's praises under:
And say no more, then all the world may see,
If Angell-woman on the Earth, 'tis shee.

Some out of *French, Italian, Dutch,* or *Spanish,*
   Doe draw discourses of most worthie creatures:
But let those fictions, all like fables, vanish,
   To shew the notes of all those gratious natures:
I goe no further then our Soveraigne Queene,
Where all in one, and one in all is seene.

For Vertue's Grace, behold hir Virgin Traine,
   Where faire demeanours put foule humours downe:
For Maiestie, what Monarch doth retaine
   So grave a Counsaile to a gratious Crowne?
And for Attendance, let Loue's Muses sing,
A Virgin Queene deserues a seruant King.

For, truely sound each point of such perfection
   As makes a Kingdome blessed in a Queene;
And let but Truth confesse without exception,
   The sacred worth in hir true wisdome seene:
And England's hart may have iust cause to say,
Blest be hir birth, and coronation-day.

A louely day, faire may it ever last,
   A sunne-shine day, whose beames are heavenly bright.
Cleere may they shine, and never overcast
   With any clowde, that may obscure the light:
That, in hir height of brightnesse not declining,
England may ioy to see hir ever shining.

Oh, could I flie with such an eagle's wings
   As could be soaring in the sunnie light;
Or, could I heere but what that Angell sings
   That never poet had the power to write:
Then should my spirit and my penne not cease
To write hir praise, that now must hold my peace.

And onely praie, that he that sits on high,
   And holds the band of Mercie's maiestie,
Our gracious God, that shee maie never die,
   But in the life of Love's eternitie;
Liue from the blot of fowle oblivion's penne,
All faithfull harts in England, saie *Amen*.

A Prayer for the prosperous Successe of hir Majestie's Forces in Ireland.

Sweet Jesus, God of mercie, Lord of compassion, regard thy seruants' humble petition, thou that didst fight the most bloodie battaile that euer was fought; that sprinkled *Golgotha* with that sacred precious effusion that flowed from thy bodie; suffer thy seruants to passe through that *Irish* red Sea of sanguin and blodie pretence, and let those rebbels be ouerwhelmed with the *Egiptian Pharo*. Circumuent that rebellious *Sissira*, that thy judgement (like a naile), may pierce into the braine of his malitious practises: that our *Soueraigne* may sing with *Debora* after the victorie, having with *Hester* preserued hir people, and with chast *Judith* cut off the head of harme pretending *Holofernes*. And as to thy seruant *Moyses*, under-prop the arme of hir Generall with thine own powre, the head corner stone of the Temple. Stand still, O Sonne of God, and give thy people victory. Let the traiterous vaissaile be confounded, thy seruant *Elizabeth* preserved, and thy selfe above all glorified. Graunt this, O Father! for thy Sonne Jesus Christ his sake. Amen R. V.

SAINT GEORGE FOR ENGLAND.

[*And below a Cut of the Saint this Motto,*]

Conculcabis Leonem et Draconem. Psal. 90.

A Virgin Princesse and a gentle Lambe,
   Doomb'd both to death to gorge this vgly beast:
This valiant victor like a Souldier came,
   And of his owne accord, without request:
With never daunted spirit the Fiend assail'd,
Preserv'd the Princesse and the Monster quail'd.

Saint George, the figure of our Saviour's force,
   Within the Dragon's jawes his speare hath entred:
Whose sword doth threaten, banishing remorce,
   And hee that on his noble part hath ventred,
Spewes forth his poyson on the sullen ground,
And stands in danger of a deadly wound.

And may my soule, oh Jesus! speake with zeale?
   Thy woord, thy swoord, will Sathan's pride consume?

So doth thy Father's holy will reveale,
  And with that beast all those that dare presume:
That peece of wood whereon thy body dide,
Hath made a mortall passage in his side.

Saint George the Dragon, Jesus Sathan kill'd;
  Saint George the Princesse and the Lambe preserv'd:
Jesus his bitter combat hath fulfill'd,
  And by the Divel's death his Church reserv'd:
That spotlesse Dame whose ravishment was sought
By tirant's rage that bloudy ruine brought.

Saint George's Knight, goe noble Mountjoy on,
  Bearing thy Saviour's badge within thy breast:
Quell that Hell's shape of divellish proud Tirone,
  And cover with the dust his stubborne crest:
That our deere Princesse and hir land be safe,
Such power to him, oh Jesus Christ vouchsafe.

And as thou hast thy glorious mercy showen
  In beating downe his foes beefore his face;
So let them still bee wholely ouerthrowen
  That seeke thy glorious words disgrace;
And give true subjects vertues true renowne
While proude rebellion headlong tumbels downe.

Oh, let him Mount vnto thy mercie's Joy,
  In name and nature make his honour one:
And in thy fury all his foes destroy,
  That are assistantes to rebellion:
And let thy sunne so on his army shine,
That he and we may praise that name of thine.

Make his young yeeres vnto the world a wonder,
  His valiant courage, vertues honours love;
His fearelesse hand, to teare those harts asunder
  That dare the issue of rebellion prove:
And make his triumph, such an English story,
That England's joy may sing thine endlesse glory!

FINIS.

A faithfull Subject's Praier.

O Glorious God, and onely King of Kings,
   Whose holie eie both Heaven and Earth beholdeth;
And from whose mercie all and onely springs
   The fayrest life that faithfull love vnfoldeth:
Mine humble spirit I beseech thee raise,
To give thy glory all eternall praise.

O gratious God, among the many graces,
   Wherein thy mercie hath this Island blest:
In whom the height of all our happie cases,
   Under thyne onely holy hand doth rest:
For our sweet, gratious, vertuous Soveraigne Queene,
Let our harts humble thanckfullnesse be seene.

Blesse hir, O Lord, with Nestor's happie daies,
   Health, wealth, and peace, and everlasting pleasure:
Let Vertue's love resound hir worthie praise,
   And thy true wisedome be hir spirit's treasure:
Hir greatest hopes vpon thy graces grounded,
Hir state preserved, and hir foes confounded.

Preserve, oh Lord, hir faithfull Counsellors,
   Hir loyall subiects, and hir true attendants:
Hir virtuous lawiers, valiant souldiers,
   And let thine Angels be hir loves defendants:
Hir state of blisse bee England's blessed storie,
And give hir soule a Crowne of endlesse glorie.   R. V.
       Amen.

Lady Dorothy Stafford *to the Countess Dowager of* Shrewsbury.

"To the Right Honorable and my verie good Ladie, the Countesse of Shrewsburie Dowager.

"Righte honorable and my verie good Lady. I have, according to the purporte of your hon^{ble} letters, presented your La$^{p's}$ New-yeres gifte, togeather wth my Ladie Arbella's, to the Queene's Matie, whoe hathe verie graciously accepted thereof, and taken an especiall likeing to that of my La. Arbella's. It pleased her Matie to tell mee, that whereas in certaine former letters of your La$^{p's}$, your desire was that her Matie would have that respecte of my La. Arbella that she mighte be carefullie bestowed to her Matie good liking, that, according to the contents of those letters, her Matie tould mee that shee would be carefull of her, and wth all hathe retorned a token to my La. Arbella, wch is not so good as I could wish it, nor so good as her La^p deserveth, in respecte of the rarenes of that wch she sente unto her Matie. But I beseeche you, good Maddam, seeing it pleased her Matie to saie so muche unto mee touching her care of my La. Arbella, that your La^p will vouchesafe mee so muche favor as to keepe it to yourselfe, not makeing anie other acquainted wth it, but rather repose the truste in mee for to take my opportunitie for the putting her Matie in mynde thereof, wch I will doe as carefullie as I can. And thus being alwaies bownd to your La^p for your hono^{ble} kindnesses toward mee, I humbly comett your La^p to the safe protection of Almightie God. From Westminster this xiiith of Januarie, 1600-1.   DOROTHIE STAFFORD.

The Earl of Essex's *Apprehension, Arraignment, and Execution.*

Sundaie the 8th of February, 1600, the Earle of Essex, uppon advise of his friends, came to London about tenne a clocke, assisted with the chiefe gallants of the time, viz. the Earle of Southampton, Sir Charles Danvers, Sir Christopher Blount, Robert Catesby, and many others; and as they passed Fleete-streete, cryed, " For the Queen; for the Queene;" and in other places they sayd, " that Cobham and Rawleigh would have murdered the Earle of Essex in his bed."

The general multitude, being entirely affected to the Earle, sayd, " that the Queene and the Earle were made friendes, and that her Majesty hadde appoynted him to ryde in that triumphant manner through London, unto his house in Seeding-lane;" and all the way he went, the people cryed, " God save your Honour, God blesse your Honor," &c. [2]

[1] There is a good account of this Lady on her monument in St. Margaret's Church, Westminster. " Here lyeth the Lady Dorothy Stafford, wife and widow of Sir William Stafford, Knight, daughter to Henry Lord Stafford, the only son of Edward the last Duke of Buckingham. Her mother was Ursula, daughter to the Countess of Salisbury, the only daughter to George Duke of Clarence, brother to King Edward the 4th. She continued a true widow from the age of 27 till her death. She served Queen Elizabeth 40 years, lying in the bed-chamber; esteemed of her, loved of all, doing good all she could to every body, never hurted any, a continual remembrancer of the suites of the poor. As she lived a religious life in great reputation of honor and vertue in the world, so she ended in continual fervent meditations and hearty prayer to God: at which instant (as all her life), so after her death she gave liberally to the poor, and died aged 78, Sept. 22, 1604. In whose memory Sir Edward Stafford her son hath caused this memorial of her to be in the same form and place as she herself long since required him."—Hunter's Hallamshire, p. 92.

[2] In 1598 the Corporation of Coventry presented £50 to the Earl of Essex.

The Lord Maior, being at Paule's Crosse, received warning from the Counsell, to looke to the Citie; and by eleven of the clocke the gates were shut, and strongly guarded. The Earle kept his course to wardes Fanchurch, and entered into Master Thomas Smith's house, Sheriffe of London, where the Earle dranke; in which space the Sheriffe went out at a backe doore unto the Lord Maior, offering his service, and requiring direction. The Earle went into an armorer's house, requiring munition, which was denyed him: from thence the Earle went to and fro, and then came backe to Gracechurch-streete, by which time the Lord Burghley was come thither, having there, in the Queene's name, proclaymed the Earle and all his company traytors, as he had done before in Cheapeside.

At hearing whereof, one of the Earle's followers shot a pistoll at the Lord Burghley; whereupon he well perceiving the stout resolution of the Earle's followers, together with the people's great unwillingness, eyther to apprehend the Earle, or ayde him, returned to the Court; assuring the Queene, that notwithstanding the great love the Londoners bare unto the Earle, yet they will not ayde him: the Court being now fortified and double guarded, the streete in divers places sette full of emptie carts and coaches, to stoppe the Earle's passage, if he should attempt to come that way.

You are to understand, before that the Earle came forth of his house, the Queene, upon jealousie that the Earle intended some practise, by reason that but the night before being by the Counsell required to come to Court, which in plaine tearmes he refused, sent unto him the Lord Keeper, the Lord Chiefe Justice, Sir W. Knowles, and the Earle of Worcester, not being then a Counsellor of Estate, to confer with him whilest some further course might be taken concerninge the Earle; the which sayd Counsellors of Estate being come to Essex-house, the Earle entertayned them kindly, saying, "He was sorry he could not stay with them, being now going to take order with the Lord Maior of London, but hee would presently returne unto them;" commanding his chiefe servants to attend, and keepe them safe until his returne, hoping to have found them there when he came backe, and by them to have made his peace with the Queene; but whilest he was in London, they were enlarged.

About two of the clocke, the Earle having passed to and fro through divers streetes, and beeing forsaken of divers his gallant followers, he resolved to make his neerest way home; and coming towards Ludgate, he was strongly resisted by divers companies of well-armed men, levyed, and placed there by the Lord Byshop of London; then he retyred thence, Sir Christopher Blunt being taken and sore wounded in the head; from thence the Earle went into Fryday-streete, and being faynt, desired drinke, which was given him; and, at his request, unto the cittizens. The great chayne which crosseth the streete was held up to give him passage; after that he tooke boat at Queene-hith, and so came to his house, where, missing the aforenamed counsellors, he fortified his house, with full purpose to die in his owne defence. But when he beheld the great artillery, and the Queenes forces round about the house, being sore vexed with the cryes of ladies, about ten of the clocke at night he yeelded himselfe unto the Lord Admirall, earnestly desiring his tryall to be speedie and honorable, which was performed.

Amongst others his faithfull followers, Captaine Owen Salisbury, seeing all hopes frustrate, stood openly in a window bare-headed, of purpose to be slaine, and one in the streets hyt him in the side of his head with a musket bullet: "Oh," quoth Salisbury, "that thou hadst beene so much my friend to haue shot but a little lower!" He died the next morning of that hurt.

From this time until all arraygnments and executions were past, the cittizens were exceedingly troubled, and charged with double watches and warding, as well about the Courte as the Cittie.

The 17th of February, Captaine Thomas Lee[1] was drawne to Tyborne, and there hanged and quartered; being before condemned for conspiracy against the Queene, about deliverance of the Earle of Essex out of the Tower: he tooke his death constantly confessing he had divers wayes deserved it; but to be innocent of that he was condemned for, &c.

The 19th of February, the Earle of Essex and the Earle of Southampton were

[1] Mr. Secretary Cecil, in a letter to Mr. Winwood, March 7, 1600-1, after giving an account of the Earl of Essex's arraignment, and of his execution in the Tower, has the following passage: "This death of his was the more hastened by that bloody practice of Thomas Lee; who, not four days after his apprehension, dealt with Sir Henry Nevill (son-in-law to the Lord Treasurer), and with Sir Robert Cross, assuring them that he would deal with some other gentlemen of resolution to the number of four, who should at supper-time (the Queen sitting in her Privy Chamber) have taken her, locked her doors, and (as he sillily pretended) only have pinned her up till he had forced her to sign a warrant for the Earl's delivery out of the Tower. Which vile purpose being discovered by those two gentlemen, and avowed to his face (he being at that very night watching at the Privy Chamber door, to discover how he might have access the next day), he was seized, and being examined confessed thus much, only vowing, that he would have forced in upon her, to hinder that course which he pretended, for their delivery." Memorials, vol. I. p. 301.

arraygned at Westminster: they were jointly and severally indited. The chiefe poynts were (for holding of private counsels, conspiring to depryve the Queene of life and government) for attempting to surprise the person of the Queene at Whitehall; the imprysoning of the Lordes which the Queene had sent unto him as his good friends upon the day of his rysing, and his perswading them to stand for him; his warlike entrance into London, and to surprise the Tower: unto all of which they pleaded not guiltie; and very willingly submitted themselves to be tryed by their Peeres. Their tryers were 24 in number, viz. 8 Earles, one Viscount, and 15 Barons: there were present divers others of right honorable ranke and qualitie, besides the reverend Judges of the Law. At this arraygnment the Lord Buckhurst, Lord High Treasurer of Englande, was then Lord Steward. The prisoners were found guilty, and the sentence of death was denounced against them. This arraygnment began about nine a clocke in the morning, and continued untill sixe at night; where there was a world of people pressing to see the event. The prisoners demeaned themselves very temperatly and discreetly, and gave the Queene and the Lordes most humble and heartie thankes for so speedie and honorable a tryall. The newes of all this dayes businesse was sodainly divulged throughout London; whereat many forsooke their suppers, and ranne hastily into the streets to see the Earle of Essex as he returned to the Tower, who went a swift pace, bending his face towardes the earth, and would not looke upon any of them, though some spake directly to him; concerning which, with other passages, and the Earles objections and answers, &c. I have written (says Stow) a more large discourse, according to the general expectation, whereunto by multitudes I have beene infinitely urged, but for divers reasons it must be omitted at this time; therefore let this suffice without tarrying.

The 25th of February, being Ash-Wednesday, about eight of the clocke in the morning, was the sentence of death executed upon Robert Devereux, Earle of Essex, within the Tower of London, where a scaffold being set up in the court, and a forme neere unto the place, whereon sat the Earles of Cumberland and Hartford, the Lord Viscount Bindon, the Lord Thomas Howard, the Lord Darcy, and the Lord Compton. The Lieutenant, with some 16 partizans of the guard, was sent for the prysoner; who came in a gowne of wrought velvet, a blacke sattin sute, a felt hat blacke, a little ruffe about his necke, accompanied from his chamber with three Divines, Doctor Montford, Doctor Barlow, and Maister Ashton his

Chaplaine: them he had requested not to part from him, but observe him, and recall him, if eyther his eye, countenance, or speech, should bewray any thing which might not beseeme him for that time. All the way he desired the spectators to pray for him; and so arryving on the scaffolde, he vailed his hat, and, with obeysance unto the Lords, to this effect he spake, viz,

"My Lords, and you my Christian Brethren, who are to be witnesses of this my just punishment, I confesse to the glory of God, that I am a most wretched sinner, and that my sinnes are more in number than the hayres of my head. I confesse that I have bestowed my youth in wantonnesse, lust, and uncleannesse; that I have been puffed up with pride, vanitie, and love of this world's pleasures, and that notwithstanding divers good motions inspired into mee by the spirit of God; the good which I would, I have not done; and the evill which I would not, that have I done. For all which I humblie beseech my Saviour Christ to be a mediator to the eternall Majestie for my pardon; especially for this my last sinne, this great, this bloudie, this crying, this infectious sinne; whereby so many have, for love to mee, beene drawne to offend God, to offend their Soveraygne, to offend the world; I beseech God to forgive it us, and to forgive it me most wretched of all. I beseech her Majestie, and the State and Ministers thereof, to forgive it us; and I beseech God to send her Majestie a prosperous raygne, and a long, if it bee his will. O Lorde, graunte her a wise and understanding heart! O Lord, blesse her, and the Nobles, and the Ministers of the Church and State! And I beseech you and the world to hold a charitable opinion of me, for my intention toward her Majestie, whose death I protest I never meant, nor violence towards her person; I never was, I thanke God, Atheist, not believing the Word and Scriptures; neyther Papist, trusting in mine owne merits, but hope for salvation from God onely by the mercie and merites of my Saviour Christ Jesus. This faith was I brought up in, and herein I am now readie to die; beseeching you all, to joyne your soules with me in prayer, that my soule may be lifted uppe by faith above all earthly thinges in my prayer; for nowe I will give myselfe to my private prayer: yet, for that I beseech you to joyne with me, I will speake that you may heare me."

And here, as he turned himselfe aside to put off his gowne, Doctor Montford requested him to remember to pray to God to forgive all his enemies, if he had any. To whom he answered, "I thanke you for it." And so turning himselfe againe to the Lords and the rest, he sayd, "I desire all the world to forgive me, even as I doe freely and from my heart forgive all the world." Then, putting off his gowne and ruffe, and presenting himselfe before the blocke, kneeling downe, hee was by Doctor Barlow encouraged against the feare of death. To whom he answered, " That having beene divers times in places of danger, where death was neyther so present, nor yet so certaine, hee had felt the weakenesse of the flesh, and therefore nowe in this great conflict desired God to assist and strengthen him ;" and so, with eyes fixed on heaven, after some passionate pawses and breathings, he beganne his prayer in effect following:

" O God, Creator of all things, and Judge of all men, thou hast let mee know by warrant out of thy Word, that Sathan is then most busie when our ende is neerest, and that Sathan being resisted will flee. I humbly beseech thee to assist me in this my last combat; and seeing thou acceptest even of our desires as of our actes, accept, I beseech thee, of my desires to resist him, as of true resistance; and perfect by thy grace what thou seest in my flesh to bee frayle and weake; give mee patience to beare, as becommeth me, this just punishment inflicted upon me by so honorable a tryall; grant me the inward comfort of the spirit; let thy spirit seale unto my soule an assurance of thy manifolde mercies; lift my soule above all earthly cogitations; and, when my life and bodie shall part, send thy blessed angels, which may receive my soule, and convey it to thy joyes in heaven."

He was wondrous patient and penitent. Then, concluding his prayer for all the estates of the realme, hee shut up all with the Lord's Prayer, reiterating this petition, " Lord Jesus, forgive us our trespasses; Lord Jesus, receive my soule." Then, desiring to be informed what was fit for him to doe for disposing himselfe fitly for the block, the executioner on his knees presented himselfe, asking him forgivenesse: to whom the Earle sayd, " I forgive thee; thou art welcome unto me; thou art the minister of justice." At which time Doctor Montford requested him to rehearse the Creed, which he did, repeating every article after the divines. So opening and putting off his doublet, he was in a scarlet wastecoate, and then readie to lye downe, he said, " he would onely stretch forth his armes, and spread them abroad, for then he was readie:" so bowing towards the block, the Doctors requested him to say the two first verses of the 51st psalme, which he did: and then, inclining his bodie, he sayd, " In humilitie and obedience to thy commandement, in obedience to thy ordinance, to thy good pleasure, O God, I prostrate myselfe to my deserved punishment: Lord, be mercifull to thy prostrate servant." So lying flatte along on the bordes, and laying downe his head, and fitting it upon the blocke, stretched out his armes with these wordes, which he was requested to say, " Lord, into thy hands I commend my spirit [1]."

His head was severed from his bodie by the axe at three stroaks, 'but the first deadly and absolutely depryving all sence and motion. The hangman was beaten as hee returned thence; so that the Sheriffes of London were called to assist and rescue him from such as would have murthered him.

The bells at Lambeth were rung on the 23d of May, and the ringers were paid 4s. "when the Queen came through Lambeth, and took horse at my Lord of Canterbury's Gate [2];" and again, on the 6th of August, they received 5s. 4d. for ringing "when she took water at Lambeth, and went to the Bishop of London's [3]."

[1] Mr. James exhibited to the Society of Antiquaries, June 28, 1781, a table-cloth and a napkin of the finest damask, ornamented with her arms, which belonged to her Majesty when confined in the Tower, and became, with all the furniture of her apartment, a perquisite to the keeper when she left, in 1558. They were then in possession of Richard Sherwood, Esq. of New Inn, maternal grandson to Lord Chief Justice Bedingfield, who was of the same family with the then Constable of the Tower.

The celebrated Ring, on which the life of the Earl of Essex is said to have depended, has been claimed by various persons. Mr. Thomas Penning, late of the Exchequer, had, in 1781, a Purse and Ring, by inheritance from Mr. Fotherby, whose sister he married, and who was related to Mrs. Cooke by long succession and inheritance from Sir Anthony Cooke, of Gidea Hall, Essex, Preceptor to Edward VI. to whose Lady, tradition says, the Queen gave them. The Purse, though small and lined with leather, was richly ornamented with four rows of gilt orrice, interleaved with pearles, spangles, and embost work, and two rich tassells appendant to the strings, and two more from the end of each side: the ring is gold, with a flat hollow surface edged with gold wire, which shews it to have been originally enamelled, and was studded at intervals with gold pins in form of roses; some still remaining. It is embellished with a pale topaz set in a silver collet.

The real Ring which in 1788 was in the possession of William Sotheby, Esq. of Bloomsbury-square, descended from Colonel William Sotheby, though no further tradition how it came there, remains, is gold, with the Queen's bust in bas-relief on a garnet, dressed as on her six-penny and three-penny pieces of 1574, with the same features in it round the garter with the motto, and fastened with a buckle composed of two diamonds, and the strap turned by another. Over the bust is the crown, composed of twelve diamonds; and on each side the collet three diamonds. On the inner surface, immediately under the bust, is the union rose.

"A belief was instilled into Elizabeth, that the distemper of the Earl of Essex had been entirely counterfeit in order to move her compassion, and she relapsed into her former rigour against him. He wrote her a letter, and sent her a rich present on New-year's Day; as was usual with the courtiers at that time; she read the letter, but rejected the present." Hume, vol. V. p. 412.

[2] Dr. John Whitgift.   [3] Dr. Richard Bancroft, then at Fulham.

Letter from the QUEEN *to Sir* GEORGE CAREW [1].

" MY FAITHFUL GEORGE,   [*June*... 1601.]

" If ever more services of worth were performed in shorter space than you have done, we are deceived among many eye witnesses. We have received the fruits thereof; and bid you faithfully credit, that whatso wit, courage, or care may do, we truly find they have all been thorowly acted in all your charge. And for the same, believe, that it shall neither be unremembered nor unrewarded; and in the mean while believe, my help nor prayers shall never fail you.

    " Your Soveraign that best regards you,   E. R." [2]

---

[1] This Gentleman had been sent, at the early age of fifteen, to Pembroke College, Oxford, but being more delighted in martial affairs than in the solitary shades of a study, left the University without taking any degree, and betook himself to travel. The first place we find he went unto was Ireland, at that time the scene of noble actions, where he had soon a command given him in the wars, which he diligently pursued against that noted rebel, the Earl of Desmond, a subdolous man; who occasioned great disturbance to the English Government in that kingdom.

This Gentleman having behaved himself very well in Ireland, his merits, at length, were made known to Queen Elizabeth: upon which she made him one of her Council there, and Master of the Ordnance in that kingdom. In which last employment he behaved himself with great renown in various actions; as he did likewise, some years after, in his voyage to Cadiz in Spain.

Some time after this, he returned to England; and coming to Oxford, he was in company with other persons of quality, as Ferdinando Earl of Derby, Sir John Spencer, &c. in the year of our Lord 1589, in the month of September, created Master of Arts, before which time he had been advanced to the degree of knighthood.

Some time after this, he went back into Ireland again; and when that unhappy kingdom was, in a manner, over-run with a domestic rebellion and a Spanish army, Sir George Carew was made Lord President of Munster for three years; at that time, joining his forces with those of the Earl of Thomond, he took divers castles and strong holds in those parts; as Logher, Crome, Glane, Carigroile, Ruthmore, &c. and at length brought the titular Earl of Desmond, one of the most active rebels there, to his trial. How greatly this carriage and conduct of his pleased his gracious mistress, Queen Elizabeth, may appear from the above Letter written with her own hand, and sent to him by her Majesty, anno 1601.—Sir George was created Baron Carew of Clopton in Warwickshire, by King James I. in 1605, and Earl of Totness, by King Charles I. in 1625. He died without issue, March 27, 1629, at the age of seventy-three.—See more of him in Prince's Worthies of Devon.

[2] From Moryson's History of Ireland, from the year 1599 to 1603, 8vo.

That which passed from the Excellent Majestie of Queen ELIZABETH, *in her Privie Chamber at East Greenwich,* 4º *Augusti* 1601, 43º *Reg. sui, towards* WILLIAM LAMBARDE [1].

He presented her Majestie with his Pandecta of all her rolls, bundells, membranes, and parcells that be reposed in her Majestie's Tower at London; whereof she had given to him the charge 21st. January last past.

Her Majestie chearfullie received the same into her hands, saying, "You intended to present this book unto me by the Countess of Warwicke; but I will none of that; for if any subject of mine do me a service, I will thankfully accept it from his own hands;" then, opening the book, said, "You shall see that I can read;" and so, with an audible voice, read over the epistle, and the title, so readily, and distinctly pointed, that it might perfectly appear, that she well understood, and conceived the same. Then she descended from the beginning of King John, till the end of Richard III. that is 64 pages, serving eleven kings, containing 286 years: in the 1st page she demanded the meaning of *oblata, cartæ, literæ clausæ*, and *literæ patentes*.

W. L. He severally expounded the meaning, and laid out the true differences of every of them; her Majestie seeming well satisfied, and said, "that she would be a scholar in her age, and thought it no scorn to learn during her life, being of the mind of that philosopher, who in his last years began with the Greek alphabet." Then she proceeded to further pages, and asked where she found cause of stay, as what *ordinationes, parliamenta, rotulus cambii, rediseisnes*.

W. L. He likewise expounded these all according to their original diversities, which she took in gratious and full satisfaction; so her Majestie fell upon the reign of King Richard II. saying, "I am Richard II. know ye not that?"

W. L. "Such a wicked imagination was determined and attempted by a most unkind Gent. the most adorned creature that ever your Majestie made."

Her Majestie. "He that will forget God, will also forget his benefactors; this tragedy was played 40tie times in open streets and houses."

[1] Communicated, from the original, by Thomas Lambard, of Sevenoaks, Esq.

Her Majestie demanded " what was *præstita ?*"

W. L. He expounded it to be " monies lent by her Progenitors to her subjects for their good, but with assurance of good bond for repayment."

Her Majestie. " So did my good Grandfather King Henry VII. sparing to dissipate his treasure or lands." Then returning to Richard II. she demanded, " Whether I had seen any true picture, or lively representation of his countenance and person ?"

W. L. " None but such as be in common hands."

Her Majestie. " The Lord Lumley, a lover of antiquities, discovered it fastened on the backside of a door of a base room; which he presented unto me, praying, with my good leave, that I might put it in order with the Ancestors and Successors; I will command Tho. Kneavet, Keeper of my House and Gallery at Westminster, to shew it unto thee." Then she proceeded to the Rolls,

Romæ, Vasoon, Aquitaniæ, Franciæ, Scotiæ, Walliæ, et Hiberniæ.

W. L. He expounded these to be records of estate, and negotiations with foreign Princes or Countries.

Her Majestie demanded again, " if *rediseisnes* were unlawful and forcible throwing of men out of their lawful possessions ?"

W. L. " Yea, and therefore these be the rolls of fines assessed and levied upon such wrong-doers, as well for the great and wilful contempt of the crown and royal dignity, as disturbance of common justice."

Her Majestie. " In those days force and arms did prevail; but now the wit of the fox is every where on foot, so as hardly a faithful or vertuouse man may be found." Then came she to the whole total of all the membranes and parcels aforesaid, amounting to . . . . , commending the work; " not only for the pains therein taken, but also for that she had not received since her first coming to the crown any one thing that brought therewith so great delectation unto her;" and so being called away to prayer, she put the book in her bosom, having forbidden me from the first to the last to fall upon my knee before her; concluding, " Farewell, good and honest Lambarde."

Lambarde survived this conversation but a few days, as appears from the epitaph hereafter inserted in p. 563.—He was " a man," says Mr. Thorpe[1], " not only

[1] Antiquities in Kent, within the Diocese of Rochester, p. 70.

eminent for his knowledge in the laws of his country, but likewise for his charity, for having founded and endowed an alms-house at Greenwich [1]; and was the first Protestant that built an Hospital [2]. So humble was his disposition of mind, that it is said the Queen (who ever carried a sparing hand in bestowing of honor, as has been elsewhere remarked [3]), would have made him a Judge, which he modestly declined. How highly he was in the favour and esteem of that great Princess, this conference will testify."

The following original Letter from this venerable Topographer to the Lord High Treasurer Burghley was also communicated by Mr. Lambard.

W. Lambarde to the Lord Treasurer, contayning reasons why her Majestie should with speed embrace the action of the defence of the Lowe Countries, 1585.

My Right Honourable good Lord,

Seguris was with me this morning to take his leave, discontented, but confessing that you alone had dealt most honourable for his King; which he would not only publish here, but assure his King that you were the sole personage to whom affairs ought to be addressed. He affirmed [4]..........

But I humblie affirme, that if her Majestie undertake not thoroughly and royallye the matter of the Lowe Countries, she consumes her treasure to no purpose; she wasteth her men; undoeth that poore people that must needs have a faithful sovereigne head (the lack whereof is their destruction, *par enim in parem non habet imperium*); she bringeth the war even to her own doore; and yet can she not provoke Spain more than she alreadie hath; she provokes all Princes (as well Protestants as others) against her; she maketh herself naked of all aide, and converteth the aides now presented to be turned against herself; she staineth her credit

---

[1] Of this Hospital see more hereafter, in p. 560.

[2] Camden's Britannia, Gibson's edit. p. 110.—In the second edition by Bishop Gibson, p. 222, Lambarde's having built an hospital at Greenwich is mentioned, without any notice taken of his being the first Protestant who raised such a charitable edifice. But in Philipott's Villare Cant. p. 163, are the following words relative to this foundation: "as the prying adversaries of our religion then observed, was the first Protestant that built an hospital." Query, however, is the observation just? If it can be truly said of a Subject, it certainly cannot of a King, because Edward VI. was the founder of the three great hospitals in London. S. Denne. [3] Regist. Roffens. p. 1044.

[4] A line and half here blotted so as not to be legible.

everlastingly, having importuned the poore people over unto her, and then to send them away fruitless (for so it is, if her Majestie become not their head to beat down the tyrannie of Spain); she abandonneth the Church of God in distresse (her best bulwarke); and enterteignes the calamities of her neighbours, not preserves them which are both in her help and near her help; she excludes all traffique at home, by despising all friends abroad; she dissolveth merchandize, breaketh the drapery of the Realm, and stirreth up all poore folkes that live of the same to a necessitie that will shake the frame of the whole state, joining the inconveniences that will therewith concur.

The gentleman shall not sell his woole, the plowman his corne, the grazier his ware, nor the artificer shall be employed; all things will be disordered, and we shall be suffocated in our own fatte, tho' wee feele not the force of any foreigne invasion. Her Majestie's Customes will be nothing: she must live of her own rentes, and how they will be answered it is doubtfull: that which she most feareth will follow, the contempt of her own Person, the reputation whereof partly hath been kept in tune these 27 years by one policie; but the date is out, and the last enterteignement had like to have proved tragical. Her Majestie shall neither have nor see any thing about her but sadness of her subjects, open discontent and murmuring of all sorts; drooping in the Nobilitie; in the rest, whispering, conspiring, and exclaiming against the Government, as Queen Marie had a little before her end, from the which God of his mercy preserve her Majestie! This only sequel is able to dissolve a greater kingdome than ours hastily, which falleth not by pushing at, but by his own weight, wanting means to resolve and to execute pregnantly, and to know and use his own forces: *Sic peribit (ni Deus avertat) regnum florentissimum summo tripudio.*

On the other side, her Majestie undertaking the cause roundly, the Prince of Parma shall mysse of Antwerp, and must then sack some of the Cities (capitulated withal) to satisfie his soldiers, which will breed a general revolt of all the Provinces named *discontented*: and yet the Nobility will be easily without this drawn to her Majestie, if she shew herself openly, not masked; a ground inconvenient for Princes to stand upon, which otherwise (to speak plainly and reverently withal) argueth fear and no policie, howsoever it may be covered or pretended.

The Subjects of England, with the contribution of the Low Countries, will abundantly defray the charges, without touching her Majestie's coffers. The matter roundly (not slowly) followed, will make a short war and a long peace, without danger to the Enterprisor. For against whome hath her Majestie to deal? With a King augmented by tyrannie and usurpation, by the sufferings of neighbour Kings—a beggar indeed! hateful to God, without people of his own—living of bankers, his dominions scattered and chargably maintained by the sword, having nothing but opinion of greatness: but now so overtaken by his overweaning to embery, but to spoil rather indeed all Nations his meaning was, whereby he is nearer ruin if it be followed. Her Majestie was miraculously advertised of his intention by his own warrant, sent in poste by God's goodnesse. His forces (if he have any) be farre from us, and the same nothing if they be looked into; his country like to be starved within this year, and his purse will be empty tyll the beginning of September. A great Colossus outwardly, but inwardly stuffed with clouts. A man subject to melancholie, and meeting in these years with disgraces, deadly and mortal passions follow; one that keeps all his owne reckonings to cover his bare estate from others. And this is the scare-crow of the world that her Majestie has to contend withal: of whome, not Kings, but mean persons have small cause to dread. His Lieutenant Parma in despair, and without pay and victuals, wherein our restraint hath done great good; his soldiers few, and worne with necessities, and he not able to bring many together for want of provision to feed them. These being the enemies and their estate, there wanteth nothing on our side but the spirit of God to incline her Majestie to that which is just and necessarie. For it seemeth that God hath delivered them into her hands already, which her faithful Counsellors (as ye be all) should pursue, till she hath yielded to the thing that concerneth her safetie and high honour. Wise Counsellors serve (under correction) as well experienced physicians, to cure the diseases of the mind by diversitie of remedies till they have expelled the griefe. This (with favour) is their office; and those that be under their charge do look for discharge thereof (with all reverence) at their hands.

In this action her Majestie shall be effectually assisted by the King of Denmark. The Princes of Germany (who never favoured the French nor the Prince of Orange's course) will back her Majestie, and join to restore Truces to the See of Colleine; a matter of high importance. Her Majestie shall be Lady of 10,000 sayle of ships in Holland and Zealand, and shall have the stable of the world in her hand, defensible against all the world, having only a head that will oppose. This will stay and divert the French King's braynsicke projects, who is both a coward and a beggar: all the provinces (named Malecontents) shall be united hereby; her Majestie shall have infinite obedience; and they shall be delivered from extreme calamitie. The glory is God's, the enterprize safe and easy, and her Majestie shall have immortal honour, wealth, and security.

For her Majestie's reason, that she would not enter into a war for displeasing of her people, that have so long lived in peace, is (with her Highness's favor) no reason at all. Her people generally desireth this war, as just and necessarie, taken in ripe season, and will hate those that do impugne it, as enemies of their countrey, condemning them of dotage, or malice, or of both. The consent (saith Cominæus) first had of the people of Ingland to allow of war, is a marvellous strength to their Kings, and is undertaken with alacrity, and supplied with abundance. The Kings were then fegne to sue for the people's favor, but this is offered ultrò with a general consent and voice of all, the Gentry, Nobility and Counsellors, concurring therein, which were most dangerous to be disappointed. The realme will discharge her Majestie of the charge of this war, for the vehement desire it hath to the preservation thereof. I dare (in fear of God) assure her Majestie, that if she deal openly in this action, she shall with facility rid the country of Parma and Spain before Christmas-day, and so quit herself of this war, more fearful in conceit, than dangerous in effect.

I have told her Majestie of late sundry things of good consequence, proving true; but I have had Cassandra's luck: I pray God to open her gracious eyes, and strengthen her royal heart in true valour, that all weak respects be chased thence: *Une bonne guerre faiet une bonne paix.*

Touching defensive playsters to be made to help and heal our sore, is a matter (in the judgement of men of gravitie) impossible by man's brain, but most dangerous to him that shall take upon him to persuade that course, and to be the author of a new counsell. Without all stop, this issue by imposthumiation breaks inwardly to our present and manifest destruction.

For this my tedious discourse, I crave humble pardon of your Lordship that I am entered so far, being transported into it ere I was aware; but it is the humble harmless opinion conceived of me, her Majestie's poor, loyal, and careful servant, uttered in all humble duty to you alone, and referred to your honourable censure, having my blood ready to seal it for her Majestie's service, and the preservation of my sweet natural country: and to you, my Lord, my assured duty and devotion to the end of my life; wherewith (weak and sick) I humbly take my leave. The 16th, and kept till the 18th of July, 1585. Your honour's ever most bounden.

"William Lambard," says Strype under the year 1587, "a learned lawyer, excellently skilled in the history and antiquities of this land, received this year, as he had done before, some favours from Lord Burghley, who valued him for great parts and deserts. He was sometime of Lincoln's-Inn; afterwards his station was at Halling in Kent; and was, by the especial order of the Lord Chancellor Bromley, put into the commission of the peace for that county for his great abilities. He was not without troubles; to which 'tis like he exposed himself the more by his care of the public service, and search after such as were disaffected persons, priests, and others. But the Lord Treasurer, well knowing the cause, and the merits of the Gentleman, had cleared him and set him free, which he styled *halcyon-days* restored to him at Halling. And the Lord Cobham of that County was also his seasonable helper, whom he called his *father-like good Lord*; who had favoured some request and petition of his to that Lord. For which restoration of those his halcyon days, he excused himself that he returned him his thanks only by writing and did not personally pay them: but the cause was, that he was busy at Rochester about the Queen's subsidy; and likewise the grief he was then under for the loss of a godly and dear companion [probably his wife]. But his own letter so well penned, and so deeply expressive of his obligation to that Lord, and his own particular circumstances, must follow in his own words: for letters to and from such persons of eminency in these days deserve to be preserved:

"Albeit, my most honourable and singular good Lord (raised unto me by God, for rescue of all my distresses), duty willeth, that I should thankfully present myself upon my knees before you, and not cover me after this sort in paper: yet may it please your good Lordship, in regard that I am perfectly closed in the midst of her Majesty's service for the subsidy, both in the City of Rochester, and in the County at large, to vouchsafe this manner of yielding my most bounden thanks, till God in further time will give me the means to perform it better.

"I have evermore, my singular good Lord, perceived a most honourable disposition of favour in your good Lordship towards me, that never did or could demerit any thing at your hands. I felt it also to my joyful peace, which for these few halcyon days I have enjoyed at my ferme in Hallying. But most sensibly do I now apprehend it in this my just sorrow for the life of the most godly and dear companion of my life; when your good Lordship granted the desire presented on my behalf by that my favourable and father-like good Lord Cobham, not only in respect of my petitions, but also pity of mine estate; and for that affection which your Lordship doth bear unto myself.

For all these I most humbly thank your good Lordship upon the knees of my heart; beseeching that Lord of all to repay unto you on the great day that comfortable kindness, which I have received from you: and assuring you, that not only myself will daily call unto God for you, but will also teach my poor sucklings to send up, and sound their praises in his ears. The same bless your good Lordship with long life, and honourable prosperity here, and take you at the last unto himself in heaven. From Hallying, this 5th of Sept. 1587.

" Your for ever most bound, WILLIAM LAMBARDE."

" I add (that I may here collect together what I have to say of this worthy Gentleman Mr. Lambarde) that after a year or two he was nominated by the said Lord Treasurer, his friend, knowing well his abilities, for a judge, or some such eminent place in the Law. And so the said Lord let him understand, which caused another grateful letter to him; shewing his thankfulness, and his modesty too, in a desire he made; *viz.* that before he should be invested in that service to be tried first for the next Term. For so ingenious and well-weighed letter ran:

" After my most humble and bounden duty, my right honourable good Lord, your Lordship's letters of the 30th of September were even now delivered to my hand, having (by whose default I wot not) suffered that great delay in the coming towards, which howsoever it may fall out to my detriment in the matter that they purport, yet came they not unseasonable to glad my poor heart, in that they were the infallible messengers, not only of the continuance, but of the encrease (if any may be) of your most honourable favours and disposition to work my good; who, as I never demerited any thing at your hands, so nevertheless have I drawn more from the fountain of your mere bounty, than from all the good wills and wyles of all the persons that be alive. Thus tyed, I may not cease to pray to God for your honour: praying withal, that he will make my prayer effectual for you.

" Betouching the matter contained in your Lordship's letter, albeit I know mine own insufficiency (now also encreased by decay of sight, and discontinuance from study) to serve in any place where wisdom or learning must be set on work; yet acknowledging that I do reap some benefit by her Majesty (which I received from the free hand of your honour) I hold myself double bounden to serve her

Highness with all the powers that I have. And the rather also, for that it hath pleased you, my most honourable Lord, to give my name, and your report of me. Therefore——Only I do most humbly beseech your Lordship to add this unto the rest of your great favours vouchsafed, that I may not be invested in the service but upon probation, and for this next Term only; to the end that, after such an experiment, and conference made of my small abilities with the office itself, I may faithfully (and in that duty which I bear to God, her Majesty, and your honour) assure your good Lordship, whether I shall find myself fit to discharge the trust that belongeth to the place.

"Thus much I most humbly pray your good Lordship to accept at this time; and until that I may, as duty bindeth, personally attend your good Lordship; which also, by the favour of God, I will not fail with all good speed to perform. And so I most humbly take my leave of you, my right honourable Lord, and do in my heartiest prayer recommend you to the gracious protection of the Almighty. From Hallying, this 4th of October, 1589.

"Your Lordship's most humble and bounden, WILLIAM LAMBARDE."

"I cannot let this man pass, without the mention of a character that Kilburne gives of him, in his "Topography and Survey of Kent;" who termed him, "That learned, judicious, and laborious Gentleman, William Lambarde, Esq. whose monuments of piety and charity in that county, his Directory of the peaceable government of the same [i. e. his book of the office of a justice of the peace], and his painful and able performance of his Perambulation [i. e. in his book of that county, so named], have rendered, and will perpetuate his memory famous." And that monument of his piety and charity above spoken of, was a college, or alms-house, for twenty poor people, founded by him anno 1560, in East Greenwich, termed The College of Queen's Elizabeth's poor people [1]."

To this account of Strype we may add, that Mr. Lambarde was son of an Alderman and Sheriff of London, eminently versed in the Armenian language, and admitted of Lincoln's-Inn, where he made a considerable progress in the Law. Tanner has enumerated several Tracts of his on this and other subjects. His principal publication is a collection of Saxon Laws, first written by Lawrence Noel, Dean of Lichfield; who, going abroad, left them to him to translate and publish,

---

[1] The building was begun in August 1575, and completed in September 1576, at the expence of £.2,642. 8s. 6d. as appears by a MS in the hands of Mr. Lambarde. See p. 561.

which he did, under the title of "Ἀρχαιονομία, sive de priscis Anglorum Legibus, London, 1568," 4to; revised by A. Wheelock, Cambridge, 1644. Of his " Perambulation of Kent," there have been four editions, 1570, 1576, 1596, 1640. His "Eirenarcha; or, of the Justices of the Peace, 1581," 8vo; his " Archion, or a Commentary upon the High Courts of Justice in England, 1591," was re-printed in 1635; his "Pandecta Rotulorum" appeared in 1600. His posthumous " Alphabetical Description of the chief places in England and Wales, 1730," 4to, has a good head of him by Vertue [1].

An Estimate of the Charges of the foundation, building, and endowment of this College of the Poore of Queen Elizabeth, in Eastgrenwich, begane to be erected in August 1575, and ended in September 1576, 18° Reg. Elizab.

Landes, and assurance thereof.

	£.	s.	d.
The Mannor of Brenchesley, alias Criels, and the lands thearwithall bought of Mr. Sydnor, together with the charges of the assurance, cost	905	0	0
The fermes of Brattels and Chelmyll, &c. bought of Mr. Wilyss, togeather with the charges of the assurance, amounted unto	605	0	0
The ferme of Beltring and Tassewood meadow, together with the assurances, amounted unto	525	0	0
Ballingboroughe and grove, with the assurance, coste	27	0	0
Shukfon's grove, with the assurance, cost	16	0	0
The patente of the incorporation did cost by all meanes	20	0	0
The purchase of the close of seven acres, wherein the College is situated, and which is not divided, did amount to	70	0	0

[1] Among the MSS still remaining in the collection of Mr. Lambard are 1. " A Charge for the Peace, by Order of the Decalogue (or Ten Commandments of Almighty God), by William Lambarde, Esq." (since printed in Bibliotheca Topographica Britannica, vol. I. p. 517.) 2. " Directions for Juries chardged to enquier on the behalfe of the Queene's Majestie, at any Sessions of Oier and Terminer, Gaole Deliverie, or of the Easter Sessions of the Peace," signed, " W. Lambarde, with the Allowance of the whole Benche, at the Easter Sessions of the Peace, 1595;" and indorsed, " Directions for Enquyrers, 1599, by W. Lambarde."

First Building, &c.	£.	s.	d.
The bricklaiers, plaisterers, and tylers had in all by their first bargaine	297	0	0
And afterwards for amending the eves, crest, and dormant wyndows	3	6	8
The carpenter had by his first bargaine, for oak tymber and workmanship	120	0	0
And afterwards for postes, spurres, the uttergate, and other things	2	10	0
Fowrtie tonnes of mine owne elme timber bestowed in the floores, rated at 9s. the tonne, amounted to	18	0	0
The free-mason had for the three stones with the inscription	1	14	0
The smithe had for the five fanes, and the locks for gates and doors	5	0	0
The plummer had for the gutters, and the apron of the pumpe	1	6	0
The pumpe cost over and besides the elme trunk	2	5	0
The glazier had for 300 foote of glass, and for the three scutcheons of arms in the house of prayer	6	6	6
Labourers and workmen had, for levelling the court, and for hedging and diching the several closes	10	0	0
The seeling of the house of prayer, with deale boord, and the table, and sixe formes there, cost	4	0	0
The paving and flinte, for the skirtes of the courte within, and the brick for the gutters thearof, cost	5	13	4
The two parts of the silver seale for the corporation coste	2	17	0
The two chestes with their locks cost	4	10	0
Summe total	£.2,600	0	0

Reparation.

Memorandum, that I payd after this, in the yeare 1579, to Lorimer and Walbanck, for new tiling of the College, and for hedding all the chimnies, and finishing the crest, &c.	32	0	0
Item, then to the plomber for leade to the dormant windos	1	5	0
Item, to Richard Jones, carpenter, for postes in the courte, for a table in the back-house, a gate at the hemplott	9	3	6
Summe	£.2,642	5	6

Note, that since anno 1576 theare have been 10 several pensioners (wheareof some marryed, and having children) continually maynteyned heare: each having house-room, a private gardene, and 5s. every month: besydes twoe loades of wood, and some profits of the common garden, that is divided amongst them.

Mr. Lambarde was one of the first Presidents of Cobham College in Kent; and the excellent rules and ordinances[1] for the election, maintenance, and well governing of the poor there, were drawn up by that learned antiquary.

The following epitaph is transcribed from a monument which formerly stood against the South wall at Greenwich[2]:

"William Lambard, of Lincoln's Inn, some time Master in Chancery, Keeper of the Rolls and Records within the Tower, of the office of Alienations to Queen Elizabeth, founded the College of the poor of Greenwich, and endowed it. Obiit 1601, Aug. 19, at Westcomb in East Greenwich.

"Sir Moulton Lambard, of Westcomb in East Greenwich, Knight, son and heir of the aforesaid William Lambard, 1634. Thomas Lambard, Esq; his only son and heir, erected this monument to Sir Moulton Lambard, his aged and dear father."

A more particular account of Mr. Lambard, communicated by Multon Lambard, Esq. his lineal descendant, may be seen in the 42d Number of the "Bibliotheca Topographica Britannica."

[1] See these in Thorpe's Registrum Roffense, pp. 242, & seqq.

[2] On pulling down the Church, in order to rebuild the present, this monument was removed at the charge of the late Thomas Lambard, Esq. and fixed in the Church of Sevenoaks; where, at the West end, on the North side, is a handsome mural monument of white marble, and on a tablet of black marble, is this inscription in gilt letters:

"Hic situs est Gulielmus Lambarde, Londinensis, in hospitio jureconsultorum Lincolniensi paredrus; in alma cancellaria magister; ad tempus custos rotulorum et recordorum infra Turrim London. ab alienationibus (quas vocant) augustissimæ Anglorum reginæ Elizabethæ, cujus sacræ memoriæ et nomini consecratum suo sumptu solus, et fundavit et annuo reditu dotavit collegium pauperum Greenovici in Cantia. Obiit anno Domini 1601, Augusti 19º die, apud Westcombe, in East Greenwiche.

Archionomia	-	-	1568.	Justice of the Peace	-	1581.
Perambulation of Kent	-		1579.	Pandecta rotulorum	-	1600.
	Archeion	-	-	1591.		

"Hic etiam situs est Moultonus Lambarde, de Westcombe in East Greenwiche, in comitatu Cantiæ, eques auratus, filius et hæres prædicti Gulielmi Lambardi. Obijt anno Domino 1634, Augusti 7º die, apud Westcombe. Hoc M. S."

Mr. Chamberlain, in his Letters to Sir Dudley Carleton, gives the following account of the Queen's Progress in this year:

"On the 13th of August the Queen came to Windsor[1]; and is expected shortly at Mr. Comptroller's[2] at Causham. And so the Progress should hold on as far

---

Underneath, on a small tablet of black marble, is this:

"Parenti grandævo colendissimo, et patri charissimo, officii et amoris ergo posuit Tho. Lambard, armiger, filius unicus et hæres prædicti Moultoni Lambardi, equitis aurati."

And beneath, on a tablet of white, is the following:

"Instauratâ funditus vetustâ Greenovicensi ecclesiâ, et exulantibus, quæ inibi erant, monumentis. Marmor hoc, abavi proavique memoriæ sacrum, huc, veluti in portum, e communi naufragio evasit, et cognati cineris libenter se in tutelam tradidit, curante Thoma Lambard, armigero, Gulielmi filio, Thomæ nepote, anno Domini M.DCC.XXXIII."

[1] Queen Elizabeth took much delight in Windsor Castle. The celebrated terrace was her work, and under it a garden, whose meanders and labyrinths are still faintly discernible. The outer gate on the hill next the town was built in her 14th year, 1572, as appears by an inscription over it. At Windsor she amused herself with translating "Boethius de Consolatione, 1593," as she had at Enfield done the like favour to Ochine's Sermon. In her way to the latter place she was pleased with Shoreditch bells. Of the Queen's early attachment to Literature, see vol. I. p. 19.—Note of the time wherein Queen Elizabeth began and ended her translation of Boethius. The Queenes Majestie being at Windsor, in the 35th yeere of her Raigne, upon the 10th of October, 1593, began her translation of "Boethius de Consolatione Philosophie," and ended it upon the eight of November then next following, which were 30 dayes. Of which tyme there are to be accompted 13 days, parte in Sondayes and other holy dayes, and parte in her Majestie ryding abrode, upon which her Majestie did forbeare to translate. So that 13 dayes being deducted from 30 remaynith 17 dayes, in which tyme her Majestie finished her translation. And in those 17 dayes, her Majestie did not excede one houer and a half at a tyme in following her translating. Whereby it apperith, that in 26 houers, or thereabouts, her Majestie performed the whole translation.—Second account by Mr. Bowyer: The computation of the dayes and houres in which your Majestie began and finished the translation of Boethius: Your Majestie began your translation of Boethius the tenth day of October 1593, and ended it the fifth of November then next immediately following, which were fyve-and-twenty dayes in all. Out of which 25 days are to be taken, fowre Sondayes, three other holly dayes, and six dayes on which your Majestie ryd abrode to take the ayre; and on those dayes did forbeare to translate, amounting togither to thirtene dayes. Which 13 being deducted from 25 remaynith then but twelve dayes. And then accompting twoo houres only bestowed every day one with another in the translating, the computation fallith out, that in fowre-and-twenty houres your Majestie began and ended your translation." W. BOWYER, Keeper of the Records in the Tower.

[2] Sir William Knollys, Knight, son of Sir Francis Knollys, K. B. who had been Treasurer of the Household, was Comptroller of the Household in 1579. He was employed by the Queen, in 1592, to negotiate between the King of Spain and the Low Countries; and on the New-year's Day follow-

as Littlecot, a house of the Lord Chief Justice [1], in Wiltshire. But there be so many endeavours to hinder it that I will lay no great wagers of the proceeding.

"About the 5th of September, certain Noblemen and others of France, to the number of 300 persons, arrived at the Tower wharf [2]; the chief of them were conveyed in coaches from thence through the City, into Bishopsgate-street, and there the principal, namely, Marshal de Biron, was lodged in Crosby-place; the other near adjoining in Cornhill.

ing presented to her Majesty " a round kirtell of ash-coloured cloth of silver, like stripes of trees, of orange-coloured silk; with eight buttons, embroidered like coronets." In return, he had 26½ ounces of gilt plate.—In 1601 he was made Treasurer of the Household; and in 1603 he was created Baron Knollys by King James, whose Queen he entertained at Causham, on her way to Bath, 1613. He was made Master of the Wards in 1614, and about the same time elected K. G. He was made Viscount Wallingford in 1616; Earl of Banbury in 1622; and died in 1631.

[1] Sir John Popham, then Chief Justice of the King's Bench. On New-year's Day 1599-1600, he presented to the Queen £10 in gold, and had in return 23½ ounces of gilt plate. He afterwards built a noble mansion at Wellington in Somersetshire. He died in 1607, at the age of 76, and has a monument in Wellington Church.

[2] The principal Noblemen and Gentlemen of France were these: Monsieur Duke of Biron, Marshal of France, the King's Lieutenant of the Countie of Burgon and Brest; Monsieur the Prince of Avergne, the King's Lieutenant in Avergne and Limosen, bastard to Charles of Valois late King of France; Monsieur Duke of Aumont, Knight of the Order of the Holy Ghost, Marshal of the Field, and Captain of 50 men of arms; Monsieur Earl of Pavabene, Lieutenant of the County of Poictou and Berie; Monsieur Earl of Croque, Lieutenant of the County Valentinois, Captain of 50 men of arms; Monsieur Earl of St. Mary, Governor of Roane, and Captain of the King's guards; Monsieur Earl of Vignolet, Camp Master and Gentleman of the King's Chamber; Monsieur Earl of Guerson, Marquis of St. Pont, and Lieutenant of the Country of Bourbon; Monsieur L. Baron of Biron, brother to the Duke of Biron, Camp Master for the King of 1500 footmen; Monsieur Baron of Tornes, Colonel of all the horsemen in France; Monsieur Baron of the Signorie, Viscount of Peaine, Captain of 1200 men; Monsieur Viscount of Sardigne, a Gentleman of the King's Chamber; Monsieur Viscount of Cassaneule, Governor of Ciquantrie; Monsieur Baron of Ferre, Captain of 50 men; Monsieur Baron of Pansack, of Ceane, upon Liere; Monsieur L. Baron de la Barre, Camp Master, and Captain of 1000 men; Monsieur Baron of Rurdire, Camp Master of 1000 men; Monsieur Baron of Cuessen, Lieutenant of the Town Teullirs; Monsieur Baron of Bullogne; Monsieur Baron of Maralles; Monsieur Baron of Delbine; Monsieur de Verdon, Governor of Barrean; Monsieur de Fraige; Monsieur de Strosse; Monsieur de Narpes; Monsieur de Padamesin; Monsieur de Gattonois; Monsieur de Peneste; Monsieur de Monplaiger; besides 30 Gentlemen attending the Duke of Biron, eight officers, three pages, and six laquies; ten Gentlemen for every Duke and Earl, four officers, two pages, and three laqueys; six for every Baron, three officers, one page, and two lacqueys; every one of the rest had three servants and three lacqueys.

"Sept. 10 1601. The Queen is now in Progress as far as Basing, a house of the Lord Marquis [1], where she entertained your Frenchmen with all favour and gracious usage. I cannot tell you the particulars [2], for I was nothing near.

[1] William Paulet, fourth Marquis of Winchester, and Earl of Wiltshire, great-grandson of William the first Marquis (who built the beautiful and magnificent seat at Basing, where he died March 10, 1571-2. This noble mansion was the largest of any subject's; was made a garrison by his great-grandson John Marquis of Winchester for Charles I.; and after enduring two sieges under its Lord, was, at length, 1645, plundered and burnt to the ground: so that nothing now remains but the garden wall).—He married Lucy, daughter of Sir Thomas Cecil, afterwards Earl of Exeter. On New-year's Day 1599-1600, the Marquis presented to the Queen £20 in gold; and the Dowager Lady Marquesse gave " a sprig of gold, garnished with sparks of rubies, a small diamond, and pearls of sundry sorts and bignesses." The Marquis had in return 29¼ ounces of gilt plate, and the Dowager Lady Marquesse 30 ounces.

[2] This portion of the Progress is thus recorded in Stow's Annals:

"The 5th of September, the Queen, in her Progress, came into Hampshire; and upon Chichester heath was received by the Sheriff of that Shire, Francis Palmer, accompanied by many Gentlemen of merit in the said Shire, so that her Majestie said, she was never so honourably received in any Shire; for as Hampshire is a county pleasant of soil, and full of delight for Princes of this land who often make their Progress therein; so it was well inhabited by antient Gentlemen, civily educated, and who live in great amity together. Her Majesty was that night attended into Basing, a house of the Lord Marquis, whereto she took such great content, as well with the seat of the house, as honourable carriage of the worthy Lady Lucie Marquesse of Winchester, that she stayed there thirteen days, to the great charge of the said Lord Marquis. The fourth day after the Queen's coming to Basing, the said Sheriff was commanded to attend the Duke of Biron at his coming into that county. Whereupon, the next day, being the 10th of September, he went towards Blackwater being the uttermost confines of that Shire towards London; and there met the said Duke, accompanied with above twenty of the Nobilitie of France, and attended with about four hundred Frenchmen, who were met by George Earl of Cumberland, and by him conducted from London into Hampshire. The said Duke was that night brought to the Vyne, a fair and large house of the Lord Sonds, which house was furnished with hangings and plate from the Tower and Hampton Court; and with seven-score beds and furniture, which the willing and obedient people of the County of Southampton, upon two days warning, had brought thither, to lend the Queen. The Duke abode there four or five days, all at the Queen's charges, and spent her more at the Vyne then her own Court for that time spent at Basing. During her abode there, her Majesty went to him at the Vyne, and he to her at Basing. And one day he attended her at Basing Park at hunting; where the Duke stayed her coming, and did there see her in such Royalty, and so attended by the Nobility, so costly furnished and mounted, as the like had seldom been seen. But, when she came to the place where the Duke stayed, the said Sheriff (as the manner is) being bare-headed, and riding next before her, stayed his horse, thinking the Queen would then have saluted the Duke; whereat the Queen, being much offended, commanded the Sheriff to go on. The Duke followed her very humbly, bowing low towards her horse's main, with his cap off, about twenty yards. Her Majesty, on the sudden, took

"Our Friend the Sheriff[1] of Berkshire was almost out of heart at the first news of the Queen's coming into the Country, because he was altogether unacquainted with *Courting*[2]; but yet he performed it very well, and sufficiently, being exceedingly well horsed and attended, which won him great commendation on all sides.

"The Queen's first remove from Windsor was to Mr. Warder's. Then to Reading. During her abode there, she went one day to dinner to Mr. Comptroller's at Causham. Mr Green, Sheriff of Oxfordshire, met her at the Bridge, very well accompanied. Mr. Comptroller made great chear, and entertained her with many devises, of singing, dancing, and playing-wenches, and such like. At her going thence, she made three Knights, your cousin Sir Edward Goodwin[3], Sir

off her mask, looked back upon him, and most gratiously and courteously saluted him, as holding it not becoming so mighty a Prince as she was, and who so well knew all Kingly Majesty, to make her stay directly against a subject, before he had shewed his obedience in following after her. She tarried at Basing thirteen days, as is afore said, being very well contented with all things there done; affirming she had done that in Hampshire that none of her Ancestors ever did, neither that any Prince in Christendom could do: that was, she lived in her Progress, in her subjects' houses, entertained a Royal Ambassador, and had Royally entertained him. At her departure from Basing, being the 14th of September, she made ten Knights (having never in her Reign made at one time so many before), whose names were, Sir Edward Cecil, second son to the Lord Burlegh; Sir Edward Hungerford, next heir to the Lord Hungerford; Sir Edward Bainton, of Wiltshire; Sir W. Kingsmil; Sir Carew Rawleigh; Sir Francis Palmer, then Sheriff of the Shire; Sir Benjamin Tichbourne; Sir Hamden Paulet; Sir Richard Norton, of Hampshire; Sir Francis Stoner, of Oxfordshire; and Sir Edmund Lutlow, of Wiltshire. That day she went from Basing toward Farnham, a Castle belonging to the See of Winchester; and in her way to Furnham, she knighted Sir Richard White in his own house, having feasted her and her train very royally; near unto which Town the Sheriff of Hampshire took his leave, and the Sheriff of Surrey met her; but the Sheriff of Hampshire and the Gentlemen of that County went to Farnham by command, and there attended the next day, where they were feasted and kindly entertained by the Learned Prelate, Doctor Bilson, Bishop of Winchester, upon whose only commendation, two ancient and worthy Gentlemen of Hampshire, Sir Richard Mill and Sir William Udall, received there the dignity of Knighthood."

[1] Samuel Backhouse, of Swallowfield, Esq. was then Sheriff. His immediate successors were Sir John Norris and Sir Edward Fettiplace, both knighted by the Queen in this Progress.

[2] i. e. with the duties and services of a Court.

[3] Of Bishop's Wooburn, Buckinghamshire. He was probably son of *John* Goodwin, and either the father or elder brother of *Sir Francis*, both of whom are mentioned by Mr. Lysons (Buckinghamshire, p. 669).—Sir Francis was High Sheriff in 21 James I. and a Representative for that County in several successive Parliaments. The dispute concerning the legality of his election in 1604 proved the cause of establishing the great constitutional doctrine, that the House of Commons have the sole right of judging and deciding on the validity of their own elections and returns. Sir Francis was a

Edward Fettiplace[1], and Sir Richard Warde. But what need I trouble you with those things, when your Brother was there in person, who can relate all at large, " et quorum pars magna fuit?" for I imagine his small troop was half drowned in the sea of such shews as the Oxfordshire men made, when Sir Anthony Cope[2], Sir Richard Waynman, and the rest, set up their sails; and Mr. Dormer, for his part, came with ten or twelve men, well mounted.

"Two or three days after, the Queen dined with Sir Edward Norris[3] at Englefield[4]; where I heard of no wonders, but that she knighted Sir Richard Stafford and his Lady's Father. Some do make much marvel that he would be the means to make such a Sir John Norris.

"From thence the Queen removed to Sir Humphrey Foster's[5]; and so meant to have gone on to the Lord Chief Justice's[6], and the Earl of Hertford's[7], if these Frenchmen had not stayed her. But now, I think, she be at the farthest for this year, and, they say, is driving back to Windsor; where, at her last being, I forgot to tell you that she made a step to Mr. Attorney's[8] at Stoke, where she was most sumptuously entertained, and presented with jewels, and other gifts, to the amount of a thousand or twelve hundred pounds.

particular friend of the celebrated John Hampden, and zealously concurred with his measures, at he commencement of the disputes between King Charles and his Parliament.

[1] An antient and numerous family in Bedfordshire.

[2] Three successive *Anthony Copes*, of Hanwell, were High Sheriffs of Oxfordshire, 1583, 1592, 1604.

[3] Youngest son of Henry Lord Norris of Ricott (where the Queen had made a visit in 1592). Sir Edward led the front at the siege of Ostend. He was the only son, out of six, that survived his parents; and died in 1606.

[4] Englefield House had belonged to a family of its own name very early. The last of them was Sir Francis, who was buried in the grave of Sir Edward Norris.

[5] Who had been Sheriff of Berkshire in 1594. His seat was at Pudworth; but he was buried in the family chapel at Aldermaston.

[6] Sir John Popham, Chief Justice of the King's Bench. See p. 565.

[7] At Elvetham in Hampshire, where the Queen was sumptuously entertained in 1591, as related under that year. On New-year's Day, 1599-1600, the Earl presented to the Queen £10 in gold; and received 21½ ounces of gilt plate.

[8] See before, p. 467.—Sir Edward Coke, some time Recorder of London, Solicitor General 1594, Attorney General 1603, Lord Chief Justice of the Common Pleas 1613; and whom Fuller quaintly styles "*our English Trebonianus*, so famous for his Comments on our Common Law." At the christening of one of his children, in 1600, the Queen presented to him a gilt bowl and cover, weighing 43½ ounces. His residence was at Stoke Pogeis in Buckinghamshire, where he died Sept. 3, 1634. His last words were, " Thy kingdom come, thy will be done."—He was buried at Tittleshall, where a sumptuous altar-tomb records his acquirements, heroism, and virtues.

THE QUEEN TO LORD DEPUTY MOUNTJOY.—AT KINGSTON, 1601.

On the 4th of October the Queen wrote the following Letter to the Lord Deputy Mountjoy, relating to the besieging of the Spaniards at Kinsale:

"Since the brain-sick humour of unadvised assault hath seized on the hearts of our causeless foes, we doubt not but their gain will be their bane, and glory their shame, that ever they had the thought there. And that your humour agrees so rightly with ours, we think it most fortunately happened in your rule to shew the better whose you are, and what you be, as your own hand-writ hath told us of late, and do beseech the Almighty Power of the Highest so to guide your hands that nothing light in vain, but to prosper your head that nothing be left behind that might avail your praise; and that yourself in venturing too far, make the foe a prey of you. Tell our Army from us, that they make full account that every 100 of them will beat a 1000, and every 1000 theirs doubled. I am the bolder to pronounce it in His name, that ever hath protected my righteous cause, in which I bless them all. And putting you in the first place, I end, scribbling in haste, your loving Sovereign,   E. R."[1]

On the 20th of October, the bells at St. Margaret's, Westminster, were rung "when the Queen came from Richmond;" and on that day passed through the town of Kingston-upon-Thames, in state; and received on that occasion a pair of gloves, and a gift of £4. 6s.[2]

"1601. Richard Butler, Mayor of Coventry.

"In his year, at the earnest suit of Mr. Tony, schoolmaster, the library was begun; and he, with Mr. Arnold the usher, made such request to gentlemen, that it was quickly furnished with books[3]."

---

[1] From Fynes Moryson's History of Ireland from 1599 to 1603.

[2] "Paid Mr. Cockes, for the gift to the Queen, £4. 6s.
To Thomas Haywarde, to pay for the Queen's gloves, 40s.
Paid to the Queen's Officers for their ordinary fees; viz.
The Serjeants at Arms, for their fees, 20s; the Trumpeters 20s; Yeomen Ushers 6s. 8d.; Gentlemen Ushers 20s.; Footmen 20s.; the Porters 10s.; Lytermen 6s. 8d.; Yeomen of the botels 6s. 8d."
From the Corporation Records of Kingston.

[3] From the Corporation Records of Coventry; whence this subsequent entry is also taken:
"1637, 17 May, Gave Mr. Burton, for making a book for the City, called 'Burton's Works,' £50."

A LOTTERY, *presented before the* QUEENES MAJESTIE, *at the* LORD CHANCELLOR's[1] *House*, 1601[2].

A Marriner with a box under his arme, containing all the severall things following, supposed to come from the Carricke, came into the Presence, singing this Song:

> Cynthia, Queene of seas and lands,
> That Fortune euery where commands,
> Sent forth Fortune to the sea,
> To try her Fortune euery way:
> There did I Fortune meet, which makes me now to sing,
> There is no fishing to the Sea, nor service to the King.
>
> All the Nymphes of Thetis' traine,
> Did Cynthiae's Fortune entertaine:
> Many a iewell, many a iem,
> Was to her Fortune brought by them.
> Her Fortune sped so well, as makes me now to sing.
> There is no fishing to the Sea, nor service to the King.
>
> Fortune, that it might be seene
> That she did serue a Royall Queene;

---

[1] At the time of this Visit, Sir Thomas Egerton was Lord Keeper of the Great Seal, not Chancellor. On the preceding New-year's Day the Queen accepted from him an amulet of gold, garnished with sparks of rubies, pearls, and half pearls, and from Dame Elizabeth Egerton, the Lord Keeper's second wife, " a round kirtell, of velvet satten, cut and embroidered all over like *Esses* of Venice gold, and a border embroidered like pyramids; and a doublet of silver chamlett, embroidered with pearls like leaves, flourished with silver." In return, Sir Thomas received $34\frac{1}{4}$ ounces of gilt plate; and his Lady $17\frac{1}{4}$ ounces.—Lady Egerton died in the month of January 1599-1600; and in the following October he married his third Lady, Alice, relict of Ferdinand Earl of Derby.—" The Lottery" was presented to the Queen in the Summer of 1601 at York House, then the town residence of the Lord Keeper; who in the following year was honoured by a Visit from his Royal Mistress at his then newly-purchased mansion at Harefield Place. See hereafter, p. 581.

[2] From Davison's " Poetical Rapsodie;" ed. 1611, pp. 1-7.

A franke and royall hand did beare,
And cast her favors euery where.
Some toies fel to my share; which makes me now to sing,
There is no fishing to the Sea, nor service to the King [1].

And the Song ended, he uttered this short Speech:

"God save you, faire Ladies all; and for my part, if ever I be brought to answere my sinnes, God forgive me my sharking, and lay vsurie to my charge. I am a Marriner, and am now come from the sea, where I had the Fortune to light upon these few trifles. I must confesse I came but lightly by them; but I no sooner had them, but I made a vow, that as they came to my hands by Fortune, so I would not part with them but by Fortune. To that end I have ever since carried these Lots about me, that, if I meet with fit company, I might deuide my booty among them. And now (I thanke my good Fortune) I am lighted into the best company of the world, a company of the fairest Ladies that euer I saw. Come, Ladies, try your Fortunes; and if any light vpon an vnfortunate blanke, let her thinke that Fortune doth but mock her in these trifles, and meanes to pleasure her in greater matters."

The Lots.

1. *Fortune's Wheeles.*

Fortune must now no more on Triumph ride;
The wheeles are yours that did her chariots guide.

2. *A Purse.*

You thrive, or would, or may: your Lot's a purse;
Fill it with gold, and you are nere the worse.

3. *A Maske.*

Want you a maske? Here, Fortune gives you one;
Yet Nature gives the rose and lilly none.

---

[1] From a passage in the Queen's Entertainment at Cowdray in 1591 (see before, p. 95), it will be seen that the burden of this song is cited as "an Olde Saying" by a Fisherman.

4. *A Looking Glasse.*

Blinde Fortune doth not see how fare you be;
But gives a glasse, that you yourselfe may see.

5. *A Hand-kerchiefe.*

Whether you seeme to weepe, or weepe indeede,
This hand-kerchiefe will stand you well in steed.

6. *A Plaine Ring.*

Fortune doth send you, hap it well or ill,
This plaine gold ring, to wed you to your will.

7. *A Ring with this poesie:* "As faithfull as I find."

Your hand by Fortune on this ring doth light;
And yet the words do hit your humour right.

8. *Paire of Gloves.*

Fortune these gloves to you in challenge sends;
For that you loue not fooles that are her friends.

9. *A Dozen of Points.*

You are in every point a louer true;
And therefore Fortune gives the points to you.

10. *A Lace.*

Give her the lace that loves to be straight-lac'd;
So Fortune's little gift is aptly plac'd.

11. *A Paire of Knives.*

Fortune doth giue this paire of knives to you,
To cut the thread of loue if 't be not true.

12. *A Girdle.*

By Fortune's girdle you may happy be;
But they that are lesse happy are more free.

13. *A Paire of Writing Tables.*

These tables may containe your thoughts in part;
But write not all that's written in your heart.

14. *A Paire of Garters.*

Though you have Fortune's garters, you must be
More staid and constant in [your] steps then she.

15. *A Coyfe and Crosse-cloath.*

Frowne in good earnest, or be sicke in iest :
This coife and crosse-cloth will become you best.

16. *A Falling Band.*

Fortune would have you rise, yet guides your hand,
From others' Lots to take the falling band.

18. *A Stomacher.*

This stomacher is full of windows wrought;
Yet none through them can see into your thought.

19. *A Paire of Sizzers.*

These sizzers doe your huswifery bewray;
You loue to worke, though you were born to play.

20. *A Chaine.*

Because you scorne Love's captive to remaine,
Fortune hath sworne to leade you in a chaine.

21. *A Praier Booke.*

Your Fortune may prove good another day;
Till Fortune come, take you a booke to pray.

22. *A Snuftkin.*

'Tis Summer[1] yet, a snuftskin is your lot:
But 'twill be Winter one day, doubt you not.

[1] August. See the Entertainment at Cowdray, pp. 90—96.

23. *A Fanne.*

You love to see, and yet to be vnseene;
Take you this fan to be your beauties skreene.

24. *A Paire of Bracelets.*

Lady, your hands are fallen into a snare;
For Cupid's manacles these bracelets are.

25. *A Bodkin.*

Euen with this bodkin you may live unharm'd;
Your beauty is with vertue so well armed.

26. *A Necklace.*

Fortune giues youre faire neck this lace to weare;
God grant a heavier yoke it may neuer beare.

27. *A Cushinet.*

To her that little cares what lot she winnes,
Chance gives a little cushinet to sticke pinnes.

28. *A Dyall.*

The dyal's yours; watch time, lest it be lost;
Yet they most lose it that do watch it most.

29. *A nutmeg with a blanke Parchment in it.*

This nutmeg holds a blanke, but Chance doth hide it;
Write your own wish, and Fortune will provide it.

30. *Blanke.*

Wot you not why Fortune gives you no prize?
Good faith, she saw you not, she wants her eyes.

31. *Blanke.*

You are so daintie to be pleas'd, God wot,
Chance knowes not what to give you for a lot.

32. *Blanke.*

'Tis pittie such a hand should draw in vaine;
Though it gaine nought, yet shall it pittie gaine.

33. *Blanke.*

Nothing's your lot; that's more than can be told;
For nothing is more precious than gold.

34. *Blanke.*

You faine would haue; but what you cannot tell:
In giuing nothing, Fortune serves you well.

Signed, I. D. (edit. 1611); Sir I: D. (edit. 1621.)

In January 1601-2 Lord Mountjoy received from the Queen this following Letter:

"ELIZABETH R. Right trusty and well-beloved we greet you well. The report which your letters by Davers have brought us of the success it hath pleased God to give you against our Rebels, and the Spaniards combined with them, was received by us with such contentment as so great and happy an accident could afford; wherefore, although we (as euer we haue done in all other happiness which hath befallen us) ascribe the highest praise and thanks to his Divine Majesty, yet, forasmuch as we do account that they who are the servants of our State, in like actions are made participant (in a second degree) of his favour bestowed upon us, by their virtue and industry, we cannot but hold them worthy of thanks from us, as they have received honour from Him, among whom, you being there the chief, not only as chiefly put in trust by us, but as we plainly perceive in vigilancy, in labour, and in valour, in this late action, we could not forbear to let you see how sensible we are of this your merit. It is true, that, before this good success upon the Rebels, we were in daily attention to have heard of some quicker attempt upon the town, than any was made, both in respect that your own letters tended to such sense, and especially because protraction of time brought with it apparent dangers, as well of access of new supplies from our foreign enemies as of defection of a people so inconstant of disposition, and so rebellious to Government, as those of that Nation ever have been. But we that time having understood by those journals (which were committed to St. John and Davers) some reasons which have moved you to the course you have taken, rather than to have used speed in attempting, seeing all assaults are accompanied with loss, and every loss (in such a time) multiplied in rumour, and wholly converted by practice to the prejudice of the cause in question, which is maintained (now as things do stand) by the reputation of your Army, we do now conceive that all your works have had their foundation upon such reasons as you thought most advantageous for our service. It remaineth therefore now, and so we desire it may be made known to our Army that have served under you, in such manner as you may think best to express it, that as we do know they have endured many incommodities in this siege (which we would have been glad they could have avoided), having made so good proof of their valour and loyalty, as they have done at this time, so as we rather seek to preserve them as the best treasure of a Prince, than to suffer them to waste, if otherwise our Kingdom could have been kept from danger of foreign conquest and intestine Rebellion, so we expect it at the hands of the better sorts of our servitors there, that it shall well be infused into the minds of the rest, that whatsoever either our own directions or expending of treasure could do (for prevention of those difficulties which follow all Armies, and are inseparable where the war is made in a climate so ill tempered for a winter's siege) hath been royally and providently afforded them; a matter of more charge and uncertainty, because all our care and direction have attended the winds and weathers curtesy. To conclude with answer to your demands for further supplies of men, although we hope at the time is so near of the final conclusion of your happy success against the remnant of the strangers in that poor town, being pressed with so many wants, and with the despair which our late victory will add hereunto, as that hardly any supplies sent from us can come before it have taken effect; yet because you may perceive how much we attribute to your Judgment, in any thing which for our affairs is there desired, we have (as by our Council hath been signified unto you) given order for 4000 men to be sent thither out of hand, with the full proportion of munition which you desire; in which kind of provisions we find so great consumptions as we must require you to take some better order with them that have the distribution thereof; for if it be observed what quantities have been daily sent over, and yet what daily wants are pretended, the expence will be found insuppportable; and so much the rather, because all men know that whatsoever the Irish companies receive (except now in this action) is continually converted for money to the use of the rebels.

> Given under our Signet at our Palace at Whitehall the 44th year of our Reign, the 12th January 1601-2."

In the beginning of this Letter, above the Queen's hand signed, these following words were over-written by the Queen's own hand, viz. "Tho' for fear of worse end you did desire (as we confess we once thought to direct) to end this work before either enemy or rebel could increase the peril of our honor, yet we hope that no such adventure shall be more made, but that their confusion be ere now lighted on their own heads: And let Clanrickard and Thomund know that we do most thankfully accept their endeavours; for yourself, we can but acknowledge your diligence and dangerous adventure, and cherish and judge of you as your careful Sovereign [1]."

April 26, 1602, Mr. Chamberlain says, "Your French Galants were gone before I came to town. They have somewhat mended the matter, and redeemed the rascal report, that Biron and his train left behind them. For I hear their carriage well commended, especially the Duke of Nevers, saving that the Queen's musicians and other inferior officers complain, that he was very dry-handed. The Queen graced him very much, and did him the favour to dance with him. We hear he is gone into Holland, and so to the Duke of Cleve his kinsman."

By the Accompts of the Churchwardens of Lambeth it appears that the ringers were paid 2s. 6d. on the 29th of April 1602, when the Queen passed through that town on a Visit to the Lord Chamberlain [2].

May 8. Mr. Chamberlain says, "On *May-day* the Queen went *a-maying* [3], to Sir Richard Buckley's [4] at Lewisham, some three or four miles off Greenwich. And this week she went to St. James's Park, where she was feasted by Mr. Comptroller [5]."

---

[1] Moryson's History of Ireland, vol. II. p. 98.

[2] Henry Carey, the second Lord Hunsdon. On the 8th of July he was at Bath, when the Queen had an intention of visiting him; see p. 578. He died Sept. 9, 1603.

[3] This appears to have been the Queen's occasional amusement on *May-day*.

[4] This was Sir Richard *Bulkeley*, of Beaumaris, ancestor of the present Lord Bulkeley.—Sir Richard was knighted in 1576; and represented the County of Anglesea in several Parliaments in the Reigns of Queen Mary and Queen Elizabeth; to the latter of whom he proved an excellent soldier, and faithful servant on many occasions; and was also Chamberlain of North Wales.

[5] Sir William Knollys. See p. 564.

Mr. Chamberlain again proceeds: "June 27. The Council have lately spied a great inconvenience, of the increase of housing within and without London, by building over stables, in gardens, and other odd corners: whereupon they have taken order to have them pulled down; and this week they have begun almost in every parish to light on the unluckiest, here and there one, which, God knows, is far from removing the mischief.

"Young Copinger[1], that was coming into France, turned his course, and went to sea with Sir Richard Levison; and being at the taking of the Carrick, was sent with the first news, and hath waited hard at Court since, in hope to be knighted; but he speeds no better than his fellows, of whom fourteen have attended all this term with great devotion to make their wives Ladies; but hitherto they have lost *oleum et operam;* and some of them, for expedition, having paid their money before-hand, are in great danger to lose their earnest.

"July 8. We speak of a Progress, to begin toward the end of this month; first, to Sir John Fortescue's[2], in Buckinghamshire; then to the Earl of Hertford's[3], and the Chief Justice [Popham]; where there were jewels and presents provided the last year[4], that would not be lost; and so to Bath and Bristol, to visit the Lord Chamberlain, that lives there for help.

In a subsequent Letter, October 2, Mr. Chamberlain says, "The Queen's Progress went not far—first, to Chiswick[5] to Sir William Russell's[6], then to Ambrose Copinger's[7], who, because he had been a Master of Arts, entertained her himself

---

[1] This "young Copinger" was probably one of the nephews (for he had many) of the "Master of Arts" who entertained the Queen at Harlington. See below.

[2] Sir John Fortescue, Chancellor of the Exchequer, was honoured by a Visit from King James I. soon after his accession to the Throne. He died in 1607, and was buried in Mursley Church.

[3] At Elvetham, where she had been splendidly entertained in 1591; see before, p. 101.

[4] See before, p. 565.   [5] See before, p. 577.

[5] This Visit is briefly noticed by Mr. Lysons, Environs of London, vol. II. p. 96; where is also the following quotations from the Sidney Papers. "I send you (says William Browne, writing to Sir Robert Sidney) all the Queen's Entertainment at Chiswick, and at my Lord Keeper's."

[6] Fourth and youngest son of Francis second Earl of Bedford, and a distinguished military character. He was knighted for his valour in Ireland; and by King James I. in 1603, created Baron of Thornhaugh. Stow, speaking of his heroic achievements at the battle of Zutphen, says, "he charged so terribly, that, after he had broke his lance, he with his cutleaux so plaid his part, that the enemy reported him to be a devil and not a man; for where he saw six or seven of the enemies together, thither would he, and so behaved himself with his cutleaux, that he would separate their friendship."

[7] Ambrose Copinger, M. A. third son of Henry Copinger, of Allhallows, Kent, and elder brother of Henry Copinger, who, in 1577, had been patronized by the Queen (see vol. II. p. 53), was presented by his

with a Latin Oration; then to Harvil [Harefield] to the Lord Keeper's, and to Sir William Clarke's by Burnham."

By a minute of the Churchwardens' Accompts at Wandsworth, it appears that the bridge over the Wandle was built, at the expence of Queen Elizabeth, between the 18th and 25th of July 1602; and on the 28th the bells at Fulham were rung, " at the remove of the Queen from Greenwich to Chiswick."

In July, Lord Mountjoy received the following Letter from the Queen:

" ELIZABETH R.—Right trusty and well-beloved, we greet you well. Although we have heard nothing from you directly since our last dispatch, yet we impute it to no neglect of yours, having so great cause to judge the best of your actions, when every dispatch from other parts of our kingdom reports of great honour in the success of our army under you, a matter specially appearing by those letters which we have seen directed to our Treasurer at War in Ireland, containing the discourse of your marches and abiding in the heart of Tyrone, and the recovery of that island, and that ours which had been fouly lost before; in which respect we value the same so much the more acceptably. We have also thought good at this time to add this further, that we are glad to find that you are joined with Dockwra and Chichester, because that is the thing which hath been long wished, often attempted, but never before effected (being indeed the true consequence of our Plantation, with great expence both at Loughfoyle and in other parts of Ulster), so as when we perceive that now the time is come, when you may make an universal prosecution, and when we find that your own words give such hope, that this ungrateful traitor shall never be able to hold up his head again if the Spaniards do not arrive, we thought it fit to touch these two things following: first, to assure you that we have sent a fleet to the coast of Spain, notwithstanding our former fleet returned with the Carrick, there to attend his coast and all such fleets as shall be prepared to annoy us. Next we do require you, even whilst the iron is hot, so to strike, as this may not only prove a good summer's journey, but may deserve the title of that action which is the war's conclusion: for furtherance whereof we have spared no charge, even now again to

Father to the Rectory of Buxhall, Suffolk, in 1569; which he resigned in 1570-1; was susequently lord of the manors of Dawley and Harlington in Middlesex; occurs as Patron of Harlington in October 1599, and August 1602; and was knighted by King James, July 23, 1603, previous to the Coronation. He married Letitia, daughter of David Earl of Kildare; but died s. p. March 17, 1603-4.—His widow was re-married to Sir John Poynter; and his estates in Harlington descended to Francis Copinger, his nephew and heir, then aged 24, who sold them in 1607, his grandmother being then living, the wife of Sir John Maurice.

send a magazine of victual and other necessaries, to those places by which you may best maintain those garrisons with which you resolve to bridle those rebels. We have heard likewise from Carew, our President of Munster, that he hath taken the Castle which was held by the rebels at Bur-haven, and defended with the Spanish ordnance. In that province we find that there is constant expectation of Spanish success, for which reason, and considering what promises the King of Spain doth make them, and with what importunity they beg it at his hands, besides one other craft they use to hide from him all fear which might divert him from that enterprise, agreeing amongst themselves, how great soever their miseries be, to conceal the same from him and his Ministers, as appeareth well by letter of O'Donnil's own hand, intercepted of late, by which he writes to a rebel called O'Connor Kelly, desiring him to advertise him of the state of Ireland, but in no sort to deliver any bad report of their losses, because he would be loth that the Spaniards should know it.

" We do require you very earnestly to be very wary in taking submissions of those rebels who ever make profit of their coming in, some let slip of purpose by the arch traitor; others, when they have compounded for their own purpose, are notoriously known to fill their countries with more cattle than ever they had in seven years before, which is a matter that most notoriously discovereth, that the great bordering traitors (whose countries are sought to be layd waste) do find a safe protection for their goods under them: a matter whereof we speake in no other sort than by way of caution, knowing that no rule is so general, either to leave or take, which may not change in respect of circumstances.

" Given under our Signet at our Manor of Greenwich, the 15th of July, in the 44th year our Reign."

To this letter, in the margin, was added these words in her Majesty's own hand: " We owe you many lauds for having so nearly approached the villainous rebel, and see no reason why so great forces should not end his days where wickedness has cut off so many, and should judge myself mad if we should not charge your authority for his life, and so we do by this, since neither Spaniard nor other accident is like to alter this mind, as she that should blush to receive such indignity after so Royal a prosecution. We have forgotten to praise your humility, that after having been a Queen's Kitchen-maid, you have not disdained to be a Traitor's Skullion. God bless you with perseverance.

Your Sovereign, E. R."[1]

[1] Moryson's History of Ireland, vol. II. p. 175.

Harefield Place, Middlesex.

Published by Nichols & Son.

Visit of the Queen to the Lord Keeper EGERTON, and his Lady the Dowager Countess of DERBY, at Harefield Place.

⁎ Harefield Place is situated in the North-western angle of the county of Middlesex, three miles from Uxbridge, and eighteen from London. It is remarkable, as Mr. Lysons observes, that the manor of Harefield (with the exception of a temporary alienation) has descended by intermarriages and a regular succession, in the families of Bacheworth, Swanland, and Newdigate, from the year 1284, when, by verdict of a jury, it appeared that Roger de Bacheworth and his ancestors had then held it from time immemorial. Mr. Lysons adds, that it is the only instance in which he had traced such remote possession in the county of Middlesex. The alienation was in 1585, when John Newdigate, Esquire, exchanged the manor of Harefield with Sir Edmund Anderson, Lord Chief Justice of the Common Pleas, for the manor of Arbury in Warwickshire. In 1601 Sir Edmund Anderson conveyed this estate to Sir Thomas Egerton, Lord Keeper; to his wife Alice Countess Dowager of Derby; and to Lady Anne, Lady Frances, and Lady Elizabeth Stanley, her daughters. Norden informs us, that "Harefield Place was a fair house, standing on the edge of the hill; the river Colne passing near the same, through the pleasant meadows and sweet pastures, yielding both delight and profit. The mansion-house[1], which is situated near the church, was the ancient residence of the Lords of the Manor. And here it was that the Lord Keeper Egerton and the Countess Dowager of Derby were honoured by a Visit from Queen Elizabeth[2]; and here, in or about the year 1635, Milton's Arcades was presented to the same Countess Dowager in her second widowhood, by some noble persons of her family[3].

Sir Thomas Egerton had been appointed Solicitor General to the Queen in 1581. He was knighted, and became Attorney General, in 1592; Master of the Rolls in 1594; and Lord Keeper in 1596.

Sir Thomas Egerton was thrice married. The first wife was Elizabeth, daughter of Thomas Ravenscroft, Esq. and mother of John first Earl of Bridgewater.

[1] Mr. Lysons says, Harefield Place was burnt down about 1660. The View which he gives (Environs, vol. V. p. 106) is of the house by which it was replaced. A more recent Picturesque View of Harefield Place accompanies the present publication.

[2] The first printed notice of this Royal Visit was in the former Edition of the Elizabethan Progresses, from a MS Letter of Mr. Chamberlain; and from the mention, in an earlier Letter, of an *intended Visit* to "the Lord Chief Justice," it was supposed (but erroneously) that the Queen had twice honoured Harefield by her presence; but the Chief Justice there meant was not *Sir Edmund Anderson* (who possessed Harefield in 1601), but Sir *John Popham*, Chief Justice of the King's Bench, who then resided at Littlecot in Wiltshire. See p. 565.

[3] "I viewed this house," says Mr. Warton, "a few years ago, when it was for the most part remaining in its original state. It has since been pulled down; the porter's lodges on each side the gateway are converted into a husbandman's dwelling-house." It is near Uxbridge; and Milton, when he wrote "Arcades," which was first performed at Harefield by the Countess of Derby's grandchildren, was still living with his father at Horton in the same neighbourhood.

His second Lady was Elizabeth, daughter of Sir William More[1], of Loseley Park, whom he married in or about 1577, she died in January 1599-1600.

In the October following the Lord Keeper married Alice[2], relict of Ferdinando fifth Earl of Derby[3]; and in the Summer of 1601 he entertained the Queen with a "Lottery."

Harefield Place was purchased by him in 1601; and the Royal Visit to that mansion was on or about the last day of July[4] 1602.

Sir Thomas Egerton, who continued in favour with King James, was appointed July 21, 1603, Lord Chancellor, and created Baron Ellesmere; and Viscount Brackley, Nov. 7, 1616. He died, at York-House in the Strand, March 15, 1616-17, in his 77th year; and was buried at Doddleston in Cheshire.

The Countess died Jan. 16, 1636-7, and was buried at Harefield[5].

[1] Of this family, and the Queen's Visit at Loseley, see before, p. 81.

[2] Sixth daughter of Sir John Spencer, of Althorpe; and married, first, to Ferdinando Lord Strange, who, on the death of his father Henry, in 1594, became Earl of Derby, but died in the next year. It has been observed by Mr. Warton, in his notes on Milton's "Arcades," that "the Peerage-book of this most respectable Countess is the poetry of her times."

Sir John Harrington, in his Third Book of Epigrams, has that which here follows:

"In praise of the COUNTESSE of DERBY, married to the LORD CHANCELLOR.

"This noble Countesse lived many yeeres
With Derby, one of England's greatest Peeres,
Fruitful and faire, and of so cleare a name,
That all this region marvel'd at her fame:
But this brave Peere extinct, by hastened Fate,
She staid (ah, too, too long) in widdowes state;
And in that state took so sweet state upon her,
All cares, eyes, tongues, heard, saw, and told her honour;
Yet finding this a saying full of verity,
'Tis hard to have a patent for prosperity,
She found her wisest way and safe to deal,
Was to consort with him that kept the Seal."

She appears to have been celebrated by nearly all the eminent poets from Spenser to Milton. "The Death of Delia, with the Teares of her Funeral, a Poetical Excursive Discourse of our late *Eliza*, 1603," which will be given hereafter, is inscribed to this noble Countess.

Mr. Todd's admirable edition of Milton's Poetical Works, a Masque by Marston is preserved, from the very curious collection of the late Duke of Bridgewater, under the title of "The Lorde and Lady of Huntingdon's Entertainment of theire right Noble Mother *Alice Countesse Dowager of Derby*, the firste nighte of her Honor's Arrivall att the House of Ashby." On this head see the History of Leicestershire, vol. III. p. 637; where the date of Marston's Masque is ascertained to have been in August 1606.—This will be more particularly noticed in the "Progresses of King James."

[3] See before, p. 570.   [4] The Queen was at Chiswick on the 28th of July; see p. 579.

[5] In Harefield Church is a handsome monument, with an elegant figure of the Countess and her three daughters. This monument is engraved in a style worthy of it, by W. P. Sherlock, for Mr. Lysons's account of Harefield.

Lady Jane Stanley, her eldest daughter, was married, first, to Grey Lord Chandos; and, secondly, in 1624, to Mervyn Lord Castlehaven. She survived her mother only ten years; and on her death, George Lord Chandos (her eldest son by her first husband) inherited the manor of Harefield under the deed of 1601. He died in February 1665, having bequeathed it to his wife Jane. This Lady was soon after re-married to Sir William Sedley, who died in 1656; and in 1657 she took a third husband, George Pitt, Esq. of Stratfield Say in Hampshire. Having vested all her estates, by a deed bearing date 1673, in Mr. Pitt and his heirs, he, in conjunction with his trustees, in the month of February 1675 (his Lady being still living), conveyed by bargain and sale the manors of Harefield and Morehall to Sir Richard Newdigate, Bart. Serjeant at Law; in whose descendants the estate remained vested till 1760, when the late Sir Roger Newdigate, Baronet, having fixed his residence in Warwickshire, sold *Harefield Place*[1] (retaining the manor and his other estates in the parish) to John Truesdale, Esquire, whose Executors in 1780 sold it to William Baynes, Esquire; from whom, or his Representatives, it passed by purchase to the Widow of the late Charles Parker, Esquire, and is now the property of her son, Charles Newdigate Newdigate, Esq. to whom the late Sir Roger Newdigate bequeathed his Middlesex estates, and also the reversion of his Warwickshire estate.

Lady Frances Stanley, the Countess's second daughter, was married to John Earl of Bridgewater; Lady Elizabeth Stanley, the third daughter, was married, in 1603, to Henry fifth Earl of Huntingdon. She died in 1632.

But we must return to the days of Masques and Chivalry. It was in July 1602, at the Visit of Queen Elizabeth to Harefield, that the Speeches, which, after the lapse of two centuries, were lately for the first time produced, were addressed to her Highness. Of this Entertainment the Publick have been informed that the late Sir Roger Newdigate once possessed an account in manuscript, but that the MS. was unfortunately lost[2].

---

[1] *Harefield Lodge*, about a mile from Uxbridge, was built by Sir Roger Newdigate in 1786. It commands a beautiful prospect, and is now the property of the above-mentioned Charles Newdigate Newdigate, Esq.—On the site of a neighbouring farm, stands *Bellamonds*, a house which was either built or much enlarged by Sir George Cooke, Prothonotary of the Common Pleas, and now the property of Colonel George Cooke.

[2] Nearly 20 years after the first notice, in Vol. II. of the first edition of these "Progresses," of the Visit to Harefield, the Editor had the satisfaction of remarking, in the Preface to the Third Volume, "that his enquiries had not been entirely unsuccessful, as the MS description of that Entertainment (though then mislaid) was possessed by Sir Roger Newdigate, who recollected that the Queen was first welcomed at a farm-house, now called *Dew's farm*, by several allegorical persons, who attended her to a long avenue of elms leading to the house, which obtained from this circumstance the name of ' The

It has also been mentioned, that the papers, which had for a time been missing, were afterwards found¹. But the history of the MS. though a matter in itself of no great moment, involves some circumstances which may serve to render it not unworthy of distinct recital.

As there happened to be in the Library at Arbury two copies of Strype's "Annals of the Reformation," the late excellent Proprietor, ever to be remembered with affectionate esteem by those who knew him, made a present of the duplicate to his Friend the Rev. Ralph Churton², who having seen in Mr. Lysons, as now quoted, an account of this lost MS., had the good fortune, in turning over Strype's second volume, to find what he supposed to be the identical papers so long missing; of which he lost no time to inform the Donor of the book, whose joy and surprize on the occasion were thus expressed: "You never were a more agreeable Correspondent than in your letter before me. I read it over and over with new amazement; and all your good faith I find necessary to confirm the good news it contains. How can it be, that papers, which for many years I have hunted, and accused all my Antiquarian Friends of purloining, and made them and their Executors search their cabinets in vain!—how can it be, that they could have crept into an old book on my shelves, which, though perhaps I have sometimes referred to, I am sure I never read? It must have been, that some of my Friends, to whom I have given them to peruse, have accidentally made use of them to keep a place, where they were reading, and on some sudden call left it, and thought no more of it³. But happy am I that it has fallen into the hands of an Antiquary, who, by a kind of habitual instinct, concludes he shall find a jewel in every torn ragged scrap of paper. I long much to see it," &c. (Arbury, 26 Nov. 1803.)

Queen's Walk.' Four trees of this avenue are distinctly represented in Mr. Lysons's View; and the greater part were standing not many years ago." But I am sorry to add that the venerable old mansion has been entirely demolished, all the trees cut down, and not a vestige of the Queen's Walk, or any part of its former magnificence remains.

¹ See the Gentleman's Magazine for 1807, vol. LXXVII. p. 633.

² Rector of Middleton Cheney, and Archdeacon of St. David's. To this learned and exemplary Divine the present Editor is indebted for the communication of this curious Royal Visit.—He would add much more on the head of obligation, for an uninterrupted and friendly intercourse of many years, if he were not confident that by so doing he should wound the feelings of unaffected modesty.

³ This conjecture is probably right. In a subsequent Letter the worthy Baronet remarked, "Your reference to Strype fairly accounts for the original concealment of the papers, whether purposely or by neglect." They were found in Strype's second volume, where (pp. 391—394) he gives an account of the sumptuous reception of Queen Elizabeth by the Earl of Leicester at Kenilworth Castle, in July 1575, from a contemporary and circumstantial detail of the whole by Master Robert Laneham, Gent. R. C.

Being thus assured that the treasure which he had discovered was the real MS. which had been so long missing, Mr. Churton returned it to its proper owner, having first, for the greater security, taken a correct copy of it.

When the packet reached its destination, the park at Arbury was occupied with Volunteers and Inspecting Colonels, and the hospitable mansion filled with guests: No room left for a single Muse! Not even for such as our great Queen could patiently sit under a tree in a shower to hear! Flattery can do much; but I will not persuade myself she had not a better motive, sensible and learned as she was, to induce her to listen to so much nonsense, that more amiable one, which Shakspeare put into the mouth of Theseus:

> For never any thing was done amiss,
> When simpleness and duty tender it." [1]

The transcript, as was desired and intended, being more legible than the original MS. was shortly afterwards dispatched to Arbury; and it was naturally concluded, that what had once so narrowly escaped, and was so much valued, would be reposited in some place, which was at once secure and obvious. But danger equally unforeseen and formidable still impended. When the incomparable Baronet, full of hope in his blessed Redeemer, had calmly breathed his last, in the 87th year of his age, Nov. 26, 1806, in due time, among other important cares and duties, which, on such sad occasions, providentially occupy the surviving Relatives of departed worth, frequent and minute search was made by Francis Newdigate, Esq. the present very worthy proprietor of Arbury, and others of the family, for the Elizabethan MSS. which could no where be found, till the Autumn of 1820, when Mr. Newdigate, by great good luck, discovered, among papers of a totally different description, Mr. Churton's copy of the Harefield Entertainment—but, alas! the original MS. is still concealed in its second hiding-place, till some successful search or fortunate chance shall bring it again to light, perhaps after many a day, or after many long years.

In the mean time the Editor of the Elizabethan Progresses is happy in being able to lay the account of this celebrated Visit before the Publick, by the kind permission of Mr. Newdigate; who, with true liberality of sentiment, judges it to be expedient that this curious relique, which has so long been a *desideratum* among Antiquaries, should be offered to their perusal, and by means of the press preserved from future risk and contingencies.   J. N.   *Feb.* 14, 1821.

[1] The Letter here quoted, which was closely written, and of considerable length, was dated, "Arbury, 28th Jan. 1804;" and ended thus: "It is near midnight. Adieu."

Copy of some Papers belonging to the late Sir ROGER NEWDIGATE, *Baronet* (7 *pages folio), lettered on the back, by a later hand*[1], " *Entertainment of* Q. ELIZ. *at Harefield, by the Countesse of* DERBY [2].

After the Queene entered (out of the high way) into the Deamesne grounde of Harefielde, near the Dayrie [3] howse, she was mett with 2 persons, the one representing a BAYLIFE, the other a DAYRIE-MAIDE, with the Speech. Her Majesty, being on horsebacke, stayed under a tree (because it rayned) to heare it.

B. Why, how now, Joane! are you heere? Gods my life, what make you heere, gaddinge and gazinge after this manner? You come to buy gape-seede, doe you? Wherefore come you abroade now I faith [4] can you tell?

Joa. I come abroade to welcome these Strangers.

B. Strangers? how knew you there would come Strangers?

Jo. All this night I could not sleepe, dreaming of greene rushes; and yesternight the chatting of the pyes, and the chirkinge of the frisketts [5], did foretell as much; and, besides that, all this day my lefte eare glowed, and that is to me (let them say what they wil) allwaies a signe of Strangers, if it be in Summer; marye, if it be in the Winter, 'tis a signe of anger. But what makes you in this company, I pray you?

B. I make the way for these Strangers, which the Way-maker himself could not doe; for it is a way was never passed before. Besides, the Mrs. of this faire

---

[1] The Speeches, &c. are in a hand a little later than the time of Queen Elizabeth. R. C.

[2] Several passages in the Speeches indicate a *Master* as well as Mistress. See p. 587, " I doubt my *Mr.* and *Mrs.* are not at home;" " my *Mr.* house," p. 588;" " mine Owners," p. 590; " my Owners," p. 593.—No doubt, the Lord Keeper, as well as the Countess of Derby his wife, was present to receive the Royal Visitor. R. C.

The Queen had honoured Sir Thomas Egerton with a Visit at his London residence (see p. 570) in the Summer of 1601. But it is remarkable that no notice is taken of either of the Queen's Entertainments in the Life of Lord Chancellor Egerton, by his learned descendant the Hon. and Rev. Francis Egerton, Prebendary of Durham. J. N.

[3] See before, p. 583.

[4] " I faith," i. e. as we now write, " i' faith," contracted for, " in faith," p. 588. R. C.

[5] Probably crickets. R. C.

company, though she know the way to all men's harts, yet she knowes the way but to few men's howses, except she love them very well, I can tell you; and therefore I myselfe, without any comission, have taken upon me to conduct them to the house.

Jo. The house? which house? do you remember yourselfe? which way goe you?

B. I goe this way, on the right hand [1]. Which way should I goe?

Jo. You say true, and you're a trim man; but I faith I'll talke noe more to you, except you ware wyser. I pray you hartely, 'forsooth, come neare the house, and take a simple lodginge with vs to-night; for I can assuere you that yonder house that he talks of is but a Pigeon-house, which is very little if it were finisht, and yet very little of it is finisht. And[2] you will believe me, vpon my life, Lady, I saw Carpenters and Bricklayers and other Workmen about it within less then these two howers. Besides, I doubt my Mr. and Mrs. are not at home; or, if they be, you must make your owne provision, for they have noe provision for such Strangers. You should seeme to be Ladies; and we in the country have an old saying, that "halfe a pease a day will serve a Lady." I know not what you are, neither am I acquainted with your dyet; but, if you will goe with me, you shall haue cheare for a Lady: for first you shall haue a dayntie sillibub; next a messe of clowted creame; stroakings, in good faith, redd cowes milk, and they say in London that's restorative: you shall have greene cheeses and creame. (I'll speake a bould word) if the Queene herself (God save her Grace) [were here[3]], she might be seen to eat of it. Wee will not greatly bragge of our possets, but we would be loath to learne to praise: and if you loue frute, forsooth, wee haue jenitings, paremayns, russet coates, pippines, able-johns[4], and perhaps a pareplum, a damsone, I[5] or an apricocke too, but that they are noe dainties this yeare; and therefore, I pray, come neare the house, and wellcome heartily doe soe.

B. Goe to, gossip; your tongue must be running. If my Mrs. should heare

---

[1] It might yet perhaps be seen on the spot (if Dew's house, *i. e.* the Dayrie house, remains) whether going to the *right* would lead to the avenue. But perhaps there is an equivoque, " I go the *right way*, which way (but the right) should I go?" R. C.

[2] " *If* you will believe me," as common formerly. So in the Verses, p. 592, " *and* she cometh," I suppose is, " *if* she cometh." R. C.

[3] The words in brackets are wanting in the MS. R. C.

[4] Q. " *Apple* Johns," that being the name of an apple? R. C.

[5] " *I* or an apricocke," *i. e.* " *aye*, or," &c. R. C.

of this, I faith shee would giue you little thankes I can tell you, for offeringe to draw so faire a flight from her Pigeon-house (as you call it) to your Dayrie-house.

Jo. Wisely, wisely, brother Richard; I faith as I would vse the matter, I dare say shee would giue me great thankes: for you know my Mrs. charged me earnestly to retaine all idele hearvest-folkes that past this way; and my meaning was, that, if I could hold them all this night and to-morrow, on Monday morning to carry them into the fields; and to make them earne their entertaynment well and thriftily; and to that end I have heere a *Rake*[1] and *Forke*[1], to deliver to the best Huswife in all this company.

B. Doe soe then: deliver them to the best Huswife in all this company; for wee shall haue as much vse of her paines and patience there as here. As for the dainties that you talke of, if you have any such, you shall do well to send them; and as for these Strangers, sett thy hart at rest, Joane; they will not rest with [thee²] this night, but will passe on to my Mr. house.

Joa. Then, I pray take this *Rake* and *Forke* with you; but I am ashamed, and woe at my hart, you should goe away so late. And I pray God you repent you not, and wish yourselves here againe, when you finde you haue gone further and fared worsse.

When her Maiestie was alighted from her horse, and ascended 3 steps neare to the entering into the house, a carpet and chaire there sett for her; PLACE and TIME present themselves, and vsed this Dialogue.

PLACE *in a partie-colored roobe, like the brick house.*

TIME *with yeollow haire, and in a green roabe, with a hower glasse, stopped, not runninge.*

P. Wellcome, good *Time.*

T. Godden[3], my little pretie priuat *Place.*

P. Farewell, godbwy[4] *Time;* are you not gone? doe you stay heere? I wonder that *Time* should stay any where; what's the cause?

---

[1] A note in the original MS. calls these " 2 Juells;" probably in the *form*, one of a Rake, and the other of a Fork; but how *elegant* such a form or shape of a jewel might be, I cannot say. R. C.

[2] The word in brackets, as before, is wanting in the MS. R. C.

[3] Meant, I suppose, for *Good e'en,* that is, *good evening,* to you. R. C.

[4] Is this meant for *Good bye,* or for *God be with you,* of which, or of *Good be with you,* Good bye is a contraction. R. C.

T. If thou knewest the cause, thou wouldst not wonder; for I stay to entertaine the Wonder of this time; wherein I would pray thee to ioyne mee, if thou wert not too little for her greatnes; for it weare as great a miracle for thee to receive her, as to see the Ocean shut up in a little creeke, or the circumference shrinke vnto the pointe of the center.

P. Too little! by that reason she should rest in noe *place*, for noe *place* is great ynough to receive her. Too little! I haue all this day entertayned the Sunn, which, you knowe, is a great and glorious Guest; hee's but euen now gone downe yonder hill; and now he is gone, methinks, if Cinthia her selfe would come in his place, the place that contaynde him should not be too little to receave her.

T. You say true, and I like your comparison; for the Guest that wee are to entertaine doth fill all places with her divine vertues, as the Sunn fills the World with the light of his beames. But say, poore *Place*, in what manner didst thou entertaine the Sunn?

P. I received his glory, and was filled with it: but, I must confesse, not according to the proportion of his greatnes, but according to the measure of my capacitie; his bright face (methought) was all day turnd vpon mee; neverthelesse his beames in infinite abundance weere disperst and spread vpon other places.

T. Well, well; this is noe time for vs to entertaine one another, when wee should ioine to entertaine her. Our entertaynment of this Goddesse will be much alike; for though her selfe shall eclipse her soe much, as to suffer her brightnes to bee shadowed in this obscuere and narrow *Place*, yet the sunne beames that follow her, the traine I meane that attends vpon her, must, by the necessitie of this *Place*, be deuided from her. Are you ready, *Place*? *Time* is ready.

P. Soe it should seeme indeed, you are so gaye, fresh, and cheerfull. You are the present *Time*, are you not? then what neede you make such haste? Let me see, your wings are clipt, and, for ought I see, your hower-glasse runnes not.

T. My wings are clipt indeed, and it is her hands hath clipt them: and, tis true, my glasse runnes not: indeed it hath bine stopt a longe time, it can never rune as long as I waite upon this M^ris. I [am [1]] her *Time;* and *Time* weare very vngratefull, if it should not euer stand still, to serue and preserue, cherish and

---

[1] The word in brackets is wanting, as before. R. C.

delight her, that is the glory of her time, and makes the *Time* happy wherein she liueth.

P. And doth not she make *Place* happy as well as *Time?* What if it she make thee a contynewall holy-day, she makes me a perpetuall sanctuary. Doth not the presence of a Prince make a Cottage a Court, and the presence of the Gods make euery place Heauen? But, alas, my littlenes is not capable of that happines that her great grace would impart vnto me: but, weare I as large as there harts that are mine Owners, I should be the fairest *Pallace* in the world; and weere I agreeable to the wishes of there hartes, I should in some measure resemble her sacred selfe, and be in the outward frount exceeding faire, and in the inward furniture exceeding rich.

T. In good time do you remember the hearts of your Owners; for, as I was passing to this place, I found this *Hart*[1], which, as my daughter *Truth* tould mee, was stolne by owne of the Nymphes from one of the seruants of this Goddesse; but her guiltie conscience enforming her that it did belong only of right vnto her that is Mrs. of all harts in the world, she cast [it[2]] from her for this time: and *Oportunity*, finding it, deliuered it vnto me. Heere, *Place*, take it thou, and present it vnto her as a pledge and mirror of their harts that owe thee.

P. It is a mirror indeed, for so it is transparent. It is a cleare hart, you may see through it. It hath noe close corners, noe darkenes, noe unbutifull spott in it. I will therefore presume the more boldly to deliver it; with this assurance, that *Time, Place, Persons,* and all other circumstances, doe concurre alltogether in biddinge her wellcome.

[1] " A Diamond." *Original MS.*
[2] This word is wanting in the MS. R. C.

The humble Petition of a guiltlesse Lady, delivered in writing vpon Munday Morninge, when the [1] *of rainbowes was presented to the Q. by the La.* WALSINGHAM [2].

Beauties rose [3], and Vertues booke,
Angells minde, and Angells looke,

---

[1] Some word wanting, probably "robe." See the two last lines of the 5th stanza. R. C.

[2] This was Elizabeth, wife of Sir Thomas Walsingham, Knight, of Scadbury, in Chiselhurst, Kent, and daughter of Sir Thomas Manhood, K. B.—On New-year's Day, 1599-1600, the Lady Walsingham *Junior*, gave the Queen part of a petticoat of clay-coloured sattin, embroidered over with branches of silver;" and "Sir Thomas Walsingham," gave also "part of a petticoat," exactly similar. The Lady had in return $27\frac{1}{4}$ ounces of gilt plate. She is called *Junior*, as in the same Roll occurs the name of "the Lady Walsingham *Widow*," who was Ursula, daughter of Henry St. Barb, of Somersetshire, and widow of Sir Richard Worsley; by whom she had two sons, John and George, who were both unfortunately blown up by gunpowder, at Apuldercombe, in the porter's lodge, their mother being then newly re-married to the famous Sir Francis Walsingham. Mr. Lysons informs us, from Stow's Annals, that this Lady died at Barn-elms, June 19, 1602; and was buried the next day privately, near her husband, in St. Paul's Cathedral.—Her death is not noticed in the Parish Register of Barnes; though it there appears that Robert Beale, who had married the sister of Sir Francis Walsingham's Lady, died at Barn-elms, 25 May 1601, and was buried in London.—This Mr. Beale was often employed by Queen Elizabeth in her negotiations with Mary Queen of Scots, and was sent with Lord Buckhurst to her to announce the sentence of her death. He was afterwards sent to Fotheringay with the warrant for beheading her, which he read on the scaffold, and witnessed the execution. He was employed on an embassy to Zealand with Sir William Winter, in 1576, and a year before his death was one of the Commissioners at the treaty of Boulogne. Several of his letters on the business of the Queen of Scots are among the Talbot Papers. Mr. Lodge, not aware that Beale died two years before the Queen, supposes he was discharged by her Successor. Camden calls him "a man of an impetuous and morose disposition." His daughter married Sir Henry Yelverton, one of the Judges in the Common Pleas. Manning and Bray's Surrey, vol. III. p. 316.—Their only surviving daughter had the singular good fortune of being wife to three of the most accomplished men of the age, Sir Philip Sydney, the Earl of Essex, and the Earl of Clanrickard. Her second husband, so well known, and so much pitied for his misfortunes, resided frequently at Barn-elms, which, after the death of Sir Francis Walsingham, was called one of his houses. "Some think," says Rowland Whyte, writing to Sir Robert Sidney, June 11, 1600, "that the Earl of Essex shall have the liberty of his houses at London (see p. 489) and Barn-elmes, and that he shall have his friends come to him."—We shall meet with this Lady again, under the year 1603, in the "Progresses of King James."

[3] Queen Elizabeth, "Beauty's Rose," &c. had now attained the blooming age of sixty-nine! She danced, however, in April 1602. See pp. 525, 577.

To all Saints and Angells deare,
Clearest Maiestie on earth,
Heauen did smile at your faire birth,
    And since your daies have been most cleare.

Only poore St. *Swythen*[1] now
Doth heare you blame his cloudy brow:
    But that poore St. deuoutly sweares,
It is but a tradition vaine
That his much weeping causeth raine
    For S^{ts} in heauen shedd no teares:

But this he saith, that to his feast
Cometh Iris, an unbidden guest,
    In her moist roabe of collers gay;
And she cometh, she ever staies,
For the space of fortie daies,
    And more or lesse raines euery day.

But the good S^t, when once he knew,
This raine was like to fall on you,
    If S^{ts} could weepe, he had wept as much
As when he did the Lady leade[2]
That did on burning iron tread,
    To Ladies his respect is such.

---

[1] Alluding to an antient prejudice, still entertained by the common people, that a rainy St. Swithin's day (the 15th of July) will be followed by forty days of the same weather. This is a confirmation, if any were wanting, of the date of the Visit. R. C.

[2] I am not clear about this Legend. Was it St. Swithin who, in 1041, led Queen Emma (wife of Ethelred the Saxon Monarch, afterwards of Canute, and mother of Edward the Confessor) over bars of burning iron? This could not literally be the case; for St. Swithin died in the middle of the ninth Century, and Emma in the middle of the eleventh: but, as she is said to have spent the night previous to the ordeal in prayers at the tomb of St. Swithin, what the Saint was, I suppose, believed to do by invisible agency, the Poet feigns him to have done personally, "leading the Lady, that did on burning iron tread."

>He gently first bids Iris goe
>Unto the Antipodes below,
>> But shee for that more sullen grew.
>When he saw that, with angry looke,
>From her her rayneie roabes he tooke,
>> Which heere he doth present to you.
>It is fitt it should with you remaine,
>For you know better how to raine.
>> Yet if it raine still as before,
>St Swythen praies that you would guesse,
>That Iris doth more roabes possesse,
>> And that you should blame him no more.

At her Maiesties departure from Harefield, PLACE, attyred in black mourninge aparell, used this farewell followinge [1]:

P. Sweet Maiestie, be pleased to looke vpon a poor Wydow, mourning before your Grace. I am this *Place*, which at your comming was full of ioy: but now at your departure am as full of sorrow. I was then, for my comfort, accompanied with the present cheerful *Time;* but now he is to depart with you; and, blessed as he is, must euer fly before you: But, alas! I haue noe wings, as *Time* hath. My heauines is such, that I must stand still, amazed to see so greate happines so sone bereft mee. Oh, that I could remoue with you, as other circumstances can! *Time* can goe with you, *Persons* can goe with you; they can moue like Heauen; but I, like dull Earth (as I am indeed), must stand vnmovable. I could wish myselfe like the inchaunted Castle of Loue [2], to hould you heere for euer, but that your vertues would dissolve all my inchauntment. Then what remedy?

---

[1] This single Speech was printed, in the Third Volume of the former Edition of the Elizabethan Progresses, from a copy preserved in the Talbot Papers, and published in Mr. Lodge's "Illustrations." It was copied from Birch's MSS. in the British Museum, N° 4173, under the title of "The Lord Keeper Egerton, visited at Harvile by Queen Elizabeth."

[2] I suppose there is here an allusion to some such "inchanted Castle" in some then popular work, as the Fairy Queen, Sir Philip Sidney's Arcadia, &c.; but I am not sufficiently learned in such lore to know where the "Castle" may be found. R. C.

As it is against the nature of an Angell to be circumscribed in *Place*, so it is against the nature of *Place* to haue the motion of an Angell. I must stay forsaken and desolate. You may goe with maiestie, joy, and glory. My only suyte, before you goe, is that you will pardon the close imprisonment which you have suffred euer since your comminge, imputinge it not to mee, but S*t* Swythen[1], who of late hath raysed soe many stormes, as I was faine prouide this *Anchor*[2], for you, when I did vnderstand you would put into this creeke. But now, since I perceaue this harbour is too little for you, and you will hoyste sayle and be gone, I beseech you take this Anchor with you. And I pray to Him that made both *Time* and *Place*, that, in all places where euer you shall arriue, you may anchor as safly, as you doe and euer shall doe in the harts of my Owners.

The Complaint of the V[3] Satyres against the Nymphes.

Tell me, O Nymphes, why do you
Shune vs that your loues pursue?
What doe the Satyres notes retaine
That should merite your disdaine?

On our browes if hornes doe growe,
Was not Bacchus armed soe?
Yet of him the Candean maid
Held no scorne, nor was affraid.

Say our colours tawny bee,
Phœbus was not faire to see;
Yet faire Clymen did not shunn
To bee Mother of his Sonne.

If our beards be rough and long,
Soe had Hercules the strong:
Yet Deianier, with many a kisse,
Joyn'd her tender lipps to his.

---

[1] See the Note in p. 592. R. C.
[2] "A Jewell." *Original MS.*
[3] This is a "*V*," and might *possibly* be meant for *Five;* but I suppose the stroke through it means to cross it out as a mistake. However, I thought it right to notice it. R. C.

If our bodies hayry bee,
Mars as rugged was as wee:
Yet did Ilia think her grac'd,
For to be by Mars imbrac'd.

Say our feet ill-fauored are,
Cripples leggs are worse by farre:
Yet faire Venus, during life,
Was the lymping Vulcan's wife.

Breefly, if by nature we
But imperfect creatures be;
Thinke not our defects so much,
Since Celestial Powers be such.

But you Nymphes, whose veniall [1] loue
Loue of gold alone doth moue,
Though you scorne vs, yet for gold
Your base loue is bought and sold.

FINIS [2].

Sir Thomas Edmonds, in a Letter to the Earl of Shrewsbury, August 23, says, "Her Majesty hath had compassion, notwithstanding her earnest affection to go her Progress, yet to forbear the same in favour to her people, in regard of the unseasonableness of the weather; and for that purpose doth appoint to return by the end of this week, and settle at Oatlands [3]. Her Highness hath been very honourably entertained at my Lord Keeper's house, and many times richly presented; yet all here are not confident that the same will procure an abolition

---

[1] This evidently should be "venal;" yet possibly it was written "venial." R. C.

[2] This "Complaint" is on a separate leaf, and seems to be in a different hand, though little, if at all, more recent than the other. It does not appear when or how the "Complaint" was introduced; and it may possibly be doubted whether it formed a part of the Entertainment, though it probably did. The title, "Entertainment of Q. Eliz.;" &c. is written on the back of this paper: but the title as already said, is in a later hand. R. C.

[3] By the Accompts of the Corporation of Kingston-upon-Thames in 1603, it appears, that another Visit from the Queen had been expected in the preceding year; as there is an entry of a payment of "5s. 3d. for a box for the late Queen Elizabeth, which was returned to the Seller."

of *former unkindness*¹."—Again, Sept. 1, " Since the writing of my other Letter, there hath been a great forwardness to have continued the Progress to my Lord of Hertford's house; but now at length it is utterly broken, in respect of the lateness of the season, and it is in deliberation to find out some place between Oatlands and Windsor, as Horsely, and Sunning Hill, and other like, where to entertain the Queen a fortnight, and afterwards to return to Nonsuch."

On the second day of September the Lord President Mountjoy received the following gracious letter from the Queen, written with her own hand:

"MY FAITHFUL GEORGE,

"How joy'd we are that so good event hath followed so troublesome endeavours, labrious cares, and heedfull travels, you may guess, but we best can witness, and do protest that your safety hath equalled the most thereof. And so God even bless you in all your actions. Your Sovereign,   E. R."²

On the 18th, William Browne thus writes to the Earl of Shrewsbury. "I send your Lordship here inclosed some verses compounded by Mr. Secretary, who got Hales³ to frame a ditty unto it. The occasion was, as I hear, that the young Lady of Darby⁴ wearing about her neck, in her bosom, a picture which was in a dainty tablet; the Queen espying itt, asked what fyne jewell that was? The Lady Darby was curious to excuse the shewing of it; but the Queen wold have it, and, opening it, and finding it to be Mr. Secretary's, snatcht it away, and tyed itt upon her shoe, and walked long with it there; then took it thence and pinned itt on her elbow, and wore it there some time also; which Mr. Secretary being told of, made these verses, and had Hales to sing them in his chamber. It was told her Ma⁽ᵗʸ⁾, that Mr. Secretary had rare musick, and song; she would needes hear them; and so this ditty was soung which you see first written. More verses there be lykewise, whereof som, or all, were lyke-wyse soung⁵. I do

---

¹ See before, pp. 442. 586.   ² From Moryson's History of Ireland.

³ One of the Gentlemen of the Chapel Royal.—On New-year's Day 1599-1600, Robert Hales presented to the Queen " a pair of perfumed gloves."

⁴ Elizabeth, eldest daughter of Edward Vere, Earl of Oxford, and wife to William sixth Earl of Derby. She is called here " the young Lady," to distinguish her from her sister-in-law, the preceding Earl's widow.

⁵ I much regret that I am unable to trace these verses to their hiding-place. It is possible, however, that they may still be preserved, either at the Marquis of Salisbury's at Hatfield, or the Marquis of Exeter's at Burleigh.—In an indorsement at the back of the title they are called " The Verses of the Picture taken from Dianae's Nymph."

boldly send these things to your Lo. which I wold not do to any els, for I heare they are very secrett. Some of the verses argue, that he repynes not, thoghe her Ma^{ty} please to grace others, and contents himself with the favour he hath.

On the 19th, the Earl of Worcester, in a Letter to the Earl of Shrewsbury, says, "We are frolick here in Court; much dancing in the Privy Chamber of country dances before the Q. M. who is exceedingly pleased therewith. Irish tunes are at this time most pleasing; but in winter, Lullaby, an old song of Mr. Bird's[1], will be in more request, as I think."

September 23, Sir Fulke Grevill[2] tells the Countess of Shrewsbury, "The best newes I can yet write your Ladyship is of the Queen's healthe and disposition of body; which, I assure you, is excellent good; and I have not seen her every way better disposed thes many years. I understand my Lord Marquis has offered

---

[1] William Bird was Organist of the Chapel Royal in this and the following Reign. Several of his compositions were published; the most considerable of which, intituled " Gradualia, seu Cantionum Sacrarum, quarum aliæ ad quatuor, aliæ vero ad quinque & sex voces, editæ sunt," was printed at London in 1610, in six volumes, quarto. He was likewise author (says Wood) of several divine services and anthems in English, of a most admired composition, in forty parts, long since lost; and, with the assistance of two others, of a collection of 20 lessons, called " Parthenia; or the Maidenhead of the first musick that ever was printed for the Virginals." Lodge, vol. III. p. 148.

[2] This Gentleman, though one of the principal ornaments of Elizabeth's Court, never held any high office of State; owing, in some measure, to a dignified indolence of temper, but more to a degree of refinement in morality, which rendered him unfit for the common pursuits of mankind. His name occurs repeatedly in the various Rolls of New-year's Gifts to the Queen. He is thus enrolled by Fuller, among the "Worthies" of Warwickshire: "Sir Fulke Grevil, Knight, son to Sir Fulke Grevil the elder, of Becham Court in this County. He was bred first in the University of Cambridge. He came to the Court backed with a full and fair estate; and Queen Elizabeth loved such substancial *Courtiers* as could plentifully subsist of themselves. He was a good scholar, loving much to employ (and sometimes to advance) learned men, to whom worthy Bishop Overal chiefly owed his preferment, and Mr. Camden (by his own confession) tasted largely of his liberality. His studies were most in Poetry and History, as his works doe witness. His style, conceived by some to be swelling, is allowed for lofty and full by others. King James created him Baron Brook of Beachamp-Court, as descended from the sole daughter and heir of Edward Willoughby, the last Lord Brook in the Reign of King Henry the Seventh. His sad death, or murther rather, happened on this occasion. His discontented servant, conceiving his deserts not soon or well enough rewarded, wounded him mortally; and then (to save the law the labour) killed himself, verifying the observation, ' that he may when he pleaseth be master of another man's life, who contemneth his own.' He lieth buried in Warwick Church, under a monument of black and white marble, whereon he is styled ' Servant to Queen Elizabeth, Counsellor to King James, and friend to Sir Philip Sidney.' Dying Sept. 30, 1628, without issue and unmarried, his barony, by virtue of entail in the patent, descended on his kinsman Robert Grevill Lord Brook, father to the Right Honourable Robert Lord Brook."

his house [1] to sale; and there is one Swinnertown, a merchant, that hath engaged himself to deal for it. The price, as I hear, is £5000; his offer £4500. So, as the one's need [2], and the other's desire, I doubt, will easily reconcile this difference of price between them. In the mean season, I thought it my duty to give your Ladyship notice, because both your house and my Lady of Warwick's are included in this bargain; and we, your poor neighbours, would think our dwellings desolate without you, and conceive your Ladyship would not willingly become a tenant to such a fellow [3]. It may therefore please you to determine of your own in your wisdom; wherein, if my travail to my Lord Marquis might do you any service, when I shall receive your directions, I shall bestow myself more contentedly in no business whatsoever. Good Madam, be pleased to resolve with my Lord, and do something in it that we may not lose you. (From the Court at Oatlands [4].)"

September 25, Mr. Secretary Cecil, in a Letter to the Earl of Shrewsbury, says, "Because you may know where to find us, this Letter comes from Oatlands; and will shortly write from Richmond.—Good Foulke, our true Friend, for so I now protest to you I cordially hold him, was about to have stolen down to you; and then should you have had our sack of news, even from the Privy Chamber door to the Porter's Lodge; but further than that, you know, we are no censurers. Well, Sir, he cannot for his life get down now from the Queen; for, though his services at such time much contented her, she now will not let him go from her."

In an undated Letter to the Earl of Shrewsbury, "From the Court of Oatlands," he says, "We were again desired on Wednesday to go onward to my Lord of Hertford's, though in my opinion we shall not much pass Windsor."

[1] This house, which was built on the site of the Augustine Friary, near London Wall, was in 1735 the birth-place of the late celebrated Antiquary, Richard Gough, Esq.

[2] The Marquis of Winchester, having been reduced to great necessities by his magnificent style of living, (see p. 566) and the burthen of a large family, was obliged to dispose of this mansion and its appendages, to raise money for the payment of his debts.

[3] The person of whom Mr. Greville speaks so contemptuously was John Swinnerton, Esq. a respectable merchant, and nearly allied to the Swinnertons of Staffordshire.

[4] The Queen was fond of hunting, and occasionaly enjoyed that diversion in various places, particularly in the Park at Oatlands, one of the Royal Palaces. She was frequently there, and is said to have shot with a cross-bow in the paddock.

A monument is preserved in the chancel of the Church, of Walton-upon-Thames, consisting of three several plates, nailed up against the South wall, the two small ones being placed over the centre of the inscription.—That they once were laid over a grave-stone is evident, but in what part of the Church is not known, neither at what time or on what occasion they were taken up; they

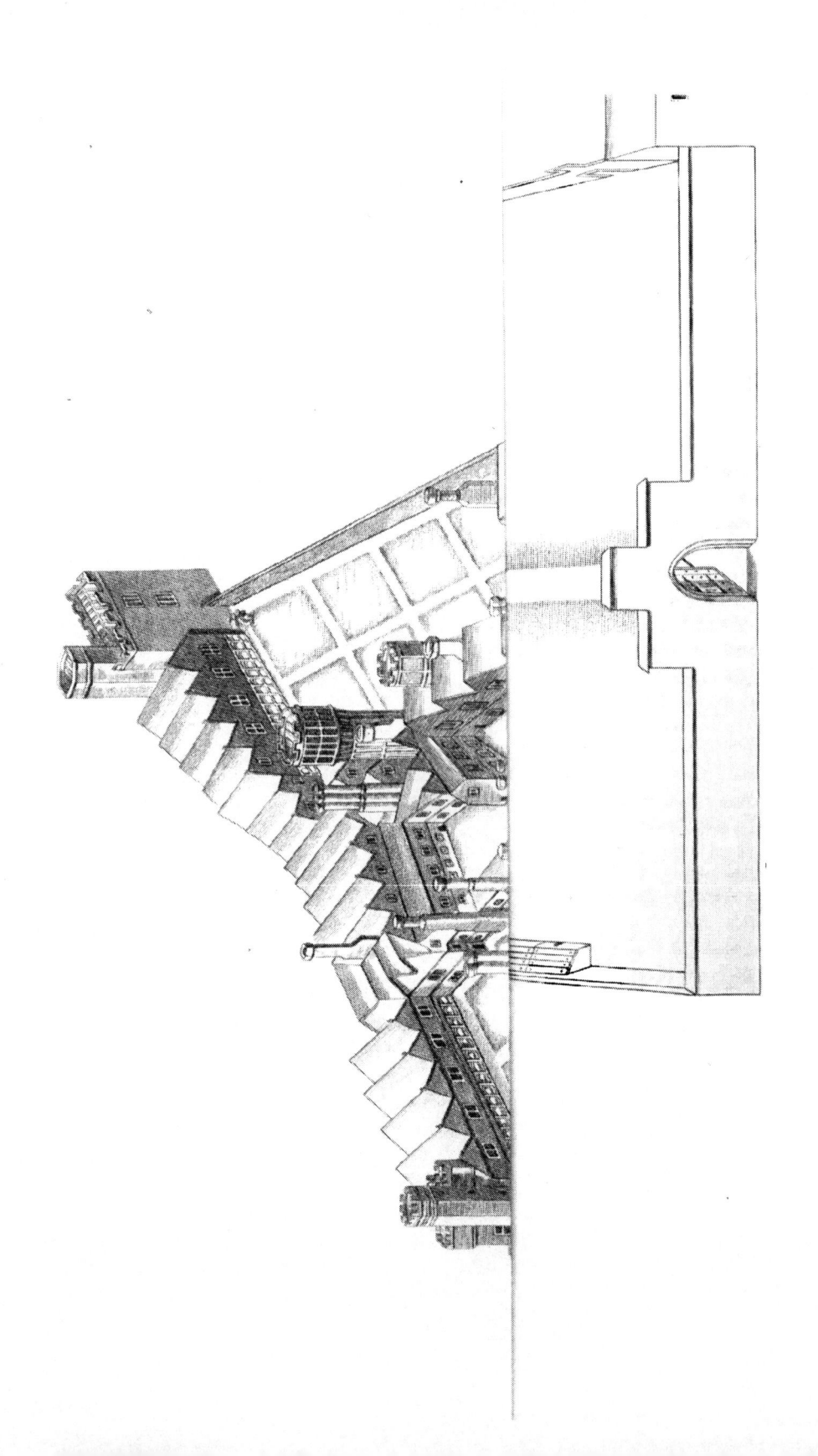

Mr. Chamberlain's Letters shall now be resumed:

October 2. "Sir William Clarke [1] so behaved himself that he pleased nobody, but gave occasion to have his misery and vanity spread far and wide. Then to

were, however, for a long time loose, and kept in the vestry. An ancient Sexton many years ago, explained to Captain Grose the figures engraved thereon by the following traditionary story, which, though strange, seems from the concurrent testimony of the monument, not to be without foundation. John Selwyn, the person represented both in the praying posture, and in the act of killing the stag was (as appears by the inscription) Under Keeper of the Park at Oatlands in the Reign of Queen Elizabeth; the bugle-horn, the insignia of his office, is apparent in both figures. This man was famous for his strength, agility, and skill in horsemanship, specimens of all which he exhibited before the Queen, at a grand Stag-hunt in that Park; where attending, as was the duty of his office, he in the heat of the chase suddenly leaped from his horse, upon the back of the stag (both running at that time with their utmost speed), and not only kept his seat gracefully in spite of every effort of the affrighted beast, but drawing his sword, with it guided him towards the Queen, and coming near her presence, plunged it in his throat, so that the animal fell dead at her feet. This was thought sufficiently wonderful to be chronicled on his monument, and he is accordingly there portrayed in the act of stabbing the beast. An extraordinary circumstance occurs in this plate, which has given rise to various conjectures. The representation of the story here related, is engraved on both sides of the same plate; in one, Selwyn appears with a hat on his head, and in the other, he is bareheaded, but with spurs on; a circumstance wanting in the former. From this double representation, some have thought he performed this feat more than once: others, with more probability, attribute it to the first engraving not having been approved of by the family, as deficient either in likeness, or some other circumstance; wherefore a second might be done, and, to save the expense of a fresh plate, was executed on the back of the former; which opinion receives some confirmation from the four holes, seen at the corners of the plate, by which it was immoveably fastened down, so that only one could be viewed. In Captain Grose's drawing, (in the Antiquarian Repertory, 2d edit. vol. I. p. 1.) both sides of the plate are shewn. Beneath his feet, and those of his wife and children is the following inscription: " Here lyeth y*e* bodye of John Selwyn, Gent.. Keeper of her Ma*ties* Parke of Otelands under y*e* Right Honorable Charles Howward, Lord Admyral of England, his good Lord et Mr.; who had issue by Susan his wife v sunes et vi daughters all lyving at his death, et departed out of this world the 27th day of Marche, Anno Domini 1587."

In the time of Queen Elizabeth, the Keeper of the House at Oatlands had the yearly fee of £5. 2*s.* 6*d.*; of the Park £3. 0*s.* 10*d.*; of the Garden and Orchard £12. 2*s.* 6*d.*; and of the Wardrobe £9. 2*s.* 6*d.* Anne, Queen of James I. was frequently there, and built a room called the Silk-worm room. King Charles I. on 14 March, *anno* 2, granted the same to his Queen Henrietta Maria for her life. His youngest son was called in his cradle *Henry of Oatlands*, being born there in 1640, in the house which Fuller, when he wrote, says " was taken to the ground." The Royal House was on low ground, near the present kitchen garden. It was destroyed in the time of the Usurpation, except some lodgings which one of the Earls of Dorset enjoyed, and the Gardener's chamber, which was the Silk-worm room, and the Park was disparked. Many foundations of buildings are to be traced in the land where the house stood, especially when sown with corn.

[1] At Burnham; see p. 579.

Oatlands, where she continues till the 7th of this month, that she comes to Richmond. The causes that witheld her from the Earl of Hertford's, and the Lord Chief Justice's were, the foul weather, and a general infection of the small-pox over all the Country.

"The Lord Hume[1] came this way home, and had audience at Court on Sunday. The Queen was very pleasant with him, and well disposed.

Oct. 15. "The Court came to Richmond the 8th of this present, where the Queen finds herself so well, that she will not easily remove."

Nov. 19. "The Queen came to Whitehall on Monday by water; and the Lord Mayor, with his troops of 500 velvet coats, and chains of gold, was already mounted, and marching to meet her at Charing Cross. The sudden alteration grew upon an inkling or suspicion of some dangerous attempt. *Her Day*[2] passed with the ordinary solemnity of preaching, singing, shooting, ringing, and running. The Bishop of Limerick, Dr. Thornborough[3], made a dull Sermon at Paul's Cross.

"At the Tilt, there were many young runners, as you may perceive by the peper of their names. Your Fool Garret made as fair a shew as the fairest of them, and was as well disguised, marry not altogether so well mounted; for his horse was no bigger than a good ban-dog; but he delivered his scutcheon with his *imprese* himself, and had good audience of her Majesty, and made her very merry. I send you here the Queen's Entertainment at the Lord Keeper's[4]. If you have seen or heard it already, it is but so much labour lost.

Dec. 6. "The Queen should have come to the warming of Mr. Secretary's[5]

---

[1] Sir George Hume, who afterwards attended King James from Scotland; and was raised to the English Peerage, as Lord Hume of Berwick; created Earl of Dunbar in Scotland, and elected K. G. He died in 1611.

[2] The day of her Accession to the Throne.—In this year was entered in the Books of the Stationers' Company, "A comfortable Song of Thanksgyvinge, to be song on the 17th daye of November, for the most gracious and happie Reigne of our Soverayn Lady Queene Elizabethe."

[3] He was made Bishop of Bristol in 1603, of Worcester 1617, and died July 9, 1641.

[4] A duplicate, probably, of the "Entertainment" now printed.

[5] Sir Robert Cecil, son of Lord Treasurer Burleigh by his second marriage, was knighted in 1591; made Principal Secretary of State, and Master of the Court of Requests. On New-year's Day, 1599-1600 he presented to the Queen "seven sprigs of gold, garnished with sparks of rubies, diamonds, and pearls pendant; and a jewel of gold like a hunter's horn, with a stone called a ...., garnished with small rubies, and a pearl pendant." In return, he had 26½ ounces of gilt plate. In 1603 King James created him Baron of Essenden in Rutland; in 1604 Viscount Cranborne; and in 1605 Earl of Salisbury. During this time he continued sole Secretary of State. On the death of the Earl of Dorset, in 1607, he was made Lord High Treasurer; and died in May 1612.

new house[1] on Monday; but then the cold weather hindered it; and on Wednesday the foul weather; and whether it is held this day is a question. The Queen dined this day at the Secretary's; where, they say, there is a great variety of Entertainment provided for her, and many rich jewels and presents."

Dec. 23. " I have pacified Wat Cope[2], in shewing what you wrote touching his papers. Mr. Secretary did him a very extraordinary favour, to admit him a partner in his Entertainment to the Queen; and to permit him to present her with some toys in his house; for the which he had many fair words, but as yet cannot get into the Privy Chamber, though he expects it daily. You liked the Lord Keeper's Devices so ill, that I care not to get Mr. Secretary's, that were not much better, saving a pretty Dialogue[3] of John Davies, ' 'twixt a Maid, a Widow, and a Wife,' which I do not think but Mr. Saunders hath seen, and no doubt will come out one of these days in print with the rest of his Works. The Lord Admiral's[4] feasting the Queen had nothing extraordinary; neither were his presents so precious as was expected, being only a whole suit of apparel; whereas it was thought he would have bestowed his rich hangings of all the fights with the

[1] " Mr. Secretary's new house" (which was annexed, on the East, to Burleigh House, see before, p. 79) is described by Stow as " *Cecil House*, built on the site of what some time belonged to the parson of St. Martin in the Fields, and by composition came to Sir Thomas Palmer, Knt. in the reign of Edward the Sixth, who began to build the same of brick and timber, very large and spacious; but of later time it hath been far more beautifully increased by the late Sir William Cecil, Baron of Burghley, Lord Treasurer, and great Counsellor of the Estate." After the mansion called Doctors' Commons, upon Bennet's-hill, London, was burnt in the Fire of London in 1666, this house was taken by the Society of the Doctors of the Civil Law, where, till the year 1672 (that Doctors' Commons was re-built) the Civilians lodged, and kept their Courts of Arches, Admiralty, and Prerogative. But now of late their house is turned into an Exchange, and called Exeter Exchange.—The names of Burleigh-street, Cecil-street, Salisbury-street, &c. &c. remain as testimonials of the residence of their original owners.

Lord Burghley, according to Norden, had also " a proper little house" at Panns in Middlesex.

[2] Son of Sir Walter Cope (Master of the Wards, and Chamberlain of the Exchequer). He was knighted by King James, April 23, 1603. He was a considerable land-owner in Kensington, and built Holland House, distinguished for its architectural peculiarities; and died August 1, 1614.

[3] I am sorry that I cannot recover this " Dialogue," which was written expressly for the Entertainment of the Virgin Queen.

[4] Charles second Lord Howard of Effingham was appointed Chamberlain of the Household in 1574. Lord Howard was appointed Lord High Admiral in 1588. He was created Earl of Nottingham in 1597.

Spanish Armada in eighty-eight [1]. These feastings have had their effect, to stay the Court here this Christmas, though most of the Carriages were well onward on their way to Richmond. The Queen christened the French Ambassador's daughter, by her Deputy the Lady Marquesse [of Winchester]; the Countess of Worcester and the Lord Admiral being the other assistants."

Jan 27, 1602-3. "The Court removed hence to Richmond the 21st of this month [2] in very foul and wet weather: but the wind suddenly changing to the North-east, hath made here ever since the sharpest season that I have lightly known. On Monday before her going, the Queen was entertained and feasted by the Lord Thomas Howard [3] at the Charter-house [4]. Two days after, the Lady of Effingham [5] was brought to bed of a daughter, altogether unlooked-for, and almost before she or any body else supposed she was with child."

[1] These seem to be the hangings, of which part is now in the House of Lords. More were preserved in the Royal Wardrobe when Pine engraved the others in 1739. They were designed by Henry Cornelius Vroom, a famous Painter of Shipping, at Haerlem, and woven by Francis Spiring.

[2] It appears by the Accompts of the Churchwardens of Fulham, that the Queen dined that day with Mr. Lacy at Putney.

[3] Son, by a second marriage, of Thomas Howard, fourth Duke of Norfolk. He was created Lord Howard of Walden in 1597, Earl of Suffolk in 1603; and died in 1626.

[4] The Queen had resided some time at this house in 1558. See vol. I. p. 31. "King James, on his accession to the Throne of England, was pleased to shew a very remarkable regard to the family of the Howards, as having been sufferers for his mother the Queen of Scots. And out of an especial respect to Lord Thomas Howard (and at the same time to imitate the steps of Queen Elizabeth) when the Lord Mayor, Aldermen, and five hundred of the chief citizens, all in velvet gowns and gold chains, met his Majesty on horseback, at Stamford Hill, on the King's approach towards London from Scotland, on the 7th of May 1603, his Majesty was pleased to be conducted in grand procession to the Charter-house, and to keep his Court there four days; and before his departure, May 11, to make more than 80 Knights, to do this Lord more abundant honour, whom he soon after created Earl of Suffolk." Bearcroft.

[5] Anne, daughter and coheir of John Lord St. John of Bletsoe, and wife of William the second son of Charles, Lord Admiral, and afterwards Earl of Nottingham; but, dying in his father's life-time, never had the title of Baron Howard of Effingham.

Sir ROBERT CAREY's *Narrative of the* QUEEN's *last Sickness and Death.*

"After that all things were quieted, and the Border in safety, towards the end of five years that I had been Warden there, having little to do, I resolved upon a journey to Court, to see my friends, and renew my acquaintance there. I tooke my journey about the end of the year 1602. When I came to Court, I found the Queene ill-disposed, and shee kept her inner lodging; yet shee, hearing of my arrivall, sent for mee. I found her in one of her withdrawing chambers, sitting low upon her cushions. Shee called mee to her, I kist her hand, and told her it was my chiefest happinesse to see her in safety and in health, which I wished might long continue. Shee toake mee by the hand, and wrung it hard, and said, 'No, Robin, I am not well;' and then discoursed with mee of her indisposition, and that her heart had been sad and heavy for ten or twelve dayes, and in her discourse she fetched not so few as forty or fifty great sighes. I was grieved at the first to see her in this plight; for in all my life-time before I never knew her fetch a sigh, but when the Queene of Scottes was beheaded. Then [1], upon my knowledge, she shedd many teares and sighes [2], manifesting her innocence that she never gave consent to the death of that Queene.

"I used the best words I could to persuade her from this melancholy humour; but I found by her it was too deep-rooted in her heart, and hardly to be removed. This was upon a Saterday night, and she gave command that the great closet should be prepared for her to go to Chappell the next morning. The next day, all things being in a readinesse, wee long expected her coming. After eleven o'clock, one of the groomes [3] came out and bade make ready for the private closet, she would not go to the great. There we stayed long for her coming, but at the last she had cushions lay'd for her in the privy chamber hard by the closet doore, and there she heard service.

"From that day forwards she grew worse and worse. She remained upon her cushions foure dayes and nights at the least. All about her could not persuade her either to take any sustenance or go to bed.

"I, hearing that neither the physitians nor none about her could persuade her to take any course for her safety, feared her death would soone after ensue. I could not but think in what a wretched estate I should be left, most of my livelyhood

---

[1] At that time, in the year 1587.
[2] They were indeed necessary upon that occasion.
[3] Of the chambers.

depending on her life. And hereupon I bethought myselfe with what grace and favour I was ever received by the King of Scottes, whensoever I was sent to him. I did assure myselfe it was neither unjust or unhonest for me to do for myselfe, if God at that time should call her to his mercy. Hereupon I wrote to the King of Scottes (knowing him to be the right heire to the crowne of England [1]), and certified him in what state her Majesty was. I desired him not to stirr from Edenborough; if of that sicknesse she should die, I would be the first man that should bring him newes of it.

"The Queene grew worse and worse, because she would be so, none about her being able to go to bed. My Lord Admirall was sent for (who by reason of my Sister's death, that was his wife, had absented himselfe some fortnight from Court); what by faire meanes, what by force, he gatt her to bed. There was no hope of her recovery, because she refused all remedies.

"On Wednesday the twenty-third of March she grew speechless. That afternoone, by signes, she called for her Councill, and by putting her hand to her head [2], when the King of Scottes was named to succeed her, they all knew hee was the man she desired should reign after her [3].

[1] Protestants and Papists unanimously allowed his right: not a murmur arose against it.

[2] The sign here mentioned is a true and indisputable fact, otherwise it would not have been inserted by the plain, sincere, and ingenuous author of these Memoirs, who was present at the time the sign was made. But it still remains a doubt whether the Queen intended it for a sign or not. The Lords pretended to think it one.—Camden's account of the death-bed sign is substantially the same with that of Sir Robert Carey; and, in point of fact, it is fully confirmed by the extracts from the Cottonian MSS. printed in p. 607.

[3] March 30, 1603, Mr. Chamberlain says, "I make no question but you have heard of our great loss before this came to you; and no doubt you shall hear her Majesty's sickness and manner of death diversely related; for even here the Papists do tell strange stories, as utterly void of truth, as of al civil honesty and humanity. I had good means to understand how the world went, and find her disease to be nothing but a settled and unremoveable melancholy, insomuch that she could not be won or persuaded, neither by Councils, Divines, Physicians, nor the Women about her, once to sup, or touch any physic, though ten or twelve Physicians, that were continually about her, with all manner of asseverations of perfect and easy recovery, if she would but follow their advice; so that it cannot be said of her, as it was of the Emperor Hadrian, *Turba Medicorum occidit Regem*; for they say, she died only for lack of Physick. Here was some whispering that her brain was somewhat distempered, but there was no such matter; only she held an obstinate silence for the most part, because she had a persuasion, that if she once lay down she should never rise; could not be got to go to bed in a whole week, till three days before her death; so that, after three weeks languishing she

"About six at night she made signes for the Archbishop and her Chaplains to come to her, at which time I went in with them, and sate upon my knees full of teares to see that heavy sight. Her Majestie lay upon her backe, with one hand in the bed, and the other without. The Bishop kneeled downe by her, and examined her first of her faith; and she so punctually answered all his several questions, by lifting up her eyes, and holding up her hand, as it was a comfort to all the beholders. Then the good man told her plainly what she was, and what she was to come to; and though she had been long a great Queene here upon earth, yet shortly she was to yield an accompt of her stewardship to the King of Kings. After this he began to pray, and all that were by did answer him. After he had continued long in prayer, 'till the old man's knees were weary, hee blessed her, and meant to rise and leave her. The Queene made a signe with her hand. My sister Scroope[1] knowing her meaning, told the Bishop the Queene desired hee would pray still. He did so for a long halfe houre after, and then thought to leave her. The second time she made signe to have him continue in prayer. He did so for halfe an houre more, with earnest cryes to God for her soule's health, which he uttered with that fervency of spirit, as the Queene to all our sight much rejoiced thereat, and gave testimony to us all of her Christian and comfortable end. By this time it grew late, and every one departed, all but her women that attended her.

"This that I heard with my eares, and did see with my eyes, I thought it my duty to set downe, and to affirm it for a truth, upon the faith of a Christian, because I knowe there have beene many false lyes reported of the end and death of that good Lady. I went to my lodging, and left word with one in the Cofferer's[2] chamber to call me, if that night it was thought she would die, and gave the porter

departed, being the 24th of this present, being on Lady's Eve, between two and three in the morning, as she was born on our Lady's Eve, in September. And as one Lee was Mayor of London when she came to the Crown, so is there one Lee now she left it. Sir Thomas Leigh was Lord Mayor in 1558-9; Sir Robert Lee in 1602-3. The Nobility and Council came from Richmond that morning; and before ten o'clock had proclaimed King James at Whitehall, Temple Bar, and so forward in Cheapside and other places. The Council went on Saturday to Richmond; and that night brought the Corpse with an honourable attendance to Whitehall, where the Household remains. The body was not opened, but wrapt up in cere cloths, and other preservatives."—Again, " April 12. The Queen's Funeral is appointed the 28th of this present month, with as much solemnity as hath been used to any former Prince, and that by the King's own direction. It shall be kept at Westminster."

[1]. Philadelphia Lady Scroope, second daughter of Henry Carey Lord Hunsdon.
[2] Sir George Cooke.

an angell to let me in at any time when I called. Betweene one and two of the clock on Thursday morning, he that I left in the Cofferer's chamber brought me word the Queene was dead[1]. I rose and made all the haste to the gate to gett in. There I was answered, ' I could not enter; the Lords of the Councill having been with him, and commanded him that none should go in or out, but by warrant from them.' At the very instant, one of the Councill (the Comptroller)[2] asked whether I was at the gate. I said, ' Yes.' He said to me, if I pleased, hee would let mee in. I desired to know how the Queen did. He answered, ' Pretty well.' I bade him good night. He replied, and said, ' Sir, if you will come in, I will give you my word and credit you shall go out againe at your owne pleasure.' Upon his word I entered the gate, and came up to the Cofferer's Chamber, where I found all the Ladies weeping bitterly. Hee led mee from thence to the Privy Chamber, where all the Councill was assembled; there I was caught hold of, and assured I should not go for Scotland, till their pleasures were farther knowne. I told them I came of purpose to that end. From thence they all went to the Secretarye's Chamber; and as they went, they gave a speciall command to the porters, that none should go out of the gates but such servants as they should send to prepare their coaches and horses for London. There was I left in the middest of the Court to think my owne thoughtes 'till they had done counsaile. I went to my Brother's[3] Chamber, who was in bed, having been over-watched many nightes before. I gott him up with all speed, and when the Councill's men were going out of the gate, my Brother thrust to the gate. The Porter knowing him to be a great officer, lett him out. I pressed after him, and was stayed by the Porter. My Brother said angrily to the Porter, ' Let him out, I will answer for him.' Whereupon I was suffered to passe, which I was not a little glad of.

" I gott to horse, and rode to the Knight Marshall's lodging by Charing Crosse, and there stayed 'till the Lords came to Whitehall Garden. I staide there till it was nine a'clocke in the morning, and hearing that all the Lords were in the old orchard at Whitehall, I sent the Marshall to tell them, that I had staide all that while to know their pleasures, and that I would attend them if they would command mee any service. They were very glad when they heard I was not gone, and desired the Marshall to send for meé, and I should with all speed be dispatched

---

[1] She died March 24, soon after the Archbishop had left her, about three o'clock in the morning.
[2] Sir Edward Wotton.
[3] George second Lord Hunsdon, a Privy Counsellor, Captain of the Band of Pensioners, Governor of the Isle of Wight, and Knight of the Garter.

for Scotland. The Marshall beleeved them, and sent Sir Arthur Savage for mee. I made haste to them. One of the Council (my Lord of Banbury[1] that now is) whispered the Marshall in the eare, and told him, if I came they would stay me, and send some other in my stead. The Marshall gott from them, and mett me coming to them between the two gates. Hee bade mee be gone, for he had learned for certaine, that if I came to them, they would betray mee.

"I retourned, and tooke horse betweene nine and ten[2] a clocke, and that night rode to Doncaster[3]. The Friday night I came to my own house at Witherington[4], and presently tooke order with my Deputies to see the Borders kept in quiet, which they had much to doe: and gave order the next morning the King of Scotland should be proclaimed King of England, at Morpeth and Anwick."

Sir Robert Carey's narrative is thus confirmed and enlarged by an article in the Cottonian MSS. (Julius, C. VII. 46):

"On the 14th of January the late Queen who had two days before sickened with a cold (being ever forewarned of Dr. Dee[6] to beware of Whitehall), removed to Richmond. But a little before her going, even the same morning, the Earl of Nottingham, High-Admiral of England, coming to her, partly to speak with her concerning her removal, and partly touching other matters wherein her pleasure and direction was to be known, she fell into some speech of the Succession; and then she told him, 'that her seat had ever been the throne of Kings, and none but her next heire of bloud and descent should succeed her.' After falling into other matters they left that speeche; and she departed to Richmond, where she was well amended of the cold: but on Monday the 28th of Februarie she began to sikken agayne, and so continued till Mondaie the 7th of Marche, at which time notice was given to the Lords of the Councel that shee was sick of a cold, and soe she continued sick till

---

[1] Sir William Knolles; of whom see before, p. 564. [2] On Thursday morning, March 24.
[3] Situated upon the river Done in Yorkshire, 155 miles from London.
[4] Then the residence of Sir Robert Carey, in right of his wife, the heiress of the Widringtons. It is a Chapelry in the parish of Woodhorn, the East division of Morpeth, county of Northumberland, where for the present we shall leave him; and resume his Narrative as an introductory article in the "Progresses of King James," where *Morpeth* and *Alnwick* will again be mentioned.
[5] Dr. Dee had been a favourite of the Queen from the time of her accession to the Throne; and was occasionally honoured by her Majesty's Visits at Mortlake. See vol. I. p. 414.

Tuesdaye the 15th of March following, being Friday, she began to be very ill: whereupon the Lords of the Councell weare sent for to Richmond, and there continued till Wednesday the 24th of Marche, about three of the clock in the morning (being our Lady even), at which time she died. But on the Tuesday before her death, being the 23d of March, the Lord Admiral being on the right side of her bed, the Lord Keeper on the left, and Mr. Secretary Cecill (afterwards Lord Burghley), being at the bed's feet, all standing, the Lord Admirall put her in mynde of her speeche concerning the Succession had at Whitehall; and that they, in the name of all the rest of her Counsell, came unto her to know her pleasure who should succeed: whereunto she thus replied, ' I told you my seat had been the seat of Kings, and I will have no rascall to succeed me; and who should succeed me but a King?' The Lords, not understanding this dark speech, and looking one on the other, at length Mr. Secretary boldly asked her what she meant by these words, ' that no rascal should succeed her.' Whereunto she replied, ' that her meaning was, a King should succeed her; and who,' quoth shee, ' should that be but our Cousin of Scotland?' They asked her, whether that were her absolute resolution? Whereunto she answered, ' I pray you trouble me no more: I'll have none but him.' With which answer they departed. Notwithstanding, after againe, about four o'clock in the afternoon the next day, being Wednesdaye, after the Archbishop of Canterbury and other Divines had been with her, and left her in a manner speechless, the three Lords aforesaid repaired unto her again, asking her, ' If she remained in her former resolution, and who should succeed her?' But she, not being able to speak, was asked by Mr. Secretary in this sort, ' Wee beseech your Majesty, if you remain in your former resolution, and that you would have the King of Scotts to succeed you in your kingdom, shew some sign unto us:' whereat, suddenly heaving herself upwards in her bed, and pulling her arms out of the bed, she held both her hands jointly together over her head in manner of a crowne: whereby, as they guessed, she signified that she did not only wish him the kingdom, but desired the continuance of his estate. After which they departed; and the next morning (as is aforesaid) shee died. Immediately after her death, all the Lords, as well of the Counsell, as other Noblemen that weare at Court, came from Richmond to Whitehall, by six o'clock in the morning, where other Noblemen that were at London met them. But as they began to sitt in Counsell in the Prince's Chamber at Whitehall, the Lord Keeper, Sir Thomas Egerton, and the rest of the Counsell that weare no

Barons, offered to sit at the lower end of the Counsell-table, and not above any of the meanest Nobility; but the Noblemen (in respect to their former authority) called them to the higher end of the table, and wished them to keep their places: whereunto the Lord Keeper made answer,—" If it be your Lordships' pleasure, we will doe soe; but that it is more of your courtizie then wee can demand of dutye;" and so they sat down, every man according to his degree, in counsell touching the Succession: where, after some speeche had of divers competitions and matters of State, at length the Lord Admiral related all the aforesayd premisses which the late Queen had spoken to him, and to the Lord Keeper, and to Mr. Secretary, with the manner thereof; which they, being asked, affirmed to be true upon their honour.

This interesting event is thus recorded in Strype's Life of Archbishop Whitgift: " The conclusion of this year, March the 24th, concluded the life and reign of the most incomparable Princess and Queen ELIZABETH; an account of the manner of whose sickness and death, one uncertain (whether some one of the Physicians about her, or some other, it is unknown) wrote the very day after, in a Latin epistle to one Edmund Lambert, in these words: ' Regina, cum per tres fere hebdomadas morbo melancholico stuporem quendam non sine læsæ phantasiæ indiciis inferente, laborâsset, nec per totum id tempus, ullis vel rationibus, vel precibus, vel fallaciis induci potuisset, ut aliquod artis medicæ auxilium experiretur, ac difficulter persuaderi sibi passa sit ut alimentum naturæ sustinendæ debitum sumeret; somnum autem quam minimum, eumque non in lecto, sed inter pulvinaria, ubi totos dies, & insomnis & immota, sedere consueverat; intelligendi autem vim ad extremum usque spiritum retineret; linguæ vero facultate tribus ante obitum diebus fuisset privata; postquam est omnibus & fælicissime Principis & Christianissimæ Fœminæ officiis, functa, die hesterno, sc. 24 Martii, hora tertia matutina, naturæ cessit.'

" But I supply, as to her religious and Christian behaviour in her last sickness, what this writer is silent in. She had several of her learned and pious Bishops frequently about her, performing the last offices of religion with her, as particularly Watson Bishop of Chichester, her Almoner, the Bishop of London [Bancroft], and chiefly the Archbishop [Whitgift]: with whom in their prayers she very devoutly, in her eyes, hands, and tongue, and with very great fervency, joined. She cared not to have any other discourse, but with them, about her spiritual estate. And though she was impatient of any speeches of others with her, yet she was ever well pleased to hear the Archbishop and the Bishop of London give her comfort and counsel to prepare herself Godward: and most heartily and devoutly prayed continually with them; and making signs and shews to her last remembrance, of the sweet comfort she took in their presence and assistance, and of the unspeakable joy she was going unto [1].

" The very prayer that was made for her but the day before her death is preserved in our Archbisop's [Whitgift] Register. Which makes it probable himself was the composer thereof. And because another Archbishop [Parker] thought it worthy his own transcribing into a printed book of Forms of Prayer in Emanuel College, where himself was once the worthy Master, I shall enter it here, taken thence by an exact hand [2].

" 'O most heavenly Father, and God of all Mercy, we most humbly beseech Thee to behold Thy Servant, our Queen, with the eyes of pity and compassion. Give unto her the comforts of Thy Holy Spirit, work in her a constant and lively Faith; grant unto her true repentance, and restore unto her, if it be Thy will, her former health and strength, both of body and soul. Let not the Enemy, nor his wicked instruments, have any power over her to do her harm. O Lord, punish her not for our offences, neither us in her. Deal not with us, O Lord, as we have deserved; but for Thy mercy's sake, and for Thy Christ His sake, forgive us all our sins; and prolong her days, that we may still enjoy her, to the glory of Thy Holy Name, and joy of all such as truly fear Thee, through Jesus Christ our Lord. Amen [3].'

" Her death drawing near [4], the Archbishop exhorted her to fix her thoughts upon God, the better to draw off her mind from other secular things concerning her kingdom and successor, that some then of her Court propounded to her. To

[1] Cott. Librar. Julius, F. VI.
[2] Rev. Thomas Baker, B. D.
[3] Regist. Whitgift, vol. III. p. 148.
[4] Sir Edward Peyton, in his " Divine Catastrophe of the Kingly Family of the House of Stuarts:" 12mo, Lond. 1652, pp. 24, 25, speaking of Queen Elizabeth, says, " She was a Lady adorned with Majesty, Learning, Languages, Wisdom, and Piety; yet fearful of death, for she hated any word that tended to it; as shall be manifest by Roger Lord North (see vol. II. p. 236), when carving one day at dinner, the Queen asked what that covered dish was; he lifting up the cover, replied, *Madam, it is a coffin;* a word which moved the Queen to anger: *And are you such a fool,* said she, *to give a pie such a name?* This gave warning to the Courtiers not to use any word that mentioned her death."

which good advice to stay her at that hour, she answered him, 'She did so, nor did her mind wander from God.' And as a sign thereof, when she could not speak, she was observed much to lift up her eyes and hands to Heaven [1].

"We have this farther passage of her religious belief, which she expressed when her Almoner waited upon her, to assist her devotions; as it was related in the Paul's Cross Sermon, preached by John Hayward, a known, wise, learned, and reverend divine of the City of London, March the 27th, being the Lord's-day next ensuing her death, whose text was taken out of the xxxivth Psalm, v. 1, 'The earth is the Lord's, and the fulness thereof, &c.' Perhaps taking those words for the subject of his discourse, that from thence he might comfort the people, that though they were left destitute of so excellent a Princess and good Governor, yet the 'Earth was the Lord's,' and that he would provide graciously for His good and pious people therein: and speaking of their late departed Queen, he shewed his auditors, 'How her Almoner rehearsing to her the grounds of the Christian Faith, and requiring her assent unto them by some sign, she readily gave it both with hand and ey: and that when he proceeded to tel her, that it was not enough generally to believe that those Articles of Faith were true, but that every Christian was to believe them true to them, and that they themselves were members of the true Church, and redeemed by Jesus Christ, and that their sins were forgiven to them; she did again, with great shew of faith, lift up her eyes and hands to heaven, and so stayed them long, as a testimony she gave of applying the same unto herself.' This remarkable circumstance of the Queen's faith and devout behaviour on her death-bed, was repeated again ten years after, in the same pulpit, at St. Paul's Cross, by Miles Moss, D. D. Pastor of Combes in the county of Suffolk, in a Sermon there preached about *justifying faith*.

"As the Archbishop had the honour thus to perform the last duties to Queen Elizabeth, so he likewise had to set the crown upon the head of King James and Queen Anne his Royal Consort, at Westminster, on St. James's day, July 25, 1603, with all the royall ceremonies accompanying that solemnity, in an august presence of the Nobility, the Lord Mayor and Aldermen, and many others of the Gentry assembled."

[1] Camden's Elizabeth.

The following strange and incredible particulars (ex Personii Jesuitæ maledictâ discussione, p. 217,) are from the Cottonian MSS. Julius, F. VI. fol. 121.

"Her Majesty being in good health one day, a Privy Counsellour presented her with a piece of gold of the bigness of an Angel, dimly marked with some small characters, which he said an ould woman in Wales bequethed her on her death-bed, and thereupon he discoursed how the said ould woman, by vertue of the same, lived to the age of an hundred and odd years, and in that age having all her body withered and consumed, and wanting nature to nourish, she said, commanding the said piece of gold to be carefully sent her Majesty, alleging further, that as long as the sayd ould woman wore it upon her body, she could not dye. The Queene, upon the confidence she had thereof, tooke the sayd gould, and wore it upon her rufle. Now, though she fell not suddenly sicke, yet dayly decreased her rest and feding, and within a few days fell sick indeed, and the cause being wondered at by a lady with whom she was very private and confidant, her Majesty tould her (commanding her to conceal the same) that she saw one night in her bed her body exceeding leane and fearful, in a light of fire; this sight was at Wighthall, a little before she departed from thence to Richmond, and may be testifyed by another lady, who was one of the nearest about her person, of whom the Queene demaunded whether she was not wont to see sightes in the night, telling her of the bright flame she had sene. Afterward, in the melancholy of her sicknes, she desired to see a true looking-glass, which in twenty years she had not sene, but only such a one as was made of purpose to deceive her sight; which glasse being brought her, she fell presently into exclayming against those which had so much commended her, and took it so offensively, that some which before had flattered her, dourst not come into her sight. Now falling into extremity, she sate two dayes and three nightes upon her stole, ready dressed, and could never be brought by any of her Councell to go to bed, or to eat or drink, only my Lord Admirall one time persuaded her to drinke some broath, for that any of the rest she would not answer them to any question, but sayd softlye to my Lord Admirall's earnest persuasions, that if he knew what she had sene in her bed, he would not persuade her as he did, and commanding the rest of the Lords to depart her chamber, willed my Lord Admirall to stay, to whom she showke her head, and with a pitiful voice said unto him, 'My Lord, I am tied with a chaine of iron about my feet;' he alleging her wonted courage, she replied, 'I am tied, tied, and the case is altered with me.'

"About the same time, two Ladyes waiting on her in her chamber, discovered in the bottom of her chaire the Quene of Hartes, with a nayle of iron knockt through the forehead of it, and which the Ladyes durst not then pull out, remembring that the like thing was reported to be used to others for witchcraft; another Lady waighting in these times on the Queene, and leaving her after in her privy chamber at Richmond, at the very first distemper of her sickness, met her, as she thought, three or four chambers off, and fearing that she would have been displeased that she left her alone, came toward her to excuse herselfe, but she vanished away; and when the Lady retourned into the same chamber where she left the Queen, she found her asleep as before; so in time growing past recovery, having kept her bed some daies, the Councell sent unto her the Bishop of Canterburie, and other of the Prelates, upon sight of whom she was much offended, cholerickly rating them, bidding them be packing, and afterwards exclaiming to my Lord Admirall, that she had the greatest indignity offered her by the Archbishop that a Prince could have, to pronounce sentence of death against her, as if she had lived an Atheist; and some Lords mentioning to have other Prelates to come unto her, she answered, that she would have none of those hedge-priests, and so none of them came to her till after she was past sense, and at the last gaspe, at which time some praiers were said not far from her.

"The Queene being departed this life, the Lords of the Councell went to London to proclaime his Majestie, leaving her body, with charge not to be opened, such being her desire: but some, for some reasons, having given a secret warrant to the surgeons, they opened her, which the rest of the Councell did not contradict. Now the body being seared up, was brought to Whitehall, where it was watched every night by six several ladies; who being all about the same, which was fast nayled up, within a brod coffin, with leaves of lead, covered with velvett, it happened that her body brake the coffin with such a cracke, that it spleated the wood, lead, and cer-cloath, to the terror and astonishment of all that were present; whereupon the next day she was fayne to be new trimmed up, insomuch as all were of opinion, that yf she had not been opened, the breth of her body would have been much worse. Divers other particularities, for that they concearne special personages, I have thought good for some causes to conceal."

Description of the QUEEN's *Funeral; by Mr.* ST. JOHN GUILLIM [1].

To his noble, worthye, generous, and most respected kinseman, Mr. John Gwyllym, of Walthamstowe. All health, happienes, and heartes content in this life, and eternall blessednes in that to come, &c.

Worthy Sir, haveinge founde some dispersed collections of my late industrious father's (who ever trewly loved and respected you for your manye kinde deserts), I have taken some paynes in re-collectinge and digestinge them into this simple forme; and am boulde to presente them unto you, who, both for name, alliaunce, and meritte (I make no doubte) will kindely accepte hereof, beinge an unworthye tetimonye of my love and service, which my sowle ever striveth to power forthe into the boundeles cisterne of your boundles and matchles goodness, wanttinge better meanes (yet) to expresse the same. Thoughe the discourse be solemne, treatinge of sixe severall funeralls, *viz.* Doctor Martyne Luther's, Hugh [2] a Bishop of Lincolne, Henry the IV's late Kinge of Fraunce, Philip's Kinge of Spaine, Queene Elizabethe's, and Prince Henrye's, besides some other occurrents worthye your observation; yet it may serve to entertaine some leasurable howers, and give you content in the readinge; which, with all other happines to yourselfe and kinde bedd-fellowe, with all yours, I most wishe, and for which, my vowes and prayers shall ever attende you, so longe as I shall be thoughte worthye to be your affectionate kinseman to comaunde, ST. JOHN GWYLLYM.

In the stately, magnificent, and solemne proceedinge of the traine that accompanyed the corpes of our late Soverigne Ladye Elizabeth (who maye without offence be paralleled with the moste renowned and famous Kinges of all Christendome for sacrednes of Relligion, hir wisdome, justice, governement, magnificence of estate, hir love and clemencye to hir subjectes, hir generall skill and knowledge in all good letters; finally, beinge a most rare, singular, and peirelesse patterne of all heroicall and princely virtues), it is to be observed, that the Knyghte Marshalls-men ledd the traine, and made waye for the more easie and orderlye passage of the mourners without throngeinge or other disturbaunce.

[What follows in the MS. of Guillim appears to have been abridged from the succeeding Narrative given in p. 621.]

[1] From a MS. in the Cathedral Library at Lichfield; communicated by the Rev. Henry White, Sacrist of that Church, and Vicar of Chebsey, in Staffordshire; whose general love for literature is well known; and to whose polite attentions I am happy thus to acknowledge repeated obligations.

[2] Probably St. Hugh, 1203.

ELIZABETHA QUASI VIVENS,
ELIZA'S FUNERALL.

A fewe Aprill Drops, showred on the Hearse of dead ELIZA: or,
The Funerall Tears of a true hearted Subject. By H. P.[1]

To the worthy and Curteous Gentleman Mr. RICHARD HILDERSHAM,
H. P. wisheth increase of worship and virtue.

I have (worshipfull and wise), contrary to the expectation of many, presumed to publish the formall maner of my private sorowes, for the great losse of your late deceased Lady-mistres, and England's Soveraigne. And knowing our Worship a sad and pensive mourner for so great a losse, I have made bold to shrowd my teares under your sad garment; which if you deigne to shadowe from the heate of envie, there is no fire of malice can have power to partch them. Shrowd them at your pleasure, keepe them no longer than you please to mourne, which I knowe will be of long continuance: not that you have cause by this late change, but that the memorial of so sweet a Princes cannot be sodainly buried in oblivion. God graunt that the auncient saying in this barter may be verified; which is, "We have changed for the better." Is it possible a better than shee should succeed? but what is impossible with the Almightie? What ELIZA was in her life, you know, nay the world knowes her fame girdles in the earth: what her Successor hath been in his kingdom of Scotland, his subjects they know, and we have heard, which hath been much to God's glory, his countries peace, and his Majesties honour; therefore, since it hath pleased God to continue his wonted favour towards us in blessing us his unworthy servants with so gracious a Soveraigne, adding unto his Royal Crowne the highest tytle of Majestie and earthlie dignitie: Graunt thou Most of Might (Almightie King) that our dread Soveraign James, the first of that name of these three united kingdoms, England, France, and Ireland, and of Scotland the Sixt, maye be so directed and governed by thy Almightie hand, that he may rule his sevrall kingdoms in peace, to thy glory; raigne in tranquility Nestor's yeeres, to our comfort; and, in the end, dye in thy favour, to live againe in glory with his æternized sister the divine ELIZA. Thus, not dreading your kinde acceptance of my love, I humblie take my leave.

Your Worship's most obsequious, HENRY PETOWE.

[1] London, Printed by E. Allde, for M. Lawe, dwelling in Paule's Church Yard, neere unto Saint Austin's Gate, 1603, quarto, 20 pages.—This little Tract is valued, in the " Bibliotheca Anglo-Poetica," at £2. 12s. 6d.

The Induction.

I that obscure have wept till eyes be drye,
  Wil teach my pen another while to weep.
Obdurant hartes that they may mollifye,
  For losse of her that now in peace doth sleep.
    Peace rest with her, but sorowe with my pen,
    Till dead Eliza doth revive agen.

Amongst high sp'rited paragons of wit,
  That mount beyond our earthlie pitch to fame,
Creepes forth my Muse; ye great ones favour it,
  Take her not up, alas! she is too tame.
    Shee 'l come to hand, if you but lure her to you,
    Then use her kindly, for shele kindly woe you.

And if this infant of mine art-lesse braine,
  Passe with your sweet applause as some have done,
And meane good favour of the learned gaine
  For showring teares upon Eliza's tombe;
    My Muse shall hatch such breed when she's of yeres
    Shall bring you comfort, and dry up your teares.

The last of many [1], yet not the least of all,
  Sing I a heavie dirdge for our late Queene:
And singing, mourne Eliza's Funerall,
  The *E per se* of all that e're have beene.
    She was, she is, and evermore shall bee,
    The blessed Queene of sweet eternitie.

With her in Heaven remaines her fame: on earth
  Each moderne Poet that can make a verse
Writes of Eliza, even at their Muse's birth.
  Then why not I weepe on Eliza's herse?
    Som-where in England shall my lines go sleep
    Till England read; and (England reading) weepe.

[1] " The 28th day of Aprill, being her funerall-day, at which time the cittie of Westminster was surcharged with multitudes of all sorts of people in their streetes, houses, windows, leads, and gutters, that came to see the obsequie; and when they beheld her statue or picture lying uppon the coffin set forth in royall robes, having a crowne uppon the head thereof, and a ball and sceptre in either hand; there was such a generall sighing, groning, and weeping, as the like hath not beene seene or knowne in the memorie of man, neyther doth any historie mention any people, time, or state, to make like lamentation for the death of their Soveraygne." Stow's Annals, p. 815.

ELIZA'S FUNERALL.

Then withered the primrose of delight,
   Hanging the head o're Sorowes garden wall:
When you might see all pleasures shun the light,
   And live obscurer at Eliza's fall.
Her fall from life to death; oh, stay not there!
   Though she were dead, the shril-tong'd trump of Heaven
Ras'd her againe, think that you see her heere:
   Even heere, oh where? not heere, shee's hence bereaven,
For sweet Eliza in Elizium lives,
   In joy beyond all thought. Then weepe no more,
Your sighing weedes put off, for weeping gives
   (Wayling her losse) as seeming to deplore
      Our future toward fortunes, morne not then:
      You cease awhile, but now you weepe agen.

Why should a soule in passion be deny'd
   To have true feeling of her essence misse!
My soule hath lost herselfe now deified,
   I needes must moane her losse, though crown'd with blisse.
Then give me leave, for I must weepe a-while,
   Till sorrowes deludge have a lower ebbe;
Let lamentation never finde a stile,
   To passe this dale of woe, untill the webbe
Appointed for my latest mourning weed
   Be spun and woven with a heavie hand;
Then will I cease to weepe, I will indeed,
   And every beating billowe will withstand.
      'Twill not be long before this web be spun,
      Dy'd blacke, borne out, and then my teares be done.

Of April's month the eight and twentith day,
   M. sixe hundred three, by computation:
Is the prefixed time for sorowes stay.
   That past: my mourning weedes grow out of fashion.
Shall I by prayer hasten on the time?
   Faine would I so, because mine eyes are drie,
What cannot prayers doe for soules divine,
   Although the bodies be mortallitie?
Divine she is for whome my Muse doth morne,
   Though lately mortall, now she sits on hie,
Glorious in Heaven, thither by angells borne,
   To live with them in blisse eternally.
      Then come faire day of joyfull smiling sorow,
      Since my teares dry, come happie day to-morow.

Yee herralds of my heart, my heavie groanes,
  My teares, which, if they could, would showre like raine;
My heavie lookes, and all my surdging mones,
  My mooning lamentations, that complayne,
When will you cease? or shall paine, never-ceasing,
  Seaze on my heart? oh, mollifie your rage,
Least your assaults, with over-swift increasing,
  Procure my death, or call on tymeles age.
She lives in peace, whome I do morne for so;
  She lives in Heaven, and yet my soule laments.
Since shee's so happie, I'le convert my woe
  To present joy, turne all my languishments.
    And with my sorrowes see the time doth wast,
    The day is come, and mid-day welnigh past.

Gaze, greedy eye: note what thou dost beholde,
  Our horizon is of a perfect hew,
As cleere as christall, and the day not olde:
  Yet thousand blackes present them to thy view.
Three thousand and od hundred clowds appere,
  Upon the earthly elament belowe,
As blacke as Night, trampling the lower sphere,
  As by degrees from place to place they goe.
They passe away: oh whether passe they then?
  Into a further climate out of sight,
Like clowds they were, but yet like clowded men,
  Whose presence turn'd the Day to sable Night.
    They vanish thence; note what was after seene,
    The lively picture of a late dead Queene;

Who, like to Phœbus in his golden car,
  Was the bright eye of the obscured day:
And though her glorious prograce was not far,
  Yet like the smiling Sunne, this semblance lay:
Drawne in a jetty chariot vayl'd with blacke,
  By foure faire palfraies that did hang the head,
As if their Lady-mistris they did lacke,
  And they but drew the figure of the dead.
Oh, yee spectators, which did view that sight!
  Say, if you truelie say, could you refraine,
To shed a sea of teares in deathes despight,
  That reft her hence, whome Art brought backe againe?
    He that knew her, and had Eliza seene,
    Would sweare that figure was faire England's Queene.

Faire England's Queene, even to the life, though dead,
  Speake if I write not true, did you not crye?
Cry foorth amaine, and say, her Princely head
  Lay on a pillowe of a crimson dye,
Like a sweet Beauty in a harmlesse slumber:
  She is not dead; no sure it cannot be:
Thus with unlikely hopes, the vulgar number
  Flatter themselves (oh sweet lyv'd flatterie).
Indeed a man of judgment would have thought,
  Had he not knowne her dead (but seene her so,
Tryumphant drawne in robes so richly wrought,
  Crowne on her head, in hand her scepter to).
    At this rare sight, he would have sworne and said,
    To Parliament rides this sweetly slumbring Maide.

But that my warrant's seald by Truthe's one hand,
  That in her counterfeit Art did excell:
I would not say that in this little land,
  Pigmalions equall doth admired dwell.
Enough of that: and now my teares are done;
  Since she that dy'd lives now above the spheres;
Luna's extinct, and now beholde the Sunne,
  Whose beames soake up the moysture of all teares.
A Phœnix from her ashes doth arise,
  A King at whose faire crowne all glory aymes.
God graunt his Royall vertues simpathize,
  With late ELIZA's, so God save King JAMES.
    He that in love to this, saies not Amen,
    Pray God the villaine never speake agen.   Amen.

The true Order and formall Proceeding at the Funerall of the most high, renowned, famous, and mightye Princesse, ELIZABETH, *of England, France, and Ireland, late Queene; from Whitehall to the Cathedral Church of Westminster; the* 28 *day of Aprill,* 1603 [1].

>Before thou reade, prepare thine eyes to weepe,
> If that thine eyes containe one liquid teare:
>Or if thou canst not mourne, fall dead in sleepe,
> For naught but death such sorrow can out-weare.
>   'Twill grieve heereafter soules as yet unborne,
>   That one soules losse, did make so many morne.
>
>Did make so many mourne? oh, heavie time,
> That brought a period to her happie life.
>But, cruell Death, the fatall stroke was thine,
> Her losse is ours, Heaven thereby gaines a Wife.
>   Yet had not Sin bin hugg'd in th' armes of Pride,
>   England had smil'd, and Heaven had lost a Bride.
>
>But now, oh now, our mourning weedes are on,
> And many thousand blacks for her are worne:
>Which do demonstrate that ELIZA's gone;
> For whose untimely losse so many morne.
>   What these sad Mourners are, good reader, see;
>   And seeing, reade; and reading, weepe with me.

[1] This Order of the Procession is exactly the same with that which is appended to a little tract entitled, "*Epicedium*: A Funeral Oration, upon the Death of the late lamented Queen of England, France, and Ireland. Written by *Infelice Academico Ignoto*," 1603, 4to.

⁂ In the Vetusta Monumenta, vol. III. plates 18 to 24 contain "The Funeral Procession of Queen Elizabeth, from a drawing of the time, supposed to be by the hand of William Camden, then Clarencieux King of Arms, which was in the possession of John Wilmot, Esq. Fellow of the Royal Society, who found it among the papers of his grandfather Peter Sainthill, Esq.; and by him since deposited in the British Museum." These engravings are illustrated by re-printing the Ceremonial here given in pages 621—626.

These Persons heereafter named came in their place and order, as was appointed. Also the names of such Noblemen and Gentlemen as caryed the Standerds and other Ornaments at the Funerall.

First, Knight Marshals men, to make roome.
Then followed 15 poore men.
Next 260 poore women, foure and foure in a ranke.
Then servants of Gentlemen, Esquires, and Knights.
Two Porters.
Four Trumpeters.
Rose Pursevant at Armes.
Two Sergeants at Armes.
The standerd of the *Dragon*, borne by the worshipfull Sir George Boucher.
Two Querries leading a horse, covered in blacke clothe.
Messengers of the Chamber.
Children of the Almondry.
Children of the Woodyard.
Children of the Scullery.
Children and Furners of the Pastry, Scalding-house, and Larder.

Then folowed Groomes; being,

Wheat Porters.	Caterye.
Coopers.	Boyling-house.
Wine Porters.	Larder.
Conducts in the Bake-house.	Kitchin.
Bel-ringer.	Lawndrie.
Maker of spice-bags.	Ewerie.
Cart-takers, chosen by the boord.	Confectionary.
Long carts.	Waferie.
Cart-takers.	Chaundrye.
Of the Almonry.	Pitcher-house.
Of the Stable.	Buttrie.
Woodyard.	Seller.
Scullery.	Pantrye.
Pastry.	Bake-house.
Scalding-house.	Counting-house.
Poultrye.	

Then Noblemen's and Embassador's servants,
And Groomes of the Chamber.
Foure Trumpeters.

Blewemantle.
A Sergeant at Armes.
The standerd of the *Greyhound*, borne by Master Herbert[1], brother to the Erle of Pembrooke.

Yeomen; being

Servitors in the Hall.	Waferye.
Cart-takers.	Purveyer of the waxe.
Porters.	Tallow-chandler.
Almonrye.	Chaundrye.
Herbengers.	Pitcher-house.
Wood-yard.	Brewers.
Scullery.	Butterye.
Pastrye.	Purveyers.
Poultrye and Scalding-house.	Seller.
Purveyers of the the Poultrye.	Pantrye.
Purveyers of the Acatrie.	Garneter.
Stable.	Bake-house.
Boyling-house.	Counting-house.
Larder.	Spicerye.
Kitchin.	Chamber.
Ewerye.	Robes.
Confectionarye.	Wardrobe.

Erles and Countesses servants.
Foure Trumpeters.

Portcullis.
A Sergeant at Armes.
Standerd of the Lyon, borne by M. Thomas Somerset.
Two Querries leading a horse, trapped with blacke velvet.
Sergeant of the Vestrie.
Gentlemen of the Chappel in copes; having the children of the Chappel in the middle of their company, in surplices, all of them singing.

Clarkes:

Deputie Clarke of the market.	Scullerye.
Clarkes extraordinarye.	Wood-yard.
Cofferer.	Poultrye.
Dyet.	Bake-house.
M. Cooke for the Housholde.	Acatrie.
Pastrie.	Stable.
Larder.	

[1] Sir Philip Herbert, created Earl of Montgomery, May 4, 1605; and, after the death of his brother, in 1630, Earl of Pembroke. He died Jan. 3, 1652.

Sergeants:

Gentlemen Harbenger.   Larder.
Wood-yard.   Ewerie.
Scullerye.   Seller.
Pastrye.   Pantrie.
Caterye.   Bake-house.

M. Cooke of the Kitchin.
Clarkes of the Equerrie.
Second Clarke of the Chaundry.
Third Clark of the Chaundry.
Second Clark of the Kitchin.
Third Clark of the Kitchin.
Supervisors of the Dresser.
Surveyor of the dresser for the Chamber.
Musitians.
Apothicaries.
Chirurgians.
Sewers of the Hall.
Marshall of the Hall.
Sewers of the Chamber.
Groom-porter.
Gentlemen Ushers, Quarter Wayters.
Clarke.
Marshall.
Avenor.
Chiefe Clark of the Wardrobe.
Chiefe Clark of the Kitchin.
Two Clarkes Controllers.
Clarkes of the Green-cloth.
M. of the Housholde.
Sir Henry Cocke, Cofferer.

Rouge Dragon.

The banner of Chester, borne by the Lord Zouch, between two Sergeants at Armes.
Clarkes of the Counsell.
Clarkes of the Privie Seale.
Clarkes of the Signet.
Clarkes of the Parliament.
Doctors of Phisicke.
Queene's Chaplaines.
Secretaries for the Latine and French tongues.

Rouge Crosse.

The banner of Cornwall, borne by the Lord Herbert (eldest sonne to the Earrl of Worcester), betweene two Sergeants at Armes.

Cheife Officers to the Lord Maior of London.
Aldermen of London.
Solicitor.
Attourney.
Sergeants at Law.
M. of the Revels.
M. of the Tents.
Knights Bachelers.
Lord Cheife Baron.
Lord Cheife Justice of the Common Plees.
M. of the Jewell-howse.
Knightes which have beene Embassadours.
Gentlemen Agents.
Sewers for the Queene.
Sewers for the Bodye.
Esquires of the Bodye.
Gentlemen of the Privye Chamber.
Gentlemen Pencioners, holding their pol-axes heades downewards, covered all with blacke.

Heere, Reader, stay: and if thou aske me whie,
'Tis to intreate thee beare them company.
But if th' high spirit cannot weepe so lowe,
Weepe with these flowers of honour that drooping goe.

Lancaster.

The banner of Wales, borne by Viscount Bindon.
Lord Mayor of London.
Sir John Popham.
Sir John Fortescue.
Sir Robert Cicill, Principall Secretarie.
Controller of the Housholde.
Treasurer of the Housholde.
Masters of Requests.
Agents for Venice, and for the Estates.

Windsor.

The banner of Ireland, borne by the Earle of Clanricard.
Barons.
Bishops.
Erles eldest sonnes.
Viscounts.
Dukes second sonnes.
Erles.

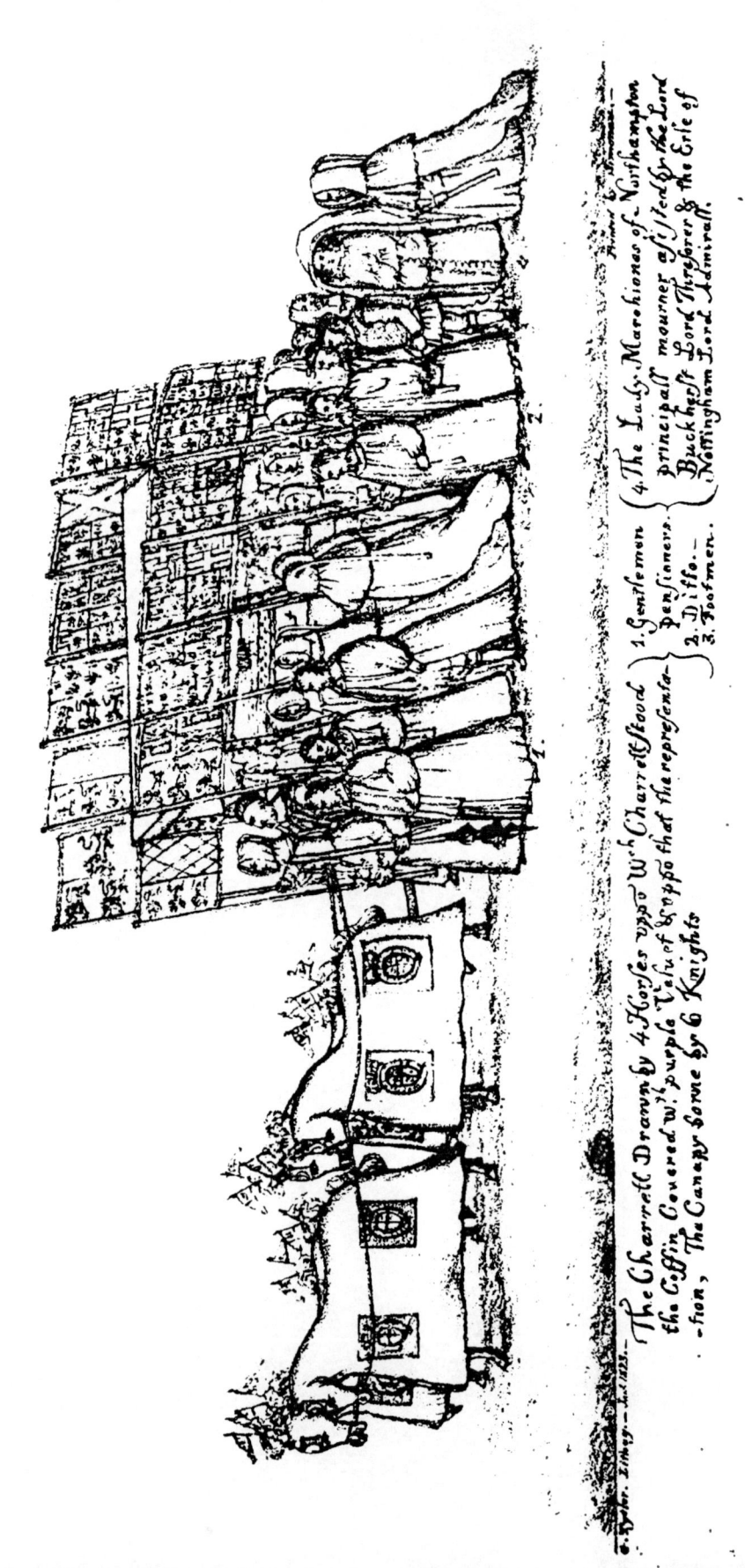

The Charrett Drawn by 4 Horses uppon w.ᶜʰ Charrett stood the Coffin Covered w.ᵗʰ purple Value of y.ᵉ y.ᵗ Suppᵒ that the representa- -tion, The Canopy borne by 6 Knights

1. Gentlemen
Pensioners.
2. Ditto.
3. Footmen.

4. The Lady Marchioness of Northampton principall mourner assisted by the Lord Buckhurst Lord Thresorer & the Erle of Nottingham Lord Admirall.

PART OF THE FUNERAL PROCESSION OF QUEEN ELIZABETH.

From a Drawing in the British Museum, supposed to be by W. Camden, then Clarenceux King at Arms.

Marquesses.
Bishop of Chichester, Almoner, and Preacher at the Funerall.
Lord Keeper.
Archbishop of Canterburie.
French Embassadour.
Foure Sergeants at Armes.
The great imbrodered banner of England, borne by the Earle
of Pembrooke, assisted by the Lord Howard of Effingham.
Somerset and *Richmond*.
Yorke, helme and crest.
Chester, target.
Norrey King at Armes, swoord.
Clarenciaux King at Armes, cote.

Art thou yet dry, as if thou hadst not wept?
Reade further then, and thou wilt force a teare.
But hadst thou seene her figure as she slept,
In memorie thou wouldst her semblance beare.
Whose deere remembrance would so touch thy minde,
That in thy passion thou no meane could'st finde.

The lively Picture of her Majesties whole body, in her parliament robes,
with a crowne on her head, and a scepter in her hand, lying on
the corpes inshrined in leade, and balmed; covered with
purple velvet; borne in a charriot, drawne by
foure horses, trapt in blacke velvet.
Gentlemen Ushers, with white roddes.
A canopie over the corpes, borne by sixe Knights.
Six Earles, assistants unto the bodye.
On each side the corpes six banerols, caryed by twelve Noblemen.
Footemen.
The Earle of Worcester, Maister of the Horse, leading the palfrey of honor.
Two Esquiers and a Groome, to attend and leade him away.
Gentleman Usher of the Privie Chamber.
Garter King at Armes.
The Lady Marques of NORTHAMPTON, Chiefe Mourner: assisted by the Lord Treasurer and the Lord Admirall; her traine caryed up by two Countesses, and Sir John Stanhop, Master Vice-chamberlaine.
Two Earles assistants to her.
Fourteen Countesses assistants.
Countesses.
Ladies of Honour.
Viscountesses.

Earles Daughters.
Baronesses.
Maides or Honour of the Privie Chamber.
Captaine of the Guard, with all the guard following, five and five in a ranke, holding their holberds downeward.

> Loe beere are all that in blacke weedes do mourne,
> And now methinkes I see thy count'nance turne:
> What trill thy teares? nay (Reader), then adon
> The firmament containes but one cleere Sun.
>
> And since that Delia is from hence bereaven,
> We have another Sun ordein d by Heaven.
> God graunt his virtues may so glorious shine,
> That after death he may be crown'd divine. Amen.

The twelve bannerols were caried by twelve Barons; beginning at the yongest first.

The first banner was of King Henry the second and Elenor of Aquitaine; caried by the Lord Norris.

The second, of King John and Isabel of Angolisme; caried by the Lord Compton.

The third, of King Henry the Third and Elenor of Arragon; caried by the Lord Chandois.

The fourth, of King Edward the First and Elenor of Castillia; caried by the Lord Rich.

The fift, of King Edward the Second and Isabel of France; caried by Lord Darcy of the South.

The sixt, of King Edward the Third and Philippa of Haynolt; caried by Lord Cromwel.

The seventh, of Edmond of Langley Duke of Yorke, and Isabel of Castil; caried by Lord Windsor.

The eight, of Richard Erle of Cambridge and Anne Mortimer; caried by Lord Darcy of the North.

The ninth, of Richard Duke of Yorke and Cicely Nevill; caried by Lord Dudley.

The tenth, of King Edward the Fourth and Elizabeth Woodvile; caried by Lord Gray.

The eleventh, of King Henry the Seventh and Elizabeth daughter to King Edward the Fourth; caried by Lord Cobham.

The twelfe, of Henry the Eight and Anne Bulleine, father and mother to our late deceased Queene; caried by the Lord De la ware.

Vivat JACOBUS, Angliæ, Scotiæ, Franciæ, et Hiberniæ, REX,

Fees given and parted betweene the Officers of Armes at the Funerall of Queene ELIZABETH [1].

"There is allowed in reward to the Officers of Armes, accordinge to auntient president, for theire attendaunce at the buriall of our late Soveraigne Ladie of blessed memorie Queene Elizabeth, the some of £40; receaved by Sr William Dethicke, Knight, als Garter, and Ralfe Brooke, Yorke Heraulte, of Steeven Thurger, servant to Sr John Fortescugh, Knight, Master of the Warderobe.

The particion of the same £40:	£.	s.	d.
To Garter	5	8	6
To Clarenceulxe	5	8	6
To Norrey	5	8	6
To Chester } To Yorke }	5	8	6
To Richemond } To Somerset }	5	8	6
To Windesor } To Lankaster }	5	8	6
To Rougecrosse } To Rougedragon } To Portcullis } To Bluemantle }	5	8	6
Geven by us in reward to Mr. Thurger that delivered us this £.40	2	0	0
	£.39	19	6

[1] Harl. MSS. 69, fo. 60 a.

ATROPOÏON DELION, or the DEATH OF DELIA:

with the Teares of her Funerall.

A Poetical Excursive Discourse of our late Eliza.—T. N. G.[1]

Quis ejus oblitus.

To the Right Honorable my Lady ALICE, Countesse of DARBIE[2], now wife to the Right Honorable Sir THOMAS EGERTON, Knight, Lord Keeper of the Great Seal of England, and one of his Majesties most honorable Privie Counsell.

Right Honorable, having no means at all to make knowne the humble affection I beare unto your good Ladyship, but in putting the patronizing of this my poore paines upon your Honour: hoping first, for the tender love you bore to the *Delia* of my sorrowing, you will deigne both to looke over it, and favour it: next, for the hartie love (in no little honourable kindnesse) your Ladyship bore to your humble servant my late uncle *Marmaduke Newton;* who in the bitter paines of his death, discoursed the bountifull affection your Ladyship bore unto him, and what losse he had sustained in losing so good a Lady and Mistris: which corsite inwardly so greeved him, that he grew weerie of the World, lamenting to his last gaspe, that he had not time to preferre me to your Ladyship's favour, that his former love towards you, and your three honourable Daughters, dying in him, might live in mee. And thus hoping that with the remembrance of both, your Ladiship will deigne to accept my paines to your favour, in the amplest hope of my desire.

Your Ladyship's devoted in all humilitie, THO. NEWTON.

To the Right Honorable my Lady ANNE STANLEY, *Lady* STRANGE.

  A Silver shower from your rich orient eyes,
  N Akte trickling downe those Alpes where beautie keepeth,
      Would more adorne the tombe where *Delia* lies,
      Since that a Virgin for a Virgin weepeth.
      Good Lady, from your heart one thought I crave,
      To thinke how poore your *Delia* lies in grave:
      And if to weepe a teare, that will not move ye,
      Infortunate was she, so deare to love ye:
      But I dare sweare your eyes have wept so many,
      That you are not a teare behinde with any.   T. N.

[1] Imprinted at London for W. Johnes, at the Signe of the Gunne, near Holborne Conduit, 1603.
[2] Of this Lady and her three Daughters, see before, p. 583.

ON THE DEATH OF DELIA, 1603.

To the Right Honourable my Lady FRANCIS.

F Ainting with sorrow this my youngling Muse,
R Equires as much of you for *Delia's* death:
A Teare is small: eyes, that are sorrowes sluce,
N Ever drops one, for one so deare on earth,
C Ould all your teares at once be dry distill'd,
I Know you would not leave one drop unshead,.
S O deare you lov'd your *Delia*, wrapt in lead.

To the Right Honourable my Lady ELIZABETH.

E Yes that before her death, did then behold her,
L Amentes in flood of teares to lose their seeing,
I N yours no lesse, I know, your teares infolde her:
S O heavie bears your heart her losse of beeing.
A Dde one (good Lady) more, at my desire,
B Ut for to give my teares a worthier shade:
E Lse shall my hopes and paynes with griefe retire,
T Hat for your Sister's sake and yours were made,
H Ere with my paynes my bounden heart I give,
E Ver to love a *Stanley*, whiles I live.

In Laudem Authoris.

Passe foorth, pure Jem, to subjects censuring;
   And what thy vertue yeelds, let subjects read:
Free is thy heart from false dissembling;
   For which, thrice happie, in so blest a deed.
Small is thy port, yet with rich Trueth art grac'd,
   Where she (great Empresse) ever singing liveth,
(Before his christal Thron, which al good giveth)
More white than snow, free'd from infirmitie,
   Crown'd with pure Lawrell of Eternitie;
Many have writ sad *Elegies* of woe:
   But these true Mourners with her *Funerall* goe.

ON THE DEATH OF DELIA, 1603.

A Poetical Excursive Discourse of our late ELIZA.

CASTITAS.

Late I sad Angell in an Angel's breast
   Inthroned late in glory, state, and blisse,
But now displac't to mourne my throne at rest,
   I see how brittle state and glory is:
My vertuous pride, so proude, was never seene,
   Nor so preserv'd from blot, from breath, or staine:
Or ever was so rich in any Queene,
   As in this *Delia* whom I thus complaine:
No stranger's eye but weepes that never knew her,
   What then can mine, that never lodge without her?
Or what can *Delos* soules that still did view her?
   Or her chaste beauteous traine that kept about her?
Ye *Nymphs* to her link't all like burnish't amber,
   Why let ye death approach her Privy Chamber [1]?

NYMPHÆ.

Mad in dispaire (poore soules) we fainting stood,
   Arm'd all with blades of hopes and speares of praiers,
Pik'd hanging down our haire to shed Death's blood,
   And drench his forces in a sea of teares.
With stormes of sighs we striv'd to weake his strength,
   And fought with earnest courage on our knee:
Yet pale-fac't hag with creeping dart at length
   Depriv'd us (wretches) of our Deitie:
When we awak't, and watcht all sleepie houres,
   That mid-night Death eche heavie braine doth cover,
That end of all usurping ending powers,
   Robb'd her of life, and us, who deare did love her.
O Lords! why let yee such a one bereave her,
   That makes us al disper'st mourn, weep, and leave her.

HEROES.

Our wits that ever were imploy'd to keepe
   Her sacred person safe and still secure:
Our eyes that now upon her Hearce do weepe,
   Scarce wink't at all, since first she seem'd unsure.

---

[1] In the hour of her departure, Queen Elizabeth ordered her musicians into her chamber, and died hearing them. Whilst in health, she had been herself a performer on the virginals. See Hawkins's History of Music, vol. III. p. 458; vol. V. p. 201.

But wandered in our wisedomes arts, and skill,
  To find a meane, by all the meanes we could,
Which meane we found, but being mortal still,
  No meane immortall could we finde for gold,
Wits, witlesse thus, ceas'd to proceed in paine:
  Eyes, eyelesse thus, ceas'd to be blinde in seeing:
Heart, heartlesse thus, ceas'd longer to maintaine
  That wrong, which had no helpe on earth a being.
O world! why didst thou foster such a foe,
  To be chast *Delia's* traytour, *Cynthia's* woe.

MUNDUS.

I Mourne for *Delia*, for I partly knew her,
  And partly knew her not; yet wholly mourne,
The part that knew her well, makes tother rew her,
  And both together, waile to be forlorne.
For in the spacious multitude of me,
  I find a great defect, though one be small,
The losse of *Delia's* crown'd Virginitie:
  But *Delia's* grace and person most of all:
In this (poor world) I differ from the skies,
  For they inlarge and never break their number,
And them they winne, to thrones eternall rise:
  And those I loose, intomb'd in claye lye under:
O Earth, why did thy wombe beare such a brood,
  That thus (remorcelesse) drank my *Delia's* blood?

TERRA.

Delia, subject of the world's lamenting,
  Was such a glorious issue of my wombe,
In her above the rest, grew my contenting,
  But now the mother, and her issues tombe:
Alas too timelesse did I bring her foorth,
  Since she too timelesse is returnde againe;
More joy I took to see her living worth
  Than thus in warping of my *Delia* slaine:
Her life, how rich a life was it to many!
  The sight of her, how rich a comfort blist it:
How then her death, is it not griefe to any?
  Yes, griefe; with crosse of hopes to them that wisht it.
Delos I wayle, and with mine eyes beweep her,
  That neither thou nor I hadst power to keepe her.

ON THE DEATH OF DELIA, 1603.

DELOS.

If any place of pleasure or delight,
   As Garden, Mount, or Vale, by River's side,
Had fed her vitall spirits, with their sight;
   Then would not I have moorn'd, nor *Delia* di'de.
The whitest [1] seat I had, my *Delia* had it.
   The greenest [2] Palace of my brest's support,
The richest [3] Mount (the richest hands had made it)
   Was hers, where she did lastly keepe her Court:
That time of last, would it had never beene!
   Then had my late dead *Delia* lasted ever.
For one poore period of *Time*, my Queene
   And me, doth both incorporate and sever.
Then woe to thee, O *Time*, for thou dost wrong us,
That wouldst not lend us time for her among us.

TEMPUS.

I was the Aseclist that did attend her,
   Weft to her vitall web, her breathing scope:
I was that *Time*, against my will, did ende her,
   And he that set the passelesse point of hope,
Along my snaylish-journey as I went.
   I led my *Delia* in a dextrous hand,
And having travel'd farre (at last a Saint)
   My chast companion, wisht me take a stand,
Till she afresh had gotten breath and winde:
   Now I that had no joynts to rest nor bend,
Constrain'd to travell, left my Saint behind,
   Els had we travel'd to our journey's end.
Thou fatall *Clotho*, to my Sacred sweet,
Wouldst not afford her *Time*, heart, breath, nor feet.

CLOTHO.

I stucke the distaffe in my bosome fast
   Whereon my *Delia's* life was wrapt in flaxe,
And duely sate, till many yeeres were past
   My distaffe bare and threed ful length was waxt:
Which threed when first my Sisters gan to spin it
   How fast they drew, so fast it rol'd and knotted,
That more their care and paine was to begin it,
   Doubting too timelesse breach to it allotted.

[1] Whitehall.   [2] Greenwich.   [3] Richmond.

But having spun a full third part and more,
  The other two it turned all to gold,
And spun not halfe so harsh as 't did before,
  Till all at last upon a knot it rold.
So, *Lachesis*, thy spinning and my paine,
Was but to put on *Time*, and done in vaine.

LACHESIS.

Alas, had I had substance whereupon to pull,
  Or where withall to adde unto her threed,
My fingers should not wearie, nor mine eies be dull,
  Nor night nor day from worke lay down my head:
For rich was he that might but kisse her hand,
  And much esteem'd that had her word of praise:
How proud was he, might at her door but stand
  And hold a Polax in her princely dayes!
Amongst these riches then, how rich was I,
  That had both twisting, twining of the Clew!
Ne greater riches with my *Delia* die,
  Then whom she lov'd, must seek their love anew.
Oh had I *(Atropos)* flax for her life,
Thou shouldst not only spin, but breake thy knife.

ATROPOS.

So Angel-like, immortal seeming Saint,
  The tract of her most chast and prosperous life,
Did make the worldlings thinke that scarce constraint,
  Could bring her threed once under yoake of knife.
I cannot chuse but mourne her death, their grief,
  Shee did so love them: they no lesse deserv'd it.
And held her next to *Jove;* on Earth for chiefe:
  Her as her love, and love as her preserv'd it.
If *Clotho's* distaffe had been still supplide,
  And *Lachesis* small fingers spinning longer:
My knife should still have hung close by my side,
  And neither edge nor poynt toucht threed nor wrong'd her.
But, *Nature*, thou art she that would't not give
Substaunce of life, to make my *Delia* live.

NATURA.

When first my curious pensill did purtraie
  The pure composed limbes of *Delia's* forme;
Meethought my fingers strived to assaie
  A worke immortall, not terrestrial borne.

And having brought it to a full perfection,
  The very Gods descended down to see
Their next celestiall shape, with such affection:
  It pleas'd them so, they would have robbed mee.
But I more glorying in my labour taken,
  Grew jealous of the same, the while 'twas mine:
Since when, my worke itselfe had me forsaken,
  The Gods have seeted her in heaven to shine:
Death was the fatall messenger that crost her,
She having spent my strength, I having lost her.

Mors.

I was that fatall executioner,
  That gave that fatall stroke of *Delia's* death:
I also was that fatall messenger
  That brought this fatall newes into the Earth.
I was that theefe which stole into her chamber;
  And first that made her faint, the *Nymphes* to wonder:
I was that traytour which did feare no danger
  For acting treason to be rent asunder:
Yet what I did was by the Gods agreed,
  And not by me, but by the Powers above her;
They, not my dart, had made your *Delia* bleed;
  But for to make her know how they did love her:
A Quier of Angels did discend beneathe,
To take her up to heaven, too good for earthe.

Angeli.

Cease, *Nymphes*, with teares to overcharge your eies,
  For *Delia* weeps not now, that she hath left ye,
Comfort yourselves in earth for she in skies,
  Comforted by them, which late bereft ye,
So many yeeres the Gods did let you keepe her,
  In tender love for to support your peace,
But being gone, it nought availes to weep her.
  Shee now enjoyes a crowne of longer lease:
Let this suffice how looth she was to part.
  So long as she had tongue, hand, eye, or breath,
Till when our Quire of Angels tooke her heart,
  She then bid welcome joyes, and farwell earth.
Where once each soule his *Delia's* soule shall see,
Crown'd in another kinde of Majestie.

FAMA.

Bright Heavens, you that enjoy our *Delia's* soule,
   And death with death that caus'd our Ladies moorne,
That did the wisedome of our Lords controule,
   And striv'd against all *Synthus'* power in scorne,
Know this, that *Fame* immortall is on earth,
   As you in heaven, and will not lose her so:
You have her substance: I a God beneath,
   Will keepe the substance of her life to shew,
I have her shape drawne in as limely die,
   As if my *Delia* were herselfe in being:
And that's her *Delia's* selfe unto my eye,
   I need no other *Delia* for my seeing:
And yet methinkes shee not in heaven essign'de,
So plaine I keepe her *Trophey* in my minde.

I have in writing Golden Pens to prayse her,
   In datelesse volumes of the silver ayre,
The very stile so loftie high shall raise her,
   That *Time* shall be too short to tear her haire:
Wherein shall first her chastitie be writ
   As pure in picture as itselfe was pure:
Next her Religion, Love, her Arte, and Wit,
   So faire, that *Delia's* life may still endure,
Then *Synthus*, thinke thou hast thy *Delia* ever:
   The Heavens do keep her soule, thou keep'st her life,
Which life (I vow) from thee shall never sever,
   Nor subject bee to Fate's Atropian knife.
Take this to wipe thy bleared eyes againe,
Her life is thine, though Heaven her soule containe.

CASTITAS.

At length to Church I brought my *Delia's* Hearse,
   Blindfolded (for my eyes were blinde with crying)
And all along the way in howling verse,
   I sung a dirge unto her utmost dying:
The birdes above, while I did sing beneath,
   With heartlesse yeelping fil'd the silver ayre,
Ne with a shriller Quier then I on earth,
   For all I sobb'd, I howl'd, and rent my haire:
But then to helpe my Song my *Delia's* Singers,
   (I meane her boyes new turn'd to blacke from red,
Like lambs by *Uthers* nurs'd, with *Orpheus'* fingers)
   Mixt teares with notes to see her buried:

And to be chang'd to clay, her robes from gould,
Her princely guard to woormes, her bed to mould.

NYMPHÆ.

Now hath attendance done the last commande,
   That love or duetie to our *Delia* ought:
It need not watch her call, or slender hand:
   The one is mute, the other wastes to nought.
Now are our Revels and our dauncing sport
   Tvrnde all to sighes, each one to private plaine:
Now *Delia* can no more remoove her Court,
   The Grave's her Pallace, and the woormes her traine.
She is arrayde in Robes, in Pearle, in Stone:
   But not so rich as she was wont to bee:
For why; shee lackes us Ladyes every one,
   The worst herselfe, shee lackes as well as wee:
Her robes are sullen, such as Earth containe:
Her Stones unpollisht, Pearle, Earthe's sinking raine.

HEROES.

Our eyes did now behold their last beholding
   Of *Delia's* shape, wrapt in obscuritie:
Till that the crummie Earth, her corpes infoulding,
   Had blinded us with his condensitie:
Returning then our thoughtes, began to paint
   Her lyvelie shape with new remberaunce:
And comming to her face, a new complaint
   Grew, thinking on so sweete a countenaunce,
That then we thought we had anew to make
   Both mourning vestments, tears, grave, hearse, and all:
For *Delia* seem'd anew in life to wake,
   When was but done anew her Funerall,
A grief unto us all, to them most wretched,
To whom our *Delia's* love and bountie stretched.

PHISICI.

With chastitie the *Nimphes* and noble Peeres,
   Our over-weeried wittes and drowsie eyes,
Restles retires with droughtlesse spring of teares,
   To thinke how *Delia* in a colde bed lyes:
We thought our Arte would have preserv'd her ever,
   But now we see his purest power and strength

Was but for to prolong (and not deliver)
  Her life, which Death did overcome at length:
No trust we put in *Phisick's* Arte at all
  But this; when alwayes we began to make it,
For life no more to be effectuall,
  Till when her stomack's strength did faile to take it:
Which weekenesse finding in her vitall veines,
Then ended she her life, and we our paines.

Sepulchrum Castitati Loquens.

Hence from my mouth, and wast no more thy teares:
  No tears prevail to take my *Delia* from me:
No sighs can make my breast that thee up-rears
  Dissolve in two; with kneeling thus upon me:
But to the greene grasse sprouted hilles be winging,
  Where pleasure doth release the time of Sorrow,
And where in pleasure Sorrow sits a singing,
  When one sad soule another's breast doth borrow:
There make a chaplet of the sweetest flowers,
  That prettie pinked grove or dale doth yeeld:
There shade thy temples in those templed bowers
  That canopize the haunters of the field;
And round about thee in the springing meedes,
The *Swaynes* will finger ditties to their reedes.

Or els, gird bow and quiver to thy side,
  And run with *Cynthia* in the *Pheboone*-parke.
To seeke the hart where he his head doth hide,
  With bended bow whiles chopping talbots barke
That after midday-heat some willow under
  You may betake yourselfe to bathe and wash
In some clear spring kept coole with such a number
  That none may see you nak'd to sport and dash,
Thou may'st be happie, that in *Brumae's* snow,
  Thy flight was not decreed nor *Delia's* death,
On every twigge a thousand pleasures grave,
  That now a Heaven doth scarce resemble Earth:
Leave kneeling teares, bid farewell Court and Trayne,
For them thou know'st not when to see againe.

ON THE DEATH OF DELIA, 1603.

SEPULCHRUM NYMPHIS LOQUENS.

As her I have dismi'st, so must I you:
    Nought can release your Queene, my armes must keep her;
No sad submission, though you bend and bow,
    Are ought of force to make ye more beweep her:
Binde up your haire, wipe both your cheekes and eyes,
    Leave wringing, kneeling, thumping of my brest;
Envy not me, though in me *Delia* lyes,
    For shee contented gives herselfe to rest,
For I am night, and bed; her life was day,
    Wherein cours'd and recours'd her cares of minde,
Which wearied her at last: but I for aye
    Am that sweete rest, wherin she rest doth finde:
O *Nymphs!* for *Delia* why so much complaine yee?
Doubtlesse as good a Queene will entertaine yee.

SEPULCHRUM HEROIBUS LOQUENS.

Assemble now no more for consultation:
    (I meane, for *Delia's* safetie, life, and state)
I take upon me now her preservation,
    All wits extending duetie comes too late;
You have committed her unto my keeping,
    Shee is my Prisoner, I am her Gaole.
The debts so great, that neither gold nor weeping,
    Nor all the world beside, can be her baile.
Bondage is judg'd to be her punishment,
    Death officer to execute her woe:
For *Time* perpetuall imprisonment.
    Perpetual to earth, to Heaven not soe.
For *Jove's* sweete *Mercurie* will from her tombe
Release your *Delia* at the day of Dome.

VERMES MEDICIS LOQUENS.

You that by Art procure the ease of man
    With short abridgement of continuance,
'Tis short, you see; for not beyond a spanne
    The greatest Prince of all you can advance:
Your ease is wasting ease, and Nature spendeth,
    Perchance you'le say it addes unto the breath;
Not so in age, for then it but befriendeth
    The heart, to bring it to a pleasant death:

For now your labours vaine you see at last,
   The leafes and rules of *Gallen* lies at rest,
And now when all your hope is dead and past,
   No more you search to finde *Probatum est.*
Now what's your art in power, ne all you have,
   Cannot preserve her bodie in the grave.

For what's her body now, whereon such care
   Was still bestow'd in all humilitie?
Where are her robes? is not her body bare,
   Respectles in the Earth's obscurite?
Now where's her Glory and her Majestie?
   Her triple crowne, her honour, state, and traine?
Are not her riches all in povertie,
   And all her earthly Gloryes past and vaine?
Now where are all her cates, her glorious dishes,
   That were by death of sundry creatures spread,
Her fowles, her fat *Quadrupidists* and fishes,
   Are they not living, now your *Delia's* dead?
And we in life too filthy for her tooth,
   Are now in death the next unto her mouth.

With that the greedy wormes their heads shrunk down,
   The grave shut close her heavie brooken ground,
And crawling crept unto her livelesse crowne
   Much like to flyes about a bleeding wound,
Then all her mourners eyes were veil'd and blinde;
   They weepe not now with passion of the sight,
But, with a true remembrance of the minde,
   They meane to mourne their *Delia* day and night:
Thence they returne, where *Delia* helplesse lyes,
   Each one betakes him to a private place,
To wipe the teares of over-delug'd eyes,
   Instead of her to welcome such a grace,
As all the boundes of *Europe*, ne the Earth,
   Affords a wiser Prince of greater birth.

A CHAINE OF PEARLE;

or, a Memoriall of the Peerles Graces and heroick vertues of Queene ELIZABETH, of glorious memory.

Composed by the Noble Lady DIANA PRIMROSE [1].

"Dat ROSA mel apibus, qua fugit ARANEA virus."

TO ALL NOBLE LADIES AND GENTLE-WOMEN.

To you the honour of our noble sex,
I send this Chaine, with all my best respects;
Which, if you please to weare for her sweet sake,
For whom I did this slender Poem make:
You shall erect a trophie to her name,
And crowne yourselves with never-fading fame.

Devoted to your vertues,
DIANA P.

TO THE EXCELLENT LADY, THE COMPOSER OF THIS WORKE.

Shine forth *(Diana)*, dart thy golden raies,
On her blest Life and Raigne, whose noble praise
Deserves a quill pluckt from an angel's wing,
And none to write it but a crowned king.
Shee, shee it was, that gave us golden daies,
And did the English name to Heaven raise:
Blest be her name! blest be her memory!
That *England* crown'd with such felicity.

And thou, the *Prime-Rose* of the *Muses* nine,
(In whose sweete Verse Eliza's fame doth shine,
Like some resplendent star in frosty night)
Hast made thy native splendor far more bright.

[1] London: Printed for Thomas Paine, and are to be sold by Philip Waterhouse, at his shop at the signe of St. Pauls-head, in Canning-street, neere London-stone, 1603. 4to, ten leaves.

Since all thy PEARLES[1] are peerless-orient,
And to thyself a precious ornament.
　　This is my censure of thy ROYAL CHAINE
　　Which a far *better censure*[2] well may claime.
　　　　　　　　　　　DOROTHY BERRY.

THE INDUCTION.

As Golden Phœbus, with his radiant face,
　　Enthron'd in his triumphant chaire of state,
The twinkling stars and asterismes doth chase,
　　With his imperiall scepter, and doth hate
All consorts in this starry monarchy,
As prejudiciall to his Soveraignty.
So great Eliza, England's brightest Sun,
　　The world's renowne and everlasting lampe,
Admits not here the least comparison,
　　Whose glories doe the greatest Princes dampe,
That ever scepter swai'd, or crowne did weare,
Within the verge of either hemispheare.
Thou English Goddesse, Empresse of our sex,
　　O thou whose name still raignes in all our hearts;
To whom are due our ever-vow'd respects!
　　How shall I blazon thy most Royall parts?
Which in all parts did so divinely shine,
As they deserve *Apollo's* quill (not mine).
Yet since the Gods accept the humble vowes
　　Of mortalls; deigne (O thou star-crowned Queene)
T'accept these ill-composed pearly-rowes
　　Wherein thy glory chiefly shall be seene.
For by these lines so blacke and impolite,
Thy swan-like lustre shall appeare more white.
　　　　Thy Emperiall Majesties eternall votary,
　　　　　　　　　　　DIANA.

---

[1] In a scarce Poem, entitled, "Newes, &c. of Sir Francis Drake," 1587, the following lines occur:
　　　Tryumph, O England, and rejoyce,
　　　　And prayse thy God uncessantly
　　　For thys thy Queene, that *Perle* of choyse,
　　　　Which God doth blesse with victory.

[2] i. e. judgment, opinion.

The First Pearle.—Religion.

The goodliest Pearle in faire Eliza's Chaine
Is true Religion, which did chiefly gaine
A royall lustre to the rest, and ti'de
The hearts of all to her when Mary di'de.
And though Shee found the realme infected much
With superstition, and abuses, such
As (in all humane judgement) could not be
Reform'd without domesticke mutiny,
And great hostility from Spaine and France,
Yet shee, undaunted bravely did advance
Christ's glorious ensigne, maugre all the feares
Or dangers which appear'd: and for ten yeares,
She swaid the scepter with a Ladies hand,
Nor urging any Romist in the land,
By sharpe edicts, the Temple to frequent,
Or to partake the Holy Sacrament.
But factious Romanists, not thus content,
Their agents to their Holy Father sent,
Desiring him, by sollemne bull, proclaime
Elizabeth an Heretike, and name
Some other Soveraigne, which might erect
Their making masse, and hence forthwith eject
The Evangelicall profession,
Which flourisht under her protection.
The Pope to this petition condescends,
And soone his Leaden Bull to England sends,
Which by one Felton on the Bishop's gate
Of London was affixed; but the State
For that high treason punisht him with death,
That would dethrone his Queene Elizabeth.
Yet was this ball of wild-fire working still,
In many Romanists which had a will;
The present state and governement to change,
That they in all idolatrie might range;
And hence it came that great Northumberland
Associate with Earle of Westmerland,
And many moe, their banners did display
In open field, hoping to win the day.
Against these Rebells, noble Sussex went,
And soone their bloudy purpose did prevent:

Westmerland fled, Northumberland did die,
For that foule crime, and deepe disloyalty;
Having engaged thousands in that cause;
After which time, the Queene made stricter lawes,
Against Recusants; and with Lyon's heart
Shee bang'd the Pope, and tooke the Gospell's part.
The Pope, perceiving that his Bull was baited
In such rude sort, and all his hopes defeated;
Cries out to Spaine for helpe; who takes occasion,
Thereby t'attempt the conquest of this nation.
But such sage Counsellers Eliza had,
As, though both Spaine[1] and Rome were almost mad
For griefe and anger, yet they still did faile,
And against England never could prevaile.

The Second Pearle.—Chastity.

The next faire Pearle that comes in order heere
Is Chastity, wherein Shee had no peere,
Mongst all the noble Princesses which then
In Europe wore the Royall Anadem.
And though for beauty shee an Angell was,
And all our sex did therein far surpasse;
Yet did pure unspotted Chastitie
Her heavenly beautie rarely beautifie.
How many Kings and Princes did aspire,
To win her love? in whom that vestall fire
Still flaming, never would shee condescend
To Hymen's rites, though much shee did commend,
That brave French Monsieur who did hope to carry
The Golden Fleece, and faire Eliza marry.
Yea Spanish Philip, husband to her Sister,
Was her first sutor, and the first that mist her:
And though he promis'd that the Pope by Bull
Should license it, shee held it but a gull:
For how can Pope[2] with God's owne law dispence?
Was it not time such Popes to cudgell hence?
Thus her impregnable Virginity,
Throughout the world her fame did dignify.

---

[1] In ultimam rabiem furoremque conversi.

[2] Yet his Canonists say, "Benè dispensat Dominus Papa contra Apostolum. Extra de Renunc. Ca. post translationem."

And this may be a document to all,
The Pearle of Chastity not to let fall:
Into the filthy durt of foule desires,
Which Satan kindles with his hell-bred fires;
For whether it be termed Virginall
In Virgins, or in Wives stil'd Conjugall.
Or Viduall in Widdowes, God respects
All equally, and all alike affects.
And here I may not silent overpasse
That noble Lady of the Court, which was
Sollicited by Taxis that great Don,
Embassador for Spaine [1] (when shee was gone)
Who to obtaine his will, gave her a Chaine
Of most rare orient Pearle, hoping to gaine
That worthy Lady to his lust; but shee,
That well perceiv'd his Spanish Policy,
His faire Chaine kept, but his foule offer scorn'd,
That sought (thereby) her husband to have horn'd;
Taxis repulst, sent to her for his Chaine,
But (as a trophie) shee did it retaine;
Which noble president may all excite,
To keep this pearle which is so orient bright.

The Third Pearle.—Prudence.

How prudent was her government appear'd
By her wise counsels, by the which shee steer'd
In the most dangerous times that ever were,
Since King or Queene did crowne in England weare.
Her choice of famous Councellors did shew,
That shee did all the rules of Prudence know.
For though her wit and spirit were divine,
Counsels (shee knew) were best, where more combine:
That for experience and deepe policy
Are well approved; whose fidelity
Retaines them in the bonds of loyall love,
And no great pensions from their Prince can move.
Thus rul'd shee prudently, with all her power,
With Argus eyes foreseeing every houre
All dangers imminent, least any harmes
Should us befall by Spanish arts or armes.

[1] Primo Jacobi; related by the honorable Knight and Baronet Sir Richard Houghton, of Houghton Tower.

This gift in her was much more emminent,
In that it is so rarely incident
To our weake Sex: and, as a presious stone,
Deepe set in gold, shines fairer then alone,
Or set in lead; so did all Graces shine
In Her more gloriously, because divine:
For Kings are Gods, and Queenes are Goddesses
On Earth, whose sacred Vertue best expresses
Their true Divinitie: wherein if wee
Them imitate, tis our Felicity.
This Pearle of Prudence then wee all should prize
Most highly, for it doth indeed comprise
All Morall Vertues, which are resident
In that blest soule, where this is president.

The Fourth Pearle.—Temperance.

The golden Bridle of Bellerephon
Is Temperance, by which our passsion,
And Appetite, we conquer and subdue
To Reason regiment: else may we rue
Our yeelding to men's Syren-blandishment,
Which are attended with so foule events.
This Pearle in her was so conspicuous,
As that the King[1] her Brother still did use,
To stile her His sweete Sister Temperance;
By which her much admir'd selfe-governance,
Her passions still shee checkt, and still shee made
The world astonisht, that so undismaid
Shee did with equall tenor[2] still proceede
In one faire course, not shaken as a reed,
But built upon the rocke of Temperance;
Not daz'd with Feare not maz'd with any chance;
Not with vaine Hope (as with an emptie spoone)
Fed or allur'd to cast beyond the Moone;
Not with rash anger too precipitate,
Not fond to love, nor too, too prone to hate;
Not charm'd with Parasites, or Syrens songs,
Whose hearts are poison'd, though their sugred tongues
Sweare, vow, and promise all fidelity,
When they are bruing deepest villainy.

[1] Edward.   [2] Semper eadem.

Not led to vaine or too profuse expence,
Pretending thereby State Magnificence:
Not spending on these momentary pleasures
Her precious time; but deeming her best treasures
Her subjects Love, which she so well preserv'd,
By sweet and milde demeanor [1], as it serv'd
To guard her surer than an Armie Royall;
So true their Loves were to her and so loyall:
O Golden Age! O blest and happie yeares!
O Musicke sweeter than that of the Spheares!
When Prince and People mutually agree
In sacred concord, and sweet symphonie!

The Fift Pearle.—Clemency.

Her Royall Clemency comes next in view,
The Vertue which in Her did most renew
The image of Her Maker, who in that
Exceeds himselfe, and doth commiserate
His very rebells, lending them the light
Of Sunne and Moone, and all those diamonds bright.
So did Eliza cast Her golden rayes
Of Clemency on those which many wayes
Transgrest Her lawes, and sought to undermine
The Church and State, and did with Spaine combine [2].
And though by rigor of law Shee might,
Not wronging them, have taken all Her right,
Yet Her innate and princelie Clemencie
Mov'd Her to pardon their delinquencie,
Which sought Her gracious mercy, and repented
Their misdemeanors, and their crimes lamented.
So doth the kingly lyon with his foe,
Which once prostrate, he scornes to work his woe.
So did this Vertues sacred Auri-flame
Immortalize our great Eliza's name.

The Sixt Pearle.—Justice.

Her Justice next appeares, which did support
Her Crowne, and was her Kingdomes strongest Fort.
For should not lawes be executed well,
And malefactors curb'd a very Hell

---

[1] Omnibus incutiens blandum per pectora amorem.   [2] Monstra, teterrima monstra.

Of all confusion and disorder would
Among all States ensue. Here to unfold
The exemplary penalties of those,
Which to the Realme were knowne and mortall foes:
And some putrid members pared away,
Lest their transcendant villainy should sway
Others to like disloyalty; would aske
A larger volume, and would be a taske
Unfit for Feminine hands, which rather love
To write of pleasing subjects, than approve
The most deserved slaughtering of any;
Which justly cannot argue Tyranny.
For though the Pope have lately sent from Rome,
Strange bookes and pictures painting out the doome
Of his pretended Martyrs: as that they
Were baited in beares skins, and made a prey
To wilde beasts, and had bootes with boiling lead
Drawne to their legges, and hornes nail'd to their head;
Yet all our British world knowes these are fables,
Chimæras, phantasms, dreames, and very bables
For fooles to play with; and right goblin sprights,
Wherewith our nurses oft their babes affrights.
His Holinesse these martyrdomes may adde
To the Golden Legend; for they are as madde,
That first invented them, as [1] he that writ
That branelesse booke: and yet some credit it:
For cruelty and fond credulity,
Are the maine pillers of Rome's Hierarchy.

The Seventh Pearle.—Fortitude.

This goodly Pearle is that rare Fortitude,
Wherewith this sacred Princesse was endu'd;
Witnesse her brave undaunted looke, when Parry
Was fully bent Shee should by him miscarry:
The wretch confest, that Her great Majestie
With strange amazement did him terrifie.
So Heavenly-gracefull, and so full of awe,
Was that Majesticke Queene, which when some saw,
They thought an Angell did appeare: Shee shon
So bright, as none else could her Paragon.

[1] Vappa Voraginosa.

But that which doth beyond all admiration
Illustrate Her, and in Her this whole nation;
Is that heroicke march of Her's and speech
At *Tilbury* [1], where shee did all beseech
Bravely to fight for England; telling them
That what their fortune was, should Hers be then.
And that with full resolve Shee thither came
Ready to win, or quite to lose the Game.
Which words, deliver'd in most Princely sort,
Did animate the army, and report
To all the world her magnanimity,
Whose haughtie courage nought could terrify.
Well did Shee shew Great Henry was Her Sire,
Whom Europe did for valor most admire,
Mongst all the warlike Princes which were then
Enthronized with Regall Diadem.

The Eight Pearle.—Science.

Among the vertues intellectuall,
The Van is lead by that we Science call:
A Pearle more precious then th' Ægyptian Queene
Quaft off to Anthony; of more esteeme
Then Indian gold, or most resplendent gemmes,
Which ravish us with their translucent beames.
How many Arts and Sciences did decke
This Heroina? who still had at becke
The Muses and the Graces, when that Shee
Gave Audience in State and Majestie.
Then did the Goddesse Eloquence inspire
Her Royall breast; Apollo with his lyre,
Ne're made such musicke; on her Sacred lips
Angells enthron'd most Heavenly Manna sips.
Then might you see her Nectar-flowing Veine
Surround the hearers: in which sugred streame
Shee able was to drowne a world of men,
And drown'd, with sweetnesse to revive agen.
Alasco, the Embassador Polonian,
Who perorated like a meere Slavonian,
And in rude rambling Rhetoricke did roule,
Shee did with Atticke Eloquence controule.

[1] See vol. II. p. 536.

Her Speeches to our Academians,
Well shew'd Shee knew, among *Athenians*[1],
How to deliver such well tuned words,
As with such places punctually accords.
But with what Oratory ravishments,
Did Shee imparadise Her Parliaments?
Her last most Princely Speech doth verify
How highly Shee did England dignify.
Her loyall Commons how did Shee embrace,
And entertaine with a most Royall Grace?

The Ninth Pearle.—Patience.

Now come we Her rare Patience to display:
Which, as with purest Gold, did pave her way
To England's Crowne; for, when her Sister rul'd,
Shee was with many great afflictions school'd;
Yet all the while Her mot was Tanquam Ovis,
Nor could her Enemies prove ought amisse
In her, although they thirsted for her bloud,
Reputing it once shed, their soveraigne good.
Some time in prison this sweet Saint was pent,
Then hastily away Shee thence was sent
To places more remote; and all her friends
Debar'd accesse, and none but such attends
As ready were with poison or with knife,
To sacrifice the sacred Princesse life,
At bloudy Bonner's becke, or Gardner's nod;
Had they not been prevented by that God,
Who did Susannah from the Elders free,
And at the last gave her her liberty.
Thus by her patient bearing of the crosse
She reaped greatest gaine from greatest losse,
(For he that looseth his blest liberty,
Hath found a very Hell of misery:)
By many Crosses thus Shee got the crowne;
To England's Glory, and her great renowne.

The Tenth Pearle.—Bounty.

As Rose and Lillie challenge cheefest place,
For milke-white lustre, and for purple grace;

---

[1] So great was her proficiency in various Languages, that Du Bartas says,
"Rome, Rhine, Rhone, Greece, Spain, and Italy,
Plead all for right in her Nativity."

So England's Rose and Lillie had no Peere,
For Princely bounty shining every-where;
This made her Fame with golden wings to fly
About the world, above the starry sky.
Witnesse France, Portugall, Virginia,
Germany, Scotland, Ireland, Belgia;
Whose Provinces and Princes found her aid
On all occasions, which sore dismaid
Spaine's King, whose European Monarchy
Could never thrive during her Soveraignty.
So did shee beate him with her distaffe; so
By Sea and Land Shee him did overthrow;
Yea, so that the Tyrant on his knees Shee brought,
That of brave England Peace he beg'd, and thought
Himselfe most happie, that by begging so
Preserv'd all Spaine from beggery and woe.
  Here all amaz'd my Muse sets up her rest,
  Adoring Her who's so divinely blest.

At nos horrifico cinefactam Te propè Busto,
Insatiabiliter deflebimus, æternumquè.

On a splendid Monument in Westminster Abbey are the effigies of the Queen[1], and these inscriptions:

1. "*Memoriæ Æternæ* Elizabethæ, *Angliæ, Franciæ, & Hiberniæ* Reginæ, R. Henrici VIII. Fil.; R. Henrici VII. Nept.; R. Edward IV. Pronept.; Patriæ Parenti, Religionis & bonorum Artium Altrici, plurimarum Linguarum peritiâ præclaris, tum animi tum corporis dotibus regiisque virtutibus supra sexum Principi incomparabili. Jacobus, *Magnæ Britanniæ, Franciæ, & Hiberniæ* Rex, Virtutum & Regnorum Hæres, benemerenti posuit.

2. "*Memoriæ Sacrum.*—Religione ad primævam sinceritatem restauratâ, Pace fundatâ, Monetâ ad justum valorem reductâ, Rebellione domesticâ vindicatâ, *Galliâ* malis intestinis præcipiti sublevatâ, *Belgio* sustentato, *Hispanicâ* Classe profligatâ, *Hiberniâ* pulsis *Hispanis*, & Rebellibus ad deditionem coactis pacatâ, Redditibus utriusque Academiæ Lege Annonariâ plurimum adauctis, totâ denique *Angliâ* ditatâ prudentissimeque annos xlv, administratâ: Elizabetha Regina victrix, triumphatrix, pietatis studiosissima, fœlicissima, placidâ morte suptuagenariâ soluta, mortales reliquias, dum Christo jubente resurgant immortales, in hâc Ecclesiâ celeberrimâ ab ipsâ conservatâ & denuò fundatâ deposuit.

"Obiit 24 Martii, Anno Salutis mdcii, Regni xlv, Ætatis lxx.

"Regno Consortes & Urnæ hìc obdormimus Elizabetha & Maria, Sorores in spe Resurrectionis."

[1] "Her Corpse was solemnly interred under a fair tomb at Westminster, the lively draught whereof is pictured in most London, and many country Churches, every parish being proud of the shadow of her tomb: and no wonder, when each loyal subject erected a monument for in his heart." Fuller.

An Epitaph vpon the Death of our late gratious and dread Soveraigne ELIZABETH, *Queene of* ENGLAND [1], *&c.*

  Sooth not thyselfe, vile dust, vile lumpe of clay,
As though thy life were leas'd for dateles day.
Man is but thing of nought: soone as he breathes,
He is exposed to a thousand deaths.
Soone as he 'gins to liue, he 'gins to die,
And wailes the time he did salute the skie.
And ling'ring on, he softly weares away,
Like timeles flowre before the skorching ray,
What ever this vast world hath or shall have,
Must be devoured by the hungrie grave.
Impartiall Fates spare none, for die must all,
Both baser Cobler and proud Cardinall.
Loe, here for signe, how Death hath equall made,
The Princely scepter and the deluers spade.
Witnesse this trophee of insulting Death,
England's great Empresse, Queene ELIZABETH.
Me list not blot whole reames with larger read
Of matchlesse graces of this Soueraigne dead.
Speake envie 'selfe, and envie will confesse,
The world ne're sawe so rare an Empresse.
Was neuer Prince which swaide Emperiall mace
Did equalize, much lesse excell her Grace.
Not that wise King of Peace, King Dauid's Sonne,
In whome great grace and wisdome great did wonne,
Had greater grace, ne more did vnderstond,
Then did ELIZA, Queene of Fayry-lond.
Oh hadst thou liu'd, great Queene, in times of yore,
When he in Palestina scepter bore;

[1] Extracted from a Tribute of the CAMBRIDGE MUSES, under the title of "SORROWE'S JOY; or, a Lamentation for our late deceased Sovereign ELIZABETH; with a Triumph for the prosperous Successe of our gracious Sovereign King James."—The whole Tract should here be given, but that it will find a more appropriate place at the commencement of the succeeding Monarch's reign.

The two following Publications should here be briefly noticed, and might not improperly be copied; but they are in Latin, and are copious enough to form an entire Volume.

1. "Oxoniensis Academiæ Funebre Officium in Memoriam Honoratissimam Serenissimæ Elisabethæ, nuper Angliæ, Franciæ, et Hiberniæ Reginæ. Oxoniæ, Excudebat Josephus Barnesius, Almæ Academiæ Typographus, 1603."

2. "Threno Thriambeuticon. Academiæ Cantabrigiensis ob Damnum Lucrosum, et Infœlicitatem fœlicissimam, Luctuosus Triumphus. Cantabrigiæ, ex officinâ Johannis Legat, 1603."

That Queene which ween'd, nor toyle, nor charges deare,
So shee mought well be learn'd in Wisdom's leere;
But crost from Saba to Hierusalem,
To heare that King discourse on deeper theame;
Had shee but heard of great ELIZAE's name
(For great was shee in power, and great in fame,)
Soone had shee left that most admired Jewe,
And shipt to Albion her wise Prince to viewe.
And soke the wisdome shee from thee did heare,
With an insatiate and greedie eare.
Shee ruled long, with peace and plentie great,
And we could wish her daies were doubled yet.
Shee which liu'd well liu'd long; for length of daies
Fond ideots count by time, wise men by praise:
Whilst here shee liu'd, shee spent her virgin yeares
In Royall pompe amongst her wiser Peeres:
Nor mought shee daygne with earthly Prince to ioyne,
To bring forth issue from her virgin loyne:
She had espoused her selfe to th' Lord of Life,
So still shee liues, a maiden, and a wife.
He bought her deare; and it was reason good
He should her wedd, who bought her with his blood.
So now shee's crown'd with blisse, amongst those spirits,
Which ransomd are, by Christ's all-saving merits.
Little shee recks this world: ne had shee losse,
Who got a crowne of blisse for one of drosse.
England, thou maist bewaile her beeing dead,
But more reioyce that her thou fostered.

J. JONES, Jun. Soc. Pemb.

BRITTAIN'S LACHRIMÆ[1].

Weepe, little Isle, and for thy Mistris death
  Swim in a double sea of brackish waters:
Weepe little world, weepe for great ELIZABETH;
  Daughter of warre, for Mars himself begate her,
  Mother of peace, for she bore the latter.
She was and is, what can there more be said,
In earth the first, in heaven the second Maid.

[1] From the Donation MSS. in the British Museum, 4712.

INDEX

TO THE

NEW YEAR'S-GIFTS PRESENTED TO AND BY THE QUEEN.

A.

Abergavenny, Henry Nevill fourth Lord i. 112, 123. ii. 70, 84
———— Catherine Lady i. 112, 123
Absolon, Rev. —— ii. 77, 88
Adams, Mr. (Schoolmaster) i. 118, 127
Adderley, Humfrey iii. 21
Alee, Sir John i. 115, 125
Allen, or Allom, Mrs. iii. 11, 19
Alley, Verney iii 456, 464
———— William, Bp. of Exeter i. 110, 121
Anes, or Amys, Dunston ii. 420. iii. 14, 21
Anthony, Anthony i. 118, 127
Antony, Mark ii 78, 79
Apparey, or à Parry, Blaunch i. 116, 125, 295, 324. ii. 52, 75, 87, 290, 301, 398, 420, 427, 499. iii. 10 19
Arabella, Lady iii 451, 462
Arundel, Henry Fitz-Alan 11th Earl of i. 108, 120. ii. 66, 82, 301, 387, 396, 426
———— Lady ii. 73, 86
———— Mrs. i. 116, 125, 324
Askewe, Lady Anne ii. 301
Asteley, John i. 117, 126. ii. 89, 452. iii. 21
———— Richard ii. 90
———— Thomas i. 127, 129. iii. 21
———— Mrs. i. 116, 125
Audley, George Lord iii. 450, 461
———— Lady ii. 71, 85. iii. 454, 462
Aylmer, John, Bp. of London ii. 69, 84. iii. 416

B.

Babington, Gervase, Bp. of Worcester iii. 449, 461
Bacon, Sir Nicholas, i. 111, 122. ii. 65, 81
———— Francis iii. 457, 465
Baker, George iii. 458, 466
Bancroft, Richard, Bp. of London iii. 448, 461
Baptest, John i. 127. ii. 89. iii. 21
———— Mrs. i. 116, 125. ii. 75, 87
Barley (alias Penne), Mrs. i. 116, 126. ii. 76, 88. iii. 12, 20, 455, 464

Barlow, William, Bp. of Chichester i. 110, 121
Barnes, Richard, Bp. of Durham ii. 69, 83
Bashe, Edward ii. 78, 88
Bassano, Andrew iii. 457, 465
———— Arthur iii. 457, 465
———— Edward iii. 457, 465
———— Jeremy iii. 24, 25, 457, 465
Bath, William Bourchier fourth Earl of iii. 2, 15
———— Countess of ii 451. iii. 4, 16, 447, 460
Bathe, Mr. i. 117, 126
Batty, Ralph iii. 457, 465
Bayly, or Bayless, Dr. iii. 13, 21
Bedford, Francis Russell second Earl of i. 109, 120. ii. 52, 66, 82, 420
———— Margaret, Countess of i. 110, 122
———— Bridget, Countess i. 294. ii. 68, 83, 398
———— Countess Dowager iii. 447, 460
———— Edward, third Earl iii. 446, 460
———— Lucy Countess iii. 3, 16, 447, 460
Bellot, Hugh, Bp. of Chester iii. 449, 461
Benger, Sir Thomas i. 115, 124, 295
Bentham, Thomas, Bp. of Lichfield and Coventry i. 110, 121. ii. 69, 84
Berkeley, Henry eleventh Lord i. 112, 122, 129. iii. 450, 462
———— Katherine Lady i. 112, 123. ii. 71, 85. iii. 7, 18
———— Jane Lady iii. 451, 462
———— Gilbert, Bp. of Bath and Wells i. 110, 121. ii. 69, 84
Betts, John i. 119, 127
Bewtricke, Dr. ii. 91
Bickley, Thomas, Bp. of Chichester iii. 5, 17
Billingsley, Sir Henry iii. 455, 463
Bishop, Mr. iii. 457, 465
Blomefield, Mr. i. 118, 127
Bowes, Ralph ii. 77, 88
Bowne, Mrs. iii. 12, 20
Bradbridge, William, Bp. of Exeter ii. 69, 84
Bridges, Elinor ii. 88
———— Elizabeth iii. 456, 464
Brissetts, Jane ii. 76, 87. iii. 11, 20
Bristow, Nicholas i. 127. ii. 90. iii. 21, 466

Brodebelt, Dorothy i. 116, 125
Brooke, Elizabeth iii. 11, 19
——— Henry iii. 13, 20
Browne, Dr. iii. 456, 465
Bruncker, Sir Henry iii. 12, 20, 454, 463
Buckhurst, Thomas Sackville first Lord (afterwards Earl of Dorset) ii. 70, 84. iii. 6, 17, 445, 459
——— Lady ii. 71, 85. iii. 7, 18, 451, 462
Bull, Randall, iii. 458, 466
Bullingham, John, Bp. of Gloucester (formerly of Bristol) iii. 5, 17|
——— Nicholas, Bp. of Lincoln i. 110, 121
Burleigh. See *Cecil.*
Butler, Lady i. 113, 123. ii. 72, 86

C.

Care, Edward ii. 89
Carew, Sir Gawen i. 115, 124. ii. 74, 87
——— Rev. Archdeacon George i. 115, 125. ii. 77, 88
——— Katherine i. 116, 125
——— Sir Peter i. 115, 125
——— Lady i. 113, 123. ii. 72, 86. iii. 8, 18
Carey, Sir Edward iii. 21, 466 *bis.*
Carmanden, Mr. ii. 499. iii. 456, 465
Caron, Mons. iii. 467
Carr, Mr. iii. 13, 21, 456, 464
Carre, Mrs. iii. 11, 20, 455, 464
Carree, Sir George i. 127
Casemere, Duke iii. 124
Cave, Sir Ambrose i. 114, 124
——— Mrs. ii. 76, 87
Cavendish, Mr. ii. 529
Caliardo, Cæsar iii. 24, 25
Cecil, Sir William (afterwards first Lord Burleigh) i. 114, 124. 128. ii. 65, 81, 420, 427, 499, 528. iii. 2, 15, 450, 461
——— Mildred Lady i. 113, 123. ii. 52, 71, 85, 289, 388, 397, 426, 451
——— Sir Thomas (afterwards second Lord Burleigh and Earl of Exeter) iii. 10, 19, 413
——— Dorothy, Nevill Lady iii. 6, 17, 451, 462
——— Sir Robert (afterwards Earl of Salisbury) ii. 528. iii. 453, 463, 600
Chaderton, William, Bp. of Chester (afterwards of Lincoln) iii. 5, 17, 449, 461
Chamberlain, Francis i. 118, 127
Chandos, Edmund Brydges, second Lord i. 112, 123
——— Dorothy Lady (re-married to Sir William, afterwards Lord Knowles) ii. 71, 85. iii. 6, 17, 451, 462
——— Giles third Lord ii. 70, 84. iii. 6, 17
——— Frances Lady, ii. 71, 85. iii. 6, 17, 451, 462
Cheeke, Lady i. 113, 123, 294, 324. ii. 52, 72, 86, iii. 8, 18, 452, 462

Cheney, Henry first and only Lord ii. 70, 85
——— Lady ii. 2, 71. 85, 300, 388, 419, 426, 451, iii. 7, 18
——— Richard, Bp. of Gloucester ii. 69, 84
Clarke, Daniel iii. 457, 465
Clere, Sir Edward ii. 77, 88. 1ii. 10, 19, 454, 463
Clinton, Edward Clinton Lord i. 111, 122
——— Lady i. 112, 123, 294
Cobham, William Brooke Lord ii. 70, 85. iii. 5, 17
——— Lady i. 112, 123, ii. 71, 85. iii. 6, 17
——— Henry Brooke second Lord iii. 450, 461
——— Sir Henry ii. 389
Coke, Edward iii. 467
Compton, Henry Compton first Lord ii. 70, 84. iii. 6, 17
Comy, Innocent iii. 24, 25. 458, 468
Constable, Lady Catherine ii. 301. iii. 7, 18
Copley, Mr. i. 128
Coppyn, Mrs. iii. 455, 464
Cordall, Sir William i. 114, 124. ii. 74, 87
——— William iii. 457, 465
Sir *Cormack,* an Irish gentleman ii. 90
Cornwallis, Sir William ii. 398, 419. iii. 454, 463
——— Lady Katherine iii. 451, 462
Cotton, Henry, Bp. of Salisbury iii. 448, 461
——— William, Bp. of Exeter iii. 449, 461
Cowper, Thomas, Bp. of Lincoln (afterwards of Winchester) ii. 69, 84. iii. 4, 16
Cox, Richard, Bp of Ely i. 109, 121. ii. 69, 83
Coxe, Mr. iii. 252
Cranmer, Robert iii. 466
Crofts, Sir James iii. 9, 19
Crofts, Lady ii. 73, 86
Cromer, Mrs. iii. 12, 20, 455, 464
Cromwell, Sir Henry ii. 74, 87. iii. 10, 19, 454, 463
——— Lady ii. 72, 86
Cropson, or Crokeson, Mrs. ii. 77, 88
Cross, Capt. iii. 14, 21
Cumberland, George Clifford third Earl of iii. 2, 15, 446, 459
——— Frances Countess of ii. 68, 83. iii. 3, 16, 447, 460
Curteys, Richard, Bp. of Chichester ii. 69, 84

D.

Dacres, Lady i. 112, 123. ii. 71, 85. iii. 6, 17
Dale, Mrs. ii. 53, 77, 88. iii. 11, 19
Damsell, Sir William i. 115, 124. ii. 74, 87
Dane, Mrs. i. 116, 126. ii. 77, 88
Darcy of Chiche, Lord i. 112, 123. ii. 70, 84, 397. iii. 5, 17, 450, 461
Darcye, Edward iii. 466
Darsey, Mr. iii. 21

Davies, Richard, Bp. of St. David's (formerly of St. Asaph) i. 110, 121. ii. 69, 84
Delaware, Lord iii. 450, 461
——— Lady iii. 451, 462
Denny, Sir Edward iii. 21, 466
——— Sir Maurice i. 114, 125
Dennys, Mons. i 128.
Derby, Edward Stanley eighth Earl of i. 108, 120. ii. 66, 82. iii. 2, 15, 445, 459
——— Lady Margaret Countess of i. 110, 122, 323. ii. 65, 81. iii. 447, 460
——— Countess Dowager iii. 447, 460
De Seure, Mons. i. 129
Dethick, Sir Gilbert (Garter King of Arms) ii. 74, 87. iii. 13, 20, 456, 464
——— Sir William (Garter) i. 115, 125, 129
Digby, Lady iii. 8, 18, 23, 452, 463
Downham, William, Bp. of Chester i. 110, 121
Drake, Sir Francis ii. 303, 420, 499
Drury, Sir William ii. 75, 87, 388, 499
——— Lady ii. 73, 86. iii. 8, 18
——— Frances ii. 389
Ducke, Thomas iii. 457, 466
Dudley, John ii. 78, 89. iii. 14, 21
——— Jane Dowager Baroness iii. 7, 18
——— Robert. See *Leicester.*
Dunstoneanus ii. 499
Dyer, Sir Edward ii. 78, 89, 290. iii. 12, 20, 454, 463

E.

Edmondes, Lady iii. 453, 463
Edmunds, Mrs. ii. 75, 87, 499. iii. 11, 19
Egerton, Sir Thomas iii. 445, 459, 570
——— Lady iii. 452, 463
Eryzo, Mark Anthony i. 118, 127
Essex, Robert Devereux second Earl of ii. 498. iii. 23
——— Frances Countess of ii. 68, 83
Eylanby, Mrs. i. 126

F.

Fitzwilliam, Lady i. 114, 124
Fortescue, Sir John iii. 453, 463
Freake, Edmund, Bp. of Rochester (afterwards of Worcester) ii. 69, 84. iii. 4. 16
French, Richard iii. 458, 466
——— Thomas iii. 457, 465
Frogmorton [Throgmorton], Lady ii. 73, 86
Fulwell, Stephen i. 128. ii. 90. iii. 22
Fyfield, Mrs. iii. 12, 20
Fynes, Mr. iii. 13, 21

G.

Gallyardo, Cæsar iii. 457, 465
Garret, Elizabeth ii. 88
Gastell, Mons. ii. 90
Gawnte, Viscount ii 90

Gheast, Edmund, Bp. of Rochester (afterwards of Salisbury) i. 110, 121. ii. 69, 84
George, Mr. iii 23
Godwin, Thomas, Bp. of Bath and Wells iii. 4. 16
Goldsborough, Godfrey, Bp. of Gloucester iii. 449, 461
Goodres, William iii. 458, 465
Gorges, Sir Thomas ii. 90. iii. 21, 26, 466
Gormanston, Viscount ii. 52
Graves, Richard iii. 458, 465
Gray, Lady Mary ii. 65, 81
Grene, Elizabeth iii. 455, 464
Gresham, Sir Thomas i. 115, 125. ii. 74, 87
——— Lady i. 114, 124. ii. 72, 86. iii. 9, 18
Greville, Fulke ii. 78, 89. iii. 456, 464
Grey, John Lord i. 111, 122
Grindal, Edmund, Bp. of London i. 109, 121
Gryffyn, Mrs. iii. 456, 464
Guildensterne, Nicholas i. 130
Guildford, Sir Henry iii. 454, 463
——— Lady iii. 452, 462
Guy, Peter iii. 457, 465
Gyfford, Dr. iii. 13, 21
Gyles, Christopher ii. 79, 89

H.

Hales, Robert iii. 458, 465
Harman, Mrs. ii. 76, 88
Harrington, John i. 117, 126, 295. ii. 1, 77, 88
——— Lady ii. 499. iii. 9, 18, 453, 463
——— Mrs. i. 116, 125
Hastings Edward first Lord of Loughborough, i. 111, 122
Hatton, Sir Christopher i. 114, 124. ii. 74, 86, 289, 300, 388, 397, 419, 424, 426, 451, 499, 528. iii. 1, 15, 23 *bis*
——— Mr. i. 295, 324. ii. 2, 52
Havering, Marquis ii. 91
Hawarde, Sir George ii. 89
——— Elizabeth ii. 76, 88
——— Frances ii. 75, 87. iii. 11, 19.
——— Katharyn ii. 88. iii. 20
——— Martha ii. 88
Hawkins, Lady iii. 453, 463
Haydon, Sir Christopher ii. 74, 87
Hemingway, John i. 118, 127. ii. 79, 89. iii. 24 *bis,* 457, 465
Hemynham, Mary iii. 466
Heneage, Sir Thomas i. 117, 126. ii. 1, 53, 75, 87, 289, 388, 397, 419, 427, 452, 499. iii. 9, 19
——— Lady i. 116, 125. ii. 53, 73, 86, 420, 452, iii. 8, 18
Henningham, Lady i. 113, 123
Hereford, Viscountess Dowager of i. 111, 122
Hertford, Edward Seymour second Earl of ii. 52, 66, 82, 388, 389, 396. iii. 2, 15, 446, 460
———Countess of iii. 3, 16

Hewycke, Dr. i. 117, 126. ii. 78, 89
Hickes, Richard i. 119, 127
Hobby, Sir Edward iii. 454, 463
—— Lady iii. 453, 463
Hope, Ralph ii. 90
Hopton, Sir Owen i. 295. ii. 74, 87. iii. 9, 19
—— Ann iii. 20
Horne, Robert, Bp. of Winchester i. 109, 121, ii. 69, 84
Horsey, Sir Edward i. 324. ii. 75, 87, 289, 301
Hottoft, Nicholas iii. 466
Howard of Effingham, Charles Lord (afterwards Earl of Nottingham) i. 324. ii. 1, 70, 84, 388, 397, 419, 426, 445, 451, 459, 498. iii. 5, 17
—— Lady i. 112, 123, ii. 1, 71, 85, 300, 388, 397, 419, 426, 498. iii. 6, 17, 447, 460
—— Dowager Lady ii. 71, 85, 300
—— Lord Henry iii. 450, 461
—— Lord Thomas ii. 388
—— Lord William i. 111, 122
—— Elizabeth i. 295
—— Sir George i. 115, 125
—— Mary i. 126
Howland, Richard, Bp. of Peterborough iii. 5, 17, 449, 461
Huggens, Frances iii. 455, 464
—— William i. 118, 126. ii. 78, 89. iii. 13, 21, 458, 465
—— Mrs. i. 117, 126. ii. 77, 78. iii. 12, 20, 455, 464
Huishe, Mr. iii 14, 21
Hunsdon, Henry Carey first Lord, i. 112, 122. ii. 1, 70, 84, 397. iii. 5, 17
—— Anne Lady i. 112, 123. ii. 397. iii. 6, 17
—— Dowager Lady, iii. 450, 462
—— George second Lord iii. 10, 19, 449, 461
—— Mary Lady iii. 450, 462
Huntingdon, Henry Hastings third Earl of i. 109, 120, 294, 323. ii. 66, 82. iii. 2, 15, 446, 460
—— Countess of i. 111, 122. ii. 67, 83, 389, iii. 3, 16, 447, 460
—— Countess Dowager of i. 111, 122, 324, 447, 460
Hutton, Mathew, Abp. of York iii. 448, 461
Hyde, Lucy ii. 88. iii. 455, 464

J.

James, Dr. iii. 456, 465
Jaromy, Mr. iii. 24, 25
Jarret, Sir Thomas ii. 289. iii. 454, 463
—— Sir Gilbert iii. 9, 19
—— Lady iii. 8, 18, 452, 463
Jerningham, Sir Henry i. 114, 124
Jewel, John, Bp. of Salisbury i. 109, 121
Jobson, Lady i. 113, 124
Jones, Mrs. iii. 12, 20 bis.

Joslyn, Sir Thomas i. 115, 124
Ipolitan, the Tartarian i. 129
Julio, Mr. ii. 78, 89
—— Mrs. ii. 77, 88

K.

Kent, Mary Countess Dowager ii. 68, 83
—— Susannah Countess ii. 68, 83. iii. 446, 460
Kildare, Earl of ii. 52
—— Countess of iii. 448, 460
Killigrew, William ii. 90. iii. 21, 466
Kirkham, Fraunces iii. 456, 464
Knevett, Katherine i. 126. iii. 455, 464
—— Sir Thomas ii. 389, 499
—— Mr. Thomas ii. 90. iii. 21, 466
Knightley, Sir Richard iii. 23
Knowles, Sir Francis i. 114, 124. ii. 73, 86. iii. 9, 19
—— Dame Elizabeth i. 113, 123. ii. 1, 75, 87
Knowlys, Sir William iii. 453, 463

L.

Lane, Lady i. 113, 123
—— Robert iii. 458, 466
Lavyson, Mr. ii. 2
Lee, Sir Henry ii. 1, 75, 87, 289, 301, 388, 397, 420, 427, 452, 499
Leicester, Robert Dudley, the celebrated Earl of i. 294, 323. ii. 1, 52, 66, 81, 289, 300, 387, 396, 419, 420, 424, 426, 451, 498
Leighton, or Layton, Sir Thomas ii. 53, 300. iii. 9, 19, 454, 463
—— Lady iii. 8, 18, 452, 462
Lenox, Lady Margaret ii. 65, 81
Lichfelde, Mr. ii. 528
—— Mrs. ii. 76, 87
Lincoln, Edward Clinton first Earl of ii. 66, 82. iii. 2, 15
—— Countess of i. 324. ii. 1, 52, 67, 83, 388. iii. 3, 16
Lobopyne, Mons. ii. 90
Longe, Lady iii. 9, 18, 453, 463
Lopus, Dr. iii. 13, 21
Lucy, Mrs. i. 295
Lumley, John Lord i. 111, 122. ii. 70, 85, 420, 499, 528. iii. 6, 17, 450, 461, 499
—— Jane Lady ii. 397.
—— Elizabeth Lady iii. 6, 17, 451, 462
Lupo, Ambrose ii. 79, 89. iii. 24, 25
—— Joseph iii. 24, 25, 457, 465
—— jun. iii. 457, 465
—— Peter iii. 24, 25, 457, 465
—— Thomas iii. 458, 465

M.

Mackwilliams, Elizabeth iii. 20

INDEX TO NEW-YEAR'S GIFTS.

Maister, Dr. i. 117, 126. ii. 78, 89
Mannors, Lady Elizabeth i. 324
Mantle, George i. 118, 127
Marbery, Mrs. i. 116, 125. ii. 76, 87
Marten, Mr. Alderman ii. 301
Marven, Mrs. i. 116, 125
Maskers, Eight ii. 389 bis.
Mason, Sir John i. 114, 124
―――― Lady i. 113, 123
Matthew, Tobias, Bp. of Durham iii. 448, 461
Matthews, Richard i. 119, 127
Mauxwell, Mary i. 126
May, John, Bp. of Carlisle ii. 69, 84. iii. 4, 17
Medilkirk, Adolf ii. 91
Mewtheus, Frances i. 126
Middlemore, Henry ii. 90
Middlemour, Mr. iii. 21
Middleton, Marmaduke, Bp. of St. David's (and of Waterford in Ireland) iii. 5, 17
Mildmay, Sir Walter i. 114, 124. ii. 74, 86. iii. 9, 19
Morett, Mons. i. 129
Morgan, Mr. ii. 79, 89. iii. 24 bis, 457, 465
―――― Mrs. iii. 12, 20
Mounsieur (Francis de Valois, Duke of Anjou), ii. 387
Mountagu, Anthony first Viscount i. 109, 121, 128. ii. 67
―――― Mary Viscountess i. 111, 122. ii. 68, 83. iii. 4
―――― Anthony second Viscount ii. 82. iii. 2, 16
―――― Jane Viscountess iii. 16, 448, 460
Mountague, Mr. iii. 14, 21, 456, 465
―――― Mrs. ii. 76, 88
Mountjoy, Geo. Lord i. 112, 122, 129. iii. 450, 462
―――― Lady i. 112, 123
Myddleton, Thomas iii. 457, 465

N.

Newton, Mr. ii. 78, 89. iii. 13, 20.
―――― Mrs. iii. 19
―――― Lady iii. 453, 463
Nightingale, Richard iii. 466
Norfolk, Thos. Howard fourth Duke of i. 108, 120
―――― Duchess of i. 110, 121
Norrys of Ricote, Lord ii. 70, 84. iii. 6, 17, 450, 461
―――― Lady ii. 71, 85, iii. 7, 18
North, Edward first Lord i. 111, 122
―――― Sir Roger (afterwards second Lord) i. 115, 125. ii. 70, 84. iii. 6, 17, 450, 461
Northampton, William Lord Parre first Marquis of i. 108, 120. ii. 300
―――― Marchioness of i. 323. ii. 67, 82, 498. iii. 2, 16, 446, 460
Northumberland, Thomas Percy seventh Earl of i. 109, 121
―――― Anne Countess of i. 111, 122
―――― Henry eighth Earl of ii. 66, 82
―――― Catharine Countess of ii. 68, 83
Northumberland, Henry Percy ninth Earl of iii. 2, 15, 446, 460
―――― Dorothy Countess iii. 448, 460
Norton, Elizabeth iii. 456, 464
Nottingham, Earl of. See Howard.
Nowell, Mr. ii. 452

O.

Odonerle, an Irish Lord i. 129
O'Raely, an Irish Lord i. 128
Ormond, Earl of i. 323. ii. 52, 66, 82. iii. 2, 15, 23 ter.
―――― Countess of iii. 3, 16
Overton, William, Bp. of Lichfield and Coventry iii. 4, 16, 449, 461
Owen, or Over, Mrs. iii. 12, 20
Oxford, Edward de Vere sixteenth Earl of i. 109, 121. ii. 289, 300, 388. iii. 660
―――― Anne Cecil Countess i. 110, 122. ii. 52, 68, 83
―――― Eliz. Trentham second Countess ii. 289, 300, 388, 397, 419, 426, 451, 498. iii. 446, 460

P.

Packington, Mr. ii. 290, 301, 389
Paget, Lord i. 111, 122. ii. 70, 84
―――― Lady i. 112, 123, 324. ii. 71, 85
Paget Caree, Lady ii. 72, 85, 289. iii. 7, 17, 450, 462
Pallat, Lady i. 113, 123
Parker, Matthew, Abp. of Canterbury i. 109, 121.
Parkhurst, John, Bp. of Norwich i. 110, 121
Parrat, Thomas ii. 389
Parrett, Sir John iii. 10, 19
Parry, or Apparey, Blaunch. See Apparey.
Paston, Katherine ii. 53, 75, 87
Paulavizino, Sir Oratio iii. 10, 19
Pawlett, Lady iii. 8, 18
Pearce, Walter iii. 458, 464
Peckham, Sir Edmund i. 114, 124
Pembroke, William Herbert first Earl of i. 109, 120.
―――― Anne Countess of i. 110, 122
―――― Dowager Countess of ii. 68, 83
―――― Henry Herbert second Earl of ii. 66, 82. iii. 215, 227, 446, 460
―――― Catharine Countess of ii. 68, 83. iii. 3, 16, 447, 460
Penne. See Barley.
Peter, Sir William i. 114, 124
Piers, John, Bp. of Peterborough (afterwards of Salisbury) ii. 69, 84. iii. 4, 16
Pigeon, Edmund i. 127
Pigeon, John i. 128. ii. 90. iii. 21
―――― Nicholas iii. 22, 466
Pilkington, James, Bp. of Durham i. 109, 121
Popham, Sir John iii. 454, 463
Prayner, Baron John ii. 90
Puckering, Sir John, Lord Keeper iii. 369,
―――― Lady iii. 452, 463

Putrino (an Italian) ii. 79

R.

Randall, or Smallpage, Mrs. i. 117, 126
Rastrop, Jacob iii. 24
Ratclif, Lady i. 113, 123. ii. 73, 86. iii. 9, 18
—— Mary i. 126. ii. 88. iii. 11, 19, 455, 464
Revell, Mr. 118, 127
Reyes, Mushac iii. 24
Rich, Richard first Lord i. 111, 122
—— Robert 2d Lord ii. 70, 84, 300. iii. 6, 17, 24
—— Elizabeth Lady iii. 7, 18
—— Dowager Lady iii. 7, 18
—— Robert third Lord iii 450, 461
—— Lady iii. 451, 462
Richardson, Ferdinand iii. 21, 466
Robinson, Henry, Bp. of Carlisle iii. 449, 461
—— Mrs. iii. 12, 20
—— William, Bp. of Norwich iii. 449, 461
Robotham, Robert i. 118, 126
Rogers, Sir Edward i. 114, 124
Roynon, John i. 127
Rudd, Anthony, Bp. of St. David's iii. 449, 461
Russell, John Lord (afterwards second Earl of Bedford) ii. 70, 85, 300
—— Elizabeth iii. 455, 464
Russie, Count i. 130
Rutland, Henry Mannors second Earl of i. 109, 121
—— Bridget Countess of i. 111, 122
—— Edward Mannors third Earl of ii. 66, 82
—— Isabel Countess of ii. 68, 83
—— John Mannors fourth Earl of iii. 446, 460
—— Elizabeth Countess of iii. 3, 16, 447, 460

S.

Sackford, Henry i. 127. ii. 89, iii. 21, 466
—— Mrs. ii. 76, 87, 397, 427. iii. 11, 19, 456, 467
Sackville, Sir Richard i. 114, 124
—— Lady i. 113, 124
—— Thomas i. 129
Sadleir, Sir Ralph ii. 74, 86
St. Barbe, William i. 119, 127
St. John of Bletso, Lady ii. 71, 85. iii. 6, 17, 451, 462
St. Lowe, Lady i. 113, 123
Sands, Mrs. i. 116, 125
Sandys, Edwyn, Bp. of Worcester (afterwards of London, and Abp. of York) i. 109, 121. ii. 69, 83
Saulte, Mons. i. 128
Savoy, Duke of ii. 301
Scambler, Edmund, Bp. of Peterborough (afterwards of Norwich) i. 110, 121. iii. 4, 16
Scory, John, Bp. of Hereford (formerly Bp. of Rochester, and Chichester) i. 110, 121. ii. 69, 84
Scudamore, Sir John iii. 454, 463
—— Lady iii. 452, 462
Scroope, Henry Lord i. 112, 123
—— Lady Margaret i. 113, 123. iii. 8, 18, 451, 462

Seymour, Lord Henry ii. 53. iii. 6, 17
—— Lady Elizabeth iii. 7, 18, 452, 462
—— Lady Mary ii. 72, 85. iii. 7, 18, 452, 462
Shandowes. See *Chandos*.
Sheffield, John second Lord i. 112, 123, 129
—— Douglas Lady i. 112, 123, 324
—— Ursula Lady ii. 72, 85. iii. 7, 18, 451, 462
Shelton, Amey i. 117, 126. ii. 77, 88
—— Elizabeth i. 117, 126
Shref, Lawrence i. 118, 127
Shrewsbury, Eliz. Countess Dowager i. 110, 122
—— George Talbot sixth Earl of i. 108, 120. ii. 60, 82. iii. 2, 15
—— Gertude Countess of i. 111, 122. ii. 67, 83. iii. 3, 16, 446, 460
—— Gilbert seventh Earl iii. 446, 459
—— Mary Countess of iii. 447, 460
Skidamour, Mr. iii. 13, 21
Skipwith, Mr. ii. 397
—— Mrs i. 116, 125
Skydmore, Mrs. ii. 75, 87. iii. 11, 19
Smith, or Smyth, Charles (Customer) i. 118, 127, ii. 79, 89, 397.
—— (Dustman) ii. 79
Smythson, Mrs. ii. 88. iii. 12, 20
—— John ii. 78, 89. iii. 14, 21
Snowe, Mr. ii. 2
—— Mrs. i. 116, 126. ii. 53, 75, 87
Somerset, Anne Duchess Dowager of i. 110, 121. ii. 67, 82, 424.
Southampton, Henry Wriothesley second Earl of ii. 66, 82
—— Mary Countess ii. 68, 83. iii. 3, 16, 448, 460
Southwell, Sir Richard i. 114, 124
—— Sir Robert, ii. 452. iii. 10, 19
—— Lady iii. 8, 18, 452, 462
—— Mrs. iii. 20
Sowche, Lady ii. 73, 86. iii. 9, 18
Speckard, Abraham iii. 457, 465
—— Dorothy iii. 456, 464
Spillman, John iii. 13, 21, 24, 456, 465
Spinulla, Benedict i. 118, 126. ii. 78, 89
Stafford, Henry first Lord i. 111, 122
—— Ursula Lady i. 1, 72, 86
—— Henry second Lord i. 294. ii. 70, 84
—— Mary Lady i. 289, 300, 426, 499. iii. 7, 18, 452, 462
—— Sir Edward ii. 290, 301, 302. iii. 454, 463
Stanhop, Sir John ii. 78, 89. iii. 13, 21 *bis*, 454, 463
Stanhope, Michael iii. 466
Stanley, Thomas i. 117, 126
Still, John, Bp. of Bath and Wells iii. 448, 461
Strange, Lord i. 112, 123. ii. 1
—— Lady Margaret i. 108, 120
Strinke, Sir Martin iii 23
Strumpe, Sir James i. 115, 125
Suffolk, Frances Duchess Dowager of ii. 67, 82

INDEX TO NEW-YEAR'S GIFTS.

Surrey, Thomas Earl of ii. 52
——— Countess of i. 111, 122
Susan, Lady (a Maid of Honour) ii. 88
Sussex, Thomas Ratcliffe third Earl of ii. 66, 82
——— Frances Countess of ii. 67, 82
——— Henry Ratcliffe fourth Earl ii. 528. iii. 2, 15
——— Honora Countess of iii. 3, 16
——— Robert Ratcliffe fifth Earl of iii. 445, 459
——— Bridget Countess of iii. 447, 460
——— Countess Dowager of iii. 3, 16
Sydney, Sir Philip ii. 77, 88, 290, 301, 397
——— Lady i. 294, 324. ii. 2, 290
——— Lady Mary ii. 1, 72, 85
——— Sir Robert iii. 10, 19

T.

Talbot, Gilbert Lord ii. 451, 499
——— Mary Lady ii. 72, 85, 451. iii. 7, 18
Tamworth, John i. 127
Tayleboys, Lady (Sir Peter Carewe's wife) i. 112, 123. ii. 71, 85
Taylor, Mrs. ii. 76
Terling, Levina i. 117, 126
Thornborowe, Sir John iii. 10, 19
Thurland, Rev Mr. ii. 2
Throgmorton, Elizabeth iii. 11, 19
Thynne, Sir John i. 115, 124. ii. 74, 87
Trayford, Henry i. 119, 127
Trentham, Mrs. iii. 20
Trochins, Mr. iii. 458, 465
Tomysen, or Tomazine, Mrs. ii. 424. iii. 12, 20, 455, 464
Townsend, Lady iii. 9, 18
——— Mr. 290, 301
——— Mrs. ii. 1, 76, 87, 420
Twyst, Mrs. ii. 76, 68. iii. 12, 20, 455, 464

U.

Ubaldino, Petruchio iii. 24, 25
Umpton, Sir Edward i. 295. ii. 301

V.

Vannes, Peter i. 116, 125
Vaughan, Mrs. iii. 12, 20
Vere, Lady Mary i. 323. ii. 72, 85

W.

Wade, Armigell i. 118, 127
Walsingham, Sir F. ii. 1, 74, 86, 388. iii. 9, 19, 28
——— Lady ii. 73, 86, 289. iii. 8, 18, 28, 453, 463
——— Sir Thomas, iii. 454, 463
——— Lady, jun. iii. 453, 463
Warner, Sir Edward i. 114, 124
Warren, William iii. 457, 465
Warwick, Ambrose Dudley second Earl of i. 109, 120, 294, 323. ii. 52, 66, 82, 300, 396, 419, 424, 426, 452, 498. iii. 2, 15

Warwick, Anne Russel (third wife) Countess of i. 294, 323. ii. 52, 67, 83, 289, 300, 396, 419, 426, 452, 498, 528. iii. 3, 16, 447, 460
Webster, George i. 119, 127
West, Lady iii. 9, 18
——— Mr. ii. 2
——— Mrs. ii. 75, 87, 452. iii. 12, 20
Westmorland, Henry Nevil fifth Earl of i. 109, 121
Weston, Mr. iii. 457, 465
Westphaling, Herbert, Bp. of Hereford iii. 5, 17, 449, 461
Wetston, Mrs. iii. 11
Wharton, Philip Lord ii. 70, 85. iii. 6, 17, 450, 461
——— Elizabeth Lady iii. 7, 19
Whitgift, John, Bp. of Worcester (afterwards Abp. of Canterbury) i. 387. ii. 69, 84, 424, 528. iii. 4, 16, 448, 461
Wickham, William, Bp. of Lincoln (afterwards of Winchester) iii. 4, 16, 448, 461
Willoughby of Eresby, Peregrine Bertie Lord iii. 450, 461
——— Mary Lady ii. 73, 86. iii. 8, 18, 453, 463
Wilson, Anthony, Bp. of Chichester iii. 449, 461
——— Thomas ii. 74, 86, 301
Winchester, Wm Pawlet first Marquis of i. 109, 120
——— William Pawlet third Marquis of ii. 65, 81. iii. 2, 15
——— Agnes Marchioness of ii. 67, 82
——— William Pawlet fourth Marquis of iii. 445, 459
——— Lucy Marchioness of iii. 446, 460
——— Winifred March'ss Dowager of ii. 67, 82
Windsor, Lord i. 111, 112. ii. 426
——— Amy i. 126
Wingfield, Mr. ii. 302
Wolley, Francis ii. 290. iii. 12, 20, 457, 465
——— Mrs. iii. 11, 19
Woodhouse, Thomas ii. 420
——— Lady i. 113, 124, 324. ii. 72, 86
Woolton, John, Bp. of Exeter iii. 5, 17
Worcester, Edward Somerset fourth Earl of iii. 446, 460
——— Elizabeth Countess of iii. 441, 460
Wotton, Nicholas i. 115, 125
Wylfords, Lady iii. 73, 86
Wynkefeld, Mrs. ii. 76, 88. iii. 11, 19, 455, 464

Y.

Yonge, John i. 117, 126
Young, John, Bp. of Rochester, iii. 5, 17, 449, 461
——— Thomas, Abp. of York i. 109, 121

Z.

Zouche of Haringworth, Lady iii. 453, 462

See also a Roll of New-year's Gifts in the reign of PHILIP *and* MARY, *in the Preface, p.* xxxiv.

ADDENDA.

Vol. I. p. 150. In the Progress of 1563 Queen Elizabeth knighted Sir Henry Cheyney, when she visited the noble mansion which he had built at *Todington* in Bedfordshire; and in 1572 he was created Lord Cheyney of Todington; but, dying without issue in 1557, the estate devolved to his wife, daughter of Thomas Lord Wentworth of Nettlested.—In the same Progress Arthur Lord Grey of Wilton entertained the Queen at Whaddon, Bucks; and, by papers in the possession of Viscount Hampden, it appears that she honoured Griffith Hampden, Esq. (High Sheriff in 1576) by visiting him at Great Hampden; and that, for the Queen's more commodious access to the house, a gap was cut through the woods, still called "The Queen's Gap."—The Queen afterwards called on Mr. Penton at Prince's Risborough. William Totehill, Esq. of Shardloes, had also the honour of entertaining her. Lysons' Beds. and Bucks, pp. 143, 496, 571, 627, 662.

P. 109. Edward de Vere, who in 1564 became the 17th Earl of Oxford, was the first person who brought perfumes and embroidered gloves into England; of which having presented Queen Elizabeth with a pair, she took such pleasure in them, that she was pictured with them in her hands.

Vol. III. p. 656. In St. Saviour's Church, Southwark, was placed the Picture of the Queen's Monument, with these verses:

> St. Peter's Church in Westminster,
> Her sacred body doth interr.
> Her glorious soul with angels sings,
> Her deeds live patterns here for Kings.
> Her love in every heart hath room,
> The only shadow o'er her tomb.

A similar inscription was placed in St. Thomas's, Southwark; Allhallows, London Wall; St. Olave, Old Jewry, and in many other London Churches.

CORRIGENDA.

Vol. I. p. xxviii. at bottom, read *her* autograph.
—— p. li. col. ii. r. Gorhambury i. 102, 602. ii. 55.
—— p. lii. add to the places visited,
Prince's Risborough iii. 660.
Shardloes iii. 660.
Todington iii. 660.
—— p. 78, l. 27. r. "Manus."
—— p. 150, note l. 17, Sussex.
—— p. 543, note l. 4, r. "*Giles* Brydges."
Vol. II. p. 54. for 1609, r. 1619.

Vol. II. pp. 297, 421, 432. The Autograph in in these pages is that of Elizabeth Queen of Bohemia, daughter of King James I.
Vol. III. p. 76, note, l. 2, for 205, r. 308.
—— p. 143, the particulars respecting the house are improperly repeated, having been before given in p. 41.
—— p. 568, l. 11, r. "Sir Humphrey Forster.
—— p. 579, l. 2, r. "Sir William Clerke's."

INDEX

OF

REMARKABLE EVENTS; OF PERSONS BIOGRAPHICALLY NOTICED; AND OF PLACES DESCRIBED, &c.

A.

Aglionby, Edward, his speech to the Queen at Warwick i. 310. the Queen's answer 315

Ailesworth, or Aylworth, Anthony, acc. of iii. 157

Alançon, Francis de Valois, Duke of (afterwards Duke of Anjou) his proffered marriage with the Queen i. 304. his offer refused 321. negociation of marriage ii. 337. his presents to the Queen ib. his visit to the Queen 343. accompanied by her to Canterbury on his departure 345. sonnet by the Queen on their parting 346. his arrival at Flushing 348. his reception and entertainment on his return 350—385. made Duke of Brabant at Antwerp 361. the Queen's parting with him 386

Alasco, Albertus, Baron Lasco, his arrival in England, and entertainments given to ii. 398, 405

Alcock, John, Bp. of Ely, founder of Jesus College, Cambridge i. 150

Ale sent to the Queen at Kenilworth i. 525. at Cowdray iii. 84. at Guildford ib. at Shalford ib. at Southampton, ib. at Portsmouth 84, 97

All Souls' College, orders for defacing plate at i. 247. for destroying superstitious books and plate 248, 249. for destroying superstitious monuments 327

Allen, Francis, letters to the Earl of Shrewsbury i. 87

Alley, Wm. Bp. of Exeter, sermon at Court i. 83

Allingbury, Morley, account of i. 99

Allington, Sir Giles, account of ii. 221

Altars, demolition of in Westminster Abbey i. 88

Althamer, Andrew, notice of i. 429

Andover, letter from the Earl of Leicester to the burgesses of ii. 422

Andrews, Thomas, account of ii. 504

Anjou, Henry Duke of (afterwards Henry III. King of France) proposed marriage to the Queen i. xxxiii

—— Margaret of, Queen of King Henry VI. founder of Queen's College i. 150

Antics, men in fantastical postures in embroidery iii. 505

Apparel, regulations and orders respecting ii. 393, 543. iii. 32

Appletree, Thomas, condemned to death, and pardoned ii. 285

Apprentices, regulations for the apparel of in London ii. 393

Archers, splendid shooting match ii. 411

Argyle, Earl of, letter from the Queen to ii. 304. his answer 305

Armada, Spanish, defeat of the ii. 537. thanksgivings on that account ib. the battles represented in tapestry iii. 602

Arthur, Prince, with his Knights of the Round Table, prolusion of ii. 529

Arundel, Henry Fitz Alan eleventh Earl of, Ambassador to the Queen i. 66

Arundel House iii. 371

Ascham, Roger, his account of the Princess Elizabeth's progress in literature i. ix. 19

Ashby, George, curious Prayer-book in his possession, bound in solid gold, with some account of its former possessors i. xxxvii

Ashby-de-la-Zouch, the house built by William Hastings destroyed in the civil war i. xix. King James entertained at ib.

Aske, James, his "Elizabetha Triumphans" ii. 545

Asteley, John, one of the Princess's attendants i. 14. appointed to an office in the Tower ib. made master of the Jewel-house ib. autograph of i. 119, 130. ii. 80, 91

Atropoïon Delion, or the death of Delia iii. 628

Aucher, Sir Anthony, letter to from Princess Elizabeth i. 3

Audley, Thomas, Chancellor of England, founder of Magdalen College, Cambridge i. 150

Audley-end, expences at i. 280, 281

Autograph of Queen Elizabeth i. x. 108, 119, 120, 130. ii. 65, 80, 81, 91, 249, 264. iii. 14, 22, 25, 445, 459, 467

——————— Mary Queen of England i. x. xxxv

——————— Mary Queen of Scots i. x

——————— Edward VI. i. x

——————— Elizabeth Queen of Bohemia (printed here by mistake) ii. 297, 421, 432

Autographs of John Asteley, i. 119, 130. ii. 60, 91. iii. 14, 22, 25
——————— N. Bristow, iii. 14, 22, 25
——————— S. Fulwell, iii. 14, 22, 25
——————— J. Pigeon, iii. 14, 22, 25
——————— N. Pigeon, iii. 14, 22, 25
Awbre, William, account of i. 231
Aylmer, John, Bp. of London, the Queen displeased with his sermon iii. 249. his death 369

B.

Babington, Gervase, Bp. of Worcester, account of iii. 449
——————— William, apprehended for treason ii. 481. letter to the Queen 482
Backhouse, Samuel, account of iii. 567
Bacon, Anthony, account of iii. 191. his situation after leaving York-house 489
——————— Sir Francis, letter on the Masques at Gray's Inn i. xxi. pleaded against his patron the Earl of Essex when arraigned for high treason ii. 58. iii. 192. his sudden retirement to Twickenham iii. 124. spent much of his time in retirement at Twickenham 190. cause of his retiring ib. Earl of Essex and Lord Burleigh solicit the Queen to promote him ib. his letter to the Queen on his disappointment ib. presents a sonnet to the Queen in honour of the Earl of Essex, and his attachment to him 191. the Earl of Essex's generosity to him; threatened with assassination; published his "Apology" 192. Speeches drawn up by, delivered before the Queen at the Earl of Essex's device 372. inhabited the Earl of Essex's house in the Strand 441. letters to the Queen, on sending New-years' Gifts 468. and on his pecuniary affairs 489
——————— Sir Nicholas, account of, and of his entertaining the Queen at Gorhambury i. 602. ii. 55. description of his house ii. 58.
——————— Nicholas, of Suffolk, knighted (afterwards a Baronet) ii. 224
Baden, Christopher, Prince of, and Cicily his wife, their arrival in England, her delivery, and child baptized, i. 198. leave England 200
Badew, Richard, and Elizabeth Countess of Clare and Ulster, founders of Clare Hall i. 150
Baker, Sir Richard, his description of the Queen i. xiii
——————— Richard, account of i. 334
——————— Dr. Vice-chancellor of Cambridge, account of i. 175
Balsam, Hugh, Bp. of Ely, founder of Peter House i. 149
Bancroft, Rich. Bp. of London, account of iii. 448

Ban-dog, description of i. 438
Barbary, King of, letter to Queen Elizabeth ii. 298
Barne, Sir George, Lord Mayor of London, the Queen's letter to respecting a conspiracy ii. 481
——————— ceremony at the funeral of his lady i. 68
Bartholomew Fair, riot at iii. 31. custom of the Lord Mayor and Aldermen of London at 31. not kept in 1592 iii. 254
Bashe, Edward, account of ii. 93
Basing, account of iii. 566
Bath, charter granted to the city of iii. 250
Battwright, John, cumptroller of mines i. 148
Bavare, Duke of. See *Cassimer*
Baylie, Henry, account of i. 232
——————— Walter, account of i. 232
Beacon, Thomas, account of i. 244
Bear-baiting, amusement of i. 67, 68, 438, 439. ii. 459
Beauchamp, William Lygon first Earl, creation of i. 541
Bedford, Francis Russell second Earl of, his death i. 274
——————— Bridget Countess of, chief mourner at the funeral of Mary Queen of Scots, account of ii. 509
Bedgbury, account of i. 334
Bedingfield, Sir Henry, Princess Elizabeth committed to his care i. 8. discharged from Court 11. visited by the Queen ib.
Bedington, the Queen's oak and wall at iii. 441
Beggars, number of ii. 303
Bell, Mr. his oration to the Queen at Worcester i. 545
Bell-house, account of ii. 94
Bellot, Hugh, Bp. of Chester, account of iii. 449
Belly, John, account of i. 236
Benedictine Nuns, Priory of, founded by William the Conqueror i. 179
Bene't College, Cambridge, by whom founded i. 150
Berkeley, Henry Lord, clothes persons on Maundy Thursday ii. 297. expence of attending the Queen at Ivy-bridge 343
Berling, account of i. 333
Bermondsey House i. 290
Betenhall, account of i. 542
Bice, a colour i. 479
Birch, Dr. Thomas, letter to Dr. Ducarel i. 396
Bird, William, account of, iii. 597
Bisham, or Bissam, description of, and of the abbey there iii. 130. entertainment given to the Queen at 131. descent of the abbey and manor ib. "Queen Elizabeth's well" at 132
Bishop's Ichington, account of i. 310
Black Book at Warwick, extracts from i. 417

Blackwood, Adam, his epitaph on Mary Queen of Scots ii. 519
Blanke, Sir Thomas, Lord Mayor of London, orders sent to respecting the plague ii. 392. presented to the Queen 399
Blunt, Sir Christopher, wounded, and taken iii. 546
Bohemia, Elizabeth Queen of, her autograph, (printed here by mistake) ii. 297, 421, 432
Bollond, a traitor, apprehended ii. 482
Bolton, Edmund, verses in praise of the Queen iii. 62
Boonen, William, introduced coaches into England, iii. 150
Borough, William Lord, account of ii. 482
Boughton Malherb, account of i. 334
Bowyer, Gentleman Usher of the Black Rod, anecdote of i. 385
Bracebridge, Rowland, letter from H. Goldwell to ii. 310
Brackenbury, Richard, his letter to Lord Talbot iii. 69
Brerewood, Edward, account of iii. 156
Bride-ale, custom of serving at marriages i. 442
Bristow, N. autograph iii. 14, 22, 25
Bristowe, Richard, account of, i. 232
Britain's Lachrimæ, on the death of the Queen iii. 652
Browne, Richard, conversation with the Queen, on her expences i. xlv.
——— William, letter to the Earl of Shrewsbury iii. 596
Brydges, Sir Egerton, his description of Sudeley Castle iii. 217. his account of the Chandos family 219
Bucer, Martin, notice of i. 208
Buckhurst, Baron. See *Sackville*.
Buckingham, Edward Stafford third Duke of, his death, with account of his family i. 532
Buckridge, John, account of iii. 153
Buck-venison, custom of rendering by tenure, ii. 238
Bulkeley, Sir Richard, account of iii. 577
Bull, John, account of, and of his skill in music, iii. 158
Bull-baiting, a favourite amusement i. 67, 68. ii. 459
Bullingham, Nicholas, Bishop of Lincoln, notice of i. 246.
Burleigh House, Northamptonshire i. 205
Burleigh House, Westminster i. 205, iii. 79
——— Lord. See *Cecil*.
Burton, Richard, Mayor of Coventry, present to iii. 569
Bushy Hill, at Rochester, account of, with the Queen's approbation of i. 354
Bust, Henry, account of i. 232. iii. 157
Bynge, Thomas, account of i. 244

C.

Cæsar, Sir Julius, his present to the Queen iii. 68. account of 428.
Caius College, Cambridge, by whom founded i. 150
Caius, John, joint founder of Gonvill and Caius College i. 150
Calais Castle, Lord Wentworth arraigned for losing i. 68. keepers of, sentenced to death for negligence 81
Calamine, patent granted for finding i. 147
Calfhill, James, Bishop elect of Worcester, account of i. 230
Calthorpe, Sir Martin, Lord Mayor of London, his letter to the Queen on the defeat of the Spaniards ii. 537
Cambricks first brought into England iii. 504
Cambridge, account of, and time of the foundations of Colleges i. 149, 150. the Queen's grand reception at 151. persons made M. A. at her visit 180, 181. her departure from ib.
——— Members of the University of, attend the Queen at Audley End ii. 111
Camden, William, his account of the Queen's parting with the Duke of Anjou ii. 386
Campion, Edmund, account of i. 232
——— Thomas, poems by iii. 349, 350
Canterbury, descent of St. Austin's Abbey at i. 340. charges on the Queen's visiting 548. the Queen's parting with the Duke of Anjou at ii. 345
Capel, account of the family of ii. 222
Carew, Sir Francis, mode of preserving cherries on the trees iii. 441
——— Sir George (afterwards Baron), letter to from the Queen, and account of iii. 551
——— Dr. George, account of i. 115
Carey, John, epitaph on, i. 288
——— See *Hunsdon, Monmouth*
Carleton, Sir Dudley, extracts from letters to iii. 428
——— George, verses to the Queen iii. 180. memoirs of ib.
Caron, Sir Noel, account of iii. 440
Cartwright, Thomas, made Master of Warwick Hospital ii. 390
Case, John, account of iii. 157
Cassimer, John Count (Duke of Bavare), entertainment of, made Knight of the Garter, and departure ii. 277. Earl of Leicester's letter respecting him ib.
Catherine Hall, Cambridge, by whom founded i. 150
Catholic Religion, amusements and festivals connected with i. 447
Catlage Hall, account of ii. 219
Cave, Sir Ambrose, account of i. 36
Cecil, Sir William (afterwards first Lord Burleigh),

expence of the Queen's visits to him i. xxvii. appointed Principal Secretary 30. Queen Elizabeth godmother to his daughter 149. letters to 301. letter to Vice-chancellor of Cambridge 151, 153. his reception at Cambridge 156. description of his houses 205. letters to Earl of Shrewsbury 255, 320, 334. great expences in entertaining the Queen 308. letter to Abp. of Canterbury, with Abp.'s answer 346. letter to from William Fleetwood, Recorder of London (City Diary for a week) 355. letter to from Bp. Cox 389. letters to from the Earl of Leicester 524. goes to Buxton for benefit of his health ii. 62. his grief on the death of his son-in-law 394 letter to him from the Queen 399. expence of his house at Theobalds 404. letter to the Earl of Leicester 440. the Earl's answer 442. his writings to the Queen on the death of Mary Queen of Scots referred to 521. his grief on the death of his wife iii. 27. letter to from the Queen 75. his death and funeral 427. words spoken by the Queen to him ib. founded an hospital at Stanford 429. letters from the Earl of Cumberland 522, 523, 524. a pistol fired at him 545. letters to from Mr. Lambarde 554, 558. letter to him from Sir Nicholas Bacon iii. 660

Cecil, Sir Robert (afterwards Lord Cecil, Viscount Cranborne, Earl of Salisbury), his Hermit's Oration at Theobalds iii. 241. letter to from Sir J. Stanhope 430. from Michael Stanhope 441. to Mr. Winwood 546. to the Earl of Shrewsbury 598

────── Sir Thomas (afterwards second Lord Burleigh, and Earl of Exeter), account of 413. elected Knight of the Garter; created Earl of Exeter; his death 414

Cecil House iii. 601

Chaderton, William, Bp. of Chester, letters to from the Queen ii. 298, 299, 453. letter to from the Lords of the Council on libellous publications 434

Chalk, carriages provided for the Queen's service from iii. 37, 253, 369, 410

Chamberlain, ──── Keeper of Calais Castle, sentenced to death for negligence i. 81

──────── Sir Thomas, sets out for Spain i. 82

──────────── John, account of iii. 428. extracts from his MS. letters 428, 564, 577, 578, 599, 604

Chandos, [Giles] Brydges, third Lord, account of i. 543

──────── family, memoirs of, by Sir Egerton Brydges iii. 219—226

Chardin, Sir Thomas, death of i. 75

Charington, or Sherington, account of the family i. xviii.

Charles I. King, birth and baptism of iii. 526
Charles the Fifth, Emperor, his death i. 34
Charter-house, the Queen entertained at i. 30. iii. 602. King James held his Court at iii. 602
Chartley, account of i. 532
Cheeke, Sir G. letter to, on the Queen's proficiency in learning i. ix.
Chelsea Place iii. 414
Cheney, Richard, Bp. of Gloucester and Bristol, sermon at Court i. 83
Chester, Christopherson Bp. of, buried with the Popish ceremonies i. 34
Chieneie, Sir Thomas, his death i. 33
Child, Sir Francis, account of ii. 280
Childerley, descent of the lordship of ii. 221
Chillington, account of i. 532
Chimney-piece, curious one from Theobalds iii. 76
Christ's College, Cambridge, by whom founded i. 150
──────── Hospital, management of carts in London given to i. 411
Christening feasts, derivation of ii. 246
Christmas, kept at the Temple i. 131
Church-ales, excesses of, described, i. 455
Church-books, limnings used in i. xxxv
Church-goods burnt i. 75
Church service, English, began at the Queen's chapel i. 67
Churchwardens' Accompts, Mr. Denne's remarks on their utility i. xlix. extracts from ib. 247, 275, 290. ii. 92, 285, 412, 431, 455, 481, 482, 507, 527, 543. iii. 27, 30, 40, 74, 124, 369, 413, 442, 489, 514, 550, 569, 577, 579, 595
Churchyard, Thomas, his account of the Queen's entertainment at Bristol i. 393. extracts from his description of the Queen's entertainment in Suffolk and Norfolk ii. 115, 133, 179—213. verses on the voyage of Sir Humphrey Gilbert 226. Welcome-home to Master Frobusher 233. A Spark of Friendship and warm Good-will ii. 582. The Benefit that Paper brings brings 592. Rebuke to Rebellion 603. Verses by when the Queen was at Oxford iii. 175. his "Challenge" 176. his "Pleasant Conceite" 232. his "Fortunate Farewell" to the Earl of Essex 433
Churton, Archdeacon Ralph, his opinion of the Queen's visit to Middleton i. xviii. acknowledgements to iii. 584. possessor of a duplicate copy of the Queen's visit at Harefield ib. annotations on that visit 584—594
Clare and Ulster, Elizabeth Burke Countess of, joint founder of Clare Hall with Richard Badew i. 150
Clare Hall, Cambridge, by whom founded i. 150
Clere, Sir Edward, account of ii. 214

INDEX.

Clergy, their wives not to live in colleges with them i. 104. proclamation respecting 600

Clinton and Say, Edward ninth Lord, created Earl of Lincoln i. 75. time of his death ib. letters to Sir William Cecil 301, 362. his departure, with other commissioners, to France 301. their entertainment at Paris described 302. letter to the Earl of Leicester 304.

Clocks, early ii. 248

Coaches, time of their introduction into England ii. 309

———— first used in England iii. 150

Cobham, William Brooke first Lord, account of i. 354. his death iii. 413

———— Henry Brooke second Lord, account of iii. 413. preparations for the Queen's reception 498

Coin, base, called in i. 87

Coke, Sir Edward, account of iii. 568

Colchester, order for the Queen's reception at ii. 286

Collyweston, account of i. 204

Colt, George, notice of ii. 224

Compton, Henry Lord, account of i. 317. ii. 93. one of the Peers on the trial of Mary Queen of Scots ii. 510

Cooke, Robert, account of ii. 512

———— Maister, speech to the Queen ii. 319

Cooper, Thomas, account of i. 236

Cope, Anthony, three of the same name Sheriffs of Oxfordshire iii. 568

———— Sir Walter, letter to Lady Kitson ii. *250. account of his son Walter iii. 601

Copinger, Ambrose, account of iii. 578

———— Rev. Henry, account of, and epitaph ii. 53, 54

———— William, account of ii. 55

Copt Hall, account of i. 253

Cordell, Sir William, account of ii. 108, 116

Coriat, George, account of i. 236

Cornhill, houses in, sold, and foundation-stone of Royal Exchange laid i. 200

Cornwallis, Richard, account of and family iii. 30

Corpus Christi College, Cambridge, by whom founded i. 150

Cotton, Henry, Bp. of Salisbury, account of iii. 448

———— William, Bp. of Exeter, account of iii. 449

Coventry, account of the Queen's entertainment at i. 192. mayor of, displaced 260. cause of decay of trade at 448. library established at iii. 569

Cowdray-house, Sussex, iii. 81. the Queen's entertainment at 90

Cowper, Thomas, Bp. of Winchester, notices of i. 361. preached at St. Paul's a thanksgiving sermon ii. 538

VOL. III.

Courts, Inns of, on education in i. xxi. apparel to be worn by members of iii. 32

Cox, Richard, Bp. of Ely, Ambassador to the Queen i. 66. letter from on providing for the poor 257. letter to the Lord Treasurer, respecting his riches, and on behalf of his fellow Bishops 389. requested to give up his house in Holborn, with his refusal 390. his letter to the Queen ib. the Queen's letter to him to give up Ely House iii. 41

———— Captain, a humorous personage in the entertainment at Kenilworth i. 449

Cradock, Edward, account of i. 232

Cranmer, Thomas, Abp. of Canterbury, godfather to the Queen i. 2

Craudene, John, founder of Trinity Hall i. 150

Cromer, William, account of i. 353

Cromwell, Sir Henry, called the Golden Knight ii. 109

Cromwell (alias Williams), account of some of the family of i. 179

Croydon, palace and gateway i. 331, 385. preparations for receiving the Queen at i. 385. Abp. Whitgift's hospital at 387. iii. 519

Cuddington, royal residence at i. 74

Cuffe, Henry, executed for treason iii. 151

Cullum, Sir John, his account of Hawsted House ii. 117

Cumberland, George Clifford third Earl of, appointed the Queen's champion iii. 44, 497. biographical account of his family 490. his great strength 492. account of his passion for nautical adventures 496. the order of the Garter conferred on him 497. his speech to the Queen, as a pensive and discontented Knight 522. letters to Lord Burleigh 522, 523, 524. to Sir Francis Walsingham 523

Cut and long tail, meaning of i. 445

Cutt, or Cutts, Sir John, account of i. 278. ii. 221

Cynthia, ode to, sung before the Queen at the Earl of Cumberland's iii. 490

D.

Dacre, Lord, letter to on Vertue's description of the picture of the Hunsdon House procession i. xvi.

Dartford Priory fitted up as a Royal Palace, and descent of i. xi. 354

Davies, John, conference between a Gentleman Usher and a Post iii. 76, 570

Davison, Mr. William, Ambassador in the Low Countries, and afterwards Secretary of State, letter to him from the Earl of Leicester ii. 277

Decanter, a curious one iii. 98

Dee, Dr. John, memoirs of i. 414.

Delia, Death of, a poem on the Queen's funeral iii. 628
Denmark, Frederick second King of, invested with the Order of the Garter ii. 392
Denne, Samuel, remarks on the accompts kept by churchwardens i. xlix. observations on the orthography of Vauxhall, or Foxhall, with the descent of the manor iii. 438
Derby, Edward Stanley fourth Earl of, sent to attend the Privy Council on the Queen's accession i 30. attends at Westminster 38
—— Alice Countess Dowager of (afterwards Lady Egerton), entertains the Queen at Harefield Place iii. 581, 586. lines in praise of 582. acrostics on her three daughters Ladies Anne (afterwards Strange), Frances, and Elizabeth 628, 629
Dering, Richard, account of i. 335
Desiderata i. xlviii
Desmond, George Earl of, anecdote of ii. 280
Dethick, Sir William, resigns the office of Garter King of Arms ii. 512
Devereux, Robert, Earl of Essex. See *Essex*
Devonshire, Edward Courtney Earl of, Queen Mary's partiality for him i. 4. sent to the Tower ib. imprisoned in Fotheringay Castle 25. his death ib.
Dew's farm iii. 583
Dimmocke, Sir Edward, champion at the Coronation i. 60
Dinners, charges for i. 71, 358
Dixie, Sir Wolstan, Lord Mayor of London, pageant of ii. 446. founder of the grammar-school at Market Bosworth ib.
Dochyn, Thomas, account of iii. 157
Doddington, account of i. 257
Dorset, Margaret Marchioness of (widow of Thomas Grey second Marquis), godmother to the Queen i. 2
Dover, visited by Henry VIII. i. 345
—— Castle, inscription on piece of ordnance at i. 336
Downes, Edward, verses by, on delivering a pair of gold spurs to the Queen at Erlham ii. 132. sent to the Tower 216
Drake, Sir Francis, visited by the Queen on board his ship ii. 303
Drayton, Michael, verses in praise of the Queen iii. 63
Drew, Edward, his speech to the Queen, when Recorder of London iii. 228
Drury, Sir William, account of ii. 117. killed in a duel in France iii. 30. epitaph 31
—— Lady Elizabeth, the Queen's letter to her on her husband's death i. xxix.

Ducarel, Dr. Andrew Coltée, letter from Dr. Birch to i. 386
Duddeley, Thomas, letter to the Earl of Leicester ii. 455
Dudley, Ambrose. See *Warwick*
—— Robert. See *Leicester*
Dunkirk, English ships pillaged, under pretence of carrying provisions to ii. 5
Durham House iii. 371
Dutch Church, oration by a minister of the, to the Queen at Norwich ii. 151, 152
Dyer, Edward, knighted, and appointed Chancellor of the Order of the Garter i. 329
—— Lodowick, account of ii. 109

E.

Edmonds, Sir Thomas, letter to the Earl of Shrewsbury iii. 595
Edward VI. his autograph i. x. used to call Elizabeth " his sweet Sister Temperance" vi. letter to from Prs. Elizabeth 3. place of his birth 75. acquainted with his father's death 101. letter from 261
Edwards, Richard, account of l. 235
Egerton, Sir Thomas, the Earl of Essex committed to his custody iii. 441. account of the Queen's visit to him at Harefield, with biographical memoirs of the family iii. 581. lines in praise of his lady (Alice Countess Dowager of Derby) 582
Egyptians, Old, described i. 440
ELIZABETH, Princess, afterwards QUEEN, her birth i. 1. ceremony of, and persons at, her christening ib. her godfather and godmothers 2. letter to Edward VI. from Hatfield 3. called by her Brother Edward his " sweet Sister Temperance" i. vi. expences of her domestic establishment at Hatfield vii. mode of gaining popularity xi. portraits of her destroyed xii. her portrait at Hatfield described ib. anecdote of ib. proclamation respecting her portrait ib. descriptions of her person by several authors xiii. character of by Fuller ib. Mr. Roger's remarks on the portraits of the Queen and the Earl of Leicester xiv. letter to Sir Anthony Aucher 3. letter to King Edward VI. on his desiring to have her picture *28. letter to Sir Francis Jernegan while she was in confinement at Woodstock *29. placed under the care of Sir Thomas Pope 4, 19. under the care of Dowager Queen Catherine Parr at Chelsea while Princess iii. 389. rode in a chariot at Q. Mary's coronation i. 4. treated with disrespect and insult by Queen Mary 5. illness of at Ashridge,

and removal to London 6. requests not to be sent to the Tower ib. conveyed to the Tower 7. committed to the custody of Sir Henry Bedingfield 8. her removal from the Tower to Woodstock ib. sonnet written by her on her window-shutter at Woodstock 9. her writing in a book while in confinement 10. embossed devices and inscriptions on the covers of a book ib. translated an Italian sermon into Latin, and wrote it elegantly on vellum ib. her removal to the Court on King Philip's interposition 11. released from guards and keepers 12. minute of her officers to the Queen's Council 13. visits the Queen at Richmond 17. suffered to make excursions ib. her progress in learning i. ix. x. 19. verses by, upon the Queen of Scots 20. reported that she had married Lord Edward Courtney, and proceedings thereon 21. Eric King of Sweden proposes marriage to her 22. her refusal ib. marriage with the Duke of Savoy proposed to her by King Philip ib. her refusal 25. her regard for, and anecdotes of her coquetry with, Lord Thomas Seymour 23. iii. 514. the King of Sweden renews his addresses to her when Queen i. 27. offended with his solicitations ib. threatens to dismiss her Privy Counsel ib. her accession to the throne 29. proclaimed Queen ib. her first Privy Council held at Hatfield 30. her Progress through London to Westminster from the Charter-house 32. preparations for her public procession through London to her Coronation 34. her attendants 36, 37. account of the procession from the Tower to Westminster 38—58. notes of her mercy, clemency and wisdom, in her procession 58. her coronation 60. her first Parliament 63. her first speech in Parliament ib. her answer to the message of the Commons respecting her marriage ib. her Ambassadors return from France after concluding a peace 66. entertained by the City of London at Greenwich 69. named a ship when launched at Woolwich after herself 73. entertainment given by her at Greenwich ib. proclamation respecting singing men and boys 81. visits the Mints, and coins pieces of gold 91. offended with the clergy, and her order respecting them 96. wives of the clergy not to reside within colleges, &c. 104. presents to her from the King of Sweeden ib. the hedges cut down to enable her to go from Islington to Charing-cross ib. present to from the King of Sweden ib. conversation with Dean Nowel respecting the Church service 105. her second Parliament 106. fac-similes of her signature x. 108, 119, 120, 130. ii. 65, 80, 81, 91, 249, 264. iii. 1, 14, 22, 25, 445, 459, 467. letter to the Earl of Huntingdon i. 142. ratifies the treaty of Troyes 149. godmother to Sir William Cecil's daughter ib. congratulated by the scholars at Eton and Cambridge xv. preparations for her reception and entertainment at Cambridge 151 —189. Latin speech of to the University of Cambridge 176. her speech epitomized 177. persons made Masters of Arts at Cambridge 180, 188. her partiality for the Earl of Leicester 190. ill of the flux 191. entertained at Coventry and Kenilworth 192. offended with the Earl of Leicester 198. godmother to the Prince of Baden's son ib. letter to the Earl of Shrewsbury 201. her fondness for music 209. questions disputed before her at Oxford 213. her Latin orations at Oxford 217, 250. refuses marriage with the Duke of Anjou (afterwards Henry III. of France) xxxiii. advice to the Duke of Norfolk on his meditated marriage with the Queen of Scots 257. her reprimand to him ib. letter to from Lord Heriz on Scottish politics 258. letter depriving the Mayor of Coventry of his office 260. letter to the Earl of Huntingdon 261. account of the office of Keeper of her Purse 264. her birth-day kept 274. carried by gentlemen in a chair of state 282. letter to from Lord Hunsdon 285. taken ill, and relieved by an emetic 291. her recovery 292. fell sick again, but soon recovered ib. her skill in music 293, 487, 529. letter to the Lord Mayor of London 296. letter staying an execution 297. Duke d'Alençon's proffered marriage with her 304. royal donation to the gentlemen of the Queen's chapel 307. entertained at Warwick 309. Latin verses presented to her at Warwick 316. her departure from Warwick 318. positive refusal of marriage 321. letter to the Earl of Shrewsbury respecting her illness 322. sick with the small-pox, and speedy recovery 322, 324. her dislike to Abp. Parker's marriage 331. preparations for her entertainment at Sandwich, when she left Dover 337. her regard for the sabbath 353, 529. her attention to business 354. list of her plate and jewels 381. her rebuke to the Earl of Leicester 385. receives presents from Mary of Scots 386. passed six days in retirement at Havering 387. her despotic temper 392. godmother to Thomas son of Lord Berkeley ib. gives orders for monuments at Fotheringay to the memory of her ancestors the Dukes of York 410. petition to, on account of the difficulty of procuring payment for goods taken by her purveyors 411. a purveyor hanged ib. attends the Countess of Pembroke when sick 416. verses in praise of 599. a prayer used by her after her progress to Bristol in 1574, 601. touched persons with the evil xxii. letter to Lady Drury on the death of her husband xxix. her great regard for the Earl of Leicester xxxii. recommends the Earl of Leicester to marry the Queen of Scots ib. displeased at the Earl of Leicester's being recommended to her for a husband xxxiii. her prayer-book xxxvii. presented with a pair of silk stockings, and never wore cloth ones afterwards xlii. the first person who wore knit stockings ib. complimented in verse by Mr. Gascoigne xliv. expences at the commencement and latter part of her reign ib. conversation with Mr. Browne, on the household expences xlv. letter to the Master and Fellows of Queen's College, Cambridge ii. 3. her speech in Parliament 1575-6 noticed ib. daily expences of her table in 1576, 8—48. incidental charges not in her diet-book 48. letter to the Earl of Shrewsbury, on his entertaining the Earl of Leicester 63. attended by the University of Cambridge at Audley End 111. dropped her fan into the moat at Hawsted 118. verses delivered to her with a pair of gold spurs 132. her reception at Norwich 133. hunts in Gossie Park 151. her entertainment in Suffolk and Norfolk 179—213. gentlemen knighted by her in Suffolk and Norfolk 224. her love of money and costly apparel 261. one of her watermen shot while she was in her barge, her clemency on that occasion 285. the King of Barbary's letter to her 288. her warrant respecting Maundy Thursday 297. letters to Dr. Chaderton, Bp. of Chester 298, 299, 453. opens the Parliament 302, 423. at the Justs in the Tilt-yard, when several persons were killed 302. letter to from the Grand Turk ib. visits Sir Francis Drake in his ship 303. disturbed by beggars at Islington ib. her letter to Sir Henry Sidney ib. letter to the Earl of Argyle 304. his answer 305. triumphal Justs before her 334. iii. 41. negociation of marriage with the Duke of Anjou ii. 337. displeased with the Earl of Leicester's marriage with the Countess of Essex 337. visited by the Duke of Anjou 343. accompanies him to Canterbury on his departure 345. sonnet by, on parting with him 346. Camden's account of her parting with the Duke of Anjou 386. Lord Burleigh petitions the Queen to permit him to retire from office 399. her humourous letter to him on the subject 400. letter to the Sheriff of Lancashire 421. sonnet addressed to 424. order of her proceeding to Parliament 433. iii. 409. letter to the Bishop of Chester to raise forces ii. 453. her jealousy of being outshone in splendour 455. letter to Sir George Barne, relating to a conspiracy. 481. her present to a young Hollander 481. letter to from Babington, the conspirator 482. King James's remonstrance with her, on account of the condemnation of Mary Queen of Scots 495. letter to from King James, on his Mother's sentence 501. her letter to King James disavowing her privity to his Mother's death 507. letters, &c. from Lord Burleigh to her, on the death of Mary Queen of Scots 521. in the camp at Tilbury 532. her speech to the soldiers 536. letter to from the Lord Mayor of London on the defeat of the Spaniards 537. went to St. Paul's Cathedral to return thanks 538. gave bond to the citizens for £.20,000 she borrowed of them 543. poems, &c. dedicated to her by Aske and Churchyard on the overthrow of the Spaniards 545—612. letter to Sir Edward Stafford 626. to the young King of Scots 627. to Mrs. Anne Talbot 628. anecdote of, respecting purveyors iii. 37. letter to Dr. Cox, Bp. of Ely respecting Ely House 41. prayer for her 48. resembled to a crowned pillar 51. to a spire 52, poems in praise of her 54, 67, 175, 250, 349, 350. grants a charter to Winchester 68. letter to Lord Burleigh 75. anecdote of 79. provisions served for her household 83. proclamation respecting the Queen of Scots' sentence 99. entertained at Elvetham 101. at Bisham, Sudeley, and Ricot 130. wells called by her name 132. her Latin speech at Oxford 147. cause of her visiting Oxford a second time 149. makes a speech at leaving Oxford 160. verses to her by Carleton 176. letter to from Mr. Francis Bacon 190. her regard for the Earl of Monmouth 246. displeased with a sermon preached by Dr. Aylmer Bp. of London 249. lines to by Sir John Harrington 250. letter to Peregrine Bertie Lord Willoughby 260. entertained by the Earl of Essex 371. her procession to Parliament 409. letter to King Henry IV. of France 412. order of receiving her in the College Church of Westminster, on the first day of Parliament 415. her conference with the Polish Ambassador 416. with the Danish Ambassador 419. with a Bohemian Baron 425. letter to Lady Norris 420. ceremonial used in decking her table 425. words spoken by her to Lord Burleigh 427. letter from the Earl of Essex, on his going to Ireland 432. present at the marriage of Mrs. Hennyngham 438. commands the Lord Keeper and others against rumourous talk of the Earl of Essex 442. letters to from Sir Francis Bacon, on New-year's gifts 468. address to her, in verse, as a New-year's gift 469—488. letter to from Sir Francis Bacon 489. Ode to Cynthia performed before her at the Earl of Cumberland's 490. letter to Lady Paget on the death of her daughter Lady Crompton 497. at Lord Herbert's wedding 498. her wardrobe in 1600, 500. her luxury in dress 504. portraits of her at Hardwick and Hatfield i. xii. iii. 506. takes the diversion of hunting in Hanworth Park iii 514. receives the Russian Ambassador 515. the Ambassador from the King of Barbary 516. compared to Cynthia's brightness 525. dialogue between two Shepherds spoken before her at the Countess of Pembroke's 529. "The Right Way to Heaven," a poem, by Mr. Vennard, in praise of her as "The Miracle of Nature" 532. acrostic on her 533. reads a letter, but rejects a present from the Earl of Essex 550. letter to Sir George Carew 551. her conversation with Mr. Lambarde on receiving a present from him 552. her improvements at Windsor Castle, and her studies there 564. her entertainment in Hampshire 566. knighted several gentlemen at Basing and at Reading 567, 568. letters to Lord Deputy Mountjoy 569, 575, 579, 596. a Lottery presented before her at Sir Thomas Egerton's 570. occasionally went a-maying on May-day 577. her visit at Harefield Place 581—595. styled "Beauty's Rose" 591. her fondness for hunting 598. delays her visits on account of the small-pox being very general 600. godmother to the French Ambassador's daughter 602. particulars of her latter days by Anne Countess of Pembroke i. xxiii. Sir Robert Carey's account of her last sickness and death iii. 603. sign made by her when speechless 604, 605, 608. confirmation of Sir Robert Carey's account of her last illness 607. her last words 608. Strype's account of her illness and death 609. character, and anecdote of 610. Jesuit Parsons's account of her sickness and death 612. description of her funeral 614. poems on her death and funeral 615, 620, 628, 640, 641, 650, 651. order of procession at her funeral 621. fees given at the funeral 627. expired while the music was playing in her chamber 630. epitaphs 650, 651

Elizabetha quasi Vivens iii. 615
Elizabetha Triumphans ii. 545—582
Elmley Castle, account of i. 543
Eltham, Royal Palace at i. 74
Elvetham, the Queen splendidly entertained at iii. 101. pond at ib.
Ely House, London, description of iii. 122

Emanuel College, Cambridge, by whom founded i. 150, 173
Enfield, account of the Royal Palace at i. 101
Eridge, account of i. 334
Erlham, descent of the manor of ii. 132
Essex, Robert Devereux second Earl of, family notices of i. 503. device exhibited by before the Queen on the anniversary of her accession iii. 371. his departure for Ireland 432. letter to the Queen, considering his going to Ireland as a banishment ib. Churchyard's "Fortunate Farewell" to him 433. his return from Ireland 438. visits the Queen at Nonsuch 441. committed to the care of Lord Keeper Sir Thomas Egerton ib. his principal residence was at York-house ib. the Lord Keeper and others persuaded against rumorous talk of him 443. permitted to return to York-house 489. his apprehension, arraignment, and execution 544—550. presented with £.50 by the corporation of Coventry 544. Sir Robert Cecil's account of the cause of his death being hastened 546. his speech at the place of execution 548. his prayer 549. his last words 550. possessors of the ring, on which his life is said to have depended 550. his illness said to be feigned ib.
Eton, verses under the arms at the school i. 142. description of 147
Evelyn, George, account of iii. 489
Euston, descent of the manor of ii. 216
Exchange, Royal, foundation-stone laid i. 200
Exchequer, Court of, necessaries furnished for in 1579-80 ii. 290
Execution, eleven persons for robbery i. 82
Exeter House iii. 79
Exeter 'Change iii. 79

F.

Fans, specimens and description of those used in Queen Elizabeth's time ii. 118
Farley Wallop, account of and its owners iii. 100
Farnham Palace, Surrey iii. 90
Faversham, extracts from the Chamberlain's book of expences at i. 352. King James's visit to ib.
Felix Hall, account of i. 95
Ferdinando, Emperor, obsequies for i. 191
Ferrers, M. verses by i. 491
Field, Rev. Mr. account of iii. 124
Finland, Duke of, a Prince of Sweden, arrival of in London i. 79. at Court 82. at Windsor 87
Fireworks introduced for the Queen's amusement i. 319, 440
Fisher, Thomas, account of i. 332
Fitz-William, Hugh, letter to the Countess of Shrewsbury i. 291

Fitzwilliams, Sir William, account of ii. 533
Fleetwood, William, Recorder of London, City Diary of i. 355
Fleming, Thomas, his speech, as Recorder of London, on presenting the Lord Mayor iii. 254. form of his discharge from the degree of Serjeant at Law, when made Solicitor-general 370
Fletcher, Richard, Bp. of London, acc. of ii. 510
Fork, a curious one iii. 370
Fortescue, Sir John, account of iii. 578
Fortunate Farewell to the Earl of Essex iii. 434
Foster, Sir Humphrey, account of iii. 568
Foulks, William, thanksgiving sermon i. 292
Fox, Samuel, extracts from his Diary i. 253
Foxhall, observations on the orthography of, and its owners iii. 438 a different place from Vauxhall gardens 440
France, Henry II. King of, cause of his death i. 73. funeral kept at St. Paul's 76
——— Henry III. King of, his proposed marriage with the Queen i. xxxiii. invested with the Garter ii. 428
——— Henry IV. King of, invested with the garter iii. 398. entertainment of Mary de Medicis his Queen 517
——— Ambassadors from entertained i. 67. their departure 68. peace with 148, 306. arrival of noblemen from iii. 565. entertained at Basing 566.
——— and Scotland, peace with i. 83
Francis, Thomas, account of i. 241
Friendship, a Spark of, and warm Good-will ii. 582
Frobisher, Sir Martin, Welcome-home to, by Church-yard ii. 233. took possession of a part of New Greenland ib.
Fuller, Dr. Tho. his character of the Queen i. xiii
Fulshart, the Queen's fool, committed to Bridewell i. 204
Fulston, descent of i. 353
Fulwell, Stephen, autograph iii. 14, 22, 25
Furth, or Ford, notice of, 245

G.

Gage, Maister (probably Sir Edward) the Queen under his care i. 12. account of, and of some of the family of ib.
Gar. Ber. See *Goldingham*.
Gascoigne, George, verses complimenting the Queen i. xliv. his Princely Pleasures at Kenilworth 485. some account of, and epitaph for ib. The Hermit's Tale at Woodstock 553
Gaudy, Sir Basing, account of ii. 225
Geason, meaning of i. 442
Gerards, Mark, account of i. 297
Gesner, Conrad, account of i. 441

Gesta Grayorum, an account of the entertainment at Gray's Inn iii. 262—348
Gibbons, Edward, account of iii. 158
Giddy Hall, account of i. 253
Gifford, John, account of i. 232
Gilbert, Sir Humphrey, account of, and verses on his voyage, by Churchyard ii. 226—232
——— Richard, account of ii. 226
Gipps, Sir Richard, account of i. xxi
Gloves, perfumed and embroidered, presented to the Queen iii. 660
Godwin, Thomas, Bp. of Bath and Wells, account of i. 230
Goldingham, Bernard, one of the contrivers of the sports at Norwich on the Queen's visit ii. 134. account of the reception and entertainment of the Queen at Norwich 137
——— Henry, account of i. 458, 502. address to the Queen prefixed to his "Garden Plot" ii. 135
Goldsborough, Godfrey, Bp. of Gloucester, account of iii. 449
Goldwell, Henry, his account of the entertainment to the Queen and the French Ambassadors at the Tilt-yard ii. 310. his dedication to Mr. Bracebridge ib.
Gonville and Caius College, Cambridge, by whom founded i. 150
——— Edmond, joint founder of Gonville and Caius College i. 150
Goodwin, Sir Edward, account of iii. 567
Gorges, Sir Arthur, presents the Queen with a jewell as she passed his house at Chelsea iii. 442
Gorhambury, the Queen's first visit at in 1572 i. 309. again in 1573 602. account of ii. 55. expences of the Queen's entertainment at in 1577, 57
Goring, Henry, letter respecting his entertainment of the Queen ii. 62
Gosfield, account of i. 98
Gough, Richard, his friendship to Mr. Nichols, and assistance in forming the Collection for this Work i. v. letter to Lord Dacre, on the picture of Hunsdon House procession xvi. bequeaths three maps in tapestry, and his valuable library to the University of Oxford xvii. Vertue's account of the painting at Hunsdon controverted by i. 289. part of a curious chimney-piece from Theobalds preserved by him in his library iii. 76. his sketch of the pedigree of the Cecil family at Theobalds 242. place of his birth iii. 598
Grafton, royal palace at ii. 6
Grammar-schools, fashionable places of education i. xi
Granville, Cardinal, account of ii. 218
Gray, James, epitaph on i. 289

INDEX.

Gray's Inn, letter on the Masques at i. xx. customs of students at xxi. orders respecting the pastimes at ii. 390. apparel to be worn by gentlemen of iii. 34. masques at for the entertainment of the Queen 262. commons at 351

Green, Richard, curious instrument of brass in his Museum at Lichfield i. 484

Greenwich, birth-place of the Queen i. 1. the Queen entertained with a military muster of the Citizens of London 69, 206. descent of the alace of, to the time of Queen Elizabeth, 69. entertainment given by the Queen at 73

Gresham, Sir John (uncle of Sir Thomas), account of ii. 279

———— Sir Richard, (father of Sir Thomas), account of ii. 279

———— Sir Thomas, founder of the Royal Exchange i. 200. ii. 283. entertains the Queen at Mayfield i. 233. Count Cassimer ii. 277. visited by the Queen at Osterley 279. manor of Heston granted him by the Queen ib. time of his birth ib. New-year's gifts presented to Queens Mary and Elizabeth, and gifts received in return ib. his will 282 founder of Gresham College 283. his death 284

———— Lady, her contribution at the threatened invasion ii. 284

Greville, Sir Fulk, letter to the Countess of Shrewsbury iii. 597. account of ib.

Grey Friars (Christ Church), sermon at i. 91

Grey, Lady Jane, her autograph i. x. beheaded 4

———— Sir John, Purgo granted to him by the Queen i. 93

Griffin, Maurice, Bp. of Rochester, his death and funeral i. 3.

Grindal, Edmund, Bp. of London (afterwards Abp. of Canterbury) the Queen displeased with i. 386. letter from respecting it 387

———————— Vice-chancellor of Cambridge, letters to i. 152

Guilford, Lord Dudley and Lady Jane beheaded i. 4

Guillim, St. John, description of the Queen's funeral iii. 614

Guldesford, Mr. account of i. 334

Gunton, Symon, particulars relating to the funeral of Mary Queen of Scots ii. 502

Gusman, ————, Dean of Toledo, the Spanish Ambassador notices of i. 207, 234

Gwin, Matthew, account of iii. 152

H.

Hadham Hall, ii. 222

Haddon, Dr. Walter, sent for to attend the Privy Council on the Queen's accession i. 30. verses in praise of the Queen 599

Hake, Edward, his speech to the Queen at New Windsor, ii. 461—480

Hallingbury, Great, account of i. 99

Hampton Court, births, marriages, &c. at i. 75. description of 274. iii. 232

Hanworth, a royal residence i. 23. iii. 513, 514

Hardwick House fitted up to receive the Queen of Scots, and a visit from Queen Elizabeth, remains in the same state ii. 543

Harefield Lodge, built by Sir Roger Newdigate iii. 583

Harefield Place, description of, and account of the Queen's visit to iii. 581—595

Harford, John, deprived of his office of Mayor of Coventry i. 260

Harrington, John, (father of Sir John) account of ii. 261. began the house at Kelveston 250

———————— Sir John, letter to from Sir Robert Sidney i. xxxix. extracts from his papers xlvii. iii. 247, 429, 443. Sheriff of Somersetshire iii. 249. lines to the Queen 250. finished the house at Kelveston ib. visits Lord Buckhurst 429. advice to 430

Harris, Vincent, account of ii. 287

Hartie, Isle of, combat to be fought for the manor and lands of i. 277

Harvey, Gabriel, acc. of, and his works ii. 110

Harwich, the Queen entertained by the borough of i. 97

Hastings, Earls of Huntingdon. See *Huntingdon*.

———— William, beheaded i. xix

Hatfield House, Prs. Elizabeth's residence i. 3, 4. new built by Robert first Earl of Salisbury 12

Hatton, Sir Christopher, memoirs of iii. 40, 123. his advice to Sir John Harrington 430

Hatton House, account of iii. 41, 122

Havering atte Bower, Dr. Fox born and christened at i. 253. description of 307. description of the Palace at iii. 70. inscription on a stone taken from the ruins of the Palace 71

Hawford, Edward, Vice-chancellor, letters to i. 151, 152, 153

Hawsted House, description of ii. 119. figure of Hercules at 121. emblems at 124

Heath, Dr. Nicholas, Abp. of York, appointed Chancellor by Q. Mary i. 28. appointed with others, to transact urgent business on the Queen's accession 30. biographical account of 250

Helmingham, account of i. 98

Hely, William, killed i. 260

Heneage, Sir Thomas, letter to Sir John Puckering iii. 129

Hengrave Hall, account of, and of some expences when the Queen visited there i. xxix

Henley, Dr. Samuel, contemplated a similar work to the present i. v.

Hennyngham, Mrs. Mary, the Queen present at her wedding iii. 438

Henry VI. King, founder of King's College, Cambridge i. 150

Henry VII. King, yearly expences of his reign i. xliv
Henry VIII. King, increasing annual expence of xliv. founder of Trinity College, Cambridge i. 150. at Dover i. 345
Henry Frederick, Prince, son of King James, ceremony of his baptism i. xlii. iii. 353
Henry II. of France, the first person who wore knit stockings in that kingdom i. xlii.
Henry III. King of France, proposed marriage with the Queen when Duke of Anjou i. xxxiii. invested with the order of the Garter ii. 428
Henry IV. King of France invested with the order of the Garter iii. 398. entertainment of Mary de Medicis, his Queen iii. 517
Hentzner, Paul, on education at the Inns of Court i. xxi. his description of Windsor and Eton 143. account of bull and bear-baitings ii. 459. of proclaiming Bartholomew fair iii. 31. description of Oxford 172. of Woodstock 174. of Hampton Court 232. of Theobalds 241. of the Queen's Court at Greenwich iii. 484
Herbert, Henry Somerset Lord, the Queen at his wedding i. xxii. iii. 498. account of i. xxii.
Herbs, distillation of ii. 123
Heriz, Lord, letter to the Queen on Scottish politics i. 258
Hermit's Tale at Woodstock, the i. 553
Hertford, Edward Seymour second Earl of, entertainment given to the Queen at Elvetham iii. 101.
———— fair and charter granted to i. 100
Hessen, Langrave of, his princely receiving and entertaining the English Ambassador iii. 380—397
Heston, grant of maner of ii. 279. Norden's description of ib.
Hicham (or Higham), Sir Robert, account of ii. 129, 224
Hide Hall, Herts, the two Hide Halls distinguished ii. 222
Higford, John, account of, and family iii. 129
Higham family, account of ii. 129
Hinchinbrook, account of i. 179
Hobbinol's Ditty, by Spenser iii. 56
Hoby, Thomas Posthumus, account of the Queen's intended visit to Bisham iii. 124. account of his entertainment to the Queen 131
———— family, account of iii. 131
Hoke-tide, elucidation of i. 446
Holdeston, or Hurleston, Keeper of a hold at Calais, sentenced to suffer death for negligence i. 81
Holland, Thomas, account of iii. 155
Hooke, Thomas, account of ii. 246
Horeham, account of i. 281
Horne, Robert, Bishop of Winchester, preached at the Queen's Chapel i. 88

Howard of Effingham, Charles Lord (afterwards Earl of Nottingham), account of iii. 414, 601
Howard, Lord Thomas (afterwards Earl of Suffolk), visited by King James, who held his Court at the Charter-house iii. 602
———— Catharine Lady, Chelsea Place granted her iii. 414
Howland, John, account of ii. 109
———— Richard, Vice-chancellor of Cambridge, letter to Lord Burleigh their Chancellor ii. 109. his answer 110. account of 510
Huicke, Robert, account of i. 231, 245
Hume, Sir George (afterwards Lord), account of iii. 600
———— David, account of the negociation of marriage with the Queen and Duke of Anjou ii. 337. his account of King James's intercession to save Mary Queen of Scots 495. account of the Queen's luxury in dress 504. account of the Earl of Essex's illness iii. 550
Humphrey, Lawrence, account of i. 207, 230. reflected upon by the Queen for his preciseness 207. his Oration at Woodstock 585
———— William, grant to i. 147
Hunnis, William, account of i. 489
Hunsdon, Henry Cary, created first Lord i. 284. anecdote of ib. letter of thanks from the Queen 285. visited by the Queen on his death-bed 286. his death 286. iii. 380. epitaph on John his second son i. 286. epitaph on his park-keeper 289
———— George Carey second Lord, account of iii. 27. his death 577
———— House, painting supposed to be a procession to described i. 283. its removal 288. description of the house ib.
Huntingdon, Henry Hastings third Earl of, the Queen's letter to, on her interview with the Queen of Scots i. 142. letter to on the Earl of Shrewsbury's illness, and on the confinement of Mary Queen of Scots 261
———— George Hastings fourth Earl of, account of ii. 511
———— Henry Hastings fifth Earl of, entertained King James at Ashby-de-la-Zouch i. xix.
Hurd, Richard, Bishop of Worcester, on trial by battle i. 277
Hutton, Matthew, Abp. of York, account of iii. 448
Hynde, John, account of ii. 109

I.

Ichington, Bishop's, account of i. 310
Ingatestone (Ingerston), account of i. 94
Invasion, Spanish, preparations for resisting ii. 531
Ipswich, assessment at, for entertaining the Queen, i. 97

Jaline, Paulus de, Ambassador from the King of Poland, his arrival iii. 416
James I. King, his dislike to tobacco ii. 125. letter to his Secretary 482. his remonstrance with the Queen in behalf of his mother 495. his letter to the Queen on her sentence 501. the Queen's letter disavowing her privity to the death of his mother 507. his letter desiring the removal of his mother's body to Westminster 520. letter to from the Queen 627. his regard for the Howard family iii. 602. held his Court at the Charter-house ib. proclaimed King 605. crowned by Abp. Whitgift 611. entertained at Ashby-de-la-Zouch by the Earl of Huntingdon i. xix. died at Theobalds iii. 76
James II. his visit at Faversham i. 353
Jermin, Sir Robert, account of, and family ii. 128, 224
Jernegan, Sir Francis, letter to from the Princess i. *29
Jesus College, Cambridge, by whom founded i. 150
Jewell, John, Bp. of Salisbury, notice of i. 214
Jones, J. epitaph on the Queen iii. 651
Justs at the Tilt-yard ii. 302, 310. iii. 41, 443, 600. a series of triumphal, with the prizes given 330—336

K.

Kelke, Roger, Archdeacon of Stowe, death of i. 167
Kelston, or Kelweston, the seat of the Harrington family ii. 250, 261
Kendal Green, a side gown of i. 461
Kenilworth, the Queen splendidly entertained at i. 197, 318, 418, 426. view of 423
Kennall, John, account of i. 231, 240
Kenninghall, description of ii. 130
Kery, Thomas, letter to Lord Talbot iii. 68
Key, or Cay, Thomas, notice of i. 239
King's College, Cambridge, by whom founded i. 150. the Queen's reception and entertainment at 163, 171
Kirtells, a garment iii 506
Kirtling, account of ii. 219, 220.
Kitson, Sir Thomas, account of i. xxix. ii. 129, 224. letter to Mr. Playter ii. *250
———— Lady, letters to ii. *250
Knevet, Sir Thomas, account of ii. 224
Knife, account of a curious one ii. 423
Knightly, Sir Richard, account of ii. 511
Knollys, Sir William, account of iii. 564
Knowlls and Norris, account of the families of iii. 420

L.

Lacy, John, account of ii. 92
Lady of the Lake i. 431, 491
Lambarde, William, his present to the Queen, and conversation with her iii. 552. was the first Protestant that built an hospital 554. letters to Lord Burleigh ib. 558. biographical memoirs of ib. expence of building his hospital 560, 561. his epitaph 563
Lambeth Palace i. 325
Laneham, John, life and character of i. 420. portrait of 425. his account of the Queen's entertainment at Kenilworth Castle i. 426
Largess, meaning of i. 466
Latimer, Dr. William, account of i. 180
Latten, mines of i. 148
Lawns first brought into England iii. 504
Lawrence, Giles, account of i. 233
Lee, Sir Anthony, epitaph iii. 45
———— Sir Henry, biographical account of, and of his family iii. 42, 125. epitaph 44. monument for his Lady 47
———— Capt. Thomas, executed at Tyburn iii. 546
Leech, James, notice of i. 232
————— William, notice of i. 232
Lees, account of i. 99
Leicester, preparations for receiving the Queen at i. 417. the corporation of splendidly entertain the Earl of Leicester ii. 421
Leicester, Robert Dudley, the celebrated Earl of, Mr. Rogers's remarks on his portrait i. xiv. recommended to marry Mary Queen of Scots xxxii. his marriages xxxiii. elected K. G. 67. installed 68. his reception at Cambridge 156. created Baron of Denbigh, and afterwards Earl of Leicester 189, 190. Chancellor of the University of Oxford 169. the Queen's partiality for him xxxii. 190. offended with him 198. Knight of the Order of St. Michael 200. letter to Abp. Parker 201. discord with the Earl of Sussex 204. reconciliation ib. on the proffered marriage of the Duke D'Alençon with the Queen 304. influence of 355. rebuked by the Queen 385. issues his warrant for furnishing horses for the Queen 411. preparations for receiving the Queen at Kenilworth 417. strengthens Kenilworth Castle 418. letters to Lord Burleigh 524. New-year's gifts presented to him by the Queen 525. physician's advice to ii. 4. his marriage with the Countess of Essex 223. letter to Mr. Davison, Ambassador for the Low Countries (afterwards Secretary of State) 277. entertained by the Corporation of Leicester 421. letter to the Burgesses of Andover

422. letter to from Lord Burleigh 440. his answer 442. letter from Thomas Duddeley to him at the Hague 455. account of his keeping the feast of St. George at Utrecht ib. letter to the Earl of Shrewsbury on the Queen's triumphal visit to the camp at Tilbury 536. biographical anecdotes and memoirs of him and his family 613—624. his epitaph 614. his character supposed to be written by himself 616. his crest 618

Leicester House iii. 371

Lesley, John, Bishop of Ross, charges against, and his supplication i. 255

Lichfield, expences when the Queen visited i. 529

Lightning, damage by i. 89. storm 96

Limbert, Stephen, his oration to the Queen on her coming to Norwich ii. 155—158. on her departure 168—173

Lincoln, Edward, first Earl of. See *Clinton and Say*

―――― Henry Clinton second Earl of, his residence i. 75. one of the Commissioners on the trial of the Queen of Scots 509. account of iii. 380 Ambassador to the Landgrave of Hessen ib. his entertainment in the Low Countries 395

Lincoln's Inn, customs of students at i. xxi. revels at 251. expences of on great solemnities ib. orders respecting 252. apparel to be worn by gentlemen of iii. 33.

Lindsay, David, Bishop of Ross, baptized King Charles 1. iii. 527

Litany, the English, used in churches and chapels i. 34

Liveries, costly ii. 244, 399

Lloyd, Hugh, account of i. 231

London, many curious wills in the records of the City of, from the reign of King John to Queen Elizabeth, with an accurate calendar kept there i. xlvi. plague in 147, 263. ii. 392. iii. 130, 190. ceased 149. a week's Diary in the city of 355. regulation for the apparel of apprentices in ii. 391. mode of nominating sheriffs 410. splendid shooting match by the citizens 411. offer of raising men, and furnishing ships, by the citizens 530. apparel to be worn by the citizens 543. the citizens lend the Queen £20,000, 543. population of, in 1588 iii. 35, 36. houses ordered to be pulled down on account of their increase 578

Long Melford Hall, owners of ii. 108

Lorde, James, notice of i. 273

Lottery, one presented before the Queen at York-house iii. 570

Lovel, Sir Thomas, account of i. 101

Lougher, or Loffer, Robert, account of i. 231

Loughton, descent of the manor of ii. 222

Lowten Hall, account of i. 94

Lucas, Sir Thomas, account of ii. 286

Ludlow Castle, Court for the Marches held at ii. 306

Lygon, Reginald, notice of i. 541

Lynn, present of the Corporation of to the Queen ii. 275

M.

Madingley ii. 109

Magdalen College, Cambridge, foundation of, and additions to i. 150

Maltravers, Anne Lady, account of, ii. 286

Man, John, sent Ambassador to Spain i. 234

Mansfield, Sir Rice, his funeral i. 66

Maps worked in tapestry i. xvii

Mark Hall, account of i. 281

Marloe, Christopher, extract from his Edw. II. i. 25

Marlow, extracts from the Churchwardens' accompts of iii. 124. "Queen Elizabeth's well" at i. 132

Marsh, Capt. Richard, account of King James the Second's visit to Faversham i. 353

Martyr, Peter, notice of i. 208

Mary Queen of England, autograph i. x. xxxv. her antipathy to Princess Elizabeth 4. her partiality for Edward Earl of Devonshire ib. the Princess visits her at Richmond 15. Sir Thomas Pope's letter to, respecting the Princess's inclinations to marry 23. her death 29. removal of her body to St. James's 33. her funeral in Westminster Abbey ib.

Mary Queen of Scots, her autograph i. x. the Earl of Leicester recommended by Queen Elizabeth to her for a husband xxxii. verses on, by Elizabeth 20. Elizabeth's letter to the Earl of Huntingdon on the intended interview with her 142. Duke of Norfolk reprimanded on his meditated marriage with her 257. letter to the Earl of Huntingdon respecting her confinement 261. plan for liberating her 263. her retinue diminished, and guard doubled ib. sonnet addressed to ii. 425. her trial and condemnation 495. interposition of the young King of Scots in her behalf ib. proclamation against 497. account of her death 502. solemnity of her funeral 508. epitaph for, in Latin and English 519. order for the disinterment of her body at Peterborough, and its removal to Westminster 520. verses on the removal of her supposed tomb 522. Hardwick House, fitted for her reception, remains in its original state 543. proclamation respecting her sentence iii. 99

Mason, Sir John, with others appointed to transact urgent business on the Queen's accession i. 30

Masque of Owls i. 447

Masques, ticket for admission to the i. xxi. the greatest indulgence that could be given xxv. performed before the Queen in 1590 and 1592 iii. 193—213

Mass, persons taken into custody for being at i. 82

Master, Richard, account of i. 232
——— William, speech to the Queen i. 161

Matthew, Tobie, Abp. of York, account of i. 246. iii. 448
——— Toby (his son), account of iii. 372

Maundy Thursday kept at Westminster i. 83. order of keeping described i. 325. ii. 297. warrant respecting ii. 297

Mayfield, description of i. 333

Medicis, Mary de, Queen to Henry IV. of France, account of her voyage from Florence to Marseilles, and entertainment there iii. 517. her entry into Lyons 520

Melford, Long, Suffolk ii. 108

Melvil, Sir James, anecdote respecting Mary Queen of Scots, and Queen Elizabeth i. xii. extract from his Memoirs, on the Earl of Leicester's being recommended to marry Mary Queen of Scots xxxii. anecdote of respecting the Queen's dresses iii. 504

Mercia, Penda King of, slain i. 428

Mericke, John, Bishop of Sodor and Man, account of i. 232

Middleton, query which, visited by the Queen? i. xix.

Mildmay, Thomas, account of ii. 287
——— Sir Walter, founder of Emanuel College, Cambridge i. 150, 173

Millicent, Lord North's kindness to him and others of his servants ii. 241

Milner, John, notice of i. xlvii.

Mineral and Battery Works, society for i. 147

Minstrels, ancient dress of described i. 460

Montmorancy, Mons. and the French Ambassadors, entertained i. 67. gentlemen who accompanied him, and presents given 305

Monmouth, Robert Carey, Lord Lepington, and Earl of, extracts from his Memoirs ii. 497, 535. iii. 214, 245. notice of iii. 27. his account of the Queen's last sickness and death 603

Montague, Anthony first Viscount, account of, and family i. xxvii. sets out for Spain 82
——— Anthony second Viscount, account of i. xxviii.
——— Elizabeth Lady, account of ii. 511

Monyns, Sir Edward, account of iii. 381

Mordaunt, Lewis Lord, sat on the trial of Mary Queen of Scots ii. 510

Morice, William, account of ii. 286

Morland, Sir Samuel, projector of Vauxhall gardens iii. 440

Morris, William, account of iii. 70

Moulsham Hall and manor described ii. 287

Mountjoy, George Lord, letters from the Queen to iii. 569, 575, 579, 596

Mowtlowe, Henry, account of iii. 149. letter to from Mr. Stringer 150

Muncaster, Dr. Richard, verses by i. 493. account of ib.

Muses, Triumphs of the i. 151

Music, the Queen's skill in i. 293, 487, 529. proclamation respecting singing boys ii. 433

N.

Naked Hall Hawe ii. 94

Neale, Thomas, description of Oxford i. 217

Netherlands, or Low Countries, entertainment of the Deputies for the States of ii. 437

New Hall, Essex, a royal mansion i. 94. inscription over the door ib. account of it; its owners; fine painted window at 95

New-year's Gift, in verse, addressed to the Queen iii. 469—488

New-year's Gifts, a roll of, in the reign of Philip and Mary i. xxxiv. practice of giving xl. ceremony in presenting ib. See also under each year.

Newberry, Jack of? i. 254

Newdigate, Sir Roger, built Harefield Lodge iii. 583. possessed the MS. account of the Queen's visit to Harefield ib.

Newton, Thomas, his Death of Delia iii. 628

Nichols, John, plan of collecting the Progresses and Processions suggested to him i. v. assisted by Mr. Gough and Mr. Steevens ib. published two volumes in 1788; a third in 1807, great part of which was destroyed by fire ib. commenced collecting for a new edition ib. acknowledgments to gentlemen for their assistance in the Work xlvi. xlvii. xlviii. not able to meet with several publications of the time xlviii. xlix.

Nine Ashes i. 288

Nonsuch (formerly Cuddington), a royal residence, and description of i. 74

Norden, John, royal palaces described by i. 83, 102, 103. description of Westminster Hall 83. of Hampton Court 274. of Gorhambury ii. 55. of Heston 279. of Osterley 280. of Highgate iii. 30. account of antient houses near the Strand iii. 371. definition of streets, lanes, and alleys 414

Norfolk, Thomas Howard fourth Duke of, elected K. G. i. 67. installed 68. godfather to the Prince of Baden's son 198. invested with the order of St. Michael 200. reprimanded, on his intended marriage with Mary Queen of Scots 257. beheaded 180. his benefaction to St. Mary Magdalen College, Cambridge 181.

———— Mary Duchess of (widow of Thomas Howard second Duke), godmother to the Queen i. 2

Norham, re-granted to the Earl of Monmouth iii. 246

Norris, Sir Edward, account of iii. 568

———— Lady Margaret, the Queen's letter to on her son's death iii. 420

———— John, sent for to attend the Privy Council on the Queen's accession i. 30

Norris and Knowlls, account of the families of iii. 420

North, Edward (afterwards the first Lord), account of ii. 219. site of the monastery of Charter-house given to 239

———— Roger second Lord, account of ii. 219. extracts from his Household-book 236—248. charges of his buildings at the Charter-house 239

———— Dudley third Lord, succeeded his grandfather ii. 241

———— Sir John, eldest son of Roger, second Lord North, his death ii. 241

———— Sir Thomas, account of ii. 241

Northampton, William Lord Parr seventh Marquis of, elected K. G. i. 67. installed 68

Northumberland, Thomas Percy Earl of, proclamation against for high treason i. 263. his death 321

Norwich, prices of provisions at i. 419. account of the Queen's entertainment at ii. 133—179. plague at 214

Nowel, Dean, sermons before the Queen i. 88, 105. dialogue with the Queen on the Church service 105

Nymphs, Complaint of the Satyrs against the iii. 594

O.

Oatlands, early descent of, and fees to the keepers iii. 599

Occhini, sermon by, translated into Latin by the Queen i. 10

Odiam, description of iii. 100

Offley, Hugh, entertainment given by, and account of him ii. 529

Oglethorpe, Owen, Bishop of Carlisle, crowned the Queen i. 60

Orator, Public, account of the office of iii. 144

Osterley, account of, and of Sir Thomas Gresham's mansion at ii. 279. described by Norden 280. descent of the manor of, and description of the mansion at ib.

Overton, William, Bishop of Lichfield and Coventry, account of i. 231

Oxford, Edward de Vere, seventeenth Earl of, account of i. 329

Oxford, particulars of the Queen's entertainment at i. 206—247. persons admitted M.A. on her visit 215. Neale's description of 217—229. the Queen's departure from 217, 250. Latin Oration by the Queen at 243. orders for defacing superstitious plate at All Souls 247. great mortality at ii. 66. Wood's account of the Queen's entertainment at iii. 144. Stringer's account of the same 149. rents of the Colleges at 160. Hentzner's description of the City and University of 178

P.

Page, dress of a i. 413

Paget, Lady Catharine, letter to from the Queen on the death of her daughter Lady Crompton iii. 497

Paper, the benefit it brings ii. 592

Paris Garden, bull and bear-baitings at i. 67. ii. 459

Parker, Matthew, Abp. of Canterbury, at Court i. 83. hospitality of 201, 208. letter for defacing the superstitious plate at All Souls College, Oxford 247. letters of, and other of the Queen's commissioners, for destroying books and plate 248, 249. memoirs of 331. married privately, and the Queen's dislike to it ib. anecdotes of 340. letter to Lord Treasurer Burleigh 346. Latin Life of 349, 384

———— Philip, account of ii. 224

Parliament, order of proceeding to i. 229, 599. ii. 433. iii. 409

Parr, Queen Katherine, married to Lord Thomas Seymour i. 23. Princess Elizabeth under her care ii. 389. her death ib.

Parry, Sir Thomas, extract from his Accomptbook of the Queen's domestic establishment at Hatfield i. vii. appointed Comptroller of the Household i. 30

Parsons, or Persons, Robert, a celebrated English Jesuit, account of, and his works ii. 434. prophecy of 1588, 535. his account of the Queen's last sickness and death iii. 612

Paston, Sir William, account of, and family ii. 224

Pavy, Salathiel, epitaph on i. 488

Peace proclaimed with France and Scotland i. 66, 83. with France concluded 306

Peacocke, Sir Stephen, Lord Mayor of London, at Princess Elizabeth's baptism i. 1
Pearl, a Chain of, a Poem on the death of the Queen iii. 640
Pembroke, Mary de St. Paul Countess of, founder of Pembroke Hall i. 150
——— Henry second Earl, account of i. 408
——— Mary Countess of, account of, and of her entertaining the Queen iii. 529
——— Anne Clifford, Countess of Dorset, and afterwards of Pembroke, her account of the family of Cliffords Earls of Cumberland iii. 491. author of a Chain of Pearl [by Diana Primrose] 640. verses to her by Dorothy Berry on it ib. particulars of the latter days of the Queen i. xxiii.
Pembroke Hall, Cambridge, by whom founded i. 150
Percy, Dr. Thomas, Bp. of Dromore, contemplated a work similar to the present i. v
Perot, Sir Thos. his speech to the Queen ii. 319
Perry Mills near Fotheringay, why so called ii. 507
Peter House, Cambridge, when founded i. 149
Petowe, H. poem on the Queen's funeral iii. 615
Petre, Sir William, appointed, with others, to transact urgent business on the Queen's accession i. 30, 94
Petworth House, account of iii. 97
Peyton, Sir Edw. anecdote of the Queen iii. 640
Pheodorowich, Lord Boris, the Russian Ambassador, entertainment given to iii. 515. rode through London, and hunted in Marybone-park 519
Philip and Mary, roll of New-year's Gifts to i. xxxiv
——— King, his intercession for the Princess's removal from Woodstock i. 11. proposes to marry the Princess to the Duke of Savoy 22
Piers, John, Abp. of York, account of i. 231
Pigeon, J. autograph iii. 14, 22, 25
——— N. autograph iii. 14, 22, 25
Pilkington, James, Bp. of Durham preached at Court i. 88
Plague in London i. 147, 263. ii. 392. iii. 130, 190. ceased i. 149. iii. 130
Plants, used in distillation ii. 123
Players, proclamation against i. 66. attached to the household of noblemen i. 463, 531. ii. 249. licence i. 489
Playter, Christopher, letter to ii. *250
Plumer, William, account of, and his son ii. 108
Poland, Ambassador from the King of iii. 416
Pole, Cardinal, his death, and order for his funeral i. 30. grant to 201
Poliphant, a musical instrument i. 293

Pope, Sir Thomas, Princess Elizabeth (afterwards Queen) placed under his care i. 4, 12. letter from the Privy Council to him 13. letter to the President of Trinity College 15. his kindness to the Princess 16. directed to learn her inclinations respecting marriage 22. his letter on that subject to Queen Mary 23. built Bermondsey House 290
Popham, Sir John, account of iii. 565
Poultry, prices of in 1572 i. 298
Paynings family, some account of i. 385
Prayer-book, a curious one bound in gold i. xxxvii
Preston, Thomas, account of i. 181, 245. ii. 481
Primrose, Lady Diana, verses to her, on composing the Chain of Pearl iii. 640
Pritchard, Humphrey, account of iii. 156
Provisions, price of in 1561, i. 419. served for the Queen's household iii. 83
Puckering, Sir John, letter to from Sir Thomas Heneage iii. 129. furniture for his house at Kew, preparatory to the Queen's visit to him 252. appointed Lord Keeper ib. some account of him ib. visited by the Queen 369
Purgo in Essex, account of i. 93
Puritans, origin of i. 150. increase of; denounce public amusements; one characterized in "The Masque of Owls" 447
Purse, account of the office of Keeper of the Queen's i. 264
Purveyors, difficulty of getting payment from i. 411. one hanged ib. iii. 37. abuses of 83
Puttenham, George, songs in praise of the Queen iii. 65

Q.

Quarendon, description of iii. 42, 126. of the chapel and monuments 127
Queen's College, Cambridge, by whom founded i. 150
Queen's Walk at Harefield iii. 584
Quintain, a martial spot described i. 444

R.

Rainolds, John, account of iii. 156
Raleigh, Sir Walter, Durham House given to iii. 371
Rambouillet, Mons. Nicholas D'Angennes, Marquis of, invests the Duke of Norfolk and Earl of Leicester with the order of St. Michael i. 200. waited on the Queen at Norwich ii. 218. account of ib.
Ramelius, Henry, a Danish Ambassador, entertainment given to ii. 458

Randolph, Mr. Ambassador to Russia and Scotland, to attend the Queen at Hunsdon ii. 99
Ratcliff, Edward, account of iii. 157
Reading, monastery at turned into a Royal Palace; royal Visits at i. 599
Rebellion, a Rebuke to ii. 603
Recorder, a musical instrument i. 433
Revels, at the Temple i. 131. at Lincoln's Inn 251. at Gray's Inn ii. 390. iii. 262
Revett, account of the family of ii. 215
Retz, Comte de, a French Ambassador, anecdote of i. 339
Rich, Robert Lord, Wansted granted to i. 93
Richmond, Princess Elizabeth visits the Queen at i. 15. account of the Royal Palace ii. 404, 412
Richmond, Margaret of, mother of Henry VII. founder of Christ's and St. John's Colleges, Cambridge i. 150
Ring, possessors of the one on which the Earl of Essex's life is said to have depended iii. 550
Roharts, John, of the Temple, speech to the Queen at Bristol i. 403
Robbery, eleven persons executed for i. 82
Robinson, Henry, Bp. of Carlisle iii. 449
——— John, account of i. 245
——— Nicholas, Bp. of Bangor, some account of i. 169. his account of the Acts at Oxford, when the Queen visited there i. 229. biographical notices of ib.
——— Wm. Bp. of Norwich, acc. of iii. 449
Rogers, Charles, his remarks on the portraits of Queen Elizabeth, and the Earl of Leicester i. xiv. anecdotes of the Earl of Leicester ii. 613
——— Sir Thomas, appointed Comptroller of the Household i. 30
Ronsard, sonnet by ii. 425
Rookwood, Ambrose, account of ii. 129. sent to the Tower 216, *249
Rosamond's Bower at Woodstock i. 9
Rowland's song in praise of the Queen iii. 63
Royal Exchange, foundation-stone laid i. 200. so named by the Queen ii. 281
Rudd, Ant. Bp. of St. David's, acc. of iii. 449
Ruffs, pains bestowed upon i. 460. reduced to legal dimensions ii. 625
Rushes, custom of strewing on floors of apartments ii. 243
Russell, Sir William, account of iii. 578
Rutland, Henry Manners second Earl of, elected K. G. i 67. installed 68
——— Edward Manners third Earl of, account of, ii. 509
Rycot, speeches to the Queen at iii. 168. descent of the manor, &c. with some account of its owners ib.

S.

Sackville, Sir Thomas, (afterwards Lord Buckhurst and Earl of Dorset) sent to congratulate the King of France on his marriage i. 275. his entertainment in France 276. letter to the Earl of Sussex ii. 60. account of 61
Sadleir, Sir Ralph, account of i. 100. epitaphs, and account of his family 104
Saffron Walden, extracts from the Corporation-books of expences at Audley-end i. 280, 281. expences of, on the Queen's visit to Audley-end ii. 114
St. Austin's Abbey, Canterbury, descent of i. 340
St. Elizabeth's day, observed at Court iii. 69. account of her canonization ib.
St. George for England iii. 541
St. George's Day, observance of i. 88, 94. ii. 455
St. Gregory's, service performed at till St. Paul's was ready i. 91
St. James's Palace, account of i. 103
St. James's Park, inscription at the entrance of i. 86
St. John, Oliver Lord, account of ii. 109. iii. 440
——— of Basing, William Pawlet Lord, account of i. xxxi. ii. 510, 511
——— of Bletso, John Lord, one of the Peers on the trial of Mary Queen of Scots, account of ii. 511
St. John's College, Cambridge, by whom founded i. 150
St. Margaret's Westminster, painted window at i. 95
St. Martin's Ludgate, church damaged by storm i. 89
St. Mary Magdalen College, benefaction to i. 181
St. Mary's Church, Cambridge, the Queen's entertainment at i. 167, 174
St. Osythe's, account of i. 96
St. Paul's, mass ceased to be said at i. 68. funeral ceremonies at, on death of Henry II. King of France 76. sermons at 82, 83, 87, 90, 91, 105, 292. ii. 537, 538. iii. 600, 611. burnt i. 89. re-building of 90. rails set up at 104. opening of after the fire 105. obsequies in, for Emperor Ferdinando 191. procession to, after defeat of the Spaniards, when the Queen went ii. 541
St. Thomas of Acre, ceremonial used in burying a gentlewoman at i. 65
St. Tibba, shrine of at Peterborough, supposed to be the tomb of Mary Queen of Scots ii. 522
Salisbury, Robert Cecil first Earl of, built Hatfield-house i. 12

Salisbury, Capt. Owen, killed by a musket-shot iii. 546
Salt-cellar, curious iii. 90, 370
Sampson, —— Dean of Christ Church, preached at Court i. 88.
Satyrs, complaint of the, against the Nymphs iii. 594
Savile, Sir Henry, his oration before the Queen at Oxford iii. 161
—— Thomas, account of iii. 151
Savoy, the, by whom built i. 92. burnt by the Kentish rebels 92. re-edified; made an hospital ib. government of ib.
—— Peter, Earl of, first built the Savoy i. 92
—— Philip Emanuel Duke of, proposes marriage with the Princess Elizabeth i. 22. her refusal 25
Scambler, Edmund, Bp. of Peterborough, preached at Court i. 88
Scotland, peace with proclaimed i. 83
—— Henry Frederick Prince of (afterwards Prince of Wales), account of the ceremonial of the baptism of iii. 353—369
Segar, Sir William, his account of the justs at the Tilt-yard iii. 41
Selwyn, John, account of, and his monument at Walton-on-Thames iii. 598. feats of agility while stag-hunting 599
Servants and Retainers in families, proclamation respecting ii. 399
Settle, Elkanah, author of " Spes Hunsdoniana," i. 287
Seymour, Queen Jane, her death i. 75. funeral of i. 88
—— Thomas Lord High Admiral, the Princess's regard for him i. 23. married to Queen Catherine Parr, ib. proposes marriage with the Princess ii. 289. further account of, and anecdotes of him and the Princess iii. 514
Sheldon, William, first introduced tapestry into England i. xvii
Shelton, Sir Ralph, notice of, and family ii. 225
Sheriffs, custom of nominating in London ii. 410
Sherington, or Charington, family of i. xviii
Sherwood, Ruben, account of i. 244
Shrewsbury, account of Sir Henry Sidney's visits to ii. 303, 309
—— Francis Talbot fifth Earl of, letters to i. 4, 201. sent for to attend the Privy Council on the Queen's accession i. 30
—— George Talbot sixth Earl of, letters to, from Robert Swift i. 4. from persons unknown 86, 274. from Mr. Allen 87. from Sir William Cecil (Lord Burleigh) 255, 334. from the Queen respecting her illness with small-pox 322. from his sons 328, 387. ii. 2, 92, 386, 625. from Mr. Topclyffe ii. 215. from the Earl of Leicester ii. 536

Shrewsbury, Countess of, letter to from her son i. 388. from Lady Anne Talbot 416. from Lady Dorothy Stafford iii. 543. from Sir Fulke Grevill 597

—— Gilbert Talbot seventh Earl of, letters from, shewing the intrigues of Court i. 328. letters to his father 328, 387. ii. 4, 92. letter to his mother i. 388. letters to from Mr. Kerry and Mr. Stanhope iii. 68. from Mr. Brackenbury 69. presents made by him in his embassage of France 408. letter to from Middle Temple Society 423. from Sir Thomas Edmonds 595. from Mr. Browne 596. from the Earl of Worcester 597. from Sir Robert Cecil 598.

Shrovetide, shews, &c. customary at ii. 278
Siculus, Diodorus, description of the Old Egyptians i. 440
Sidney, Sir Henry, account of his visit to Shrewsbury ii. 303, 309. letter to from the Queen 303. his death, and inscription on an urn 309
—— Sir Philip, dramatic interlude written by, for the Queen's entertainment at Wanstead ii. 94—99. letter to Lady Kitson 248. his death, and funeral procession 483—494. epitaph 494
—— Sir Robert, letter to Sir John Harrington i. xxxix. created Lord Sidney and Earl of Leicester ib. letter to from Sir Thomas Wilkes iii. 74. extracts from Rowland Whyte's letters to iii. 73, 442, 498, 513, 519, 591
Sidney College, Cambridge, by whom founded i. 150, 173
Singing boys, proclamation respecting i. 81. ii. 432
—— men and boys, proclamation respecting i. 81. on the Queen's establishment 487
Siradia, account of the palatine of ii. 407
Slawata, W. a Bohemian Baron, introduced to the Queen iii. 425
Small-pox, the Queen afflicted with i. 322. the Queen's visits delayed on account of the general infection of iii. 600
Smith, Sir Thomas, account of i. 281, 531. amusements at Christmas described by 324
—— Thomas, account of iii. 152
Smalridge, account of i. 98
Somerset, Anne Dutchess of, inventory of her jewels ii. 525. substance of her will ib.
Somerset-house, who built by i. 92
Southampton, the Court held at i. 259. account of the town 261. ale sent to for the Queen's use iii. 84
Southampton, Henry Wriothesley second Earl of, confinement of, by order of the Queen ii. 6. arraigned at Westminster with the Earl of

Essex iii. 546. found guilty, and sentence of death denounced against him 547
Southwell, Sir Robert, funeral of i. 80. account of ii. 214
Southwick, account of iii. 122
Spain, Philip King of, his marriage with Elizabeth, daughter of the King of France i. 73
Spaniards, thanksgivings for the defeat of ii. 537
Spencer, John, account of iii. 156
Spenser, Edmund, Hobbinol's Ditty, in praise of the Queen iii. 55. imitation of it by Webbe 58
Spilman, John, erected a paper-mill at Dartford ii. 592. obtained an exclusive grant to buy linen rags, and make paper iii. 431
Spoon, a curious one iii. 370
Spring, Sir William, account of ii. 116, 129, 224
Squire of Low Degree, The, i. 421
Squyre, Adam, account of i. 232
Stafford, Sir Edward, letter to from the Queen ii. 626
——— Lady Dorothy, letter to the Countess of Shrewsbury iii. 543. her epitaph 544
Stage-plays, licence granted for i. 531. theatres for ii. 459
Stamford, view of the White Friary at i. *199. fall of the White Friery 205. the Queen entertained at the Grey Friery ib.
Standen House, account of i. 100. ii. 107
Stanhope, Sir John, letter to Lord Talbot iii. 68. to Sir Robert Cecil 430
——— Michael, letter to Sir Robert iii. 441
Stanstead, description of iii. 97
Stapleton, Sir Robert, account of ii. 628
Stationers' Company, books relating to the Queen entered with the i. xvi. xvii. ii. 211, 395, 527, 530, 544. iii. 123, 379, 600. letter to them to attend the Queen iii. 26
Steevens, George, assisted in forming the present Work i. v.
Still, John, Bishop of Bath and Wells, account of iii. 448
Stokelees, John, Bishop of London, at the Queen's christening i. 2
Stone, Nicholas, monuments executed by iii. 30
Storms, damage by i. 76. violent 89, 96
Stow, John, his account of the Queen's progress into Hampshire in 1601 iii. 566
Strange, Ferdinando Lord Stanley, letter from the Lords of the Council to him and Dr. Chaderton, respecting libels ii. 434
Strangways, and others (sea-rovers), sent to prison i. 75. sentenced to suffer death 79. punishment stayed ib.
Streatham, the manor-house at supposed to be one of the Queen's palaces iii. 68

Stringer, Philip, his account of the Queen's reception and entertainment on her second visit to Oxford iii. 149. letter to Mr. Moutlowe 150
Strype, John, memoirs of Mr. Lambarde iii. 558. his account of the Queen's last illness and death iii. 609
Style, Lady, notice of ii. 132
Sudeley Castle, account of i. 543. speeches delivered to the Queen at iii. 186. Sir Egerton Brydges's description of 217
Surrey House ii. 130
Suffolk, Frances Duchess of, widow of Henry Grey Marquis of Dorset and Duke of Suffolk, her funeral i. 80
Sussex, Thomas Ratcliffe third Earl of, discord with the Earl of Leicester i. 204. reconciliation ib. account of i. 290
——— Lady Frances Sidney, Countess of, founder of Sidney College, Cambridge i. 150
Sutton Place, description of iii. 121
Sweden, Eric King of, proposes maariage with the Princess Elizabeth i. 22. his proposal rejected ib. renews his addresses to her when Queen 27. the Queen's refusal ib. expected in London 87. arrival of his brother at Windsor ib. presents to the Queen 104
——— Prince of (Duke of Finland), arrives in London) i. 79. goes to Court 82. at Windsor 87
Swift, Robert, letter to the Earl of Shrewsbury i. 4
Swinnerton, John, account of iii. 598
Swithin, St. conjectures respecting iii. 592

T.

Tachebrok Episcopi, account of i. 310
Talbot, Francis Lord, letters to his father ii. 2, 386, 625
——— Lady Anne, letter to the Countess of Shrewsbury i. 416. letter to from the Queen ii. 628
Tapestry, first introduction of in England i. xvii. curious ornaments on ib. iii. 505, 602
Temple, customs by students at i. xxi. Christmas kept at the 131
——— Inner, orders respecting apparel to be worn by the gentlemen of the iii. 32
——— Middle, apparel to be worn by gentlemen of the iii. 33. letter purporting to be from the students of to the Earl of Shrewsbury 423
Theobalds, description of i. 205, 291, 308. iii. 241. rooms in ii. 404. curious chimney-piece at iii. 76. Hermit's Oration to the Queen at

241. ancient pedigree of the Cecil family in the gallery at ib.
Thetford, a Royal residence ii. 275
Thompson, Giles, Bishop of Gloucester, account of iii. 156
Thornborough, John, Bp. of Limerick (afterwards of Bristol and Worcester), account of iii. 600
Thornton, Thomas, account of i. 232
Throgmorton, Sir John, Recorder of Coventry, his Oration to the Queen at Coventry i. 193. Recorder of Worcester 534
Thynne, Sir Thomas, his great wealth i. 408
Tichfield House, description of iii. 98
Tilbury, camp at ii. 532
Tilt-yard, Justs before the Queen at the i. 276. iii. 443. several persons killed ii. 302. the Queen and French Ambassadors entertained at 310. triumphal Justs at in 1590, iii. 41; in 1602, 600
Ton-sword explained i. 451
Topclyffe, Richard, letter to the Earl of Shrewsbury ii. 215. account of 219
Tower of London, Princess Elizabeth confined in i. 7. her removal from 8
Traitors apprehended ii. 481
Trinity College, Cambridge, by whom founded i. 150
——— Hall, Cambridge, by whom founded i. 150
Tufton, John, account of i. 335
Tuke, Sir Brian, account of ii. 286
Turk, the Grand, letter from to Queen Elizabeth ii. 302
Tunstall, Dr. Cuthbert, Bp. of Durham, arrives in London i. 73. notice of ib.
Tuthill-fields, combat appointed to be fought at i. 277
Twickenham Park, Sir Francis Bacon's favourite place for study iii. 190
Tyson, Michael, designed forming a collection similar to the present i. v.

U. and V.

Vavasor, Anne, account of iii. 69
Vauxhall, origin of the gardens at iii. 440. See *Foxhall.*
Vernard, Richard, his " Right Way to Heaven," calling the Queen " The Miracle of Nature " iii. 532—543. prayer for the success of the forces in Ireland 541
Vertue, George, description of the painting of the procession to Hunsdon House i. 282—289. controverted by Mr. Gough 289
Vyne, The, the Court held at i. 261
Unton (or Umpton), Sir Edward, account of i. 391
——— Sir Henry, sent Ambassador to France iii. 85. character of ib. expences of his embassy 86
Utrecht, the feast of St. George kept at ii. 455

W.

Wages, rates of iii. 411
Wales, Henry Frederick Prince of, ceremonial of his baptism i. xliii. iii. 351—369
Walsingham, Sir Francis, account of his death, and inscription for iii. 28. verses occasioned by his death 29. letter to from the Earl of Cumberland 523
——— Elizabeth, wife of Sir Thomas, her petition to the Queen at Harefield, as a guiltless lady iii. 591
——— family, some account of iii. 591
Walter, Sir William, notice of ii. 280
Wanstead House, its owners i. 93. ii. 94. descent of, after the Earl of Leicester's death ii. 223
Warwick, account of the Queen's entertainment at i. 309
——— Ambrose Dudley, created Earl of i. 318. his death iii. 39. epitaph ib.
——— Ambrose Dudley second Earl of, his marriage i. 199. time of his creation 313
——— Anne his Countess, account of iii. 381
Watson, Thos. verses in praise of the Queen iii. 66
Watts, Richard, account of i. 354
Webbe, George, imitation of Spenser's Hobbinol's Ditty iii. 58
Wentworth, Lord, arraigned for losing Calais i. 68
Westenhanger, account of i. 335
Westminster, painted window at St. Margaret's church i. 95. order of proceeding to Parliament at i. 299, 599. ii. 433. iii. 409. formerly the Archbishops of Canterbury resided in i. 324. noblemen's houses in iii. 371, 414
——— Abbey, altars in demolished i. 88
——— Hall, Norden's description of i. 83. stalls for sale of goods in ii. 247
Weston House, account of i. xvii.
Westphaling, Herbert, Bp. of Hereford, account of i. 231. the Queen sent to him to shorten his oration at Oxford iii. 146
Wharton, Thomas Lord, his death i. 307
Whitacre, ———, where buried i. 150
Whitaker, Dr. Thomas Dunham, biographical memoirs of the family of George Earl of Cumberland iii. 490
White, Henry, notice of iii. 614
Whitehall, Justs at i. 80. curiosities in 85
White Ladies, The, account of i. 552. the property of the Somers' family ib.
Whitfield, Arnald, Ambassador from the King of Denmark, arrival of iii. 419

Whitgift, John, Abp. of Canterbury, preached before the Queen when Dean of Lincoln i. 384. built an hospital and school at Croydon 387. iii. 519. attends the Queen in her last moments 610. placed the Crown on King James and Queen Anne 611

Whyte, Rowland, extracts from his letters to Sir Robert Sidney iii. 73, 442, 498, 513, 519, 591
——— Thomas, notice of i. 239

Wilkes, Sir Thomas, letter to Sir Robert Sidney iii. 74. died at Paris 430

Williams, Lord, of Thame, burial of i. 80
——— John, account of iii. 156
——— Thomas, chosen Speaker of the House of Commons, and presented to the Queen i. 107

Williams (or Cromwell), Sir Henry, highly respected by the Queen, account of i. 179
——— (or Cromwell), Richard, Hinchinbrook priory granted to i. 179

Willoughby, Peregrine Bertie Lord, letter to from the Queen iii. 260. account of ib.

Wilson, Anthony, Bishop of Chichester, account of iii. 449
——— Dr. Thomas, account of, and his works i. 245. verses on the New-year (1570) 274

Winchcombe, John, called Jack of Newbery? i. 254

Winchester, charter granted to iii. 68. confirmations of former favours 99
——— William Paulet, first Marquis of, sent for to attend the Privy Council on the Queen's accession i. 30. death of 258. appointed Lord High Treasurer 273. built the magnificent seat at Basing iii. 566
——— William Paulet fourth Marquis of, and Earl of Wiltshire, account of iii. 566. reduced by his magnificent style of living 598

Windows, large ones fashionable ii. 127

Windsor Castle, description of i. 143. the Queen's delight in, and her studies there iii. 564

Wingham, account of i. 339

Winwood, Sir Ralph, account of iii. 152. letter to from Sir Robert Cecil 546

Witherington, the seat of Sir R. Carey iii. 607

Wolley, Sir John, account of iii. 81

Wolley, Francis, account of i. 232

Wood, Anthony, account of the entertainment of Baron Alasco at Oxford ii. 406. his account of the Queen's entertainment on her second visit to Oxford iii. 144
——— Sir Robert, his oration to the Queen on her coming to Norwich ii. 139, 140. on her departure 166

Woodhouse, Sir Henry, account of ii. 225
——— Sir Roger, account of ii. 214, 225

Woodlake, Robert, founder of Catherine Hall, Cambridge i. 150

Woodstock Palace, the Queen in confinement at i. 8. besieged, and much damaged 9. the gate-house converted into a dwelling-house ib. Fair Rosomond's bower at ib. residents at ib. the Queen's well at ib. sonnet on a window-shutter at, by the Queen ib. description of iii. 174. Ethelred held a parliament at iii. 174

Worcester, charges on the Queen's visit i. 548
——— Edward Seymour third Earl of, letter to Earl of Shrewsbury iii. 597

Wotton, Rev. Dr. Nicholas, Ambassador to the Queen i. 66
——— Thomas, account of i. 334

Wray, Christopher, Lord Chief Justice, his additions to Magdalen College, Cambridge i. 150

Wreast, description of a i. 463

Wyat, Sir Thomas, breaking out of the rebellion under him i. 6. a second insurrection attempted 20

X.

Xarife, Mully Hamet, Ambassador from the King of Barbary, entertainment of iii. 516. rode through London, and hunted in Marybone park 519

Y.

Yarmouth, preparations for entertaining the Queen at ii. 275

Yeldard, Arthur, account of i. 231

Yeoman of the Guard, frontispiece to vol. II.

York House iii. 79, 371, 441

Young, John, Bishop of Rochester, account of iii. 5, 449

FINIS.